JUAN GRIS

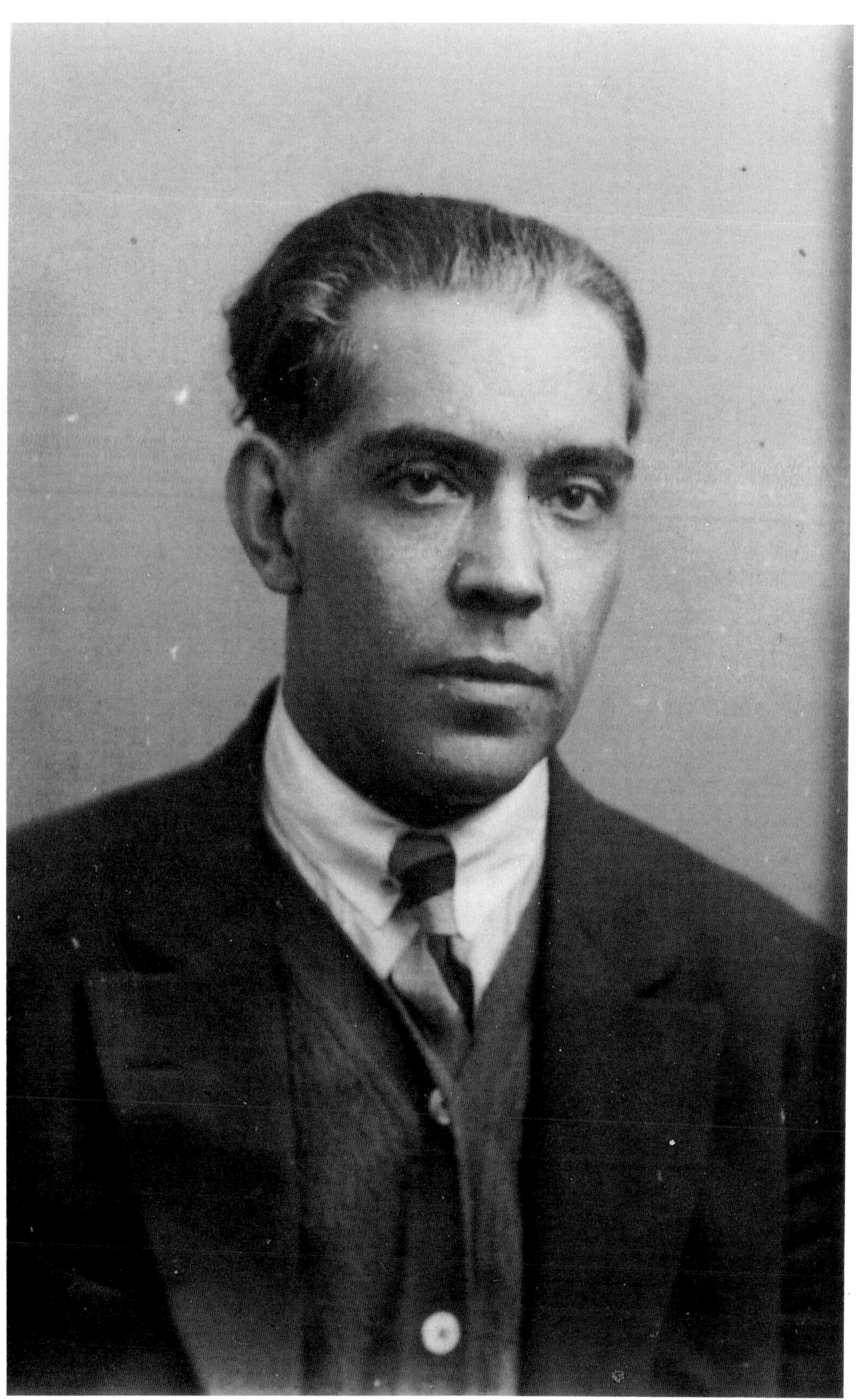

JUAN GRIS

Christopher Green
with contributions by
Christian Derouet
and
Karin von Maur

Whitechapel Art Gallery, London
in association with
Yale University Press
New Haven and London
1992

An exhibition organised by the Whitechapel Art Gallery

Whitechapel Art Gallery, London
18 September – 29 November 1992
Staatsgalerie Stuttgart
18 December 1992 – 14 February 1993
Rijksmuseum Kröller-Müller, Otterlo
6 March – 2 May 1993

In association with the European Arts Festival with support from the Baring Foundation

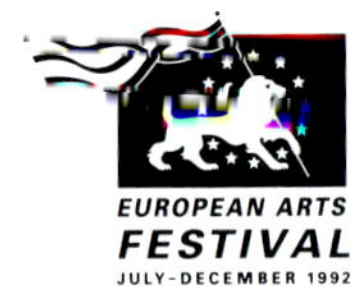

The Whitechapel Art Gallery is grateful to Her Majesty's Government for its help in agreeing to indemnify the exhibition under the terms of the National Heritage Act 1980 and to the Museums & Galleries Commission for its assistance in arranging this indemnity

Printed in Germany by Dr. Cantz'sche Druckerei, Ostfildern-Ruit bei Stuttgart

ISBN 0300053746
Library of Congress Catalog Card No.: 92-56394

Contents

Foreword

In March 1914, the Director of the National Gallery, J. B. Manson, warned the Whitechapel's then Director, Gilbert Ramsey, who was organising a show of the 'modern movements' against letting the selection fall 'too much into the hands of the Cubists and other charlatans'. He was speaking of the British artists who, like their other European counterparts, had became rapidly and irreversibly challenged by the artistic developments in Paris in the previous five years. Indeed, one of the original converts was Juan Gris who made his first avant-garde paintings in 1910 – much influenced by the work of Picasso and Braque – and within months was finding how potent and how intellectually and visually flexible the Cubist idiom might be. Some eighty years later Cubism is still a 'modern movement', alive to artists who continue to relish the irreducible fact that the canvas is a flat plane which can accommodate subjects that might nominally be inspired by anonymous and mundane objects, but quickly become highly metaphorical and demanding.

The structure and content of this exhibition were devised by Professor Christopher Green of the Courtauld Institute of Art who, with unflagging curiosity and fresh enquiries, has been researching and contemplating the artist's work for some thirty years. Paul Bonaventura, the Whitechapel's Senior Exhibitions Co-ordinator, and I decided to take advantage of his knowledge by inviting him to organise a Gris exhibition for the Whitechapel and its European partners and he early on promised to question the standard view of Gris as the 'logician' of Cubism by using the evidence of a more open-ended approach which the individual pictures proffer. The paintings and drawings chosen include not only most of Gris's acknowledged masterpieces, but also clusters of works which chronicle what was happening in his studio at any particular time, sometimes by reference to partially finished compositions. The selection includes, for example, some fifteen pictures from the period October 1915 through October 1916 which travel across three distinct styles of Cubism, starting with a solid extrapolation of the structures and materials of objects, moving into the placement of brilliant coloured dots drifting across flat signs for still-life objects, and culminating in a flattened 'chiaroscoro' realised in planar contrasts of a monochromatic palette. The rather disrupted and dismissed last period, before Gris's early death in 1927 at the age of 40, produced intervals of strong and beautiful works, not least the open window paintings and still-lives and those dedicated to the theme of the arts of painting, music and theatre.

There have been very few attempts in the last thirty years to organise exhibitions of the work of Gris. Notwithstanding, those arranged for Baden-Baden in 1974, for Berkeley in 1983 and for Madrid in 1985 have served as helpful models. The early offers and repeated extensions of personal help which came from Georges González Gris and from Quentin Laurens and his staff at the Galerie Louise

Leiris have been much called upon as have the goodwill and counsel of various scholars, collectors, dealers and admirers of Gris. From a very early stage, Peter Beye and Karin Frank von Maur at the Staatsgalerie Stuttgart and Evert van Straaten and Jaap Bremer of the Rijksmuseum Kröller-Müller in Otterlo shared our enthusiasm for the exhibition and began working closely with us on the format of the show. We in turn joined Christopher Green in his visits to as many owners of the works by Gris as possible. Without exception they volunteered their particular knowledge and personal generosity to such a degree that these meetings became an important part of the formation of the show. To those who were able to part with their works, the majority for a period of nine months, the Whitechapel and its partners owe an immense debt.

The concept for the catalogue which Christopher Green introduces has been enhanced significantly by the contributions of Karin von Maur and Christian Derouet. Most of all, it is a book of seven formidably analytic and personal essays by Professor Green which scrutinise the evidence and opinion about Gris, contemporaneous and contemporary, in a way that deliberately stimulates the reader into comparing such interpretations with the works themselves. The personal involvement of Gerd Hatje and his colleagues at Verlag Gerd Hatje which directly links the publication to Gris's principal dealer, Daniel-Henry Kahnweiler, and indeed to the artist himself, has been very gratifying, as has the involvement of John Nicoll and his colleagues at Yale University Press. All of the staff at the Whitechapel have contributed to the organisation of the show, most significantly Paul Bonaventura assisted by Rebecca Hurst. Together with Christopher Green we have benefitted from the unstinting help offered throughout by many organisations and individuals, most particularly those mentioned in the acknowledgements and the list of lenders.

It is a challenge for a relatively small institution such as the Whitechapel to initiate such an exhibition with the major financial and organisational demands which inevitably accrue. The early promise of support from The Baring Foundation which allowed us to progress with confidence was therefore especially welcome and in that respect we should like to thank Barry Till, Sir Nicholas Baring and David Carrington for their commitment and foresight. Equally, the contribution of the European Arts Festival came at a critical moment in the genesis of the show and gave us the financial means to make and promote this exhibition to a much wider audience. For their part, we are grateful to John Drummond and Tim Renton and also to Tony Dyer.

To present this exhibition in Britain, Germany and The Netherlands at this moment seems relevant to the surfeit of creative directions of our time insofar as Gris worked for his whole career in the midst of a formidable group of poets, critics, painters and dealers, arguing the choices for ground-breaking art to a degree that anyone as severely honest in their self-assessment as Gris might have lost courage. Instead, this reticent Spaniard, without attempting extreme feats either formally or episodically, gave us a legacy perhaps actively inspirational. The best pictures and drawings trigger spine-chilling pleasures. For me and many others, this is so partly because of Gris's adroit balancing and splintering and re-hingeing of forms, definitely engendered from the marvellous rhythms of colours, limpid to garish, so impossible to reproduce in print. His voice also derives from the slivers and hints of notations which in their restraint are all the more confessional, romantic and esoteric.

Catherine Lampert
Director, Whitechapel Art Gallery

The Whitechapel Art Gallery wishes to express its gratitude to all those who have participated in the elaboration of this project:

Alison de Lima Greene
André Straatman
Angela Schneider
Ann Temkin
Anna Maria
Anna Zissimatou
Anne d'Harnoncourt
Anne London
Antony Langdon Down
A. Tarica
Brian Boylan
Carl Belz
Carole McNamara
Christian Jenny
Christina Fässler
Cora Rosevear
David Britt
Dawn Ades
Diana Kunkel
Dieter Schwarz
Doris Ammann
Duncan MacGuigan
Edna Moshenson
Eliza Rathbone
Elvira González
Emily Braun
Ernst Beyeler
Esther Grether
Eugene Thaw
Felipe Vicente Garín Llombart
Fiona Bradley
Francis Briest
Frank Meyer
Gary Tinterow
Germain Viatte
German Ancochea Soto
Gregory Eades
Heather Kelly
Heather Wilson
Hubert Neumann
Isabel Mignoni
Isabelle Monod-Fontaine
Jan Krugier
Jan Runnqvist
Jane Brenton
Jeanne Vaughn
Jim Moyes
Joachim Pissarro
John Botts
John Bull
John Elderfield
John Golding
José Capa Eiriz
Juliette Laffon
Karin Hämmerling
Kate Moore
Kate Stephens
Kim Vick
Kirk Varnedoe
Klaus Perls
Leeann Risch
Luis García Velarde
L. Ishi-Kawa
Manuela Mena
Marc Blondeau
María de Corral
Mark Rosenthal
Marta Elorriaga
Martin Owen
Maurice Jardot
Michael Shapiro
Mrs Georg Guggenheim
Nathalie Karg
Patricia Tang
Paul Winkler
Peter Nathan
Phillip Young
Robert Evren
Robert Graham
Robert Rothschild
Rosalie Cass
Rudolf Koella
Samuel Botero
Sasha Newman
Sheila Murray
Stephen Hahn
Suzanne Pagé
Tanja Van Steenkiste
Thomas Ammann
Tomás Llorens
Ulrike Gauss
Victoria Combalia Dexeus
Violaine de la Brosse
William Acquavella
Xenia Wörle
Ylva Rouse

JUAN GRIS

Christopher Green

Introduction

Juan Gris is an artist who, more than most in the twentieth century, has encouraged the illusion of a clear object for analytical writing. His work has been presented predominantly as an orderly sequence of *tableaux objets* made by a man dedicated to reason whose life was short, but long on commitment and consistency. Yet, Gris was not detached from his painting. A theme of this catalogue is his insistence that his specific "aesthetic" and "sensibility" is the determining factor in all that he produced. And both emotionally and intellectually Gris was a complex man, not at all so simple in his rationalism as to avoid contradiction, even conflict, always open to new possibilities. Any writer on Gris's painting is engaged in a subjective encounter with a strong subjective presence that changes as the paintings change. I have tried not to retreat into the detachment of the analytical observer in this catalogue, but rather to acknowledge my own subjective engagement with Gris.

The structure of the text follows from a determination to avoid the impression of a life and work objectively and definitively surveyed. My aim is to pose questions about Gris and his work and to suggest ways of looking at the "facts" and the paintings. I have decided not to write a chronological narrative of Gris's "development", as if there is a coherent line to be drawn and an easily characterized artist and *oeuvre* to be described. Instead the chapters of the catalogue have been conceived as a series of essays which approach Gris's work from different angles. They can be read in sequence (as they were written), but need not be. If they add up to a view of Gris and Cubism, it is one view, not the "total picture".

Any text that deals with Juan Gris accepts as perhaps the major intermediary the monograph by his dealer Daniel-Henry Kahnweiler, first published in 1946 in French and translated into English in 1947. What perhaps more than anything allows that book to retain its significance now is its refusal of a simple "objective" narrative. It is the result of a close relationship between two powerful and open personalities and its tone and its structure say as much. Its sections record a *rapport* between individuals which was many-layered: affectionate, respectful, emotional, intellectual and, of course, commercial. The stories it tells bring together the voice of Gris from the letters with the voice of Kahnweiler, for whom Gris's painting is above all the vindication of deeply-held beliefs explored in long passages of reflection. Kahnweiler's beliefs were formed *with* Gris. No text written now can approach so close and so full a relationship. The example left by Kahnweiler's book remains, however, compelling.

The catalogue is completed by two further new contributions on Gris. They both offer the results of new research and I am especially grateful for the ways in which they add to the diversity of the image of Gris given here. Karin von Maur's essay deals with music and theatre, a theme that is central to Gris's work, but which is otherwise only touched on in my essays. It presents new evidence of his activities as a theatrical designer. No previous text on this topic has discussed the musical analogy or Gris's collaboration with Diaghilev's *Ballets Russes* so fully. Christian Derouet's essay is the first discussion of a major new discovery of letters written by Gris to his war-time dealer Léonce Rosenberg. These letters fill a crucial gap in our knowledge of Gris between 1915 and 1920 that Kahnweiler and Douglas Cooper were forced to leave. They offer new and fascinating glimpses into a whole range of relationships between Gris and such figures as Picasso, Braque, Lipchitz, Reverdy, Apollinaire and Cocteau.

There is one final relationship with Gris to acknowledge. It is between the painter and his son, Georges González Gris. Now, in the early 1990s, the closest anyone can come to Juan Gris is through his son. All of us who have worked on this exhibition and on the texts for this catalogue owe a debt to the benevolent care with which Monsieur González Gris protects and supports the memory of his father.

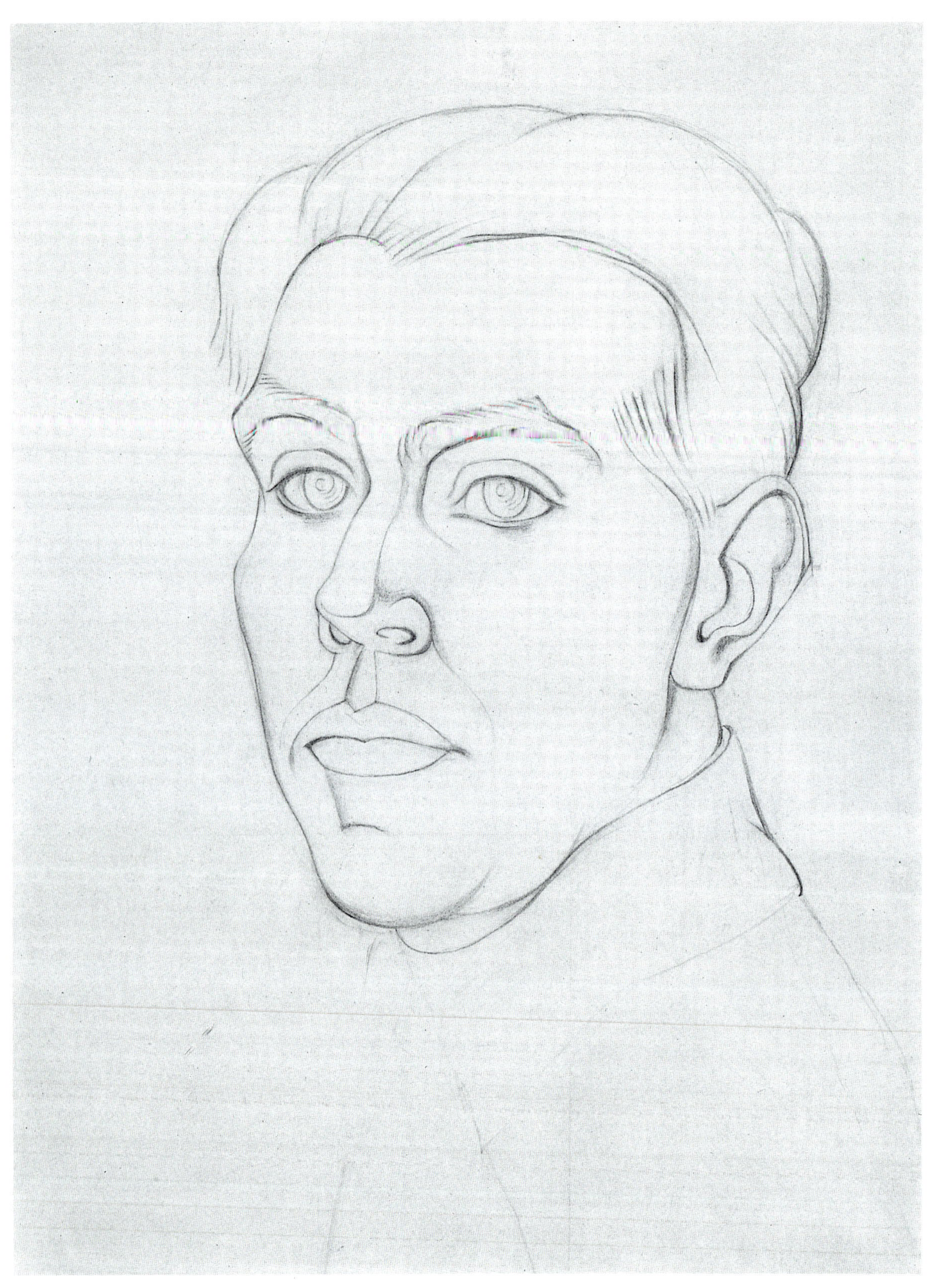

1. The Making of "Juan Gris"

In 1926 Christian Zervos opened an essay on Juan Gris with a fable. Its theme was the inevitability of death and the danger that we might reach it with nothing said. It was almost diabolical in its prescience. A year later Juan Gris died; he was 40. The point of Zervos's fable was simple: it was that most of all what counted was "to find the words, ... here below", to be understood by oneself and by others. Gris, he claimed, was "always in search of a new language in order to make of it the clothing of thought..."[1]. Zervos was to announce Gris's death thus: "On the 11th May last Juan Gris died, one of modern painting's artisans"[2]. The choice of the word "artisan" was enhancing, not demeaning: it connoted a humble, but profound integrity[3].

The clear thought in painted form, profound integrity in a human form resolutely resistant to glamour; these are two generalisations often made about the pictures and the personality of Juan Gris. The name (John Grey) seems to sum it up, even though it was the invention of one who was actually named by his *Madrileño* bourgeois parents, José Victoriano Carmelo Carlos González Pérez. When in 1933, Zervos introduced the special number of his periodical *Cahiers d'Art* dedicated to the artist, he set this image of clarity and humility in a precise context, one that constituted, judgmentally, a field of values: "Alongside the two great masters of Cubism each of whom is unique and irreplaceable, Jean (sic) Gris plays the role of a brilliant second. For having been eclipsed by the marvellous lustre of Picasso and the rare qualities of Braque, his works must not any less be considered of high quality"[4]. By the time Zervos so explicitly situated Gris in this way, Picasso, Braque and Gris were the accepted leaders of a Cubist movement about which histories could be written, with Léger often added to make the trio into a quartet[5]. The dealer Daniel-Henry Kahnweiler's selection of four "masters" from among the many to have been called Cubist had come to form the Cubist canon[6]. Gris was always to be placed *after* Picasso and Braque, his reputation elevated with theirs, but often hedged about with qualifications. He and his work could not be thought of without them, above all, not without Picasso.

The year 1933 was also the date of the publication of Gertrude Stein's *The Autobiography of Alice B. Toklas*. She recalls Gris's entrance into the 'milieu' of Picasso before 1910 thus: "It was in these days that Juan Gris, a raw rather effusive youth, came from Madrid to Paris and began to call Picasso *cher maître* to Picasso's great annoyance"[7]. Wryly she acknowledges deference as the function of his humility, but, for her, deference does not mean subservience. "The only real Cubism," she writes, "is that of Picasso and Juan Gris. Picasso created it and Juan Gris permeated it with his clarity and his exaltation"[8]. If Gris cannot be thought of without Picasso, she suggests, Cubism cannot be thought of without Gris: their complementary relationship is fundamental to Cubism. Picasso "creates" Cubism, which is completed by the "clarity" and "exaltation" of Gris. Clarification, of

Self-portrait, 1920–21
Pencil on paper,
33 x 25 cm
Georges González Gris

course, comes *after* creation, but it is something distinct, and in Gris's case, as Stein words it, "clarity" is in his very being: *he* (clarification) is added to Picasso (creation) to produce "the only real Cubism".

This conviction that Gris's art was an essential component of Cubism, and that it was independent, original, even though it followed Braque's and especially Picasso's, has become another constant. In 1950, Marcel Duchamp summed up what Gris added thus: "Gris immediately imposed his conception of Cubism on his work. This was rather an explanation of forms than a complication of forms... He pursued this line of expression to the end and methodically polished one of the purest facets of Cubism"[9].

The private Gris of his letters (intimate, professional or both) was certainly sometimes humble: he often mentions his failings. But he reveals also an awareness of strengths: there is no false modesty. Indeed, by 1918 he could assess his role as a Cubist with an appreciation of its importance, its "place" in things, that anticipates Zervos's positive yet qualified view of fifteen years later. The occasion came of financial disagreements with Léonce Rosenberg, the dealer who took over from Kahnweiler between 1915 and 1920[10]. Gris was furious at what he felt was inferior treatment. "I believe," he wrote firmly to Rosenberg in November 1918, "setting aside Braque and Léger, that I have more rights than all the others"[11]. By "all the others" he meant Metzinger, Herbin, Severini, María Blanchard, Lipchitz and Laurens; Picasso is not mentioned because he was above such equations[12]. Gris had no doubts: he was worth more "per canvas" than any of the Cubists but Picasso, Braque and Léger. He knew where he stood. He would have been willing to accept Zervos's "brilliant" second place.

Integrity, clarity and deference were all, at the time, acknowledged features of Gris's public entrance as a Cubist in 1912. The poet and critic André Salmon was briefly, like Picasso, a neighbour of Gris's at 13, rue Ravignan (the ramshackle studio-building dubbed the "Bateau-Lavoir"); later he was to claim that he was the author of the captions for some of Gris's pre-Cubist caricatures[13]. On 2 January 1912 it was Salmon who announced in *Paris-Journal* the Spaniard's switch from the caricature magazines to the profession of painter. "A quantity of his canvases and numerous drawings are now gathered," he wrote, "in the Galerie Sagot. It is probable that collectors will next be invited to a very important exhibition of works by this disciple of Picasso"[14]. Salmon welcomes him both as a "disciple of Picasso" and as capable of something "very important". Two months later, in March 1912, Gris made his debut at the Salon des Indépendants. He showed three pictures; the one that attracted most attention was a portrait of Picasso (Plate 10)[15]. In the bottom right corner he inscribed it carefully, in a copy-book hand, pupil to master: "Homage to Pablo Picasso, Juan Gris". Salmon commented: "This evidence of good faith will not deny him his personality. Certainly, it is not yet with reference to Juan Gris that the question of Cubism should be re-opened; the work of those who have made researches for five years will be the pretext for discussion. But one must recognize immediately the taste and the clear sense of direction of this new painter, in whom one must have confidence"[16]. Already in 1912 Gris the follower is promoted as simultaneously Gris the clear-thinking independent.

Especially before 1910 Salmon had been one of the circle around Picasso in Montmartre. It was another of that circle who most memorably set up Gris's reputation in all its essentials as it has been shaped and re-shaped ever since: Guillaume Apollinaire. He did so with typical insouciance in a couple of throw-away comments. The first was his response in the newspaper *L'Intransigeant* to Gris's debut at the Indépendants of 1912. "Juan Gris," he wrote, "is exhibiting an *Homage to Picasso* that reveals a praiseworthy effort and a noble disinterestedness. Juan Gris's exhibit could be entitled "Integral Cubism"..."[17]. That phrase, "Integral Cubism", with its essentialist inference, anticipates, of course, Gertrude Stein's talk of "real" Cubism. Gris's work was said to be *basic* Cubism on its very first Salon showing. The second of his comments came in response to Gris's contribution to the co-ordinated exhibition of Cubist art (rather widely defined) held in Paris in October 1912, the Salon de la Section d'Or. Apollinaire supplied *L'Intransigeant* with a mock dialogue between two "elegant young women" present at the hanging. "Louise", the one in the know, mentions in passing: "Jean Gris, the demon of logic"[18].

The prolix anti-Cubist critic Louis Vauxcelles had called Gris's *Homage to Pablo Picasso* a portrait of "Père Ubu-kub", connecting Cubism and Picasso with Alfred Jarry's grotesque champion of scatalogical nonsense "Père Ubu"[19]. To equate Picasso and the "pataphysician" Jarry was to equate Picasso's Cubism with the *anti*-logical[20]. Vauxcelles did so in bad faith, but the equation has held with the construction of Picasso's massive reputation. To equate Gris with logic was to distinguish him and his Cubism sharply from Picasso. This equation too has held, as we shall see.

Gris's sense of his own importance as a Cubist brought him to remonstrate with Léonce Rosenberg in 1918. His desire both to recognise the primacy of Picasso and Braque, and to count himself as one of a trio at the centre of something led him to paint or even write them into his pictures. His *Homage* does both for Picasso, and more than once, less directly, he used the labels and press-cuttings that added a scattering of words to his *papiers collés* of 1914 to declare his loyalty.

In June 1914, at Collioure, he cut and glued together a small composition around the crux of the label of an Anis del Mono bottle (Plate 43). The label can be read as an heraldic device marking his sense of *esprit de corps* with Picasso and Braque. The contents of the bottle are declared a "special distillation", and so are the contents of the work. Below, as today, the Anis del Mono label gives the place of manufacture, the Barcelona suburb of Badalona; on either side are two medallions inscribed: "El major premio/Paris 1878" and "Primer premio/Madrid 1877". A pattern of references to Barcelona, Paris and Madrid is easily read as a pattern of references to the alliance with which Gris identified, and which he believed to be the core of the "special distillation", Cubism: Picasso (from Barcelona, the "place" of manufacture) and the two prize-winners, Braque (then currently from Paris) and Gris (from Madrid). Also in June 1914 Gris made *The Packet of Coffee* (Plate 41). Here, stuck right at the heart of the shadowy cluster of cut-out and over-drawn surfaces, is a head-line which reads: "ces explor...eurs!" Above it, symbol of progressive communications, is a telegraph post, part of the mast-head of the newspaper *Le Matin*. "These explorers", dabbling in progressive communications on a daily basis, surely included, for Gris, himself alongside Picasso and Braque[21].

Such references, to be read obliquely from the verbal fragments in the *papiers collés* of 1914, signified only for a small circle of knowing viewers/readers, the most privileged being Picasso and Braque. Gris made them as one of Kahnweiler's Cubists, having withdrawn from the open, public world of the annual Salon des Indépendants. The compliments he paid his acknowledged guides were usually not so indirect, but neither were they to be again as open and direct as *Homage to Pablo Picasso*. Painted to mark a debut anticipated with such interest by André Salmon, it was, as we have seen, decisive in cementing Gris's public position after but alongside Picasso. It marked without doubt an intimate and actual relationship between Picasso-as-leader and Gris-as-follower, but, just as plainly as Gris's *papiers collés* of 1914, it marked also his distinctness from both Picasso and Braque. A debt was acknowledged, but, to use Salmon's word, a "personality" was to be "seen" in the painting, at least by those who knew well the work of the "personality" honoured by it.

It is not difficult to establish the closeness and the habitual deference of Gris's relationship with Picasso. Salmon moved into 13, rue Ravignan in 1908, and his autobiography strongly suggests that Gris's studio there was then occupied by another young painter, "the frenetic Jacques Vaillant"[22]. This, coupled with the evidence of Gris's long-standing friend Enrique Echea and the painter Vázquez Diaz, with whom Gris lodged on his arrival in Paris in 1906, confirms that he did not move into it immediately[23]. But he was certainly there, the neighbour of Picasso and Salmon, for some of the period 1908–9, years when the cohesion of the group centred on Picasso, Braque, Salmon, Apollinaire and Max Jacob was particularly solid. That cohesion began to loosen a little when first Salmon left Montmartre for Montparnasse in the spring of 1909, and then Picasso, newly affluent because of Kahnweiler's backing, moved down the hill with Fernande Olivier to a more spacious apartment on the Boulevard de Clichy in the autumn[24]. Gris, however, stayed in touch, and in November 1911 Picasso took a studio again in the "Bateau-Lavoir", so that they were in close, daily proximity throughout the four months leading up to the Indépendants of 1912[25]. Indeed, when in May that year Picasso wrote from the French Catalan town of Céret to Kahnweiler of the need to "fix" the "canvases which are only drawn in charcoal" then stored in the rue Ravignan studio, he suggested Gris to do the "fixing"[26]. He might have been annoyed at the title "cher maître", but he did not hesitate to treat Gris as his assistant.

An attempt to see how this new deferential, but distinct "personality" could be found in the *Homage* and the other pictures that made up Gris's contribution to the Indépendants of 1912 can as well start by looking at them in contradistinction to Braque as to Picasso. 1910–12 were the years of Picasso's and Braque's most productive working relationship.

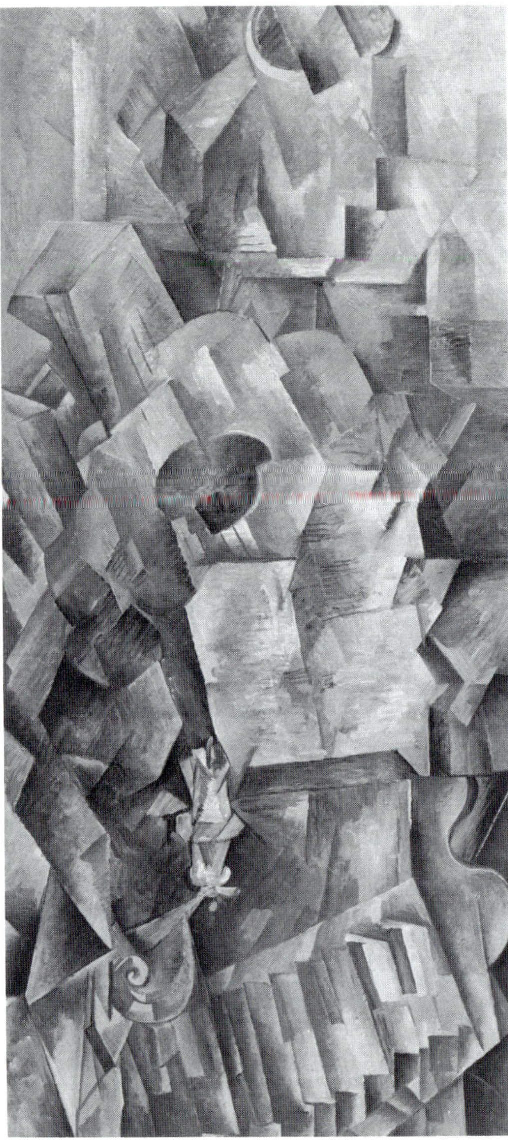

Figure 1
Georges Braque
Piano and Mandola,
1909–10
Oil on canvas,
91.8 x 42.9 cm
The Solomon R. Guggenheim Museum, New York
© ADAGP, Paris and DACS, London 1992

They saw each other, wrote to each other, and followed each other's painting in a quickening rhythm of exchange[27]. Gris had known Braque from his arrival in the "Bateau-Lavoir" at least. To follow Picasso's Cubism as closely as he did between 1910 and 1912 was to follow Braque's too. Indeed, it seems at least possible that he accompanied his explicit homage to Picasso at the Indépendants with a more covert homage to Braque as well.

One of the two pictures recorded to have been hung with *Homage to Pablo Picasso* at the Indépendants was a "still-life". The most ambitious still-life that Gris completed early in 1912 is *Still-life with Flowers* (Plate 8). Its size, elaboration and immaculate finish encourage the idea that this picture was the Indépendants still-life, and there is new evidence that makes it almost certain[28]. Unmistakeably, it takes up the theme announced by one of Braque's musical instrument still-lives from the major series of 1909–10, *Piano and Mandola* (Figure 1). Gris's vertical format is a more moderate version of Braque's, but it too is a possible figure format on a figure scale, unusual for still-life[29]. More telling, the central set-up of sturdy water-jug frontally placed behind a guitar whose arm is swung diagonally to the left, exactly repeats the configuration of Braque's water-jug and mandola. Even the placing of the glass below and to the left of the guitar carries an echo of Braque's candle. *Still-life with Flowers* is Gris's response to Braque's musical still-lives of 1909–10 as much as his *Homage* is a response to Picasso's portraits of 1910 (especially the Vollard portrait (Figure 2)). By responding Gris pays a compliment.

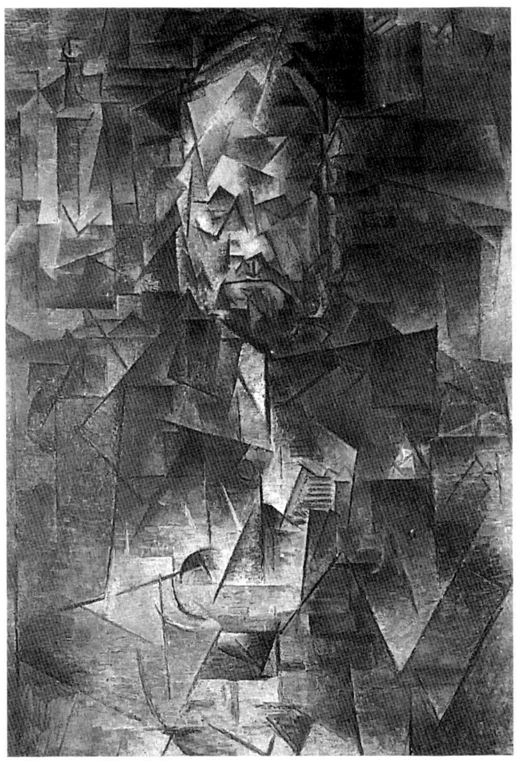

Figure 2
Pablo Picasso
Portrait of Ambroise Vollard, 1909–10
Oil on canvas, 92 x 65 cm
Pushkin Museum of Fine Art, Moscow

The invitation to make comparisons is, however, an invitation to make distinctions too.

Braque's *Piano and Mandola* displays an understated, but evident care. Especially around the candle and its holder, the vestiges of a considered pencil outlining are visible. The configuration of jug and instrument are almost repeated, in reverse, in another of the series; they are clearly thought out as well as crisply painted. The facetted structure of planes operates about an undeclared, but inferred central axis: competing diagonals in equipoise.

Care is something deliberately stated in Gris's response, something that is not a matter of vestiges of pencil. There are no such vestiges visible, but every edge has a decisive finality found nowhere in the Braque. Gris uses block-like touches of warm and cool colour, a technique used too by both Picasso and Braque from late 1910, but he places them with an even regularity they rarely approached. Where Braque's objects, however sharply conceived, are left open and vulnerable to their flickering surroundings, Gris's are, each one, firm, closed, frozen definitions. The highly specific combination of arc and triangle that describes the top and foot of the glass, and the base of the fruit dish that partially occludes the face of the guitar, applies a simple geometric construction. This expresses the ratio of the area of a circle and the area of a square inscribed, which Gris sketched with the ratio written alongside (1:1.570 or π2) in a drawing of around the same date (Figure 3)[30]. The definitions can be mathematically controlled. The placing of objects and the facetting of surfaces resolves into a stable structure of diagonals about a central axis. But the central axis is explicit, and exactly halves the format; it is crossed by horizontals that divide the format proportionally and halve it as well, and there is an inferred combination of regular orthogonal and diagonal grids. Care and clarity signify as method: logic.

The same kind of points are to be made, of course, about Gris's *Homage to Pablo Picasso* in

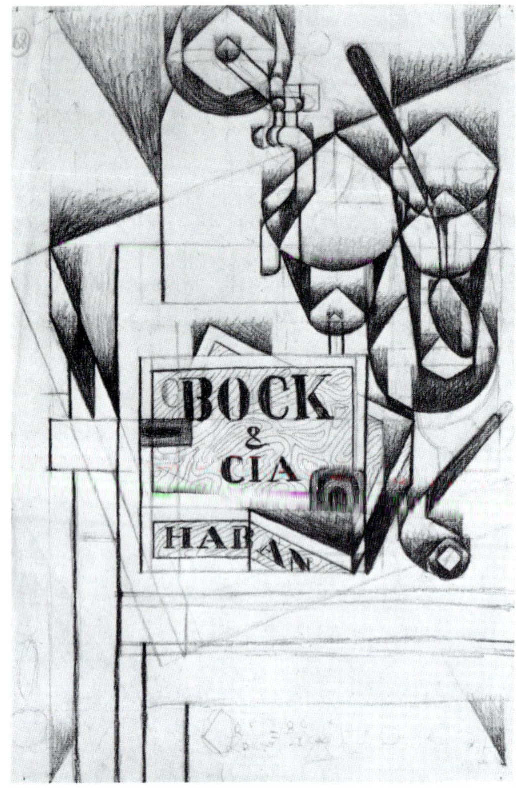

Figure 3
Still-life, 1912
Pencil and
charcoal on paper,
dimensions unknown
Galerie Louise Leiris,
Paris

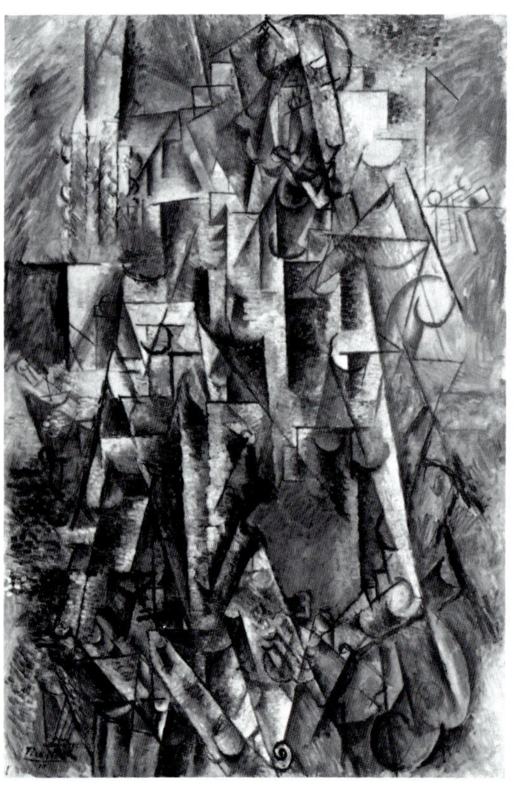

Figure 4
Pablo Picasso
The Poet, 1911
Oil on canvas,
131.2 x 89.5 cm
Peggy Guggenheim
Foundation, Venice;
The Solomon
R. Guggenheim Foundation, New York
© DACS 1992

contradistinction to its most obvious point of reference, the *Portrait of Vollard*, although in the last but one of these essays I shall argue that Gris leaves Picasso, on his own terms, *un*defined. Manifestly, however, the Picasso in the painting is in the grip of another intelligence, another "personality" in which the ordering and defining characteristics of logical *intelligence* are declared. But the distinctness of Gris's *Homage* in the context of the work of its subject is even more clearly delineated if one looks at Picasso's then current work. *The Poet* (Figure 4) was painted in Céret in August 1911, just before Picasso returned to work next door to his admirer. At the same time, Picasso was making drawing after drawing of related figures (Figure 5). These drawings were not studies for this or any other painting. Rather, they ran together into suites of connected ideas generated in parallel.

The Poet, like all the paintings of this phase, combines a broken line (the quick sum of black strokes discontinuously put together) with a surface broken up into varied areas of brushing, dabbing or streaking. There is an unevenness of finish that declares a refusal of definition, and that invites the unravelling not merely of the figure, but of the *process* that has built it. Process as an active, volatile pursuit of figural representation by mark-making is left deliberately exposed, and painting is allowed to become an on-going mode of "study" on the same level as drawing. Indeed, in some cases the drawings in the parallel suites, however small, are far more decisively resolved[31]. In painting, Picasso resists finish as much as definition. Carelessness is made a virtue to be seen.

No drawings survive specifically for *Homage to Pablo Picasso*, but a delicately resolved drawing does exist for *Still-life with Flowers*[32]. As Gris worked alongside the Picasso of *The Poet* towards his debut at the Indépendants, he kept the activities of drawing and painting strictly separate: he studied by drawing and he made studies for his paintings[33]. With the clarity and definition this encouraged went an

Figure 5
Pablo Picasso
Man with Clarinet,
1911
Pen, Indian ink and
conté crayon on paper,
30.8 x 19.6 cm
Musée Picasso, Paris
© DACS 1992

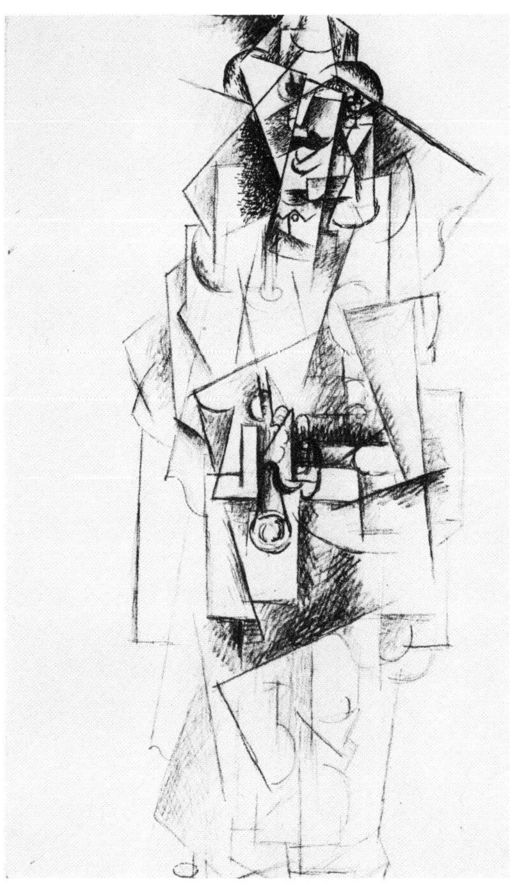

immaculacy of oil technique that masked utterly the traces of process. The pictures shown in 1912 were whole, finished conceptions. Manifest care went with finish as the complement to definition. The results were still more distinct from the Picasso (and Braque) of 1912 than from the Picasso they most obviously answered, that of 1910.

The open windows of 1921–22 could be called Gris's responses to Picasso's open window gouaches painted at St Raphael in 1919 (Plates 99, 100, 101 and 102), his later Pierrots and Harlequins to Picasso's, but it is clear that Gris most explicitly and deferentially paid his pictorial compliments to Picasso and Braque before the Great War. One sequence of pictures, however, is worth mentioning as an exception, because it makes the link between Gris the "definitive" Cubist aware of his debts before the war, and Gris the accepted leader among leaders of the post-war decade. An example from this sequence is *The Guitar* dated March 1918 (Plate 79).

This is one of a long line of vertical guitars, usually placed on tables or chairs leaning against walls. Gris was to paint variants on the theme right through to 1927[34]. He painted the very first early in 1913 and *The Guitar* of May 1913 is one of them (Plate 28). The more complex, heteroclite *Guitar on a Chair* painted at Céret in September 1913 (Plate 31) is an early sequel. A feature of the Céret picture is a small area of *trompe l'oeil* painting depicting the chair-caning of the chair on which the guitar sits. Like the words "ces explor... eurs", it brings Gris together with Picasso at the heart of the painting for, notoriously, oil-cloth printed illusionistically to represent chair-caning had been the crucial element stuck onto Picasso's first *collage* in the spring of 1912[35]. And beside the painted chair-caning there is a fragment of wood grain wallpaper collaged onto the canvas.

Yet, still more resonant with the name of Picasso within the small circle of "explorers" by the summer of 1913 was the guitar on the chair. It stands and leans, but in July Gris had painted a violin very like it hung from a nail on the wall, as perhaps the guitar is in the painting of May[36]. The reference would certainly have been clear to Picasso himself: it is to the cardboard and string guitar, probably made in October 1912, which served as a maquette for the steel version in New York, and with which he generated his first series of constructed sculptures (Figure 6)[37]. The reference is still there, acting across a distance of half a decade, in *The Guitar* of March 1918.

Much has been claimed for Picasso's cardboard *Guitar*. Most recently it has been claimed, persuasively, to mark the beginnings of a modernism whose semiotic openness and "self-reflexivity" is of a different order from that of pre-1912 Cubism (something to which I shall return in a later essay)[38].

More obviously and often it has been claimed to mark the beginning of a "new

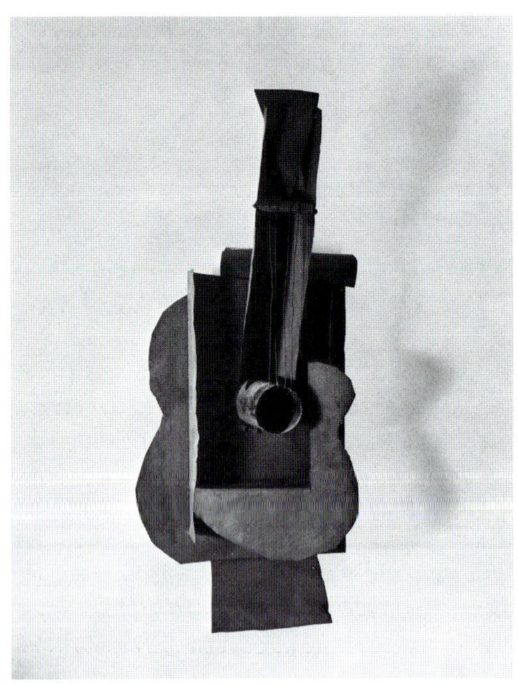

sculpture", constructed and inclusive of space[39]. It is in both these contexts that Edward Fry has connected it with the most tonal and sculptural of Gris's vertical musical instrument pictures of 1913, the *Violin and Guitar* in the Colin collection (Plate 32), but what is striking about Gris's vertical guitars of 1913 is more often their *refusal* of the illusionistically sculptural[40].

The most illusionistically sculptural elements in the May 1913 *Guitar* are the fragments of picture frame and the figure in the cheap engraving stuck, as it were, into that frame. Both are, in a simple sense, routine depictions of solid form. The guitar is an arrangement of lines and flat surfaces, set in a flat pattern of strips. The chair in the Céret picture is placed above a patterned floor and in front of a pocket of recessive depth made credible by a naïvely modelled table leg and corner. The *possibility* of depicting sculptural form is affirmed. Yet, again the guitar is almost entirely an arrangement of flat, jig-saw planes, and by mixing sand or earth into the paint Gris has manifestly wedded it to the flat picture surface.

Gris responds to Picasso's card-board sculpture, but without turning painting over to the mock-sculptural. The distinctions between the media are kept clear. In May 1918 they were clearer still. The suggestion here of tonal modelling on the curved flank of the guitar can still be read as an allusion to sculptural illusionism, but it is strictly contained in a structure of planes that otherwise nowhere alludes to depth or weight in illusionistic terms.

Gris's extended meditation on Picasso's card-board *Guitar* can be seen, often in contradistinction to Picasso, as an affirmation of his clarity of purpose. With firm definitions go clear distinctions at the level of fundamentals. Picasso "creates"; Gris "clarifies". Wherever Gris embeds into his work deferential references to Picasso (and Braque), he asks to be counted with them, but as "Juan Gris". The briefest look at his overt or covert "homages" can quickly establish the firm basis on which his image as the one who tidied up Cubism was constructed. Repeatedly, explicitly, his work confronted the mercurial (above all Picasso) with the methodical.

If from the very beginning, his 1912 debut, Gris painted an image of himself in relation to Picasso and Braque into his pictures, and got a ready response from Salmon and Apollinaire, it was not until around 1920, with his role much more widely acknowledged, that criticism really made the "Juan Gris" of later histories of Cubism. Two critics were above all responsible: Waldemar George and more especially Maurice Raynal. Both, as will emerge more fully later in these essays, were personally and intellectually closer to Gris himself[41].

This is George, writing in 1921 in *L'Esprit Nouveau* no. 9: "A work by Gris is always a rigorous demonstration. Only a very great artist, a perspicacious theoretician too, confronts, as he does, plastic problems. Gris consecrates the triumph of clarity"[42]. He backed this up with a major monographic article in

Figure 6
Pablo Picasso
Guitar, 1912
Sheet metal and wire, 77.5 x 35 x 19.3 cm
Collection, The Museum of Modern Art, New York. Gift of the artist
© DACS 1992

the November 1921 number of *L'Amour de l'art*, where Gris becomes "one of the most orthodox grammarians of the Cubist school", "honest" enough and "perspicacious" enough to welcome the analysis of his paintings[43]. But Raynal's was the more suggestive contribution because it so acutely anticipated not only Gris's characterisation as the thinking Cubist, but also the quality as well as the shape of the Picasso-Braque-Gris configuration later to become historical orthodoxy.

A few months before Waldemar George's talk of "the triumph of clarity" in no.9, Raynal published his own extended monographic essay on Gris in *L'Esprit Nouveau* no.5. It was a demanding piece, which made extensive metaphysical claims for Gris's painting (I shall return to it in the later essays), and it defined Gris clearly as, in Raynal's terms, an "artist", not a "painter". "The work of Juan Gris, replete with modesty, respectability, if you will, instantly touches the special nerve-endings of those spectators who, most purely and most zealously *artists* rather than *painters,* demand from the severe control of a picture nourishment for a more exigeant, a more balanced sensibility, one less fictive and less impetuous"[44]. The distinction between the *artist* and the *painter* was, for Raynal, basic. It was the difference between controlled understanding and unknowing spontaneity, between, most obviously, a figure like Gris and such so-called "naturalists" as, say, Matisse or Vlaminck[45]. It distinguished Gris as a *type*. But, as an individual, he was to be distinguished too from other *artists* (Raynal considered all Cubists *artists*), and it was looking at him thus as one of the group included by Léonce Rosenberg in a gallery show that the critic sketched out (perhaps for the first time so completely) the classic configuration of relationships. He did so in his regular art column for *L'Intransigeant* on 3 January 1922. Picasso is "unceasingly re-juvenated"; Braque has "delicacy" and "charm", "so very French"; Léger's is "a totally modern activity", all "force"; and Gris is summed up with the two words "engaging austerity"[46]. The valencies of that interactive field of contrasting characterisations which has become a given in historical assessments of the four Cubist "masters", Kahnweiler's Cubists, are all there, succinctly evaluated one against the other: the restless Picasso, on the move; the tasteful Braque, being "French"; the "modern" Léger, being forceful; and the "austere" Gris, engaging serious attention.

Gris never supplied so full a picture of himself as a personality integral to the central Cubist configuration, but, in the 1920s, he did offer a sequence of verbal statements that more than adequately substantiated the image of modesty, method and "austerity", to be set against the contrasting images of Picasso, Braque and Léger. Most comprehensively he did so in the lecture he gave in 1924 to Dr René Allendy's "Société des études philosophiques et scientifiques pour l'examen des idées nouvelles" at the Sorbonne. This lecture, Kahnweiler later claimed, in its published German and English translations, did more to establish Gris's reputation than any exhibition in his lifetime[47].

Strikingly, Gris placed his thoughts in three contexts: art, of course, but also philosophy and especially mathematics and science. His metaphor for the constants of pictorial structure is the "painter's mathematics"; his metaphor for the total pictorial conception, what he calls "architecture", is the synthesis of a chemical compound. Clarity is one of the declared principles that guides the entire text. In 1925 Gris answered the request for a statement on Cubism from the *Bulletin de la vie artistique* with a short account of his "evolution" as a Cubist. With great cogency, he describes it as a single, straight line of development, from "a purely descriptive and analytic representation" of things to an art that deals with "the relations between the things in themselves". He then encapsulates his entire career in a single, containing scientific metaphor: "Before the existence of physics as a science," he writes, "physical phenomena were described and classified"[48]. His evolution has been, he suggests, from a simple taxonomy to a "physics" of painting.

When, in February 1920, Gris answered a request for a few biographical facts from Kahnweiler, he opened his chronology thus: "born on March 23, 1887; studied something of physics and mathematics"[49]. It has now been established that Gris actually studied at the School of Arts and Industries in Madrid, an education that could take him only as far as a certificate of aptitude, not a full technical qualification, and in which he probably learned the skills necessary to be an illustrator and caricaturist[50]. Yet, however preliminary his technical training, he saw to it that his origins, as well as his painting, would always be connected with mathematics and science. Consistently, he built on Apollinaire's phrase, "the demon of logic", to complement the lucid immaculacy of his pictures and the harmonious chimings of Raynal and George.

By the date of his death, in May 1927, his work, his statements and those of his critic-friends had constructed a "Juan Gris" who could be accepted not merely as one of the core Cubist quartet, but actually as *the* leader of a Cubist second phase. In 1918–19 Léonce Rosenberg put together a series of exhibitions of work by the leading Cubists at his newly opened Galerie de l'Effort Moderne. Gris showed around fifty pictures in April 1919, following exhibitions of Laurens, Metzinger, Léger and Braque. In June Picasso marked the climax of the campaign, for campaign it was: a well-planned and disciplined campaign to demonstrate that Cubism had survived the war in a new "collective" form, marked by a new intellectual rigour[51]. The Cubism of what was already dubbed the "call to order" was promoted, in a sense, in the image of "Juan Gris"; if Picasso always remained Cubism's accepted "creator", Gris was easily placed in the role of the instigator behind its later development.

Interviewed in 1926 by Jacques Guenne for *L'Art Vivant*, the painter-writer André Lhote (briefly in 1916–17 one of Rosenberg's Cubists), identified a "second Cubism", "invented by Picasso", but "reduced to formulas by Juan Gris and Diego Rivera"[52]. By the date of Rosenberg's L'Effort Moderne exhibitions Rivera, like Lhote, had rejected this "second Cubism". So the inference was clear: Picasso, being beyond "schools", left Gris the leader. It was a Catalan, Sebastiá Gasch (friend and ally of Miró and Dalí), who wrote perhaps the fullest endorsement of Gris's leadership of a second Cubism during the 1920s. He did so in *Le Veu de Catalunya* in January 1928, and Zervos published a French translation simultaneously in *Cahiers d'Art*. Gasch wrote as a committed opponent. For him, Surrealism and most uncompromisingly Miró's "assassination" of the formal values in painting was an anarchic reaction against the cold logic of a "second period of cubism", for which Gris was *the* exemplar. Gasch's text respects Gris, but dismisses what he is seen to stand for: intellectual "abstraction" "logically" imposed upon things. Gris has led Cubism into the "impasse" of the cerebral[53].

It is, then, clear that by 1933, the date of Gris's Zurich retrospective, of Zervos's special Gris number of *Cahiers d'Art*, and of Gertrude Stein's *The Autobiography of Alice B. Toklas*, the humble "artisan" Juan Gris who represented "the triumph of clarity" was firmly established as a Cubist who had followed only to become a leader. The ground was well prepared for the extensive cultivation of this "logical" Cubist as the necessary complement to the divergent historical images of Picasso, Braque and Léger. The cultivation of that image as part of a whole took place most influentially between the late 1950s and the early 1970s (it was done with respect, indeed affection).

Kahnweiler's second monograph of 1946 gave considerable encouragement. It re-published most of Gris's statements of the 1920s and, in the context of a metaphysical discussion that ranged from philosophy in the Kantian tradition to non-Saussurean linguistics, insisted on a Gris who could not tolerate "equivocation"[54]. The Gris of Douglas Cooper's extensive writings on the artist and on Cubism is emphatically Waldemar George's and Raynal's "austere" painter-thinker. This is how he sums him up in contrast to the "intuition" and "fantasy" he finds in Picasso and Braque: "Gris's work reflects his intellectual lucidity and integrity, as well as his scientifically conditioned mind." He extended the "possibilities of Cubism in a limited field of his own until he arrived at a logical conclusion"[55].

Still more influentially, this too is the Gris of John Golding's crucially formative history of Cubism, although he resists such bald encapsulating judgements[56]. And this is the Gris that still emerges in discussions of Cubism when the attention of specialists switches momentarily away from Picasso and Braque. Thus Edward Fry, in his major re-thinking of Cubism in terms of the conventions of classicism, can decisively differentiate the flexible relativism of Picasso and Braque from what he calls the "affinity" of "such artists as Gris" for "Cartesian *a priori* thought, a tendency that may be traced back through Seurat or the Ecole des Beaux-Arts and even David to the long tradition of French classicism itself"[57]. There have been recent attempts to play down the method and the "purity" of Gris, the "integral Cubist"[58], yet the Gris made by the finished definition of his painting, by the clarity of his statements and by the criticism that sustained him is the Gris we still can but see and with whom I must contend.

I end this essay by pointing to a few signs left by those most responsible for the formation of the "Cartesian" Juan Gris that a more complex, open, contradictory, even equivocal Gris was to be experienced in his painting and that, despite the tenor of so much said about him, they knew this Gris well.

First, there is Waldemar George in his little monograph of 1931. "A dualist principle," George writes, "ruled his work and life. This aetheist, this revolutionary, this absentee from the Spanish army, had a singular penchant for alchemy and astrology. This doctrinaire, this acerbic logician, transgressed the accepted limits of rational logic. Juan Gris, the calculator, was only such in exact measure with the extent to which his calculations served the ends of poetic expression"[59]. Perhaps George knew that in February 1923 Gris had been initiated into the Grand Orient of France as a Free Mason. In fact, as I shall show more fully in my essay on the figure, Free Masonry in France was at this time dominated by an ethos of secular rationalism. Nonetheless, it is probable that, for Gris, a crucial attraction was its deep tradition of mysticism, connected as it was with Alchemy and the hermetic sciences[60]. Whatever George had specifically in mind, this is the preface to a passage in which he treated Gris the theoretician (whose perspicacity he had so praised in 1921) with something close to contempt. For George now, Gris's theoretical justifications are a pretence: "His actions, his pictures, found their *raison d'être,* their justification, not in the vain commentaries to which he gave himself, but in their own law and their own context". What mattered was that Gris "could express himself frankly, spontaneously"[61].

Then, perhaps most surprisingly, there is Raynal. As we shall see, Raynal, one of Gris's closest and most loyal friends, was very like him as writer and theoretician in the 1920s. Yet, he used the preface he wrote for the exhibition at the Galerie Balaÿ et Carré in 1938 to discount utterly Gris the intellectual and the theorist. He wrote acidly of "a naïve thirst for meta-understanding", of the "laboured construction" of theories that distracted from the "magnificent plastic achievements that he had imagined altogether without them"[62]. He made, publicly, a retraction.

Then finally there is Carl Einstein, one of Kahnweiler's closest intellectual confidants and another tried admirer of Gris. In 1929 Einstein reviewed an exhibition in Zurich that placed the Cubists in relation to "abstract art". Gris, here, is named as one of the core Cubist quartet in strict opposition to an abstraction which is to be aligned with science. "The pictures of Picasso, Braque, Gris, Léger constitute the inventories of experiences, rich and audacious. For them it is never a case of illustrating programmes, but of discovering particular solutions; and, in the domaine of art, only the particular and the exception are decisive, contrary to what occurs in the domaine of science, where the scientists make of their discoveries metaphysical facts, helped by their limitless generalisations"[63]. Gris too was presented as committed first to "experience", *against* the abstractions of science.

I have mentioned the words "special distillation" on the label of the bottle of Anis del Mono in Gris's *papier collé* of June 1914 as a phrase that applies to his, Picasso's and Braque's Cubism. Another label that he stuck onto more than one of his *papiers collés* in 1914 came from cigarette packets; it referred to taxation with the words: "indirect contributions" (Plate 45)[64]. After his death, George, Raynal and Einstein could all evoke a Gris more concerned with experience than with logical thinking. In 1914 Gris himself could even suggest the possibility of equivocation.

1 Christian Zervos, 'Juan Gris et l'inquiétude d'aujourd'hui', *Cahiers d'Art,* Paris, 1926, no. 10, pp. 260–74.
2 C(hristian) Z(ervos), 'Juan Gris', *Cahiers d'Art,* Paris, 1927, no. 6, p. 170.
3 Especially relevant here is Léger's positive use of the term "artisan" in the subtitle of his lecture 'L'Esthétique de la machine'. See Fernand Léger, 'L'Esthétique de la machine', lecture given in June 1923, first published in *Der Querschnitt,* Berlin, vol.III, 1923 and *Bulletin de l'Effort Moderne,* Paris, nos. 1 and 2, January and February 1924; in Fernand Léger, *Fonctions de la Peinture,* Paris, 1965.
4 'Juan Gris', *Cahiers d'Art,* Paris, 1933, no. 5–6, p. 177.
5 Daniel Robbins has claimed that the "serious historical study of Cubism" begins in the late 1920s. He cites Guillaume Janneau, *L'Art cubiste,* Paris, 1929. If a distinction is made with partisan criticism, this seems tenable. See Daniel Robbins, 'Abbreviated Historiography of Cubism', *Art Journal,* Winter, 1988, pp. 277–83.
6 Gris's contract with Kahnweiler is dated 12 February 1913, Léger's 20 October 1913. Agnès Angliviel de La Baumelle has pointed out, however, that Gris is unexpectedly not included in the Munich edition of Kahnweiler's *Der Weg zum Kubismus* in 1920, although Léger is. Despite this, Gris's contract with Kahnweiler was renewed by 23 December 1920. From that date the dealer certainly had no doubts about his importance. See *Donation Louise et Michel Leiris, Collection Kahnweiler-Leiris,* Centre Georges Pompidou, Musée National d'Art Moderne, Paris, 1984, pp. 52–61 and 114.
7 Gertrude Stein, *The Autobiography of Alice B.Toklas,* New York, 1933, p. 111.
8 Ibid., p. 259.
9 Marcel Duchamp, 'Juan Gris', *Catalogue of the "Société Anonyme",* New Haven, 1950.
10 Gris's dealings and relationship with Léonce Rosenberg as a whole are best followed in Christian Derouet, *Juan Gris: Correspondance, Dessins 1915–21,* IVAM Centre Julio González, Valencia and Centre Georges Pompidou, Musée National d'Art Moderne, Paris, 1990–91. For a discussion in relation to the letters published there and to newly discovered correspondence between Gris and Léonce Rosenberg, see Christian Derouet's essay below.
11 Beaulieu-lès-Loches, 26 November 1918. Ibid., p. 67.
12 Picasso was in a strong enough position not to have needed a contract with Léonce Rosenberg.
13 See André Salmon, *Souvenirs sans fin, Deuxième époque (1908–1920),* Paris, 1956, p. 246 and *Troisième époque (1920–1940),* Paris, 1961, p. 277.
14 'La Palette' (André Salmon), 'Courrier des ateliers: Exposition probable', *Paris-Journal,* Tuesday, 2 January 1912, pp. 4–5.
15 The portrait was no.1426 in the catalogue.
16 André Salmon, 'Le Salon des Indépendants', *Paris-Journal,* Tuesday, 19 March 1912, p. 5.
17 Guillaume Apollinaire, 'Le Vernissage', *L'Intransigeant,* 25 March 1912; in *Apollinaire on Art: Essays and Reviews* 1902–1918, edited by Leroy C. Breunig, translated by Susan Suleiman, New York and London, 1972, p. 214.
18 Guillaume Apollinaire, 'La Section d'Or', *L'Intransigeant,* 10 October 1912. Ibid., p. 254.
19 Cited in Judith Cousins, with the collaboration of Pierre Daix, 'Documentary Chronology'; in William Rubin, *Picasso and Braque: Pioneering Cubism,* The Museum of Modern Art, New York, 1989, p. 389.
20 Jarry was firmly associated with the anti-logical because of his satire of 1898, *Gestes et opinions du docteur Faustroll, pataphysicien.*
21 This genre of reading Cubist papiers collés is indebted initially to Robert Rosenblum. See Robert Rosenblum, 'Picasso and the Typography of Cubism'; in *Picasso 1881–1973,* ed. Roland Penrose and John Golding, London, 1973, pp. 49–73.
22 See especially Salmon (1956), op.cit., p. 93. Referring to this period in the "Bateau-Lavoir", Salmon writes: "Dans mes derniers de Montmartre, la vie changeait beaucoup. Picasso allait laisser bientôt le Bateau-Lavoir pour le boulevard de Clichy. L'austère Juan Gris allait, dans le même batiment, remplacer le frénetique Jacques Vaillant..."
23 Enrique Echea, 'En la ruta de la Celebrad', *ABC,* Madrid, 28 August 1951; Vásquez Diaz, 'Juan Gris o la Creciente Vocacion', 'Sus Primeros Dibujos en las Prensa de Paris', and 'Juan Gris y Nustra Vieja Amistrad', *ABC,* 5 May 1957, 8 March 1966, and 27 September 1966.
24 See Pierre Daix and Joan Rosselet, *Picasso, the Cubist Years, 1907–1916, A Catalogue Raisonné of the Paintings and Related Works,* London, 1979, p. 247.
25 See Judith Cousins (1989), op.cit., p. 384.
26 Cited, ibid., p. 391.
27 The closeness of their relationship emerges clearly in Rubin (1989), op.cit., see especially 'Picasso and Braque: an Introduction', pp. 15–53.
28 The near certainty that *Still-life with Flowers* was the still-life exhibited at the Indépendants of 1912 is established by the new correspondence discovered by Christian Derouet and discussed by him in his essay below. The evidence is in a letter detailing pictures sold and exhibited, sent by Gris to Léonce Rosenberg on 10 August 1917. Gris refers to the Indépendants pictures as size 40 in format. In fact, neither *Homage to Pablo Picasso* nor *Still-life with Flowers* is size 40, but *Homage* is a little smaller and the *Still-life* a little larger (110x68 cm as against 100x81 cm, 100x73 cm or 100x65 cm), and no other still-life is as comparable in scale. I am grateful to both Georges González Gris and to Christian Derouet for allowing me to see the correspondence in question before its full publication as part of an edition of Gris's writings planned by the publisher of this catalogue in the near future. This important newly-discovered correspondence has been consulted for factual and corroborative material, but will not be quoted in these essays. Significant quoted passages from it are, however, to be found in Christian Derouet's essay below.
29 The format is 110x68cm. Braque's *Piano and Mandola* is 91.8x42.9 cm, but his *Violin and Pitcher* of the same series compares closely to the Gris: 117x75 cm. Braque painted several vertical still-lives on this scale in 1910–11. These are often standard landscape format canvases stood on their heads, as it were, and never standard "figure" formats (following the system used early in the century), but they remain figurative in size and vertical in orientation. Significantly, *Still-life with Flowers* is actually more vertical and larger than *Homage to Pablo Picasso,* see note 28 above.

30 Lucy Adelman and Michael Compton were the first to publish this drawing and note its inclusion of the ratio. See Lucy Adelman and Michael Compton, 'Mathematics in early abstract art'; in *Towards a New Art: Essays on the Background to Abstract Art, 1910–1920,* ed. Michael Compton, Tate Gallery, London, 1980, pp. 76–7.
31 One such resolved drawing in the collection of the Musée Picasso is *Woman Playing a Guitar* of summer-autumn 1911, M.P. 662.
32 *Flowers in Vase,* 1911–12, charcoal on paper, Indiana University Art Museum, Bloomington, Jane and Roger Wolcott Memorial.
33 See Chapter 2 below for a fuller discussion.
34 The latest that can be loosely related are Cooper nos.586 and 619, dated by him November-December 1926 and February–April 1927.
35 For the dating of Picasso's *Still-life with Chair Caning,* see William Rubin, *Picasso in the Collection of The Museum of Modern Art,* The Museum of Modern Art, New York, 1972, p. 207, note 1.
36 Cooper no. 44, dated by him July 1913.
37 The crucial discussion of the dating of the card-board Guitar is Edward Fry, 'Picasso, Cubism and Reflexivity', *Art Journal,* Winter, 1988, pp. 305–6, note 24.
38 The most important recent discussions are Ibid, and Yves-Alain Bois, 'Kahnweiler's Lesson', *Representations,* Spring, 1987, pp. 33–68. See also chapter 4 below.
39 This claim was most tellingly made by D.-H. Kahnweiler in 'L'Art nègre et le cubisme', *Présence Africaine,* Paris-Dakar, no. 3, 1948; in *Confessions esthétiques,* Paris, 1963, pp. 222–36.
40 The other work to stress the sculptural by tonal modelling is Cooper no. 54, also dated September 1913.
41 Their contribution is discussed fully in later chapters.
42 Waldemar George, 'Une Exposition du groupe', *L'Esprit Nouveau,* Paris, no. 9, June, 1921, n.p.
43 Waldemar George, 'Juan Gris', *L'Amour de l'art,* Paris, November 1921, p. 351.
44 Maurice Raynal, 'Juan Gris', *L'Esprit Nouveau,* Paris, no. 5, 1921, pp. 540–9.
45 C.f. Green (1987), op.cit., p. 178 and p. 312, note 59.
46 Maurice Raynal, 'Les Arts: Exposition de l'Effort Moderne', *L'Intransigeant,* Tuesday, 3 January 1922.
47 Gris, Lecture (1924); in Kahnweiler (1968), op.cit., p. 53.
48 Gris (1925); in ibid., p. 203.
49 Ibid., p. 31.
50 Although archives for this school do not survive, since it was later divided into two, this much has been established by Gaya Nuño. See, Juan Antonio Gaya Nuño, *Juan Gris,* translated from Spanish by Kenneth Lyons, London, 1975, pp. 36–50.
51 For the military character of Rosenberg's campaign, see *Correspondance* (Derouet), 1990-91, op.cit., p. 25 (Letter 1).
52 Jacques Guenne, 'André Lhote', *L'Art Vivant,* Paris, 1926, p. 179.
53 Sebastiá Gasch in 'Journaux et périodiques', *Cahiers d'Art,* Paris, no. 1, 1928, p. 48.
54 The monograph did not include the text of Gris's interview with Georges Charensol, published in *Paris-Journal,* 25 April 1924.
55 Douglas Cooper, *The Cubist Epoch,* New York, 1971, pp. 229–30.
56 John Golding, *Cubism: a History and an Analysis, 1907–1914,* London, 1959, 1968 and 1988.
57 Fry (1988), op.cit., p. 297.
58 See especially Mark Rosenthal, *Juan Gris,* Berkeley University Art Museum, 1983.
59 Waldemar George, *Juan Gris,* Paris, 1931, p. 6.
60 My thanks are due to Georges González Gris, who has given me invaluable help with the bibliography for Gris and Free Masonry. The Grand Orient de France has put on its own exhibition of Gris for which a catalogue was published: *Hommage à Juan Gris (1887–1927),* Grand Orient de France, 16 rue Cadet, 75009 Paris, 3–26 June 1987. The most comprehensive, but still a distinctly preliminary treatment of the topic is José A. García Diego, *Antonio Machado y Juan Gris, Dos artistas masones,* Madrid, 1990. Ishi-Kawa discusses, in a suggestive but still preliminary way, the theme of mysticism and numerology in Free Masonry in relation to Gris. See L. Ishi-Kawa, *Aproximación a Gris: ocho marcos para once cuadros,* Fundación "Arte y Technología" for Telefónica de España, S.A., 1990, pp. 37–38. For further discussion, see chapter 6 below.
61 Waldemar George (1931), op. cit., pp. 7–8.
62 Maurice Raynal, 'Juan Gris'; in *Juan Gris,* catalogue of the exhibition held between 13 June and 3 July 1938, Roland Balaÿ et Louis Carré, Paris, 1938, pp. 5–6.
63 Carl Einstein, 'L'Exposition de l'art abstrait à Zurich', *Documents,* Paris, 1st Year, no. 6, 1929, p. 342.
64 See Cooper no. 101 also.

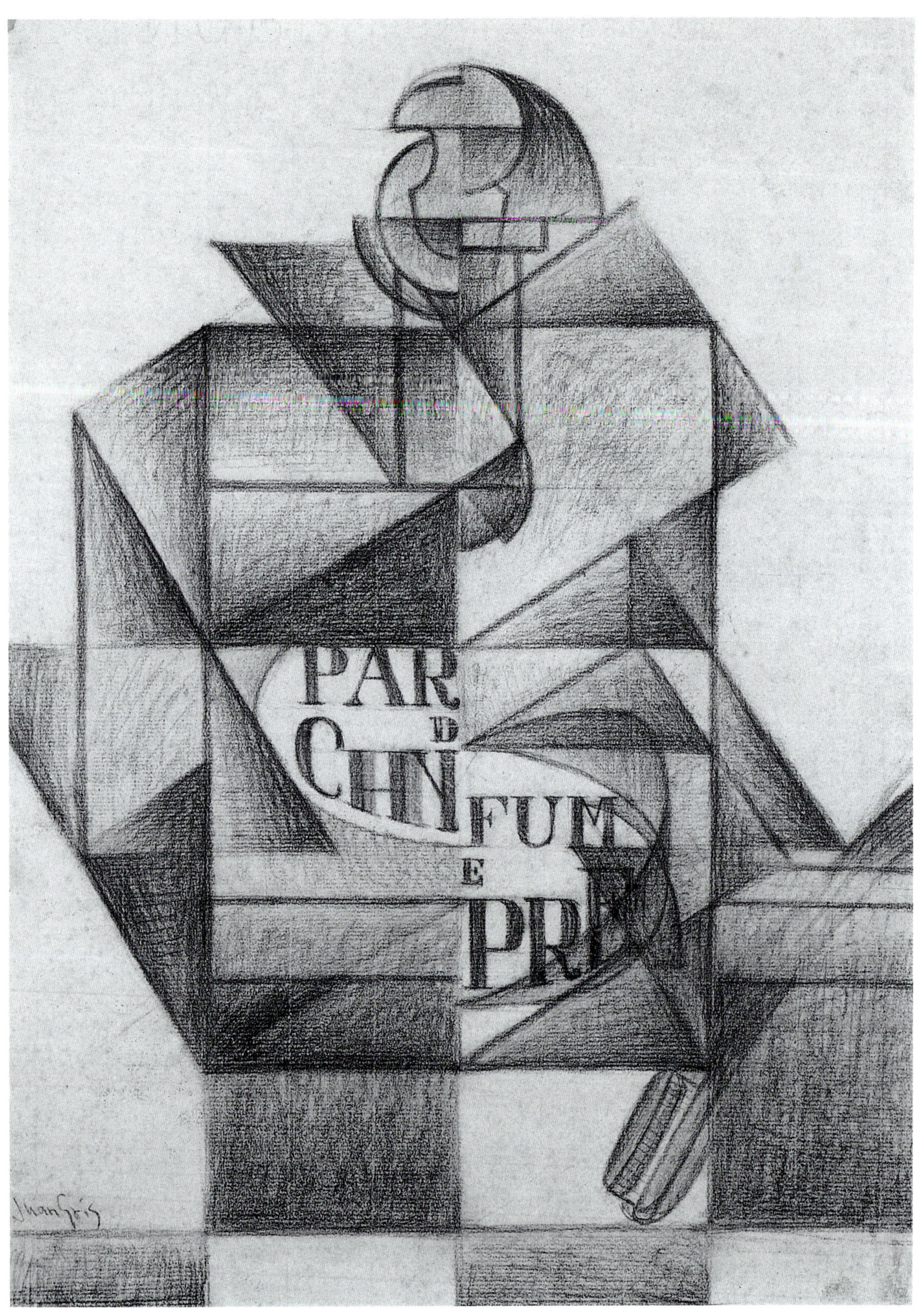
PAR
D
CHN
FUM
E
PRE
Juan Gris

2. 1910–1916: The Demon of Logic?

The tendency to contain Juan Gris in a circle circumscribed by the names Picasso, Braque and (sometimes) Léger is inadequate in one obvious way. He moved in other circles too.

When Gris made his debut at the Indépendants of 1912, he instantly became engaged with the group of "Salon Cubists" around Jean Metzinger, Albert Gleizes, Henri Le Fauconnier and the Duchamp brothers that met regularly in the suburban studios of Courbevoie and Puteaux. Metzinger was to remain a friend[1]. Historically "Cubism" is as much to be identified with the growing sense of a common pursuit of the structural in painting generated by Metzinger, Gleizes and Le Fauconnier between 1910 and 1912 as with the extraordinary pictorial inventions of Picasso and Braque before 1910[2]. When Gris began seriously to work alongside Picasso at the end of 1911, Picasso was acknowledged by Apollinaire and Salmon to be the originator of Cubism, but Jean Metzinger was considered a leader too. The Salon group first came together at the Indépendants of 1911, showing in the notorious "Salle 41". Apollinaire's response was to underline Picasso's precedence, but he allowed that Metzinger was "a cubist in the proper sense of the word"[3]. Responding to the group's second showing at the Salon d'Automne of 1911, Salmon called Metzinger: "the young prince of Cubism"[4]. Five months later, Gris's *Homage to Pablo Picasso* (Plate 10), with its clear combination of geometric structure and "analytic" depiction, unmistakably responded to the Picasso of the Vollard portrait (Figure 2) through an intermediary. That intermediary was Metzinger's *Tea-time* (Figure 7), his contribution to the 1911 Automne; it had widely been acknowledged the key Cubist exhibit[5].

Just before the opening of the 1911 Automne, Gleizes published a major article on Metzinger in *La Revue indépendante*. The Metzinger he characterized is an uncanny anticipation, in certain essentials, of the Gris who was to be given the role of Cubist "logician" from 1912. Metzinger, he writes, is "haunted by the desire to inscribe the total image". Further, "to purely objective truth he wishes to add a new truth, born from what his intelligence permits him to know". This "truth" permitted by "intelligence" was embodied, for Gleizes, in the multiplication of "the visual field" (that is, the combination in a single image of many view-points) and was given "equilibrium" by a geometric structure of "cubes"[6]. Metzinger, incidentally, had been the first to write about "mobile perspective", as early as 1910 and in connection with Picasso[7]. Here, the action of intelligence in painting is firmly attached to mobile perspective controlled by a simplifying "cubic" geometry. Metzinger's *Tea-time* is like a pictorial demonstration of Gleizes's text.

At the same time this picture can seem the outcome of a meditation on intelligence and the senses, conception and sensation. The word in French for tea-time is "le goûter"; as a verb, "goûter" refers to the experience of tasting. Metzinger's simplistic geometric depiction gives us a "pretty" woman naked to the waist, her left hand lightly touching the

Parfum de Chypre,
1911–12
Pencil on paper,
41.9x30,5 cm
Private Collection

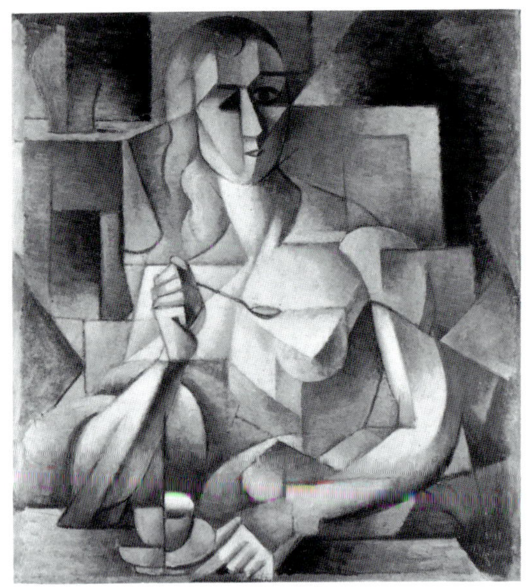

Figure 7
Jean Metzinger
Tea-time, 1911
Oil on wood,
75.6 x 69.5 cm
Philadelphia Museum of Art: The Louise and Walter Arensberg Collection

saucer of a cup, her right hand holding a spoon suspended between cup and mouth. Phenomenologically, touch and taste are states of such immediate intensity that the subject (the toucher or taster) and the object become indistinguishable in the moment of sensation[8]. The suggestion of the senses in a state of activation is acute here. But mobile perspective and geometry signify the total control of intelligence. The tasting and touching of the woman is something known, not felt, and a clear division is erected between sensation and conception. It is stated as the formulation of a problem.

Gris's *Homage to Pablo Picasso* certainly signifies the control of intelligence through mobile perspective and geometric structure, but it does not allude to the problem of sensation except indirectly by the colours on the palette. Occasionally, however, in 1912–13 Gris set up the basic confrontation between intelligence and the senses in a way distinctly reminiscent of Metzinger's picture. He approaches such a thing in *Man in the Café* (Plate 21), one of the Gris's in the Section d'Or of 1912 that excited Apollinaire's remark "the demon of logic". But perhaps most plainly of all he does so in *The Smoker*, painted at Céret in 1913 (Figure 8). The right hand of the earlier man in the café is in the act of resting and touching, while in front of him anticipated pleasures are signalled: the open box of cigars, the glass. A cigar is in the mouth of *The Smoker*. It swings up as the head rocks to the left (the images repeated), and the lazy curl of its smoke transgresses the strict regulatory order of a geometric structure. That wisp of smoke wittily attests to the light pleasures of smoking as Gris "intelligently" takes apart his smoker and puts him back together again.

Gleizes's text on his friend Metzinger was one of the first to outline what has been called the conceptual view of Cubism. It was Maurice Raynal, already the close friend of Gris, who most influentially codified the view, and he did so in the summer that separated Gris's *Homage to Pablo Picasso* from his showing of *Man in the Café* at the Section d'Or, with the publication of his article 'Conception et vision' in the newspaper *Gil Blas*. As Metzinger and Gris set up conception and sensation in diametric opposition, so did Raynal, and he too placed mobile perspective at the crux, as the means to a conceptual

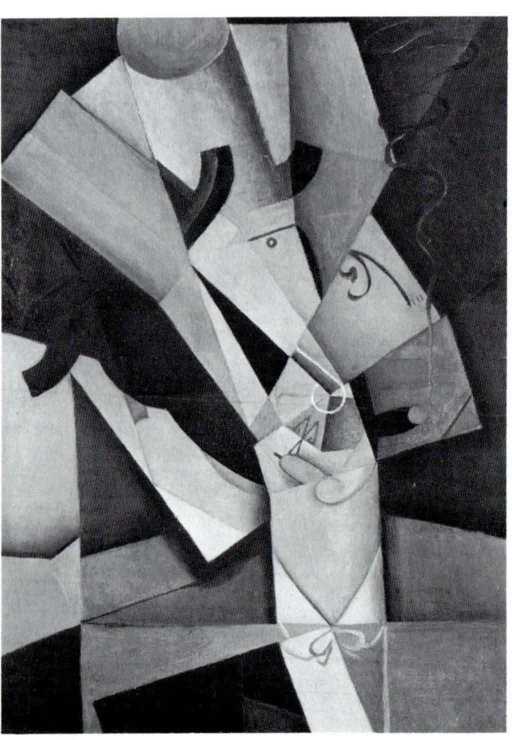

Figure 8
The Smoker, 1913
Oil an canvas,
73.5 x 54.5 cm
Private Collection

representation of things in painting beyond the simply visual. "We never, in fact, see an object in all its dimensions at once," he argues. "Therefore what has to be done is to fill in the gap in our seeing. Conception gives us the means. Conception makes us aware of objects that we would not be able to see... and so, if the painter succeeds in rendering the object in all its dimensions, he achieves a work of method which is of a higher order than one painted according to the visual dimensions only"[9]. By 1919, having returned from the front to the Paris of Léonce Rosenberg's "call to order" with Gris at its head, Raynal had taken this to the extent of a radical Idealist division between conception and sensation. He quoted Plato in his pamphlet *Quelques Intentions du cubisme*: "The senses perceive that which passes, the understanding that which endures"[10]. And he, like Gris, found support in scientific analogy, remarking: "In the sciences, hypothesis is everything, the senses operate only as "tools". To discover the laws of the decomposition of light, Newton saw no more clearly than anyone else. Huber, the great observer of bees, was blind"[11].

In Cubism, intelligence in painting was first thought of thus: it was the application of the artist's conceptual powers to go beyond sensation, and it implied the strict division of pictorial thinking from simple sensation; hence the poignancy of Metzinger's and Gris's allusions to the most immediate of sensations, touch and taste. From the beginning, fundamental to this notion of conceptual painting was mobile perspective, the practice of the part-by-part dissection of things from different view-points that Gris himself later called "analysis". Conceptual painting was strictly divorced from the so-called painting of "vision", but it was understood to use vision, analytically, like the apparatus of a scientist. This was one elementary level on which Cubist painting could be considered logical, and it was initially formulated precisely as Gris worked through his first Cubisms in 1911–12. If Gris was the Cubist logician, he was the one seen most clearly to divide "conception" from "vision", and the one thought most rigorously to "analyse" the things he painted. On the day that Apollinaire coined the phrase "the demon of logic" for Gris, he opened a piece on "Cubism" published elsewhere with his own gloss on Raynal's formulation: "Cubism," Apollinaire wrote, "is the art of painting new configurations with elements borrowed not from visual but from conceptual reality"[12].

There was, however, another direction from which the conceptual, the logical, the scientific and the mathematical could be read into Cubist painting. There is a clear hint of it in Gleizes's 1911 article on Metzinger when he suggests a two-stage process in pictorial conception: first, the multiplication of the "visual field" (analysis) but then the controlling use of "the cube... to re-establish... equilibrium". Visual dissection takes things apart; pictorial structuring (a painter's "mathematics") puts them together again[13]. Raynal echoes this two-stage understanding of picture-conception when, in the essay he wrote for the *Bulletin de la Section d'Or* in 1912, he explains that the "analysis" of things into their component parts is to be followed by "a synthetic task", the bringing together of these elements into a "new whole"[14]. The other direction from which a conceptual order could be seen in Cubist painting was that of pictorial structure, considered as an abstraction, on the same level as number and geometry. It went with that version of Cubism that accentuated "pure" painting, the autonomy of the work of art. The conceptual version of Cubism placed representation at the centre of painting, whereas the "pure" version can seem to deny it. The conflict was resolved (effectively but not altogether convincingly) by the two-stage theory of process.

Gris's *Man in the Café* and the most recent of his contributions to the Salon de la Section d'Or, such as *The Watch* (Plate 22), have been shown to be carefully modulated displays of proportional composition using squares and Golden Section rectangles[15]. That summer of

1912, when these more recent pictures were painted[16], had seen much discussion of systems of proportion, supported by reference to Leonardo, Alberti and others[17]. In *L'Intransigeant*, as well as the *Bulletin de la Section d'Or*, Apollinaire stressed the linkage between the new Cubist "salon" and "antiquity's Measure of Beauty"[18]. More or less rigorously, Gris was to apply the flexible methods of Golden Section composing periodically throughout his career, to control or later to generate pictorial ideas. Almost certainly they are in use late in 1916 in establishing the geometric armatures of *Woman with a Mandolin, after Corot* and *Portrait of Madame Josette Gris* for instance (Figure 9 and Plate 66), and at the end of 1917 and during 1918 in, for example, *Pipe and Fruit Dish with Grapes* and *The Guitar* (Plates 78 and 79)[19].

Besides his friendship with Maurice Raynal, Gris kept another close friendship with a writer unbroken from his earliest Cubist studies around 1911 until his death. This was with the poet Pierre Reverdy. Despite the periods of high tension typical of Reverdy's relations with people, their relationship was generally close and positive, especially between 1917 and 1920, a period when Reverdy explored flexible metric rhythms in his poetry as Gris explored proportion[20]. It is Reverdy who most succinctly connects the notion of compositional structure with the notion of logical order. He does so in his little book *Self Defence* which was published in 1919 with a dedication to Gris. "The logic of a work of art," he writes, "is in its structure. The moment the ensemble holds together and is balanced, it is logical"[21].

Two directions from which to scrutinize Gris as "the demon of logic" are, then, conception and structure, as they were thought of in the circles he frequented. Those circles, and therefore the most immediate of the contexts for any scrutiny, were not restricted to Picasso, Braque and Montmartre, even before the 1914–18 war. They included, importantly, Metzinger and the Puteaux group (especially in 1911–12), and from 1916 Léonce Rosenberg's "L'Effort Moderne", along with Pierre Reverdy and many others.

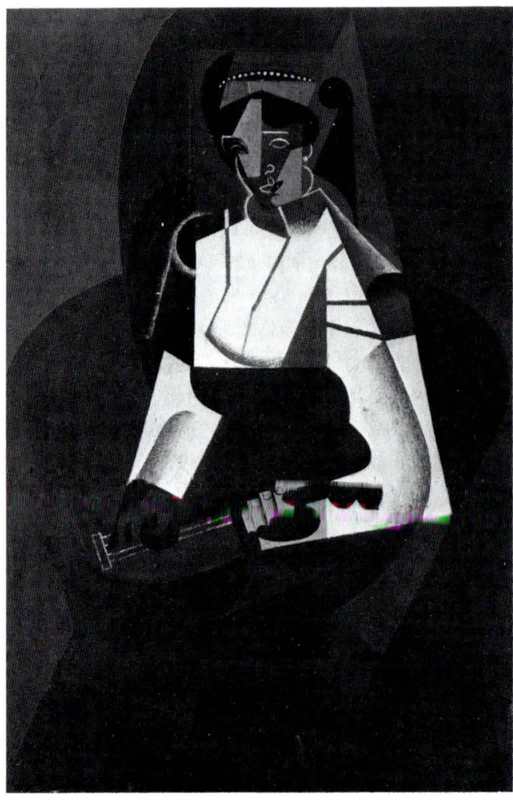

Figure 9
Woman with a Mandolin, (after Corot), 1916
Oil on plywood,
92 x 60 cm
Öffentliche Kunstsammlung Basel, Kunstmuseum

The number and diameter of the circles that can be taken to form the context(s) of an artist's work are not easy to fix. Recently William Rubin has remarked that the appalling French revealed by Picasso's correspondence before 1914 establishes that he could not have read any of the authors usually considered significantly contextual to Cubism: Bergson, Poincaré, Lévy-Bruhl, Mauss, etc. The sophisticated French of such texts was simply beyond his capabilities at this stage[22]. These are areas, he infers, clearly outside the circles of Picasso's context. The French revealed by Gris's correspondence is not perfect, but it is more than adequate, and Josette Gris told me that he was distinctly proud of it. Even before 1914 he could certainly have read the "difficult" French of Mallarmé's late poetry, which he seems to have done, as well as Bergson, Poincaré, Lévy-Bruhl and Mauss, which he probably did not[23].

So narrow a fixing of contextual limits argues a peculiarly one-dimensional view of painting. It takes as relevant only the immediate relationship between the painter and the painting, as if the meanings of paintings are (*can* be) discovered only by the reconstruction of the painter's specific attitudes and intentions at the moment of its making. Yet, the painting, once made, carries its meanings into the various social milieux in which it can be seen. The meanings it can convey are increasingly determined by the experience and knowledge, the mentalities of its viewers. Especially after he signed his contract with Kahnweiler in February 1913, Gris's "audience" was limited, but Kahnweiler himself, the other painters close to Gris, the writers (Apollinaire, Salmon, Reverdy, Raynal, Jacob *et al*), the collectors initiated by Kahnweiler, like Rupf, and the enthusiasts, like Wilhelm Uhde and Gertrude Stein, certainly brought more than Gris alone could to pictures like *Man in the Café* (purchased by Léonce Rosenberg in 1914) or the *papier collé Fruit Dish and Carafe* (purchased by Uhde) (Plate 40). Further, the image once made exists not only in actual exchanges with its viewers, but also in a field of *possible* conception and experience, as a product of its time and society. It is a statement that enters current discourses of not only, say, culture, but also perhaps science. Gris's paintings, seen as logical conceptions and structures, had much wider ramifications than he, intentionally, could put into them.

I shall return, however, for the moment, to the narrower context of Gris's milieux and to the discussions of conception and structure that went on in it. Towards the end of the 1914–18 war, and immediately afterwards, the two-stage theory of process in Cubist art, beginning with "analysis" and ending with "synthesis", was modified in a highly significant way. It was applied as a principle of all artistic development, making possible the construction of a new story-line for the history of Cubism altogether: earlier Cubism would be called "analytic", later Cubism "synthetic". The development from analysis to synthesis was seen to characterize an historical as well as a picture-making process.

Gris himself was to insist on his personal development as a development from "analysis" to "synthesis" in his statements of the 1920s (his account of a move from a taxonomy to a "physics" of painting, for instance)[24], but in doing so he applied a general periodizing principle then widely established. Whatever Raynal might have said about analysis as the conceptual mode in art, by the 1920s it was often associated with a commitment to the flux of visual experience, and set against the synthetic which was considered *fully* conceptual. By 1922, Waldemar George's reading of Heinrich Wölfflin's *Principles of Art History* had led him to see "conception" and "vision" in painting as cyclical phases which inevitably succeed one another: Impressionism becomes a cyclical return to the painting of appearances whose beginnings are seen to lie in the Baroque; Cubism becomes a cyclical return to the painting of the "intrinsic quality" of things, to a "Classic" art[25]. In the particular context of the Great War and vanguard culture, analysis was not merely identified as the necessary preliminary to synthesis; it was also identified with a notion of pre-War dissolution to set against subsequent integration: the collective "call to order" of L'Effort Moderne. In 1919, Paul Dermée, one-time colleague of Reverdy on *Nord-Sud* and another of Gris's writer friends, prefaced a planned series of articles on the Cubists thus: "Analysis before synthesis! And first the individual aesthetic attitudes of each of the cubist painters... Then the search for what is common to all – what essentially constitutes Cubism"[26].

This adaptation of the two-stage theory of process in painting to an equally reductive theory of historical development was the ground on which first Carl Einstein in 1930 and then Alfred Barr (with a succinct sweep which was irresistable) periodized the history of Cubism in terms of pre-1912 Analysis and post-1912 Synthesis[27]. It is fundamentally in these terms, following Gris himself, that historians have written of the "straight line" of his personal development. Logic has been found here too[28].

"Analysis" and "synthesis" are words that will always tend to figure in discussions of Cubism. They were words used by the Cubists, especially Gris, and by those who defended them. Now, however, their use as tools for gaining a purchase on Cubist painting and history has been rendered near obsolete either by criticism or neglect[29].

The neglect of the distinction is most obvious in the recent attempts to read Cubist painting, especially Picasso's, in the light of Structuralist and post-Structuralist theory. Rosalind Krauss's and Yves-Alain Bois's re-reading of Cubist works has gone beyond analysis and synthesis on to a meta-perceptual plane. What matters to them is the way Cubist images operate on the spectator as clusters, as systems of signs to be read. Intention and process do not matter, so neither does the analysis/synthesis distinction[30]. Yet, what this latest by-passing of the analysis/synthesis distinction has done is actually to deepen awareness of a change in Cubist art, still to be dated 1912, between something more perceptual and something more conceptual. It is as the emblem of this change that Picasso's cardboard *Guitar* of 1912 (Figure 6) has acquired almost sacred status. Using a late twentieth century terminology, Raynal's adamant division of conception from vision has been reinstated. Bois in particular takes the 1912 cardboard *Guitar* as not merely an assertion that a representation can be obviously unlike what it denotes, but as an assertion that the practice of art is artificial, the *conceptual* production of signs (a word Kahnweiler used rather differently)[31]. Because of its relation to other elements in the piece, empty spaces in Picasso's *Guitar* can designate fullness of form in the same way as a cylindrical projection can designate the sound-hole. The arbitrariness and the structural interdependency of the Saussurean sign is exposed, and what Raynal called the "visual" is cast adrift once again. The old story is told a new way.

There is another odd symmetry between the recent re-reading of Cubism around 1912 and the original formulation of the division between conception and sensation. The change to the conceptual is closely identified in both cases with so-called "primitive" art, especially African. The key stimulus for the change is now specifically pin-pointed to Grebo masks, an example of which, with projecting eye-cylinders, was probably bought by Picasso in Marseilles, in August 1912[32].

At that time, the so-called "primitive" was invoked in relation to Cubism in many forms, and more as analogy than as stimulus or source. The point is, however, that the conceptualism of Cubist painting was habitually aligned in 1912 with the presumed conceptualism of African and pre-Renaissance "primitive" images. Raynal refers to Giotto, as a European "primitive", depicting cities from more than one vantage-point. It is, for him, a model of analytic conception[33]. Apollinaire, also in autumn 1912, celebrates a "god of war" from Dahomey in the Trocadero Museum precisely as if it is a Cubist conception. "The human figure," he writes, "certainly provided the inspiration for this singular work. And yet, by a stroke of invention as funny and profound as a page of Rabelais, not one of the elements that compose it resembles any part of the human body. The African artist was obviously a 'creator'"[34].

The linkage of Cubist conceptualism to the so-called "primitive" is immensely suggestive. It parallels or echoes the then current convergence in ethnology of the question of logic and the question of the "primitive". Logic was the key concern in all the major debates about the notions of magic and "primitive mentality" from the late nineteenth century, especially in France. Marcel Mauss and Lucien Lévy-Bruhl, by far the most respected writers on the subject in France from the early twentieth century into the 1920s, both took as a starting-point J.G.Frazer's contention that magical thinking in primitive societies was a kind of logic based on mistaken premises (that the dead live because they appear in dreams, for instance)[35]. Lévy-Bruhl, in particular, argued against this in a way highly relevant to the question of logic in Cubism, as we shall see. But by far the most astonishing parallel with Cubism is found in another quarter: a short study of child-drawing made as a contribution to "developmental psychology", G.-H.Luquet's *Dessins d'un enfant* published in 1913, the year after the Section d'Or and Raynal's 'Conception et vision'.

None of the Cubists or their supporters ever mention the name Luquet before 1914, so there are no direct links here. Further, the inferred connection made by Luquet between the mentality of children and so-called "primitive mentality" has now rightly been discredited[36]. But the point remains that it was possible in 1913 for a psychologist to look at child drawing with almost exactly the same distinction between conception and vision structuring his understanding as Raynal and Apollinaire applied to Cubist painting. For what Luquet observed in the drawings of his little girl Simone was what he called a "logical realism", a realism of conception, which he placed in radical opposition to what he called the "visual realism" of adults. And he observed in this "logical realism" of children all the characteristics then and now identified as basic to Cubist analysis. Mobile perspective, the "hinging" of one aspect swung forward onto the picture-plane alongside another, transparency – all were included[37]. In child drawing, according to Luquet, analysis operated "logically" to describe the known just as Gris was to suggest it did in his earliest Cubisms.

Yet, by 1912 the word logic could as well be placed in *opposition* to the notion of primitive conception, and most of all responsible for this was Lévy-Bruhl's major book, *Les Fonctions mentales dans les sociétés inférieures*, published in 1910. For Lévy-Bruhl, thinking did not necessarily work according to the laws of logic. Indeed, what he later termed "primitive mentality" fundamentally contradicted logic. The test he applied was simple. If logic could be defined as founded on the "law of non contradiction", then the exposure of contradiction in "primitive mentality" established the operation of different laws. In magical thinking, Lévy-Bruhl had no difficulty in showing that things in different places at different times could be treated as causally connected (a spell can act across time and space). The law of non-contradiction was simply over-ridden. He proposed instead the "law of participation" as the law of "primitive mentality". Anything, according to this law, could "participate" in anything else at any time, in any place. He established the logic of European thinking in opposition to the otherness of a non-European thinking based on *non*-logical principles[38].

Juan Gris's reputation as the Cubist logician was formed in milieux that made of logic, like conception, an issue almost as central as it was for Lévy-Bruhl. Rubin is right: Picasso's rudimentary French probably did not equip him for Lévy-Bruhl, and there is no clear evidence that even such figures as Apollinaire and Raynal were aware of the "law of participation" before 1914. Yet, the conceptual and the so-called "primitive" *were* thought of together, and there is no mistaking both a positive awareness of profound issues and a negative irony directed at European *hubris* in Picasso's remark, reported by Salmon, about the "reasonableness" of African sculpture[39]. There is no mistaking either the fact that contradiction as such becomes, from 1912, an increasingly manifest feature of the work of Picasso, Apollinaire and perhaps most plainly of all, Max Jacob[40]. Cubist painting and sculpture, the card-board *Guitar* and the *papiers collés* of 1912 made it possible to build contradiction literally into the repertoire of Cubist technique: emptyness as fullness, projection as recession, wall-paper cut out to denote a guitar or the wine in a glass while remaining wall-paper. The "law of participation" operates, even if it is not invoked. Anything can be anything else anywhere.

Of all the Cubists, Gris is perhaps the one least readily associated with African sculpture and the notion of "the primitive". He never gave his work recognisable African features, and he always resisted the rough insouciance of a mask-maker's technique. It is tempting to conclude that the sheer European-ness of his work endorses his reputation as a painter-logician, that in its ordered clarity it signified for a eurocentric rationalism against the contradictoriness of magic. Yet, it is known that his interest was aroused by Picasso's and Braque's collections of African sculpture because he made his own replica of the Kota reliquary figures so in vogue with them, a joke which borders on a gesture of sympathy[41]. And, as we shall see, he too embedded contradiction into the very basics of his technique, explicitly, provocatively.

In the first of these essays, I mentioned the critic Vauxcelles's reference to the Picasso who sat for Gris's *Homage* in 1912 as "Père Ubu-kub"[42]. Picasso might have talked of the *raisonable* in African sculpture, but he was publicly associated with an assault on logic by satire and ridicule, with the Alfred Jarry of "Dr Faustroll". Indeed, the entire vanguard intellectual drift from Symbolism into Cubism, shared by the milieux of *La Plume*, *Vers et Prose* and the "Bateau-Lavoir" group before 1910, and afterwards by those around Picasso and Apollinaire, could be characterized as a profound reaction against the "law of non-contradiction", against the commonsense logics that ruled the mechanistic mentalities dominant in Third Republic France[43]. So, as we shall see, could the Bergsonism that accompanied the attraction to "antiquity's Measure of Beauty" in the Puteaux group, Metzinger included. This was the context in which, working as a knowing insider, Gris became "the demon of logic". It seems hardly likely that what he did with logic, what his paintings said about logic, was simply a straightforward endorsement of the "law of non-contradiction" and all it stood for in his liberal bourgeois society. If clarity was from the beginning a virtue of Gris's painting, the operation and the meanings of the "logic" that has for so long been found there are not necessarily clear at all.

An encounter with the logical in Gris's painting before 1916 generates the following questions: how does "conception" relate to "vision" (if Raynal's terms can still be applied); how arbitrary or how rigorously controlled is his working-practice; and how consistent (how far *without* contradiction) is both the practice and the pictorial result? These questions overlap, but they can be kept, each distinctly, in mind.

When Gleizes wrote of "cubes" giving "equilibrium" to the fragmented image in Metzinger's *Tea-time*, he supplied terms that can easily be applied to the ordering of Gris's painting throughout 1912. The word "grid" substituted for "cubes" does the trick: Gris's grids can be said to give "equilibrium" too. Like Metzinger, and unlike Picasso and Braque, Gris combined mobile perspective and grids to move towards greater lucidity of depiction as well as structural regularity; his work became clearer, not more obscure[44]. His use of grids from 1912 (and of geometric armatures later) focuses attention on all the questions I have raised.

A sensitive visual empiricism opened the way to the generation of these apparently *a priori* geometries. "Vision" precedes "concept" (analysis before synthesis) in 1911–12. Gris may have been the "disciple" of Picasso, and he may have learned from Metzinger's intelligent if repressed Cubism, but it is well known that he began as a Cubist in 1910 by setting up his own arrangements of objects in his rue Ravignan studio to apply what he had learned for himself by looking and drawing. He seems to have switched his attention away from the tricks of caricature which had earned him his living since his arrival in Paris, by deliberately returning to the practice of the academy (he had received the beginnings of an academic training in Madrid from the painter Moreno Carbonero). Large charcoal drawings, heightened with white gouache, and the paintings *Siphon and Bottles* and *The Eggs* were the first results of this studious return (Plates 2 and 3). By the end of 1911 he had followed these with canvases like *Bottles and Knife* and *Still-life with Oil Lamp* (Plates 7 and 6), the preludes to *Still-life with Flowers* (Plate 8), which were pictorial glosses on a continuing stream of drawings based on looking, now in pencil (Plate 5 and *Kettle and Milk Bottle*, see page 146).

The Eggs reveals something of how the activity of looking worked in combination with a Picassian determination to arrive at a facetted arrangement of flat surfaces. Most obviously there is a connection with a specific charcoal drawing (Figure 10), whose gouache high-lit bottle is the stimulus for the blurring here of the edges of bottle and white tablecloth, as if the glass division has vanished. More generically the patterning of light and shadow across the porcelain breakfast bowl clearly follows from more than one of the charcoal drawings (Plate 1). Here the bowl is gently fragmented as if by a partial tipping up onto the picture plane of its base and its hollow inside. But, most tellingly of all, there are just a couple of indications that the observed fall of light has itself begun to suggest the possibility of a flat linear geometry which can press everything together onto the picture-plane. Shadows with sharp straight edges suggest the tentative cutting of facets to the left of the bowl and the dish.

Similar facettings break up, delicately, much of the surface of the probably contemporary watercolour *Three Lamps* (Plate 4). Something approaching an all-over pattern of diamond facets seems to have been suggested by the very way Gris has recorded the action of light forming, yet disintegrating these fragile objects. The sheer controlling regularity of the diamond grid used in *Bottles and Knife* and its contemporaries, and the arbitrary lighting of edges to give it the appearance of facetting cut directly into the surface, together encourage the conclusion that the grid is a wholly artificial structure imposed upon still-life analyses. In fact, the indications offered by the charcoal drawings, *The Eggs* and *Three Lamps* suggest that even the grids had their origins in looking. And the pencil drawings that accompany the pictures of late 1911 often betray relatively open, sketchy beginnings, where the adjustment of objects to grids is far from planned[45]. The irony of these pictures is that they declare their artifice (conceptual control) by the dramatic artificiality of their lighting within a structure suggested by the conscientious observation of light in nature.

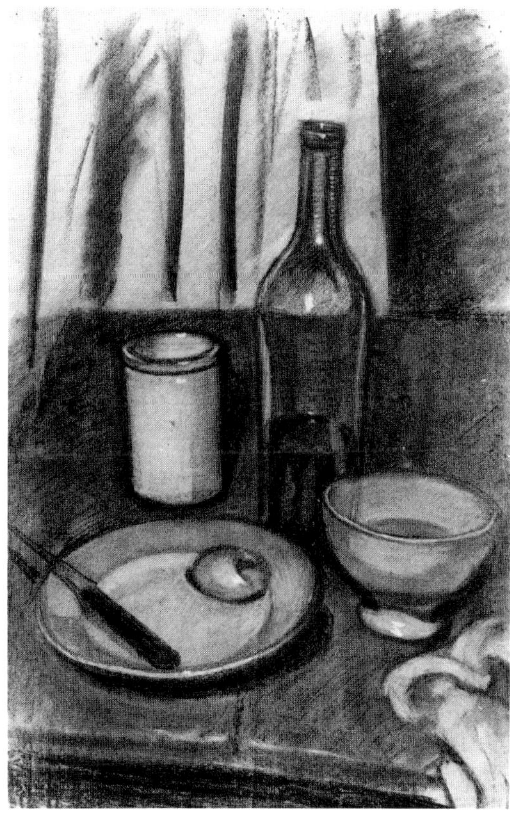

Figure 10
Still-life, 1910
Charcoal and gouache on paper, 48 x 32 cm
Private Collection

Yet, two points have to be made that initially seem to accentuate the willed abstractness of the grid as Gris used it in 1912. First, it was often modular and regular, and as such was easily fitted to the demands of Golden Section composing in the pictures of the summer, such as *Man in the Café* and *The Watch* (Plates 21 and 22). Second, immediately after *Still-life with Flowers* and *Homage to Pablo Picasso* Gris made it the organising principle for analysis itself, that is, the process of conceptualising by the compiling of different views. The synthetic and the analytic were visibly fused. In the Golden Section paintings and in the *Portrait of Germaine Raynal* (Plate 13) he laid the grids like systems of fault-lines across things, fault-lines on either side of which view-points switch. The drawing in Basel, *Head of a Man* (Plate 14), made, it seems, immediately after *Homage* and *Portrait of the Artist's Mother* (Plate 11), is an early, if remarkably resolved, instance of the procedure[46]. An immaculate drawing like *Parfum de Chypre* (see page 28), a charcoal study for one of the items in another of the more recent Section d'Or pictures, displays it in more complex form: the diagonal and orthogonal grids are not merely overlaid, they shunt across one another and lock together[47]. And a comparable complexity is achieved in a charcoal drawing closely related to the *Head of Germaine Raynal* where a system of interlocking arcs cuts across an orthogonal grid (Plate 16)[48].

So complete in such images is the integration of the grids and analysis that indeed there is the *look* of strict geometric regulation. And the academic use of studies to finalize the parts of the painting, as in *Parfum de Chypre* and the drawings for *Man in the Café* (Plate 18, 19 and 20), shows a planner at work. Yet, even here procedures were not rigidly systematic, and the grid was not altogether *a priori*. One of the most closely related drawings for the head of *Man in the Café* reveals multiple erasings, as does the drawing related to *Portrait of Germaine Raynal,* so there was considerable room for *ad hoc* adjustment[49]. In *Man in the Café,* as in the other Golden Section pictures, the complications of the grids were obviously developed in *response* to the structure of things analysed. Gris did not merely overlay a unitary grid, determined by the rectangle of the format to guide his dissection, as he did in *Head of a Man*, he also elaborated one slanting grid controlling the fragmentation of collar and lapel, another orthogonal one for the idiosyncrasies of the face (supplemented by a proliferation of arcs), and a combination of another slanting one and another orthogonal one for the hat, besides others still for the table-top still-life and the view across the street. The procedures of figure analysis and grid genesis are impossible to separate; the grid is not a separate construction which imposes an abstract conceptual order.

From the grids of 1912 Gris worked his way through the post-*papier collé* development of broad structures first of vertical (Plate 24), then of fanned strips in 1913 (Plate 30), always using them in integration with the part-by-part fragmentation or unfolding of his subjects. Geometry continued to signify with apparently little ambiguity the operation of a controlling intelligence in the face of the phenomenal world, the subordination of the "visual". But John Golding long ago pointed out the lack of fully co-ordinated proportional or geometric systems in the few surviving measured drawings, evidently made with the use of divider and set-square as the adjuncts to pictures like the *Violin and Guitar* (Plates 32 and 36) and *Three Cards* in Bern[50].

It was at the end of 1913 that Gris re-stated the theme of the grid as such, and he did so while introducing it into his pictures in the guise of a new object, the chequerboard, sometimes accompanied by a dice-cup[51]. These chequerboard grids are so complex in the overlappings of their modules that they defy a simple grasp of their inter-relations. Suggestively, they bring together method, apparently in the process of disintegration, with the throw of the dice: logic with games of chance.

In 1916 Gris started to make drawings again from set-ups of objects in the studio of the "Bateau-Lavoir". Once more he followed with infinite sensitivity the fall of light and shadow across things, but this time from the start looking for hints that might suggest a framework of light and dark planes to bind objects and setting together, and from the start translating objects into simple flat configurations (Plates 67 and 69). These meticulous drawings anticipated and accompanied a sequence of severe paintings that summer which set still-life objects, not in grid-structures, but in broad geometric armatures whose diagonals and orthogonals linked the four sides of the format. One of the most coherent of these is *Fruit Dish, Glass and Lemon* of August 1916 (Plate 58). Pictures like this display a mode of analysis rather different from the grid pictures of 1911–12, one that could be called logical in a distinct way.

The fruit dish and glass in the picture of August 1916, the central items on display, are given in triplicate, their component images locked, one by one, to the major lines of the geometric armature. Their profiles are defined in shadow silhouette on the vertical axis; they appear again, on a tilted axis, as flat, angular emblems, altogether unlike their actual shaping; and they emerge as partial, modelled forms, on a slightly differently tilted axis. Gris does not break his objects down by combining different view-points. He offers instead three versions in one, each version isolating a different property: profile, surface (the white porcelain of the fruit dish), density or volume. The geometric armature is integrated with an analysis that proceeds by the clear separation of qualities.

A little less than a year after Gris painted *Fruit Dish, Glass and Lemon*, one of his new allies in the circle of Léonce Rosenberg, the ex-Futurist Gino Severini, published a manifesto-article in *Mercure de France*. Linda Henderson has noted the central role Severini gives here to the analytical separation of qualities, and its justification in a late essay by the important scientific writer Henri Poincaré[52]. Poincaré had suggested that certain senses should be abstracted to clarify understanding of things. On this basis Severini writes: "... If we sometimes place colour, for example, outside its "local form", it is solely in order to preserve the sensation of it in all its force... As with everything in our aesthetic, this separation is extremely logical; because... we do not want to represent the accidental, the momentary, but the essential, the eternal, and for this reason, when an object presents itself to our mind, it is, above all, its essential qualities that we see..."[53]

Poincaré seems to have been one of the enthusiasms of a well-remembered associate of the "Bateau-Lavoir" group, repeatedly credited with introducing Picasso and his friends (including Gris) to new mathematical thinking: Maurice Princet[54]. Henderson has shown too that Gleizes and Metzinger used Poincaré's *La Science et l'hypothèse* extensively in their tract *Du "Cubisme"* of 1912 (to which I shall return)[55]. It could well be that Gris was himself aware of analysis by the separation of qualities as a "logical" procedure from before 1914. Indeed, the procedure relates also to a philosophical source which, probably unknown to Gris, Kahnweiler brought to bear during 1915 in writing the study that was to become *Der Weg zum Kubismus*: Locke's *Essay on Understanding*. In the 1920 version of his book, Kahnweiler claimed that the Cubists endeavoured "to present the primary... qualities as exactly as possible". These qualities were defined by Locke, who Kahnweiler cites, as those that "are utterly inseparable from the body in what state so ever it be..."[56]. They include size, form, density, local colour, the kind of properties isolated so clearly by Gris in *Fruit Dish, Glass and Lemon*.

Gris began to apply the basic techniques essential to this "logical" practice at the beginning of 1913, and between then and 1916 periodically returned to them with more or less rigour. They are used first in the post-*papier collé* strip paintings, in *Guitar on the Table* (Plate 25), *The Guitar* (Plate 28) and especially *The Siphon* (Plate 26), for example. In the last of these, the siphon stands beside a glass with fluted bowl on the marble top of a cafe table, its spout echoing the curve of a bent-wood chair-back. The spout and the transparent tube in the soda are both given three-dimensions by schematic modelling. So is the top of the glass's bowl. Otherwise, the profile and section of glass and siphon, and indeed of most of the things on the table, are given in only two-dimensions, by the barest linear diagramming. There is a high level of simplification here, but every denotative element is clearly descriptive of one or more "quality".

A pair of ambitious still-lives dated March 1915 (Plates 46 and 49) use the same array of linear and modelled means in richer compositional and chromatic circumstances. Here, anticipating Severini, the surface qualities of materials and local colour are decisively separated from local forms, appearing in their own angular framing planes: the porcelain caught by sun-light of cups and fruit dish, the brown and red of the stout bottle and label in the former, the grained brown of the coffee-mill in the latter.

The procedure is, as Severini and Raynal were to stress, analytical[57], but the simplification of Gris's modes of depiction sometimes goes with a refusal of descriptive likeness that suggests synthesis: a realisation of the arbitrariness of the signifier's relation to its referent that is now more fully conceptual. The elementary containing shapes for the surface and colour qualities of porcelain, bottle-glass or wood, are not at all *like* cups, bottles or coffee-mills[58]. This willingness to ignore likeness and to stress artificiality in the forming of signs was again something that emerged in 1913 (immediately after Picasso's card-board *Guitar*, of course): one can see it in the line and dot of *The Smoker's* eye (Figure 8), and the decorative twirl of *The Bull-fighter's* nostrils (Plate 30).

The separation of qualities could go with the combination of different idioms for sign-making, some more iconic or descriptive (analytic), some more arbitrary (synthetic). Things were taken apart and put back together again in conflicting dialects, sometimes refined, sometimes matter-of-fact, the distinctions clear. Astonishingly, the result was usually free of confusion. To assemble figures or still-lives in different dialects, as Picasso did from 1912, is one thing; to take them apart again analytically, is another, with its own difficulties, above all the danger of disintegration into babble. Gris rarely, if ever, succumbs.

Despite the role of looking in the genesis of Gris's grids and his geometric armatures, and despite the evidence that he left space for options as he fitted analyses to grids, my scrutiny of the way he analysed and the way he structured compositions between 1911 and 1916 leaves an overwhelming impression of clarity of purpose and intellectual control. The pictures say this still, certainly to me. The questions then remain. First, is this clarity and control simply a matter of appearances? And second, acknowledging that the paintings repeatedly signify clarity and control, do these characteristics serve consistency? Put another way, do Gris's Cubisms engage with or avoid contradiction, and if they do engage with contradiction, what ultimately could the logic so often "seen" in his pictures amount to? What might it have meant in a context of critical scepticism?

There can be no doubt that we are concerned here with appearances. The thick, opaque surfaces and the thin paper cut-outs of certainly the paintings and *papier collés* of 1913–14 are screens drawn across a surprisingly open-ended practice, full of the tension of uncertainty. A central principle of Gris's working procedures in these years was erasure: he rubs out, over-paints and covers up in constant pursuit of the appearance of perfection.

The vertical strip structure and the separated views and "qualities" of the early 1913 pictures might declare a firm conceptual certainty, in pictures like *The Siphon*, but the finished paint surface masks a complex, vacil-

Figure 11
Guitar and Pipe, 1913
Oil an canvas, 65 x 50 cm
Private Collection

Figure 12
Guitar, 1913
Pencil on paper,
65 x 50 cm
Jasper Johns

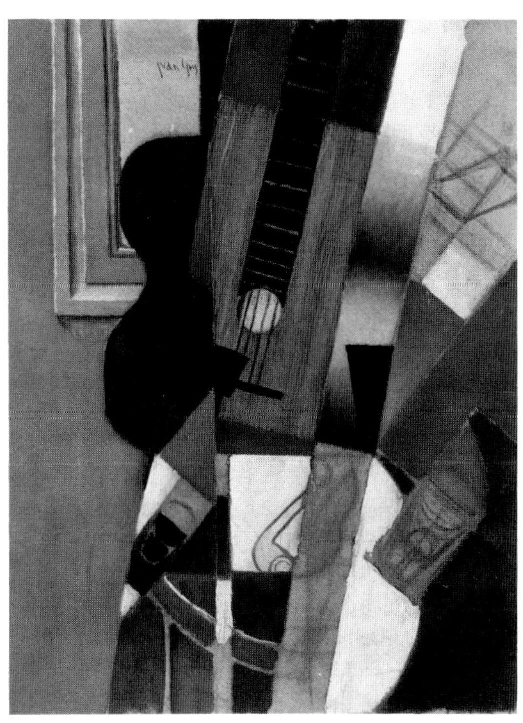

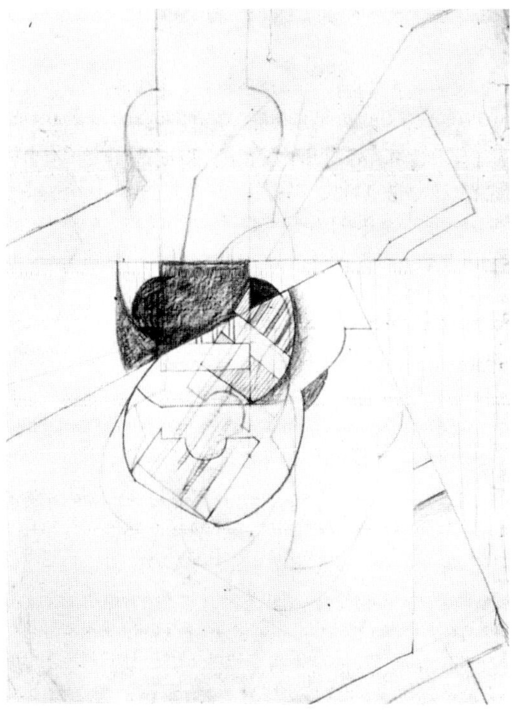

lating process. A close look at *The Guitar* of a month later reveals that the broad, lime green plane beneath the engraving has been painted over a far more complicated structure, probably not unlike the structure of charcoal lines exposed in a rare canvas, *Guitar and Pipe,* left at a relatively early stage from about the same date (Figure 11). Such charcoal outlinings, left in varying states of complication, obscurity or even confusion, are found in several unfinished and rejected compositions on the backs of re-used canvases[59]. At this moment Gris seems not merely to have been willing to re-build his strip architecture as he worked on the canvas, but to have offered himself a plethora of options for how to denote every aspect of every object or figure, selecting in the end only a very few. The anxieties and excitements of this process of hypothesizing in charcoal before perfecting in colour are there to invite our empathetic response in both *Guitar and Pipe* and the *collage* and gouache compositions that accompanied the strip paintings, above all *Glasses, Newspaper and Bottle of Wine* (Plate 23).

That processes of a comparable openness and complexity are concealed by the still more immaculate resolution of the Céret pictures of summer 1913 is demonstrable too. But now Gris turned to drawing with well-sharpened pencils and geometers' instruments to explore possibilities.

As I have mentioned before, where measurement can be seen to be used in the drawings made alongside paintings (Plates 35 and 36), there is no over-all system at work, and a few surviving drawings leave no doubt as to the intricate openness of Gris's graphic activity. I illustrate here one side (the least resolved) of a sheet drawn on both sides (Figure 12). It is literally covered with holes from divider or compass points, and by the traces of abandoned calculations. This sheet could precede the summer, but it seems at least likely that phases of comparable openness[60], when uncertainty was *enjoyed,* accompanied the smooth certainty of most of the violins and guitars painted in Céret (Plate 32). *Guitar on a Chair,* by contrast, preserves some trace of creative *effort* in the worked roughness of its surfaces, but it is very much the exception, not the rule (Plate 31).

At the turn of 1913–14 erasure seems actually to have become, for Gris, a means of exploration, not merely of getting rid of unwanted options. There are a few coloured drawings which are almost certainly the product of partial tracings. Omission has become as positive an act as inclusion, giving results whose arbitrary incompleteness is itself arresting[61]. The painting *Bottle and Glass on a Table* (Plate 38) could well be a transference of the technique onto canvas; the neck of the bottle is a palpable, almost troubling absence[62].

Papier collé was, of course, by its very nature a technique of covering up, and the lifting of the cut papers from the exactingly intricate *Flowers* (Plate 44) has revealed a careful preliminary outlining in pencil, not unlike the drawings made by partial tracing[63]. Such a covering up of what were probably divergent, open-ended processes by which options were offered and then withdrawn is almost certainly one function of the precisely cut-out paper masks that conceal these canvases. The sheer tidiness of *papiers collés* like *The Packet of Coffee* and *Fruit Dish and Carafe* (Plates 41 and 40) contrasts with the crudity of fabrication in many of Picasso's and Braque's (Figure 13), but their appearance of certainty *is* a mask as oil-paint always had been in Gris's painting.

Most obviously it is in the *papiers collés* that Gris engages with contradiction before 1916 and, as obviously, their technical precision does not go with the making of clear, unambiguous distinctions. The ambiguities are often underlined by the words in the fragmentary head-lines and texts pasted on. Besides "indirect contributions", there is "the true and the false" and, more than once, the pages from books concern disguise and identity[64]. The very look of the earlier *papiers collés*, made in the first six months of 1914, is that of the shadowy hermeticism of pre-*papier collé* Picasso and Braque. The objects that surround "ces explor... eurs" in *The Packet of Coffee* are not at all explicit in their every feature or their spatial relationships. Their dissolution into open fragments floating in a shallow pool of deep blues, greys and browns has none of the sharp clarity of especially Picasso's most recent *papiers collés* and constructions. Gris responds to the echoes of hermeticism still present in Braque's earliest attempts with *faux bois* from over a year before[65].

Contradiction is also verbally underlined by, for instance, that phrase "the true and the false", but it is concretely there to be seen, even touched, in the material parts of the *papiers collés* and their relations, especially when these turn out to conflict with the relationships they designate in the still-life (all but one are still-lives)[66]. Thus, when one begins by just identifying the parts of the elegant paper jig-saw of *Fruit Dish and Carafe* and the things they designate, one ends by finding a succession of unexpected contradictions between the relatively true and the relatively false. The cloth, which can be read as *on* the checked surface (table and/or floor) is the primed canvas drawn on with pencil and red oil paint. The checked surface is blocked out on paper stuck onto the canvas (*over* the cloth).

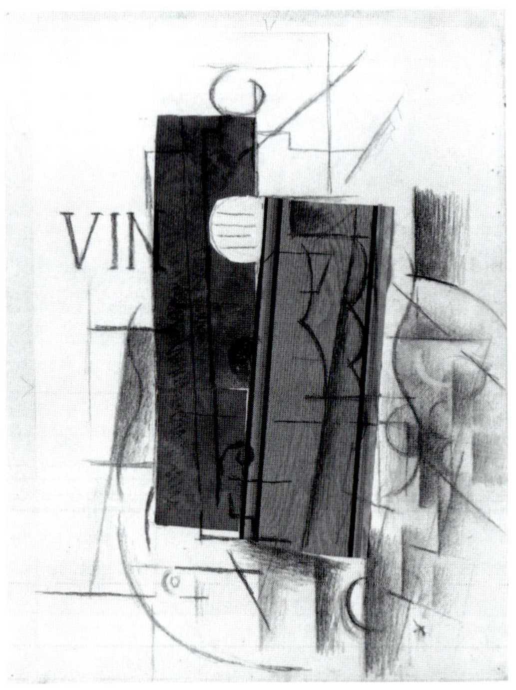

Figure 13
Georges Braque
Still-life with Guitar (Wine), 1913
Papier collé, pencil and wash on canvas
63.5 x 48.3 cm
Philadelphia Museum of Art: The Louise and Walter Arensberg Collection

The yellowed fragment of newspaper, which can appear as if showing through a gap from behind, is stuck *onto* the checked surface. The knife on the plate on the cloth is drawn tangibly enough to invite picking up, only to be overlaid by an arching strip of paper treated to be like the porcelain of the plate. Everywhere, material relationships (what is in front or behind) contradict denoted still-life relationships. Appearances are false, like the deliciously convincing false marble.

Contradiction, of course, was built into the very terms of Cubist picture-making, before, during and after the development of *papier collé,* and this is certainly the case with the "logical" Juan Gris. The separation of qualities and the multiplication of idioms led directly to the confrontation of contradictory signs in pictures like *The Siphon* and the multiplication of perspectives led to comparable conflicts. Especially after Picasso's card-board *Guitar*, emptiness could signify fullness, and from the pictures of late 1911 that prefaced *Homage to Pablo Picasso* body and depth were given by flat facets on or at least close to the picture-plane. It is almost a truism to say that Cubist painting made a key virtue of the contradictoriness inherent in the practice of depicting three dimensions on two.

Far from minimizing conflict, the sheer clarity of Gris's practice could be and was used to accentuate contradiction. The most obvious instances before 1916 are the vertical strip pictures of early 1913 (Plates 25 and 26), where the different aspects of objects in their different idioms are made to slip out of alignment with each other, enhancing the difficulty of reading objects as wholes and even in some cases rendering it almost impossible. This introduction of difficulty to invite active spectatorship relates to a well-known passage written by the supporter of the Puteaux Cubists, Roger Allard, in autumn 1912: "The pleasure of a work of art involves two creative beings: one is the artist... the other is the viewer, whose mind finds a way back to the natural object. The further both of them travel, ... the more creatively both are working"[67]. It could be argued that Gris presents us with contradictions to resolve into consistent, whole ideas and this is certainly how Kahnweiler thought about both the contradictory and the fragmentary in all of Cubist painting by 1915[68]. Yet, it cannot be denied that consistency co-exists with the clear declaration of contradiction in his work and that in the *papiers collés* Gris did not merely expose the contradictory, he revelled in it.

If Gris's pictures repeatedly signify clarity and control, and so have been seen to possess logic, what they said about logic was never very straightforward.

Perhaps the most comprehensively logical of all Gris's applications of the grid and analytical method came, as we have seen, with the most recent of pictures shown at the Section d'Or (Plates 13 and 21). In their proportional structuring and their diligent compilation of view-points, there is something like consistency. Two of them are Gris's first *collages,* of which *The Watch* is one (Plate 22). It incorporates fragments of pages from two poems by Apollinaire with a single title clearly legible: 'Le Pont Mirabeau'.

For Kahnweiler, writing in his first monograph of 1929, the decison to "introduce foreign materials into his canvases" was one of Gris's most logical. "Why, he said to himself, give the illusion of things that can be displayed in their actuality?"[69] There is evidence enough that this kind of matter-of-fact reasonableness was indeed associated with the introduction of *collage* at the beginning. As early as 1914 Salmon recalled discussions about what "cannot be imitated in painting",[70] and in September 1913 Gris himself wrote to Kahnweiler about the other early 1913 canvas besides *The Guitar* (Plate 28) to which he had stuck an engraving, with the suggestion that, since the engraving was not integral to the pictorial conception, any new owner could change it[71]. Yet, there is a good deal more evidence that *collage,* from the beginning, was simultaneously associated with surprise, the subversion of aesthetic hierarchies and *un*reasonableness. Both reasonableness and unreasonableness are there in Apollinaire's memorable response to Picasso in March 1913. Picasso, he writes, "has grown accustomed to the immense light of unfathomable spaces. At times, he has not hesitated to entrust real objects to the light – a two-penny song, a real postage stamp, a piece of newspaper, a piece of oil-cloth imprinted with chair-caning. The art of the painter could not add any pictorial element to the truth of these objects. Surprise laughs wildly in the purity of light, and the numbers and block letters insistantly appear as pictorial elements – new in art but long imbued with humanity"[72]. The later reputation of *collage* was to be far more one of unreasonableness, of subversion. The surprises of conflictual juxtaposition were, of course, to make the "collage principle" central to Surrealism and its derivatives, as Tzara, Aragon and Breton all realised by the early 1930s[73]. In 1930, even Kahnweiler's friend Carl Einstein could stress that *collage* had played "the destructive role of acids", corroding certainties[74].

And all is not entirely resolved, entirely matter-of-fact, entirely without conflict in *The Watch*. There is, for instance, nothing consistent about the placing of real fragments of pages from Apollinaire alongside *painted* wall-paper, both material "objects" to which the artist obviously cannot "add". There is, too, nothing consistent about the jarring juxtaposition of the naively represented curtain and the sophisticated Cubist representation of the still-life it has been drawn back to reveal: idioms are already in conflict. And on this carefully measured, proportionally divided plane, the clock and the vestiges of poems alongside the bottle invite reading as well as looking, verbal as well as visual engagement. The time of clocks, like poems, is read.

René de Costa has pointed out that, while the title 'Le Pont Mirabeau' can be read whole, the other fragments of Apollinaire are from another poem, 'L'Enfer', as it appeared in May 1912 in *Les Soirées de Paris*. He has argued that the clock and the book are the generative core of the entire picture, whose conception revolves around the central themes of the poems read *as texts*: on the one hand the metaphor of love as a dream of hell, on the other the metaphor of the Seine at night passing under the Pont Mirabeau and becoming one with the endless flow of time. He reads the time from the clock at five minutes or a quarter to twelve, and links it with Apollinaire's refrain "Let the night come: strike the hour/The days go past while I stand here"[75].

The hour strikes in 'Le Pont Mirabeau', but time both passes and stands still; its flow escapes measure. Gris's clock has one hand, the hour hand, but it might be five to, it might be quarter to, it might be morning, it might be night. By placing time clearly yet unmeasurably at the centre of *The Watch*, Gris, in company with most who pondered the nature and the status of logic around him, gave time in space a key role.

I have mentioned the centrality of the question of logic to Lévy-Bruhl's division of European "scientific" from so-called "primitive" thought (mentality). In making this division in 1910, Lévy-Bruhl followed the clear distinction made between the logical positivism of science and art as "intuition" by Henri Bergson. For Bergson, logical thought had no more than a restricted pragmatic role, it could not penetrate to essences. Such penetration was only possible if the logical measuring of time could be ignored and "our inner experience of time" regained as the ground for contemplation. If, he wrote in 1889, "we penetrate into the depth of organized and living intelligence, we shall witness the joining together or rather the blending of many ideas which, when once dissociated, seem to exclude one another as logically contradictory terms"[76]. The artist's capacity for intuition beyond logic offered, he suggested, a kind of access to "living intelligence", to a grasp, however momentary, of one's "unmeasurable duration in which nothing is repeated"[77]. The parallel between his notion of artistic "intuition" and Lévy-Bruhl's notion of an *a*-logical "primitive mentality" is plain enough.

The Bergsonian notion of artistic intuition and of unmeasurable duration as the essence of being was the very basis of the entire argument developed by Gleizes and Metzinger in *Du "Cubisme",* which was being written throughout the period that took Gris from *Homage to Pablo Picasso* to the Section d'Or as an associate of the Puteaux group[78]. 1911–12 were years when Cubism not only emerged as a public phenomenon through the activities of the Salon Cubists, but when, as I have suggested, it was linked, from inside the circles of the Salon Cubists themselves, with "Bergsonism"[79]. It might seem strange that the distinctly measurable "cubic" geometry of Metzinger's *Tea-time* (Figure 7) could be the product of an artist who made the *un*measurable a fundamental tenet of Cubism, but the fact is that, following Bergson, it could be argued that space, in essence, was always quantitative (measurable), and that only time was, in essence, "qualitative", to be experienced as beyond measure.

Edw. Hopper?

Most directly, time became a factor in Cubist painting, for Gleizes and Metzinger, through the act of multiple view-point conception. To "synthesize", in Raynal's terminology, different views and aspects of things in a single image was to bring time into pictorial space[80]. The logic of analysis becomes the tool for reaching, intuitively, *beyond* logic towards "duration". What Gris said by placing a clock that has ceased to tell time, and the flowing, measureless time of Apollinaire's poems at the centre of the measured grids and the analysed objects of *The Watch* could not have been simply an affirmation of logic. A month or so after he showed the picture in the Section d'Or, *Du "Cubisme"* appeared. Apollinaire had already dubbed him (perhaps affirmatively, perhaps provocatively, perhaps ironically) "the demon of logic".

It is, ultimately, in time that the metaphor of logic least satisfactorily applies to the work of Juan Gris; when one considers change through time, the invention and re-invention of his Cubisms. Talk of straight lines, of a logical working through of problems, is hard to equate with a "development" so open to change in often so unpredictable a way. The story of the grid can appear a simple progression from single to double grids, from unitary to plural grids, from grids to vertical strips to fanned strips, from strips to geometric armatures. But how logical is the return to *papier collé* in the guise of a new hermeticism early in 1914? Perhaps the most remarkable demonstration of how the open-endedness of Gris's working practice, its endless generation and withdrawal of possibilities, was carried through into the proliferation of his Cubisms is the sequence of changes in his work over the fifteen months between June 1915 and October 1916. In that brief time, he set up a more and a less "conceptual" Cubism as clear alternatives with the near abstract Berlin *Still-life* and the far from abstract *Still-life and Townscape (Place Ravignan)* (Plate 48)[81], generating not one, but two "lines" of development through the *Guitar on a Table* and *Breakfast* of October 1915 (Plates 50 and 52). He then switched unaccountably into a dazzling *pointilliste* Cubism at the turn of 1915–16 with pictures like *Fruit Dish on a Blue Tablecloth* and *Newspaper and Fruit Dish* (Plates 57 and 54), and finally, but not of course conclusively, to the flattened *chiaroscuro* of *Fruit Dish, Glass and Lemon* (Plate 58). Juan Gris was not, in the end, so much of a logician that he lost the capacity to surprise himself.

When Kahnweiler wrote his first monograph in 1929, he sustained whole-heartedly the image of Gris as one who could not tolerate in his work "anything confused, anything obscure". In doing so, he confirmed Waldemar George's "triumph of clarity". He was also one of the first to find that straight line in Gris's development from the fragmentation of analysis and *collage* to the unity of synthesis. But he qualified the image of the logician thus: "Juan Gris always thought an idea through to the end, with an inexorable rigour. Not that he was a flat rationalist, set on cold logic. This was a Spaniard, with a fanatical, passionate temperament"[82].

Quick conclusions and simple characterisations are to be resisted in front of so complex an achievement, even when, before 1916, logic was so obviously a central issue.

1 For the "Salon Cubists", see Daniel Robbins, *Albert Gleizes, 1881–1953,* Solomon R. Guggenheim Museum, New York, 1964, and especially Daniel Robbins, 'Jean Metzinger: At the Centre of Cubism'; in *Jean Metzinger in Retrospect,* edited by Ann Moser, The University of Iowa Museum of Art, Iowa City, 1985. For Gris's connection with Metzinger, see *Juan Gris: Correspondance, Dessins 1915–21,* IVAM Centre Julio González, Valencia and Centre Georges Pompidou, Musée National d'Art Moderne, Paris, 1990–91, p. 83 (Letter 32, note 5). Madame Josette Gris told me that Metzinger was a friend, although not so close as Lipchitz, Reverdy, Dermée or Raynal. Conversation, 20 July 1977. For further observations on Gris's and Metzinger's relationship, see Christian Derouet's essay below.

2 The case for this view is persuasively argued in Robbins (1985), ibid.

3 Guillaume Apollinaire, 'Le Salon des Indépendants', *L'Intransigeant,* 21 April 1911; in Guillaume Apollinaire, *Apollinaire on Art: Essays and Reviews, 1902–1918,* edited by Leroy C. Breunig, translated by Susan Suleiman, New York and London, 1972, p. 151 (the translation given above is the author's).

4 'La Palette' (André Salmon), *in Paris-Journal,* 3 October 1911; cited in Lynn Wissing Gamwell, *Cubist Criticism: 1907–1925,* thesis submitted for the degree of Ph. D., University of California, Los Angeles, 1980, p. 155, note 29.

5 See for example John Golding, *Cubism: a History and an Analysis, 1907–1914,* London, 1968, p. 158 and Robbins (1985), op.cit.

6 Albert Gleizes, 'Art et ses représentants, Jean Metzinger', *La Revue Indépendante,* September 1911, pp. 161–72. Cited by Robbins (1985), op.cit., p. 19.

7 Jean Metzinger, 'Note sur la peinture', *Pan,* October-November 1910.

8 I am grateful to Michael Stone-Richards for having pointed out to me Alphonse Lingis's discussion of Husserl's term Empfindrisse (states of contact: touch, pressure, heat, cold, etc., and of "being moved" in the kinaesthetic and affective sense: states in tension and relaxation). See Alphonso Lingis; in *For Roman Ingarden, Nine Essays in Phenomenology,* Martinus Nijhoff, 1960, pp. 79–80.

9 Maurice Raynal, 'Conception et vision', *Gil Blas,* 29 August 1912. Translated into English in Edward F. Fry, *Cubism,* London, 1966, p. 95.

10 Maurice Raynal, *Quelques Intentions du cubisme,* Paris, 1919; in *Bulletin de l'Effort Moderne,* no. 2, February 1924.

11 Ibid.

12 Guillaume Apollinaire, 'Le Cubisme', *L'Intermédiaire des chercheurs et des curieux,* 10 October 1912; in Apollinaire (1972), op.cit., pp. 257–8.

13 See note 6 above.

14 Maurice Raynal, 'L'Exposition de la Section d'Or', *Bulletin de la Section d'Or,* 9 October 1912.

15 See William A. Camfield, 'Juan Gris and the Golden Section', *Art Bulletin,* March 1965, pp. 128–34.

16 The newly discovered correspondence between Gris and Léonce Rosenberg provides evidence concerning Gris's contribution to the Salon de la Section d'Or in the list referring to sold and exhibited pictures sent to Rosenberg. This is in a letter of 10 August 1917. Among the 13 pictures he sent to the Section d'Or were, according to this list, the 3 shown at the Indépendants earlier in the year and, it can be inferred, several more that were completed before the summer.

17 See George Heard Hamilton and William C. Agee, *Raymond Duchamp-Villon, 1887–1918,* New York, 1967, pp. 59 and 69.

18 Apollinaire (1972), op.cit., pp. 252–8.

19 This is revealed by analysis following the indications provided by Camfield (1965), loc.cit.

20 For a fuller discussion of their relationship during this period, see Christopher Green, 'Purity, poetry and the painting of Juan Gris', *Art History,* June, 1982, pp. 180–204. See also Christian Derouet's essay below where important new material is used for the first time.

21 Pierre Reverdy, *Self Defence,* Paris, 1919; in Pierre Reverdy, *Oeuvres Complètes, Nord-Sud, Self Defence et autres écrits sur l'art et la poésie,* edited with notes by Etienne-Allain Hubert, Paris, 1975, p. 108.

22 William Rubin, 'Picasso and Braque: An Introduction', *Picasso and Braque: Pioneering Cubism,* The Museum of Modern Art, New York, 1989, pp. 54–5, note 3.

23 There is no evidence that he read the latter. Kahnweiler, in particular, has insisted that he was already reading Mallarmé before 1914, and that he read the prose as well as the poetry. Conversation, 14 April 1977. See D.-H. Kahnweiler, *Juan Gris, His Life and Work,* translated by Douglas Cooper, London, 1969, pp. 48–9 and 98. Kahnweiler's recollections and assessment were corroborated by Madame Josette Gris. Like Kahnweiler, she considered his French good. Conversation, 20 June 1977.

24 Juan Gris, 'Reply to a Questionnaire', *Europa-Almanach,* Potsdam, 1925, pp. 34–5; translated by Douglas Cooper in Kahnweiler (1969), op.cit., pp. 202–3.

25 Waldemar George, 'Kisling', *L'Amour de l'art,* January 1922, p. 26.

26 Paul Dermée, 'Orientation', *S.I.C.,* nos. 42 and 43, 30 March and 15 April 1919, p. 12.

27 Anon., 'Notice Documentaire'(probably Carl Einstein), *Documents,* 2nd Year, no. 3, 1930, pp. 180–2. Alfred H. Barr, *Cubism and Abstract Art,* The Museum of Modern Art, New York, 1936.

28 The idea of a coherent, logical development is already clear in Kahnweiler's first monograph, *Juan Gris,* Leipzig and Berlin, 1929. Published in French translation in D. H. Kahnweiler, *Confessions esthétiques,* Paris, 1963, pp. 42–51. It is explicitly stated in Anon., 'Exposition Juan Gris' (probably Carl Einstein), *Documents,* 2nd Year, no. 4, 1930, p. 243. A particularly plain statement of the view in the later literature is to be found in Douglas Cooper, *The Cubist Epoch,* New York, 1971, pp. 229–30.

29 Paul Crowther's has been the most comprehensive critique. He has exposed the inadequacies of the Cubist theorists' adaptations of Immanuel Kant's basic distinction between "analytic" and "synthetic" judgements from the late eighteenth century, establishing that it has been too rigidly applied and that the objectivity required by the notion of analytical dissection cannot be assumed in any Cubist painting. See Paul Crowther, 'Cubism, Kant and Ideology', *Word and Image,* April–June 1987, pp. 195–201.

30 Rosalind Krauss, 'In the Name of Picasso'; in *The Originality of the Avant-Garde and Other Modernist Myths,*

Cambridge, Mass. and London, 1985, pp. 23–40; Yves-Alain Bois, 'Kahnweiler's Lesson', *Representations,* Spring, 1987, pp. 33–68.

31 For a discussion of Kahnweiler's use of the term "sign", see chapter 4 below.

32 See Bois (1987), loc.cit., pp. 37 and 40–8. For the probable date of purchase, see Judith Cousins with the collaboration of Pierre Daix, 'Documentary Chronology'; in Rubin (1989), op.cit., p. 401.

33 Maurice Raynal *(Gil-Blas,* 1912), loc.cit.; in Fry (1966), op.cit., p. 95.

34 Guillaume Apollinaire, 'Exoticisme et ethnographie', *Paris-Journal,* 12 September 1912; in Apollinaire (1972), op.cit., p. 144.

35 See Marcel Mauss and H. Hubert, *Esquisse d'une théorie générale de la magie,* Paris, 1902–3; in Marcel Mauss, *Sociologie et Anthropologie,* Paris, 1966 and L. Lévy-Bruhl, *Les Fonctions mentales dans les sociétés inférieures,* Paris, 1910.

36 Luquet took his ideas about the contiguity of child and "primitive mentality" to their most developed conclusions in the later book *L'Art primitif,* Paris, 1930. An early and trenchant criticism is Georges Bataille's review in *Documents,* 2nd Year, 1930, no. 7, pp. 389–97. Kahnweiler does mention Luquet in his monograph of 1946, and is strongly critical in very much the same vein as Bataille. See Kahnweiler (1969), op.cit., pp. 113–114.

37 G.-H. Luquet, *Dessins d'un enfant, étude psychologique,* Paris, 1913, especially pp. 145–225.

38 Lévy-Bruhl (1910), op.cit., especially chapter II, pp. 68–110.

39 André Salmon, 'Petite Histoire anecdotique du cubisme'; in *La Jeune Peinture Française,* Paris, 1912. The use of the term "raisonable" here is too often uncritically accepted as positive and without irony because it is not placed contextually. It should also be realized that in French the meaning of this term concerns correctness as much as reason.

40 Contradiction is a basic principle in Jacob's prose-poems for *Le Cornet à dés.* Most were written before 1914. See Max Jacob, *Le Cornet à dés,* Paris, 1917 and Gerald Kamber, *Max Jacob and the Poetics of Cubism,* Baltimore and London, 1971.

41 Rubin illustrates Gris's rather flat replica in William Rubin, 'Modernist Primitivism, An Introduction', *"Primitivism" in 20th Century Art,* The Museum of Modern Art, New York, 1984, vol. 1, p. 14.

42 See chapter 1 above.

43 Molly Nesbit, in her Durning-Lawrence Lectures, given at University College, London in Summer 1991, has argued that the geometric and projective character of Cubist painting acted to signify a Positivist notion of knowledge, although she is well aware of the complexities and the ironies of the relationship with Positivist assumptions thus established. Especially if one takes into account attitudes to logic in the milieux of the Cubists, it is difficult to associate their work with a simple attempt to explain things on the basis of empirical evidence. As Nesbit suggests, however, it has to be accepted that one reason for the hostility to the geometric in Cubism could well have been that it appeared profoundly anti-artistic precisely because geometry and projection were practices considered basic, not to "art", but to mechanistic "common sense", a fact underlined by the rigidly programmed teaching of drawing in French primary schools at this time. Henderson has comprehensively placed Cubist interest in the fourth dimension and non-Euclidean geometry in the context of a strong reaction against nineteenth century Positivism. See Linda Dalrymple Henderson, *The Fourth Dimension and Non-Euclidean Geometry in Modern Art,* Princeton, New Jersey, 1983.

44 See J()M(),'Cubist Works, 1910–1921'; in Moser (*Metzinger,* 1985), op.cit., pp. 43–7.

45 See, for example, *Glasses,* 1911 (charcoal, 34x29cm); reproduced in *Juan Gris,* Kunsthalle Baden-Baden, 1974, Z. 4. Here initial pencil sketching is visible at the base of both glasses and the bowl of the left hand glass.

46 This drawing is sometimes referred to as *Head of a Woman.* Its relationship with *Portrait of the Artist's Mother* seems to be the justification for this. The indication of a masculine hair-line at the back of the neck, and the lack of ear-rings, suggests to me that the subject is male.

47 The drawing relates to Cooper no. 26.

48 For further information on this drawing, see R. Stanley Johnson, *Cubism and La Section d'Or: Reflections on the Development of the Cubist Epoch: 1907–1922,* Chicago-Düsseldorf, 1991, p. 62.

49 This drawing is reproduced in Juan Antonio Gaya Nuño, *Juan Gris,* translated from Spanish by Kenneth Lyons, London, 1975, p. 27, no. 43.

50 Golding (1968), op.cit., pp. 130–1.

51 See Cooper nos. 60, 62 and 71.

52 Poincaré's essay is titled 'Pourqoui l'espace a trois dimensions'. See Henderson (1983), op.cit., p. 305.

53 Gino Severini, 'La Peinture d'avant-garde', *Mercure de France,* June 1917, pp. 465–6; cited ibid.

54 Princet's connection with "modern painters" who questioned the principles of perspective is mentioned as early as 1910 by Salmon. See "La Palette" (André Salmon), 'Courrier des ateliers', *Paris-Journal,* 10 May 1910; cited Ibid, p. 68. Gris was directly implicated as one who learned from Princet in "Pinturicchio" (Louis Vauxcelles), 'Le Carnet des ateliers: Le Père du cubisme', *Le Carnet de la semaine,* 29 December 1918, p. 11. Gris was quick to deny Vauxcelles's account, however. See Letter to Maurice Raynal, 15 February 1919; in *Letters of Juan Gris (1913–1927),* edited and translated by Douglas Cooper, London, 1956, pp. 62–3 (Letter LXXVII).

55 Ibid., pp. 72–3 and 81–3.

56 Daniel Henry (Daniel-Henry Kahnweiler), *Der Weg zum Kubismus,* Munich, 1920; translated into French in Kahnweiler (1963), op.cit., p. 33. Crowther has established the source in Locke as the *Essay on Understanding,* vol. 1, London, 1974, p. 104; see Crowther (1987), p. 196.

57 C.f. above and Raynal (1919), op.cit.; in *Bulletin de l'Effort Moderne,* no. 1, January 1924.

58 On a particularly striking occasion, Gris omitted the white outlines that give specificity in these two pictures and the result was as close to non-objectivity as he ever came. The work in question is Cooper no. 130. For a fuller discussion, see Christopher Green, 'Synthesis and the "synthetic process" in the painting of Juan Gris', *Art History,* March 1982, pp. 89–90.

59 A particularly telling instance is Cooper no. 43 on whose verso is an unfinished composition reproduced as no. 43a. There ia an abandoned painting on the verso of

Guitar and Pipe. Curiously, it reveals less than the recto, and comes close to resolution.

60 The drawings on this sheet relate most closely to the large watercolour, *Guitar and Glasses,* of 1913 in the Sandra Payson Collection. See *Juan Gris (1887–1927),* edited by Gary Tinterow, Ministerio de Cultura, Madrid, 1985, p. 338, no. 127. It is unlikely that this could be as early as the vertical strip pictures of the period up to May 1913.

61 A striking case is the coloured drawing, *Still-life,* now in the Thyssen-Bornemisza collection. This is identical, except for a few omissions, to a charcoal drawing of exactly the same dimensions across which Gris has written "Esquisse". The latter drawing was in the collection of Maurice Raynal. See Juan Antonio Gaya Nuño, *Juan Gris,* translated from Spanish by Kenneth Lyons, London, 1975, pp. 20–21. The coloured drawing must have come second (in view of the omissions). It is not on tracing paper, but a tracing could have been made against the light with the first drawing fixed to the studio window.

62 Cooper titles this picture *Glasses on a Table.* The cone rising from the bottom of the tall cylinder on the left can clearly be read as the cone at the bottom of a bottle, and the two disc shapes above are then most convincingly to be read as its top and cork. Gris's omission of the neck seems to have been troubling enough to have misled Cooper in his titling.

63 The drawing on the canvas, as revealed by lifting off the paper, is reproduced as Cooper no. 95b.

64 "Le vrai et le faux" is a newspaper head-line found in Cooper no. 90, where the pages from a novel concern one "Fandor" dressing up in the uniform of a "caporal Vinson". Vinson also figures in the page cut out for Cooper no. 83, where we find him on the Côte d'Azur.

65 Especially relevant are Braque's *Fruit Dish and Glass* and *Man with a Pipe,* both of late 1912; see Nicole Mangin (Worms de Romilly), *Catalogue de l'œuvre de Georges Braque, Peintures 1908–1915,* Paris, 1982, nos. 150 and 159.

66 The one exception is Cooper no. 76.

67 Roger Allard, 'Die Kennzeichen der Erneuerung in der Malerei', *Der Blaue Reiter,* Munich, 1912; translated in Fry (1966), op.cit., p. 71.

68 As shown by the texts that led to *Der Weg zum Kubismus.*

69 Kahnweiler (1929 and 1963), op.cit., p. 44.

70 André Salmon, *La Jeune Sculpture française,* Paris, 1919; translated in Fry (1966), p. 140. Fry points out that Salmon's text was written in 1914.

71 Letters (1956), op.cit., p. 2 (Letter III). See Cooper no. 38. Raynal took up the issue with specific reference to the use of real fragments of mirror in *The Wash Basin* (Cooper no. 26) as early as 1912. See Maurice Raynal, 'L'Exposition de La Section d'Or', *La Section d'Or,* Paris, 9 October 1912; in ibid., p. 100.

72 Guillaume Apollinaire, 'Pablo Picasso', *Montjoie!,* 14 March 1913; in Apollinaire (1972), op.cit., p. 279.

73 See for instance André Breton, 'Max Ernst' (1922); in *Les Pas perdus,* Paris, 1930 and Tristan Tzara, 'Le Papier Collé ou le proverbe en peinture', *Cahiers d'Art,* no. 2, 1931.

74 Carl Einstein, 'Exposition de collages (Galerie Goemans)', *Documents,* 2nd Year, no. 4, 1930, p. 244.

75 "Vienne la nuit sonne l'heure/les jours s'en vont je demeure." See René de Costa, 'Juan Gris y la poesia'; in *Gris* (1985), op.cit., pp. 75–7. For further discussion of this work, see Lewis Kachur, 'Gris, Cubismo y Collage'; in *Gris* (1985), p. 34.

76 I have returned to my earlier interest in Bergson and Cubism with the important stimulus of a fresh look at the topic provided by the article by Robert Mark Antliff, 'Bergson and Cubism: A Reassessment', *Art Journal,* Winter, 1988, pp. 341–9. The passage quoted here is from Henri Bergson, *Time and Free Will: An Essay on the Immediate Data of Consciousness,* authorised translation by F. L. Pogson, London and New York, 1959 (first French edition, 1889). Antliff cites it on p. 343.

77 The theory of duration is central to Bergson's thought. It is discussed in many of his major texts, most influentially perhaps in *L'Evolution créatrice,* Paris, 1907. The phrase quoted here is cited by Antliff. Ibid., p. 342.

78 The chronology of *Du "Cubisme"* is fully set out by Cousins and Daix in Rubin (1989), op.cit., pp. 389–409.

79 This is very fully discussed in Antliff (1988), loc.cit. The key writers involved in making the connection were Salmon and above all Tancrède de Visan, especially the latter's article 'Le Philosophie de M. Bergson et le lyrisme contemporain', *Vers et prose,* April–May–June 1910.

80 C.f. my discussion in Christopher Green, *Léger and the Avant-Garde,* New Haven and London, 1976, p. 24 and Gleizes's account of multiple view-points in Albert Gleizes (1911), op.cit., pp. 165–6.

81 The Berlin *Still-life* is Cooper no. 130. I have decided to call the picture originally titled by Cooper *Still-life and Landscape (Place Ravignan), Still-life and Townscape (Place Ravignan)* because of its Montmartre setting.

82 Kahnweiler (1929 and 1963), op.cit., p. 44.

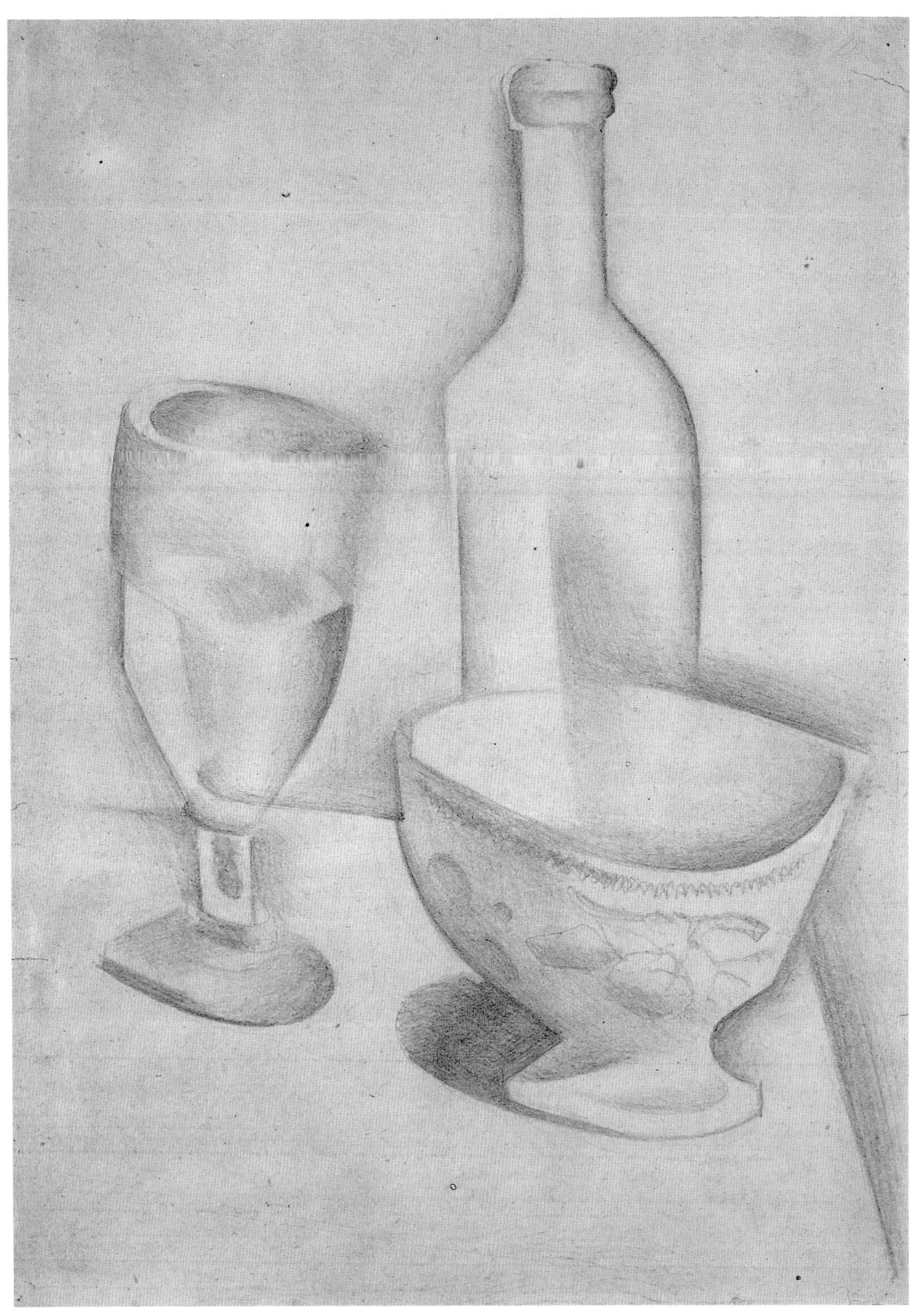

3. 1916–1921: Platonic Absolutes?

When, in 1929, Kahnweiler sketched his brief straight-line account of Gris's development out of analysis into synthesis, he isolated a particular causal factor behind it, a problem to which Gris's brand of synthesis was a solution. The problem was that *collage* and *papier collé* exposed the conflict between things from the world outside – labels, newspapers, wallpaper – and painting. He wrote that Cubism was too realist in the most profound sense of the term not to formalize the things it assimilated. They could be assimilated, but they remained "foreign". For Kahnweiler, Gris's move into synthesis *resolved* the contradictions of *collage* and *papier collé*[1].

At the same time, Kahnweiler separated Gris's "solution" from that of Picasso and Braque and, despite Gris's repeated use of the term "synthesis" in his statements of the 1920s, the dealer called their solution "synthetic cubism" and implied that Gris's was something else. This something else was defined by Gris's particular approach to the "problem" which, according to Kahnweiler, was not in the first place a matter of inventing new signs for things, but of developing a new procedure. This procedure gave precedence to painting by subordinating subject-matter *to* painting. It started with the basic elements of painting, "a sort of flat, coloured architecture", and allowed this "architecture" to suggest the things that finally became the subject-matter of the work[2]. The inference is that, where Picasso and Braque started with sign-making (subject-matter), and built compositions with their signs, Gris started with composition and allowed it to generate signs. The results, however, were comparable since all three jettisoned the "analysis of the depicted object" as starting-point; and in his second monograph of 1946 Kahnweiler was to embed his discussion of Gris's "solution" in a far wider series of reflections on all such painting as the return of the visual arts to their essential condition, that of the invention of signs. For him painting was defined as a kind of writing[3].

In the second of his monographs, Kahnweiler gave prominence in his account to a couple of letters written to him by Gris during and just after the Great War. He took the first, a letter of 26 March 1915, to mark the beginning of the move away from analysis. Gris wrote: "I think I have really made progress recently and that my pictures begin to have a unity which they have lacked till now. They are no longer those inventories of objects which used to depress me so much"[4]. He took the second, a letter of 15 August 1919, to offer a clear insight into the character of Gris's solution: it stressed form and intellect while rejecting both "the exaggerations of the Dada movement" and "abstract painting". Gris wrote of stripping his painting of "too brutal and descriptive a reality" and added: "I hope to be able to express an imagined reality with great precision using the pure elements of the mind"[5].

Kahnweiler dated the move (at least implicitly) to the months following the *pointilliste* canvases of early 1916, that is, to the summer and autumn when *Fruit Dish, Glass and Lemon*, *Woman with a Mandolin (after Corot)*

Bottle, Bowl and Glass, 1918
Pencil on paper,
43.1 x 31.5 cm
Graphische Sammlung
Staatsgalerie Stuttgart

and the *Portrait of Madame Josette Gris* were painted (Plates 58, 66 and Figure 9). "Gris finally gave up presenting the beholder with a great variety of information (acquired by empirical observation) about the objects which he displayed. He now offered a *synthesis*: that is to say, he packed his knowledge into one significant form, a single emblem. True conceptual painting was born"[6]. For Kahnweiler, as for the post-War defenders of the Cubist "call to order", synthesis was a higher condition of conceptualism than analysis; at the same time it offered the resolution of the contradictions exposed and left un-resolved by *collage* and *papier collé*.

Kahnweiler's account will always carry conviction because it fits so completely with Gris's own. Gris's statements are vague and vacillating about when the move occurred, but they are clear and consistent about the rejection of analysis and what it entailed. They are clearest of all about procedure. From the statement published in *L'Esprit Nouveau* early in 1921, with its famous example of bottles made from cylinders rather than cylinders from bottles, he repeatedly insisted that his composition (a flat planar "architecture") came first and that his subject-matter was *always* the result, not the cause of it[7]. The model for Kahnweiler's exegesis of the procedure in 1929 was the lecture given in 1924 at the Sorbonne. It was especially this lecture that Waldemar George and Maurice Raynal were to scorn as irrelevant to a grasp of his painting when they looked back from the 1930s, but when they wrote in Gris's defence during the 1920s they invariably talked of "the deductive method", the "purity" it guaranteed Gris's practice, and the "monstrousness" that it avoided by starting from the harmonies of "the painter's mathematics" rather than "distorting" from subject matter.

In the making of "Juan Gris" then, synthesis went together with a procedure, "the deductive method" (one that moved from the general to the particular, not the particular to the general). This was presented as the resolution of a problem and as a return to consistency that restored the aesthetic cohesion, the formal wholeness and independence, of the art of painting.

That Gris did come to use a "deductive method", at least sometimes and to some extent, can be demonstated[8]. The key to its development was pictorial rhymes. Especially from mid-to-late 1917, the simplicity of the flat configurations by which he could denote the features of figures and things increasingly meant that very similar configurations could denote different things. The inference, of course, was that the moment he set down on paper or canvas a pattern of planes within a geometric armature, he offered himself a whole range of possible signs and referents: the options he could accept or reject were not merely formal. Kahnweiler is right, he could indeed turn a simple white shape into a "plate", and it required certainly the merest of "stimulants", "a few parallel black lines on a white ground", for him to be able to turn the plate into a "music sheet"[9]. Elsewhere, I have argued that the process was often more complicated than the accounts make it seem and, as we shall see here, sometimes it cannot have operated in the manner claimed to be invariable. I have argued too that Gris is unlikely to have worked in such a way before 1917[10]. But, indisputably, he was often working broadly in such a way when he painted *The Man from the Touraine* in September 1918 and *Guitar and Fruit Dish* at the end of 1921 (Plates 83 and 89); he certainly believed he was by 1921. Rhymes abound in both: the eyes rhyme with the buttons of the peasant figure, his hand with his sleeve, the structure of his brow, cheek and nose taken together with the neck and square-rimmed top of the bottle. The fruit dish and the glass rhyme in the still-life, their tops and the sound-hole of the guitar. A single shape or type of configuration can "become" more than one thing, a point perhaps especially clear in the almost interchangeable rhyming guitars and fruit dishes of *Guitar and Fruit Dish* of 1919

Figure 14
Jacques Lipchitz
Bas Relief I, 1918
Painted plaster,
55.9x35.6x6 cm
Private Collection

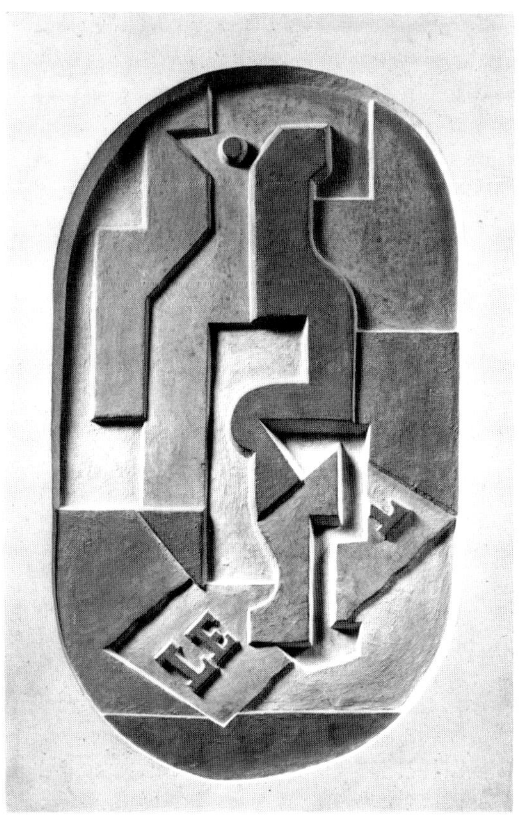

and its distant descendent *The Book of Music* of April 1922 (Plates 98 and 97).

Gris did not make this change and develop the rhetoric of purity that went with it all alone. Paul Dermée had been one of the circle around the poet Pierre Reverdy and his periodical *Nord-Sud* in 1917–18; Gris was a close friend of Dermée as well as Reverdy, and a committed supporter of *Nord-Sud*. In 1919–20, the criticism of Paul Dermée clearly infers a deductive practice both in the painting of Metzinger and in the sculpture of Jacques Lipchitz; he sees it as crucial to the "purity" of both (Figure 14)[11]. The younger Lipchitz had become a far closer friend of Gris's than Metzinger from 1916, and all three had been together with Gris and María Blanchard in the Touraine, escaping from the bombardment of Paris, during the summer of 1918. They were key figures in Léonce Rosenberg's plan to re-establish Cubism at the end of the war as a collective synthesis rather than a fragmentary sum of disconnected individuals[12]. Further, both Metzinger and Lipchitz were also in the circle, which in 1917–18 included, besides Dermée, the Chilean poet Vicente Huidobro. Huidobro was another who spent the summer of 1918 with Gris and Josette at Beaulieu. It was Gris who helped him translate his poems from Spanish into French at that time. When Gris wrote to Kahnweiler on 25 August 1919 about working with "the pure elements of the mind", he followed up on 3 September with a letter that placed his new work in relation to Lipchitz (along with Braque, Léger and Severini), but also to "the sudden crop of poets", singling out Reverdy and "the Reverdy following" as most akin to "our painting"[13].

Between 1918 and the early 1920s responses to the new Gris, exponent of "deductive method", were unquestionably bound up with responses to what was taken to be a group phenomenon, a tendency, which before 1921 was firmly associated with Léonce Rosenberg's Galerie de l'Effort Moderne and with the poetry of the "Reverdy following". I have referred already to the "order" as well as the "collective" group unity identified with this perceived phenomenon, but it had another basic feature. It was called idealist, the name of Plato often invoked, and its representatives supplied both friendly and hostile critics with the most explicit idealist assertions.

When André Lhote talked about a "second Cubism" in 1926, naming Gris, he did so while rejecting what he called "a priorism"[14]. This was a reference to a distinction he had first made in 1920 in response to the group showing of the L'Effort Moderne Cubists, including Gris, at the first Indépendants after the War. At this time he had written of the "pure Cubists", and of Metzinger loving "to speak of "pure effusion", and he had coined the term "*a posteriori* Cubism", where the analytical procedures of the earlier Cubists were still applied. He even anticipated, with a detailed account of processes, Gris's own explanation of "the deductive method" in *L'Esprit Nouveau*[15]. Lhote's use of the term *a priori* was a pointed attempt to associate "pure Cubism" with Kant's "synthetic *a priori*", with the aspiration to grasp the eternal in things, the essence believed to be there before and beyond empirical experience.

A little earlier in 1920, the still vigorously anti-Cubist critic Louis Vauxcelles wrote the following in his rumbustious weekly column for *Le Carnet de la semaine*: "We have just read a cubist manifesto. This is not the first, for there is much theorizing in the bosom of this school... Who is the author of this paper... where the *Philebus* (of Plato), and Epicurus, the Sphinx of Gisah, the Median wars in Chaldea at the time of Goudea, the aesthetic of locomotives, of Emerson, and of Apollinaire, are all spoken of? This aesthetician who leads the troops of the Cubists into the assault (the assault on what?)... is it a painter? Is it a critic? A poet? No. It is Léonce Rosenberg, an art-dealer"[16]. He had just read Rosenberg's text *Cubisme et tradition*, published to serve as the preface to an exhibition of the L'Effort Moderne Cubists in Geneva. Here, indeed, Rosenberg cited the passage from *The Philebus* of Plato, where Socrates tells Protarcus of forms that are not merely relatively beautiful, like those that give pleasure to the senses, but which are "always beautiful in themselves": "straight and circular" lines, figures "made with ruler and set-square", geometric forms. And here, indeed, Rosenberg claimed that Cubist art possessed "a strictly intrinsic value", that it was "beautiful in itself"[17].

The recent emergence of much of the correspondence between Gris and Léonce Rosenberg during the Great Wat has underlined the dealer's role in giving so emphatic an idealist cast to the "second Cubism" that emerged in those years. In a "confidential circular", dated 3 September 1917 and sent to all the artists of L'Effort Moderne, Rosenberg based his order (and it was an order) that they resist the temptation to follow Picasso and Serge Férat into designing for the theatre on the following unbending declaration: "Great art knows neither laughter, nor tears, it is serene. It does not see the joy of the instant, the sadness of the moment, but rather that which Humanity confines to the absolute and the eternal. It leads to God"[18]. It was by means of such a transcendental view of the "eternal" that Rosenberg fastened his link between the "collective" Cubism of L'Effort Moderne and the arts of the past he most admired, back from Cézanne through Giotto to the Chaldeans[19]. Cubism as idealism was in easy reach of "tradition" in its many French or European forms.

As Léonce Rosenberg issued orders to what he plainly thought of as his platoon of Cubists in France, in Bern the exiled dealer Kahnweiler pondered the Cubism he had so effectively supported until the declaration of war, in terms of a far more rigorous and far more sophisticated consideration of idealist philosophy. When he returned to Paris early in 1920, the year of the Munich publication of *Der Weg zum Kubismus*, he had just seen a sample of Gris's war-time work in Léonce Rosenberg's show of L'Effort Moderne in Geneva. He recalls being struck by Gris's "progress" (one wonders what he thought of Rosenberg's text)[20]. It was with his return, from 1920, that Kahnweiler's friendship with Gris deepened, and it did so as a meeting between intellects as well as between personalities and tastes. In the brief period between his arrival and the first, near fatal onset in May of the illness that would eventually kill Gris, there was certainly one long, searching discussion when their intellectual proximity struck at least Kahnweiler[21]. The idealism of Gris's own statements in the 1920s carries echoes more of the sceptical, measured idealism of Kahnweiler than of the doctrinaire Platonism of Rosenberg.

Something of the authority the German dealer carried as a far more than merely commercial presence is conveyed in the recollections of the "Sundays" in Kahnweiler's house and garden left by Armand Salacrou. From Gris's move in 1922 out of the "Bateau-Lavoir" into a house close by in Boulogne-sur-Seine, these "Sundays" were to become a feature of his life. Salacrou recalls the rather unappetising suppers that sometimes followed the excitements of the afternoon, evenings lifted, however, by the pleasure of being "close to the wisdom, the curiosity and the intellectual assurance of Kahnweiler..."[22].

For Kahnweiler, in both the 1929 and the 1946 monographs Gris is emphatically a Platonist. "No-one was as pure as him," he wrote in 1929, and concluded his short text by claiming for Gris's art the highest transcendent status, "alongside those painters he loved... Jean Fouquet, Mathieu Le Nain, Boucher, Ingres and Cézanne"[23]. In 1946 he identifies Gris's Platonism more precisely with the "synthetic Cubism" that emerged, as he saw it, after 1916. Mentioning *The Peasant in a Blue Smock* (called by him *The Miller*) alongside *The Man from the Touraine* (Plate 84 and 83), the Pierrots and the Harlequins of 1919 (Plates 86 and 88), he wrote: "The objects which he created are no longer those we meet with on a given day at a given time: they have been raised to the dignity of the type, redeemed from particular fortuities... These figures and objects remind one of the Platonist "idea""[24]. We shall see that Kahnweiler's (and Gris's) idealism was not so very "pure", but these claims are unequivocal enough.

The other close friendship maintained by Gris until his death which, as a meeting of intellects, seems to have deepened his sense of the idealist in him was with Maurice Raynal (Plate 12). They had met as members both of the Picasso and the Puteaux circles before the war, and had kept in touch throughout Raynal's time at the front[25]. In 1918, when Rosenberg was contemplating a periodical to accompany his planned sequence of Cubist exhibitions, Gris, with quiet determination, made sure that Raynal remained first choice for editor, keeping him throughout apprised of his manoeuvring. "Nothing," he wrote to Rosenberg in October 1918, "gives me more pleasure than the choice you seem to have made of Raynal... This is my oldest friend and for years, perhaps ten, we have lived as brothers... This is an intelligent man, and steady and very energetic and serious..."[26]. During the 1920s, alongside Kahnweiler's, it was Raynal's opinion of his work that he most eagerly awaited, if we are to believe the letters[27].

Raynal has lately been accused of ignorance in philosophical matters, but his more pondered texts on Cubism and the Cubists from the period 1919–27 reveal a knowledge of German philosophy and especially of Kant that is far more profound than the mere citation of names[28]. He lacked the cogent rigour of Kahnweiler, but he too resisted the unproblematized Platonism of Léonce Rosenberg, as we shall see. Yet, he too was capable of apparently unequivocal assertions about the idealism of his Spanish friend's art, and indeed about Cubism altogether, something for which he was challenged at the time[29]. "Juan Gris," he writes in his *L'Esprit Nouveau* article of 1921, "contemplates his unquantifiable sensibility in the things that surround him as others contemplate it in the sky or in their mirror, and it is thus that he invites us to take part in an intimate communion with the very essence of the objects that he aims to paint". He goes on to align Gris's art with Greek art before Phidias, quoting Winckelmann: "The ancient style of the Greeks... is founded on a system of rules taken from nature, but which afterwards became separated from nature to become *ideal,* in such a way that one worked less after the nature one had to imitate than after an ideal system with which one had substituted it"[30]. The great eighteenth century idealist historian, looking at pre-Hellenic Antiquity, is found to have anticipated Gris's "deductive method" in the name of the "ideal".

I have mentioned, in the last essay, the idealist clarity of Raynal's division between concept and sensation in *Quelques Intentions du cubisme* of 1919. By the time, in 1927, he summed up his view of art in France "from 1906 to today", he was to see everything in terms of a division between the "Idealists" and the "Realists", between the painters of "concepts" and the painters of "sensation", "artists" and "painters". For Raynal, Cubism had become the most extreme form of "Idealism" in art[31].

It has often been argued that from the beginning, from before 1914 and even before 1910, Cubism was always fundamentally idealist. Not only have later idealist readings of Cubist art been blamed on the determining role of Kahnweiler as dealer and writer (to which now the role of Rosenberg should be added), but a proliferation of idealist statements about Cubism from such figures as Apollinaire, Salmon and Olivier Hourcade, besides Raynal, has been taken to demonstrate an actual and a dominant idealism as an attribute of pre-War Cubism. This is seen to follow from the links between the late Symbolist and the early Cubist milieux, especially between the circles of Picasso and Apollinaire, and those of *La Plume* or *Vers et Prose*. The Gris who in 1911–12 probably read Mallarmé is identified with a rampantly idealist late Symbolism[32].

There is over-simplification of a thoroughly misleading kind here. Of course, idealist statements from the period about the painting of the "thing in itself" (the *nuomenon*) abound. Certainly, as Linda Henderson has established, a profound idealist aspiration pervaded the talk of the fourth dimension and non-Euclidean geometries (in which Gris was probably involved)[33]. Yet, this was but one facet of a bewildering, contradictory bustle of assertions, another facet of which was the diametrically opposed talk of empirical analysis. As early as July 1911, Michel Puy could write: "Cubism seems to be a system with a scientific foundation, which enables the artist to support his effort with reliable data"[34]. Gris's own characterisation of his first Cubisms as analytical taxonomies based on empirical observation stresses the analogy with a kind of elementary logical Positivism in contradistinction to his later synthesis. At a profound level, certainly in his case, the linkage between "deductive method", synthesis and idealism clearly *separated* the work he produced after 1916 from all he produced before. Logic was applied in the service of an idealism that denied not only his earlier "analytical cubism", but all that nineteenth century Positivism in twentieth century industrial Europe represented.

This is not to say that the "purity" of Gris's post-1916 Cubisms can effectively be separated from the social and political in the France of the War years and their aftermath. We know well enough that the Cubist "call to order" was part of a major ideological shift that went with the formation of the "Union Sacrée", and that set France up as a "Latin culture" against the habitually designated "barbarous" culture of Germany. The idealism and the focus on collective discipline that characterised Rosenberg's L'Effort Moderne and Kahnweiler's "Classicism accomplished" of 1918–22 were easily appropriated by the traditionalist and even the fascisizing Right[35]. Indeed, in November 1922, just after the Fascists' march on Rome, Rosenberg could publish a letter in *Le Carnet de la semaine* declaring that Mussolini was "a 'cubist' hero". He quoted himself on Cubism from the Geneva preface of 1920: "But, by its doctrine, it leads us back to order, establishing, by an hierarchy of values, the discipline thanks to which it has been able to organise with a view to the creation of a new unity". Add, he remarked, "national" to "a new unity" and "it is Mussolini who speaks"[36]. It should be emphasized, however, that a classical notion of Cubism was just as easily appropriated by the "collectivist" Left, as witness the cases of Léger and Gleizes (the latter's Cubism could be called "Communist" in 1924)[37]. The Kahnweiler who placed Cubism in so clear an idealist context during the war-years was actively engaged with the Socialist Left in Bern[38]. He was not in the least attracted, like Rosenberg, to the Fascist "new man". Neither was Gris.

I opened this essay with Kahnweiler's observation that Gris's "deductive method" was developed in order to resolve the contradictions exposed by *collage* and *papier collé*. A primary underlying theme of his 1929 monograph was the transcendent significance that he claimed for the unity and the completeness he found in Gris's solution to this problem. He approached the final cadence of his text thus: "If, in the frame of the history of art, one of the essential aims of cubism consisted in the return to the unity of the work of art, in the desire to create not sketches, but autonomous and accomplished organisms, then no cubist has pursued this aim with more success... than Juan Gris"[39]. Tradition and the ideal were most completely manifest, he suggested, in the cohesion and the finish of Gris's pictures. Alongside "organism", "architecture" was perhaps the most favoured epithet applied by Gris and his supporters to his work. Because they were not merely additive, but totally transformed *wholes,* Gris's paintings were not "constructions", but "architectures"; this was Gris's contention in the lecture of 1924[40].

The issue of logic, the question most importantly of the law of non-contradiction, has to be central in any encounter with the analytical work Gris produced before 1916 in the context of his reputation as Apollinaire's "demon of logic". It is not so much the issue of logic that is central to an encounter with the post-1916 painting. The questions to be asked follow from the idealist claims that were made for it. The relationship of "concept" to "vision" remains central and so does the question of control in working practice, but above all what matters is the question of how far his work can be called integrated, whole, the contradictions declared, but then resolved with conclusive finality.

Kahnweiler's first monograph stressed equally the importance of both Gris's "deductive method" and his assertion of "the unity of the work of art" to the resolution of contradictions in his painting. Elsewhere I have given close attention to the question of Gris's "deductive method", how and whether it actually worked as he claimed it did[41]. My concern here will be more with the *results* than the processes believed to guarantee their "purity". I want to explore the theme of unity, and with it that of resolution and conclusiveness. It was, after all, in the appearance of a conclusive wholeness that Gris's finished pictures signified transcendence.

I closed my last essay by pointing to the extraordinary open-endedness of Gris's work through the brief period between June 1915 and October 1916; the fact that its technical finish conceals a willingness to leave conclusions open. He was always ready to surprise himself. This openness to change was not extinguished after 1916, although the rhythm of his switches of direction slowed, especially from 1920. At the same time, there is one phase after 1916 when, as with the *papiers collés* of 1914, Gris's painting can seem to equivocate, on this occasion without the anchorage of firm compositional stability. It comes in

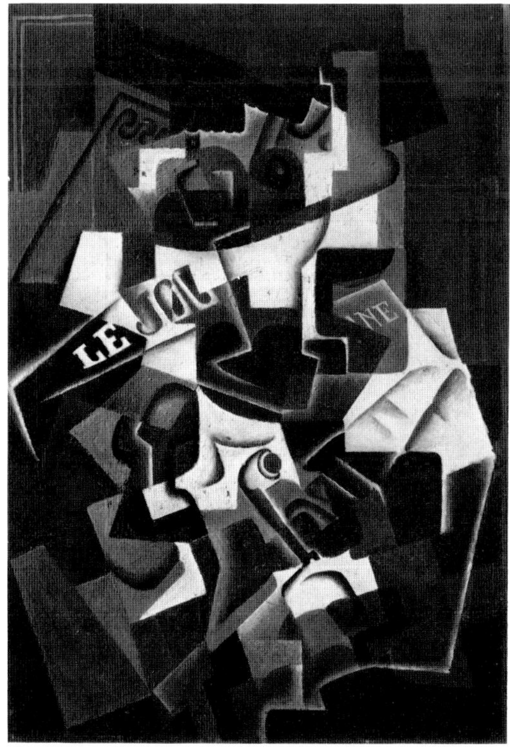

Figure 15
Fruit Dish, Pipe and Newspaper, 1917
Oil on plywood, 92x65.5 cm
Öffentliche Kunstsammlung Basel, Kunstmuseum

November-December 1917, and one of the pictures implicated is *Fruit Dish, Pipe and Newspaper* of November (Figure 15).

This was a clearly formulated still-life idea, developed from a theme Gris had already explored, and its geometric armature is another demonstration of the Golden Section ratio flexibly applied[42]. Yet, the proportionate simplicity of the geometric structure is concealed by the sheer complexity of its elaboration, and the multiplication of obliques threatens equilibrium. Such also is the openness of the relationships between objects, and between objects and setting, that confusion is often a possibility when the signs are read. Thus, the black curved shape above the letters "NE" can either be the profile of the fruit dish overlapping the bottle or the level of the wine inside the bottle and, below, the shaping of the crumpled cloth above the pipe so obviously echoes the shaping of the glass that it can be read *as* a glass. Signs are not always definitive; there are ambiguities. The label "indirect contributions" would not be entirely out of place.

Such equivocation and instability is, however, a factor for no more than a few months at this time, and what this phase seems to mark is the moment of transition from the development of a simple vocabulary of flat planar signs denoting a range of different things to something like the "deductive method" proper. For what is revealed in the few pictures of late 1917 like *Fruit Dish, Pipe and Newspaper* is the sheer capacity of simple configurations to take on identities, to "become" objects. It was a semantic flexibility that, briefly, Gris did not always tie down by making definitive decisions; more than one option was sometimes left to the spectator. By the end of 1918 and Gris's return to Paris from his long summer and autumn at Beaulieu-lès-Loches, the referents to the signs in his pictures were invariably unequivocal. The rhymes in *The Man from the Touraine* or *Harlequin at a Table* (Plates 83 and 88) never confuse identities. The Harlequin's leg rhymes with the table leg, but there is no doubt which is which. And, where orthogonals are dominant in the peasant picture, the obliques are precisely balanced about a clear vertical axis in the *Commedia dell'Arte* picture. Stability is regained. Indeed, both clarity and stability are dominants in almost all of Gris's painting associated with the "call to order".

There is one other basic feature of the pictures he produced between 1916 and 1921 that needs to be mentioned before looking more closely at the "architecture" in them and beginning to consider the question of wholeness and finality. This is the restrictiveness of their subject-matter.

Gris's subjects are of importance, even in this period, and I shall argue the case for them in the last two of my essays. From time to time he was, in fact, willing to take on new kinds of figure and object and the work he produced on his visits to Beaulieu-lès-Loches is demonstration enough of that. There are wholesome heritage landscapes from the visits both of 1916 and 1918, clearly inspired by specific *motifs* (despite in 1918 the emerging deductive method). There are groups of new still-life objects in 1918. And, again both in 1916 and 1918, there are new figures with specific models (the subjects "found" in Gris's pictorial architecture were not necessarily general types).

In 1916 he painted the ramparts and the keep of the castle at Loches, probably from the Boulevard Philippe-Auguste (what had been the encircling ditch), as well as a wrought-iron gate possibly close by (Plate 65)[43]. In 1918 he painted an old stone house opposite the Abbey in Beaulieu with a quaint corner turret, often the picturesque subject of tourist postcards (Plate 81 and Figure 16)[44]. In 1918 he drew and painted new kinds of cup and porcelain-container, as well as tobacco pouches (Plate 93), to join the established repertoire of musical instruments, bottles, glasses, fruit dishes and so on (Plates 80 and 89). In 1916 he used drawings after postcards of "master" paintings by Corot, Velázquez and Cézanne (Plates 62, 63 and 64) as the basis for a new, explicitly

Figure 16
Postcard image of the house in Beaulieu-les-Loches
(Photograph: Courtesy Christopher Green)

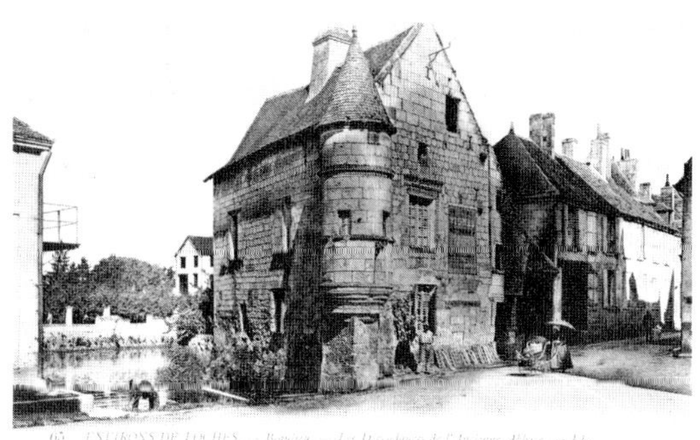

traditionalist series of Cubist figure-paintings, including *Woman with a Mandolin (after Corot)* and the *Portrait of Madame Josette Gris* (Figure 9 and Plate 66). In 1918 he painted peasant figures, *The Peasant in a Blue Smock*, *The Man from the Touraine* and *Seated Peasant Woman*[45] (Plates 84, 83 and 82), which seem to have been modelled on actual peasants (as we shall see in the essay on Gris's figures).

New *motifs* and new models were demonstrably taken on by Gris after 1916 when the occasion presented itself. But it is obvious, nonetheless, that Gris's restricted range of simplified pictorial elements and signs was the counterpart to a carefully restricted range of subjects, certain kinds of still-life set-up and figure above all. The *quid pro quo* of strict structural control was strict control of subject-matter. Both facilitated the accomplishment of cohesive resolution. Indeed, between 1918 and 1921 the restriction of subject-matter was repeatedly picked out as an essential feature not only of Gris's, but of all the L'Effort Moderne Cubists' "call to order". It was, in fact, the least acceptable of their restrictions.

By 1918, André Salmon was not numbered among the loyal supporters of L'Effort Moderne Cubism[46]. That year, with heavy irony, he wrote in *L'Europe Nouvelle* an appreciation of what he called "the latest discovery of our painter-abstractors of the quintessence". This discovery turns out to be a new way of treating the letters of the word "Journal" (newspaper), and the entire article ridicules the "pure Cubists'" refusal of "impure" subjects. Salmon titled the piece 'The Pure and the Impure'. "These gentlemen," he writes, " organised into a company by a dealer who equals them in subtlety, licence only restricted themes. They banish the nude because it is impure". He continues mockingly: "Among the themes allowed the still-life comes first, but reduced to a limited selection of objects: the newspaper, the packet of tobacco, the glass, the pipe, the mandolin and the siphon. It is to Juan Gris that is due the enthronement of the siphon in cubism, and this audacity was not accepted without discussion"[47].

The tone and the topic of Salmon's attempt to deflate Rosenberg, Gris and the others is found again, a few months later, in Louis Vauxcelles's even more mischievous series of articles in *Le Carnet de la semaine*, which through the summer and autumn of 1918 declared Cubism dead, and announced a return to nature led by André Lhote and Diego Rivera. We know from Gris's correspondence how this series irritated him at Beaulieu[48]. Vauxcelles's starting-point was precisely Lhote's and Rivera's refusal to keep to Cubist subject-matter as stipulated by Rosenberg, and this refusal is directly linked to a desire to break out of the doctrinaire idealism associated with L'Effort Moderne, its insistance on conceptual purity. In the first of the articles, Vauxcelles quotes Lhote thus: "I am, ultimately, free to marvel everyday at the freshness and the variety of nature. I have, ultimately, the right to concern myself with flowers, naked flesh, landscapes..."[49]. According to Vauxcelles, the sin of Lhote and Rivera had been Lhote's readyness to paint nudes, and Rivera's to paint portraits.

Gris's traditionalist figure paintings of late 1916 included, of course, portraits: the two portraits of Josette and what could be a self-portrait[50]. And they represented a widening of his range, in a sense. But the traditionalism of these new subjects was itself explicitly restrictive. Both on the level of pictorial architecture and on that of the restriction of subjects, these pictures and the drawings related to them set

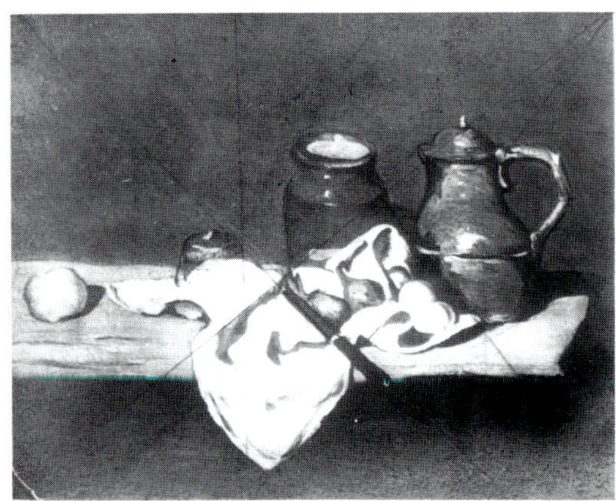

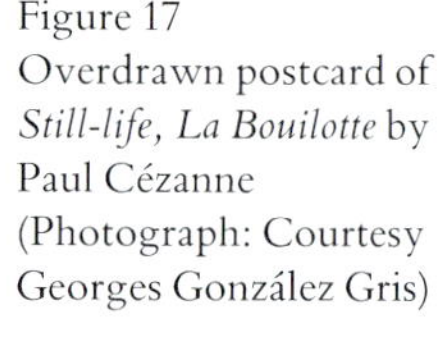

Figure 17
Overdrawn postcard of *Still-life, La Bouilotte* by Paul Cézanne
(Photograph: Courtesy Georges González Gris)

the terms for Gris's pursuit of an ideal unity over the next half-decade.

The drawings "after" Corot, Velazquez and Cézanne were based on black-and-white postcards. Recently it has emerged that some of these have survived. Several are divided by the "organising lines" of analyses in pencil using set-square and ruler (Figure 17)[51]. These analysed postcards underline, literally, a central area of signification opened up by the explicitly traditionalist figure paintings of autumn 1916. Gris's use of clearly recognisable subject-types (Josette as a "Corot subject") to emphasize the linkage between his Cubism and what he considered *the* tradition was integrated with a basic analysis of the geometry of structure, whose "organising lines" were made an explicit pictorial feature.

As I have contended elsewhere, it was just such an architecture of organising lines, using overlapping triangles drawn from the sides of the format, that seems to have established the main planar divisions of *Woman with a Mandolin (after Corot)* and *Portrait of Madame Josette Gris*, right down to the detailed dividing up of the faces[52]. The abstract geometry first suggested to Gris in his drawing from new still-life set-ups earlier in 1916 (Plates 67 and 69) became the formative architecture of these declarations of the transcendence of painting. The themes of pictorial architecture and the "constants" of tradition were consolidated and integrated. The inference was there to be drawn: to restore tradition was to restore not only an old subject-matter in new terms, but to find the unchanging principles of structure in painting. Cohesion in space (composition) and cohesion in time (Corot *in* Gris) were presented as a single, fundamental truth.

The aspiration to compositional cohesion was the complement to a comprehensive notion of the French tradition; indeed, it was an integral feature of it. Cohesion was certainly a central theme for Gris from 1916, and nothing demonstrates it more clearly than a look at the question of the separation or integration of figure and ground, object and setting.

In May 1916 Gris painted his first war-time siphon (the "innovation" on which Salmon was to comment later) (Figure 18). If the siphon was a new war-time subject to him, the glass he placed beside it was not, and he used it as the central *motif* in another picture dated May 1916, the perversely titled *The Packet of Tobacco* (Plate 73). This elaborate sign for a glass, angular yet cursive, closed yet open, had been taken through a sequence of variations since its arrival in the *pointilliste* gouaches around March (Plates 53 and 55)[53], and this fact underlines the primacy of both these

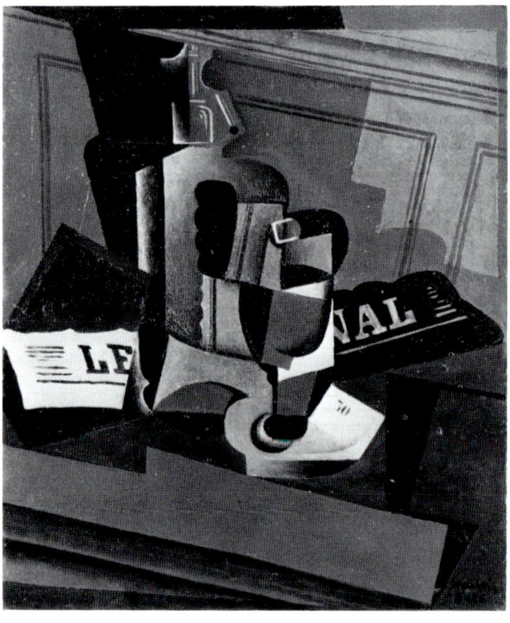

Figure 18
The Siphon, 1916
Oil on canvas,
55 x 46,5 cm
Museum Ludwig, Cologne

objects when Gris actually conceived and put the composition of *The Siphon* together. The glass and the siphon obviously came first, not the pictorial structure of "organising lines" and, consonant with this, there is a certain twofoldness in *The Siphon* which is found in *The Packet of Tobacco* too. Certainly the objects are snugly enough fitted in to the geometric armatures formed by Gris's "organising lines", much as in many of the drawings of the time. And, in fact, a large drawing in pencil and gouache was made preparatory to *The Siphon*[54]. Yet, the objects remain to be read as discrete items placed on a table-top in a space: there are things and there is the setting, a clear *two*fold unity. Glass and siphon are not so opened up that the lines of the over-all structure can penetrate them fully. Colour stresses division.

By mid-1917, a year later, Gris had succeeded in getting rid of this two-foldness without compromising the lucidity of his signs. And one of the earliest pictures of which this can be said is the tiny, chunky *Carafe and Bowl* dated May 1917 (Plate 72). Still here, however, Gris was working with variations on signs that he was exploring in drawings as well as paintings, and still, therefore, he was starting not with "organising lines", but with a limited range of subjects. This painting gives in reverse variants on the signs used in a *conte* and pencil drawing (Plate 70) which, although inscribed to mark the date in July when Gris gave it to Jean Cocteau ("7–17"), was almost certainly done at the time of or before the canvas. It is clear that by now, both in drawing and in painting, Gris had effectively fused the structuring of his signs and his compositions; one cannot be conceived any more without the other. Even in the less pared down syntax of the drawing, so completely is the planar division of objects and setting fused that figure/ground distinctions become nearly impossible to make, however crisp the definition of objects.

From that moment, in the spring of 1917, certainly until the end of 1922, the fusion of

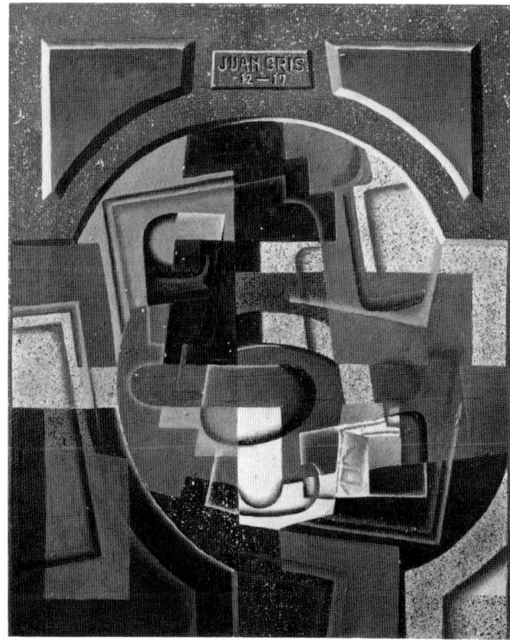

Figure 19
Still-life with Plaque,
1917
Oil on canvas,
81 x 65.5 cm
Öffentliche Kunstsammlung Basel,
Kunstmuseum

figure and ground, object and setting, is a constant and primary theme of Gris's painting, and at the turn of 1917–18 he re-introduced a *motif* that gave this theme of cohesion a particular inflection and emphasis. The *motif* in question is the frame. Among the pictures of late 1917 and early 1918 to make the most overt use of it are *Still-life with Plaque* and *Pipe and Fruit Dish with Grapes* (Figure 19 and Plate 78). All offer objects and settings as one, and all give us frames within the frame.

Gris had put frames into his pictures before. *Still-life with Flowers* (Plate 8) has a painted band to frame the still-life. Frames accompany *collage* early in 1913 (Plate 28) and in 1914 (Figure 20), picking up the talk then current about *collage* being a sort of "internal frame" to mark the limits of the flat surface and so of pictorial depth[55]. Picasso's and Braque's oval formats are quoted in certain *papier collés* of 1914 (Plate 44) and in, say, *Book, Pipe and Glasses* of 1915 (Plate 49)[56]. But in these cases frames are either conventional boundaries or act not to enhance cohesion at all, but to bring out the contradictoriness so central to the whole Cubist enterprise, especially after 1912. In the *papiers collés* they add another

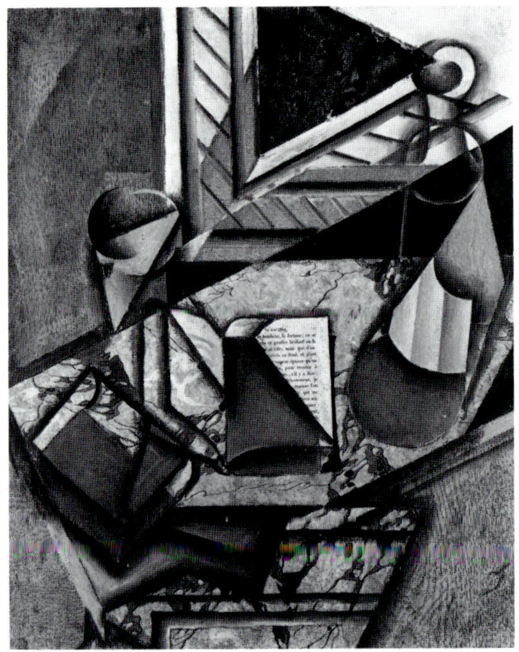

Figure 20
The Marble-topped Console Table, 1914
Oil, paper and glass on canvas, 61 x 50.2 cm
Private Collection

layer of irony, one that "frames" the entire "conception" and insists on that *refusal* of resolution that Kahnweiler was to pose as a problem to be solved. In the 1915 ovals, they bring the basics of pictorial composition into conflict: the framing ovals are *negated* by overriding pictorial structures.

In 1917–18, the frames in Gris's paintings are neither conventional, ironically contradictory, nor in conflict. Instead they function as powerful signifiers of cohesion. In fact, they are integral elements of pictorial structure, literally produced by it in such a way that this can be seen as a simple fact. They declare not merely the limits of flatness, but the *precedence* of format. The flat rectangle or oval comes first. If, for Kahnweiler, the key to the "deductive method" was that the picture took priority, these frames said so more clearly than anything in Gris's painting hitherto. Thus, in *Still-life with Plaque* the swivelling arcs that seem to pull objects together into a measured vortex are a function of the oval frame of the plaque, whose stone texturing, achieved with wonderfully controlled flicks of paint, fastens it to the surface. The tilted stem of the fruit dish in *Pipe and Fruit Dish with Grapes*, along with the dominant orthogonals, are a function of the framing panel and its triangular corner-features.

Conventionally frames are thought of as decorative additions that mark completion. And what is known of the way that Kahnweiler and his German agent Flechtheim showed Gris's pictures in the 1920s demonstrates that his work was certainly given a decisive completeness by its framing. Broad, dark mouldings, without too many decorative excresences were usual; they contrast with the heavily gilded frames often used for Picasso[57]. Gris's frames within frames signify completion too, but at the same time they have become, themselves, starting-points, and say so. The architecture of these pictures, turned into frames, declares the *primacy* of the *tableau-objet* as well as Gris's commitment to completion. Framing devices, incidentally, and the decisive concluding image are a feature of many of the poems written by Reverdy, Dermée and Huidobro between 1917 and 1920[58].

Gris's painting is more often associated with a particular framing *motif* other than the frame within the frame: the open window. It was his most compelling metaphor of a pictorial architecture that could contain things and yet be open. Again, there are echoes in the poetry of the "Reverdy circle". There are a proliferation of windows in Reverdy's *Ardoises du toit*, published just before Gris left for Beaulieu in 1918[59]. The closed and the open play against one another in Gris's painting as in Reverdy's poetry. While Gris worked on the open windows of 1921–22 at Bandol and Céret (Plates 99, 100, 101 and 102), he was working also with shallow, "closed" surfaces where depth was shut out. *Guitar and Fruit Dish* of December 1921 (Plate 111) is patently *without* an internal frame, a lack which draws attention to the unrelieved flatness of the surface on or in front of which the cluster of signs for objects is hung. The openness of the open windows was one of two options, the other was to close in the objects.

The first of Gris's open windows was one of his most ambitious and best known paintings, *Still-life and Townscape (Place Ravignan)* (Plate 48). It was painted in June 1915, but it was not to have its sequel until the views onto a tourists' Mediterranean painted at Bandol in 1921. I shall return to the open windows because their openness has many senses that invite exploration. For the moment, however, I stress them as metaphors of openness architecturally contained. Their pictorial architecture is read *as* architecture, the architecture of the window frame that contains and the shutter that can be opened.

If it is in the frame within the frame, and pictorial architecture *as* architecture that Gris made the containment of coherence most explicitly the theme of his post-1916 painting, it is perhaps most pervasively in the cueing of associations with Cézanne that he associated this architectural Cubism with an idealized French tradition. Between 1918 and 1922 the words "construction" and "constructive" were, in fact, more used about painting that gave priority to structure than "architecture" and "architectural". By the early 1920s a broad trend towards "constructive" painting was diagnosed in French independent art[60]; "pure Cubism" was taken to be its most extreme manifestation. Cézanne was often identified as its model, and indeed the crucial link between vanguard painting and the French tradition.

Perhaps Gris's most explicitly Cézannist still-life of the 1918–19 period is *Bottle and Fruit Dish* of January 1919 (Plate 90). The napkin that gently softens its architecture of pale yet luxuriant green, of warm brown and steely grey surfaces unmistakably invokes Cézanne. This is a painting without an inner frame, or even framing devices; Cézanne provides by allusion another kind of frame, one that contains Gris's pictorial architecture temporally in an ideal of tradition.

Is this all? Do I simply have to re-assert, in the end, what Kahnweiler gave us to start with; a simple straight-line development towards a "deductive" kind of painting, whose structural and traditional imagery of cohesion signifies an actual working commitment to completeness? Is there nothing that tempers the ineluctable finitude of these pictures or that can qualify the idealism for which they were believed to stand?

One should recall, first, the elementary point made at the outset, that Gris's conclusions did, in fact, remain open. He could still manage surprising switches, for instance in the few months between the chromatic stridency of his painting early in 1918 (Plate 80) and the subdued *Guitar and Fruit Dish* of August 1918 (Plate 89). Yet, far more profoundly important, the point has to be made that change was itself a central feature of the "deductive method", and that this was something that was signified as unmistakably as framing could signify cohesion, and an unfurled napkin could allude to Cézanne. It was signified above all by Gris's rhymes.

Just as the open windows can infer possible closure, Gris's rhymes can signify both structural cohesion and conceptual openness at once. This dual signification is clear in by far the most remarkable text written on his rhymes in the 1920s, an essay written in response to Gris's solo exhibition at Kahnweiler's Galerie Simon in April 1923 by Maurice Raynal. Like the piece in *L'Esprit Nouveau* two years earlier, it seems again to have been written from the vantage-point of an insider[61]. Here Raynal used the term "metaphor" for Gris's particular kind of visual rhyming, which was, as we have seen, the key to the deductive method. His notion of metaphor was adapted from Pierre Reverdy's notorious 1918 definition of the poetic "image" as the product of the meeting of two more or less distant "realities"[62].

In Gris's case, the guitar is a poetic "image" or "metaphor", not because in *Guitar and Fruit Dish* of 1919 (Plate 98) it is *like* the bunch of grapes, but because it can *become* the bunch of grapes, so patently do the two share just one form.

Like Reverdy's notion of the image, Raynal's notion of the metaphor in Gris's painting simultaneously stressed openness and closure. Reverdy insists that a new, indivisible whole is the result of the meeting of "distant realities" in the image. Raynal expands on the cohesiveness, the closure of the metaphor, thus: "The metaphor does not merely compare, but draws out of the affinity in the relations between certain objects an essentially new object endowed with its own existence... On this basis, comparison is the work of the dictionary, but the metaphor is the work of creation; the first is a heap of stones, the second is a house constructed"[63]. Raynal sees not geometry or proportion, but Gris's rhymes (metaphors) as the essence of his pictorial architecture. For him, it is metaphor that holds Gris's pictures together at a deep conceptual level, and Gris himself was to use precisely the distinction between additive accumulation (the pile of bricks) and architecture (the house constructed) in the Sorbonne lecture of 1924, switching to an analogy with chemical compounds[64]. Yet, as we shall see, the metaphoric was also always open to metamorphosis; new wholes were "constructed", but one thing always *became* another.

Gris's rhymes operate cohesively in his paintings of 1918–22 as an underpinning of compositional geometry, much as they do with rhythm in Reverdy's and Huidobro's poetry of the time[65]. They amplify structural relations as they bring "distant realities" together. Thus, in *Harlequin at a Table* (Plate 88), the rhyming elipses of the knotted cord, the glass-top, the eyes and the mouth draw the gaze to different points on the canvas to tie a simple network of connections. And the rhyming of leg and table-leg makes metaphor and structure signify together: the figure, the object on the table and the pictorial architecture all "stand" upon a rhyme. *Guitar and Fruit Dish* was painted in July 1919, one month after the *Harlequin*. They were both the product of Gris's first extended phase of pictorial rhyme-making, which followed his return from Beaulieu in November 1918. Here again simple shape-rhymes, the elipses of guitar sound-hole and glass-top, the softer ovals of grapes and carafe-top, threaded together by the frieze-pattern above (a sequence of ovals), encourages a pattern of movement for the eye, reinforcing the poised symmetry of the composition. And, at the heart of the picture, the complex configurational rhyme between the guitar and the fruit dish (with its bunch of grapes), establishes a metaphor of fusion, not merely linkage, about the central axis that otherwise threatens to divide one from the other.

Gris did certainly use rhyming cohesively, and Raynal recognised the fact. But Raynal made far more of its other, its metamorphic aspect. Metaphor, he said, did not merely fuse things into one more effectively than likeness (comparison), it was also "more lyrical, more inventive": it produced *new* forms. Bringing to mind the open windows of Bandol, he writes : "Since Gris has in him the sinusoid of the guitar and that of the hill (i.e. since Gris finds the *a priori* form of the *sinusoid* in both), one can become the other and vice-versa..."[66]. Such "lyrical illusions" (his phrase) of flexible identity have a parallel in grammar, which he uses to draw out the openness of the inventive processes released.

"Among the figures of rhetoric," Raynal writes, "*catacresis* is that which allows the imagination to choose a known word in order to contribute to the designation of a new thing. Thus, in saying "leaf of paper", "table-leg", "mill sail", the inventive spirit takes from two different things the necessary resources to construct a third... The principle is always the same: it is only the imagination that gives lyrical variety to more or less happy discoveries"[67]. Raynal was careful to separate the imaginative openness basic to the invention of metaphors from the technical procedures that gave Gris's painting its perfected completeness. The metaphors, he said, came first; only afterwards came the "arranging"

Figure 21
The Glass, 1919
Oil on canvas,
33 x 18.5 cm
Whereabouts unknown

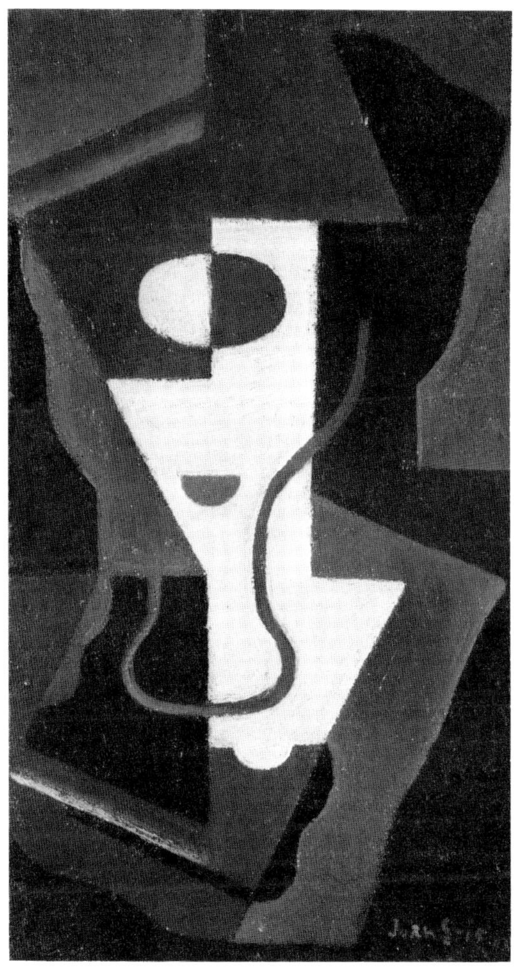

and "co-ordinating" that characterised Gris's "mechanical preparations". Imagination preceded control; it was primary[68].

Raynal's remarkable discussion (almost certainly a gloss on his continuing conversations with Gris) does not fit altogether snugly with the account left us by Kahnweiler of the way Gris actually worked from the time they renewed their friendship early in 1920. In the monograph of 1946, Kahnweiler asserts that the deductive method entailed a starting-point in drawings which used, for example, "a proportion (a Golden Section, say)" as the stimulus for a "coloured architecture". These initial drawings, which he and Josette destroyed after Gris's death at his request, were without objects and therefore without metaphors. The objects and the metaphors, he said, only came as Gris worked on the canvas, "qualifying" the coloured architecture, turning it into signs for things[69]. This is an extreme simplification of what were clearly far less straightforward processes of interaction between the "abstract" and the "concrete", syntax and semantics, but Gris would surely have substantiated Kahnweiler's account in principle. He repeatedly insisted that the objects came only when the coloured architecture was "qualified" at a later stage. Raynal was either already persuaded that the theory did not fit the practice or he used the idea of the precedence of metaphor to stand, *symbolically,* for its primacy: the primacy of metaphoric invention was his key point.

Whatever actually happened as Gris drew and then worked up his paintings after 1917–18 (and we shall never know)[70], it is possible to see how the invention of one metaphor could lead both to refinements and to the generation, through further metamorphoses, of other metaphors.

Guitar and Fruit Dish of July 1919 was an idea generated by a much smaller and simpler picture painted in March, *The Glass* (Figure 21). Its germ is the pipe and glass of the earlier canvas, which remain the hub. The guitar seems to have been generated by the shadow shape that echoes the glass's profile above and to its right in the earlier composition, and then to have generated the rhyming fruit dish, in equilibrated response[71]. The July picture had its own sequel in a succession of later variants, both refinements and sometimes new ideas. The first was Gris's contribution to the Indépendants of 1920, *Guitar, Book and Newspaper* (Figure 22), where the arm of the guitar is swung the other way, so that the bunch of grapes and the tuning keys can overlap and fuse, while a book replaces the glass and pipe below. There were angular and cursive variants in March 1920[72]. Then, after the enforced break caused by his illness, there came a further pair of responses, the first in December 1921 (Figure 23), the second in April 1922, *The Book of Music* (Plate 97)[73]. First the guitar,

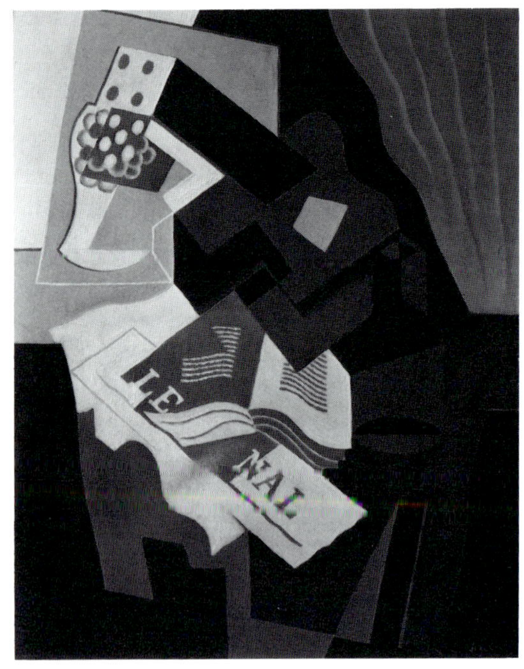

Figure 22
Guitar, Book and Newspaper, 1920
Oil on canvas,
92 x 73 cm
Öffentliche Kunstsammlung Basel, Kunstmuseum

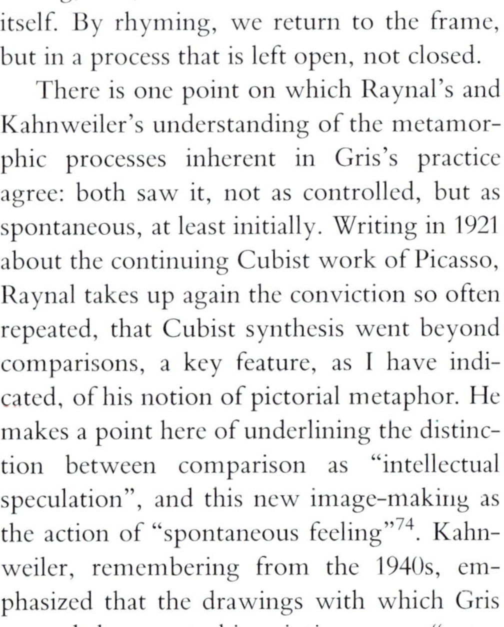

made now fluidly sinuous, generates a new rhyme with an equally fluid carafe, whose oval top doubles with the sound-hole; then the book of music is placed between guitar and carafe, producing another new rhyme with the table, the major containing plane of the setting, and, of course, with the tall format itself. By rhyming, we return to the frame, but in a process that is left open, not closed.

There is one point on which Raynal's and Kahnweiler's understanding of the metamorphic processes inherent in Gris's practice agree: both saw it, not as controlled, but as spontaneous, at least initially. Writing in 1921 about the continuing Cubist work of Picasso, Raynal takes up again the conviction so often repeated, that Cubist synthesis went beyond comparisons, a key feature, as I have indicated, of his notion of pictorial metaphor. He makes a point here of underlining the distinction between comparison as "intellectual speculation", and this new image-making as the action of "spontaneous feeling"[74]. Kahnweiler, remembering from the 1940s, emphasized that the drawings with which Gris opened the way to his paintings were "automatic", by which he meant undirected. The use of geometry and proportions ("a Golden Section, say") was, he acknowledged, "a conscious choice", but from this "spring-board" Gris at first worked "automatically". Only afterwards, he says, with the arrival of the objects, did he move into "the logical stage" of the process[75]. There is no such thing, of course, as *absolute* automatism, total lack of conscious direction, and none of these "automatic drawings" survive from which to judge the degree of their automatism, but again, it seems, the perfect painted surfaces of Gris's canvases screen a practice that put open-ended exploration before logical control.

Kahnweiler could not refrain from remarking on the irony of so "classical" an art whose "spring-board" was a process comparable with Surrealist automatism. It is indeed an irony of Gris's vanguard position in Paris in the 1920s that this acknowledged Platonist with a gift for the rigours of logic was, in fact,

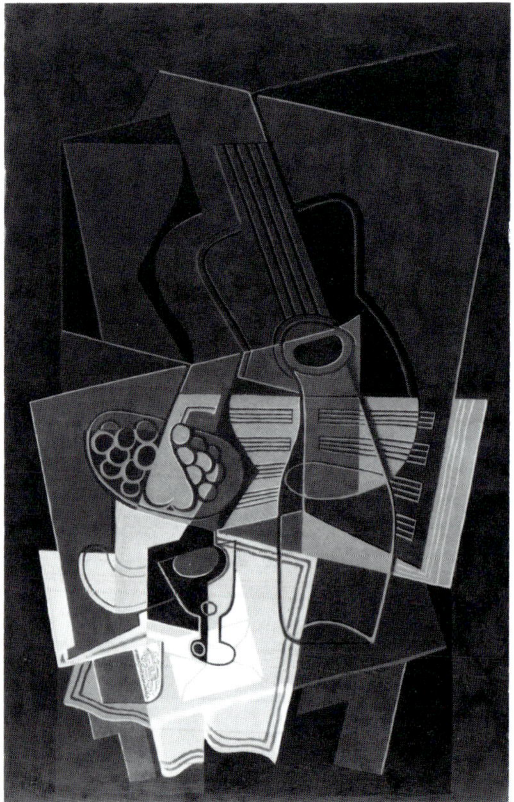

Figure 23
Guitar, Carafe and Fruit Dish, 1921
Oil an canvas,
100 x 65 cm
Kunstmuseum Bern, Hermann and Margrit Rupf Foundation

close to certain of the early Surrealists, and that the way the deductive method worked was actually relevant to the way Surrealist automatism worked in painting from 1923–4.

Through Kahnweiler's "Sundays" Gris made friends with the two allies from the rue Blomet group, Michel Leiris and André Masson. He spent a relaxed holiday with Masson, visited by Leiris, in the summer of 1924[76]. Masson's particular kind of working procedure, whereby he started with "automatic drawings" and then controlled the results in paintings which achieve a dry immaculacy of finish, was obviously like Gris's, and the drawings show how he too discovered his subject-matter in abstract configurations, sometimes explicitly architectural[77].

In 1929 Leiris wrote a "definition" of metaphor for the section called 'The Dictionary' in the dissenting Surrealist periodical *Documents*. The metaphor, he declared, revealed the impossibility of reaching the thing-in-itself, the essence. No word or sign can definitively correspond to it, and so all language and indeed all "intellectual life rests on a play of transpositions, symbols, which one can call metaphoric". Knowledge altogether is based on the linking, by analogy, of one thing to another in "interdependent relationships," so that knowledge itself is metaphoric. "As the sky is a subtle terrain, the terrain is a heavy sky". Clear distinctions are lost in metaphoric fusions, there are *no* definitions, least of all Leiris's definition of metaphor. He ends: "This article itself is metaphoric"[78].

Gris's metaphors, like the images of Rimbaud or Breton, Mallarmé or indeed Reverdy, allow the sign to become detached from its referent. The single shape like the single word can denote more than one thing. Manifestly his metaphors evade the conclusiveness of final definition. Yet, Raynal's article of 1923 suggests that there was a considerable difference of degree between Gris's pictorial metaphors, kept so firmly within so restricted a range of possible identities, and the uncompromising denial of certainty on any level conveyed by Leiris's brief text. For Leiris, metaphor, by exposing the thing-in-itself to be an illusion, transgressed against idealism; for Raynal, metaphor in Gris was fundamentally compatible with idealism. Like Reverdy, Raynal insisted on the "purity" of the "creation" of metaphor (Reverdy had called it "a pure creation of the spirit")[79]. It was a matter of conception not vision. And further he implied that Gris's metaphors brought out *essential* rapports between things that were, for the painter, true. This was why he could not accept the term "pun". "Puns", he wrote, "have been spoken of and rather in error. The pun responds to no constructive necessity; it results from no observation, no judgement. On the contrary, the plastic metaphor, in itself, contains a true judgement; it is a sort of synthesis that flows legitimately from the confrontation of elements of the same quality"[80]. In the end, at their most profound, Raynal believed that Gris's metaphors, despite their "lyrical" openness to "invention" delivered definitions of things that approached essences. He was able to adapt even the notion of the visual rhyme as metaphor to the idealist language of the "call to order". Metamorphosis opened up new possibilities, but repeatedly it led back to *stasis*.

What of Gris himself? Did the theories he set out, especially in the Sorbonne lecture, leave room for something other than the closure of cohesiveness and of a transcendent idealism legitimized by tradition? The short answer is, they did.

And they did so because he was not a simple-minded, doctrinaire idealist in the image of Léonce Rosenberg, but, as a painter directly engaged in looking and picture-making, an infinitely more subtle thinker. Kahnweiler followed Kant far enough to believe that the *nuomenon* was thinkable, but not knowable[81]. Gris, who talked often to Kahnweiler, but never read Kant[82], stressed, like Kahnweiler, that the "truth" he could grasp in the world and in painting was relative, contingent. Any *stasis* he found was always provisional, a function of him, of his society, culture and time. In his lecture he made a clear distinction between the consistency of pictorial architecture (the link between old and new), and the always changing character of what he called the painter's "aesthetic". Pictorial "technique" was governed by a constant set of laws, he argued, by which the flat, coloured "elements" basic to painting would always be structured; the painter *saw* the world in terms of these elements. But the painter's "aesthetic", claimed Gris, can always be dated; it was without constancy[83]

Gris's notion of the "aesthetic" was intellectual: it projected the shaping power of knowledge onto perception. Its "sole function" was to reveal "the world of ideas which exists purely in the mind"[84]. It was, for Gris, the particular form taken by the Platonic Idea within the limits set by current knowledge. The painter working in the ideal deductive way might start with a vocabulary of abstract coloured shapes, but the special character of that vocabulary depended on looking guided by the "aesthetic". However *a priori* it might be (to use the term as Lhote did), the painter's *particular* coloured architecture was abstracted from things *seen*.

If the principles basic to "technique", to all coloured architecture, were, for Gris, constant, both the "aesthetic" and the vision basic to *his* painting were not. At one point in his lecture he quotes "a philosopher" thus: "The senses provide the substance of knowledge, but the mind gives it form". He returned to Raynal's distinction between conception and vision, and placed them in relation. For him, "mind" was the province of "technique" *and* the "aesthetic"; it had a constant foundation, but was always changing. The senses could only be ephemeral, yet it was the senses ultimately that gave "substance"[85].

Gris argued that all painting was based on unchanging principles of colour and form, but he did not argue that art could actually achieve in any particular image the total *stasis* of the Platonic ideal. He argued that the painter could only reveal "the world of ideas" in terms of his or her very specific experience of the visual, an experience that was unmeasurable, always open to change. In the end, he placed himself and his own experience at the centre of his work. He made himself, not any Platonic Absolute, the origin of its capacity to move.

1 Daniel Henry (D.-H. Kahnweiler), *Juan Gris,* Leipzig and Berlin, 1929; in French translation in D.-H. Kahnweiler, *Confessions esthétiques,* Paris, 1963, pp. 44–5.
2 Ibid.
3 D.-H. Kahnweiler, *Juan Gris: His Life and Work,* translated by Douglas Cooper, London, 1969, pp. 63–74. For further discussion of this, see chapter 4 below.
4 *Letters of Juan Gris (1913–1927),* translated and edited by Douglas Cooper, London, 1956, p. 26 (Letter XXXI)
5 Ibid, p. 65 (Letter LXXX).
6 Kahnweiler (1969), op.cit., p. 126.
7 See especially 'Notes', *Der Querschnitt,* Frankfurt-am-Main, Summer, 1923 and 'On the Possibilities of Painting', lecture delivered 15 May 1924 to the 'Société des études philosophiques et scientifiques pour l'examen des idées nouvelles' at the Sorbonne, Paris; both texts in Ibid. See also the interview with Gris published by *Paris-Journal:* Georges Charensol, 'Chez Juan Gris', *Paris-Journal,* 25 April 1924.
8 I have attempted to demonstrate this in Christopher Green, 'Synthesis and the 'synthetic process' in the painting of Juan Gris, 1915–19', *Art History,* March 1982, pp. 87–105.
9 See Kahnweiler (1929 and 1963), op.cit., p. 46.
10 See Green (March 1982), loc.cit.
11 According to Josette Gris, Dermée was a good friend, not merely an acquaintance. Conversation, 20 July 1977. See for example Paul Dermée, 'Jean Metzinger', *S.I.C.,* nos. 42 and 43, 30 March and 15 April 1919 and 'Lipchitz', *L'Esprit Nouveau,* no. 2, November 1920.
12 Josette Gris stressed Gris's closeness to Lipchitz. Ibid. This is corroborated by the newly discovered letters from Gris to Léonce Rosenberg discussed in Christian Derouet's essay below. Gris's relationship with María Blanchard seems to have been particularly positive in 1918–19.
13 *Letters* (Cooper, 1956), op.cit., pp. 66–8 (Letter LXXXI).
14 André Lhote; in Jacques Guenne, 'André Lhote', *L'Art Vivant,* 1 March 1926.
15 André Lhote, 'Le Cubisme au Grand Palais', *La Nouvelle Revue Française,* 7th Year, no. 78, 1 March 1920, pp. 467–71.
16 "Pinturrichio" (Louis Vauxcelles), 'Le Carnet des ateliers', *Le Carnet de la semaine,* 22 February 1920, p. 8.
17 Léonce Rosenberg, 'Cubisme et tradition', Geneva, 1920; in *Bulletin de l'Effort Moderne,* no. 25, May 1926.
18 Léonce Rosenberg, 'Circulaire confidentielle', Paris, 3 September 1917; in *Juan Gris: Correspondance, Dessins 1915–1921,* edited with an introduction and notes by Christian Derouet, IVAM Centre Julio González, Valencia and Centre Georges Pompidou, Musée National d'Art Moderne, Paris, 1990–91, pp. 42–5 (Letter 20).
19 This is especially clear in 'Cubisme et tradition' (1920), op.cit.
20 Kahnweiler (1969), op.cit., pp. 32–3.
21 The date he gives is 13 March 1920; he failed to keep notes. Ibid., p. 144.
22 Armand Salacrou, *Dans la salle des pas perdus, C'était écrit,* Paris, 1974, p. 132.
23 Kahnweiler (1929 and 1963), op.cit., p. 51.
24 Kahnweiler (1969), op.cit., p. 130.
25 See Raynal to Gris, 15 February 1915 to 6 November 1918; in *Letters* (Cooper, 1956), op.cit. For further observations on the relationship between Raynal and Gris, see Christian Derouet's essay below.
26 *Correspondance* (Derouet, 1991), p. 61 (Letter 43).
27 See *Letters* (Cooper, 1956), op.cit., p. 97 (Letter CXVI), p. 136 (Letter CLIV), p. 138 (Letter CLVIII), p. 143 (Letter CLXIV).
28 The accusation comes from Bois. See Yves-Alain Bois, 'Kahnweiler's Lesson', *Representations,* Spring, 1987, p. 35. It is certainly true that Raynal's bracketting of Kant and Berkeley in 'Conception et vision', *Gil Blas,* 29 August 1912, reveals ignorance, but his writings of 1919–21 can be taken as a demonstration that this should not be given too much weight.
29 See my discussion in Christopher Green, *Cubism and its Enemies: Modern Movements and Reaction in French Art, 1916–1928,* New Haven and London, 1987, p. 152.
30 Maurice Raynal, 'Juan Gris', *L'Esprit Nouveau,* no. 5, February 1921, pp. 537–8.
31 See Maurice Raynal, *Anthologie de la peinture en France de 1906 a nos jours,* Paris, 1927.
32 The Symbolist connection and the idealist view of Cubism is especially comprehensively argued in Christopher Grey, *Cubist Aesthetic Theories,* Baltimore, 1955. It is sustained also in J. M. Nash, 'The Nature of Cubism: A Study of Conflicting Explanations', *Art History,* December 1980, pp. 435–447. Taking a different vantage point, and giving special prominence to scientific and popular theories of the fourth dimension, Cubism is again linked above all to Symbolist Idealism in Linda Dalrymple Henderson, *The Fourth Dimension and Non-Euclidean Geometry in Modern Art,* Princeton, New Jersey, 1983.
33 Ibid.
34 Michel Puy; in *Les Marches du Sud-Ouest,* July 1911; cited in Edward F. Fry, *Cubism,* London, 1966, p. 65.
35 See especially Kenneth E. Silver, *Esprit de Corps, The Art of the Parisian Avant-Garde and the First World War, 1914–1925,* Princeton and London, 1989. For a less convincingly substantiated, but more emphatic view, see also Benjamin H. D. Buchloh, 'Figures of Authority, Ciphers of Regression: Notes on the Return of Representation in European Painting'; in ed. Benjamin H. D. Buchloh, Serge Guilbeaut and David Solkin, *Modernism and Modernity: The Vancouver Conference papers,* Halifax, Nova Scotia, 1983, pp. 81–115.
36 Léonce Rosenberg, Letter to *Le Carnet de la semaine,* in "Pinturrichio" (Louis Vauxcelles), 'Le Carnet des ateliers', *Le Carnet de la semaine,* 26 November 1922, p. 12.
37 Gleizes: "voyait dans le cubisme l'expression souhaitable d'un art communiste". Florent Fels, 'Le Cubisme', *Les Nouvelles Littéraires,* Saturday, 4 October 1924.
38 See Pierre Assouline, *L'Homme de l'art: D. H. Kahnweiler, 1884–1979,* France, 1988, pp. 166–7.
39 Kahnweiler (1929 and 1963), op.cit., p. 51.
40 Gris, Lecture (1924); in Kahnweiler (1969), op.cit., p. 197.
41 Green (March 1982), loc.cit.
42 This can be verified by applying the principles set out in William Camfield, 'Juan Gris and the Golden Section', *Art Bulletin,* March 1965. Josette Gris recalled that Gris was especially interested in the Golden Section towards the end of the war, and discussed it especially with Paul Dermée at this time. Conversation, 20 July 1977. The

theme of this still-life is introduced in Cooper no. 232, and an associated drawing.

43 Cooper no. 201. The juxtaposition of vegetation, walls and keep in this picture is close to views from the Boulevard Philippe-Auguste, which remains very much a broad encircling ditch and not a boulevard. The wrought iron gate echoes a similar feature found in the drawing of the Place Ravignan of 1917, but its setting is quite different and it was painted at Beaulieu.

44 The first to point this out was Philippe Carton in an unpublished lecture, 'Le Peintre Juan Gris et sa rencontre fortuite avec Le Pays Lochois', delivered at Loches, 11 May 1991. He was the first to find postcards of this building, which is now demolished, although its corner-turret still survives, re-situated in a suburb of Loches. I am grateful to Monsieur Carton for his generous help and support.

45 The titling of *Seated Peasant Woman* is discussed in chapter 6 below.

46 I discuss Salmon's position more fully in Green (1987), op.cit., pp. 9–10. He came out publicly against Cubism as an end in itself in a lecture delivered late in 1917.

47 André Salmon, 'Le Pur et l'impur', *L'Europe Nouvelle,* no. 14, 13 April 1918, p. 679.

48 See Christian Derouet's essay below.

49 Lhote cited in "Pinturrichio" (Louis Vauxcelles), 'Le Conflit du peintre et du marchand', *Le Carnet de la semaine,* 2 June 1918, p. 8. Vauxcelles's major articles in this series appeared in *Le Carnet de la semaine* under his pseudonym, "Pinturrichio", on 2, 9 June, 28 July, 18 August, 1, 15, 22 September, 6, 13, 27 October, and 10 November 1918. For Gris's response, see *Correspondance* (Derouet, 1991), pp. 52–55 (Letters 32, 35 and 36).

50 The picture thought to be a self-portrait is Cooper no. 170.

51 These postcards are in the archives of Georges González Gris. They are published in *Correspondance* (Derouet, 1991), op.cit.

52 See Green (March 1982), op.cit., pp. 92–3 and Green (1987), op.cit., p. 194.

53 The gouaches referred to here are the 11 made in connection with Rosenberg's plan to illustrate an edition of poems by Reverdy. These gouaches are published as illustrations to the much later edition published as *Au Soleil du plafond,* Paris, 1955. The glass idea developed in *The Packet of Tobacco* appears in both *The Fruit Dish* and *The Pipe* (Plates 55 and 53). See my discussion in Green (March 1982), loc.cit., p. 91 and also *Correspondance* (Derouet, 1991), pp. 78–9, note 14.

54 The drawing was exhibited at the Galerie Louise Leiris, Paris, in 1965. Its whereabouts are now unknown.

55 "L'objet réel ou en trompe-l'œil est appelé sans doute à jouer un rôle de plus en plus important. Il est le cadre intérieur du tableau et en marque les limites profondes de même que le cadre en marque les limites extérieures". Guillaume Apollinaire, 'Pablo Picasso', *Montjoie!,* 14 March 1913; in *Apollinaire on Art: Essays and Reviews 1902–1918,* edited by Leroy C. Breunig, translated by Susan Suleiman, London, 1972, p. 279.

56 See Cooper nos. 89, 90, 91, 95, 112 and 130.

57 For typical framing and hanging of Gris in a different context, see the installation photographs of the Hamburg exhibition 'European Art Today', illustrated in *Cahiers d'Art,* Paris, vol. II, no. 8, 1927, 'Feuilles volantes', p. 5. Here, Gris's *The Painter's Window* (Plate 118) is hung between a Cézanne and a Léger. The Picassos in this installation are as usual in heavily gilded frames, the Gris's as usual in dark wooden frames.

58 An instance from the poetry of Vicente Huidobro, with whom Gris collaborated on the collection *Horizon carré* (1917), helping with the translations from Spanish into French, as well as supplying illustrations, is 'Globe Trotter'. This is a poem of 1918–21; it is framed by the opening, "Ton regard bleu/ton regard bleu" and the ending, "Au bord de tes yeux bleus". See *Saisons choisis,* Paris, 1921, 'Section III, 1918–21'. An instance from Dermée is the poem he published in *Nord-Sud,* no. 10, December 1917, which is framed by the lines, "Rose éblouie dans la main" and "Une lumière ébouie dans la main". Of the concluding image in Reverdy's poems from *Les Ardoises du toit* (1918), Louis Aragon remarked: "Progressivement nous sommes entraînés vers la phrase terminale, ample, définitive, solution du problème". 'Les Ardoises du toit', *S.I.C.,* no. 29, May 1918, p. 4.

59 Aragon summed up the imagery and mood of the collection thus: "Quelques tableaux de plein soleil (...) ne mettent que mieux en valeur ceux d'ombre où chantent les nuits sans lune, trouées de fenêtres dont battent les volets". Ibid.

60 The criticism of Louis Vauxcelles in *Le Carnet de la semaine* and *L'Amour de l'art,* or Waldemar George in *L'Amour de l'art,* or J.-G. Lemoine in *L'Intransigeant* (until the end of 1921), among others makes this clear.

61 The piece was first published in *Feuilles libres,* no. 31, April 1923. It was adapted for re-publication in Raynal's *Anthologie de la peinture en France de 1906 à nos jours* (Paris, 1927), forming there the section on Gris, a demonstration that the discussion still seemed valid to Raynal at the end of Gris's life.

62 Pierre Reverdy, 'L'Image', *Nord-Sud,* Paris, no. 13, March 1918; in Reverdy *(Œuvres complètes),* op.cit.

63 Raynal (1923); in Raynal (1927), op.cit., p. 174.

64 Gris, Lecture (1924); in Kahnweiler (1969), op.cit., p. 197.

65 See my discussion of rhyme in Christopher Green, 'Purity, poetry and the painting of Juan Gris', *Art History,* June 1982, pp. 197–8.

66 Raynal (1923); in Raynal (1927), op.cit., p. 174.

67 Ibid, p. 176.

68 Ibid, p. 178.

69 Kahnweiler (1969), op.cit., p. 146.

70 For a fuller discussion, see Green (March 1982), loc.cit.

71 C.f. Ibid.

72 Cooper nos. 329 and 330.

73 From August 1921 Gris had been producing variations on the idea, playing with the guitar/fruit dish rhyme. See Cooper nos. 374, 376, 380. A further variation, using a mandolin, was painted in June 1922 (no. 397). The theme was to return, with a guitar again, in 1923 (no. 416). Echoes of the idea continue to appear after 1923. *The Painter's Window* (Plate 118) could be called an angular variant. I discuss further ramifications of this rhyme, see chapter 7 below.

74 Maurice Raynal, 'Picasso et l'impressionnisme', *L'Amour de l'art,* July 1921, pp. 215–6.

75 Kahnweiler (1969), op.cit., p. 146.
76 For the stay at Nemours, and the presence there of Leiris, see André Masson, *Les années surrealistes: Correspondance, 1916–1942,* edited with notes by Françoise Levaillant, Paris, 1990, pp. 60–70, especially p. 69, note 3. It is possible that the Kahnweilers visited too.
77 C.f. Green (1987), op.cit., p. 101.
78 Michel Leiris, 'Métaphore', *Documents,* 1st Year, no. 3, 1929, p. 170.
79 Reverdy (March 1918), loc.cit.
80 Raynal (1923); in Raynal (1927), op.cit., p. 174.
81 "'The thing in itself' (the nuomenon), since it is timeless, is not within the art-historian's competence; nor is it capable of any investigation, since it is unknowable and indefinable". According to Kahnweiler, however, the nuomenon is realizable in painting. It is that "element, which we can neither define nor analyse, but of whose presence before our eyes we are conscious; and which we call beauty". Kahnweiler (1969), op.cit., p. 88.
82 Kahnweiler states that Gris never read Kant. Ibid, p. 152.
83 Gris, Lecture (1924), loc.cit.
84 Ibid.
85 Ibid.

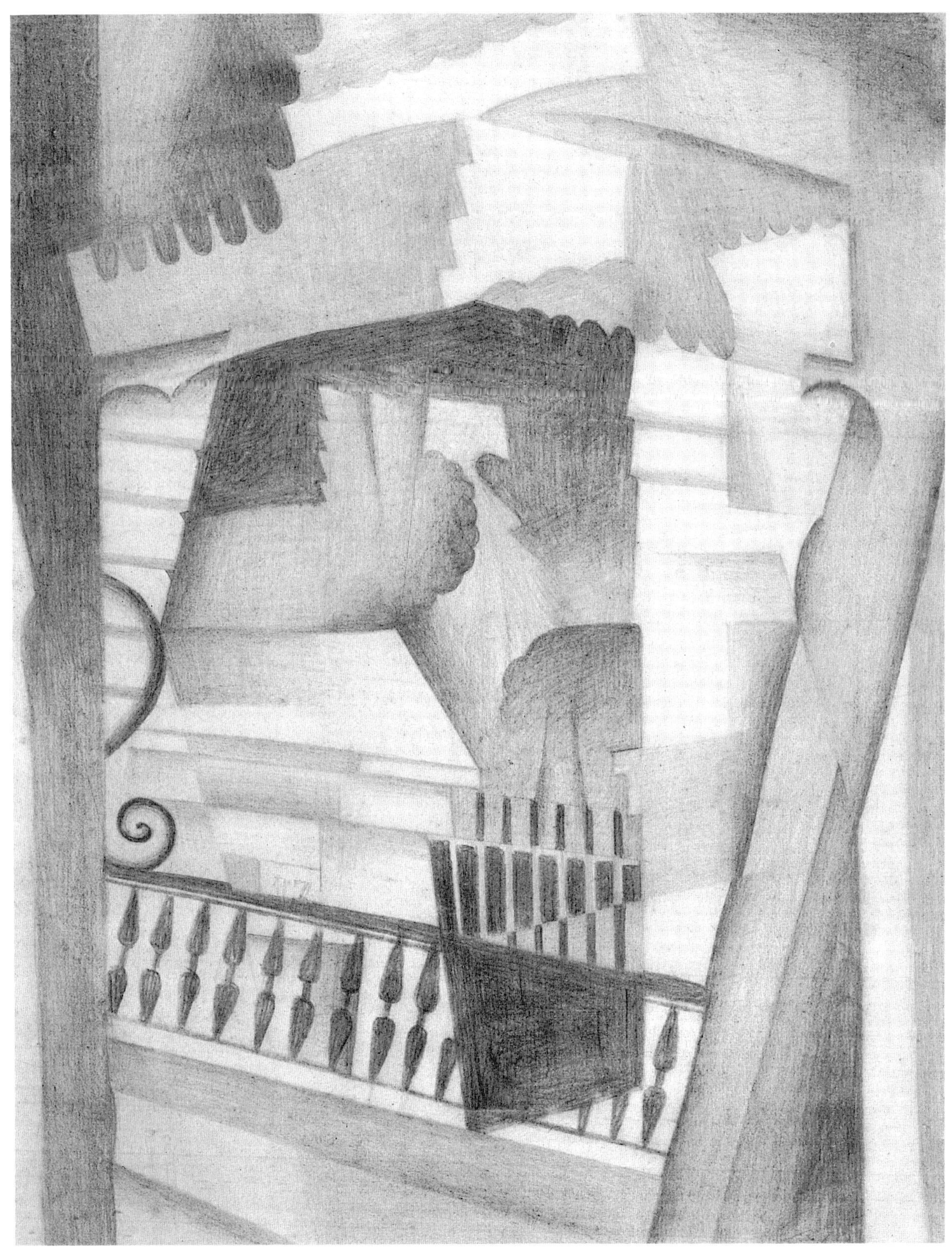

4. "One must after all paint as one is oneself"

In Juan Gris, the most "logical" of the analytical Cubists, is often seen a dispassionate observer; in Juan Gris, the "purest" of the synthetic Cubists, is often seen an artist engaged with universals, not with the individual. This "Gris" is said first to have pursued total objectivity and then to have pursued the *nuomenon,* the Platonic ideal; in both cases at the expense of himself.

What he called those "inventories of objects", *Bottles and Knife* of 1911–12, for instance, or *Still-life with Checked Tablecloth* of March 1915 (Plates 7 and 46), can seem to put the "reality" of objects before the actuality of his, Gris's, experience: object before subject. What he called the "poetry" of pictures like *The Guitar* of March 1918 or *Guitar and Fruit Dish* of December 1921 (Plates 79 and 111), can seem to put a claim to timelessness before any pretensions to personality: the universal before the individual.

In this context, it is striking to find Gris including oblique references to himself in his *papiers collés* of 1914, and on one occasion even his name[1]. There is, for instance, the placing of the page-heading "de l'auteur" (of/by the author) close to dead centre in *The Marble-topped Console Table* (Figure 20). It is striking to find him also, not only signing his work routinely, but for long periods (first, between February and December 1913) giving its exact date to the month, pin-pointing a particular moment as well as a particular individual (himself). And it is striking to read him writing regretfully in December 1915 to Kahnweiler about the lack of the "sensitive and sensuous side" in his painting, and ending: "Well, it can't be helped! One must after all paint as one is oneself"[2]. In practice as well as theory, before and after 1916, Gris placed himself, as subject, in his work.

The solo exhibition held by Kahnweiler at the Galerie Simon in April 1923 included work from across his entire career as a Cubist up to that point. Maurice Raynal's most immediate response was not his discussion of metaphor, looked at in my last essay, it was a more succinct notice in his weekly *L'Intransigeant* column. Invoking, as he loved to, Immanuel Kant, he took up the question of Gris and the "deductive method" (the finding of subject-matter in "abstract" shapes) with a particular slant. "Gris exclusively practices that cult of the laws of painting, properly so described, which leads to the creation of a reality of the imagination. In the manner in which Kant said that there is no need to know the name of a rose in order to experience it, he is given the denomination and the adjective of an object by its quality or its dimension. And the subject-matter of his picture emerges of itself solely by virtue of the harmonies of which it is composed"[3]. In his lecture of 1924, Gris was to talk of "the senses" giving his painting its "substance", stressing the primacy of his direct experience of things in the world; here Raynal talks of that experience as one of "quality" and "dimension", a knowledge that comes before the names are attached to things. He amplifies the immediacy of this knowledge of qualities by using the verb "goûter" (taste) for experience[4].

Place Ravignan, 1917
Pencil on paper,
39.7x28.2 cm
Georges González Gris

Although Kant is the philosopher Raynal acknowledges, there is in his language a clear echo of pre-1914 Bergsonism, of the debates that dominated the meetings of artists and writers at Puteaux and Courbevoie in the months that led up to the Salon de la Section d'Or and the publication of Gleizes's and Metzinger's *Du "Cubisme"*. There is a suggestion that the idealism of the "second Cubism" and the "call to order" was not altogether separate from the attitudes associated with pre-war Cubism.

The key word in making the link is "quality"; it is a key word in *Du "Cubisme"* too. For Gleizes and Metzinger, the Cubists substitute the quantitative observations of science with the qualitative vision of art. They write of "a qualitative possession of the world" and remark: "Geometry measures, the painter savours"[5]. I have already described how, in 1912, this qualitative vision was connected by Gleizes and Metzinger to the temporal rather than the spatial in experience, to the "intuition" of change in "duration" which they, following Bergson, believed was the essence of being[6]. Gris, of course, brought out what he thought of as the changing, durational character of "the aesthetic", which, he argued in 1924, patterned the artist's visual experience of the world. Indeed, the way he opened his Sorbonne lecture by distinguishing the artist's qualitative (aesthetic) vision from that of most people, takes up and gives a new inflection to another major point made in *Du "Cubisme"*. Gleizes and Metzinger insisted that "the crowd" can only grasp form in what they see "through the adopted sign" (conventional forms), and that only the artist can see *new* forms in things[7]. Gris's opening argument was that only the artist can see nature aesthetically, and therefore only the artist can see nature anew, in a manner consistent with the time, beyond convention[8].

The qualititative vision which Gleizes and Metzinger called Cubist in 1912 was, they claimed, fundamentally and intensely a *personal* vision. They contended that the artist could go beyond "the adopted sign" (convention) because the artist above all could make contact with the personal. Again, they followed Bergson, for whom the intuition of duration was only open to those who went beyond the "passive, fragmentary view of the self" established by intellect to achieve a deep level of subjective awareness, a role he gave especially to artists[9]. Their aspiration in *Du "Cubisme"* was to an art which could be, in their words, "a fixation of our personality" and consequently "unmeasurable, nothing being repeated in it ever"[10]. And, presenting Cubist painting as a product of personal intuition which invites a personal intuition from the spectator in response, they refer to pictorial space as a "sensitive passage between two subjective spaces"[11]. Their accenting of "quality", "duration" and the "unmeasurable" was the function of a profoundly subjective view of painting. And, despite the talk of conception against vision, they gave the senses a crucial initiatory importance in endowing painting with the personal. "To establish pictorial space, we must have recourse to tactile and motor sensations, and to all our faculties. It is our whole personality which, contracting or expanding, transforms the picture-plane"[12]. The conception of paintings was associated with an extreme immediacy of phenomenal experience where the subject, as in tasting and touching, could not be separated from the object[13]. The Gris who, as we have seen, placed time at the centre of *The Watch* in the Section d'Or (Plate 22), must have been alert to such thinking. It remains surprisingly relevant to the Gris of the Sorbonne lecture in 1924.

A consistent feature of Raynal's defence of Cubism in the period following the Great War, and Kahnweiler's writing on Gris in the 1946 monograph, is their common refusal of number, measurement, indeed all aspects of mathematics as of more than secondary importance in art. Gris himself was quick to play down the earlier role of "the mathematician" Princet when Vauxcelles satirized Cubism in

1918 as the formulaic application of Princet's teaching concerning "n-dimensional" geometry[14]. In 1921 Gris wrote to Ozenfant discouraging the rigid application of proportional systems in painting, while confessing that he had "passed on the 'golden section' to some nice young fellows"[15]. Kahnweiler confined Gris's use of such proportions to the initial generation of ideas; he did not present them as a mode of ensuring compositional perfection[16]. Raynal was decisive and comprehensive in his dismissal. He reacted thus in 1922 against Gino Severini's assertion that "no serious constructive basis (in art) can be established without geometry and numbers": "M. Severini seems to forget that man was a painter before he was a geometer, that art existed before mathematics, that before being rational, our ancestors first had sensibilities"[17]. For Raynal, as for Kahnweiler (and Gris), art was beyond measurement. For him, as before 1914 for Gleizes and Metzinger, art was unmeasurable because it was a matter first for the senses and intuition, however conceptual. In his *Anthologie* of 1927, he dismissed what he called the "Cubism of the senses" associated with André Lhote, where "an aspect of reality" is "transcribed", "disguised beneath the cast-off clothing of Cubism"[18]. But when he defined Cubism as the creation of "new compositions" free of the "sensual, decorative (or) psychological", he was careful to add that its components were "elements known from reality"[19]. Individual experience – "sensibility" – was fundamental. And for him, like Kahnweiler, the *nuomenon* was out of reach of human perception and therefore knowledge[20].

Perhaps the most searching of Maurice Raynal's reflections on the individual and the universal in painting was his article on Gris for *L'Esprit Nouveau* in 1921. I have already quoted his talk here of "an intimate communion with the essence itself of objects" and his adaptation to Gris of Winckelmann as evidence of an *apparently* unqualified idealism. In fact, these passages are the sequel to a long exegesis on "the unquantifiable sensibility" that Gris brings to things; and this contains a revealing critique of Kant's assertion that judgements of "Beauty" are universal. Raynal finds Kant's theory of the Sublime altogether more applicable to Gris's art than his theory of Beauty, hence the analogy he draws between Gris's "unquantifiable sensibility" and the contemplation of the infinite in the sky. He cannot accept the universality that Kant claims for judgements of Beauty, because for him, "Each man creates his special beauty, the beauty which he loves... and not which others love". It is Gris's "sensibility", which he calls "infinite like the sky", that allows him to create *his* "special beauty"[21]. When Raynal brings in essences and Winckelmann's notion of ideal systems, like Gris's coloured architecture of shapes, imposed upon nature, he does so having established the "infinity" of "sensibility" as ultimately what matters: Gris's sensibility.

My concern in this essay is Gris as the subject in his painting. I do not want to imply that this Gris is some unitary self, the unchanging essence to be found in all his painting (rather than the essence of the *things* they depict). I want to ask how he could (and can) be thought of as in his work at all. Bergson, Gleizes and Metzinger offer a starting-point by giving primacy to immediate experience (qualitative vision) in their profoundly subjective view of art, a view some of whose assumptions still inform the statements of Gris and Raynal after 1918. I shall begin, too, with this issue by considering the relationship between Gris's painting right across the years 1910–21, and the kinds of experience with which it engages. My focus will be on two areas: drawing as the record of looking, and colour.

There were distinct phases when Gris used drawing as a direct means of recording an intense scrutiny of appearances. There was the period of the large charcoal and gouache and then the smaller pencil drawings that prefaced and accompanied his public debut early in

1912 at Clovis Sagot's gallery and the Indépendants (Plates 1 and 5). There was the period of still-life set-ups and drawing from the model that prefaced, accompanied and followed his adaptations of the "masters" in 1916–17 (Plates 67 and 69). Then came the often comparable, but still more "naturalistic" drawings of still-lives, figures and even landscapes that accompanied the critical move into rhyming syntheses in the summer and autumn of 1918 at Beaulieu-lès-Loches (Plates 92 and 93)[22]. Finally came a further sequence of such drawings made, according to Kahnweiler, to mark his return to life from illness and the threat of death, during the later months of 1920 at Beaulieu and through 1921 at Bandol on the Mediterranean (Plates 91, 94 and 95)[23].

After the initial phase of studious inquiry in the "Bateau-Lavoir", Gris seems to have drawn most from nature when he was away from Paris, especially when he was in Josette's country, the Touraine. His letters suggest that these were periods of high activity and, often, increasing confidence when he was aware of "progress" in his work.

Drawing from life, however, was something he thought of and practised separately from painting, a fact indicated by a passing remark in a letter written to Paul Dermée from Beaulieu in May 1918: "Work goes ahead and I paint for eight or nine hours each day, except for two hours which I spend drawing from nature"[24]. Further, Christian Derouet has pointed out that drawing altogether was left an area of relative freedom when Léonce Rosenberg drew up his singularly tight contracts of April 1916 and November 1917. A clause was added in the second to cover it, but with none of the precise specificity of the clauses covering painting. Gris was discouraged from selling his drawings elsewhere, but things were left vague enough for him to be able to draw for himself as well as Rosenberg[25]. It is perhaps telling that so many of the drawings to have survived were gifts inscribed, often affectionately, to friends, and that in 1916 and 1921 he used drawings to make the portraits of himself and those closest to him that he only very exceptionally now made in oils (pages 12 and 112 and 96 and 76). He allowed drawings to be published as illustrations to the writings of friends like Reverdy, Dermée and Huidobro in 1917–19[26]; he published others as lithographs with Kahnweiler in 1921 (Figure 43); and he answered requests from Kahnweiler to illustrate Jacob, Tzara, Salacrou and Gertrude Stein[27]. But drawing was undoubtedly his most private and most immediate activity as an artist; certainly his least consciously, least theoretically mediated.

This is not, of course, to say that his (or any artist's) drawings could ever be a simple record of retinal sensations, and thus unmediated. In 1910–12, as after 1916, they always declare the fact that Gris has directed their making. This is obviously so when he extracts, as we have seen, hints of a flattened geometry from what he depicts, both in 1910–12 (Plates 4 and 5) and in 1916 (Plate 67). It is most obviously so when in 1916–17 he draws a subtle, interlocking arrangement of shaded planes and white paper as an equivalent of either a still-life or, say, the view of the Place Ravignan from the "Bateau-Lavoir" (page 12). But it is obvious, too, in the least transformed of the post-1916 drawings. The crisp, controlled line, the carefully modulated shading, the slightly or grossly distorted details, all make it so, especially in the pencil drawings he perfected as gifts with such conscientious attention in 1920–21: for instance, *Still-life with a Garlic Sausage, Still-life with Eggs, Fruit Dish, Glass and Knife* and the *Portrait of Daniel-Henry Kahnweiler* (Plates 94, 95, 91 and 96). Here Gris plainly extracts forms in rhyming relationships. The pears in *Fruit Dish, Glass and Knife* rhyme with the bowl of the glass and the softened stem of the fruit dish; the grapes rhyme with the oval incised or embossed on the bottom of the glass's bowl. In *Still-life with Eggs*, the breakfast bowl becomes a rhyme for the eggs: its eliptical top picks up the eggs' ovals and its surface is shaded to give an egg-shell finish.

Yet, in these later drawings especially (and it is so of the 1918 drawings too), Gris uses naturalistic shaping and surface to signify the immediacy of contact with the *motif*. The pears, the grapes and the rucked cloth, the eggs and the bowl are offered to the touch as well as the eye. In *Still-life with Garlic Sausage*, the sausage has been cut to reveal the coarse texture of the meat, with its smooth marbling of fat and its grit of pepper corns, while the string top-knot has been delineated and modelled with great care, as if to invite the fingers to take hold of it and lift it off the plate. Looking, touching, even tasting are all commemorated, and their immediacy evoked.

Within the post-1916 framework of theory built up around the idea of a "pure Cubism", Gris's more "naturalist" drawings had a clear enough rationale to go with the room left for personal sensibility. They were the analysis that preceded synthesis, the prose to his poetry. Their separateness from the activity of painting was underlined by the fact that they hardly ever led directly to paintings[28]; such a practise would not have fitted well with the claims for a deductive procedure, working *back* to objects from the abstract. But it was acknowledged that "the abstract" (coloured architecture) could only be developed according to an individual aesthetic by testing that aesthetic *against* nature; such an architecture had to be based, in Raynal's terms, on "elements known in reality". Reverdy suggested as much in relation to the poet's use of words in his crucial theoretical texts for *Nord-Sud* in 1917–18[29], and throughout the period 1915–22 he continued to write prose-poems, where the images are less condensed than in his poetry proper, and where an "I" remains, apparently as the single vantage-point from which the actuality of experiences is evoked[30].

If Gris's drawings cannot ever be called objective, unmediated, neither can their declaration of his directorial role ever be called simply idealizing. Gris himself firmly resisted such an idea about his practice on any level. Speaking, in the lecture of 1924, about the capacity of artists to be moved by nature, as if by art, he referred to what he thought of as their ability to re-arrange the elements of nature, like a pack of cards. He insisted that artists *see* nature personally; nature is neither out there as object nor something from which to idealize, it is from the moment of perception invested with the aesthetic of the artist (the subject). Gris believed that he brought his aesthetic, as a personal repertoire of graphic techniques, *to* what he saw when he drew. He believed that he could actually *see* in an idiom which brought together clear lines, simple contrasts of curved and straight, shallow surface modulations achieved by tone, patterns of light and dark, and patterns of rhyming and echoing surfaces. No wonder he considered seeing "aesthetically" to be beyond most people.

The drawings of 1920–21 especially can often *appear* idealizing, and nowhere is this more pronounced than when Gris actually did put himself into one: the pencil *Self-portrait* that he drew as he convalesced after his illness (page 12). He drew himself as Platonist, the ideal hero of a transcendent art. The drawing partners the smooth bronze busts of Cocteau, Radiguet and Gertrude Stein that his close friend Lipchitz was currently modelling[31]. It is similarly fleshless, and the appropriation of so explicit a neo-classical vocabulary for Gris's fine, symmetrical features clearly brings *him* together with a classical ethos of idealism. But, in public (this is one of Gris's most private drawings), he always repeated his refusal to idealize, to abstract from the particular to "an ideal type", and usually, even in the figure drawings of 1920–21, he allowed that quickening of the sense of surface to which I have pointed in the still-lifes to signify that the aesthetic and the sensual had come together, had fused in the act of looking and drawing. Nowhere is this more so than in the *Portrait of Josette Gris*, a drawing which may be contemporary with the *Self-portrait* (page 112).

The drawings of 1920–21 are, it seems, the records of Gris's determination to prove, at least to himself, that he could *see* the world as art, that his aesthetic could shape vision, however immediate, and that in doing so it could make the visible world his own. He placed himself, by drawing, in that world.

Gris made a number of coloured drawings, but his drawings are, of course, mostly in black and white. Conversely, he also used black as a colourist in his painting. After 1912, when he used black as a painter, he never did so as he did in his drawing (although he sometimes actually drew with pencil and charcoal on canvas). He used black flat, usually without tonal modelling, with and against colour. It is a function of colour.

The later months of 1912 and especially the beginning of 1913 was the moment when, following Picasso and Braque, Gris moved from the subdued tints and tones of his first pictures into a positive commitment to colour. It came with his first use of *collage* and *papier collé*. A cool, Mediterranean blue dominates *Guitar on the Table* of April 1913; a similar blue and a lime green dominate *The Guitar* of May 1913 (Plates 25 and 28). In both cases the colour is brushed flatly across the surface. The blue stimulates atmospheric associations (sea, sky), but it does not hole the picture-plane; it lies on the canvas beside the surfaces of false marbling, false wood, false wallpaper and real engraving. The overpainted green planes in particular read at first like stuck-on pieces of material. In *The Guitar* especially areas of white and black amplify the impact of the blue against the browns.

In January 1913 Robert Delaunay published 'Light' in the German periodical *Der Sturm*. Delaunay had been one of the Salon Cubists, a well-known figure at the Puteaux studios, but he had not taken part in the Salon de la Section d'Or. His *City of Paris* had been, for Apollinaire, the star-turn at the Indépendants of 1912, where Gris made his Salon debut. He had followed it throughout 1912 with pictures whose *motifs* were outdoor (open windows), where the Divisionist colour theory of simultaneous contrast was applied in terms not of divided colour dots or *tessurae,* but of divided colour planes. By January 1913 Apollinaire was a committed supporter. For Delaunay, simultaneous contrasts in colour were the essence of vision, and in their movement Bergsonian duration was rendered immediate by vision. "Simultaneity...", he wrote in 'Light', "creates *Man's Sight*". "The Eye... communicates most closely with... *our consciousness,* the idea of the vital movement of the *world,* and *its movement is simultaneity*"[32].

There can be little doubt that Gris's decision to take on colour relates to Delaunay's attempt to chromaticize Cubist painting, and to tackle the old Divisionist problem of finding pictorial equivalents for the intensity of chromatic experience. His response, however, was profoundly oppositional (more so even than Picasso's)[33]. His colour in 1913 is not prismatic. It does without Delaunay's delicate atmospheric nuances. But, most telling of all, it declares the irrelevance of the naturalist dimension in the Divisionist theories revived by the re-publication of Signac's *D'Eugène Delacroix au néo-impressionnisme* in 1911, and it does so by means partly of that positive use of black. For Signac and Delaunay, light and colour marginalized black in painting[34].

In Céret in the summer of 1913, black is given a still more positive role by Gris to enhance an enriched colour range. There are six paintings dated September 1913; they include *Violin and Guitar, Guitar on a Chair* and *Landscape with Houses at Céret* (Plates 32, 31 and 29). Black is a factor in the colour of all of them, most positively perhaps in the landscape where it is used not merely to give the trees below negative haloes, but actually to form the trees above in silhouette. Patently, these are pictures where a degree of chromatic equivalence to experiences of colour in nature is asserted. *Landscape with Houses at Céret* was painted alongside *Violin and Guitar*, the one brilliant in its clashes of hot yellow and cool green or blue, the other resonant in its deep crimson, its blues and browns, brightened only by the two vermillion triangles in the centre. The indoor painting is warm and shadowy; the outdoor painting is hot and sunny. Both, however, use only local colour or, where the atmospheric is included (the sky in the landscape), contain it within a plane alongside other planes, as if between inverted commas. Atmospheric colour is only quoted.

At one stage, of course, Gris was to bring the recognized mark of Divisionist theory in practice, the coloured dot, into his painting with the brief sequence of *pointilliste* pictures that culminate in the group dated March 1916. Black again is a factor, but what is most striking in the context of Divisionism is the fact that the workings of simultaneous colour contrast on the picture surface have altogether supplanted any pretence to an equivalence with light in nature. *Fruit Dish on a Blue Tablecloth* (Plate 57) offers a green that is the ground to flickering red dots, and then the same green in dots on a grey ground, while the red dots cross from the green to a grey ground too. It is possible to see how what Delaunay called the "movement" of simultaneous contrasts happens, that is, how a single colour changes value as the colours juxtaposed with it change. The control of the artist, Gris, is exposed in terms of colour. The elements of vision are given as the elements of an entirely artificial conception, directed by a *pictorial* understanding of colour contrast.

Black is not a function of brilliant or resonant colour in the pictures that followed Gris's reply to Signac, it is dominant. When Gris returned to Paris from Céret at the end of October 1913, he had brought with him another batch of strongly coloured pictures where black was used still more positively in silhouette than in September[35]. Strong colour is not a factor in the austere pictures of spring and summer 1916, but the black silhouettes of October 1913 are back again to give one of the aspects of the objects in *Fruit Dish, Glass and Lemon* (Plate 58). Here, however, and in *Playing Cards and Siphon* (Plate 61), black is used not simply in shadow-silhouettes, but as the signifier of cast shadow or of a background space without light. The table with its freight of objects in *Playing Cards and Siphon* is thrown forward, as it were, by its own shadows. Black works with and against the light to give a relief-like definition to things.

I have called these pictures an exploration of *chiaroscuro* in the flat terms of a Cubist idiom. It is their uncompromising flatness, their refusal of *modelling* by light, that keeps them separate from Gris's drawings of 1916. Like the *pointilliste* pictures, they allow the elements of a pictorial mode of illusionism, dependent on light, to become primarily *pictorial* elements by which signs can be given presence. The shift from the dazzle of the *pointilliste* to the gloom of the *chiaroscuro* pictures is surprising in its suddenness, but it can be seen as a straightforward switch from one system for the representation of things in light to another, one founded on colour, the other not.

There is another phase during the Great War when artificiality and chromatic stridency come together in Gris's work: it is at the very beginning of 1918 and just anticipates the second of his stays at Beaulieu lès Loches. For a short while he was ready to use strong clashes of hue, as he does in *Violin and Glass* (Plate 80)[36]. Black had resumed its role as the amplifier of colour. That long summer and autumn in Beaulieu, however, saw another shift from stridency to something more sombre. This re-introduced the theme of equivalence with particular subtlety in the context of a debate that, as I have already suggested in the last essay, raised the issue of Cubism in terms of the issue of vision ("naturalism") with a new vigour. The debate in question was the one about the so-called return to nature and the "death" of Cubism in which Vauxcelles embroiled Léonce Rosenberg, Lhote, Rivera and indeed Gris himself in 1918. It was carried on in the pages of *Le*

Carnet de la semaine, and Gris provided his own private commentary in his letters to Rosenberg and Raynal.

Both what happened to colour in Gris's painting in 1918 at Beaulieu, and the echoes of this debate in Gris's letters, allow an especially clear appreciation of the status he was prepared to give "sensibility" (directed by the aesthetic) in his Cubism. This, of course, was precisely the moment when he was developing his so-called deductive method as a guarantee of conceptual "purity".

In August 1918 Vauxcelles followed up his claims of June that "Integral Cubism" was "exhausted" by announcing that Picasso saw value in Rivera's portraits and that Gris had written to Rosenberg of how "he was fed up with mechanical fabrication"[37]. Vauxcelles, as ever well-informed yet economical with the truth, misquoted here a letter that Gris had indeed written to his dealer (in July), a letter in which he certainly does seem to set up nature – the loveliness of the Touraine countryside – as an urgent, new chromatic stimulus much more compelling than technical control. He mentions to Rosenberg a "size 30 picture with a peasant woman", *Seated Peasant Woman* (Plate 82), and goes on: "but I would like to make [this picture] come alive through the actual paint. I am fed up with laying on colours in a cold and mechanical way and I would like to be able to produce brushwork. In the countryside I see such solid and materially sumptuous tones and such perfect harmonies, that they carry within themselves a far greater force than all the combinations on the palette. A walk in the country is not only a source of elements but also of means... Once the dazzle of the picturesque has disappeared, its perfect, solid relationships are even more enhanced. And without any need to be a landscape painter, to understand the relationships there is (sic) in a field is to extend and verify your painting"[38].

Appalled by Vauxcelles's distortion of what he had said, Gris wrote to Rosenberg in August blaming the critic's mischievous ignorance, and tried to put things finally beyond doubt. What concerned him, he insisted, was colour as "a technical means", when he talked of making it "come alive" or of brush-work. At the deepest level, he concluded, Cubism was far more than that, it was "an aesthetic emerging out of a mental attitude that is very profound, very human and very much of its day"[39]. Yet, the fact is that he had acknowledged the possible precedence of vision (nature), however much this was informed by, shaped by "an aesthetic". And the fact is that his walks in the forests and the fields around Les Fourneaux, and in the old quarters of Beaulieu, did have a visible chromatic effect on his work; something which the pictures declare plainly enough.

Different sky blues and a field green appear in both *Houses in Beaulieu* and the *Harlequin* of April and May 1918 (Plates 81 and 85). Like the pictures of 1913, they quote sky, but in even flatter terms, with no modulation (and none of the airy brushing for which Gris expressed a need in the letter of July). There is also in *Houses at Beaulieu* a very particular combination of cool slate grey, paler grey, in places touched with cream, and a warm chestnut brown. This combination re-appears repeatedly in the paintings between July and September. It is there in *Guitar and Fruit Dish* of August and *The Man from the Touraine* of September (Plates 89 and 83), with the creamy grey warmed more towards ochre. It is there also around the deep blue of the smock in the other painting of a male peasant (Plate 84).

Houses in Beaulieu explicitly relates the combination, set among blues and greens, to the traditional stone architecture of the Touraine and, in fact, it is a combination found in the old buildings around the *château fort* at Loches, in Beaulieu and all over the immediate region. That cool slate grey is precisely the grey of the *ardoises*, the chestnut brown, the brown of the equally common vernacular tiled roofs, and the paler grey touched with cream, sometimes warmed to ochre, approximates the bleached limestone of the Loire and the Indre valleys. Les Fourneaux, the large house that Gris rented with Josette in 1916, 1918 and later in 1920, was just such a stone house with a tall grey *ardoise* roof, and beside it were farm buildings whose warm chestnut tiles add an accent of contrast against the grey slates and the shading foliage of the trees.

Appropriately, as Gris emphasized the architecture of his painting at Beaulieu, the generative role of its geometric structure, he took on a kind of colour combination that strongly suggests equivalence with the buildings around him. These are not the colours of space as coloured air, they are the colours of durable surfaces that support and protect, stone, tile and slate. The connotations are there in the figures and still-lives as much as in the townscapes.

Black plays its part in the paintings of summer and autumn 1918, and it plays its part also in the series of canvases that more than any after the *Landscape with Houses at Céret* in 1913 made a point of the chromatic equivalence of pictorial experience and the experience of nature: the open windows painted at Bandol and Céret. Here Gris worked with both the colours of atmospheric depth and of surfaces offered to the touch, and his subject-matter said so.

This series is the belated sequel to two of the most ambitious still-life paintings made by Gris during the Great War, *Still-life and Townscape (Place Ravignan)* of June 1915 and *The Pot of Geraniums* of the month after (Plates 48 and 47). The two, though on different scales, form a dramatically contrasting pair, like the indoor *Violin and Guitar* and the outdoor Céret landscape of 1913. *The Pot of Geraniums* has a speckling of dots, pink on blue, red on pink, which add vibrancy to the summer blue and green that dominate beneath a disc of yellow. This is one of Gris's first attempts to expose the colour changes of simultaneous contrasts by using Divisionist dots; it comes in a painting where a plant and the sunlight that makes it grow form Gris's subject-matter. The Place Ravignan still-life is a night picture. The light that catches the orange in the fruit-bowl and the checked curtain tacked to the open window can only be artificial. The black is darkness without the sun.

Light had, in fact, been itself a theme in Gris's painting since a *collage* made at Collioure in 1914, using a wall-paper imitation of a venetian blind[40]. These two open window pictures accompany pictures where objects are placed in front of sun-blinds pulled down, and where the background presence of a brilliant light that has been shut out of the painting threatens to burst through[41]. The blinds have been pulled up to let in, first the darkness of the Place Ravignan, and then the sun.

Gris's open windows of 1915 had anticipated Picasso for once, but his Mediterranean open windows of 1921 are sequels not only to his own of six years before, but to a new series of Picasso's painted in the summer of 1919 not far away from Bandol at the resort of St Raphael (Figure 24). He too takes the *motif* south to the sea-side. Paintings like *The Bay* and *The View Across the Bay* (Plates 100 and 99) develop the chromatic theme announced at the outset of the series. The warm/cool contrasts confront, even merge, indoors and outdoors. The light and dark of the indoor and outdoor pictures from 1913 at Céret, the dazzle and the cool of the geranium and the Place Ravignan open windows, seem to have been brought together. The warmed surfaces of table and guitar confront and merge with the cool yet sun-lit spaces of sea, mountains and sky. The theme of light, let in and closed out, is an obvious common denominator; black works as shadow, contour and as the framing darkness of the interior.

Picasso's St Raphael series were small-scale gouaches, but they figured in the highly successful exhibition put on by Paul Rosenberg in May 1921[42]. Responding to the exhibition, André Lhote let himself imagine possible Picasso windows opening onto gardens, and in doing so made of these little things the return of a Cubist to nature. He writes of a

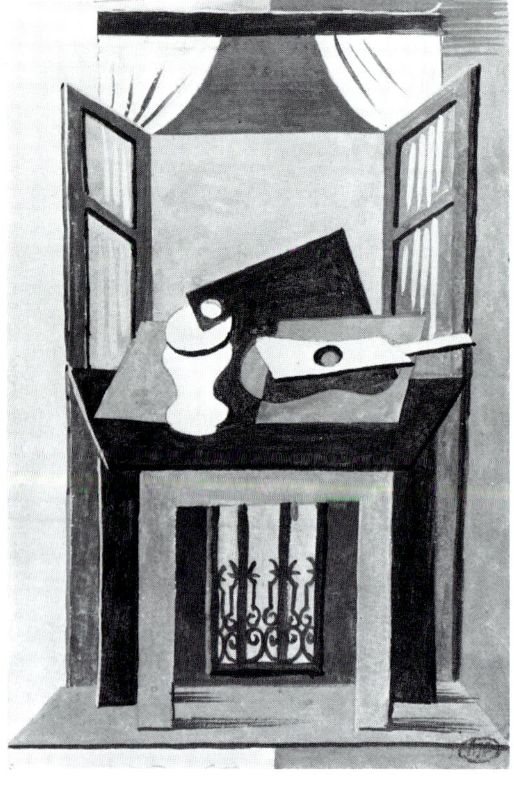

Figure 24
Pablo Picasso
Still-life in Front of a Window, 1919
Gouache on paper, 16.5 x 11 cm
Musée Picasso, Paris

"sensuous gaze" that exceeds the visual, one that absorbs not only "the perfume of the fruit" in the bowl, but "that of the garden onto which the window opens... To dare to paint as subject, not the material fruit-bowl..., but the green growth of trees behind the balcony grill, and the brilliance of the blue sky... is this not also to respect Nature"[43].

Gris included all the Bandol open windows and *Le Canigou*, a sequel painted at Céret in the winter, in his 1923 exhibition at Kahnweiler's Galerie Simon. There was also a later sequel with the same format, *Open Window with Hills* (Plate 112), a picture which shared the sweetened, sensual colour range of the new figure paintings of 1922–23, like *Seated Harlequin* (Plate 105). One critic at least saw this show as further evidence of a return by the Cubists to nature; predictably this was Louis Vauxcelles. He called what he saw "delicious", and remarked: "Gris thinks he's still a Cubist; don't let's fool outselves!" He is frankly incredulous about Gris's claims to purity: "When he explains to me – or asks his *prefacier* [Raynal] to explain – that he does not depart from the subject to end with his picture, but from the picture to end with his subject, I listen to his opinions, which I would call childish, with an inattentive ear... Gris might well say to me: "When I take my brush, I do not know what is going to happen...", I don't believe it, I cannot believe it... Gris knows very well where he's going"[44].

And indeed the sheer immediacy of the open windows, as much as the sensuality of pictures like *Seated Harlequin*, must raise the question of just how far they *could* have started, not with a view across the bay at Bandol, but in Gris's coloured architecture. There is a suggestion, indeed, that Gris himself could associate them at least with the *look* of "naturalism" in its then current more traditionalist guise. The second of the series is the only one in which the window opens onto verdure: the blue-grey of an olive tree (Plate 101). When he finished it, he wrote early in April 1921 to Kahnweiler that it was "much looser in execution" with "a sort of popular look which I rather like, but which is not due to using popular means". He claimed "purity" for his means, but acknowledged a rather different "look". "It has," he said, "... a sort of Derain air"[45]. Derain, of course, was the acknowledged leader of the return to a "traditional naturalism" in France.

The subject-matter of the Bandol open windows is in general terms what was there when Gris looked out from his attic studio across the bay, but only in the most general terms. The shutter forms and the mountain outline change from picture to picture (Plates 99 and 102). It seems clear that the blue presence of that view, with a still life in front of it, *was* in mind, as Vauxcelles insisted, from the outset, and so that these cannot have been the result of any straightforward process of *finding* subject-matter in pictorial architecture. But it remains so that the *specific* qualities of form and colour, the contrasts and the patterns of rhyme, could have emerged in the weeks of each canvas's making. Gris himself did *not* think of these paintings as derived *from* their *motif,* and it was in 1923–4, when they were first shown, that his Platonism and the "purity" of his pictorial "metaphors" was most insisted upon, as Vauxcelles found.

These pictures, however, like the open windows of 1915 and the Céret landscape of 1913, represent undoubtedly a further assertion that even the work of a "pure Cubist" like Gris took its presence and quality from the special character of his "sensibility" before nature. When seen in a context that included the flashy naturalism of Vlaminck, the "traditional naturalism" of Derain or the subtle naturalism of Bonnard, the control of what Gris called his aesthetic is evident enough and so is the artificiality of his signs and his technical means. These are consumately theatrical pictures, something that will be discussed in the last of these essays.

Yet, still, he can put himself in the picture as an artist who responds to the light in the world: a sensibility.

Recent re-readings of Cubist painting have made a point of excluding the artist. This has been above all a reaction against the domination of biography in writing about Picasso, and it has, as I remarked in the second essay, given emphasis to the changes in Picasso's and Braque's Cubism of 1912, Picasso's cardboard *Guitar*, the first *collages* and *papiers collés* being the major reference points (Figures 6 and 13). With the exposure of the arbitrariness of the sign, it has been argued, Cubist *collage* and *papier collé,* indeed all Cubist art, could be read as a play of language in the largest, most impersonal sense. These were no longer, in Saussureian terms, to be taken as the utterances of individuals (*Parole*), they exposed above all the workings of language itself, the semiotic structuring of all knowledge (*Langue*). From this perspective, Picasso and Braque (with Gris) become no more than inessential referents in their work which, in a sense, can "speak" *without* them. For Rosalind Krauss, the Picasso of the *papiers collés* of 1912–13 does not speak. *Langue* is "a repertory of terms into which each individual must assimilate himself, so that from the point of view of structure, a speaker does not so much speak as he is spoken by language"[46]

I have argued here that Gris's later theory of the aesthetic and Gleizes's and Metzinger's 1912 emphasis on qualitative experience clearly associate Gris (in his Cubist context) with a dominant subjectivism. I have further argued that colour as a function (by equivalence) of *motif* becomes a sign whose immediate signified is Gris's "sensibility", his particular individual experience of vision. And I have shown how this view is even supported by that apparently dogmatic conceptualist prone to idealist declarations, Gris's close confidant, Maurice Raynal. The question remains: how, in the light of recent re-readings of Cubist image-making, can one sustain such an argument?

The first point to make is that the arbitrariness of the sign (exposed by the "freedom", for instance, of the word from a single referent) was something routinely discussed in the context of both Cubism and post-Mallarméan poetry by the late 1910s and the early 1920s, and that this connected with a broad-based interest in language which Gris certainly shared[47]. Major sections of Kahnweiler's second monograph are taken up with searching discussions of Cubist painting in terms of post-Mallarméan poetry and a theory of the "sign". Kahnweiler's discussion of poetry stresses the autonomy of poetic imagery more than the separation of word from referent, but his discussion of the sign is certainly relevant here. Moreover, Kahnweiler told me that it was based on conversations that he had with Gris in the 1920s, and that the texts to which he refers in this foot notes were almost certainly read by Gris too at the time. These texts, Jacques de Morgan's account of the development of writing in the third part of his *L'Humanité préhistorique, Esquisse de préhistoire générale* and Joseph Vendryes' *Le Langage, Introduction linguistique à l'histoire*, both of 1921, were highly respected in the 1920s[48].

As we shall see, Vendryes' *Le Langage* throws considerable light on the attitudes to language shared not only by Gris and Kahnweiler, but by many in the milieux of the Cubists at the time. Gris's and Kahnweiler's conversations about art, language and writing were clearly related to wider discussions, the echoes of which are there in the frequency of the use of terms like "hieroglyph" and "sign" in much contemporary commentary on Cubism. With reference to Lipchitz, Raynal could say in 1920: "Artistic expression is certainly but a form of language...", and could go on to call Lipchitz's first stone carvings a search for "a new vocabulary"[49]. In 1921 Waldemar George, as we have seen, called Gris himself "one of the most orthodox grammarians of the Cubist school"[50]. He was often to apply the term "hieroglyph" to Cubism.

In his second monograph, Kahnweiler does not see any painting as mere *mimesis*: light is not *in* painting because it too is simply a referent of coloured pictorial signs. His theory of signs in painting is founded on a distinctly original application of Vendryes' analysis of language to de Morgan's account of the development and character of writing. He connects painting with "ideographic writing", that is, the making of graphic signs (either hieroglypic or cuneiform) which do not merely denote *things,* but also signify "ideas". Applying Vendryes' notion of the capacity of language to convey "images", he sums up: "Painting, in so far as it is writing, transcribes images, not words. The painter tries to transmit images; the spectator first "reads" them and then transforms them into ideas. The process of the message could be shown as follows: Graphic sign / Image / Vocal sign / Idea"[51].

Yves-Alain Bois has maintained that Kahnweiler's theory of the sign and of painting as writing was inadequate because it implied too fixed a relationship between signifier and signified, and minimized the arbitrariness of the sign as brought out by Ferdinand de Saussure[52]. The graphic sign is *definitively* connected through the vocal sign for the "image" to the "idea". The insistence on a clear, unambiguous relationship between sign, referent and idea is certainly shared by Gris himself in his statements of the 1920s; he contends that his sign for a fruit-bowl, say, can *only* be read as a fruit-bowl. This echoes Vendryes' observation that, especially in speech, words are used with as unequivocal a relationship to their referents as possible[53].

Yet, such a conviction did not follow from a lack of awareness of the arbitrariness, in general terms, of the sign, and when Vendryes published *Le Langage* he was well aware of Saussure's posthumous *Cours de linguistique générale* (which had appeared in 1916). Although Vendryes did not develop a tripartite theory of the sign, he still could define language as a "system of signs". Further, he considered the realisation of the "independent value" of the sign in relation to "its object" the first and essential step in the development of language, and he described that development as a process of "successive differentiations"[54].

If the sign's relationship to its referent was fundamentally arbitrary, however, it did not mean that, when actually *used,* it remained open and therefore ambivalent. Kahnweiler's and Gris's stress on the clarity of the relationship between sign and referent in painting did not imply a naïve failure to recognize on a theoretical level the arbitrariness of the sign, but only a focus on usage, and certainly for Gris, as for Vendryes, it was above all the contextual placing of signs that gave them clear denotational meaning. A circle in a painting by Gris denotes an eye or a button only in context[55]. Kahnweiler, when he read Vendryes, must have been made fully aware of the arbitrariness of the sign; his stress on fixed meanings indicates a concern with the analogy between painting and language on the level not of general *structures,* but of *utterance.* If he and Gris thought of painting as language (writing), they thought of it, most immediately, as *Parole* not *Langue*.

Kahnweiler's emphasis is on the invention of *new* signs. So is that of George or Raynal or any of the others who looked at the "second Cubism" in terms of writing and sign-making. This emphasis on the invention of new signs is aligned with the endemic use of the metaphor of new "vocabularies"; it confirms the continuing dominant subjectivism of the Cubists and the Cubist milieu. George calls Gris an "orthodox Cubist grammarian" to draw attention to his situation within the collectivity of the "call to order", and indeed Gris liked to explain his paintings as if simple grammatical rules applied (to inflect coloured forms so that they denoted things was to "qualify substantives" or, as Vendryes would have said, to make them adjectival)[56]. Yet, these were rules that applied whatever the "vocabulary" in question and, of course, Gris's theory of the aesthetic insisted on the development of specific technical means, a specific *personal* vocabulary. Raynal's talk of Lipchitz's pursuit of a new "vocabulary" could as easily have been applied to Gris.

There is a clear analogy here with the way that Vendryes understood linguistic change, for he made a simple distinction between structural changes in systems of signs, which he noted were slow and broad-based, and changes in the signs themselves *as used* (the vocabulary or *lexicon*), which were fast-moving, continual and individual. "New vocabularies", for Vendryes, were a feature of language in use, particularly spoken language, utterance. He argued that, whereas the phonetic and grammatical systems of language, their "morphology", was stable once acquired, "vocabulary", by contrast, "is never fixed because it depends on circumstances. Each speaking subject puts together his vocabulary from one end of his life to the other by means of a series of borrowings from his fellows. Vocabularies are added to, but also diminished and transformed". The intelligence constantly "works over... vocabulary" following the imperatives of social and physical change[57].

This argument was based on work on the dynamics of spoken language carried out at the end of the nineteenth and the beginning of the twentieth centuries under the auspices of Saussure's mentor, Michel Bréal[58]. Following these findings, Vendryes made a basic distinction between written language and spoken language. Written language observes the logical rules of grammar and conforms to language as it is held in common; it changes slowly. Spoken language is fragmented, a-grammatical and, especially in the case of slang, develops new vocabularies in direct opposition to language held in common. It was not with written language held in common that Vendryes associated the languages of art, but, very pertinently, with spoken language at its most volatile and personal: slang. He notes how "men of letters" tend to form groupings set apart: "their language, therefore, has all the characteristics of a special language", one that is set against the "common" because it is a "personal instrument". He even goes so far as to call it a "literary slang" [argot littéraire][59]. For Vendryes, the language of art is categorically a language of utterance. It is, therefore, by definition constantly renewed at the level of vocabulary, and profoundly subjective in its particularity.

Just as Kahnweiler's and Gris's stress on the fixed meanings of signs confirms their focus on usage, so their concern with the invention of new signs, the development of new vocabularies, underlines their commitment ultimately to the individual, to the artist as speaking subject. Kahnweiler might have worked through the analogy between painting and language in terms of writing, but it is clear that he conceived of the "written" sign in Cubist painting as operating with all the unambiguous clarity yet openness to change characteristic of spoken language, even "literary slang". Certainly Gris wanted his painting to "speak" about transcendence, at least after 1916, but his wish was for it to do so at the level of highly personal utterance, of *Parole*.

These observations, prompted by Vendryes' *Le Langage*, apply most directly to Gris's work after 1920 and the commentary that it generated then. As I have acknowledged, the association between Cubism and the Saussureian notion of *Langue* at its most impersonal has been made specifically with reference to Cubist *collage* and *papier collé* around 1912–13. The re-reading of these Cubist images on a plane beyond and embracing all individual utterance is underpinned, perhaps most crucially of all, by the assumption that these practices effectively got rid of personal "touch". The anonymity of press-cuttings, cheap wallpaper, false marbling and so on is seen to go with a graphic and painterly anonymity: the scissors or the blade replacing the brush, the diagrammatic line replacing the sketched, responsive line. The disappearance of the signature from the *recto* aids such conclusions[60].

The sheer precision of Gris's *collages* and especially his *papiers collés* of 1914 certainly places them in such a context of anonymity, and in 1913–14 his conscientious habit of signing and dating is almost always confined to *versos*. Further, although we have seen how he puts himself in the *papiers collés* by means of verbal inference, he always does so in 1914 to expose his role and his status in the work as problematic, never simple. I return to the label "indirect contributions". The phrase "de l'auteur" (of/by the author) in *The Marble-topped Console Table* (Figure 20) invites the addition of a question-mark. What *of* the author? And, indeed, what is *by* the author?

The first major phase of *post facto* recuperative writing about Cubist *collage* and *papier collé* came around 1930. It was provoked by the exhibition of *collages* put together in 1930 at the Galerie Goemans in Paris. Here Cubist *collages* and *papiers collés* of 1912–14 were hung together with the latest Surrealist products of Dalí, Arp, Miró and others and examples by Picasso, Braque and Gris were also included[61]. The erasure of the artist's touch was a central issue, as it had been in Surrealist milieux since 1924. Louis Aragon's preface to the catalogue 'La Peinture au défi' saw to that. Aragon imagined a time when the practice of *collage* would make painters feel it "childish" to put together their own pictures, just as they already no longer mixed their colours. He wrote of "the negation of technique" and, above all, of the end of "personality-in-technique". But he added a vital further dimension to his conclusion with the point that there would follow instead the assertion in *collage* of "personality-through-choice"[62]. The artist's hand might no longer matter, but the choice of elements could still be "personal". This was, of course, demonstrably the case in Picasso's, Braque's and Gris's early *collages* and *papiers collés*. Both the others *could* have made *papiers collés* like *The Bottle of Anis del Mono* or *Fruit Dish and Carafe* (Plates 43 and 40); neither would have. Each cultivated difference in the way they chose combined items.

Even the assumed *technical* anonymity of their early *collages* and *papiers collés* is open to question. Salmon certainly liked to encourage a belief in the artisanal skills of Braque, with his professional painter-decorator background, and his proven skills with the steel combs used to scratch false wood-graining into paint[63]. And this has led to a continuing stress on the artisanal anonymity of both Braque's and Picasso's *collages* and *papiers collés*. Yet, Braque habitually left visible vestiges of the rough blue chalk guide-lines drawn on the paper before he cut it to shape, along with pencil dashes that indicated where it was to be stuck, and his scissoring was often careless.

A *papier collé* like *Wine* (Figure 13) is entirely without the immaculate precision and the efficient covering up of all preparations that might have met the professional standards of his painter-decorator father[64]. He, and even more, Picasso, tended to leave plain enough the marks of *personal* agency. And, although their charcoal drawing can be highly schematic, it does without the impersonal instruments of the diagrammer, the set-square, the compass, the dividers.

Gris used these instruments, of course, and, as we have seen, he cut out with precision and used his paper surfaces to cover over his preparations thoroughly. His *papiers collés* often do meet high standards of artisanal care, far higher than Braque's. They *are* technically anonymous. And yet, the irony is that it is precisely in the exactitude of their intricacies that they signify their differences from Picasso and Braque. "Personality-through-choice" is asserted in the wry wit of their visual and textural materials: at the level of utterance, one of their signifieds is specifically Gris's wit. The very impersonality of their finish asserts "personality-in-technique".

There can be no doubt, as Rosalind Krauss and Yves-Alain Bois have contended, the *collages* and *papiers collés* of Picasso, Braque and Gris can indeed be read as *exposés* of the workings of *Langue,* to whose stucture all utterance (*Parole*) must be subordinate in the largest sense. If the artist is in the work it is not as some essential giver of meaning through expression, but as a signified in a play of signifiers. My contention is that even in the "anonymous" assembled images of 1912–14 the artist is a central not a marginal signified: the selection and juxtaposition of items along with the way they are cut out and fixed act together to construct a "personality", a speaking subject. The signification of a personality or a sensibility with the name "Juan Gris" is, of course, still clearer and more emphatic in the paintings that preceded and succeeded the *collages* and *papiers collés,* especially after 1920.

Finally, it should be stressed that, in terms of Michel Bréal's late nineteenth and twentieth century analysis of spoken language, *collage* and *papier collé* themselves are far more to be associated with utterance (*Parole*), than with the grand structures of language (*Langue*). They are as such distinctively individualized, set apart from language held in common both despite and because of their inclusion of mass-media fragments. Looking back to Bréal, Vendryes concluded: "The elements that written language bring together into a coherent ensemble, appear in spoken language, separated, disjointed, disarticulated: even the order is altogether different". Indeed, what we have come to call the "collage principle" is aduced as the principle of spoken language itself: "juxtaposition" is found to be fundamental to it, a "spontaneous" use of juxtaposition that is affective and highly subjective[65].

In one manifest sense, the rickety structures of Picasso's, Braque's and Gris's *collages* and *papiers collés,* so full of surprises as Apollinaire said, declare in all their transience a *refusal* to elevate the work onto the gravely impersonal plane of *Langue.* They are utterances, and as such the artist (the individual artist) is to be seen in them.

The finished perfectionism of Gris's *collages* and *papiers collés* is a quality shared by the vast majority of his oil-paintings between 1910 and 1921. Although presented proudly as fine art, not the work of an artisan, they are commonly anonymous in technique and their anonymity can always be read as the mark of the "personality" in them, of Gris. It was perhaps in Gris's Cubisms that the notion of the autonomy of the picture, the *tableau objet* (picture-as-object), was most effectively reconciled with a dominant subjectivity. It could be said that "Juan Gris" is absorbed *into* the perfection of the *tableau objet,* that by seeming to disappear he is made a part of it: the subject *in* the object.

Writing of Braque in 1929, Carl Einstein returned to the theme of anonymity and his vaunted artisanal skills: "Whoever wants perfect accomplishment no longer cares about himself and thus are born works that dissemble personality. It might be said perhaps that Braque thus becomes the more invisible to the extent that his works are the more perfect, to the extent that his marvellous skill succeeds in obscuring the great adventure of invention"[66]. The same might have been written about Gris;

but it should be added that most who responded to his work then saw him, the subject, in it. He disappeared only to reappear as the subject in the object.

At the beginning of 1918 Pierre Reverdy published a poem called 'Note'. It is a poem which can be read as an allegory of the autonomy of the art-work, an allegory of its independence from the quotidian, and of the "purity" of the "emotion" it ideally excites[67]. It is also an allegory of the disappearance of the artist into the work. I end by quoting it in full:

Note

Twelve notes vibrate in the silence
and the night will produce emotion

Another all alone in the square of the sky
detached itself
Words shone on the table

Whence this sentiment

Sometimes the author has none and his
work transports us

The assembled words formed a whole more
living than a music-hall character

The spectators were turning around the table
brushing the walls
They were looking
The band of light came from behind
and nailed the table to the floor
Music

Words
Artificial light
And the Author has disappeared
Taking his secret with him
Each spectator knows what he
wanted to say
A unique emotion grips them
Soon they will forget the Author the table the
words and the light"[68]

1 Cooper no. 92.
2 *Letters of Juan Gris (1913–1927),* translated and edited by Douglas Cooper, London, 1956, p. 34 (Letter XL).
3 Maurice Raynal, 'Les Arts: Exposition Juan Gris', *L'Intransigeant,* Sunday, 1 April 1923.
4 See chapter 2, note 8.
5 Albert Gleizes and Jean Metzinger, *Du "Cubisme",* Paris, 1912, re-issued with a preface by Gleizes and a postface by Metzinger (both dated 1947), Paris, 1980, pp.63 and 72.
6 See chapter 2 above.
7 Gleizes and Metzinger (1912 and 1980), op.cit., pp. 45–6.
8 Juan Gris, 'On the Possibilities of Painting', lecture delivered 15 May 1924 to the 'Sociétés des études philosophiques et scientifiques pour l'examen des idées nouvelles', at the Sorbonne, Paris; in Daniel-Henry Kahnweiler, *Juan Gris: His Life and Work,* translated by Douglas Cooper, London, 1969, p. 195.
9 This argument is most fully developed in Henri Bergson, *L'Evolution créatrice,* Paris, 1907. Again, in this respect, the work of Antliff is important. See Robert Mark Antliff, 'Bergson and Cubism: A Reassessment', *Art Journal,* Winter, 1988, pp. 341–9.
10 Gleizes and Metzinger (1912 and 1980), op.cit., pp. 341–9.
11 Ibid., p. 50.
12 Ibid.
13 See note 4 above.
14 "Pinturrichio" (Louis Vauxcelles), 'Le Carnet des ateliers: Le Père du cubisme', *Le Carnet de la semaine,* 29 December 1918, p. 11. And Letter to Maurice Raynal, 15 February 1919, *Letters* (1956), op.cit., pp. 62–3 (Letter CXXIV).
15 Letter to Amédée Ozenfant, c. 25 March 1921, ibid., pp. 104–6 (Letter CXXIV).
16 See Kahnweiler (1969), op.cit., pp. 146 and 148.
17 Maurice Raynal, 'Les Arts', *L'Intransigeant,* Monday, 7 August 1922.
18 Maurice Raynal, *Anthologie de la peinture en France de 1906 a nos jours,* Paris, 1927, p. 32.
19 Ibid., p. 26.
20 "La face de Dieu change tous les jours et ce que l'artiste est en droit de considérer comme la vérité se rencontre, mais assez difficilement au point mobile que relie le passage d'une face à l'autre". Maurice Raynal, *Lipchitz,* Paris, 1920, n.p.
21 Maurice Raynal, 'Juan Gris', *L'Esprit Nouveau,* no. 5, February 1921, pp. 535–7.
22 The most "naturalistic" of all, perhaps, is a landscape, which is illustrated in *Juan Gris: Correspondance, Dessins 1915–1921,* edited with notes and an introduction by Christian Derouet, IVAM Centre Julio González, Valencia and Centre Georges Pompidou, Musée National d'Art Moderne, Paris, 1991, no. 14, p. 128.
23 See Kahnweiler (1969), op.cit., p. 33.
24 Letter to Paul Dermée, 13 May 1918, *Letters* (Cooper, 1956), op. cit., p. 54 (Letter LXVI).
25 For the two contracts, see *Correspondance* (Derouet, 1991), op. cit., no. 6, pp. 27–9 and no. 21, p. 45. Derouet discusses the implications for drawings of the contracts in his introduction, see p. 15.
26 A drawing by Gris was used as the frontispiece of Vicente Huidobro's *Horizon carré,* Paris, 1917. Three drawings by Gris illustrated Paul Dermée's *Beautés de 1918,* Paris, 1919. Four drawings by Gris illustrated Pierre Reverdy's *La Guitare endormie,* Paris, 1919.
27 For a listing of the illustrated books, see Kahnweiler (1969), op. cit.
28 I have discussed one case of a drawing directly related to a painting executed at Beaulieu-lès-Loches in 1918. The drawing is reproduced here (Plate 93). See Christopher Green, 'Synthesis and the 'synthetic process' in the painting of Juan Gris 1915–19', *Art History,* March 1982, p. 97. For another case, see chapter 6 below, and Plate 86.
29 See especially Pierre Reverdy, 'L'Emotion', *Nord-Sud,* no. 8, October 1917, and my discussion in Christopher Green, 'Purity, poetry and the painting of Juan Gris', *Art History,* June 1982, pp. 188–9.
30 For a discussion of the prose-poems, see Emma Strojkovic, *L'Œuvre poétique de Pierre Reverdy,* Padua, 1951, pp. 41–48. A good instance of a prose-poem published in the period which has these characteristics is 'Compagnons' which appeared in *S.I.C,* nos. 47–48, 15 and 30 June 1919, p. 8.
31 For Lipchitz's portrait series, see Alan G. Wilkinson, *Jacques Lipchitz: A Life in Sculpture,* Art Gallery of Ontario, Toronto, 1989, p. 91.
32 Robert Delaunay, 'La Lumière', first published in *Der Sturm,* Berlin, January 1913; in Gustav Vriesen and Max Imdahl, *Robert Delaunay, Colour and Light,* Cologne and New York, 1967, p. 6.
33 Picasso produced one or two works whose prismatic colour does echo Delaunay's. See Pierre Daix and Joan Rosselet, *Picasso, the Cubist Years, 1907–1916, A Catalogue Raisonné of the Paintings and Related Works,* London, 1979, no. 570 especially.
34 Gleizes and Metzinger devoted a section of *Du "Cubisme"* to a critique of Neo-Impressionism. They go so far as to declare: "A l'idée de lumière nous ne rattachons pas mécaniquement la sensation de blanc, non plus qu'à l'idée d'ombre celle de noir. Nous admettons qu'un bijou noir et d'un noir mat soit plus lumineux que le satin blanc ou rose de l'écrin". Gleizes and Metzinger (1912 and 1980), pp. 57–8.
35 See especially Cooper nos. 59 and 61.
36 Other instances are Cooper nos. 247 and 248. The specific clashes of colour used in these pictures, especially the figure painting (no. 248) relate especially to those used by Georges Braque in *The Musician* of 1917–18 (Kunstsammlung Basel).
37 "Pinturrichio" (Louis Vauxcelles), 'Perplexité', *Le Carnet de la semaine,* 18 August 1918, p. 7.
38 Letter to Léonce Rosenberg, 10 July 1918, *Correspondance* (Derouet, 1991), op.cit., p. 51 (Letter 29). The emergence of Gris's correspondence with Rosenberg, thanks to the tenacious commitment of Christian Derouet, has led to a necessary reassessment of my previous reading of Vauxcelles's article as almost entirely fanciful and mischievous. C.f. Christopher Green, *Cubism and its Enemies: Modern Movements and Reaction in French Art, 1916–1928,* New Haven and London, 1987, pp. 8–9. In the translation given above, "I would like to be able to produce brushwork" is translated from "je voudrais pouvoir brosser".

39 Letter to Rosenberg, 22 August 1918. Ibid, p. 52 (Letter 32).
40 Cooper no. 119.
41 Cooper nos. 137 and 138. No. 137 is dated July 1915. No. 138 is undated, but dated by Cooper July, presumably because of its closeness to no. 137. Josette Gris told me that the wallpaper in a venetian blind pattern used in Cooper no. 119 was bought at Collioure. It seems likely that it was the initial stimulus behind the introduction of the window motif. Conversation with Madame Josette Gris, 20 July 1977.
42 Being in Bandol, Gris could not have seen this exhibition, but one of the St Raphael gouaches was reproduced in *L'Amour de l'art* in July 1921, and Gris could, of course, have known them from 1919–20. During the war-years, and especially in 1917–18, his relations with Picasso were mutually respectful and friendly. As the newly discovered correspondence between Léonce Rosenberg and Gris reveals, Picasso actually sought him out on returning from Rome in 1917 (see Christian Derouet's essay below). They continued to see something of each other in the 1920s. Armand Salacrou recalls visiting Picasso at 21, rue La Boétie in the early or mid-1920s: "posée sur un plateau près de la porte d'entrée, unique carte de visite, celle de Juan Gris, jaunie et recouverte de poussière. Oubli? Négligence? Désir de se souvenir que Juan Gris était venu l'adorer?" Armand Salacrou, *Dans la Salle des pas perdus, c'était écrit,* Paris, 1974, p. 138. At the time of the open window pictures of 1921, Gris does not seem to have felt very positive about Picasso, since in April he was invited to Monte Carlo by Diaghilev to design sets and costumes for the Ballets Russes only to find that Picasso "had stepped in". See Letters to Kahnweiler, 14, 15 and "probably" 21 April 1921, *Letters* (Cooper, 1956), op.cit., pp. 108–111 (Letters CXXVII, CXXVIII, CXXIX). Picasso would be one of the chief mourners at Gris's funeral, however.
43 André Lhote, 'Picasso et le "respect de la nature"', *La Nouvelle Revue Française,* 8th Year, no. 84, 1 July 1921, pp. 111–2.
44 "Pinturrichio" (Louis Vauxcelles), 'Mort de quelqu'un', *Le Carnet de la semaine,* 1 April 1923, p. 8. The title of this article, a reference to Jules Romains's novel of 1911, suggests, of course, the "death" of the Cubist Gris.
45 Letter to Kahnweiler, 19 April 1921, *Letters* (Cooper, 1956), op.cit., p. 108 (Letter CXXVI).
46 Rosalind E. Krauss, 'In the Name of Picasso'; in *The Originality of the Avant-Garde and Other Modernist Myths,* Cambridge, Mass., and London, 1987, p. 39. Also highly relevant in this context is Yves-Alain Bois, 'Kahnweiler's Lesson', *Representations,* no. 18, Spring, 1987, pp. 33–68.
47 Telling instances are Reverdy's articles in *Nord-Sud* and other publications where Mallarmé is invoked, and Jacques Rivière's 'Reconnaissances a Dada', *La Nouvelle Revue Française,* August 1920.
48 Kahnweiler (1969), op.cit. Also conversation with D.-H. Kahnweiler, 14 April 1977. Space was given to a report on Vendryes' book in *L'Intransigeant,* for instance. See "Les Treize", 'Les Lettres', *L'Intransigeant,* 27 August 1922.
49 Maurice Raynal, *Lipchitz,* Paris, 1920, unpaginated.
50 Waldemar George, 'Juan Gris', *L'Amour de l'art,* November 1921, p. 351.
51 Kahnweiler (1969), op.cit., p. 71. C.f. the discussion on "la phrase" and "l'image verbale"; in Joseph Vendryes, *Le Langage, Introduction linguistique à l'histoire,* Paris, 1921, p. 85 and Jacques de Morgan, *L'Humanité préhistorique, Esquisse de préhistoire générale,* Paris, 1921, Troisième Partie, chapter III, 'La Figuration de la pensée', pp. 273–285.
52 Bois (1987), loc.cit., p. 56. Bois considers it to have been an error to have believed the pictogram possible, since it is supposed to operate with fixed referents, outside systems. My view is that Kahnweiler was thinking in this instance on the level of the pictogram as a working element in the usage of specific languages, i.e. on the level of Parole. It is, in fact, likely that he was able to conceive of Langue as a system of signs, see note 54 below.
53 "Dans le langage courant, un mot n'a qu'un sens à la fois". See Vendryes (1921), op.cit., pp. 99–100.
54 Bois laments Kahnweiler's ignorance of Saussure (Bois, 1987, loc. cit., p. 56). Kahnweiler's reading of Vendryes, in fact, establishes his awareness, at least indirectly, of Saussure, and his access (with Gris) to a theoretical position with regard to the structure of language broadly in tune with the *Cours de linguistique générale.* Vendryes claims that his own book is the first to have appeared: "où le programme d'une linguistique générale fut complètement réalisé". A post-scriptum added just prior to publication reads: "Celà n'est plus tout à fait vrai depuis la publication en 1916 du livre de F. de Saussure, *Cours de linguistique générale;* mais cet ouvrage posthume, malgré l'abondance de vues qu'il présente, n'est pas un exposé méthodique et complète de linguistique générale". For Vendryes on language as a "system of signs", see especially Ibid, pp. 19–28. On the arbitrariness of the sign, he contended (p. 27): "Entre le signe et la chose signifiée, entre la forme linguistique et la matière de la représentation, il n'y a jamais un lien de nature, mais seulement un lien de circonstance". Incidentally, bearing in mind the reputation and availability of this book, it seems likely that the Surrealists and such figures as Jean Paulhan were aware of it; links of some kind between the Saussureian theory of the sign and Surrealist theory are, therefore, distinctly possible.
55 "Dans tous les cas que nous venons d'examiner, ce qui détermine la valeur du mot, c'est la contexte". Ibid., p. 202.
56 Vendryes points out that adjectives are often one-time substantives. In Latin "uber" (fruitful) is the substantive "uber" (breast). This is directly relevant to my discussion of Gris here because the adjectival is the qualitative. See Ibid., pp. 149–50.
57 Ibid., pp. 215–241.
58 In his discussion of linguistic change, Vendryes footnotes Michel Bréal's *Essai de sémantique,* 3rd edition, Paris, 1904 and E. Littré's *Comment les mots changent de sens,* Paris, 1888.
59 Ibid., pp. 279–80 and 299–300.
60 C.f. Krauss (1987), loc.cit., and also Pierre Daix's discussion of *collage* and *papier collé* in Daix and Rosselet (1979), op.cit. Most recently, William Rubin has put together a comprehensive case for anonymity as a guiding principle in the work of Picasso and Braque. See William Rubin, 'Picasso and Braque: an Introduction'; in William Rubin, *Picasso and Braque: Pioneering Cubism,*

The Museum of Modern Art, New York, 1989, pp. 19–20.

61 Cooper nos.84 and 94 are both illustrated in a suite of illustrations, apparently of *collages* and *papiers collés* from the Galerie Goemans exhibition, in *Cahiers d'Art,* no. 2, 1931.

62 Louis Aragon, *La Peinture au défi,* Paris, 1930; in Louis Aragon, *Ecrits sur l'art moderne, écrits d'Aragon sur l'art publiés sous la direction de Jean Risart,* Paris, 1981, pp. 34–35.

63 See especially André Salmon, *La Jeune Sculpture française,* Paris 1919; in Edward F. Fry, *Cubism,* London, 1966, p. 140. Fry points out that this text was written in 1914. Still in 1919, Salmon could write: "Une tradition de métier l'a..., toujours dirigé". André Salmon, 'Georges Braque – L'Artiste et l'artisan', *L'Europe nouvelle,* no. 13, 29 March 1919, p. 625.

64 In fact, despite this, Braque's relations with his family and specifically his father seem to have been good, and indeed his father was a founder of the Cercle de l'Art Moderne at Le Havre in 1906. This is revealed by Braque's correspondance as published in Judith Cousins, with the collaboration of Pierre Daix, 'Documentary Chronology'; in Rubin (1989), op.cit.

65 Vendryes (1921), op.cit., p. 165. For Bréal, see note 56 above. To my knowledge, Molly Nesbit is the first to have suggested a relationship between Michel Bréal's theories and *collage* and *papier collé.* She did so in her Durning-Lawrence Lectures of 1991 at University College, London. Interestingly, André Salmon was a friend of Bréal's son Auguste, and recalls visits to the house and encounters with "l'éminent philologue, père de la sémantique". See André Salmon, *Souvenirs sans fin, Première Epoque (1903–1908),* Paris, 1955, pp. 207 and 242.

66 Carl Einstein, 'Tableaux récents de Georges Braque', *Documents,* 1st Year, no. 6, December 1929, p. 296.

67 I discuss this poem as an allegory of the autonomy of the art-work in Green (June 1982), loc.cit., p. 199.

68 "Les douze notes en vibrent dans le silence/et la nuit produisirent une émotion // Une autre tout seule dans la carré du ciel/se détacha // Les mots rayonnaient sur la table / D'où vient ce sentiment // Quelque fois l'auteur n'en a pas et son oeuvre nous emporte // Les mots assemblés formaient un tout plus vivant qu'un personnage de music-hall // Les spectateurs tournaient autour de la table / en frolant les murs / Ils regardaient / Les bandeaux lumineux venait de derrière / et clouait la table au sol / La Musique // les mots / la lumière artifielle / Et l'Auteur avaient disparu / emportant son secret / Tous les assistants comprenait ce qu'il / avait voulu dire / Une émotion unique les étreignait / Bientôt ils oublièrent l'Auteur la table les / mots et la lumière".

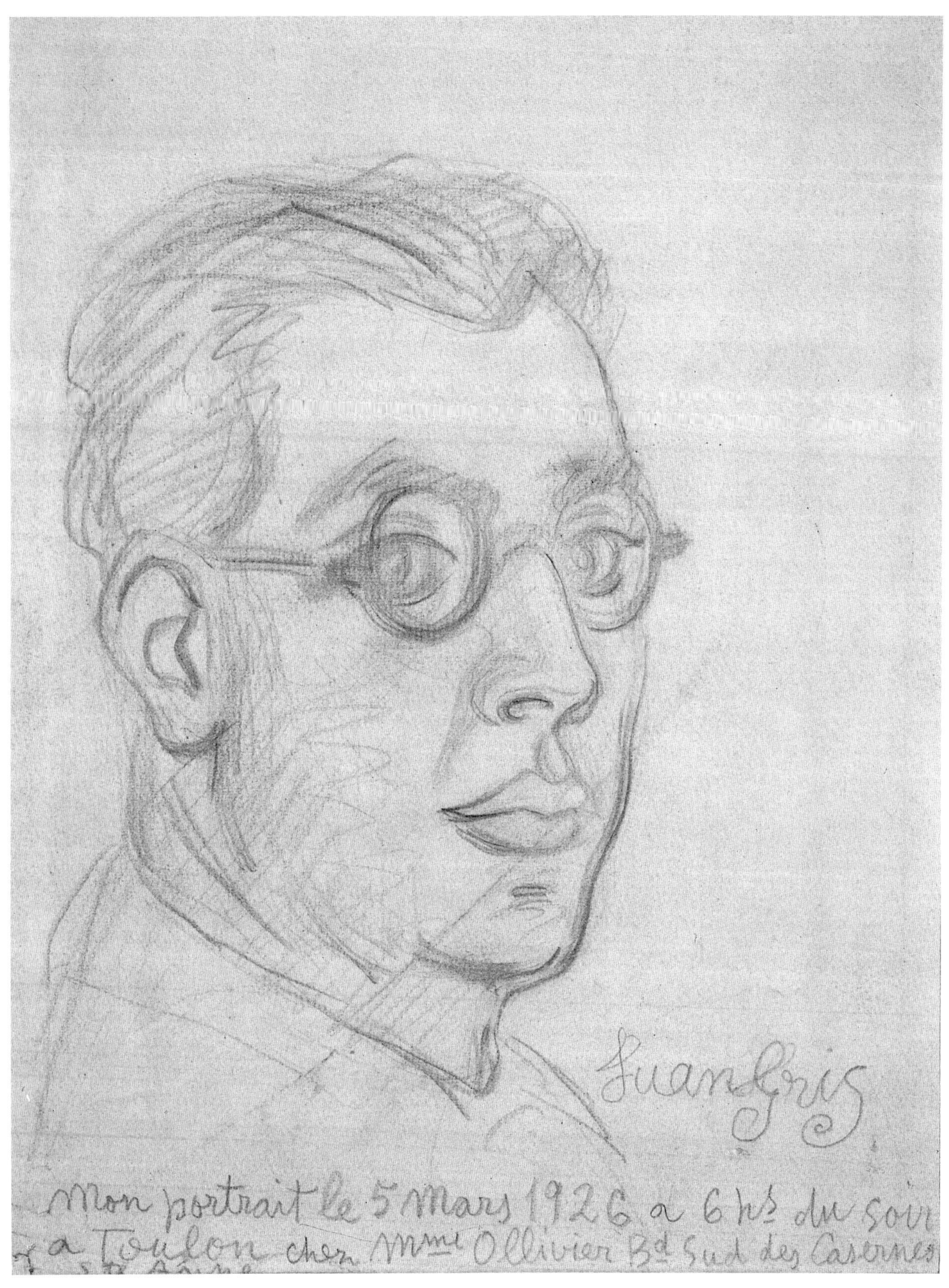
Juan Gris
Mon portrait le 5 Mars 1926 à 6 hs du soir
à Toulon chez Mme Ollivier Bd Sud des Casernes

5. Gris after 1920: Negative Events, Positive Outcomes?

Self-portrait, 1926
Pencil on paper,
31.5 x 24 cm
Georges González Gris

"Does the proximity of death accelerate latent artistic evolution or does it promote an entirely new style? There could but be a vast difference between the outlook of an artist who knows in the prime of his life that his days are numbered and one who is still healthy in body and soul". (Ethelyne J. and Germain Seligman, 1949)[1]

"The second half of 1922 saw the beginning of a weakening and a decline in the painting of Juan Gris which would not cease until 1925. Its forms become soft and passive, its colours become tired and lustreless, its technique laboured... For these three years, Gris lacks conviction". (Douglas Cooper, 1977)[2]

"Certainly Gris's illness was disastrous for his art, but neither his health alone nor any other aspect of his biography seen in isolation can account for the low quality of his late work". (Kenneth E. Silver, 1984)[3]

When Kahnweiler returned to Paris in February 1920, he recalls finding Gris ill. By early May he was thought to have pneumonia, which developed into "pleurisy". He spent over two months in Tenon hospital before being seen off from the Gare d'Orsay by Kahnweiler *en route* for four months of convalescence in the "hunting lodge" at Les Fourneaux, a kilometre outside Beaulieu-lès-Loches. He was still complaining of shortness of breath as late as May 1921 in his letters from Bandol, where his convalescence continued, but by February the next year at Céret he reported that he was regaining weight, working hard and going dancing with Josette[4].

Gris spent the late autumn and early winter of 1923–24 in Monte Carlo working on the set-designs and costumes for three productions put on by Diaghilev's *Ballets Russes*: Montéclair's *Les Tentations de la bergère*, Gounod's *La Colombe* and Chabrier's *L'Education manquée* (the last two operas). These productions are discussed in Karin von Maur's essay. The frenetic activity left him exhausted, he wrote to Kahnweiler early in January 1924[5]. December 1925 brought more signs of fatigue and weakening health, which persuaded him again to spend the winter in the South, this time at Toulon, but on 6 February 1926 he wrote that his temperature was rising to 38 °C every afternoon, and asked the medical advice of Dr Allendy. There are reports of spitting blood, bronchitis and serious anaemia[6]. In Paris through the spring and summer of 1926 Gris was strong again, but still there were days "when he was sick". The final onset of his illness came in the South, where again he had gone for the winter. A "touch of bronchitis" was followed by terrifying attacks of cardiac asthma at night in December 1926 which continued unabated. He came back to Paris at the end of January 1927; high blood-pressure and "uraemia" had been diagnosed. There was a brief, partial remission, before kidney failure killed him on 11 May 1927[7].

There is no disputing the negative events that began with that severe case of "pleurisy" in 1920 and culminated in the shattering decline to death in the winter and spring of 1926–27. There were others. Besides the experience of his collaboration with Diaghilev, which he seems to have found a threat to his equilibrium on every level, there was the derisory failure of his earlier Cubist work to achieve anything like respectable prices at the sales of Kahnweiler's sequestered pre-War stock in 1922–23[8]. Between 1925 and 1927 he knew the beginnings of commercial success, but it came perhaps too late[9]. As we shall see, by no means everything about Gris's life after 1920 was negative, but the question remains: does this accumulation of negative events corrolate straightforwardly with a depressing sequence of negative outcomes in his work?

In the end, this is, of course, a matter of opinion, but there can be no doubt that from as early as 1926 many have thought so. The diagnoses of weakness and decline in the painting are usually similar. The look of naturalism in the open window pictures, which I have discussed in the last essay, is said to be "compromise" in the later work[10]. The lack of "commitment" is said to go with a lack of cohesive rigour, a tame obedience to deadening notions of tradition, and sentimentality in his figures, repetitiveness in his still-lives, and a misplaced hedonism in his colour. The "demon of logic" and the Platonist betrays himself.

Most vilified are the paintings between late 1922 and 1924, for instance *Open Window with Hills* (Plate 112) and *Seated Harlequin* (Plate 105), although the latter has been called an exception[11]. These are certainly the kind of paintings that led Vauxcelles to talk of a Cubist returning to nature in 1923, as we have seen[12]. Curves and softened surfaces are dominant where the angular and the flat had been; the Harlequin invokes the figures of the *Commedia dell'Arte* in Cézanne and Watteau; the still-life repeats the Bandol formula with the mountains reduced to softened hills; and the cool sun-lit colours have come indoors, transformed to a rich *syrop de menthe* green and a cosmetic lilac. Less vilified are the paintings of 1925–27, especially the still-lives, for instance, *The Open Book* (Plate 113), *The Painter's Window* (Plate 118) and *The Table in Front of the Picture* (Plate 114). Yet, although these are angular and make a virtue of cohesion, there are rich colours, softened surfaces and even, as we shall see, that quality Gris had thought beyond him in 1918, "brushwork".

If there tends to be agreement about the fact and the character of "decline", there is little agreement about exactly the period of decline and exactly which paintings are "weak". The Seligmans are in no doubt that it started immediately after the first bout of illness in 1920 and was unrelieved. Kenneth Silver excuses the open windows of 1921, and dates it from 1922 right through to his death in 1927. Mark Rosenthal, in the catalogue-book of the exhibition that led to Silver's commentary, follows Douglas Cooper and most others in seeing a return to high quality between 1925 and 1927 after an enfeebled phase between 1922 and 1924. For what it is worth, my opinion is closer to Rosenthal's and Cooper's than Silver's. As we shall see, however, I feel the blanket negativity that has been applied especially to the work of 1922–24 has led to a failure to grasp its capacity for meaningful utterance in its historical situation, although this is more so in the case of the paintings made after 1924.

Criticism of Gris's later work from otherwise sympathetic quarters surfaced first in 1926, with Christian Zervos's article 'Juan Gris and the Anxiety of Today'. Zervos wrote of a "third period" in his painting, a period of reaction against the "Jansenism" of his earlier Cubism, when he worked for a richer, more brilliant palette. "Left to his instincts Gris lost his way. The drawings, the colour and the many nuances are not happy. They express themselves very badly, they speak without competence". The current work of 1926, he said, demonstrated a return to conviction and vigour[13]. Zervos's colleague on *Cahiers d'art*, Tériade, followed this, in an article published to recognize Gris's achievement the year after his death, by echoing the view that conspicuous failures precede a late burst of successful pictures, and he takes further the inference to be drawn from Zervos's article that the key to the failures is a betrayal of Gris's "true" nature. His diagnosis is worth looking at more closely; it anticipates many that have followed.

Austerity and rigour, Tériade asserts, were inate to Gris. "The logic of Gris is not dry, systematized and cold. It is on the contrary anxious, warm, spontaneous. It is in him... "natural". Gris did not wish to be logical. He was thus through physical necessity. What he "wanted", himself, was life and emotion". This desire to transgress his logical "nature" had led him to "the fugitive happiness of painting in a state of casual insouciance. What a tragic moment it was when the end of Cubism was laboriously anticipated; tragic as well because of the effort one senses in the painter to be or to appear carefree". Yet, Tériade sees this as the prelude to the "triumph" of the last paintings, which are "free" while returning to "simplicity", thus allowing us "to understand the whole of his effort" as a painter. They are "natural conclusions", the product of a Gris restored to himself, reconciled to his logical "nature"[14].

One other early diagnosis of the "failure" of Gris's late work is worth considering for it offers a suggestive gloss on that given by Tériade. It is found in Waldemar George's little monograph of 1931. George tackles the problem not so much as a betrayal of Gris's logical "nature", but as an attempt to confront the contradiction between intellect and sensibility at the heart of all of his activity. He puts the case thus: "The ideas, the notions with whose help he had built up his magnificent doctrine, crumbled between his subtle fingers. Having built the solid scaffolding of his mental universe, Gris had the impression that he was turning over the ashes. It is not that he doubted the future of his working method, the vision of his art. He saw clearly into himself, he kept a precise sense of his own value, his role, his mission. But he put in question painting as "the product of the spirit" such as he had conceived and applied it. Gris was nostalgic not for the object, not at all for the direct appeal of optical memory, but rather for living, active matter, matter which transmits the sensations of touch, odour and taste. The crisis of Juan Gris, a crisis that unfolded over four years before his death, had its origin in the tendency to endow painting with qualities and properties that it could acquire, but that remained at bottom foreign to him"[15].

The character thesis has joined the sickness thesis as a common explanation of Gris's "decline": along with the sick art of a sick man, we have the forced painting of a man who is untrue to himself. Two other diagnoses should be mentioned, one of which is not deserving of much comment, the other of which is perhaps the most far-reaching and important of all. The first comes from Léonce Rosenberg; it is clearly informed by the bitterness of his rivalry with Kahnweiler, to whom Gris returned for commercial management late in 1920, dropping Rosenberg abruptly[16]. For Rosenberg, writing in his translator's English to A. E. Gallatin in 1934, Kahnweiler was an unscrupulous Svengali, who "pushed the few cubist painters which returned to him [including Gris] to return to realism and lead, together with his agent Flechtheim, in Germany, a violent campaign against cubism". In later correspondence with Cooper and Gallatin, Rosenberg also wrote of a betrayal of "his nature", but he accused Kahnweiler of being directly culpable[17]. The second explanation is more recent; it is implicit in Kenneth Silver's assertion, quoted at the beginning of this essay, that Gris's health alone and indeed no "other aspect of his biography" can "in isolation" be the cause of any decline. Silver has been the one most responsible for giving currency to this larger alternative.

For Silver and many others, Gris's "decline" after 1922 is part of a general decline of the Parisian cultural vanguard. It is the "call to order" deprived of the earlier sharp clarity and rigour that Gris and L'Effort Moderne had been able to give it; a phenomenon which produced "a lot of bad, lifeless art" made by painters as varied as Severini, Matisse and Metzinger. And this general decline "is not merely a question of simultaneous... midlife crises", it is the result of a shift in "the cultural terrain" which restored "traditionalist values" and created "a postmodern moment"[18]. The "horizon-blue" government of the Right, elected in 1919 as the first post-war French administration after the Armistice, is seen to find a cultural counterpart in the serene stability, "Latin" allusions and unchallenging hedonism of Gris's late painting with its recurrent openings onto horizon-blue space.

Patricia Leighten, following this line, takes as a model by which to judge many failures of vanguard nerve, the case of Picasso. "He distorted," she writes, "his complex and allusive pre-war project, reducing it to a game of line, colour and form, devoid of social critique and programmatic animus towards the past (...) or any other engagement with the iconography of contemporary life"[19]. In both Picasso's and Gris's case, hers is a series of charges that are open to question, especially the charge of formal games-playing and lack of "contemporaneity", but the argument that the shift to a traditionalism which reassures rather than provokes embodies a deep ideological shift which is persuasive, and I have sustained it myself[20]. Whether it is straightforwardly aligned with a *political* shift to the Right, comparable with Léonce Rosenberg's adulation of Mussolini is, however, very doubtful, and whether it necessarily entails a weakening of commitment and a decline of quality remains a matter of opinion dependent not just on personal aesthetic response, but on whether one believes that *good* art in the twentieth century must involve "social critique" and a "programmatic animus towards the past". Where innovation is joined by effective social radicalism as a criterion of value, then Gris's late work from at least 1920 and possibly even 1916, obviously fails.

My intention in this essay is to ask not whether it failed or why, but how it could be thought to have succeeded at all. The detractors have always been opposed by supporters, and not just among those recently, like myself, who have found "quality" in the paintings of 1925–27. What was it that Gris himself and those who defended the late work believed it could say in the France not only of the "horizon-blue" administration of 1919–24, but of the formation of the French Communist Party at the Congrès de Tours in 1920 and of the centrist "Cartel des Gauches" administration of 1924–28?

The first point to make is that a qualitative judgement of Gris's work after his bout of illness in 1920 cannot convincingly be based on a simple equation between his illness and visible evidence of "weakness" in his painting. The positive judgements are not merely a matter of being kind where there is obvious enfeeblement; there is no obvious enfeeblement.

The paintings even of 1922–24 are often exhaustively deliberated and brought to as high a degree of resolution as ever in 1913 or 1919. And there is little fit between known periods of physical debility and either lower productivity or lesser resolution. The energy of commitment was often there when Gris was a sick man. Moreover, throughout the period 1922–27 there were intervals of months and even years at a time when Gris seems not to have been sick at all: between early 1922 and late 1923, and between early 1924 and late 1925 there is no evidence of illness and much evidence of vigour. If his condition was tuburcular in origin, as is very possible, such long remissions are not unusual[21].

The most obvious incidences of lack of fit between the "condition" of the work and Gris's condition are in the convalescence period between August 1920 and his departure from Bandol in June 1921, and in the period of good health between 1922 and late 1923.

The extraordinary sustained effort of the Bandol open windows was completed against a background of letters complaining of shortness of breath and a whole range of disruptive anxieties caused by an affair with a local woman of means which threatened his relationship with Josette, and by Josette's health as well as his own[22]. The "weak" paintings of the year from late 1922 were painted when all these anxieties had been resolved, against a background of new comforts afforded by the new home next door to Kahnweiler, the exhilaration of Kahnweiler's "Sundays", the continuing pursuit of Gris's craze for learning all the newest dances, and the public accolade of commissions from Diaghilev which included the spectacular *Fête merveilleuse* put on by the *Ballets Russes* in the Hall of Mirrors of the Palace of Versailles[23]. There are patently "complete" pictures from this period, including *Seated Harlequin* and *Open Window with Hills*, but there are summary, unresolved pictures too that could be seen as "symptoms" of debility. Doubtless Diaghilev provided distractions and temptations, but he did not undermine Gris's health, at least before the over-excitement of the final preparations for the Monte Carlo productions of January 1924[24].

That Gris was positive and vigorous in his periods of remission is clear from his letters and from the recollections of Kahnweiler, Armand Salacrou and Gris's son, Georges González Gris. As he recovered at Beaulieu and Bandol in 1920–21, he took immense pleasure in his work. At Bandol the craze for dancing was launched, to be followed by Carnival balls at Céret early in 1922, and his involvement in the fancy dress balls of Montparnasse, the "Bal Suédois" in the Maison Watteau and the balls at the Salle Bullier[25]. He is recalled as an irrepressible entertainer at Kahnweiler's "Sundays", a man with an infectious laugh who often used it[26]. Salacrou recalls the plenitude of the weeks spent with Gris and Josette on holiday in a Nemours mill in the summer of 1924 with André Masson and his wife Odette and with Leiris as a visitor. He remembers a routine that found time for a great deal of work and a great deal of eating and drinking[27]. They holidayed, just the Salacrous and the Gris's, the next summer too, taking a river boat down the Seine to Le Havre. This time Gris was pursued by a determined German woman who clearly did not think him a man in decline[28]. When his son Georges arrived to live with him in the spring of 1926, Gris had already suffered the set-back of the winter in Toulon, but Georges González Gris's recollection is not of a man sickening towards death, but of a man who was mostly energetic and optimistic until the rapid onset of crisis at the turn of 1926–27. He remembers the pleasure that his father took in the beginnings of success, his will to work, and the fact that he never mentioned the possibility of death[29].

Not to mention death does not mean that mortality is forgotten, of course. Gris fell ill less than two years after the flu epidemic that swept Europe in 1918, killing millions in France. In October 1918 he had nursed both Josette and María Blanchard through it[30]. In November Apollinaire had been one of those to die; Metzinger's much loved wife had also died that same year. Gris's bronchitis followed by "pleurisy" must have triggered memories of the coughing and high temperatures that went with the murderous flu of 1918; he must certainly have been aware too of the danger of tuberculosis. Nearly a year after he left the Tenon hospital, he wrote in a moment of depression to Maurice Raynal: "I am so fed up, old friend, that I regret having cheated death last year"[31]. His illness had, it seems, been for him a direct encounter with mortality, and to that extent the Seligmans were right to emphasize that Gris, after 1920, can only have had a deepened awareness of the proximity of death.

It has been accepted, however, in recent stress research that negative events, like a life-threatening illness, can have positive outcomes, especially where the stresses are not multiple and overwhelming in the long-term. Evidence has been cited of such longer term positive outcomes as heightened awareness, sense of challenge, feelings of competence and positive self-esteem arising from successful coping, virtuosity of performance following set-backs, and a strengthened sense of social identity and cohesion due to adversity. The notion of a simple linear relationship between negative life events and negative outcomes has been dismissed[32]. In Gris's case the evidence is far too vague and often indirect to come to confident conclusions, but there is much to indicate that, as his convalescence progressed after his health returned apparently fully in 1922 there *were* positive outcomes.

The "naturalist" drawings of 1920–21 (Plates 94, 95 and 96) certainly signify a reassertion of Gris's immense graphic competence, as well as of his cognitive faculties in the world. Kahnweiler recalls that when he gave them to his friends, it was to mark his re-emergence into life[33]. The Bandol open windows, and indeed many of the paintings of the 1920s, calm and stable as they were, need not only be aligned with the traditionalist "call to order" and its ideological grounding; on the micro-level of the case of Gris, they can also be read as highly personal reassertions of continuity. The timeless, Platonic Gris of the self-portrait of 1921 (page 12) can be read as an image of a desire to transcend which is not only rooted in idealist metaphysical leanings. The pleasure-principle paintings of 1923–24 can be read on a similar level as corroborations of vitality. Such readings are, of course, as subjective as the meanings they impute. That they are possible, however, warns against the equally intuitive assumption that Gris's sickness produced sick paintings.

As I have suggested, it is certainly true that Gris's late work *could* be seen as a positive outcome. I have indicated some such responses, notably Zervos's and Tériade's praise for the last paintings of 1925–27. The other such responses that anticipated or closely followed Gris's death were Gertrude Stein's, Carl Einstein's and Kahnweiler's.

From 1921, Gertrude Stein was as close and supportive a friend to Gris as Kahnweiler or Raynal. They saw a lot of each other in Paris, and in the south at Bandol, Monte Carlo and Toulon. Besides *The Table in Front of the Window* (Plate 101), she bought two of Gris's major pictures of 1924–25[34]. She had no reservations even about the work of 1922–24, something that is clear from the article she wrote on him for *The Little Review*, published at the turn of 1924–25, and from the article she wrote to mark his death, published in *Transition*. Both her pieces hint at a positive relationship between his confrontation with mortality in 1920 and his work. In the first, she writes: "Let me tell all I know about Juan Gris. To begin with he has black thoughts but he is not sad. To begin with he is complete and not completed. To begin with he is necessary and not destroyed". She calls him "a perfect painter"[35]. In the second, she writes of the 1920s: "Four years partly illness much perfection and rejoining beauty and perfection and then at the end there came a definite creation of something. This is what is to be measured"[36].

"Perfection" and "perfect" are key words in Gertrude Stein's texts, just as the theme of mastery and resolution is primary in both a laudatory article of 1930, probably by Einstein, and Kahnweiler's first monograph of 1929. In the article of 1930 the "last great figure compositions" are called "definitive solutions, achieved with the premonition of approaching death"[37]. Kahnweiler, as we have seen, aligned Gris's mastery of his means and the "unity" of his paintings with the masterworks of the museums. He also gave a special prominence to the pictures produced between the winter of 1925–26 at Toulon and his death. "More strongly structured than ever, they yet carry the touching imprint of a calm serenity"[38].

This stress on resolution and the perfecting of images was, in fact, something that Gris himself underlined in the interview with

Georges Charensol published by *Paris-Journal* in April 1924. He linked it to a notion of internal equilibrium. "I love to paint," Charensol quotes Gris saying, "for me, it is a real delight, but once a canvas is finished it pleases me no longer, for I am never satisfied and I try constantly for perfection ... Sometimes I go for months without working. When I notice a fissure in the construction I want to establish, I put down the brushes and I do not take them up again until I sense that my interior equilibrium is regained"[39]. Such a public perfectionist stance was by 1924 a commonplace in the defence of Cubism and Cubists, and in the defence by Ozenfant and Le Corbusier of their still more dogmatic version of Léonce Rosenberg's "call to order", Purism. The technical immaculacy and conceptual coherence which had been a feature of Gris's painting since 1911–12 had by the mid-1920s become a quality thought essential to modernity in the widest sense as well as to current painting, at least by a writer like Raynal alongside the Purists.

Gris's insistence on his need for perfection identifies him and his work as modern in a particular, self-conscious sense; it is a statement among many statements. By 1923–24, it is clear from Raynal's regular column as art-critic of *L'Intransigeant* that a guarantor of quality for him is accomplishment; "experiments" tend to be denigrated, as do hurry or summariness. In this Raynal echoes not only the Purists' conviction that precision was a necessary condition of the modern, but also the campaign carried on just after the war by the anti-Cubist critics Vauxcelles and Jean-Gabriel Lemoine (Raynal's predecessor on *L'Intransigeant*) for "accomplishments" ("réalisations") and against "experiments"[40]. In his study of French painting after 1906, published at the time of Gris's death in 1927, the statement from the painter that he printed (his last) again made a point of "the well-thought-out, the well finished"[41]. Raynal used distinctly comparable terms in summing up not just Gris's achievement in the 1920s, but the "evolution" of Cubism as a movement after 1921. He used the vocabulary of innovation and modernity, writing of the "rejuvenated spirit of painting", but he wrote also of a mastery of "secrets" from the "Ancients" to build "finished works". "The period of fragments is succeeded by the period of complete pictures..."[42]. Perfectionism was, of course, old as well as new, considered a feature of "tradition" as much as modernity. In 1924 Léonce Rosenberg quoted Ingres dismissing "anti-classical art". "It is the doctrine of those who wish to produce without having laboured, to know without having learned"[43]. These were words that fitted well a shared scorn of "experiments", the demand for "accomplishment".

Alongside the theme of mastery, the other major theme that surfaces in the earliest positive responses to Gris's late paintings is that to which Kahnweiler gave the name "polyphony". No sympathetic (or unsympathetic) critic uses the word for Gris's work in the 1920s, and Kahnweiler was not to apply it until his second monograph in 1946, but there are striking anticipations of the sense that he gave it in the context of Gris. They are there both in the 1929 monograph, and in Zervos's response to the late work (Zervos's before Gris's death). Indeed, they are there in Gris's last statement, as published by Raynal.

Kahnweiler amplifies his notion of polyphony thus, taking some time in 1924 as its point of departure: "Whereas from 1916 to 1919 the balance had swung in favour of Architecture (the mould), and from 1920 to 1923 in favour of Poetry (the content), the arms of the balance now stood level. He achieved equilibrium. Architecture and Poetry were blended in what I have already called Polyphony, and his work attained a magnificent amplitude"[44]. Such a balance is clearly suggested as the nub of Gris's accomplishment towards the end of the 1929 monograph in the passage: "I love the rule that corrects emotion," writes Braque. "I love the emotion that corrects the rule," replies Gris. This is to say that this painting, starting from the "rule" which aspires to order, clarity, is permeated with the deepest feeling, the poetic creation of an authentic painter"[45].

Zervos's article of 1926 follows his dismissal of the paintings of 1922–24 with, as we have seen, praise for the current work. He praises it as a return to Gris's "intellectuality" that has balanced the "sensibility" released in the failed excursion into "instinct"[46]. He sees what Kahnweiler saw and later called "polyphony". To use the vocabulary that had been established in the Cubist milieux of 1912, they both saw the accomplishment of Gris at the end in the total resolution of "concept" and "sensibility". Moreover, they both imply that such a resolution, in the fullness it was seen to achieve by 1926, could not have happened without the release from conceptual control that preceded it. The balance was lost before it could be regained in its final "polyphonic" completeness. The way Gris himself put it in the statement of 1927 was that a period of "composition" followed by one of "colour" had come after 1918, leading to their combination one with the other. He claimed for his latest painting not only "finish", but what he called "expression", a word to which I shall return[47].

The reconciliation of Cubist conceptualism to the sensuousness of experience was, like finish and resolution, a major concern of both pro- and anti-Cubist critics from 1918. It is embodied in the claims for a humanized Cubism, in Vauxcelles's desire to see wherever possible Cubists returning to nature, and in André Lhote's advocacy of a "Cubism of sensibility" against "pure Cubism"[48]. What Kahnweiler celebrated as "polyphony" in Gris was what Léonce Rosenberg later deplored as a betrayal by Gris both of his *own* "logical" character and of Cubism (*pure* Cubism). Such a reconciliation was certainly modern for a Lhote who resolutely painted modern subject-matter, but it was more often judged an essential feature of "tradition". The basis of accomplishment in both Lhote's and Bissière's influential analyses of the European "tradition" in the early 1920s was the coming together of concept and sensibility in equilibrium[49]. In 1920 Lhote made of Raphael *the* model of the artist who combines "a human sentiment" with "constructive necessity"; Raphael, first George and then Kahnweiler have said, became one of Gris's great enthusiasms, one that, I have argued elsewhere, left its mark on his painting in 1922–23 especially. The way that the *Seated Harlequin* is fused with a structure of curves obliquely alludes to the Raphael of the "Alba" *Madonna*[50]. The qualities found by Kahnweiler, Zervos, Einstein and Gertrude Stein in Gris's late work were indeed traditionalist. They involve neither a "programmatic animus towards the past" nor "social critique". They are the qualities inevitably associated with the "call to order" as a shift away from the disruptive or subversive to the socially adaptive. This is not, however, to say that they are the qualities of a kind of painting that lacked contemporaneity. In their very traditionalism, Gris's late Cubisms are thoroughly of their time, both as products of his particular milieux and as manifestations of the ethos of reconstruction after the Great War. And, despite the talk of the 1922–24 paintings as being in some profound way untrue to the "real Juan Gris", all of his late work was presented at the time as distinctly his; he put himself in it. The importance Gris attached to that word "expression" in the statement of 1927 is the last demonstration that this is so.

A look at Gris's late Cubisms in the light of the qualities that have been found in them cannot evade the most usually assumed failures, the work of 1922–24. Resolution and completeness are not issues in such paintings as *Seated Harlequin*, *The Three Masks*, *Open Window with Hills* or even the smaller, more freely handled *The Small Table*, also of 1923, and *The Bunch of Grapes* of 1924 (Plates 105, 106, 112, 109 and Figure 25). Most of Gris's production in the two years between late 1922 and late 1924 fits well enough with the perfec-

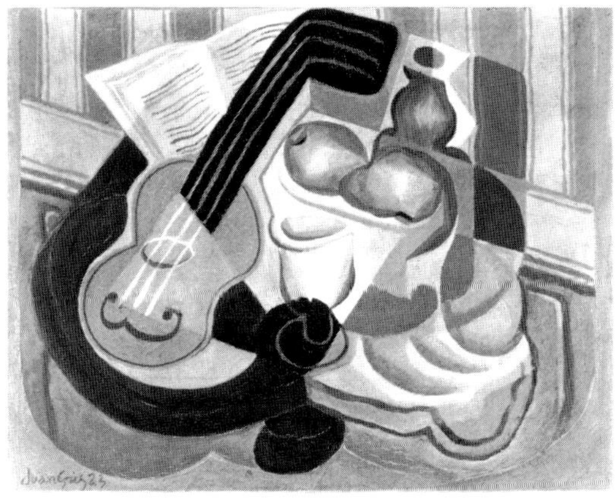

Figure 25
The Small Table, 1923
Oil on canvas,
50 x 61 cm
Kunstmuseum Bern,
Hermann and Margrit
Rupf Foundation

tionism Gris claimed in his comments to Georges Charensol right in the middle of the period. Beyond the questions of failure and compromise, the question I want to address here is this: were these paintings made with so excessive a commitment to the sensuous that they cannot be aligned with what Kahnweiler later called polyphony? There is, in fact, a case for considering them a first try to achieve such a thing, a brave try which has never achieved critical acceptance because it transgressed too radically the critical expectations already firmly attached to Cubism and above all to "Juan Gris". It ignored, indeed challenged, the vanguard assumption that Cubism, especially Gris's Cubism, signified a tough, intellectually elevated austerity, without room for simple visual pleasure.

The last paintings that Gris finished before his solo exhibition at the Galerie Simon in April 1923 included *Seated Harlequin, The Three Masks* and *Open Window with Hills.* All three are compositions which display elaborate rhyming structures. The bumpy hills seen through the open window in the still life rhyme with the rhythmically strung-out curlicues of the balcony grill. The fruit-bowl on the left is a variant on the tightly drawn shape of the violin. A chain of rhymes circles around and through the figure of the seated Harlequin: the head, the mask, the knee, the plate. But in *The Three Masks* the rhymes are not merely elaborate, they are of a new, more all-pervasive kind; one can talk of major structural rhymes and minor shape rhymes, all of which overlap and fuse to set up shifting relationships of the greatest subtlety. There are two dominant structural rhymes. Most obviously, the flanking Pierrots are each other in reverse. They are drawn together by a taut network of diagonals across a more surprising central rhyme between the head, hat and shoulders of the central Harlequin and a configuration below it made up of the Harlequin's hand (an echo of his head), and the right forearm of the figure on the left combined with the right hand and glass of the figure on the right (an echo of his shoulders). The minor rhymes bring into play the central glass, the turned chair backs, the folds of sleeves, tablecloth and curtain.

A feature of the pictures Gris painted after the Galerie Simon exhibition until late 1924 is that formal rhymes are no longer a crucial factor, certainly not in so elaborately developed a way. There is a generalized echoing of forms across the surface of *The Small Table* (Figure 25); the bowl of the glass has a squashy softness of shape generally like that of the fruit, as does the bottle-neck. But these are more similes than the metaphors Raynal discussed. There is merely likeness not virtual repetition. At the same time, however, a different kind of rhyming has been developed, a rhyming not just of forms, but of coloured surfaces, a kind of rhyming that evokes not just a visual experience of cohesiveness, of linkage, but a tactile one. Waldemar George's conclusion that in these paintings intellectual control was challenged by a desire to stimulate all of the senses, smell and taste as well as touch, comes to mind. Gris paints glasses and bottle-necks as if they *feel* like fruit, and might therefore share the taste and the delicate scent of fruit.

Shape, colour and suggested surface-texture often work together like this in the pictures painted after the Galerie Simon exhibition. They offer a different kind of structural cohesion, one that engages surface and form together. This is a long way from the analysis by the separation of "qualities" that produced the objects in triplicate of 1916 (Plate 58). There is an insistence on *fusing* qualities in forms that are given volume.

The question of the relationship between colour, surface and the depiction of volume is of particular importance here, since to approach the pictorial simulation of volume was obviously to threaten the long established Cubist insistence on the flatness of the *tableau objet*. It is this, of course, that has opened these pictures, from a Modernist viewpoint, to the charge of compromise by giving them the look of "naturalism".

To see how Gris attempted to answer the threat, it is necessary to look again at the most recent pictures shown in April 1923. Apart from the use of a deliberately naive modelling for the curtains, Gris's colour in *Open Window with Hills* is no more tonal than in the Bandol open windows. But this not so in *Seated Harlequin* and *The Three Masks*. In *Seated Harlequin* Gris uses tonally modulated colour to suggest a shallow yet substantial modelling of forms in relief. In *The Three Masks* he uses both passages of tonal modelling and carefully graded modulations. The heads of the two Pierrots are built up of facets graduated between a cool blue, a mid-brown and a pale ochre. It is this use of graded cool/warm and tonal modulations that dominates in the post-Galerie Simon exhibition pictures. The surfaces of the fruit and the bottle-neck in *The Small Table* are "cut" like the surfaces of jewelstones, and the colouring follows the facetting, from deep lilac, through emerald green to lights of paler lilac. Volume is given by tonally graded hues kept within what can be seen as flat facetted structures. Technically, this is, of course, a transposition of Cézanne's use of coloured facets and warm/cool contrasts to denote volume in space.

Light had been a dominant factor in the Bandol open windows. In the paintings of 1923–24 it is a dominant factor again, but now it is present not just as space and atmosphere, but also as a builder of volumes. The result, however, is not necessarily to be seen as increased naturalism, certainly not if that misleading term is used as it was in the 1920s[51]. Gris rejects the atmospheric colours of the Bandol open windows for a range of colours which is conspicuously artificial: mauves, purples, emerald greens, coral pinks. Although there are exceptions, he often ignores the local colour of his subject-matter as well as the atmospheric colour of its ambiance. Yet, the clarity with which he grades hues and tones and pulls the cool and the warm together repeatedly produces the effect of things grouped in a particular coloured atmosphere lit in a particular way. Once again, the integration of objects and setting over-rides the tendency for facetting to fragment. The geometry of armatures drawn from the edges of the format retains its unifying role, especially clearly in *The Small Table* for instance, but it has become the basis for a cohesiveness that operates on multiple levels: light, colour and surface-texture as well as form. In 1929 Kahnweiler was to see Gris as *the* Cubist to have reasserted "the unity of the work of art" in "autonomous and accomplished organisms". In their patent artificiality and their multi-level cohesiveness, both "autonomy" and "unity" are as much the declared themes of these pictures as they had been in 1918–19 or were to be afterwards. If they fail, it is because they fail other kinds of expectation.

Gris was not the only recognized Cubist to cultivate a more assertive and more sensuous chromaticism from the early into the mid-1920s. Both Braque and Louis Marcoussis especially did something comparable and excited critical responses that stressed the sensuory, even the pleasurable. Braque marked his move most memorably with the showing of his *Canéphores* as "decorative panels" at the Salon d'Automne of 1922, just as Gris was making his move as well. Braque's and Marcoussis's painting was perceived as part of a shift away from the austerity of the "constructive" painting that had been associated with the "call to order" of the immediate post-War years, and Vauxcelles at least recognized the role of one writer in encouraging it, Gris's committed supporter Waldemar George. In October 1923, with his customary generosity to colleagues, Vauxcelles congratulated George for having accepted for the past two years the "useful and difficult role" of persuading painters to "get out of black"[52]. When later George wrote of Gris putting in question the purity of his Cubism by engaging the most immediate sensuous responses, he did not mention how he had himself pressed hard for a switch at least out of "black" into colour.

George's campaign began early in 1921 with an argument for the precedence of Renoir over Cézanne. He contended that Renoir had achieved the architectonic with colour, whereas in his view Cézanne had never been able to. He remarked, further, that the Cubists too had achieved the architectonic, but without colour. Gris's admiration for Cézanne seems to have been unqualified; there is new evidence too that he admired Renoir, though not so unreservedly[53]. The way that George wrote about colour as constructive and above all as the vehicle of cohesiveness in Renoir is obviously relevant to the way Gris was to use colour to build volumes and to integrate atmosphere in light from the turn of 1922–23. George writes of light penetrating the "interior of his [Renoir's] volumes, circulating there, enveloping them in an invisible mesh" to situate them "in the atmospheric ambiance". He writes of light determining "the inflexions" of form "without breaking it up"[54]. Gris's graded warm and cool hues so carefully contained in his facetted structures are scarcely comparable with the broken touches of late Renoir (George particularly admired the late nudes), so the metaphor of the mesh is ill-fitting; but nothing else is.

The central thrust of George's campaign from that moment on is an anticipation of the polyphonic as Kahnweiler was to define it. George argued for a return to colour that would bring together the results of post-fauve French chromaticism, from Renoir and Bonnard to the Delaunays, with the results of Cubist structural innovation: a constructive merger of "conception" and "vision", the intellectual and the sensuous.

In the third of these essays I mentioned the way that George adapted the shift from "analysis" to "synthesis" to Wölfflin's historical notion of cyclical stylistic shifts from the "painterly" to the "linear". At the beginning of 1922 he made this Wölfflinian view of change by reaction and counter-reaction applicable also to the possibility of a switch to the ephemeral effects of the "painterly" that could even involve the Cubists. He noted how the Cubists excluded "the notation of those ephemeral effects, which give a work of art its evocative power", adding that such "effects" *could* be used as "simple artistic means" and so become "intrinsic" to paintings. He inferred, therefore, that a move into a "painterly" style, committed to such effects, was possible within the terms of the Cubist *tableau objet*[55]. This was precisely what he found had happened in Braque's showing at the Salon d'Automne nine months later, except that now George argued for it, not merely as a cyclical return to a stylistic alternative, but as marking the restoration of painting to a wholeness lost in the solely geometric.

"Now the picture," he declares, "must be a living and palpable organism and not a geometric diagram, a plan, a geographical map or an ideogram. Braque therefore takes care to enliven surfaces by every means at his disposal (pictorial and artisanal), surfaces whose simple arrangement reveals the spirit of a mathematician, but he never puts together a combination of geometric figures which, introduced into the body of the picture, risk becoming foreign, supplementary and inorganic elements there"[56]. In Braque he finds structure and surface to be one, and goes on to claim that a "humanized" colour, free of the "atmospheric" and therefore the naturalistic, is part of this "organic" oneness. Again, the way he writes, this time about Braque, obviously anticipates what was to happen almost at once in Gris's painting. The Braque of the *Canéphores* is the model for a new fusion of "the spirit of the mathematician" and the sensuous, the latter made a property above all of surface and colour.

By the Indépendants of 1923, when Gris was finishing the last of the paintings to be shown at the Galerie Simon, George was able to add Marcoussis as another model for a new painterly Cubism. Having insisted on the continued validity of Paul Signac's Divisionism, he writes of Marcoussis's contribution: "The most painterly of all, that is to say the one with the most sensitivity to harmonious relationships of tones and lines is Louis Marcoussis. While keeping his aesthetic principles intact, he exalts colour..."[57]. Once more, he claims that the painting of "ephemeral effects" does not mean a betrayal of principle.

We know from that notorious letter to Kahnweiler of 1915, where Gris talks of the lack of "the sensitive and sensuous side" in his pictures and his desire for insouciance, that he could think of his rigour and his austerity as a failing[58]. We also know it from Léonce Rosenberg's recollections in the 1930s, as well as that letter Gris wrote to him from Beaulieu in 1918 where he aspires to "brushwork"[59]. Tériade remembered it too, of course, as the besetting sin that diverted him from his "inate" rigour, and Kahnweiler saw it as *the* crucial impetus behind the move towards the sensuous in 1922–23[60].

Yet, the fact is that, whether he thought his "coldness" a failing or not, he did not allow an overt sensuousness in colour and handling to temper the austerity of the great majority of his paintings from 1915 through 1918 at least until 1921, the year of the Bandol open windows, pictures which might seem to suggest the possibility. Gris surely needed to convince himself that such a move could be made without betraying his commitment to an *a priori* purity and to the structural unity of the *tableau objet*. It is likely that George and the cases of Braque and Marcoussis were a sufficient demonstration.

George may or may not have helped open up a space into which Gris could take his painting. There can be no doubt, however, that Braque, Marcoussis and George provided his heightened commitment to colour and surface effects with the support of a context. More important, the terms of George's campaign for "getting out of black" into colour corroborate a reading of Gris's paintings of 1922–24 as a real attempt to reconcile the control of Cubist conceptualism to the sensuous qualities of experience at its most immediate, while enhancing that immediacy. The Sorbonne lecture, like Gris's interview with Charensol, was given in the very middle of this period. It balances talk of "architecture" and form with a precisely equivalent concern for colour, thought of in terms of contrast: the "mathematics of painting" is a *coloured* architecture[61]. Gris seems to have prepared for the Galerie Simon exhibition (and to have set out again afterwards) in pursuit of an equilibrium which clearly conforms to the notion of a more complex wholeness, the kind of unity that Kahnweiler later called polyphony.

Many of the paintings he produced in this first try for polyphony do not offer the qualities that I have found in the paintings analysed here. And these are, of course, images of comfortable resolution amplified by supportive allusions to the art of the past; they replace the challenge of rigour with the reassurance of validated pleasures. I believe, however, that they are and were challenging, because they represented a rejection of what had become in Gris an *acceptable* Cubist austerity. In the context of the post-War "call to order", they continued to sustain a dominant ethos of traditionalism; but in the context of the established public images both of Cubism and of Gris, they marked a break.

Their obliging traditionalism can be considered a response to Gris's failure in the market before 1922, one that is of a piece with his *Ballets Russes* collaborations from late 1922 through to early 1924. It was a response that worked, since 1924 marked the beginning of

Gris's success commercially; some of the bigger collectors of modern pictures (Alphonse Kann, Dr Reber from Lausanne) started to buy, and they, along with Gertrude Stein, found the paintings of 1922–24 attractive[62]. Gris risked ingratiation and, as a result, actually succeeded in ingratiating himself with an audience that mattered. His figure painting after 1922 even came to celebrate the leisured milieux of that audience, in which he now mixed easily, a point I shall return to in my last two essays. Yet, he took other risks when he painted these pictures. He put at risk not only the resolution of each canvas to his own demanding standards, but his very image as an artist in his painting. For many, he went too far.

Since Kahnweiler and so many others have said where and how to look for it, there is little difficulty in finding the features of the polyphony that has been claimed for Gris's painting after 1924.

Much in the paintings of 1925–27 can compare with the less summary and more ambitious paintings of the period 1922–24. Usually, they share that well-designed, thoroughly worked through resolution spoken of in the Charensol interview. *The Guitar with Inlay*, *The Painter's Window* or *The Open Book* (Plates 115, 118 and 113) are "finished" pictures. They too stand, not for experiment, but for certainty, for perfection. Coloured surfaces often still evoke touch, smell and taste, especially where fruit can be treated lushly: the pears of *The Painter's Window* and the fruit of *The Table in Front of the Picture* (Plate 114), for instance. The rich emerald greens and coral pinks return.

There are two obvious areas of difference, and they are on both sides of Kahnweiler's "balance". The colour is often stronger and less resolutely artificial, and the structure is often more assertive. Gris returns to generalized naturalistic equivalents in his use of local and atmospheric colour, and in certain paintings he is prepared to set up areas of intense local colour as key chromatic incidents. Where he uses that rich emerald green, it is usually in graded relation to more foliate greens (the fruit and the conifer greens of the cloth in *The Painter's Window*), and it serves a quasi-naturalistic purpose as ever. The quasi-naturalism of the leaf greens which provide the violet of the flower in *The Flower on the Table* (Plate 117) with its expected complementary foil in *The Flower on the Table* is obvious.

Where he uses that coral pink, it is often as a framing ground-plane on which the flat, graduated surfaces of his coloured objects can be spread out (in *The Guitar with Inlay*, for instance); it is an artificially coloured setting for colour combinations that can once again evoke the experience of things in light and atmosphere. The "sensibility" that Gris's colour offers as a referent in these pictures is a sensibility excited by the lived experience of nature again, not one focused exclusively on the artificiality of aesthetic confection. The pink has a role in declaring that this is *quasi*-naturalism, not naturalism, that local and atmospheric colour are always offered in flat pictorial terms as the elements of a fundamentally artificial coloured architecture. In the open windows the views of sea and sky are more than ever pictorial quotations.

What has mostly been emphasized in these last pictures is the other side of Kahnweiler's "balance", the renewed accenting of architecture in terms of formal structure. The less broken areas of colour and their heightened tonalities match planar structures which can have much of the assertiveness of the most architectural compositions of 1918–19, and which integrate geometric armature and objects even more unbreakably. As Zervos, Tériade and then Kahnweiler all claimed, the architecture of the L'Effort Moderne "call to order" was re-introduced and so balanced the new sensuousness of surface and colour allowed from late 1922. At the same time, formal rhymes returned to further tighten compositional cohesion.

Gris's painting in 1925–27 still declared him to be a devotee of sensual indulgence, responding to colour and touch and to the promise in them of taste and odour. But it declared as much as ever in 1918–19 the directive role of intelligence and the conceptual openness of metaphor-making. There was a return to the architectural and poetic in their L'Effort Moderne incarnations, and with it, at least sometimes, the re-statement of familiar themes, most strikingly, of course, the open window, or in the case of *The Table in Front of the Picture*, its relative the picture-frame. It is easy to understand how Kahnweiler could formulate his notion of an equilibrium between "Architecture and Poetry", where "the arms of the balance... stood level".

I have two final points to make about these last paintings. The first simply demonstrates more clearly their availability to Kahnweiler's polyphonic interpretation. The second opens the way to another kind of conclusion. The first concerns a factor that had been central to Gris's work at least since 1916: cohesiveness. The second concerns a factor that challenges cohesiveness, as we shall see.

The first is that Gris's last paintings introduce both another kind of structure and another level of fusion between object and setting. The new kind of structure is anticipated at the end of 1917 by Gris's brief investigation of rotating arcs as framing and controlling devices in, for instance, *Still-life with Plaque* (Figure 19). It is dominated by curves, and comes out of the structures of arcs developed at the turn of 1922–23 in, for example, *Seated Harlequin*. The jagged geometry of *The Open Book* or *The Painter's Window* is opposed to a sinuous geometry of curves in *The Guitar with Inlay*. The new degree of fusion is the result of a fuller integration of rhyming and structure; it centres on types of rhyme that had been used in 1919–22, but which were now developed so that they were often dominant.

In *Guitar and Fruit Dish* of 1919 (Plate 98), the major rhyming relationship between guitar and fruit dish is set up, as I have shown, around the virtual merger of their flanks in a double-S curve. In the variant of March 1920 the merger is complete[63]. This merger of the contours of rhyming objects produces a kind of fused rhyme. Also in *Guitar and Fruit Dish* of 1919, the carafe on the right is so completely synonymous in its angular shaping with the main lines of the geometric armature that it can be seen to have been generated by them (as Gris would have put it, "deductively"). The object repeats the structure, and *vice versa*, so that metaphorically object *is* structure and structure object. A kind of *architectural* rhyming is produced, something distinct from the structural rhymes already discussed.

In 1925 *The Painter's Window* and *The Open Book* both present at the very heart of the composition rhyming guitars and fruit dishes that are simultaneously fused and architectural, so interchangeable with each other and with the main lines of the pictorial geometry that one cannot be separated from the other formally or conceptually. Fusions of different kinds fuse to signify even more comprehensively the theme of unity.

My second point is about "touch", about what Aragon was soon to call "personality-of-technique". Gris's last pictures are the furthest he got from the technical anonymity of *collage* and *papier collé*. Their immaculacy of finish does not go with an evenness of painted surface; texturally there is a gentle challenge to the chromatic and formal cohesion of Gris's architecture. Gris allows "touch" to lend to his edges and his brushed lines a slight but noticeable waver, a waver that unmistakably says "sensitivity". And there is across every surface "brushwork", never *bravura* brushwork, but brushwork which is always apparent and always varied from surface to surface.

With the palette, a brush is placed at a key point in the middle of *The Painter's Window*. The slim, tapered form of its bristles rhymes with the streaked smudges of colour on the palette. All around is the evidence of the brush's activity, of the way it has pushed and kneaded and moulded the pigmented medium in more or less viscous states into smooth or slightly coarsened surfaces. The "touch" of the artist, Gris, is made a feature of coloured surfaces that appeal to *our* touch. The sensual is declared through handling to be a function of the personal. Gris for the first time uses handling as signature.

The other kind of conclusion opened up by these observations about "touch" allows me to return to the question of the subject in the *tableau objet,* of "Juan Gris" as a major theme of his last paintings. To consider this question it is useful to look once again at the last of his statements, the one that Raynal published in 1927, and to focus on his use of the word "expression". Given *in toto,* the sentence where he uses it runs as follows: "Today, at nearly forty years old, I believe that I am approaching a new period of expression, of pictorial expression, of picture-language; a well thought-out and well finished unity"[64]. Perfection, cohesiveness and "expression" were put into close conjunction with one another.

In 1926–27 "expression" was one of the key terms in the writing of the critics who found quality in Gris's latest work; it was a word that went with one of the first attempts to articulate the emergence of a post-Cubist situation that did not entail the rejection of the principles agreed to be basic to Cubist synthesis. By this date those who had welcomed the purity of the "second Cubism" were beginning to join Vauxcelles in believing that Cubism was in the past, and was giving way to something else. The something else hypothesized was no less anti-naturalistic, but it was altogether less austere, intellectual and impersonal. At precisely the moment that André Breton and *La Révolution Surréaliste* were campaigning for the final evacuation of the subject, the artist, from the image, others who considered Surrealism an aspect of a new revival of "expression" were campaigning for an art whose subjectivity would be amplified. For them, the subject, the artist, was to be more than ever the giver of meaning.

In the analysis of current painting with which Raynal preceded his publication of Gris's last statement, he wrote that Cubism had "evolved gradually towards an art of expression"[65]. But it was not Raynal who gave the word "expression" its currency, it was Zervos and Tériade in *Cahiers d'art.* Zervos actually applied the term specifically to the Gris of 1925–26 in his monographic article of 1926: "In order to find the expression right for him," he said, "Juan Gris needed to hasten back to become himself again"[66]. Zervos called the return of the "logical" Gris the rediscovery for him of self-"expression": Gris "himself" re-appeared in his work. A short time later, at the beginning of 1927, Tériade applied the term with wider implications to what he thought of as a new, post-Cubist Picasso. He wrote of a Picasso liberated by the fact that his "architecture" was now "so deeply inate" in him. It was this that made him capable of using with a fresh openness, "a language of colours and signs", thus giving him a "marvellous means of expression". This Picasso, he claimed, had entered on a new "poetic period which will be, without any doubt, the immediate future, the great future of modern painting"[67]. What he found very differently in both Picasso and Gris was a release that went with the discovery of a "means of expression"; ironically, in Gris's case it meant a return of control.

I mentioned at the start of this essay Tériade's diagnosis of the "failure" of Gris's paintings of 1922–24 as a failure to be "true to himself", and the "triumph" of the last paintings as made possible by a return to the logic of his "nature". It was Tériade, in 1928, who made most of the irony of paintings which were believed to be logical and yet at the same time freely self-expressive. His conclusions about the late work as the truest to Gris's nature go with definitive and wide-ranging remarks about the essentially expressive character of all painting. For Tériade here, painting puts us in contact directly with the "secret forces" at work in the painter. "The man alone matters," he writes, "but the man in his work"[68].

This seemingly expression*ist* theory of the relationship between the painter, the work and the spectator is actually a gloss on a series of commentaries he had written in 1927 on current developments. In these he connected the manifest subjectivity of much recent painting with, remarkably, a notion of the creative process extremely close to Gris's by now familiar "deductive method". Without acknowledgement, he took over Gris's theory of the "aesthetic" and adopted it to form his own expressive theory of art. The term he used for the result was "subjective realism".

For Tériade, the "subjective realist" is "To depart from the plastic idea to rediscover... a lyrical reality... The painter does not depart from direct, from objective reality. He departs from an inspiration in search of its form and pictorial expression. It must end in reality, but a subjective reality"[69]. For Tériade, a clear derivation from Gris's "deductive method" is the foundation in practice of a new expressive painting to be seen in the emerging work not only of Picasso, but also of younger artists very well aware of Gris's contribution, including his two friends in the Kahnweiler circle at the end of his life, André Beaudin and André Masson[70].

When Gris died, he was not alone in believing that "expression" was essential to his latest paintings. And those who stressed *his* presence as subject in the paintings thought of them as part of a broad new move into an art of expression. Georges Charensol even wrote of a new "Romanticism"[71].

Gris's death marked the end of seven difficult years. Illness and, at least until 1924, neglect dogged them. Negative events often took over. The last phase of uninterrupted activity, between early spring and early winter 1926, was bracketted by periods of illness that first threatened and then brought collapse. But until his final winter, negative events never took over altogether and incontrovertibly they left him space to think he had a future and the energy to use it. His work was a proof of continuing vitality, a constant reassurance that so far death *had* been cheated. There were many positive outcomes.

On a personal level, the impression left by the later paintings is indeed of retrenchment. In 1925–27 old certainties and old themes return and are made even more definitive. His painting certainly continues a wider retrenchment that had engaged most of the old Cubist vanguard from the end of the Great War into the 1920s. Whether the results were positive outcomes in some deeper and more far-reaching sense, as Kahnweiler above all believed, must be for us to judge anew for ourselves. Whether the "man in the work" (to use Tériade's phrase) is more or less "the real Juan Gris" is, of course, unanswerable. But one thing is clear: however obsessively perfectionist he became, Gris kept his conclusions open right up to 11 May 1927. Within the limits he set for himself, he continued to be an innovative painter.

1 Ethelyne J. and Germain Seligman, 'Of the Proximity of Death and its Stylistic Activations – Roger de la Fresnaye and Juan Gris', *The Art Quarterly*, Spring, 1949.

2 Douglas Cooper, 'Introduction', *Juan Gris*, Catalogue raisonné de l'oeuvre peint établi avec la collaboration de Margaret Potter, Paris, 1977.

3 Kenneth E. Silver, 'Eminence Gris', *Art in America*, New York, May 1984.

4 This account is put together above all with the help of two sources: Daniel-Henry Kahnweiler, *Juan Gris: His Life and Work,* translated by Douglas Cooper, London, 1969 and *Letters of Juan Gris (1913–1927),* translated and edited by Douglas Cooper, London, 1956.

5 See *Letters* (Cooper, 1956), p. 182.

6 Ibid., pp. 180–5.

7 See Kahnweiler (1969), pp. 53–62.

8 For a fuller discussion of this see Christopher Green, *Cubism and its Enemies, Modern Movements and Reaction in French Art, 1916–1928,* New Haven and London, 1987, pp. 82–4.

9 Ibid., p. 138.

10 I have argued as much. Ibid., pp. 82–4.

11 See for example Mark Rosenthal, *Juan Gris,* New York, 1983, p. 128.

12 See chapter 4 above.

13 Christian Zervos, 'Juan Gris et l'inquiétude d'aujourd'hui', *Cahiers d'Art,* no. 10, 1926, pp. 272–3.

14 E. Tériade, 'Juan Gris', *Cahiers d'Art,* no. 5–6, 1928, pp. 231–5.

15 Waldemar George, *Juan Gris,* Paris, 1931, pp. 9–10.

16 For information on this see *Donation Louise et Michel Leiris, Collection Kahnweiler-Leiris,* Centre Georges Pompidou, Musée National d'Art Moderne, Paris, 1984, pp. 55–9 and Christian Derouet, *Juan Gris, Correspondance, Dessins 1915–1921,* IVAM Centre Julio González, Valencia and Centre Georges Pompidou, Musée National d'Art Moderne, Paris, 1990–91.

17 *Correspondance,* Ibid., pp. 94–5.

18 Silver (1984), loc. cit.

19 Patricia Leighten, 'Editor's Statement', *Art Journal,* Winter, 1988, p. 270.

20 Green (1987), op. cit.

21 For two medical opinions based on the evidence concerning Gris's illness from the letters and from Kahnweiler's 1946 monograph, see my footnote in Ibid, p. 305 (note 27).

22 See *Letters* (Cooper, 1956), op. cit., pp. 89–124 (Letters CVIII-CXL). The woman in question was Marcelle Brune ("Marcelle la Blonde") (Figure 43). Gris wrote to Kahnweiler on 23 June that she had "gradually edged her way into my life until I have discovered that I am in love with her" and suggested that he had decided to leave Josette. He confessed with typical candour and self-awareness: "She's a very rich only child, and to someone like myself who has never had anything this represents the true happiness and comfort which I have never possessed". The affair led to a temporary break-up with Josette, and Gris spent most of the rest of the summer, until his departure for Céret that October, in Paris without her. See Kahnweiler (1969), op. cit., p. 40.

23 Gris's work on the Fête is reported by Maurice Raynal in *L'Intransigeant,* Friday, 29 June 1923. For a full account of this and of Gris's work with Diaghilev, see Karin von Maur's essay below.

24 For Monte Carlo, see *Letters* (Cooper, 1956), pp. 154–166 (Letters CLXXXI–CXLV).

25 Klüver and Martin publish a poster by Lhote for a "Fête de nuit à Montparnasse, Bal costumé", to be held on 30 June 1922, with Gris named among the artists involved. The celebrity barman was Kisling. See Billy Klüver and Julie Martin, *Kiki's Paris, Artists and Lovers 1900–1930,* New York, 1989, p. 95. The event is reported in *L'Intransigeant,* Saturday, 1 July 1922, with Gris mentioned. Paintings were on sale and prizes given for the best costumes. The proceeds went to "l'Oeuvre d'entre'aide de l'art français à l'étranger". The "Bullier" re-opened 2 December 1921 and offered both a venue for artists' balls and regular evening dancing. For Kahnweiler's and Gris's nights out, see Kahnweiler (1969), op. cit., pp. 46–8.

26 Ibid., pp. 43–5.

27 Armand Salacrou, *Dans la salle des pas perdus, C'était écrit,* Paris, 1974, p. 146.

28 Ibid., pp. 160–1.

29 Conversations with Georges González Gris, 1991.

30 See *Correspondance* (Derouet, 1991), pp. 61–4 (Letters 44–48).

31 Letter to Maurice Raynal, 1 June 1921, *Letters* (Cooper, 1956), op. cit., p. 119 (Letter CXXXVI).

32 See Carolyn Aldwin and Daniel Stokols, 'The Effects of Environmental Change on Individuals and Groups: Some Neglected Issues in Stress Research', *Journal of Environmental Psychology,* Academic Press, 1988, pp. 57–75. I am grateful to Carolyn Aldwin for drawing my attention to the work in this area.

33 Kahnweiler (1969), op. cit., p. 33.

34 Cooper nos. 456 and 522.

35 Gertrude Stein, 'Juan Gris', *The Little Review,* New York, Autumn-Winter, 1924–25, p. 16.

36 Gertrude Stein, 'The Life of Juan Gris. The Life and Death of Juan Gris', *Transition,* Paris, no. 4, July 1927, pp. 160–2. The relationship between Gris and Gertrude Stein is discussed in Douglas Cooper, 'Gertrude Stein and Juan Gris', *Apollo,* London, January 1971, pp. 28–35.

37 Unsigned, 'Exposition Juan Gris (Berlin, Galerie Flechtheim)', *Documents,* 2nd Year, no. 4, 1930, p. 243. Conceptual framework, style, the fact that this is a report on a Berlin exhibition, and Einstein's position as a regular contributor to *Documents* all point to his authorship.

38 Daniel Henry (D.-H. Kahnweiler), *Juan Gris,* Leipzig and Berlin, 1920; in D.-H. Kahnweiler, *Confessions esthétiques,* Paris, 1963, p. 49.

39 Georges Charensol, 'Chez Juan Gris', *Paris-Journal,* 25 April 1924.

40 Lemoine ended his welcome to the arrival of the Purists at the Galerie Thomas exhibition of late 1918 with the words: "Il n'y a si longtemps qu'on nous fait prendre des intentions pour des réalisations". J.-G. Lemoine, 'Les Arts: Le Purisme (Galerie Thomas)', *L'Intransigeant,* Thursday, 26 December 1918. Raynal's laudatory response to Gris's exhibition at the Galerie Simon in his regular *L'Intransigeant* column sets his dedication to the "laws of painting" against the "demolitions" of Dada. See Maurice Raynal, 'Les Arts: Exposition Juan Gris', *L'Intransigeant,* Sunday, 1 April 1923.

41 Maurice Raynal, *Anthologie de la peinture en France de 1906 à nos jours,* Paris, 1927, p. 172.
42 Ibid., p. 29.
43 'La Bonne Parole: Ingres' (from *Pensées d'Ingres,* Paris, 1921), *Bulletin de l'Effort Moderne,* Paris, no. 3, March 1924.
44 Kahnweiler (1969), op. cit., p. 144. Polyphony in relation to the musical in Gris's painting is discussed in Karin von Maur's essay below.
45 Kahnweiler (1929 and 1963), op. cit., p. 50.
46 Zervos (1926), loc. cit., p. 273.
47 Gris in Raynal (1927), op. cit., p. 172.
48 The attempt to adapt the abstract emphasis in "pure Cubism" to the "human" is initiated especially by Waldemar George. An important early instance of this is his article 'Georges Braque' in *L'Amour de l'art,* October 1922, where he writes of Braque's determination to "faire oeuvre humain". By the late 1920s George's belief in what he came to call "neo-Humanism" had led him to dismiss "pure Cubism" for its "purity". Lhote's advocacy of a "Cubisme sensible" relates to this. It is carried through in his articles for *La Nouvelle Revue Française* from 1919 onwards.
49 Roger Bissière, 'Notes sur Ingres', *L'Esprit Nouveau,* no. 4, January 1921 and Roger Bissière, 'Corot', *L'Esprit Nouveau,* no. 9, June 1921.
50 See Green (1987), op. cit., pp. 78–9.
51 I have discussed "naturalism" in French usage and practice during the 1920s in Ibid, Chapter 11.
52 "Pinturricchio" (Louis Vauxcelles), 'Dans les sous-sol', *Le Carnet de la semaine,* 28 October 1923, p. 13.
53 This evidence is in the newly discovered correspondence between Gris and Léonce Rosenberg, specifically in Gris's account in a letter of 28 July 1917 of a visit to an exhibition held by Paul Rosenberg which included both Cézanne and Renoir.
54 Waldemar George, 'Renoir et Cézanne', *L'Amour de l'art,* February 1921, p. 57.
55 Waldemar George, 'Kisling', *L'Amour de l'art,* January 1922, p. 26.
56 George (Braque, 1922), loc. cit., p. 300.
57 Waldemar George, 'Le Salon des Indépendants', *L'Amour de l'art,* February 1923, pp. 462–3.
58 Letter to D.-H. Kahnweiler, 14 December 1915, *Letters* (Cooper, 1956), op. cit., p. 33 (Letter XL).
59 Letter to Léonce Rosenberg, 10 July 1918, *Correspondance* (Derouet, 1991), op. cit., p. 51 (Letter 29).
60 Tériade (1928), loc. cit., pp. 231–5 and Kahnweiler (1969), op. cit., pp. 133–4.
61 Juan Gris, 'On the Possibilities of Painting', lecture delivered 15 May 1924 to the 'Société des études philosophiques et scientifiques pour l'examen des idées nouvelles', at the Sorbonne, Paris; in Kahnweiler (1969), p. 198.
62 Kann, in fact, bought a work of 1925, Cooper no. 530. Reber bought extensively from this period. His purchases included *Seated Harlequin,* 1923 (Plate 105).
63 Cooper no. 330.
64 Gris in Raynal (1927), op. cit., p. 172.
65 Ibid., p. 29.
66 Zervos (1926), loc. cit., p. 273.
67 E. Tériade, 'Les Peintres nouveaux', *Cahiers d'Art,* no. 1, 1927, p. 31.
68 Tériade ('Gris', 1928), loc. cit., p. 232.
69 E. Tériade, 'Réalisme subjectif ou peinture d'imagination', cited in *Cahiers d'Art,* no. 6, 1927, 'Feuilles volantes', p. 8.
70 C.f. E. Tériade, 'Documentaire sur la jeune peinture, V – Une nouvelle heure de peinture?', *Cahiers d'Art,* no. 4, 1930, p. 172.
71 "Notre époque est incontestablement caracterisée par un retour au drame, à l'expression; après trois ou quatre années empoisonnées par les systèmes et les théories voici enfin que le romantisme triomphe de nouveau!" Georges Charensol, 'Aix et Cézanne', *L'Art Vivant,* 1 December 1925, pp. 7–8.

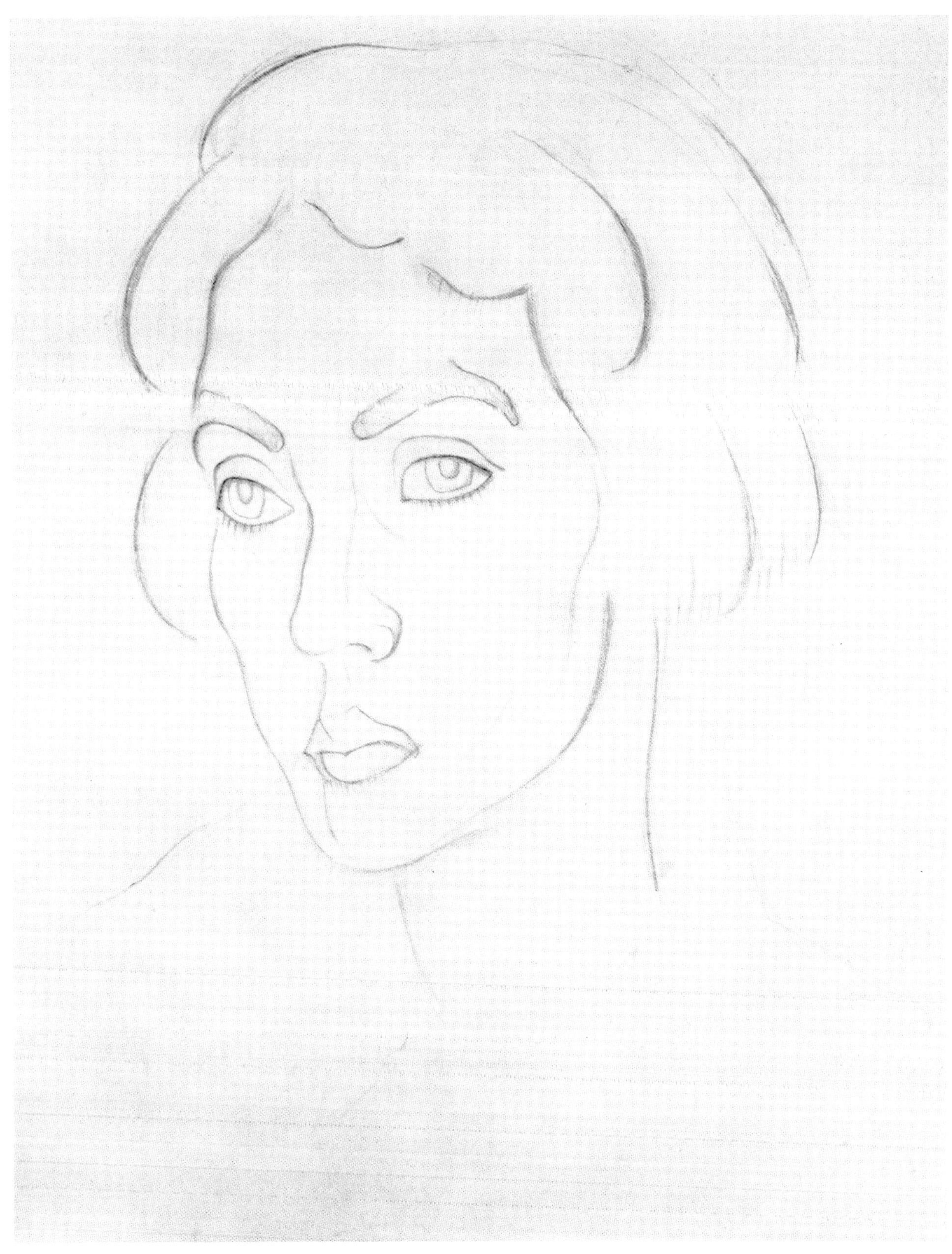

6. Figures of Artifice and Substance

Portrait of Josette Gris, 1919–21
Pencil on paper, 21,5 x 17,5 cm
Georges González Gris

At the end of his life, Gris had just completed a large figure painting, *Woman with a Basket* (Figure 26), and was at work on another, *Woman with a Guitar* (Figure 27), which he left no more than roughed out[1]. The female figures of these pictures are generalized to the point of stereotype. Both can be seen as idealizations at once of woman and of painting. A generalized ideal of female beauty is conflated with a generalized ideal of pictorial beauty and, at the same time, the sensual is balanced against the intellectual. The flushed softness of the peach in *Woman with a Basket* holds out a promise for touch and taste, the line is given a sensitive quiver, but the classicized head is sightless and the pictorial means are bare in their simplicity. *Woman with a Guitar* is shaped to give a "pretty" performance, but under the control of "organizing lines" (pencil drawn) which are still visible. Both figures are plainly artificial: the representations of notions of beauty dressed up in stage costume.

Towards the end of 1926, a few months before Gris's death, Zervos used the metaphor of stage costume revealingly in his *Cahiers d'art* discussion of the painter. He wrote of modern pictorial innovation as a new range of "brilliant costumes... invented... for our plastic ideal", and of "a prodigious capacity... to dress up the multiple aspects of thought". Taking the case of Gris himself, he wrote: "He is one of those who say to themselves with reason that the more this costume of thought is rich and varied of aspect the more the thought will become clear for himself and others"[2].

The way that Zervos uses the metaphor carries several inferences: it links style to artifice (costume), it gives ideas ("the thought") the weight of substance (that which is costumed), and it stresses the transcience of pictorial language (a costume for thought that can always be changed). He leaves no room for subject-matter as such, and nowhere in the article does he find it necessary to consider the actual objects or figures that Gris painted. In this context, the artificiality of *Woman with a Basket* and *Woman with a Guitar* has much to say. These are obviously not depictions of particular women; as types, evacuated of personality, they have been dressed up to perform on a pictorial stage. If there is substance, Zervos would have argued, it is not in the figures, but in the idea costumed by their flattened pictorial forms. Their stagey artifice complements a notion of painting as pure artifice too.

This marginalisation of the figure as such (the particular figure) is a central theme in much writing about figure-painting from within the idealist milieux of the "pure Cubists" after 1916. It is given perhaps its earliest explicit statement in Reverdy's unequivocal prohibition of the portrait in his first and most comprehensive essay on Cubism, 'On Cubism', published for the opening number of *Nord-Sud* in March 1917. Here Reverdy argues that only the "eternal and constant" should be detached from subject-matter by the Cubist painter, and concludes therefore that the specificity of the portrait cannot be admissable. "What is created is a work, ... not a head

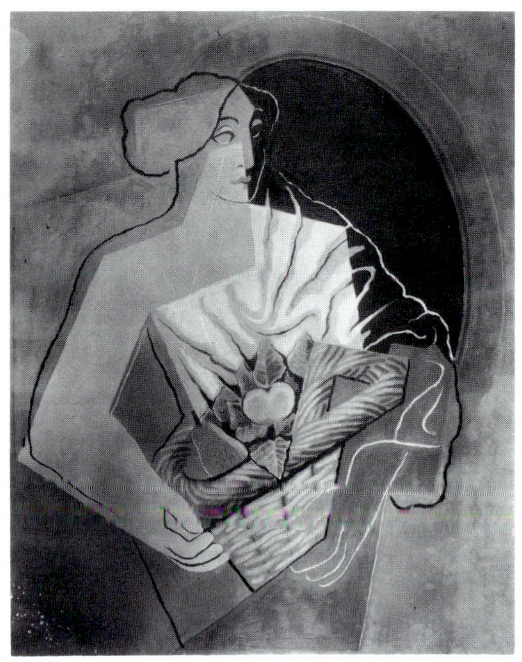

Figure 26
Woman with a Basket,
1927
Oil on canvas,
92 x 73 cm
Private Collection

or an object"[3]. Besides Léonce Rosenberg's authoritarian dogmatism, Vauxcelles must have had this text in mind when in the summer of 1918 he attacked the refusal of the L'Effort Moderne Cubists to accept that Lhote's nudes or Rivera's portraits could be pure enough to be Cubist[4].

Indeed, ultimately so inessential were the figures of Cubist figure-painting for those sympathetic to "pure Cubism" after 1916 that even the most distinctive figures could simply be ignored. The formalist imperative could make almost any subject seem to vanish from the face of the painting. Gino Severini's solo exhibition in Léonce Rosenberg's series of Cubist shows of 1919 included a picture entitled evocatively *The Old Bohemian Musician.* Writing in *S.I.C.*, Maurice Raynal allowed himself the tongue-in-cheek idea that Severini's "old bohemian" stares so fixedly at the wallpaper because he might find there "the date of his death". But he follows this up by instantly shutting out the possibility of such fancies. "In reality," he writes, "the "Old Musician" thinks of nothing of the kind, for he is not there. In front of a good picture, never try to look behind the canvas"[5].

In this essay, I start from the assumption that even after 1916, when Gris gave the painting as a flat arrangement of coloured shapes precedence over his subject-matter, the figures in his figure-paintings *are* there to be looked at, and that they, as well as their forms on the picture-plane, encourage us "to look behind the canvas". Gris's figures have been written about. His portraits of 1911–12 have been written about in terms of the traditions of portraiture[6]. Caricature has been mentioned in the same breath as *Man in the Café* (Plate 21)[7]. The *Portrait of Madame Josette Gris* has been acknowledged to be a portrait with a sitter who matters[8]. This and the *Commedia dell'Arte* figure-paintings have been discussed alongside the traditionalist drawings after the "masters" as cyphers of tradition[9]. Yet, such writing is relatively limited alongside analyses or accounts of style, process and theory in Gris, and the tendency to follow the restrictive idealist side of Reverdy or Raynal and to play down the role of the figures in the figure-painting has often been evident. Thus, Douglas Cooper made a point of stating that Gris's Harlequins and Pierrots do not conform (in his view) to the characters of Harlequin and Pier-

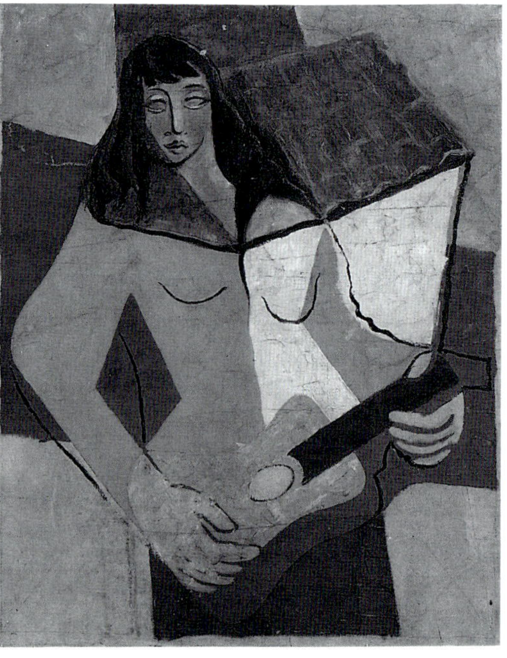

Figure 27
Woman with a Guitar,
1927
Oil on canvas,
92 x 73 cm
Georges González Gris

rot and so should not be seen as such at all. For Cooper, the *Commedia dell'Arte* is merely a traditional vehicle for making paintings; it provides the "elements", as Reverdy would have put it, for what have become *tableaux objets*[10].

Gris himself, however, did allow room in his statements of the 1920s for subject-matter, including figures, to have a role. The "deductive method" meant that he moved from the general to the particular. Certainly the general, the ideal, had theoretical precedence, and gave the particular its form, a decisively pictorial form, but the particularity of the subject-matter "found" in the "abstract" configurations from which Gris insisted he started was not in question. "I want," he said in the *L'Esprit Nouveau* statement of 1921, "to arrive at a new specification: starting from a general type I want to make something particular and individual"[11]. If a cylinder could become a bottle – "a particular bottle" – so too, could it become a particular figure, even a portrait. As such, necessarily, it took on meanings in the social world of objects and people, meanings that embodied the character of the generalities, the "thoughts", that were said to come first. Raynal's idealism, as I have shown, was not absolute, and in the same way he too left room for subject-matter to signify in his writings on Gris. The notion of metaphor that he applied to Gris's pictorial rhymes invites the spectator to see formal relationships as relationships between features and things on the level of subject-matter: the head as a head, the fruit dish as a fruit dish, eyes and buttons as eyes and buttons[12]. Even for him, Gris's figures did not vanish to become merely the pictorial costume of some abstract thought.

My contention in this essay and the last is that the figures and objects in Gris's paintings throughout his career as a Cubist, from 1910 to 1927, matter and that they matter not just because of the *way* they are conceived and painted, but because of *what* they are. The two cannot be separated. From the *Portrait of Maurice Raynal* and *Homage to Pablo Picasso* in 1911–12 to *Woman with a Basket* and *Woman with a Guitar* in the last months of his life, Gris's figures carried meanings *as* figures. Those last two figures might appear reduced to the level of stereotype, but it is as figures of a particular kind, dressed and posed in a particular way, that they signify ideals of art as artifice and of female beauty, ideals which are specific to their society and time, which, as Gris said of any painter's "aesthetic", must "bear a date"[13].

On 15 October 1911 the popular illustrated magazine, *Fantasio*, dedicated as it was to amusement, published an article by Roland Dorgelès, 'What the cubes say...', inspired by the laughter of the "visitors without culture" before Metzinger's, Gleizes's, Le Fauconnier's and Léger's Cubist canvases at the Salon d'Automne. This was an early instance of the foreign language metaphor applied to Cubism. Ironically, accepting claims that to see nothing in these pictures was merely not to speak their "language", Dorgelès and *Fantasio* undertook to give the necessary translations. They illustrated, among others, Gleizes's *Portrait of Jacques Nayral* and Metzinger's *Tea-time* alongside photographs of their subject-matter "after nature" (Figure 28). Tongue-in-cheek, the question was posed: would not seeing the "translations" in "current vision" (photographs) stop the laughter? The assumption, of course, was that it would transport the all-round hilarity to a new pitch[14].

The *Fantasio* for 1 November 1911 followed up with 'A Consultation at the Salon d'Automne' by Roland Catenoy, a putative report of a trip around the Grand Palais in the company of two medical men, whose diagnoses of the figures in the paintings are offered. The climax is reached in front of Metzinger's *Tea-time* (Figure 7), a "cubistically nude woman" who presents all the symptoms of "lithopoedion", otherwise only previously seen in petrified foetuses; she is beyond treatment and close to death[15].

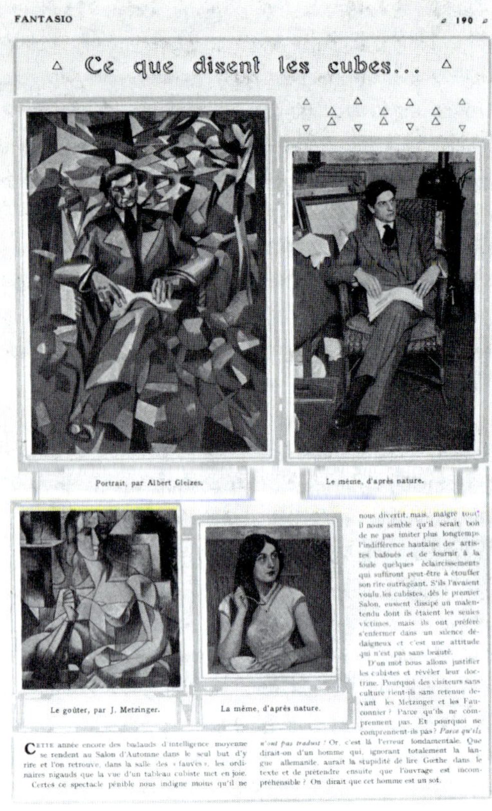

FANTASIO — 190

Ce que disent les cubes...

Portrait, par Albert Gleizes.

Le même, d'après nature.

Le goûter, par J. Metzinger.

La même, d'après nature.

Cette année encore des badauds d'intelligence moyenne se rendent au Salon d'Automne dans le seul but d'y rire et l'on retrouve, dans la salle des « fauves », les ordinaires nigauds que la vue d'un tableau cubiste met en joie.

Certes ce spectacle pénible nous indigne moins qu'il ne nous divertit, mais, malgré tout, il nous semble qu'il serait bon de ne pas imiter plus longtemps l'indifférence hautaine des artistes bafoués et de fournir à la foule quelques éclaircissements qui suffiront peut-être à étouffer son rire outrageant. S'ils l'avaient voulu, les cubistes, dès le premier Salon, eussent dissipé un malentendu dont ils étaient les seules victimes, mais ils ont préféré s'enfermer dans un silence dédaigneux et c'est une attitude qui n'est pas sans beauté.

D'un mot nous allons justifier les cubistes et révéler leur doctrine. Pourquoi des visiteurs sans culture rient-ils sans retenue devant les Metzinger et les Fauconnier ? Parce qu'ils ne comprennent pas. Et pourquoi ne comprennent-ils pas ? *Parce qu'ils n'ont pas traduit !* Or, c'est là l'erreur fondamentale. Que dirait-on d'un homme qui, ignorant totalement la langue allemande, aurait la stupidité de lire Gœthe dans le texte et de prétendre ensuite que l'ouvrage est incompréhensible ? On dirait que cet homme est un sot.

Figure 28
Reproduced page from *Fantasio* (15 October 1911) featuring *Tea-time* by Jean Metzinger and *Portrait of Jacques Nayral* by Albert Gleizes

These two responses to Metzinger and the Cubists at the 1911 Automne have one theme in common: the absurdity of the gap between Cubist painting and appearance. Just as Louis Vauxcelles made the Cubists' repudiation of "current vision" (appearances in nature) the crux of his attacks[16], so most jokes in the press at the expense of Cubism centred on the question of likeness. If Metzinger's *Tea-time* was not like its sitter, what could it mean? Surely nothing[17]. The Salon Cubists in 1911, including both Gleizes and Metzinger, stressed their commitment to the representation of experience, as we have seen; and "realism" was to be a central concern in Gleizes's and Metzinger's *Du "Cubisme"* in 1912. It might appear that in showing portraits at the Salon d'Automne of 1911 they invited ridicule and fell into a trap of their own making, but for the Cubists as much as Vauxcelles or the readers of *Fantasio* the issue of likeness was crucial as well. To paint portraits (that *genre* where likeness could seem the sole criterion of judgement) was to say so[18].

Strictly speaking *Tea-time* is not, of course, a portrait; it is a domesticated nude. The *Portrait of Jacques Nayral* is, and writing in *L'Intransigeant* a few days before *Fantasio's* spoof, Apollinaire made a point of calling it both "a very good likeness" and a canvas where "not one form or colour" is not "invented by the artist". It is, for Apollinaire, at once very like and very unlike[19]. Later, in his *Souvenirs*, Gleizes claimed that Metzinger's "multiple" representations were controlled by the "cubic" structures (the grids) of his paintings, where he, Gleizes, allowed his response to the "accidental episodes" of his subject an over-riding importance. In the case of Nayral, he recalls especially the determining role of the "well-defined planes" of his sitter's face, the "undulations of his forehead" and the "dark masses" of his hair[20]. The head is indeed the crux of likeness in portraiture, and the year before Roger Allard had brought out the central significance of the head and the face in negotiating the relationship between painting and figure when responding to Gleizes, Metzinger and Le Fauconnier at the Automne of 1910. He had remarked that the public found the "deformation of lines" in their new paintings less funny than the deformation of colour, "except" in the case of "the human face"[21]. The "deformation of lines" allowed by mobile perspective in the head of Metzinger's nude in *Tea-time* and Gleizes's Jacques Nayral have seemed tentative to historians of Cubism. In 1911, as the key area of likeness and unlikeness, they more than anything released the laughter.

This was the wider context of Gris's decision at the Indépendants of 1912 to make his debut with a *Homage to Pablo Picasso* (Plate 10) which was a portrait, and to do so with a portrait that responded to Picasso's portraits of 1910 through the intermediary of Metzinger's *Tea-time*. In 1911–12 he painted six figure-pictures, of which five were portraits.

They include the *Portrait of Maurice Raynal* and the *Portrait of Germaine Raynal* (Plates 12 and 13), but, of course, the *Homage* had the highest public profile.

The *Portrait of Maurice Raynal* is manifestly a likeness put together from an "analytical" study of the sitter strongly lit against shadow. The fact that this is a representation of a friend, one of the "Bateau-Lavoir" milieu, matters: it is a record of an individual from a specific vanguard circle, as well as the result of analytical investigation. Gris gave it to Raynal, as he did the later portrait to Germaine. *Homage* also represents, of course, a sitter who matters. It does not merely seal a bond of friendship, however, it states a commitment to Picasso *as* Cubist on a public stage, something discussed in the first of these essays[22]. Many commented on its sitter as much as on Gris. And yet, that crux of likeness, the head, is the one area that lacks depictive lucidity, especially when it is considered alongside a drawing which can be loosely related to it (Plate 15). This lack of depictive lucidity is shared by the one portrait that Gris painted which isolates the head alone, the *Portrait of the Artist's Mother* (Plate 11).

In the drawing, probably made after *Homage* was exhibited, the head (not Picasso's and possibly Gris's own)[23] is the sole concern, as in the *Portrait of the Artist's Mother*, and it too is controlled by a combined orthogonal and diagonal grid. But the lines of the grid are kept everywhere clearly separate from the features its units contain, so that they each can be read distinctly: the eyes, the mouth, the individual parts of the nose and the right ear. This is not so in the head of Picasso painted for Gris's *Homage*. Here some features of the face actually fuse misleadingly with the grid (especially on the left of the jaw), and the nose (a key to likeness in the portraits of Jacques Nayral and Maurice Raynal) is so fragmented and splayed out that only disconnected vestiges remain. The distinctive lock of black hair is there to say "Picasso". Recognition is ensured for any familiar with Picasso's looks, but the keys to likeness are otherwise neglected or disrupted. By exhibiting *Homage* Gris certainly raised the issue of likeness; he did so with a portayal that was explicitly *un*like its sitter on one obvious level. The orderliness of the grid here is confounded, at least in the face of "Père Ubu-Kub", by an image of disintegration[24].

That image of disintegration is taken to an extreme in the *Portrait of the Artist's Mother*. Here, although a combined full-face and profile depiction of the upper part of the head can be read easily enough, the grid appears to have slid across the mouth and jaw below partially rubbing them out; only traces of willful obliteration remain. Above, as with the lock of Picasso's hair, the invitation to see a likeness is offered, below, it is decisively denied. Even in the *Portrait of Maurice Raynal*, where the results of analysis are offered without equivocation, the treatment of the left eye shows a willingness to introduce distortion where it most disrupts likeness, and an unfinished head on the back of another canvas of 1911 shows how the disruption of likeness was at work from the earliest stages of depiction at the very beginning of Gris's first Cubist campaign (Figure 29)[25].

The separation of individual features from the units of the grid is the principle behind both the *Portrait of Germaine Raynal* (Plate 13) and the *Man in the Café* (Plate 21). These pictures are, especially in the heads, each open to rather literal readings, as the results of a systematic part-by-part analysis of their sitters. Yet, the fragmentation that this entails and the geometry by which it is ordered ensures results that are as grotesquely *un*like what *Fantasio* called "current vision" as *Homage to Pablo Picasso* and even *Portrait of the Artist's Mother*. *Man in the Café* is the one figure-painting of 1911–12 that is not a portrait. It raises the issue of likeness as central again by inviting comparison not with the conventions of portaiture, but with another kind of representation altogether: caricature. For, as we shall see, in the decade before 1912 caricature was considered the quintessential art of "realism", a specialists' province of heightened likeness.

When Gris made his Cubist debut at the Indépendants, the caricature weekly *L'Assiette au beurre* signalled the fact. Reporting on the Salon, its correspondent James Burkley wrote thus of the rooms that showed Gleizes, Metzinger, Léger *et al*: "Here are registered the names of *messieurs* the Cubists, for whom I shall not supply unremunerative publicity! I draw attention only to the humourist Juan Gris who has portrayed the "master" Pablo Picasso"[26]. By 1912, those who took the wave of caricature in France seriously preferred to call caricaturists "humourists"[27]. Gris was, indeed, an established humourist. The recent research of Marilyn McCully and Raymond Bachollet has shown his production in the caricature magazines to have been enormous from 1907. Bachollet has traced some 468 drawings (not including vignettes) in both Barcelona and Paris-based magazines, 149 of them (the most) for the anarchist *L'Assiette au beurre*[28]. He drew four special numbers for *L'Assiette au beurre*, and drew covers for it along with *Le Charivari*. Further, despite the impression given by Kahnweiler later of a complete break with caricature when he turned to "serious" painting in 1910–11, Gris was, in fact, heavily committed as a humourist right through 1911, and his drawings continued to appear in *Le Charivari* into 1913, and *Le Rire* and *Le Frou-Frou* into 1914[29]. When *L'Assiette au beurre* introduced him as both a humourist *and* a Cubist in 1912, this was certainly the case. Gris the debutant Cubist was still well-known as an active and successful caricaturist.

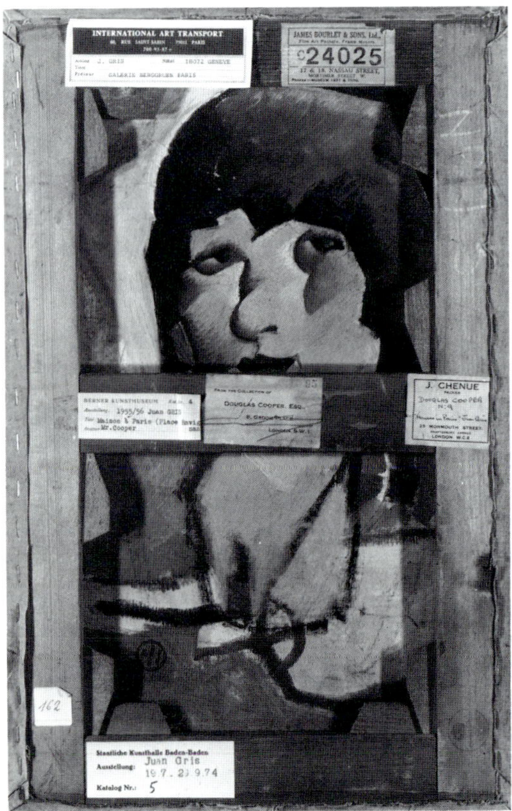

Figure 29
Portrait of a Woman
(verso of *Houses in Paris [Place Ravignan]*), 1911
Oil on canvas,
52 x 34 cm
Private Collection

Homage to Pablo Picasso observes the staid conventions of portraiture in the post-Renaissance tradition (at least so far as pose, setting and attributes are concerned); it resists, therefore, immediate comparison with caricature. *Man in the Café* does not. The café scene populated by city types, like Gris's own 'Friendship', published in *Le Charivari* in April 1910 (Figure 30), was a routine resource of the caricaturist's repertoire. What is missing (crucially) in Gris's picture is the companion to supply an anecdotal situation and the caption to give it comic point. The setting, the sharply characterized individual, the eloquent pose, the off-centre placing, all invoke the pages of *Le Charivari* or *L'Assiette au beurre*. We (the viewer) have become the companion[30].

The proximity of Cubist painting and caricature has been discussed intensively over the last decade, notably by Adam Gopnik[31]. It is indisputable that very quickly after the emergence of Cubism as a public phenomenon in 1911 it became not only the butt of innumerable caricature attacks (to accompany the satirical spoofs of magazines like *Fantasio*), but itself had an effect on caricature idioms[32]. It could even be argued that there was a real similarity between the way that Cubism and caricature aroused the hilarity of their audiences (even if the laughter was on the one

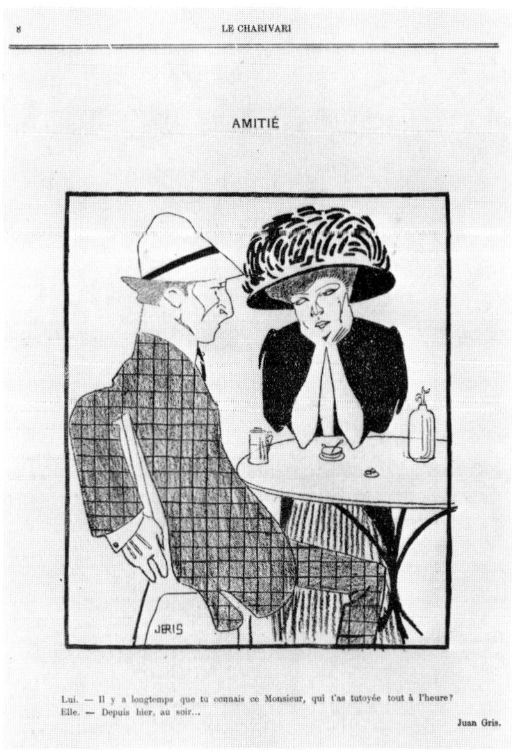

8 LE CHARIVARI

AMITIÉ

Lui. — Il y a longtemps que tu connais ce Monsieur, qui t'as tutoyée tout à l'heure?
Elle. — Depuis hier, au soir...

Juan Gris.

Figure 30
'Friendship',
Le Charivari
(April 1910)

hand hostile and on the other a matter of collusion).

There is agreement that on one level caricature works by deviation from norms, the norms of perception and the norms of accepted graphic representation. It exploits deformation knowingly[33]. In 1906, the year of Gris's arrival in Paris as an aspirant caricaturist, Paul Gaultier published a scholarly study, *Le Rire et la caricature*, itself a mark of the importance of the caricature phenomenon, and argued there (on Bergsonian premises) that the key to the laughter generated by caricature was the excess, the monstrosity of its deformations[34]. As we have seen, the joke in Cubist painting for the readers of *Fantasio* was precisely its excessive deformation of "current vision". Caricaturists dwelled on the obviousness of Cubism's deviation from norms of perception and depiction, yet caricature, like Cubism, could itself be at once very like and very unlike. Indeed, late in 1912 *Fantasio* published a page of early nineteenth century geometric caricature heads with the caption "A Cubist in 1820"[35]. The affinities were not lost, nor the fact that likeness was at the heart of the matter.

It is the affinities above all that have drawn the attention of Gopnik. He, most recently with Kirk Varnedoe[36], has argued for the role of caricature in Cubist painting, and has focused especially on the function of caricatural simplifications and exaggerations in the development of Picasso's painting through the "primitivism" of 1907–8 into the Cubist portraits of 1909–10, the reference-points for Gris's *Homage to Pablo Picasso*. Gopnik has traced what he has called "a *pas de deux* between high and low", "a complicated exchange of dialects", and has done so revealingly.

For him too, a central issue has been likeness. Both caricature and Cubist painting ask us to find likeness in "abstract" shapes, and Picasso's portraits of 1910, for instance the *Portrait of Ambroise Vollard* (Figure 2), show him using caricatural techniques to arrive at likeness[37]. In *Man in the Café* Gris explicitly invoked caricature far more obviously than Picasso had in 1910, and in 1913 he was to follow this figure-painting with others, *The Smoker* (Figure 8) and *The Bull-fighter* (Plate 30) which did so again, this time by actually incorporating an undisguised caricatural idiom into the treatment of the faces, an idiom comparable for instance with Paul Iribe's[38].

The question is did so direct a reference to the exaggerated simplifications of caricature signify in 1912–13 a blurring of the hierarchical boundaries between "high" and "low" culture? Was it the sign of an acknowledged affinity and indeed debt at a profound level? Was Gris the Cubist figure-painter saying "thank you" to the lessons of his old career?

There are two factors to be considered here: status and the debates concerning "realism" and "idealism". The latter, of course, raise the issue once again of likeness. Before returning to that issue, the question of status needs to be addressed.

Adolphe Willette, a leading figure in late nineteenth and early twentieth century caricature, was perhaps the first to insist on the inadequacy of the term caricaturist for "an artist of talent, who produced what is called caricature"[39]. He did so around the date of the first "Salon des Humoristes", organised by the magazine *Le Rire* from 1906 as a new addition to the annual series of Salons that included the Indépendants and the Automne alongside the more officially recognised Salon des Artistes Français and Salon de la Société Nationale. This was the moment of Gris's arrival in Paris and his career as a humourist between 1907 and 1912 coincided with the high period of caricature in France, when not only a book by a heavyweight academic like Gaultier's *Le Rire et la caricature*, but books by respected leaders from the Symbolist and post-Symbolist vanguard, like Gustave Kahn's *La Femme dans la caricature française* of 1907 and Mécislas Goldberg's *La Morale des lignes* of 1908, added to the case for caricature to be taken seriously[40].

That so many among the Cubists besides Gris (Kupka, Marcoussis, Villon, Duchamp) started as humourists in the period before 1912 testifies both to the success of the illustrated magazines in supplying work, and to the acceptance of them as a serious alternative for the "artist of talent". Writing of the foundation of the Salon des Humoristes, Gustave Kahn insisted on the significance of this new phenomenon given its new prominence alongside the "official Salon". "This is the celebration... of the victory of a light and mobile art... and, its manifestation being very serious and very modern in tone, there is no doubt that its importance will continue to augment like everything... that corresponds well with the needs of the times"[41].

Gris was himself a partisan of the new status accorded the humourists. The cover that he drew for *Le Charivari* on 18 December 1910, no doubt as he worked on his first Cubist drawings in charcoal and gouache, shows Willette (now aging) in his preferred costume as "Pierrot", standing in front of the

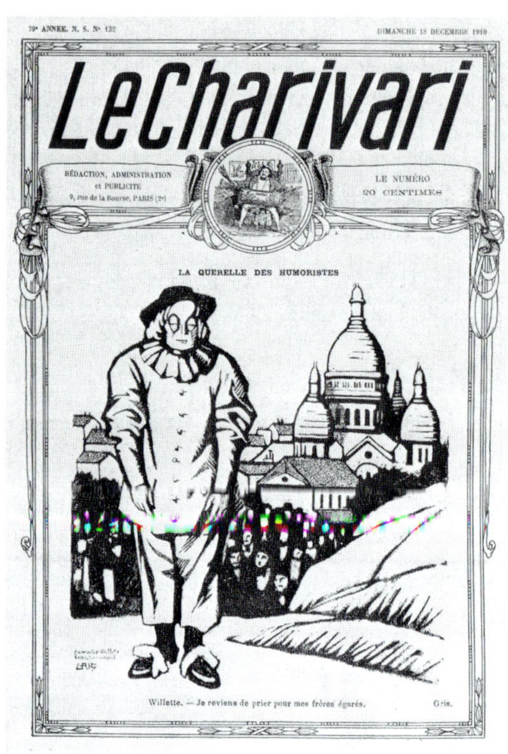

Figure 31
'To the Master Willette with respect'
Le Charivari
(18 December 1910)

bohemian multitude of Montmartre's assembled caricaturists, beneath the heading: "The quarrel of the Humourists". The caption has him announce: "I return to plead for my distraught peers" (Figure 31). The leading article, by Louis Villaret, reports on the "war" declared by the caricaturists, with the support of such major figures as Forain and Léandre besides Willette, against the dominance of *Le Rire*. It resulted in the decision to found their new magazine, *Les Humoristes*, to which Gris contributed in 1911. As he worked towards his homage to the young "master" of Cubism, Picasso, he left a homage to the old "master" of caricature. His signature on the cover of *Le Charivari* is accompanied by the inscription: "to the master Willette, with respect"[42].

Les Humoristes survived for only eleven issues. Its speedy demise is one sign of the fact that by 1912 the high period of caricature in France was beginning to wane. Paul Iribe's *Le Témoine* ceased publication in 1910, and, most telling of all, *L'Assiette au beurre* in 1912. Marcoussis, Villon and Duchamp, along with

Gris, made their switch from humourist to Cubist just at the moment when the market for the humourists began to contract, and Bachollet has been right to suggest that commercial pressures must have been a factor[43]. Yet, it remains clear that, despite the continued publication of Gris's drawings after 1911, despite his solidarity with the caricaturists against *Le Rire* in 1910–11, and despite his homage to Willette, Gris's switch from caricature to Cubist painting *was* perceived as a shift of status; it was idealized as a move away from commodity commercialism, a move "up" from the "low" to the "high" that had nothing to do with material factors. This is one of the messages carried by the account in Kahnweiler's second monograph, with its stress on a total break with caricature and its refusal to take the caricature drawings seriously[44]. But it is evident too in Gris's own tendency to ignore his beginnings as a humourist, and in, say, André Salmon's carefully contrasted respect for his "austere" Cubist work and contempt for his contributions to *L'Assiette au beurre*[45].

For all the efforts of Willette, Forain, Léandre, Goldberg and Kahn, there remained, as Gopnik and Varnedoe have put it, a "caste system" that separated caricature from the art of the Indépendants or the Automne[46]. When Gris showed *Homage to Pablo Picasso* early in 1912, both he and James Burkley in *L'Assiette au beurre* knew that he had not only taken on a new "master" in Picasso, but had applied for membership of a higher caste in the institutions of art. The status of caricature in relation to vanguard culture was certainly one factor in Gris's decision to allow the recognisably caricatural into *Man in the Café*, *The Smoker* and *The Bull-fighter*. But the question remains: in doing so, did he break down the boundaries in the cultural caste system by flagging the affinities between Willette and Picasso, between the old and the new Gris? In this connection the issue of realism, of likeness, is central.

For Gaultier, if the "belly laugh" was to be associated with the excessive deviation from the norms of appearance found in grotesque "fantasies", the category of caricature that generated it was to be distinguished from another category which provoked, rather, a moral response by stressing "truthfulness". This latter category, which he called "the comic", used exaggeration certainly, but did so to express, by retaining only the physiologically "indispensable", "the vices of the mind or of the heart"; it was a "realism" of a profound, penetrating kind, and for him, since Daumier it had been in the ascendancy[47]. Kahn too contended that "with the moderns", "deformation" and "fantasy" had been supplanted by "exact reproduction", a "truthful" realism which he called "comic" as well[48]. He picked out Steinlen (Figure 32), Léandre, Forain and Huart and wrote of a "return to lived experience", "the study of the street", whose impetus had come from Degas and the Impressionists and whose focus was on "character"[49].

Mécislas Goldberg's *La Morale des lignes* offered a distinctly alternative view of the possibilities opened up by caricature, one that was inspired by the *Carcasses divines* of Apollinaire's caricaturist friend André Rouveyre. He and Rouveyre stood for the extreme Symbolist conviction that the ultimate goal of caricature was to achieve, through simplification, images of the "quintessential" in the real (something loosely comparable to some notions of Cubism, as Neil Cox has pointed out)[50]. But there can be no doubt that Rouveyre's books of drawings backed by such idealist notions were exceptions, and that the "truthfulness" celebrated by Gaultier and Kahn continued, almost unopposed, to dominate the pages of *Le Charivari*, *Le Rire*, *L'Indiscret* or *L'Assiette au beurre* throughout the period from 1906 to 1914. Gris's relatively abstracted caricature style, to be aligned more with Iribe (a friend) or d'Ostoya than with Steinlen or Léandre, was nonetheless very much "truthfully" comic in these terms, not at all idealist: it was concerned with isolating the features of character to sharpen the point of the stories

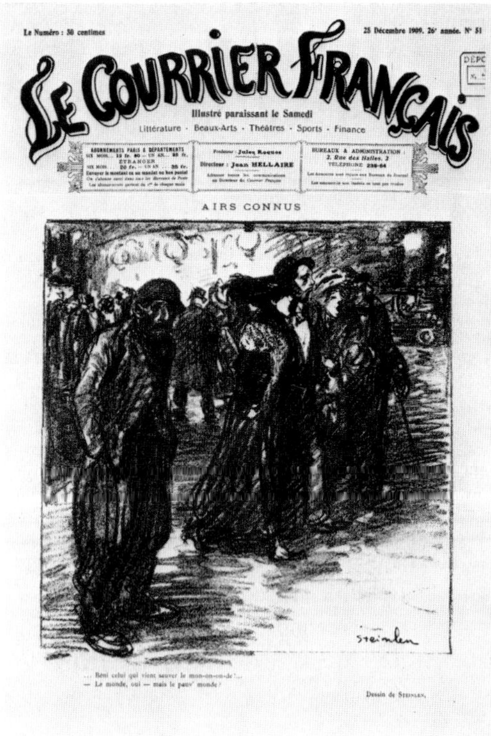

Le Numéro : 30 centimes

25 Décembre 1909. 26ᵉ année. Nº 51

LE COURRIER FRANÇAIS

Illustré paraissant le Samedi

Littérature · Beaux-Arts · Théâtres · Sports · Finance

Directeur : Jean HELLAIRE

BUREAUX & ADMINISTRATION : 2, Rue des Halles, 2

AIRS CONNUS

Figure 32
Drawing by
Théophile Steinlen
Le Courrier français
(25 December 1909)

contained in the captions (Figure 30). Gris the humourist was another demonstration of the near synonymity of caricature and "realism", the perceived continuation of the Impressionist ethos in caricature.

By invoking caricature in *Man in the Café*, *The Smoker* and *The Bull-fighter*, Gris referred, as he had with the portraits of 1911–12, to the issue of likeness, but to the issue of likeness as it was raised by caricature's affirmation of the "realist" aspiration in its quasi-Impressionist guise. And in the same way, by asserting through the caricatural the possiblity of likeness, the very *un*likeness of these figures to any imaginable sitter was enhanced. Everything about these paintings denied their viewers the pleasure of viewing them as caricature in the mode of "the comic". They speak not of the aptness of simplification to "truthful" characterization, but of the distance between the patently artificial vocabulary of Gris's pictorial signs and the sitters to whom they might refer. The excessiveness of Gris's deformations in the interests of pictorial invention remains over-riding.

Gopnik and Varnedoe have written of the deviation from the norm in caricature as a factor that exposes the arbitrariness of the workings of pictorial signs, the distance between the codes of depiction and their referents[51]. This is certainly true of the deliberately artificial signs that Gris lifted from the idioms of caraicature to give us the eyes, the nostrils and the mouths of his smoker and his bull-fighter, but it did not mean that an invitation was issued to ignore the distinction between Cubist painting and caricature and so to look at Cubist painting *as* caricature. Gris the Cubist returns to the caricatural tradition of grotesque deformation ("fantasy"), and risks the release of the "belly laugh". He denies uncompromisingly the current caricatural tradition of "truthful" realism and all that it entailed in terms of moral engagement with the social and political questions of the day. One norm, indeed, is replaced by another: that supplied by the geometry of the systematically fanned structures. As these figures depart from one norm ("current vision"), they conform to another ("pictorial mathematics"), one that breaks apart and over-turns all those criteria of "truth" that had been fundamental not only to caricature but to verist painting of every kind, especially portraiture[52].

Both the scale of these pictures (particularly *Man in the Café*) and the immaculacy of the oil technique (at least in the two of 1913) underline the fully sustained gap in status between them and the flimsy lithographed pages of the illustrated magazines. No commentator then or since has considered it appropriate to supply captions. If Gris's past as a humourist comes back into view, it is a past plainly rejected, left a long way out of reach in the new, "higher" pursuit of the conceptual. To see the portraits of 1911–12 in terms of portraiture and these figure-paintings of 1912–13 in terms of caricature was to be be either challenged or discomfited by *difference*, not to be reassured by affinities. In both cases it mattered greatly that these were figures of very particular kinds.

If it mattered that these pictures were recognisably portrait and caricature figures, it mattered too that they depicted, in the way of caricature, recognisable types. Kahn had commented on the *genre* of caricature that sharpened awareness of particular social types on the Parisian scene[53].

The *Portrait of Germaine Raynal* is the only female figure-painting that Gris executed between 1911 and 1914. The others are all male and conform in plain terms to obvious male types. Maurice Raynal is the critic-intellectual of the acute, deliberating gaze. *Man in the Café* and *The Smoker* are the drawling habitués of café-life[54]. Picasso, with his palette and brushes, in one of the eccentric blue suits coloquially called "Singapores" that he and Braque bought from 'La Belle Jardinière', is the new bohemian "master"[55]. *The Bull-fighter* is the Spanish embodiment of bravura male courage in ritual dress, complete with pig-tail and suit of lights. Although Metzinger painted a female smoker, tobacco in particular had decisively masculine connotations at this time. Gris himself never worked without a cigarette, it seems, and in May 1909, with Salmon helping on the captions, he drew a special number of *L'Assiette au beurre* devoted to "Le Tabac" mostly peopled by male smokers[56]. Molly Nesbit has linked the geometric and projective character of pre-1914 Cubist "analysis" to a controlling male notion of vision formed on the mechanical model, according to the directives of late nineteenth century Comte-ian Positivism. Certainly at first, Gris's explicit geometric rigour was applied in his figure-painting to the dissection and structuring of strongly masculine types[57].

It is, therefore, striking that when he returned to figure-painting in 1916–17, it should be almost completely dominated at first by female subjects. There are drawings from this period of male subjects (Plates 62 and 63), but the early traditionalizing figure-pictures are all but one of women. New evidence makes it clear now that the *Portrait of Madame Cézanne (after Cézanne)* was painted before spring 1917, not in 1918; it joins *Woman with a Mandolin (after Corot)* (Figure 9), the *Portrait of Madame Josette Gris* (Plate 66), the portrait head related to it, and *Seated Woman* in the Thyssen-Bornemisza collection[58]. When Gris took up a figurative subject-matter manifestly connected with notions of the French tradition and fused it with an increasing commitment to structural integration, he did so by painting a suite of female figures. Two of these, and possibly three, are portraits, so they raise again the issue of likeness, this time just a few months before Reverdy issued his prohibition of the portrait for Cubists. Gris's companion, Josette, is their sitter[59].

Information about Josette Gris is sparse, but recent investigations in Beaulieu-lès-Loches have begun to fill in the gaps. She was born in Loches in 1894, daughter of a bank employee and a school-teacher. Her background seems to have been petty-bourgeois with aspirations, for she boarded at the "école Riart" in Loches, a school designed for the daughters of the provincial "bonne bourgeoisie". Her upbringing seems to have been partially Parisian, but she retained close ties with her family in Beaulieu and Loches, for her paternal grandfather, the retired financial administrator of the hospital at Loches, was the one who found her and Gris their accomodation just outside Beaulieu (where he lived) at Les Fourneaux in 1916, 1918 and 1920[60]. She never married Gris officially, although he always referred to her in his letters to Kahnweiler and Léonce Rosenberg as "my wife", and she did not use the names with which she was christened (Charlotte Augusta Fernande Herpin), but her bohemian Montmartre life does not seem to have marked a break with her class or her origins. Her relationship with Gris was at times threatened in the 1920s, as we have seen in the last essay, but it was close and loyal, and Gris's obvious sense of well-being when he was in Beaulieu, communicated by his letters, indicates that he was accepted there by her family.

At the time of Gris's humourist career, the woman in the painter's studio was a staple of caricature. As Kahn noted with a liberal's regret, the early successes of the feminist movement in nineteenth and early twentieth century France had met with no positive recognition in the illustrated magazines. The woman as writer or painter was mercilessly ridiculed in terms of blue-stocking stereotypes in such series as Léandres's *Les Femmes peintres*, and the woman in the artist's studio was predominantly the model or companion, stereotyped in images of sexual availability and vanity, domesticity or impulsiveness, by such caricaturists as Roedel, Metivet, Mirande and Carlègle (Figure 33). The model or companion was habitually represented between 1906 and 1912 as mindless and either ludicrously ugly or frivolously desirable. The artist's bohemia was an image of male sexual liberation where problems proliferated because of what were perceived as the petty foibles of the "feeble sex"[61]. Again as Kahn pointed out, caricature altogether maintained a largely negative, misogynist view of woman, one that sustained the stereotypes of female dishonesty, selfishness, maliciousness, modishness and silliness maintained by such vicious anti-feminist publications as William Vogt's *Sexe faible* of 1908[62]. Its currency *was* stereotype after all.

The fact that Josette's mother was a schoolteacher is evidence that she actually came from that liberal sector of the petty-bourgeoisie that took the education of women seriously. Yet, when I asked her whether she discussed Gris's painting with him, her reply was that he did not like "intellectual women", and indeed "avoided them".[63] She was someone of whom his circle always took notice, but her situation and her role was not different essentially from that of, say, Fernande Olivier and "Eva" with Picasso, or Marthe with Braque. None of these women took any part in the intense intellectual life of their milieux; all of them were unmarried bohemian companions (Braque did not marry Marthe at first)[64].

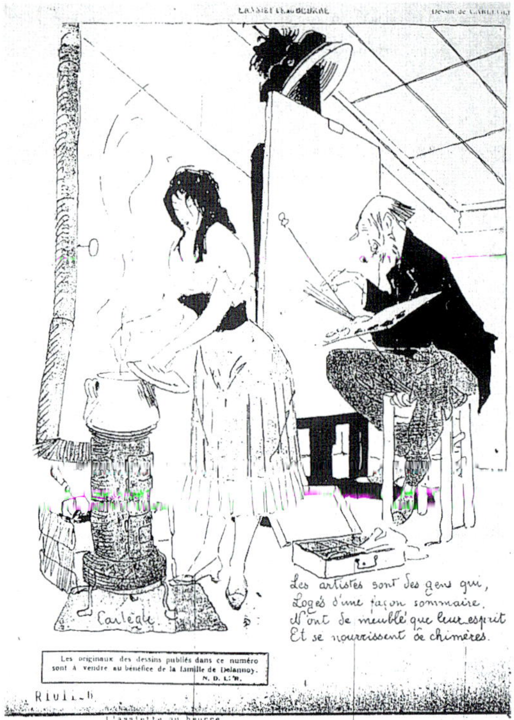

Figure 33
Drawing by Carlégle
L'Assiette au beurre
(May 1909)

Gris had, in fact, had a previous companion, Lucie Belin, whom he had married and who was the mother of his son Georges, born in 1909. But by the time Josette moved in with him at 13, rue Ravignan early in 1914, Lucie Belin was long gone, and Georges had been dispatched to Spain to be brought up by Gris's sister Antonieta[65]. The one-room studio home in the "Bateau-Lavoir" had returned fully to the non-familial condition of bohemia.

Professional caricaturists between 1907 and 1914 consciously adapted their drawings to the politics of the magazines. This was obviously so, to some extent, of Gris. In October 1908 he drew the cover for a violently anti-militarist special number of *L'Assiette au beurre* ("Noises of war and noises of peace"), in line with the required anarchist stance[66]. In October 1910 he drew a cover for *Le Charivari*, supplying a mischeivous joke at the expense of Socialist and anarchist anti-militarism, Jaurès announcing to an audience of helmetted "Prussians" that "we are now ready

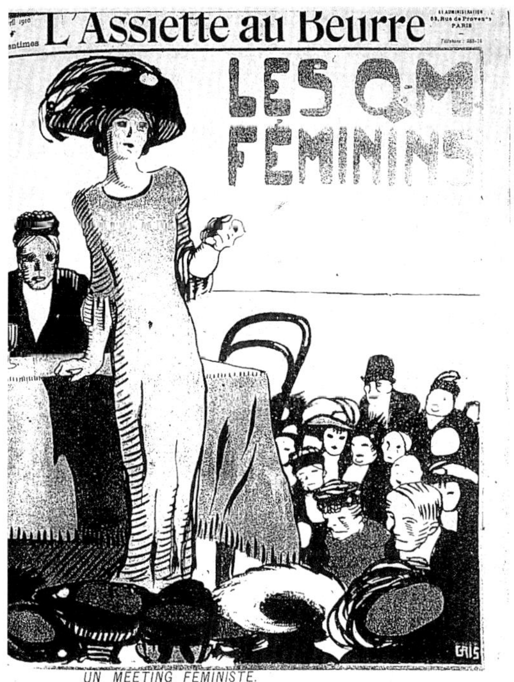

Figure 34
'Les Q-M Féminins'
L'Assiette au beurre
(April 1909)

to disarm so that you [the Prussians] can keep the peace in Europe"[67]. But, whatever the magazine, the image of women that his drawings offered was consistently stereotypical and negative. In fact, in April 1910 and September 1911 he provided sequences of drawings, including the covers, for two anti-feminist numbers of *L'Assiette au beurre*, the untranslateable 'Les Q-M Féminins' (Figure 34) and 'Honest Women', where he used anecdotes, apparently taken from the life, to illustrate the "selfishness" and "dishonesty" of women just as Vogt used anecdotal narratives in *Sexe faible*[68]. Passionate anti-feminism went with the anarchism of *L'Assiette au beurre* (at this time, it could be Politically Correct on the Left); and Gris responded with a will.

There is nothing at all misogynist about the *Portrait of Madame Josette Gris*. This is a positive image of female beauty translated into clear, stable, far from frivolous pictorial terms. And it has been possible to write of it as a likeness that transcends stereotype. It is, however, an image that relates to, even if it cannot be reduced to, stereotype, and the type to which it relates (or better, types) signified powerfully in the context of the War generally and particularly the situation then of women. By painting this calm female figure and so explicitly linking her to an ideal of the French tradition carried by Corot, Gris said a great deal that went further than the intimacy of his relationship with Charlotte Augusta Fernande Herpin.

On the 7 August 1914, René Viviani, "président du conseil", issued a call that quickly became famous, his "Call to French Women". "Stand up, French women, young children, daughters and sons of the homeland. Replace in the field of work those who are on the field of battle"[69]. In the four and a half years of the War, eight million Frenchmen were mobilised, more than sixty per-cent of the entire male population[70]. The need for the "feminization" of labour behind the front was obvious, and it happened at astonishing speed, nowhere more so than in the countryside, in areas like Indre-et-Loire where Loches is situated. Peasant women had long had an active role in French rural society, but immediately after the declaration of War and Viviani's "Call", they suddenly were largely responsible for getting the harvest in, as they would be until 1918, helped only by children and the old men. Heavy industry too was "feminized". Before the War 17,731 women were recorded as employed in the metalurgical industry; by July 1916 the figure was 104,641[71]. The crucial productive role of women was recognised widely. The 'Section cinématographique des armées' made a film to document and celebrate it, packed with shots of women in the factories and the fields, minding machinery and driving carts[72]. And a literary *genre* emerged to deliver breathless eulogies, among them Léon Abensour's *Les Vaillantes* and the well-known novellist Marie de La Hire's *La Femme française, son activité pendant la guerre*, both of 1917. Leading feminists set aside their campaigns for equality under the law, for education and the vote, and it was repeatedly claimed that the fact of war-time feminization at every level of social activity would ensure the gains that activism had not[73].

The sudden frenetic onset of feminization has, of course, nothing to do with the reserved, elegant image Gris constructed of Josette. She certainly took no part in all the activity. But there was another aspect to the war-time development of a role for women, one that complemented the ideal of forceful action while being equally powerful.

The film made by the film-unit of the armies in recognition of women's contribution culminated in the image of the "woman of the hearth", the woman who is there to restore the strength of the man who has returned from the front. The complement to the robust woman of action was the soft, but resilient ideal of the woman left behind as guardian of the home. It often merged with the figure of the nurse caring for the wounded, and could have the force of a symbol of the entire "Union Sacrée", the political unity of France in the face of invasion. Thousands of women, especially from the aristocracy and the bourgeoisie, became Red-Cross nurses under the 'Société de Secours aux Blessés Militaires', the 'Associations des Dames françaises' and the 'Union des Femmes de France'. "Thanks to the Red Cross," wrote Léon Abensour in *Les Vaillantes*, "hundreds of thousands of the wounded have been restored to life, thanks to it hundreds of thousands of men deprived for months of feminine company have found it again, have been able to have for a few moments the illusion of the family regained, an image at least of their mothers, sisters, fiancées. And often these dear images will symbolise for them the Homeland as a whole, that for which you fight and which consoles you when you are struck down"[74]. For another eulogist of women at war, Louis Barthou, the "smile of the French nurse" would, in the aftermath of War, seal "national unity"[75].

Josette, certainly, was neither a nurse nor one of those left behind. Gris himself was not a soldier. But his letters reveal his feeling for those like Apollinaire, Braque, Rosenberg and Raynal who joined up. He followed Raynal's sufferings with particular sympathy and anxiety, and he knew many who were left behind, among them Germaine. He even gave a small work for a tombola held to supply funds for the 'Union des Femmes de France'[76]. He must have been aware of the force of a female image of calm resilience in 1916, and there can be no doubt that his stable, traditionalist rendering of Josette accorded well with the virtues routinely associated with the nurse and especially the woman of the hearth. Marie de La Hire might have celebrated the forcefulness of the women who ran the charities or the nursing associations, who took over mayoral duties for the men, who produced munitions and took in the harvest, but her praise for the French woman in 1917 opened with long passages devoted to the woman of the hearth. "More than ever during the war," she writes, "the place of woman is in the home: at the hearth, of which she has become all at once the guardian and defender, after having been only the soul and the heart". The virtues she singles out are "calm courage", "resignation" and "tenderness", to sustain "the grave thoughts" provoked by absence[77]. These are all epithets that fit Gris's figure of Josette.

Perhaps the oddest war-time manifestation of the woman of the hearth as an ideal was the organisation called the "marraines de guerre" (the god-mothers of war). It brought together women volunteers of all ages, who took under their protection soldiers at the front without means or without families, sent them food-parcels, clothes, letters and photographs, and took them out when they were on leave[78]. There is no evidence whatever that Josette was a "marraine de guerre", but Gris's portrait comes uncannily close in pose and figure-type to a postcard that was printed with the heading, "the soldier's little god mother" ("la petite Marraine du Poilu") (Figure 35)[79]. The postcard carries an extra charge of sexual innuendo (the cat on the lap and the caption that puns

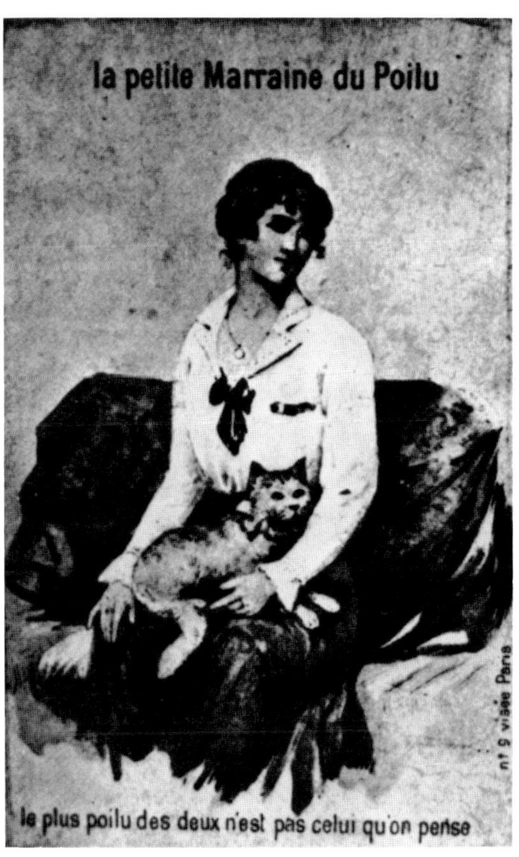

Figure 35
'La petite Marraine du Poilu'
First World War postcard

"Poilu" (front-line soldier) with "poilu" (hairy)); but the "little god-mother" is represented, however ironically, as the image of enduring gentleness and yet feminine elegance, almost the twin of Josette.

Reverdy's prohibition of the portrait in 1917 hinged, as we have seen, on his insistance that the particular should give way to the "eternal and the constant". The particularity of likeness is a factor in Gris's *Portrait of Madame Josette Gris*, and indeed one of the ironies of Gris's move towards the formal imperatives of the "deductive method" was that it went with an increased clarity in the depiction of things, including figures. The clear assertion of links with the French tradition came of a clear presentation of traditional subjects, like the Corotesque female subject, controlled by a stable compositional order. Yet, although so plainly a portrait with a sitter, in a much wider sense Gris's Josette was a type of great signifying power, a type which manifestly embodied in the most idealist way, the "eternal and the constant". This is the French woman as timeless presence: dependable, unchanging, always there.

It is worth mentioning that, despite the hopes aroused by the feminization of labour during the War, the gains made by women were only meagrely consolidated in France after the War[80]. The image of the woman of the hearth quickly displaced again the image of the woman of action. The anti-feminists, like Gris, prevailed once more.

Between late 1917 and his first bout of illness in 1920, Gris painted two broad categories of figures: the *Commedia dell'Arte* Harlequins and Pierrots, the first of which he painted in November 1917, and the peasants, a trio of which he painted at Beaulieu-lès-Loches between May and September 1918. The Harlequins and Pierrots are self-evidently character types; so, albeit less self-evidently, are the peasant figures. The two categories are, as we shall see, linked at a deep level of connotation, but they set up at the same time an obvious opposition between artifice and substance, the theatrical and the "real" world.

I have commented already on the dominance of women in the peasant life of the countryside during the War. It was calculated that in the Charente women replaced men to the extent of eighty, and in the Basses-Pyrénnés ninety per-cent. The proportion was high everywhere[81]. *Seated Peasant Woman* (Plate 82) is Gris's one attempt to construct an image of a peasant woman; in a letter of July 1918 he was explicit on the fact that she was a *peasant* woman[82]. She makes a striking contrast with the *Portrait of Josette*. Gentleness and elegance are hardly epithets that apply, and her hugely enlarged hands are signs of raw physical strength to go with the stolid stability of her thick torso, which is firmly wedged into an architecture of "organising lines". Here the "eternal and the constant" in woman is connoted with a strength that is capable of action, in the fields as much as in the kitchen. The fact remains, however, that two of Gris's three peasant figures of 1918 are male: *The Peasant in a Blue Smock* (usually called *The Miller*) and *The Man from the Touraine* (Plates 84 and 83)[83].

It could well be that these two highly "synthetic" Cubist representations, with their still emphatic concentration on the "eternal and the constant", had, like the portraits of Josette, specific subjects. If they are to be considered peasant types, they too are very possibly generalisations as such from the particular. In a letter of 4 June 1918 to Léonce Rosenberg, Gris refers to the first of the pictures as "a peasant in a blue smock", and talks of a curious "two-hundred-year-old" building, "one would say the interior of a mill". The letter also talks of his studio as a "beautiful, well-lit room", its walls white-washed, so it is clear that he and Josette were living in the spacious "manoir" at Les Fourneaux just outside Beaulieu, and it seems that the curious mill-like building to which he refers could be the little circular "colombier" (dovecot) that still stands close by, now a dwelling (Figure 36)[84]. The evidence is that it had already been converted for habitation, and it is its internal curving stone stair that can be seen through the open door behind the peasant, who stands with his bread-basket in front of a fence of palings positioned much as the modern wire fence of the "colombier" is now[85]. This is, it seems, an actual peasant neighbour of Gris's who happened to live in a dwelling "like a mill". If the picture of May 1918 could have had a particular peasant subject, so too could *The Man from the Touraine*; we have seen how responsive Gris was to his actual country surroundings at Beaulieu. As I have suggested, Gris was to contend that the cylinder became a "particular bottle"; here, his flat coloured architecture has almost certainly become particular peasants.

Yet, the figures are patently presented as generic: *The Man from the Touraine* and, as Gris first referred to the earlier picture, not a named individual, but simply "the peasant in a blue smock"[86]. Gris's traditionalist call to order here is explicitly aligned with an image of the stability and sturdy strength of the ideal French peasant man. How such representations might have signified in the months of 1918 that led up to the Armistice is less easily approached than the generally positive connotations carried by the representation of female resilience and gentleness in Josette. By 1918 a certain ambivalence had surfaced in response to the peasantry in war-time France.

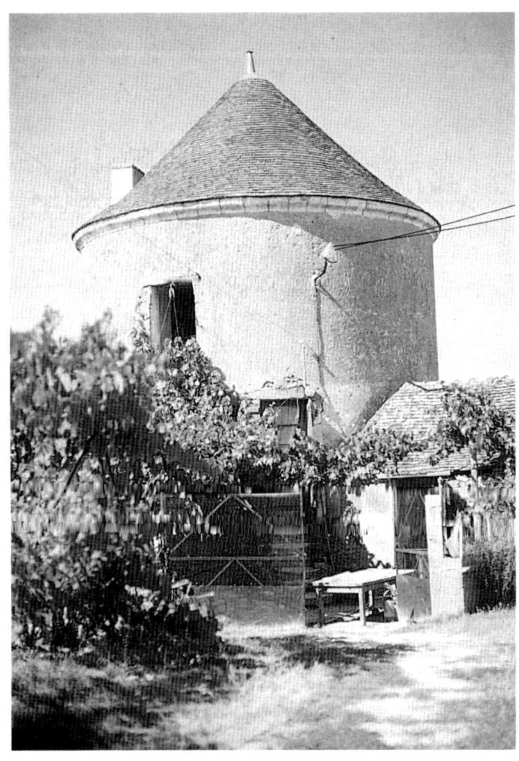

Figure 36
The dovecot at Les Fourneaux, Ferrière-sur-Beaulieu
(Photograph: Courtesy Christopher Green)

If Abensour's and de La Hire's eulogies celebrated the success of peasant women in getting in the harvest, 1917–18 saw developments in French agriculture that opened the way to growing resentment, especially from the white-collar petty bourgeoisie of the towns, against peasant success. Whatever the sacrifices and the effort, harvests actually dropped between 1914 and 1918, and some land did go out of cultivation. Demand was unchecked. The result was, on the one hand, shortages and, on the other, domestic price rises in 1917–18. While consumers paid more, the peasants did well, despite the fact that profits were creamed off by the distributors[87]. In 1917 total agricultural receipts increased by fifty per-cent; in 1918, they doubled. The benefits meant that more peasants were able to re-pay their debts and to save, and they reached farm workers too. Agricultural wages shot up between 1915 and 1920 all over France. In the Touraine, so specifically referred to in Gris's *The Man from the Touraine*, daily rates went up from 4.00 to 13.00 francs in Indre, and annual rates from 1,300 to 3,500 francs in Indre-et-Loire, the *département* for Loches and Beaulieu[88]. The peasants were suddenly well-off, as others felt the pinch, and Jean-Jacques Becker has noted that by 1917–18, official reports on morale across the country drew attention to their "selfishness" and "indifference"[89]. The peasant was not necessarily to be seen as heroic.

And yet, such indications as postcards and drawings in the mass-dailies consistently gave the peasant a positive image throughout the war-years, and the reason was simple: the disproportionate number of peasants serving as poilus on the front was quickly recognized[90]. If the peasantry at home was resented, the peasant-poilu was heroized. Nearly three-quarters of the agricultural work-force was mobilised: 3,700,000 out of the total of 5,237,000 calculated for 1914[91]. Where key industrial workers were sent back to the factories from the front, only from 1917 were peasants demobilized, and then only if they were more than 46 years old or the fathers of more than five children[92]. The high casualties on the front left, indeed, a disproportionate mark on the younger male population of the countryside. The sacrifice of peasant lives was manifest and devastating.

Gris's *The Peasant in a Blue Smock* and his *The Man from the Touraine* are ageless. By 1918, the blue smock was probably worn only by older peasants in the Touraine, and it is likely, of course, that Gris's neighbour in the "colombier" at Les Fourneaux was not a young man, otherwise he too would have been on the front. Yet, neither of these peasant figures is necessarily beyond fighting age. They are types whose agelessness encourages a merger of the notion of the peasant at home in his region and of the peasant soldier, the poilu. Just as Gris painted Josette with Corot in mind, he painted these peasant figures with the fifteenth century Touraine painter Jean Fouquet in mind. Christian Derouet has pointed out his deep awareness of Fouquet on his first visit to the region in 1916[93]. Especially in *The Man from the Touraine*, the pose and the figure type signal the connection with such pictures as the *Portrait of Charles VII*, to be seen at Loches, and the Louvre's *Man with a Glass of Wine*, then attributed to Fouquet (Figure 37). As with the image of Josette, connotations with an idealised "French tradition" combine with strict compositional control to signify a timeless, ordered continuity: in this case a male resilience. These are unequivocally positive images of male peasant strength conceived as complementary to the equally posi-

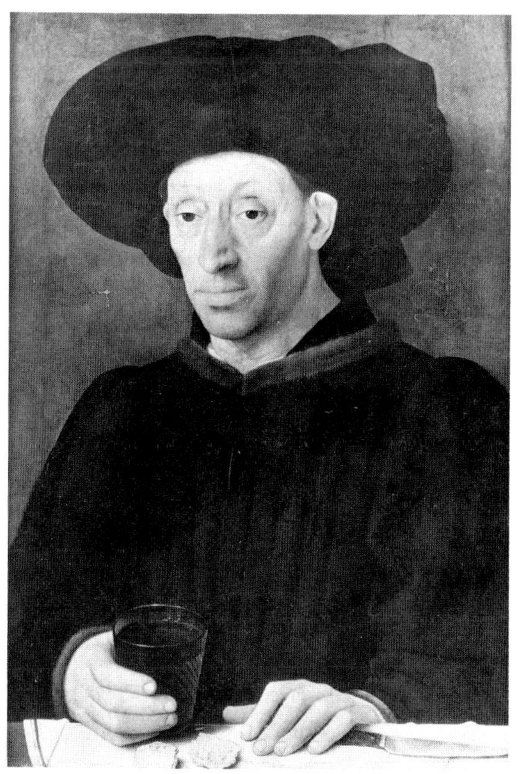

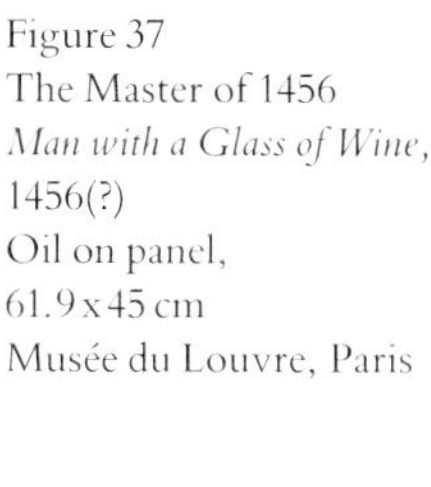

Figure 37
The Master of 1456
Man with a Glass of Wine,
1456(?)
Oil on panel,
61.9 x 45 cm
Musée du Louvre, Paris

tive image of female peasant strength represented in *Seated Peasant Woman*. They were altogether unavailable to the possible negative responses to which a more specific placing in terms of age and circumstance could have left them open.

Kahnweiler might later have talked of works like *The Peasant in a Blue Smock* and *The Man from the Touraine* as Platonic "ideas", but in 1918 when they were painted they represented on one level at least the idealism very specific to war-time. Their virtues are not only those of Fouquet's fifteenth century Frenchmen, but plainly those of the poilu as he was idealized in everything from songs to postcards: above all, simplicity, loyalty and stubborn endurance[94].

The image of the peasant in *The Peasant in a Blue Smock*, *Seated Peasant Woman* and *The Man from the Touraine* is, then, an image of honest solidity; the metaphor of construction, of architecture, fitted well the idealized virtues of these figures. At Beaulieu in 1918 Gris painted just one *Harlequin* (Plate 85). He structured it as solidly, and gave it, alongside the peasant figures, a colour range that relates to the colours of the old regional architecture of Touraine, of lime-stone, slate and tile[95]. Yet, this is a figure from the stage, and as such, like all the Harlequins and Pierrots Gris was to paint from this moment until 1925, it announces instantly that it is without "reality", a figure not of solid substance, but of artifice, a figure given identity by its costume and its mask-like face.

I introduced these two figure types, the peasants and the *Commedia dell'Arte* characters, as linked at a deep level of connotation. This is so, but the connections are of an exclusively and rather generally artistic kind. They were both explicitly traditionalizing, and signalled as much by the very fact of their figure-subjects, always so clearly designated. Gris's peasants connect with a notion of the French tradition represented by Cézanne as well as Fouquet; his *Commedia dell'Arte* figures connect with one represented above all by the Watteau of *Gilles* as well as Cézanne. Among his drawings "after the masters" of 1916 are drawings not only of Cézanne's peasants, but of the Harlequin from his *Mardi Gras* (Plate 62). As I have noted elsewhere, at the Automne of 1919 Lhote made the figure of Harlequin the crux of a *Homage to Watteau*[96]. But, where Gris's peasant figures invoke Fouquet and Cézanne while opening up a wide range of connotations outside the sphere of art, the *Commedia dell'Arte* figures seem to exclude extra-artistic meanings. Especially in the context of the Reverdian "call to order", with its stress on aesthetic autonomy, they can appear to embody the ideal of art about art, of art as a kind of costume governed by the conventions of tradition. The fact that between October 1918 and mid-1922 the *Commedia dell'Arte* figures accounted for all but one of the fifteen figure-paintings that Gris finished can appear telling indeed. Among these pictures were *Harlequin at a Table* and the *Pierrot* in Winterthur of 1919, and the *Pierrots* in Dublin and Paris of 1921 and 1922 (Plates 88, 86, 104 and 103). All fuse the architectural with the artificial. In the Dublin *Pierrot* of 1921 curtains frame a stage as the frame does the canvas, a theatrical *tableau* within a pictorial *tableau*.

During the 1920s, the figure of Harlequin came to be used itself as a metaphor of "pure Cubism" in its distilled post-1916 form. For Apollinaire, as early as 1905, Harlequin's long-established connections with the figure of Mercury (Hermes) and so with the magical metamorphoses of Alchemy had been something on which to play. Alluding to the Alchemist Hermes Trismigestus, he had invented the personnage Harlequin Trismigestus[97]. Mercury as Harlequin in a setting of mythical metamorphoses made his appearance in the ballet *Mercure* produced by Massine and the Comte Etienne de Beaumont with music by Satie and decor by Picasso in 1924. That year, the critic Claude Roger-Marx could talk of Cubism as "the cloak of Harlequin", a sort of "disguise"[98]. And in 1930,

Figure 38
Young Girl and Guitar, 1918
Pencil on paper, 48 x 37 cm
Private Collection

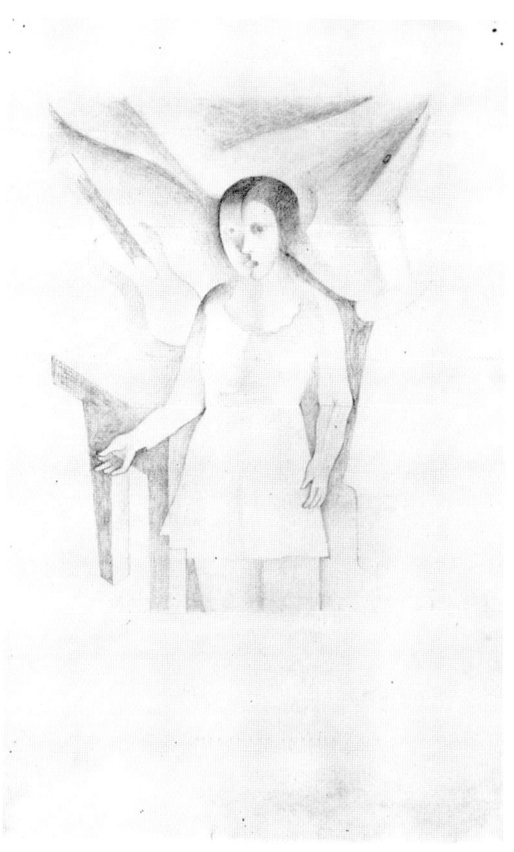

writing of Gris's last Cubist figure compositions, an anonymous contributor to *Documents* (probably Carl Einstein) could write of pictures "in the manner of Harlequins"[99].

The alchemical Harlequin was the symbol of incessant metamorphosis, of an art where subject-matter and form were one, where no identity was fixed. And it is demonstrably true that, when one looks at Gris's *Commedia dell'Arte* figures of 1918–19 in sequence, one finds abrupt switches of identity between Pierrot and Harlequin, as if their particular identities do not matter by comparison with the openness of Cubist configurations to metamorphosis. The masks and the costumes are easily changed when poses are not.

The Winterthur *Pierrot* of 1919 (Plate 86) is one of three closely related Pierrots all finished in May, whose origins lie in a delicately nuanced pencil drawing (Figure 38); this Pierrot is the closest to it[100]. The pose and the positioning of table, guitar and curtain with tasselled cord all echo the drawing, although the sense in the drawing of immediate contact with a *motif* has given way, because of the elementary clarity of the painted shapes, to a sense of arbitrary manipulation. The cut of the costumes also relates, but what was a little girl introducing her act, has become a male Pierrot, as if by quick change. Also in 1919 Gris produced a series of crisp charcoal drawings of Harlequins, one of which is *Harlequin with a Chair* (Plate 87). The pose in *Harlequin with a Chair* repeats in general terms that of this Pierrot; a prop, which could be read as a scroll or Harlequin's baton, replaces the guitar, and the gap on the right is filled by the chair. The Harlequin drawings in turn relate to the *Harlequin at a Table* of 1919 (Plate 88), whose stance is close to that of *Harlequin with a Chair* and whose hands, now held as if to declaim, evoke the positioning of the hands in the guitar-playing Harlequins from the same series (Figure 39). Pierrot was once a little Saltimbanque girl and then himself becomes a Harlequin, sometimes with guitar, sometimes with scroll or baton. The costume changes can make it seem, as Cooper suggests, that the characters of Harlequin and Pierrot do not matter, that, since one can metamorphose into the other, they as such are figures without substance: they are pure artifice just as this painting is "pure Cubism".

To take the *Commedia dell'Arte* figures as the insubstantial metaphors of "pure Cubism" is to give them a fully integrated role in the wider readings of the character of post-1916 Cubist and classicizing art that have taken hold over the last decade. They can be considered to sum up a deliberate withdrawal from the social into an idealized notion of aesthetic "creation", one that left behind the pre-war engagement with the ephemera of mass-culture (newspapers, labels, advertisements)[101], and even the war-time engagement with "real" types, the woman of the hearth and the peasant-poilu. Further, they can be considered in their thoroughly aestheticized traditional-

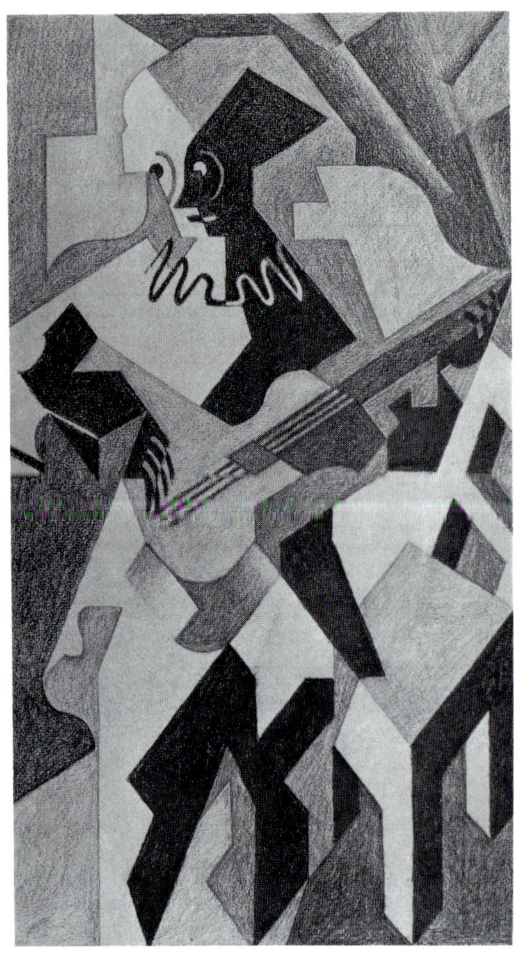

Figure 39
Harlequin with a Guitar, 1919
Pencil on paper, 42.5 x 23.5 cm
Private Collection

ism to signify the abject willingness of one-time subversive radicals to throw in their lot with the figures of authority. As cyphers of an idealized French tradition brought to such an orderly condition, they can be taken to be part of a cohesive, repressive post-war order in France that aligns the conservatism of the "call to order" with that of the "horizon blue" Chamber of Deputies[102].

In the very broadest terms these are valid readings, and there can be no doubt that the stress Gris placed from 1916 on the past, especially the French past, went at a personal level with a strong sense of his commitment to the French and to France, which was amplified by his foreignness and echoed the passionate patriotism of those close to him, like Reverdy, Ozenfant and Léonce Rosenberg[103]. But to leave these figure-paintings to be analysed only at this level of generality is to ignore the specific force and the sheer flexibility of the *Commedia dell'Arte* as a carrier of meanings in French culture from the late nineteenth century right through the 1920s.

This has been called a "redundant" imagery, recovered to give a spurious authority to cultural reaction[104]. In fact, it was a contemporary imagery with an immense signifying capacity, a well-used code whose signifiers were character-types and whose usage was not confined to one cultural sector or level. Further, however freely Gris switched Pierrot into Harlequin, it was simply not possible to use these character-types without them, as such, carrying meanings. Gris the former caricaturist must have known this, for at a far more popular level than the cultural vanguard, *Commedia dell'Arte* had been another staple of the humourist magazines. No one was more responsible for its currency in caricature than Adolphe Willette; when Gris paid him his respectful homage in 1910, he acknowledged the meaningfulness of Pierrot too (Figure 31). How could he have thought of his Cubist Pierrots and Harlequins as mere cyphers of tradition evacuated of all but aesthetic meanings?

There are innumerable indications of the currency of *Commedia dell'Arte* characters, especially Pierrot, after 1918 in France. Willette's immensely successful illustrated Pierrot books continued to be published. The carnivals of "mardi gras" in Paris and provincial France continued to be peopled by the *Commedia dell'Arte* masked characters. Gris wrote from Céret in 1922 of Josette shyly dressing up for carnival as Pierrot[105].

There are, however, two indications that deserve special attention. The first was a strange event held in April 1922 at the Montparnasse cabaret the 'Camélion' and organised by the actress Suzanne Tissier and the art-critic of *Paris-Journal*, Paul-Sentenac. A lecture given by Paul-Sentenac dressed in full Pierrot costume accompanied a performance of Théo-

Figure 40
Paul-Sentenac and Suzanne Tissier as Pierrots
Paul-Sentenac, *Pierrot et les artistes, Mémoires de l'ami Pierrot,* Paris, 1923

dore de Banville's *Le Baiser* (a short lyrical piece centred on the kiss by which Pierrot releases the beautiful fairy Urgèle from the haggish appearance to which she has been cursed) and readings from a roll-call of poets, including Paul-Sentenac himself, who had written about Pierrot: Verlaine, Catulle-Mendès, Francis Carco and Alexandre Mercereau among them. *Paris-Journal*, of course, gave full coverage, and in 1923 Paul-Sentenac's lecture was published complete with a frontispiece photograph of the "lecturer-Pierrot" alongside Suzanne Tissier who is costumed to play Banville's Pierrot (Figure 40)[106]. The second indication was the publication in 1925 of Pierre-Louis Duchârtre's *La Comédie italienne*, a comprehensive history, which went into the origins and character of the *Commedia dell'Arte* personnages.

Duchârtre's study is focused on the past, especially the period between the sixteenth and late eighteenth centuries when the *Commedia dell'Arte* moved from Italy to the French court. Paul-Sentenac's *Pierrot et les artistes, Mémoires de l'ami Pierrot* illustrates artists from well outside the Cubist milieux, like Jacques Drésa, André Fraye and Pierre Laprade; his criticism was often anti-Cubist and it seems he had no Cubist connections. But the event at the 'Camélion' and Paul-Sentenac's text makes it absolutely clear that Pierrot (and by implication Harlequin too) once represented, in any context, could not remain neutral; he demanded very specific responses and carried connotations that were too insistant to be ignored.

Whiteness is basic to Pierrot. Writing of Banville's Pierrot, Gaston Ragcot claims in 1924 that "Pierrot's sole function was to be white"[107]. Looking to his own verses of 1911, to Watteau, Banville, Edmond Rostand, Carco, Verlaine, Willette and many others, Paul-Sentenac associates this whiteness of the moon-gazer with purity and dreams[108]. Certainly if Harlequin could stand for invention and metamorphosis in Cubism, Pierrot could stand for "purity" in his whiteness. But that

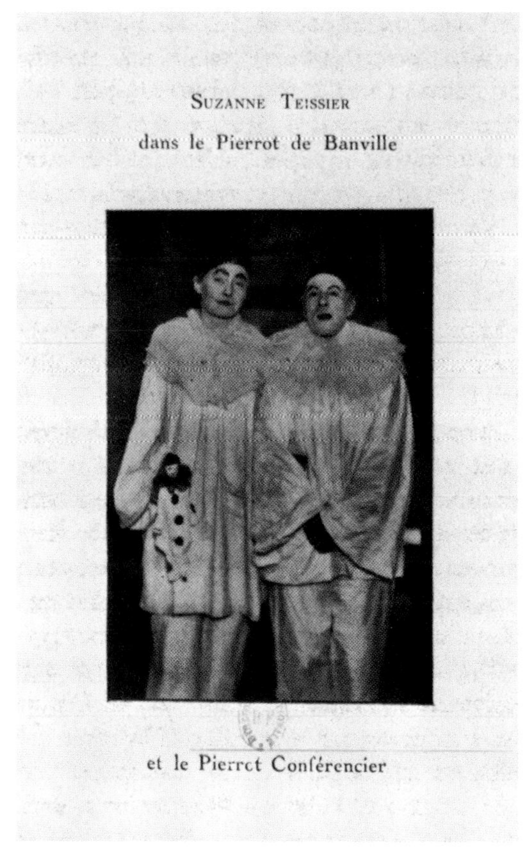

"purity" is connoted with a child-like innocence, not with artifice, and that innocence goes, not with manipulative trickery, but with a direct naiveté of sentiment. Banville's or Rostand's plays, Willette's or Drésa's drawings, substantiated Paul-Sentenac's characterisation of himself as the "lecturer-Pierrot": "I personify the type of the dreamer... This poor Pierrot still believes in those things that the scepticism of fashion forbids... He believes in love. He believes in elevated, generous feelings... I remain candid, opening always fresh eyes on life, wondering like a child. Pierrot is a grown-up child"[109]. Pierrot stands for an acute condition of receptiveness and sensitivity; he is simple in his purity, but complex because he combines opposing emotions as he responds to the cruelties of Colombine. He is sad *and* happy, and as such becomes two Pierrots in Rostand's immensely successful piece, *Les Deux Pierrots*[110]. He could even be read as a personification of the polyphonic ideal of thought and sensibility fused, since he meditates as well as feels. "I am gripped . . .," says Paul-Sentenac as Pierrot, "by an acute and trembling sensibility. I have a heart open to pity". And yet, "I have a lively intelligence. I reflect and I meditate"[111]. Paul-Sentenac's text establishes that, with the figure of Pierrot, came a complex set of characteristics and associations; that, like Harlequin, he had become a sign packed with possible significations.

In the context of Picasso's post-1915 *Commedia dell'Arte* figures, it has often been observed that they can be read as representations of Picasso himself (Harlequin) and such close friends as Max Jacob or Guillaume Apollinaire (Pierrot)[112]. It is worth remarking that between the late nineteenth century and the mid-1920s it had become habitual to read the figures of Harlequin and especially Pierrot as representations of the artist. Théodore de Banville and Willette had by the end of the nineteenth century persuaded their audiences that they had *become* their Pierrots. When Paul-Sentenac put on the mask and white costume of Pierrot to lecture on Pierrot in 1922 he followed a convention[113]. It was usual to see the writer or the artist *in* Pierrot and Harlequin. They had come to represent opposing notions of creative personality. The mercurial inventiveness and agile trickery of Harlequin was opposed to the "pure", direct sensitivity of Pierrot: the one cruel, the other vulnerable, but both equally impulsive and child-like. Despite Cooper's dismissal of their *Commedia dell'Arte* identities as irrelevant, it is easy to read Gris's *Harlequin at a Table* in terms of the vivacity and bravura of Harlequin, or his *Pierrot* in Winterthur in terms of the fragile openness of Pierrot. These figures would conventionally have been read as cyphers not only of the authority of an idealized tradition, but of Gris the artist. Harlequin and Pierrot put Gris (or distinct ideas of Gris's creative personality) into his paintings. Between 1917 and 1925 he painted about the same number of both; he oscillated between the signs for opposing creative personalities.

There is a further point to make about the way that these figures signified; it underlines the fact that they demanded responses to them *as* distinctly Pierrots or Harlequins.

They were, as I have said, character-*types*. Duchârtre stressed the importance of the formulaic in them. The origins of *Commedia dell'Arte* in theatrical forms where there was little or no scripting of parts had led to the establishment of such formula-characters so that performers could easily improvise within them. Conventionally, Pierrot and Harlequin were empty vessels, given a distinctive shape, into which the actor fitted. The actor became Pierrot or Harlequin, not *vice-versa,* hence the straightforwardness with which they could be taken over and re-invented by Willette, Picasso or Gris, and so appear manifestations of *their* identity[114].

At the same time, as Duchârtre pointed out, the formulaic masks and costumes of Pierrot and Harlequin function in relation to the spectator in a particular way, one unusual in masking. "The masks of the *Commedia dell'Arte,*" writes Duchârtre, "do not laugh, do not cry, they express no definite emotions by comparison with most antique masks, or Chinese or Japanese masks. They have an indefinable expression, as full of possibilities . . . as that of the Joconde (. . .)". He makes the analogy with the "play" of light on a jewel, "because it is surely true that the expression given by each one of us to these masks varies according to the angle at which it is seen"[115]. The costumes of Harlequin and Pierrot were cues to certain readings; the blankness of their masks acted as a screen for a further, emotive stage of reading-in.

The *Commedia dell'Arte* figures, culminating in *The Three Masks* of 1923 (Plate 106), at times allow the suggestion of anecdotes of the kind supplied by Rostand, Catulle-Mendès or Willette, especially in 1922–23. At this moment, Gris himself, as Karin von Maur is the first to point out, wrote a scenario for a ballet featuring Pierrot which is precisely of this anecdotal type[116]. In a couple of paintings we have drunken Pierrots and, in *The Three Masks*, Pierrots carousing with Harlequin[117]. Yet, most often, and without exception before 1922, they are simply stage performers whose costumes invited their audiences to read in meanings within a clearly established set of theatrical conventions. After 1922 Gris's Harlequins and Pierrots are often unmasked. In *Seated Harlequin* of 1923 he gives us Harlequin in the very act of unmasking, revealing, however, expressionless neo-classical features (another kind of mask). Before 1922 their faces *are* unequivocally masks (Cubist masks), invariably without a trace of expression. It is easy, with the cue supplied by costume to read *Harlequin at a Table* or the Winterthur *Pierrot* as I have read them; in both cases, their sightless, dumb faces-as-masks, make it still easier.

Gris's *Commedia dell'Arte* figures were never neutral. They could stand for Cubism and competing idealizations of Gris the Cubist "creator", but they could not stand for the irrelevance of the figure in Cubist figure-painting. The costumes and the masks said too much for that.

The portraits of Josette and the peasant figures of 1918 could represent the aspects of a war time idealism embodied in complementary stereotypes. The pre-war portraits and caricatural figure-paintings could set up a tension between the thrust of avant-garde Cubist painting towards a denial of likeness and the commitment of portraiture and the so-called "comic" in caricature to likeness. In all these cases the figure acted in Gris's work as a positive, sometimes challenging stimulus. The *Commedia dell'Arte* figures might have mattered as specific character-types and as masks that invited certain kinds of response, but the fit between their highly conventionalized theatrical artificiality and the ethos of post-1916 "purity" was so snug that they served to corroborate the pictorial rather than to provoke tensions in relation to it. As Gris's Cubist paintings became a series of new performances played out with a strictly limited vocabulary of elements, he peopled them with a cast-list of formulaic performers cut down to just two, Pierrot and Harlequin. The figure before 1914 and in the persons of Josette and the Beaulieu peasants had never given the impression of being merely a vehicle for pictorial manipulation; as we have seen, the *Commedia dell'Arte* figures could certainly give that impression to many, at least superficially.

From 1922 until Gris's death in 1927, the cast-list of his figures expanded once again. There were more *Commedia dell'Arte* figures besides *The Three Masks* and the *Seated Harlequin* of 1923. But there were also bourgeois women with musical instruments, paintings or books, usually in decorous postures; there were bourgeois men eating, smoking, thinking and otherwise taking it easy; there were popular musicians (the unfinished *Woman with a Guitar* of 1927 is one (Figure 27)), a fisherman, a groom, a village drummer-boy; and there were country women (the *Woman with a Basket* is one (Figure 26)). They are all, however, performers who perform in various shapes of artifice. This is obviously so of the café musicians and, as I showed at the beginning of the essay, of figures like *Woman with a Basket*, where country costume has become fancy-dress. But it is so too, if in a less obvious way, of the bourgeois figures like *Woman with a Guitar* and *Man in Front of a Window* of 1924 (Figures 41 and 42).

The idling or sometimes contemplative bourgeoisie of Gris's mid-1920s figure-painting is the prosperous bourgeoisie of France in the boom years that followed the Armistice[118]. Again Gris, the one-time caricaturist, works with types, types that represent social comfort and ease in a period of release after the austerity of war-time. The types he paints are, in fact, comparable with those he satirized as a humourist before 1912. In his earlier career Gris had depicted the stylish bourgeoisie (Figure 30) from the outside vantage-point of a ramshackle Montmartre bohemia (his *Le*

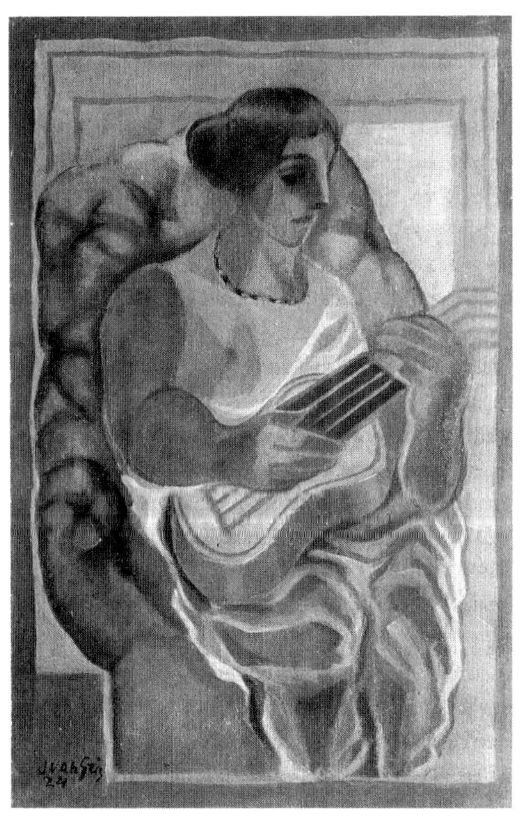

Figure 41
Woman with a Guitar, 1924
Oil on canvas, 41 x 27 cm
Private Collection

Charivari homage to Willette (Figure 31) presents the multitude of humourists as an exclusively Montmartrois profession, scrutinizing Paris from the shabby heights around Sacré-Cœur). After 1922, the boom-time bourgeoisie that Gris depicted was his society. His figures confirm his arrival as one of its members for, despite his relative lack of commercial or critical success compared especially to Picasso and Braque, he had become one of those taken on by Diaghilev's *Ballets Russes* and his place as a Cubist painter who counted for collectors was increasingly acknowledged[119]. The society he depicted from within was at ease, but it existed on the edges where a cultivated middle-class overlapped with a neo-bohemia. Gris's letters, especially from Bandol and Céret in 1921–22, have left a glimpse of the kind of people they were, the individuals behind the types in the pictures.

When he "cheated death" in 1920, Gris regained his vigour by living as hard as his health allowed. As I showed in the last essay, he worked compulsively, and he amused himself with a will. Until that first bout of serious illness, he and Josette had continued to inhabit his one-room studio in the rickety "Bateau-Lavoir", and to live among the shifting cluster of bohemian groupings that revolved around the studios of Montmartre and Montparnasse, meeting at poetry-readings, lectures and exhibitions, and in the pavement cafés. After 1920, he returned only briefly to 13, rue Ravignan before settling down with Josette next door to the Kahnweilers in Boulogne-sur-Seine. Otherwise, as he got back to painting in Beaulieu, Bandol and Céret, he moved between the "manoir" of Les Fourneaux, hotel rooms and rented rooms in distinctly different milieux.

The clearest picture of these milieux emerges in the letters he wrote to Kahnweiler from Bandol between the end of 1920 and June 1921. By Christmas Eve 1920 he was well enough to enjoy a 10 franc dinner with Josette at the Grand Casino. By February dancing had become a regular feature of his evening life. There was a Carnival fancy-dress ball, and he and Josette began to go every Sunday night to the 'Bal des Joyeux Bandolais'. By March he is writing to Kahnweiler of dinners and parties, of a veritable social whirl into which he had thrown himself with Josette. Individuals are sketched. There is "Jean the Musician", "a young man from a family which is very

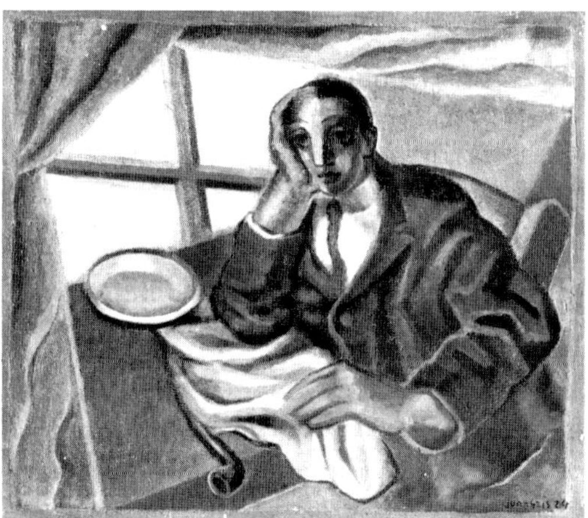

Figure 42
Man in Front of a Window, 1924
Oil on canvas, 46 x 55 cm
Private Collection

Figure 43
Marcelle la Blonde, 1921
Lithograph,
29.5 x 22.5 cm
Galerie Louise Leiris,
Paris

important locally – he's the son of a *conseilleur général* of this department… He's a good musician and a very intelligent boy who I think would like to own something by myself". On 30 March 1921, he writes of a Sunday ball followed by supper for "12 or 14 of us, with 'Marcelle la blonde'", where they stayed dancing "till 3 o'clock in the morning. Marcelle is the cousin of the young musician… They are very rich and very hospitable people such as one only finds in these parts"[120]. "Jean the Musician" and "Marcelle la Blonde" (Jean-Claude and Marcelle Brune) were both recorded in a suite of lithographs drawn on the stone for publication by Kahnweiler in 1921 (Figure 43). Gris became involved enough with Marcelle Brune to put his relationship with Josette in jeopardy that summer. He even contemplated marriage with her, tempted partly, he confessed, by the material well-being that she could bring him[121].

Back with Josette at Céret in the early months of 1922, dancing again featured prominently in their lives, and they moved in a milieu, comparable with the Bandol set, led by the family of the local sub-prefect[122]. At Céret there was also the one-time, now more comfortable bohemian, Manolo Hugué, who was seriously contemplating having Le Corbusier build him a smart modern villa, with Gris as intermediary[123]. And back in Paris between 1922 and 1927, Gris moved in a society around Kahnweiler that mixed a bourgeois intelligentsia with old and new bohemians, one-time Montmartre figures like Jacob and Gris himself, and young Left bank figures like Michel Leiris, Armand Salacrou and André Masson.

An especially telling manifestation of Gris's engagement with a progressive bourgeois intelligentia was his decision to be initiated into the Free Masons on 2 February 1923 at the Parisian Loge Voltaire of the Grand Orient de France. The research of José García Diego has established how seriously Gris took this commitment. By January 1924 he had been elevated to the grade of "companion",

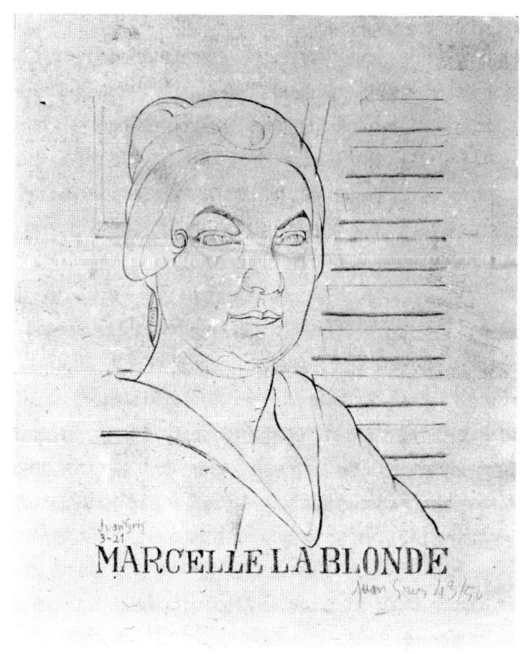

and on 1 May 1925 he reached the grade of "Master"[124].

It is clear that one of the attractions of Free Masonry was its long-lived mystical tradition (dating from the late eighteenth century), with its stress on numerology and its connections with Alchemy[125]. Indeed, his elevation to "Master" indicates that Gris studied Masonic symbolism in depth. Yet, it has to be realised that from the later nineteenth century through the 1920s, French Free Masonry had become associated above all with the Positivism of Auguste Comte, along with political anti-clericalism and progressive Republicanism. Gris was initiated the year before the election of the Cartel des Gauches, which brought into the Chamber of Deputies and into government an unprecedented number of Free Masons under the umbrella of the centrist Parti Radical (the connections between the "brothers" and the Parti Radical were closely enough knit to form a strong network of influence). There was, coincidentally, a particularly strong contingent from Josette's region, the Touraine, led by Auguste Chautemps, a "brother" who became both

1 This unfinished canvas remained in the possession of Madame Josette Gris after Gris's death. It is now in the collection of Georges González Gris by whose kind permission it is reproduced here for the first time. It is not included in Douglas Cooper's Catalogue Raisonné.

2 Christian Zervos, 'Juan Gris et l'inquiétude de l'aujourd'hui', *Cahiers d'Art,* no. 10, 1926, p. 269.

3 Pierre Reverdy, 'Sur le cubisme', *Nord-Sud,* no. 1, 15 March 1917; in Pierre Reverdy, *Œuvres Complètes: Nord-Sud, Self Defence et autres écrits sur l'art et la poésie (1917–1926),* edited with notes by Etienne-Alain Hubert, Paris, 1975, p. 19.

4 For further discussion of this, see chapter 3 above.

5 Maurice Raynal, 'Severini', *S.I.C.,* nos. 45 and 46, 15 and 31 May 1919, p. 3.

6 See for example Mark Rosenthal, *Juan Gris,* New York, 1983, p. 24.

7 Instances are Juan Antonio Gaya Nuño, *Juan Gris,* translated from Spanish by Kenneth Lyons, London, 1975, pp. 86–91; ibid., p. 29; and Marilyn McCully, 'Los Comienzos de Juan Gris como dibujante' in *Juan Gris (1887–1927),* ed. Gary Tinterow, Ministerio de Cultura, Madrid, 1985, p. 22.

8 Although Cooper, for example, insists that the portrait conveys nothing of Josette to us. See Douglas Cooper, 'Introduction' (Catalogue Raisonné), p. XXX.

9 Especially significantly in Kenneth E. Silver, *Esprit de corps: The Art of the Parisian Avant-Garde and the First World War, 1914–1925,* Princeton and London, 1989.

10 See Cooper (Introduction), op. cit., pp. XXIV–XXV.

11 Juan Gris, Statement (published as a statement made to "Vauvrecy" (Amédée Ozenfant)), *L'Esprit Nouveau,* no. 5, pp. 533–4. Translated by Douglas Cooper in D.-H. Kahnweiler, *Juan Gris, His Life and Work,* London, 1969, p. 193.

12 See my discussion of metaphor in chapter 3 above.

13 Juan Gris, 'On the Possibilities of Painting', lecture delivered 15 May 1924 to the 'Société des études philosophiques et scientifiques pour l'examen des idées nouvelles', at the Sorbonne, Paris; in Kahnweiler (1969), op. cit.

14 Roland Dorgelès, 'Ce que disent les cubes...', *Fantasio,* 15 October 1911, pp. 190–91.

15 Roland Catenoy, 'Une Consultation au Salon d'Automne', *Fantasio,* 1 November 1911.

16 "Je crois savoir que les cubistes veulent réagir au nom de la volonté contre la sensibilité... Et qu'est-ce-qu'un artiste insensible?", Louis Vauxcelles, *Gil Blas,* 30 September 1911, p. 1. For a full discussion of Vauxcelles's anti-cubist position, taken up from 1910, see Lynn Wissing Gamwell, *Cubist Criticism: 1907–1925,* thesis submitted for the degree of Ph. D., University of California, Los Angeles, pp. 32–3.

17 Gopnik has discussed the contemporaneous anti-Cubist caricatures of Luc Metivet, which also poke fun at Cubism for its supposed refusal of the model or *motif* from life. He picks out a drawing published in the *Journal Amusant,* 28 October 1911. See Adam Gopnik, 'High and Low: Caricatures, Primitivism, and the Cubist Portrait', *Art Journal,* Winter, 1983, p. 371.

18 Portraits figure importantly in the early history of Cubism. Besides Picasso's series of 1910, including the *Portrait of Ambroise Vollard* (Figure 2), and Gleizes's *Portrait of Jacques Nayral* (Figure 28) of 1911, it is worth mentioning Metzinger's *Portrait of Apollinaire,* and Gleizes's *Portrait of Arcos,* both exhibited at the Indépendants of 1910.

19 Guillaume Apollinaire, *L'Intransigeant,* 10 October 1911; in Guillaume Apollinaire, *Apollinaire on Art: Essays and Reviews, 1902–1918,* edited by Leroy C. Breunig, translated by Susan Suleiman, New York and London, 1972, p. 182.

20 Albert Gleizes, *Souvenirs* (1957), cited in Daniel Robbins, 'Jean Metzinger: At the Centre of Cubism'; in *Jean Metzinger in Retrospect,* edited by Ann Moser, University of Iowa Museum of Art, Iowa City, 1984, p. 20.

21 Roger Allard, 'Au Salon d'Automne', *L'Art Libre,* no. 12, November 1910. Cited in ibid., p. 15.

22 See chapter 1 above.

23 For the male identification of the subject in this drawing, see chapter 2, note 46 above.

24 The force of the received idea of Gris as the model of lucidity is, to my mind, demonstrated by the fact that this head has been written about as actually exemplary in its lucidity. Gaya Nuño, for instance, writes of: "a geometrical conciseness that merely increases the likeness of the subject". Gaya Nuño (1975), op. cit., p. 82.

25 This head is on the back of *Houses in Paris – Place Ravignan,* 1911, Cooper no. 9. It is reproduced here for the first time with the kind permission of Leonard Lauder. I am grateful to Dr Emily Braun for drawing it to my attention.

26 James Burkley, 'Les Indépendants (Suite)', *L'Assiette au beurre,* no. 572, 30 March 1912.

27 According to Kahn, it was Adolphe de Willette who was behind the promotion of the term "humoriste". See Gustave Kahn, *La Femme dans la caricature française,* Paris, 1907, p. 20.

28 McCully (1985), loc. cit. Also see Raymond Bachollet, 'Juan Gris, Dessinateur de presse'; in *Juan Gris et les dimanches de Boulogne,* Musée Municipale, Boulogne-Billancourt, 1987–8, pp. 15–26.

29 See Bachollet, ibid.

30 McCully claims a specific "punto de partida" for *Man in the Café* in a caricature published by *Papitu* (Barcelona, 26 January 1910); see McCully (1985), loc. cit., p. 22. Gris's drawing 'Friendship' (Figure 30) introduces another point, also made by other caricatures that he published. The check of the man's jacket is rendered by a simple grid of squares which remains absolutely flat and regular. It is, of course, an anticipation of the grid that has taken over the figure altogether by the date of the Section d'Or.

31 Gopnik (1983), loc. cit.

32 Gopnik argues as much, ibid.

33 This is discussed, notably, by Arnheim. See Rudolph Arnheim, 'The Rational of Deformation', *Art Journal,* Winter, 1983, p. 319ff.

34 Paul Gaulthier, *Le Rire et la caricature,* Paris, 1906. A note at the end of the preface (which is by "M. Sully Prudhomme de l'Académie Française") informs us that Henri Bergson was invited to write the preface, but was "empêché par un accident de santé". The reason for the invitation to Bergson was his study *Le Rire, Essai sur la signification du comique,* Paris, 1900.

35 *Fantasio,* 15 December 1912, p. 360.

36 See Kirk Varnedoe and Adam Gopnik, 'Caricature'; in *High and Low, Modern Art and Popular Culture,* The Museum of Modern Art, New York, 1990.
37 Gopnik (1983), loc. cit., pp. 372–3.
38 The idiom, for instance, of Paul Iribe's advertisement for the Boulevard des Italiens jeweller "Maxima", used more than once in *Le Charivari* in 1911–12. In fact, Gris's decision to incorporate an undisguised caricatural idiom into the treatment of faces closely relates to a parallel move made by Picasso. This is clear in the two "student" heads painted in Paris at the end of the summer of 1913, and is introduced by three figure-paintings executed when Picasso was in Céret with Gris earlier that year. See Pierre Daix and Joan Rosselet, *Picasso, The Cubist Years, 1907–1916, A Catalogue Raisonné of the Paintings and Related Works,* Paris, 1979, nos. 616, 617, 618, 620 and 621. Caricature is more easily to be seen in Picasso's work in this sequence of figures of 1913 than in the portraits of 1909–10.
39 See note 27 above.
40 Mécislas Goldberg's *La Morale des lignes* is considered at length in Neil Cox, *La Morale des lignes: Picasso 1907–10: Modernist Reception; the Subversion of Content; and the Lesson of Caricature,* thesis submitted for the degree of Ph. D., University of Essex, 1991. The book was written, largely, while Goldberg was awaiting death in a sanatorium at Avon, south of Paris, financed by the caricaturist André Rouveyre, whose drawings served as its pretext. Both Goldberg and Rouveyre were close to the circle of the Abbaye de Créteil and to Apollinaire and Salmon. Goldberg was an habitué of the soirées of *La Plume.* Cox analyses his theories in the context of Symbolist Idealism and the position of Picasso after *Les Demoiselles d'Avignon;* his conclusions are highly suggestive, and very different from Gopnik's.
41 Kahn (1907), op. cit., p. 406.
42 Louis Villaret, 'Chronique Charivarique', *Le Charivari,* Sunday 18 December 1910, p. 3. For Gris and *Les Humoristes,* see Bachollet (1987–8), loc. cit. Bachollet was the first to publish Gris's cover featuring Willette as Pierrot. He does not, however, note its function as a "homage" complementary to the "homage" to Picasso.
43 Ibid.
44 "Then Clovis Sagot bought some of them [Gris's first canvases], and from that moment Gris gave up his old livelihood for ever". Kahnweiler (1969), op. cit., p. 16. Bachollet invokes also Cooper's total lack of interest in Gris's caricatures. Ibid.
45 When Salmon writes of Marcoussis switching away from his successful career as the caricaturist "Markous", he talks of him "par adhésion au cubisme, haussé à l'art majeur". Writing of Gris, he recalls his conviction initially that he would never "dépasser le niveau artistique du laborieux dessinateur de *l'Assiette au beurre*". André Salmon, *Souvenirs sans fin: Deuxieme Epoque (1908–1920),* Paris, 1956, p. 283 and *Troisieme Epoque (1920–1940),* Paris, 1961, p. 277.
46 Varnedoe and Gopnik (1990), op. cit., p. 123.
47 Gaultier (1906), op. cit., pp. 19–21.
48 Kahn (1907), op. cit., pp. 434–5.
49 Ibid., pp. 278 and 306.
50 For a full discussion of this, see Cox (1991), op. cit. This analysis is imaginative and profound in its implications for understanding Picasso between 1907 and 1910. I believe, however, that it tends to over-state the impact of Rouveyre and Goldberg on the theory and practice of caricature. Cox does not discuss the distinction (crucial I believe) between "fantasy" and the "comic" as applied by Kahn and Gaultier and, like Gopnik, he does not look at the relevance of caricature to Cubist practice in 1912–13.
51 Gopnik calls caricature "a working code that comments on the way representational codes work". Gopnik (1983), loc. cit., p. 373. See Gopnik and Varnedoe (1990), op. cit.
52 One should remember Gaultier's point that "fantastical" caricature (based on extreme deviation) is not concerned with "reality" and therefore is not concerned with moralistic (or political) comment. See Gaultier (1906), op. cit., pp. 19–21. Gris's switch from politically engaged caricature to Cubist painting is a manifestation of the broad tendency for once politically committed artists to move into more thoroughly aesthetic forms and practices that Cottington outlines. See David Cottington, *Cubism and the Politics of Culture,* thesis submitted for the degree of Ph. D., Courtauld Institute, University of London, 1985.
53 "La caricature d'aujourd'hui abonde en ingénieux notateurs de physiognomies contemporaines". Kahn (1907), op. cit., p. 415.
54 Another case is *Portrait of Sr. Legua,* 1911, Cooper no. 5.
55 For the blue "Singapores", see Judith Cousins, with the collaboration of Pierre Daix, 'Documentary Chronology'; in William Rubin, *Picasso and Braque, Pioneering Cubism,* The Museum of Modern Art, New York, 1989, p. 399.
56 *L'Assiette au beurre,* May 1909, no. 426. Metzinger's *Woman Smoker* was probably painted in 1913, like Gris's male *Smoker.* See J().M()., 'Cubist Works, 1910–1921'; in *Jean Metzinger in Retrospect,* edited by Ann Moser, University of Iowa Museum of Art, Iowa City, 1985, p. 43. Vogt, campaigning against feminism, takes the lack of smoking compartments in French trains and the hostility to smoking in non-smoking compartments to be an attack against a healthy male habit. See William Vogt, *Sexe faible, Une riposte aux exagérations et aux utopies du féminisme,* Paris, 1908, p. 12.
57 Nesbit argued her case in her Durning-Lawrence Lectures of 1991 at University College, London, as well as in her earlier lecture, 'The Body in the Line', given at the Courtauld Institute in 1989.
58 The evidence for the re-dating of *Portrait of Madame Cézanne (after Cézanne)* (Cooper no. 257) is in a reference made in a letter of 9 June 1917 from the newly discovered correspondance between Gris and Léonce Rosenberg.
59 Besides the full-length portrait, there is the bust (Cooper no. 202). Further, *Seated Woman* of May 1917 (Cooper no. 223) is considered a portrait of Josette by Cooper, although there is no corroborating evidence known to me of this. Gris also painted a male figure in May 1916, which Cooper refers to as "Auto-portrait?"; see Cooper no. 170.
60 This information about Josette (Charlotte Augusta Fernande Herpin) has been gathered by Philippe Carton. It was made public at a lecture, 'Le Peintre Juan Gris et sa rencontre fouituite avec Le Pays Lochois', delivered in Loches, 11 May 1991. I am grateful to Monsieur Carton

for making available to me the typescript of his lecture, which has made a very valuable contribution in an area that needs more research.

61 Kahn illustrates as especially telling Roedel's series *Femmes d'artistes*. See Kahn (1907), op. cit.

62 Ibid., pp. 82–91, 343, 431–3. See also Vogt (1908), op. cit. It is relevant to Nesbit's argument concerning Positivism and the reformed education system of the Third Republic that Vogt launches his attack by quoting a letter from Auguste Comte to John Stuart Mill on the "infériorité naturelle" of women.

63 Conversation with Madame Josette Gris, 20 July 1977.

64 A further insight into the kind of women taken into these milieux and attitudes to their role is to be gained from Salmon's memoirs. See especially André Salmon, *Souvenirs sans fin, Première Epoque (1903–1908)*, Paris, 1955, p. 345 ff.

65 See especially Georges González Gris, 'Jean, mon père', *Hommage à Juan Gris (1887–1927)*, Grand Orient de France, 16 bis rue Cadet, 75009 Paris, 1987, pp. 5–6.

66 He depicts an olive-branch waving militarist in frock-coat at a lecturn from which projects, in place of his phallus, a canon. *L'Assiette au beurre*, 3 October 1908, no. 391.

67 Juan Gris, 'M. Jaurès en Prusse', *Le Charivari* (cover), Sunday, 2 October 1910. Besides being against Jaurès's passivism, *Le Charivari* was more generally against the Republican secular rationalism of the Parti Radical and the old "Cartel des gauches". In particular, it presented Radical politics as a sinister conspiracy involving Free Masonry (and the links were indeed real). See *Le Charivari*, 27 March 1910.

68 For instance, the series of conversations (said to be reported *verbatim*) used as "une démonstration" of the pettyness and self-centredness of women. Vogt (1908), op. cit., pp. 128–34.

69 Cited in Françoise Thébaud, *La Femme aux temps de la guerre de 14*, Paris, 1986, p. 25.

70 Ibid., pp. 29–30.

71 Jean-Jacques Becker, *The Great War and the French People*, translated by Arnold Pomerans, with an introduction by Jay Winter, Leamington Spa, Heidelberg and Dover, New Hampshire, 1985, p. 22.

72 Described in Thébaud (1986), op. cit., p. 43.

73 See Thébaud's discussion of this, Ibid, p. 38.

74 Léon Abensour, *Les Vaillantes*, Paris, 1917. Cited in ibid., p. 95.

75 Louis Barthou, 'L'Effort de la femme française pendant la guerre', lecture published by the 'Comité l'Effort de la France et de ses Allies', 1917. Cited Thébaud (1986), op. cit., p. 98.

76 The evidence of this is in a letter of 23 April 1917 in the newly discovered correspondence between Gris and Léonce Rosenberg.

77 Marie de La Hire, *La Femme française, son activité pendant la guerre*, Paris, 1917, p. 16. The image of the lone woman left at home is developed from p. 10, after citing Viviani's "Call". Its function is to qualify it with recognition of the role of women who remain passive. La Hire was another who declared that she had set aside campaigning Feminism for the duration of the War, although the later sections of the book are an attempt to capitalize on the *de facto* changes achieved by "feminization".

78 See André Ducasse, Jacques Meyer, Gabriel Perreux, *Vie et Mort des Français, 1914–1918: Simple Histoire de la Grande Guerre*, Paris, 1962, new edition, Geneva, 1978, p. 232.

79 This card is published in Serge Zeyons, *Le Roman-photo de la Grande Guerre*, Paris, 1976, p. 112.

80 By 1921, the massive war-time shift to female employment had been redressed, and legislation in 1921 and 1923 backed a powerful pro-natalist campaign aimed at recovering the demographic situation in France. In 1922 the Senate threw out a bill, voted by the Chamber of Deputies, to give women the vote. Opposition to it came not only from the Right, but from the liberal Left which feared that the enfranchisement of women would strengthen anti-Republican clericalism. McMillan discusses this topic more fully in James F. McMillan, *Dreyfus to De Gaulle, Politics and Society in France, 1898–1969*, London, 1985.

81 These figures were given by the correspondents of 'L'Effort féminin français' and published in Mme Borel, *La Mobilisation féminine en France*, Paris, 1919. They are cited in Thébaud (1986), op. cit., p. 149.

82 See Letter to Léonce Rosenberg, 10 July 1918; in *Juan Gris: Correspondance, Dessins 1915–1921*, edited with an introduction and notes by Christian Derouet, IVAM Centre Julio González, Valencia and Centre Georges Pompidou, Musée National d'Art Moderne, Paris, 1991, p. 51 (Letter 29).

83 On grounds of costume, it seems that the other female figure painting of this period, *Seated Woman* of 1917, is not a peasant subject. See Cooper no. 223.

84 Letter to Léonce Rosenberg, 4 April 1918; in *Correspondance* (Derouet, 1991), p. 46 (Letter 22).

85 Madame Josette Gris told me that "the miller" was an actual neighbour, although she said he did not pose for Gris. Conversation, 20 July 1977. A recent visit to the "colombier" with Monsieur Philippe Carton has confirmed the probability that a neighbour lived there, and that it was the basis for the building in the background of the painting.

86 Letter to Léonce Rosenberg, 4 June 1918; in *Correspondance* (Derouet, 1991), p. 50 (Letter 26).

87 See Becker (1985), op. cit., pp. 217–235.

88 Michel Augé-Laribé, *L'Agriculture pendant la guerre*, Paris, 1925, pp. 85–6. Augé-Laribé gives detailed figures for prices.

89 Becker (1985), op. cit., pp. 226–35. The evidence here came from replies sent by prefects in all *Départements* to a request for such reports sent out by the Minister of the Interior on 10 June 1917. More than half the total (44 *Départements*) reported morale to be "poor" or "indifferent". The prefect of Isère used the term "indifferent" in the other sense, to indicate lack of solidarity with "the idea of collective effort". Becker also records the opinion of the inspector of police at Noirétable in the Loire, not far from Loches: "Agricultural workers seem to ignore the war... cupidity having apparently supplanted everything else".

90 Thébaud notes that newspaper caricatures presented a generally positive image of the peasant, as did postcards. See Thébaud (1986), op. cit., pp. 147–8. This is confirmed, for instance, by Zeyons (1976), op. cit.

91 As a proportion of the men mobilized, this was around half and, in fact, the population of France was (unusually

for industrialized Europe) split 50:50 between towns of more than 2,000 inhabitants and the country. See Augé-Laribé (1925), p. 66. The relationship between the catastrophic casualty rates of the peasants and the representation of peasant and landscape subjects in the decade following the war has been explored exhaustively in Romy Golan, *A Moralized Landscape: The Organic Image of France between the Two World Wars,* Ph. D. thesis, Courtauld Institute, University of London, 1989. I am indebted to the important stimulus provided by her work

92 See Thébaud (1986), pp. 147–8.

93 *Correspondance* (Derouet, 1991), op. cit., pp. 17–18. Derouet points out that in the churches of Loche, Gris found "des peintures de tourangeaux contemporains de Fouquet". He illustrates (p. 49) a postcard of the Crucifixion triptych, then in the church of Saint Antoine, on the back of which Gris sketched combinations of fruit, glass and fruit dish.

94 Zeyons illustrates a postcard featuring "Les Dix Commandements du Poilu". They include: "Du Courage, tu montreras, / Jour et nuit, tout simplement"; "A la bouche, tu auras / Ta Bouffarde constamment"; "Persévérant, tu seras, / Jusqu'au bout, énergiquement"; and "En faissant ça, tu obtiendras / La Victoire, certainement". See Zeyons (1976), op. cit., p. 75.

95 See chapter 4 above.

96 See Christopher Green, *Cubism and its Enemies: Modern Movements and Reaction in French Art, 1916–1928,* New Haven and London, 1987, p. 65.

97 "Arlequin Trismégiste" appears in the last stanza of the 1905 version of Apollinaire's poem "Les Saltimbanques", and in the published version of 'Crépuscule' which first appeared in *Les Argonauts,* no. 9, February 1909. See Marilyn McCully, 'Magic and Illusion in the Saltimbanques of Picasso and Apollinaire', *Art History,* December 1980, pp. 425–34.

98 Claude Roger-Marx, 'Chronique Artistique', *Les Nouvelles Littéraires,* Saturday, 12 January 1924, p. 5.

99 Anon., 'Exposition Juan Gris (Berlin, Galerie Flechtheim), *Documents,* 2nd Year, no. 4, 1930, p. 243. See also chapter 5, note 37 above for authorship.

100 The other two Pierrots of May 1919 are Cooper nos. 302 and 306.

101 I have argued along these lines myself. See Green (1987), op. cit. Also see Kenneth E. Silver, *Esprit de corps: The Art of the Parisian Avant-Garde and the First World War, 1914–1925,* London, 1989.

102 Buchloh is the one to have presented this case most strongly. Unfortunately, he takes little account of the specific complexities and ambiguities offered by the material he discusses. It is as if the same conclusions will emerge whatever the raw material; like a production process that will turn anything and everything into, say, hats. See Benjamin H. D. Buchloh, 'Figures of Authority, Ciphers of Regression: Notes on the Return of Representation in European Painting'; in ed. Benjamin H. D. Buchloh, Serge Guilbeaut and David Solkin, *Modernism and Modernity: The Vancouver Conference Papers,* Halifax, Nova Scotia, 1983, pp. 81–115.

103 Both Ozenfant's periodical *L'Elan* and Reverdy's *Nord-Sud* were assertively patriotic. Apollinaire praised *Nord-Sud* for being "résolument françaises et nationales" in *L'Europe Nouvelle,* 15 June 1918, pp. 1106–7. Léonce Rosenberg volunteered for the Somme campaign in 1916–17, and served as a military interpreter with the English forces. He pressed Gris's graphic talents into use, asking him to design heraldic devices based on military insignia for his officer friends during the summer of 1918. He also had Gris reading Marshall Foch's *Des Principes de la guerre* that summer. As a foreigner, Gris certainly felt threatened in France, however supportive he was towards his friends on the front. See *Correspondance* (Derouet, 1991), op. cit., pp. 13–18, 47–59, and 81–84. Also see Christian Derouet's essay below.

104 Buchloh (1983), op. cit.

105 *Letters of Juan Gris (1913–1927),* translated and edited by Douglas Cooper, London, 1956, p. 142 (Letter CLXIII). In the same letter Gris mentions a *Pierrot* painting with which he is "rather pleased". It is probably Cooper no. 385, a development of the 1921 Dublin Pierrot (Plate 104).

106 See reports in *Paris-Journal,* Sunday 18, 25 June and 2 July 1922. Also Paul-Sentenac, *Pierrot et les artistes, Mémoires de l'ami Pierrot,* Paris, 1922.

107 Gaston Rageot, *La Beauté: Essai d'esthétique historique,* Paris, 1924, p. 295.

108 Paul-Sentenac (1923), op. cit., p. 20.

109 Ibid., p. 24.

110 Here Colombine is courted by a sad and a happy Pierrot. See Edmond Rostand, *Les Deux Pierrots ou le souper blanc* (Luchon 1890, first performed 21 May 1894 at the Comédie-Française).

111 Ibid., pp. 19–20.

112 See especially Theodore Reff, 'Picasso's Three Musicians: Maskers, Artists and Friends', *Art in America,* New York, December 1980, pp. 124–42.

113 It is a convention that he constantly mentions. See Paul-Sentenac (1923), op. cit.

114 See Pierre-Louis Duchârtre *La Comédie italienne,* Paris, 1925, pp. 17 and 31–2.

115 Ibid., p. 32.

116 See Karin von Maur below.

117 In Catulle-Mendès's *Le Docteur Blanc* (Paris, 1893), Pierrot is hypnotist, drunkard and murderer, caught up in a complex story that exposes his weakness and susceptibility.

118 The economic boom in France is surveyed in Alfred Sauvy, *Histoire économique de la France entre les deux guerres,* Paris, 1965, 1967 and 1975. One of its manifestations was a boom in the art-market, which was first surveyed by Gee. See Malcolm Gee, *Dealers, Critics and Collectors of Modern Painting: Aspects of the Parisian Art Market between 1910 and 1930,* thesis submitted for the degree of Ph. D., Coutauld Institute, University of London, 1977 (subsequently published in its thesis form by Garland Press, London and New York).

119 See Green (1987), op. cit., p. 138

120 *Letters* (Cooper, 1956), op. cit., p. 107 (Letter CXXV).

121 See chapter 5, note 22 above.

122 *Letters* (Cooper, 1956), op. cit., pp. 138 and 140 (Letters CLVIII and CLXI).

123 The evidence for this is in the Fondation Le Corbusier, Paris. Le Corbusier gives the approximate cost of construction as 50,000 francs in a letter to Gris dated 24 January 1992, and Gris replies in an un-dated note that the

price is "au dessus de ce que Manolo veut dépenser".

124 See José A. García Diego, *Antonio Machado y Juan Gris: Dos artistas masones,* Madrid, 1990, chapter 8. García Diego illustrates the documentation from the Loge Voltaire relating to Gris's initiation and elevation to "companion" and "master".

125 Especially important in this connection was Louis-Claude de Saint-Martin, who took on the name "Philosophe Inconnu" and who was founder and great sovereign of the order of "Elus Cohen" in the 1760s. Numerology and Alchemy were fundamental to Saint-Martin who was well versed in the works of Jacob Boëhme and Cordonnier de Gorlitz. Further research is needed on the relevance of Masonic symbolism to Gris's painting. Some suggestions have been made in L. Ishi-Kawa, *Approximación a Gris: ocho marcos para once cuadros,* Fundación "Arte y Technología" for Telefonica de Espana, S. A., 1990, pp. 37–38.

126 For Free Masonry in the Touraine, see Jacques Fenéant, *Histoire de la Franc-Maçonerie en Touraine,* C.L.D, France, 1981.

127 García Diego (1990), op. cit., p. 109.

128 "En considérant socialement la question: / La société ne peut pas suprimer la vie de ces individus qui refusent le travail. / Car la société suprimerait leurs vies si elle ne subvenait pas aux besoins de leur existence. La société peut priver des avantages sociaux ces individus, elle ne peut en aucune manière les detruire. La société n'a d'ailleurs aucun intérêt à les laisser perir. Parmi ces individus refractaires au travail, il peut s'en trouver des utiles éventuellement à la société. Des hommes d'une inactivité et d'une inutilité apparente peuvent arriver parfois a être des grandes bienfaiteurs d'une société et même de l'humanité. / . . . / Tous les hommes du fait qu'ils vivent ont une activité a depenser. Si cette activité ne se depense pas dans des agrements sociaux, comme il arrive couramment aujourd'hui avec les gens fortunés qui ne travaillent pas mais qu'ils depensent une activité, elle s'emploie sous forme de production intellectuelle ou musculaire. Elle sera peut-être un travail deguisé et apparemment inutile, mais utile parfois a l'avenir". The entire paper in the original imperfect French is published in García Diego (1990), op. cit., pp. 121–125. No attempt has been made here to correct the French.

129 "Aujourd'hui on accepte parfaitement que l'homme fortuné puisse ne rien faite, mais si un homme sans fortune ne travaille pas et ne peut pas justifier des moyens d'existence, on le punit pour vagabondage". Ibid., p. 123.

130 This drawing is published on the cover of the catalogue of the exhibition organized under the auspices of the Grand Orient de France. See Grand Orient de France (1987), op. cit.

131 Letter to Kahnweiler, 30 March 1921. Ibid., p. 107 (Letter CXXV).

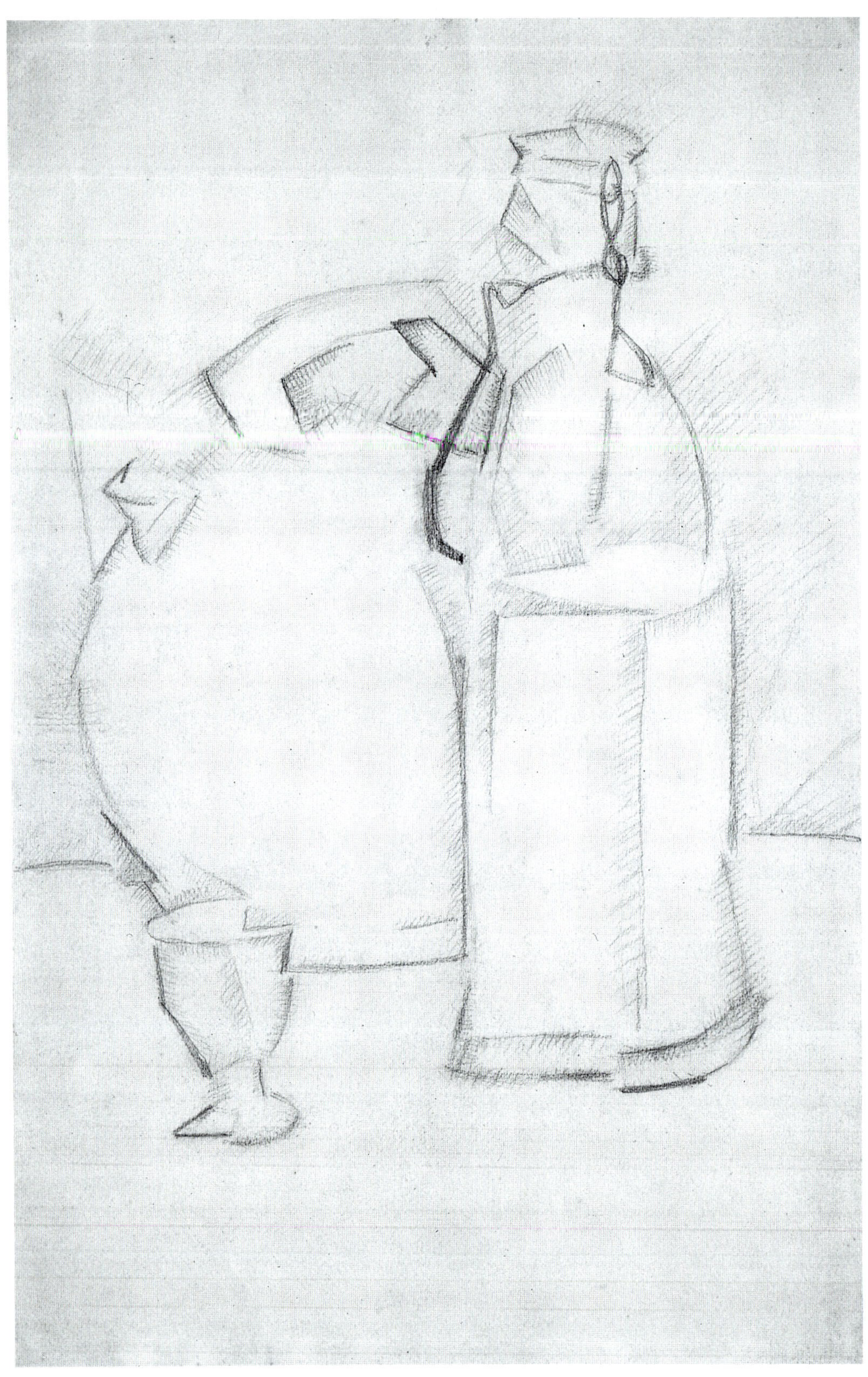

7. Gris's Objects

"Juan Gris, painter of still-lives, dealt with a limited number of domestic utensils... Sweet desserts are rare on the kitchen table". (André Salmon, 1961)[1]

Gris the still-life painter of humble objects has often been aligned with Gris the humble purist. André Salmon's muted, but respectful eulogy of the "painter of still-lifes" devotes equal attention to the poverty of his repertoire of objects and the role of white in his painting. White, he remarks, was one of the most expensive of a painter's colours. Gris used it liberally; it transformed, says Salmon, the ordinariness of his objects and delivered him from his "consuming humility". "With his bargain-basement fruit dish, his sugar-dish in thick moulded glass, his sugar-lump, all with their white lustre, Juan Gris proudly gives us luxury"[2]. Salmon resolves an antithesis between the simple things Gris painted and his aspiration to an elevated, a delicious purity (the luxury of white).

The distinction between the early "artificial" and the later "synthetic" still-lives that Gris painted in his short Cubist career can easily be articulated in these terms. Pictures like *Still-life with Oil Lamp* and *Bottles and Knife* of 1911–12 (Plates 6 and 7), as well as the first oil, *Siphon and Bottles* (Plate 2), display translations into orderly pictorial idioms of ordinary everyday objects. These are certainly the humble vessels and utensils of the kitchen table, and the metaphor of "purification" can certainly be applied to their transformation, which has indeed given a determining role to white, for it is white that lightens the shadows. In their very puritanism, these cheap oil-lamps, this very basic crockery, glass and cutlery, do not draw attention to themselves, but their unmistakable presence as objects is a reminder that they were there at the beginning. They can even be read as representations in themselves of a commitment to studious analysis. Their careful placing, but most of all the evidence they retain of first-hand observation, signify the primacy of patient, item-by-item study. These are the objects of "objective" analysis, and their total lack of preciousness situates Gris, the ultimate "Analytic Cubist", in the setting of dedicated asceticism.

The objects of objectivity, their connotations with high seriousness undiminished, return repeatedly in the still-lifes of the war-years from *Breakfast* of late 1915 to *Bottle and Fruit Dish* of early 1919 (Plate 52 and 90). By 1919, however, Gris's aspiration to purity had, of course, taken precedence over his commitment to the still-life object of study. The total integration of semantics and syntax, signs for objects and structural elements, says as much, but perhaps more telling is the removal from every object of the last trace of evidence of first hand observation. The regular block-like *tessurae* or the diagonal hatched strokes that break up the surface of the "analytic" pictures in 1911–12 approximate the look, on the one hand of the Divisionist mosaic, and on the other of Cézanne's "constructive stroke". As such, they signify in themselves painting as a response to light in nature,

Kettle and Milk Bottle, 1910–11
Pencil on paper, 48 x 31 cm
Galerie Louise Leiris, Paris

"sensation". Pencil is used to give gently nuanced gradations to light and dark across the creased surface of the cloth in *Breakfast*. It is used more blandly to model the bowl and glass on the right. The connection is made thus between every passage of tonal modelling, painted or drawn, and the practice of drawing "from nature" as a necessary starting point. Again, the precedence of vision is asserted. But in *Bottle and Fruit Dish* of 1919, typically for the period, Gris has got rid of the *tessurae,* the hatched strokes and nuanced modulation in favour of wide planes of green, brown, white, grey and black, occasionally edged by highlights and tonal gradations of the most reductive kind. The shaping of objects is either geometric (the fruit dish) or highly conventionalized (the glass, carafe and bottle). The objects of objectivity remain (this is certainly a bargain-basement fruit dish), and the fall of the cloth over the edge of the table invokes Cézanne, but what they signify now is the dominance of the shaping will of the artist over even them, and so over everything.

By the mid-1920s this is still more explicit, and the objects of objectivity are joined increasingly by objects that in themselves signify the artist as subject. Gris turns to the symbolic attributes of the arts. Musical instruments and music-sheets are placed alongside busts, suggestive of Apollo or Orpheus, as for instance in *The Musician's Table* of 1926 (Plate 116), and the painter's palette and brush is placed between the guitar and the fruit dish in *The Painter's Window* of 1925 (Plate 118). Especially in the still-lives with the attributes of the painter, the dominance of the artist over things, the precedence of the subject over the object is unqualified[3]. In these later still-lives white is subordinate to colour, but, in the sense of Salmon's metaphor, the humble utensils of the kitchen table have given way to the "white" of aesthetic "purity", to the "luxury" of art. Just as Gris's Pierrots and Harlequins, surrogates of the idealized artist, placed him, the painter, in the painting, so did the Orphic or the Apollonian bust and the artist's palette.

This kind of account of Gris's objects on either side of the supposed divide between analysis and synthesis does not ignore the objects of the still-lives. It allows them, indeed, to signify as objects either of objectivity or of subjectivity. But the stress on both sides of the divide is not on the objects as such; it is on the process of their translation (analysis or synthesis) and the "purity" of the result. The objects are seen to signify in relation to those processes or to that "purity".

If it was possible in the Cubist milieu to treat the figure in Cubist figure-painting as if it could simply be discounted, this was even more the case with still-life, especially after 1916. Still-life, not unlike the costume of Harlequin, came to be taken as the sign for the *disappearance* of all subject-matter from painting, except as pretext. When in 1918 André Lhote wrote an open letter to *Le Carnet de la Semaine* justifying his decision to break away from the limited subject-matter prescribed by the Cubists of L'Effort Moderne, he summed up what he took to be their over-riding commitment to still-life themes: "To each pictorial movement, it is said, corresponds a subject. The impressionists will choose the "banks of the Seine". The Cubists elect the guitar, the bottle, the pipe and the packet of tobacco, which are at the same time, noble "pretexts"[4].

From a more sympathetic vantage-point, Tériade and Zervos took this view of still-life in Cubism, and indeed in much twentieth century painting, to extreme conclusions at the end of the 1920s and the beginning of the 1930s in *Cahiers d'Art*. Like Gris, they picked out Cézanne's still-lives as the basic model on which Cubism was built. Reflecting on the possibility in 1931 of yet another "return to the subject", Zervos made the claim that Cézanne, finally, had vanquished "the obsession with the subject". He went on to set out the argument in full.

"The world," he wrote, "being an indissoluble unity, any object can express it in its entirety. Why choose? A painter must paint everything, so that his art remains entirely objective, submissive to that which he sees, obedient to whatever the gaze chances upon, docile before the world. The artist's temperament guides his choice and stops only at that which is open to bringing it out and reinforcing it. Only the temperament can endow the figurative with significance and express the whole world in the perception of an instant. It is thus that Cézanne has made magnificent canvases out of the most humble facts: a great artistic temperament sees nothing that is either ugly or mediocre. And the artist when he has truly achieved profundity is inevitably detached from subject-matter;... To the extent that the epoque widened his vision and confirmed his ideas, Cézanne convinced himself... that the picture represents nothing, that from the outset it must represent nothing but colours"[5].

So idealistic a view inevitably makes of Cézanne's fruit and kitchen utensils abstract absolutes, "an indissoluble unity" of colour that stands for "the world... in its entirety". How much easier was it to do this with Gris's *Bottle and Fruit Dish* and *The Painter's Window*. The still-life in Cubist painting (*all* Cubist painting) came to be treated by some as *non*-subject, or even in the case of Waldemar George, writing on Picasso's achievement, as the symbol of an art altogether detached from the actuality of "human" experience, the symbol of abstraction[6].

Using the term "decoration" almost as if it was synonymous with abstraction, Gris wrote thus to Kahnweiler in 1921 about a batch of still-lives just sent to the dealer from Bandol: "Obviously it is decoration. One must not be afraid of words when one knows what they mean, but all painting has always been decoration"[7].

Yet, as in the case of the figures, I return to the point that the "deductive method", despite the precedence it gave to "coloured architecture", actually restored the object as subject-matter. There can be no disputing the secondary status, not only as pretext but as mere after-thought, given subject-matter in Gris's lecture of 1924. He speaks of pictorial "architecture" giving "birth to the subject" and remarks: "It seems to me more natural to make subject "x" coincide with the picture that one has in mind than to make picture "x" coincide with a given subject"[8]. But the subject-matter generated is definitive both in theory and in practice: the cylinder, as we have seen, becomes a "particular bottle"[9].

The objects of objectivity so scrupulously "analysed" before 1916 are often, for all their ordinariness, highly distinctive: the "Peugeot" coffee-mill of *Breakfast* is a case in point. The objects of the still-lives after 1916 are often less distinctive, and yet they have very specific qualities of colour, consistency and shape, and they always belong to a clearly recognisable class of objects. They are unequivocally bottles or carafes, fruit dishes or breakfast bowls, just as the figure paintings are specifically bourgeois-bohemians, Harlequins or Pierrots. The figures signify *as* figures no more assertively than the objects of the still-lives *as* objects.

Even the objects of objectivity could carry strong connotative charges. I have mentioned already connotations of deprivation, isolation and high seriousness, connotations aligned with the asceticism of the analytic project. That they too could be read allusively on different levels, like the palettes and brushes or the busts and music sheets that represented the attributes of the arts, is established by the still-life poems of the "Reverdy circle", written between 1915 and 1919.

The coffee-mill is among the most used of Gris's repertoire of "humble domestic utensils". It appears from the earliest of the large charcoal and gouache drawings of 1910. In February 1918 Paul Dermée published a poem in *Nord-Sud*, whose chain of images is set going by a coffee-mill. Dermée's text switches from the coffee-mill to the sails of the windmill, wings ("ailes" in French) which become flared nostrils shivering ("ailes de nez", wings of the nose, are nostrils in French), evoking romance, a sky that turns, a wheel[10]. The humble fact of the coffee-mill is just a starting point.

Late in 1915 or early in 1916 Gris gave Reverdy's wife Henriette a gouache (Plate 51) which featured the Peugeot coffee-mill from the closely related oil *Breakfast*. He was probably on the point of beginning the series of *pointilliste* gouaches for the illustrated edition of Reverdy's prose-poems planned, but never published by Léonce Rosenberg (Plates 53, 55 and 56)[11]. To Henriette's gift Gris attached one of Reverdy's prose-poems. It was later included, in an amended form, in *Au Soleil du Plafond*. It also starts with the humble fact of the coffee-mill. In this early state, as complement to the gouache, it begins: "On the tablecloth / There are a few/grains of powder / or of coffee./The war or calm; but why / all together? The odour guided us in the evening more / than our eyes, and the mill ground our heads / with black"[12].

Gris's ordinary domestic utensils on the kitchen table of the studio at 13, rue Ravignan do not draw attention to themselves, but even these objects could not be, in themselves, simply stripped of meaning. They, like the attributes of the arts, are always there to be read. It is my intention in this essay to begin to read them.

Gris was probably not joined by Josette until the beginning of 1914[13]. She was, therefore, not with him at the time of his most solitary investigations of the object in 1910–12. It is, however, still significant that, where she could confirm that the carafes, coffee-pots, breakfast bowls, sugar-dishes and coffee-mills of Gris's still-life repertoire were indeed the everyday bric-a-brac of life in the one-room studio at 13, rue Ravignan, the guitars and violins were not. Braque, of course, surrounded himself with musical instruments in the studio, and liked to make music; Gris did not[14]. He saw musical instruments and heard music outside the studio, probably most of all in the cafés and, after 1920, in the dance-halls of Paris and the south. It is, therefore, not surprising perhaps to find only two musical instruments, both guitars, among the nineteen still-lives Gris painted between 1910 and the end of 1912, the years of his most intensely focused analytical enquiry. The pictures in question are *Still-life with Flowers* and *Guitar and Glasses* (Plates 8 and 9).

The near uniqueness of the musical instrument in *Still-life with Flowers* strengthens my earlier argument that its inclusion is a kind of homage to Braque[15], but *Guitar and Glasses* cannot, like the larger still-life, be related so easily to Braque's series of musical instrument paintings of 1910. For reasons that are not clear, this picture has always been known as *Banjo and Glasses*[16]. In fact, it is more straightforwardly read as a view down onto a table set at an angle, with the falling folds of a curtain on the left, and a guitar (only partly visible), pipe, glasses and a container (perhaps earthenware) set out upon it. What has been read as the body of a "banjo" is, on this reading, the sound-hole of the guitar, whose left shoulder and curved flank echo the lines of the curtain on the left. In the hole, beneath the strings, are words in Spanish, most legibly: "...de Guitarra de...".

This is Gris's first use of lettering (as distinct from his own hand-writing) in a painting. Coupled with the odd, elongated horizontal format, it is the cue for making connections, not just with Braque, but with Picasso who used such a format for some of his earliest still-lives to include lettering, most importantly *Still-life on a Piano*, which was probably begun at Céret in the summer of 1911 and finished around the date of *Guitar and Glasses* in spring 1912[17]. Where Braque's musical still-lives invoke the studio of the musical painter, Picasso's more often invoke the salon or especially the café (a place where songs are sung, newspapers are read and drinks consumed). Yet, whatever the setting, musical instruments are objects which have one crucial property not possessed by, say, a coffee-mill. They exist for performers and for listeners. They exist in a social setting. They signify not so much an object out there to be analysed by the studious observer in isolation, but an object that invites both immediate physical and psychological contact, and that engages the attention of many. Gris's guitars and violins are not simply more objects of objectivity; they represent something positively antithetical to the model of ascetic study, a move outside the studio. *Guitar and Glasses* must have been just completed when Gris began on *Man in the Café* (Plate 21). All his previous figure paintings had, of course, been studio portraits.

Especially in 1913, the guitar and violin are a ubiquitous feature of Gris's still-lives. Twenty out of the thirty-three still-lives of 1913 involve music, most of them guitars and/or violins. The proportion is far fewer in 1914, but musical instruments and music sheets are supplanted by a range of objects that hardly connote deprivation, isolation and high seriousness. There are open and closed books, but, although Max Jacob's *Saint Matorel* gets a mention, they are otherwise popular mysteries and adventures. The rest of the reading matter, especially in the *papiers collés,* is from the mass-circulation dailies, above all *Le Matin* and *Le Journal*. Domestic utensils including the coffee-mill return, but more often the ordinary objects on table-tops are objects of conviviality[18]. Cups and glasses come in pairs or clusters, rarely alone. There are packets of tobacco and cigarettes as well as pipes. There are cards, dice and board-games, all requiring players. And the settings are now often explicitly café settings. This is most apparent where the wooden is replaced by the marble table-top, for instance, in *The Siphon*, as early as April 1913 (Plate 26), and in *Fruit Dish and Carafe* (Plate 40). The table-top has become no longer the studio prop providing a neutral site for analytical investigation; it has become a concentrated focus for relaxation and conversation.

The social circle brought into play could be thought of as restricted: the circle within which the "private" word-games and personal allusions of the *collages* and the *papiers collés* have currency. It is nonetheless a circle that expands outside the studio into a public sphere of leisure, and it connects with others that spread far wider. The vanguard milieux of Montmartre and especially Montparnasse in 1913–14, the milieux of Paul Fort, Apollinaire, Serge Férat, the Baroness d'Oettingen or Picasso, were, after all, within that many-facetted bourgeois café society which Gris had so often caricatured as a humourist (Figure 30). To make images that evoked café worlds was to invite the spectator to step imaginatively outside the closed cultural circle of the vanguard into a social space where the seemingly oppositional categories "bohemian" and "bourgeois" overlap, indeed fade into each other under the sign of the "flaneur" (the strolling spectator). Men like Frank Haviland, Picasso's and Gris's acquaintance in Paris and Céret, come to mind[19].

There is no speech in the *papiers collés,* only writing. But, as I argued in the fourth essay, the conflicting idioms that they juxtapose so abruptly encourage an analogy with the babble of many voices, while their lack of clear syntactical cohesion, their fragmentariness, encourages an analogy with the language, not of writing, but of speech, especially the kind of volatile, spontaneous speech that must have been current in the cafés of Montmartre, Montparnasse or Céret[20]. As the fragments of newspaper, the labels, the wood-graining, the false-marbling and the objects of the *papiers collés* work metonymically to signify the noisy social arena of the cafés, the *papiers collés* themselves become a kind of visual chatter: a chatter whose preoccupations (from the Cubists, "ces explor... eurs", to pulp novels or the Balkan Wars) switch constantly from those of the avant-garde to those of the many other converging social groups that brushed against one another in the cafés[21].

Salmon's itemization of the humble objects of Gris's still-lives picks out, as we have seen, the bargain-basement fruit dish with its "white lustre". He does not mention the fruit offered in it. Gris included fruit and fruit dish in his still-lives for the first time in the autumn of 1913. In the earliest, painted at Céret in October 1913, fruit are, for the most part, black silhouetted voids, deprived of tactile substance[22]. The fruit dish with fruit reappeared in one or two of the *papiers collés* of 1914, including *Fruit Dish and Carafe* (Plate 40), and then, increasingly, in the paintings of 1915. An orange in a fruit dish glows, capturing light in front of the darkness outside in *Still-life and Townscape (Place Ravignan)* (Plate 48). The fruit of the compositions of 1914–15 are softly modelled, sumptuously coloured and sometimes gleam with highlights. The cheap porcelain fruit dish in *Still-life with Checked Tablecloth*, overflowing with grapes, is a kitchen cornucopia.

Fruit and fruit dishes figure still in the series of *pointilliste* still-lives that culminate in the pictures of March and April 1916, like *Fruit Dish on a Blue Tablecloth* (Plate 57). There is, however, a telling change now in their treatment, brought out by the relationship between *Fruit Dish on a Blue Tablecloth* and the gouache most closely connected to it from the group designed to illustrate Reverdy's prose-poems (Plate 55). I have remarked elsewhere on the fact that in the oil, the hat-shaped area of orange brushed across the piled fruit in the dish is painted over what originally were fruit modelled to give substance, more as they are in the gouache. Gris flattened the colour and set it among equally flat signs for apples rendered in negative[23]. He masked and voided the fruit in the dish, returning to the empty silhouettes of the autumn 1913 still-lives. The fruit in the *pointilliste* oils is always deprived of substance. It is offered as the crowning feature in *Newspaper and Fruit Dish* (Plate 54), but it has become a flat, highly abstracted symbol, without iconic force.

When, in the spring and summer of 1916 Gris switched to his austere chiaroscuro mode, he continued to paint fruit and fruit dishes, the apples, pears and grapes kept away from touch and emptied out into silhouette. *Fruit Dish, Glass and Newspaper* of July 1916 is a striking example (Plate 59). The canvas of a month later, *Fruit Dish, Glass and Lemon* (Plate 58), might be claimed as an exception: we are given, after all, the colour and even a suggestion of the texture of the lemon, and the solid forms of the fruit in the fruit dish. Yet, even here the presentation of the fruit can be read as a progressive removal of its substance from our grasp. The lemon is closest to us, but an angled brown plane juts up in front of it, and its faintly textured colour is allowed to seep into the grey surfaces around it. The modelled fruit in the dish occupies a middle ground, further away from touch, and all that is offered are shadowed volumes. At the furthest remove, behind the bowl, they have become empty shadow silhouettes. At each step they are less tangible, more an idea trapped in the insubstantial dimension of Socrates' shadows. Where fruit dishes do appear in the paintings of 1917, their fruit is consistantly without colour, texture or substance; the bowls can even be empty[24]. The drawings and paintings of 1917 (Plate 72 and Figure 19) repeatedly feature vessels that appear to be empty.

With this shift away from a still-life imagery of abundance late in 1915 and through 1916 and 1917, there is detectable in Gris's painting of objects a re-orientation from the convivial social space of the café back into the studio and the home. I have mentioned the domesticity of the coffee-making paraphenalia in *Breakfast*, and both *Still-life and Townscape (Place Ravignon)* and *The Pot of Geraniums* (Plates 52, 48 and 47) suggest unequivocally a domestic, not a café setting[25]. Furthermore, although the use of multiple idioms in 1915 continues to encourage the analogy with many voices, the fragmentary multifariousness of the *papiers collés* has been replaced by homogenous surfaces of oil-paint and, through 1916–17, as I have shown, would be succeeded by a growing commitment to compositional cohesion. The metaphor of café conversation is increasingly

Figure 44
Prose Poems, 1915
Gouache, pencil, charcoal and papier collé on paper, 18.5x27.5 cm
Private Collection

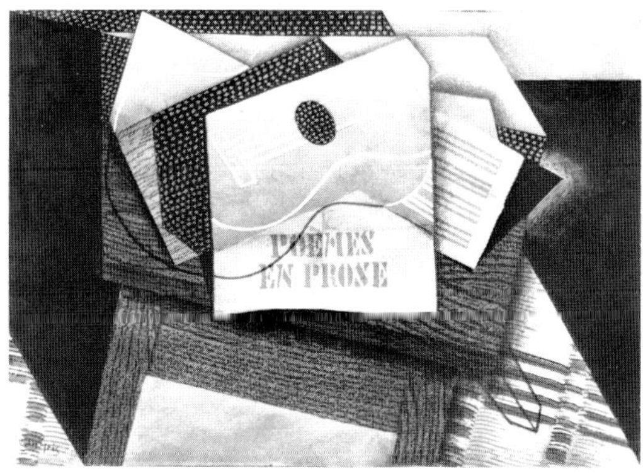

inapplicable. At the same time the sheer profusion of information, verbal as well as visual, is severely curtailed until there is not much chatter left. Newspapers do feature in the paintings that follow the *papiers collés* from early 1915 through the war years, but, beneath the single announcement *Le Journal* or *L'Intransigeant*, the words have been reduced to lines. There is nothing to be read.

Throughout 1916–17, the violins and guitars return regularly, alongside the emptied out fruit-bowls and newspapers. But they too have become further removed. Most noticeably, just as the newspapers are deprived of copy, the music sheets are deprived of music. The major musical instrument painting of late 1915, *Guitar on a Table* (Plate 50), is accompanied by open music sheets without a single note: there is nothing to perform. In one still-life of December 1917 musical notation does appear[26], but on the two occasions that music sheets are included in the still-lives between *Guitar on a Table* of October 1915 and the December 1917 picture more than two years later, they are also without music. Inevitably, the allusion to the possible encounter between player and listener in performance is reduced. Indeed, on one occasion the guitar is specifically, even deliberately placed in the solitary space of the studio or home rather than the social space of the café. Like *Breakfast*, *Guitar on a Table* is directly related to a gouache that forms virtually a pair with it (Figure 44). This gouache too is connected with the prose-poems of Pierre Reverdy; below the instrument are the words "Poèmes en prose". It seems to have been projected as a possible title page for Léonce Rosenberg's putative edition. In this case, anyway, the guitar is aligned with the intensely inward, contemplative pursuit of reading poetry. The social noise of the café is shut out.

The voided objects of the still-lives painted by Gris between late 1915 and late 1917 are easily read in terms of the encroaching "white" of purification. I have alluded to Plato's shadows of things that cannot be grasped, and there is no doubt that these fruits without substance, these empty vessels and these pages without content can signify a refusal of the transcient and the "real" for an espousal of the transcendent and the "ideal". The relegation of the object to secondary status in relation to pictorial "architecture" is plainly declared. The object is *visibly* pretext or afterthought. These still-lives can be read, however, in terms of much wider connotations that, as in the case of the portraits of Josette and the peasant figure-paintings, take in the themes and preoccupations of war-time on the home-front in the broadest sense.

In a straightforward, even obvious way, Gris's still-lives of this phase give us objects that signify the bleak deprivation of war-time. Reverdy's image, in response to the coffee-mill – "The mill ground our heads/with black" – is indeed in tune with them. I noted in my last essay the fact that agricultural production dropped and prices rose significantly from the first harvest of the war in August 1914. Between summer 1914 and summer 1918, the price of a kilo of steak rose from 3.80 to 7.80 francs in Paris, a kilo of bread from 40 to 47 centimes, and a "quintel" of potatoes from 13 to 50 francs. The rises accelerated especially through 1917–18. In the town food costs had more than doubled by the end of the war, eggs and cheese had more then tripled in price[27]. The shortages led to regulations curtailing the opening hours of hotels and restaurants, and the prohibition of the consumption of butter, milk, cream and cheese in public places. It was forbidden, as well, to serve sugar[28].

On a personal level, Gris's correspondence makes it clear that, certainly in 1915, before the lack of support from the exiled Kahnweiler was made good by Léonce Rosenberg, and early in 1917, when the cold coincided with serious coal shortages, he felt the effects of austerity. As for most, it was less a feature of his life, it seems, in the country at Beaulieu[29]. If the appetizing abundance of the fruit in the fruit dishes of the still-lives of 1915 can suggest hope combined with a vain wish for plenty, the lacks in the still-lives of 1916–17 can suggest the resignation of hard realizations. That their austere emptiness is combined with a "classic" orderliness in a framework of allusions to the "French tradition" as represented by Chardin or Cézanne gives a positive, sustaining tone to the theme of deprivation. These still-lives can be read as assertions of the enduring firmness of French resolve. They complement well the sturdy stability of *The Peasant in a Blue Smock*, *Seated Peasant Woman* and *The Man from the Touraine*. They too are consonant with the themes of national strength in adversity, of the "Union Sacrée".

A fruit dish with pears stands as the crux of the most elaborate and resolved of the still-lives Gris painted at Beaulieu-lès-Loches in 1918 (Plate 89). Dish and fruit combine rather differently from previously. Black, brown and warm ochre are used to give tonal values that model the pears; their forms have weight and substance. At the same time, the bowl of the fruit dish takes on the ogee curves of the pears. Bowl and fruit fuse as they echo each other in rhyme. On the level of the metaphor, the bowl becomes the fruit and the fruit the bowl. Colours remain within a restricted range; neither they nor the surface suggest the qualities of fruit, but rather, as I have argued, the hard materials of vernacular construction: stone, slate and tile. But the pears have become a tangible presence, and their forms are determining.

From 1918 and especially from 1920 the fruits in Gris's still-lives were to have their body, lushness and surface texture restored. But the rhyming of pears and dish in *Guitar and Fruit Dish* introduces another factor in Gris's use of objects which was to become central to the way they signify in the paintings of his last seven or eight years: pictorial metaphor as a mode of linkage, indeed of fusion.

In his important discussion of Gris's pictorial metaphors, published at the time of the Galerie Simon exhibition in 1923, Maurice Raynal stressed the point that, in metaphor, so complete is the similarity drawn out between one thing and another that they become one and the same, a new, *composite* thing[30]. The pears in the fruit-dish-as-pears deliver a clear demonstration of what he meant. The implications of this are inescapable: such a metaphorical representation gives the qualities of one thing to another, and *vice-versa*. The pears have fruit dish curves, the fruit dish has the soft swelling body of pears.

In this case, the objects fused to construct a new metaphorical object are directly related by contiguity. Fruit dishes are designed to hold fruit, including pears. From 1918 on, Gris's metaphors, like the image-making of the poets of the Reverdy circle, often fused objects whose relatedness was not a given in this way. The structural rhyme that brings together in metaphor the guitar and the fruit dish loaded with grapes about the axis of *Guitar and Fruit Dish* in July 1919 makes it possible to respond to the idea of two very different things, as if they can share each other's qualities (Plate 98). These grapes are hard and flat, this guitar is soft. Both classes of objects invite touch, but differently: the grapes can be plucked, so too can the guitar strings. Each suggests a different area of sensation: one taste, the other sound. The metaphor can seem to fuse even these sensations: both the sound and the taste could be sweet. Raynal was to write of the "truth" of Gris's metaphors as residing in the rightness with which "elements of the same quality" are brought out in different things[31].

Gris's return, especially after 1920, to objects of conviviality and abundance presented in emphatically substantial forms went with a use of metaphor that worked continually to connect and fuse not merely different classes of object, but different categories of sensation: taste, sound and vision. The musical and the edible (or drinkable) are repeatedly brought into metaphorical conjunction by visual rhyming.

This is perhaps most clearly demonstrable if one looks at the proliferation of rhyming lips and mouths in the still-lives of 1920–22. The *Guitar and Fruit Dish* considered in relation to a couple of contemporary images from 1919 provides a good preface to them. The glass of the still-life, as we have seen in a previous essay, has been developed from the glass *motif* of an earlier gouache and painting (Figure 21)[32]. The shaping of the glass with its setting of planes in this earlier state almost doubles that of the head in the *Harlequin at a Table* of around the same date (Plate 88). In this case, the mouth of the glass makes a single elipse of the Harlequin's eyes, but in *Harlequin at a Table*, the un-masked Harlequin's eyes in the mask-like face rhyme with his mouth, which rhymes with the mouth of the head-like glass on the table. The mouths of glasses from which lips drink come together with a mouth that can speak or sing, and eyes that see. In French and Spanish as in English, mouth ("bouche", "boca") is synonymous with opening, all vessels or containers can have mouths.

In both the closed and open still-lives of 1920–22 a play on openings as mouths links musical instruments and vessels or containers related to drinking or eating, everywhere, especially guitars and glasses. *Guitar, Pipe and Sheets of Music*, painted just before Gris's first bout of illness (Figure 45), takes up the rhyming fusion of guitar and fruit dish from the picture of 1919, and underpins the linkages by a chain of ovals: the sound holes of the guitar and the mouths of the glass and fruit dish. The vertical orientation of the sound-hole oval simulates the wide open mouth of the singer. Comparable patterns of mouth-like ovals encourage the imaginative fusion of guitars that "sing" and glasses for the lips to touch in *The Bay*, *The View Across the Bay* and *The Cloud*, among the open window still-lives of 1921, and in *Guitar and Fruit Dish* of December 1921 among the closed still-lives (Plates 100, 99, 102 and 111). The later developments from the vertical still-life fusion of the musical and the edible first mooted in *Guitar and Fruit Dish* of 1919 include *Guitar, Carafe and Fruit Dish* of December 1921 and *The Book of Music* of 1922 (Figure 23 and Plate 97). In the first picture, the open mouth of the carafe, with its thick lips of glass, is placed to double for the guitar's sound-hole. The sound is to be drunk from the instrument and from the carafe: both have the quality of fluidity. In the second picture, the play on mouths has been replaced by a simple fusion of shape that includes the book, coloured the blue of sky or water, and then set within it, the word "Musique". The sound-hole is masked, but the word is enough to signify sound.

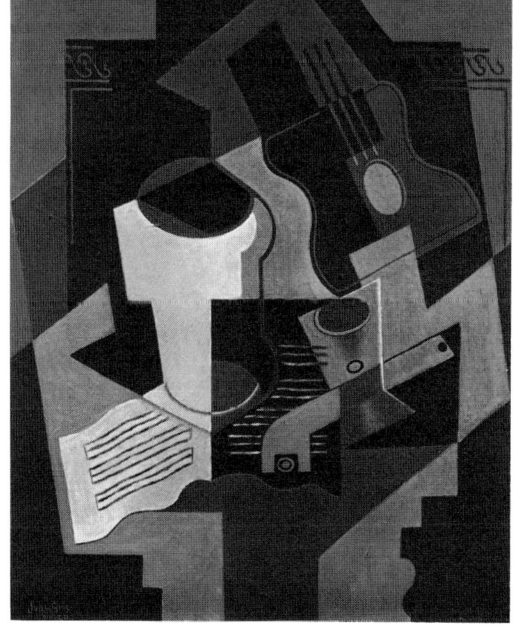

Figure 45
Guitar, Pipe and Sheets of Music, 1920
Oil on canvas,
81 x 65 cm
Van Abbemuseum,
Eindhoven

The linkages offered, then, by visual rhymes as pictorial metaphors worked by the early 1920s in Gris's still-lives to amplify an engagement not only with cohesive construction (the binding properties of metaphor), but also with the senses. There is a repeated linking of things that are to be touched, heard or tasted as well as seen. This gives obvious force to the contrast between the war-time still-lives of austerity, characterized by the removal of things from direct contact with the senses (as the shadows of "ideas"), and the still-lives that Gris painted especially after his first illness of 1920. There is more to the contrast than simply a restoration to things of colour, surface-texture and substance.

A further point needs to be made about the still-lives of 1920–22 and indeed later, one which underlines their contiguity with the figure-paintings that were produced alongside them, especially the *Commedia dell'Arte* figures, and one which distinguishes them still more sharply from the images of war-time deprivation. They are theatrical. By this I do not mean that their objects evoke the theatre or theatrical characters, I mean that the use of internal framing devices, most obviously the open window, and the scaling of objects together with their positioning on the table-tops within their "frames" is often manifestly stage-like. The curtains drawn back to display the objects and the landscape back-drops of *The Table in Front of the Window*, *The Bay* and *Open Window with Hills* (Plates 101, 100 and 112) makes the analogy with the prosenium stage almost explicit. Like Gris's Harlequins and Pierrots, his still-lives after 1920 can often be seen as highly conventionalized pictorial dramas frozen into the immobility of *tableaux,* where the characters are objects and the *dramatis personae* are restricted to a few, easily recognised character-types established by tradition. The guitars and violins, glasses, bottles and carafes, fruit and fruit dishes – in fact all of his normal still-life repertoire – are as familiar as the masks and costumes of the Italian comedy.

In a particular case, indeed, it is possible to read one of Gris's still-life objects as a surrogate *Commedia dell'Arte* character. At the turn of 1925–26, he painted *The Flower on a Table* (Plate 117). Here a single flower shaped like a rose in a bed of leaves is substituted for the sound hole of the guitar, while the vase in which it stands merges with the body of the instrument. We have a guitar-flower, or a flower-guitar. From the early days of 1912–14, Picasso especially had established the guitar as an analogue of woman[33]. The rose too has often been associated with woman, and indeed when Gris first took roses as his subject in the *papier collé Flowers* in 1914 (Plate 44), he may well have done so with a particular woman in mind, Josette. It was made three months after Josette moved in to 13, rue Ravignan, and the incorporation so legibly of the words "La Merveill(e) aérienne" (Aerial Marvel) and "Déclaratio(n)" gives it a strongly personal, even intimate tone, as if these roses are an offering, a "declaration" of commitment to her[34]. In the context of the *Commedia dell'Arte* the rose is the attribute of Colombine especially as Adolphe Willette characterized her. The one character in the *Commedia dell'Arte* triangular relationship between Harlequin, Pierrot and Colombine that Gris never painted was Colombine. In Willette's depictions, the transcience of the love-wish is symbolised by Colombine's love for her rose. To see her here in the rose-like bloom of *The Flower on the Table* is fanciful, as is my reading of the *papier collé Flowers,* but metaphors stimulate fancy.

Gris had used framing devices, of course, in earlier still-lives, once in a way that does anticipate the theatricality of the pictures of the 1920s with the open window of *Still-life and Townscape (Place Ravignan)* (Plate 48), where the objects are even spot-lit, as if by stage lighting. Most significantly, however, he had used pictorial framing in the way that I have discussed previously with reference to the *papiers collés* of 1914 and the "architectural" pictures of the turn of 1917–18, and in both these phases the frame in the picture had functioned as the sign of painting as a high art: something to be challenged by the "low" in 1914, as in *Flowers,* and to be embraced in 1917–18. The theatrical analogy is not a factor.

The contrast between the *papiers collés* of 1914 and the stagey still-lives of the 1920s is particularly revealing of the way theatricality functions in the later pictures. If Cubist art, like Brechtian theatre, revealed the artificiality of art as a representational process of sign-making, it did so most unmistakably in the *collages* and *papiers collés* of 1912–14. As I have remarked, it did so by the very plurality of its idioms, which, of course, expose them all as signs arbitrarily related to their referents. The roses in *Flowers* appear simultaneously in cheap colour-reproduction and in meticulously drawn pencil renderings. The post-1916 stress on compositional integration in Gris's work went, of course, with an insistance on a homogeneity or at least a cohesiveness of idiom. The signs for objects are increasingly unified within the unity of the pictorial architecture. Other means are required to expose the essentially artificial, arbitrary status of the painting, its semiotic workings. The theatrical analogy was perfectly adapted to this.

Since the first attempts of the Prague School theorists in the 1930s to systematize a semiotics of the theatre, it has been argued that one of the effects of the stage is to semiotize everything on it, that is to lift things out of their practical situations in life and turn them into signs, representations. This applies to the simplest objects. A table on the stage is no longer that actual table, it *represents* the class of tables generally, and specifically has a role in setting the scene or even, like the actor, in developing the action[35]. By playing on the theatrical analogy in his still-lives of the 1920s, Gris drew attention to the semiotization of all his objects, to the fact that they function linguistically as signs (what Kahnweiler was to call painting as writing)[36]. His coloured pictorial elements do not *become* objects, they *perform* as objects, just as they can perform as Pierrots or Harlequins.

The theory of the sign in the theatre has further been developed by Tadeusz Kowzan in a direction that makes of artificiality a fundamental principle of theatre. Kowzan distinguishes between what he calls "natural" and "artificial" signs. Natural signs operate where signifier and signified are linked by physical laws (smoke signifies fire, a certain colour and texture in fruit signifies a certain taste). Artificial signs depend on human volition (most obviously, they include languages developed for signalling purposes, for instance semaphore). Kowzan's point is that, on stage, even *natural* signs are artificialized; they become signs that are willed. "Even if they have no communication function in life," he writes, "they necessarily acquire it on stage"[37]. Such, evidently, is the case of Gris's "natural signs", above all his fruit in the stage-like spaces of his still-lives. Their semiotic artificiality is strikingly enhanced by their theatricality.

Considered as utterances (*Parole*), the theatrical still-lives of the 1920s are again sharply distinct from the *papiers collés* of 1914. If *collage* and *papier collé* is to be thought of as conversational, the theatrical still-lives certainly are not. They are characterized not by the fragmentary disjunction of elements, but by their structured *con*junction. They relate to the "textual control" of highly conventionalized dramatic discourse, like that of the *Commedia dell'Arte* where, despite the accent on the invention of the actors in each performance, the play of character and the development of plot are strictly determined. As Keir Elam has put it: "digressions, redundancies, *non-sequitors,* sudden changes of topic and even an overall inconclusiveness are often permitted without detriment to the *purpose-success* of the conversation. Dramatic dialogue, on the other hand, is normally powerfully constrained throughout by various levels of textural coherence". Among the levels he defines are "rhetorical and stylistic coherence", and "semantic coherence", the one referring to the idiom, the other preventing diversionary ambiguities; both are found in Gris's theatrical still-life "performances"[38].

Finally, the theatricality of these pictures encourages another kind of response that semioticians of the theatre have isolated, what has been called the "making of worlds". On stage, the part the audience sees is taken to signify an enormously larger whole: a room can signify an entire house of a certain class in a certain kind of place where a certain kind of life is led, outside as well as inside it. Using a term borrowed from the classical rhetoricians, this signification of larger wholes by parts is dubbed *synecdoche*. It is a common feature of the theatrical stage-set. It is, in fact, a feature of most Cubist still-lives (we have seen already how they can evoke the studio or the café), but, because of their theatricality, it is more strikingly a feature of many of Gris's still-lives of the 1920s.

Of all his theatrical synecdoches, the most effective are, of course, the open window still-lives (Plates 99–102 and 112). And the world that they allow us to construct imaginatively from their interiors and especially from their views outside is a world that inevitably complements, indeed helps determine the expectation signified by the objects they contain. In those that look out onto sea and sky it is a world of leisure and syberitic indulgence, the world of the post-war Riviera. Beneath the window-sill there are to be imagined the café-terraces of the promenade at Bandol (or it could as well be St. Raphael or Juan-les-Pins or Nice). There is the sun and the cooling breeze, and besides the sailing boat coaxed by the wind in *The Bay*, there are the beaches for the sun- and sea-bathers. This is the world where Marcelle and Jean "the Musician" Brune invite Gris and Josette to dine and then to dance until 3 o'clock in the morning. It is a world that offers great and varied pleasures to the senses, like everything in the paintings. We need only to see a slice of it as a picture-postcard back-drop and the tonic tone is set. These objects are there to be enjoyed and relished: to be touched, played with, listened to.

There remain still-lives by Gris painted after 1920 which continue to suggest by synecdoche the closed world of the studio, and where the controlling geometry and the cool greys, blues and browns discourage anything that could be called hedonistic indulgence. Pictures like *Guitar, Carafe and Fruit Dish* of 1921 and *The Music-book* of 1922 are still related to the austere "constructions" of war-time. Yet, even here, as I have shown, the objects work through metaphoric fusion to generate connotations of touch, taste and sound. It is the potential for pleasure that is controlled. Maurice Raynal wrote that Gris's metaphors were constructions: not "a pile of stones", but "the house constructed"[39]. What Gris built in most of his still-lives after 1920, and especially in the open windows, set aside austerity altogether: they were, following Raynal's terminology, edifices of pleasure. Their linkage of sensations in metaphor, their direct appeal to the senses by surface texture and colour, and their theatricality mounted a challenge against the self-denying ethos of war-time and against Gris's own fear of death that was comprehensive and profound. Much in these still-lives actually denies the "white" of purification. Theirs is an imagery of release and recovery. They invoke the life of the senses *against* the abstractions of the intellect and offer resolution. Salmon's "sweet desserts" were, after all, placed on the table.

Gris continued to build edifices of pleasure to the end of his life. There are no still-lives of the phase between late 1922 and late 1924 that can be effectively linked to the austerity of war-time, but in his last two or three years Gris added to this range of pleasurable still-lives pictures that include objects which generate rather different connotations. These objects include those that I called objects of subjectivity at the beginning of this essay, in contradistinction to my category, objects of objectivity: the painter's palette and brushes are among them, and so are the busts which allude to either the Orphic or the Apollonian artist. Certainly, as I contended, these are objects which place Gris, the idealized artist-subject, in the picture. On a different level, however, they are objects which confront the indulgence of the senses with the idea of art as something elevated and pure. I am tempted to call them edifices of cultural value.

The linkages of metaphor work, as they had in 1920–22, in *The Musician's Table*, *The Painter's Window* and *The Open Book* (Plates 116, 118 and 113). Furthermore, in all three they link the musical to the edible or drinkable. A flask of water echoes the curves of the guitar in *The Musician's Table*, its mouth responding to the sound-hole, while in both the others musical instruments are locked to fruit dishes, the sound-hole of the guitar in one echoing the pears in the bowl, the guitar's sound-hole in the other echoing the mouth of the fruit dish. *The Painter's Window* gives us a stage-like table and an allusion to the proscenium. But built into the structure of metaphor in all these cases are symbols of enduring value. Wedged between the guitar and the fruit dish in *The Painter's Window* is, as we have seen, the painter's palette and brush. Touching both guitar and water flask in *The Musician's Table* is the bust of Opheus or Apollo, his eye doubled by the mouth of the flask (aesthetic vision as the taste of "pure" water). Jutting up against the guitar and the fruit-bowl in *The Open Book* is a heavy book, open face-upwards on the table. How we read these conjunctions between objects is, of course, open. We could read them as the placing of cultural value in the province of pleasure, especially in *The Painter's Window* and *The Open Book*. And we could read them as the *submission* of the pleasurable to the transcendent ideal of cultural value. Either way, they signify validation, and suggest an anticipation of the commitment to Humanist values that would become evident in the writings of the established defenders of the Cubist vanguard in the years immediately following 1927, most notably Waldemar George and D.-H. Kahnweiler[40].

But, for Gris himself, perhaps more than anything they were talismans: his defence against death.

1 André Salmon, *Souvenirs sans fin, Troisième Epoque (1920–1940),* Paris, 1961, p. 278.

2 Ibid.

3 For further discussion, see chapter 5 above.

4 André Lhote, Letter (1918); in "Pinturrichio" (Louis Vauxcelles), 'Le Carnet des ateliers: Au pays du cube', *Le Carnet de la semaine,* 6 October 1918, p. 7.

5 Christian Zervos, 'Les Problèmes de la jeune peinture, II. Le retour au sujet est-il probable?', *Cahiers d'art,* no. 4, 1931, p. 198.

6 Waldemar George, 'Les Cinquante ans de Picasso et la morte de la nature-morte', *Formes,* no. 14, April 1931, p. 56.

7 Letter to D.-H. Hahnweiler, 10 February 1921; in *Letters of Juan Gris (1913–1927),* translated and edited by Douglas Cooper, London, 1956, pp. 93–4 (Letter CXIII).

8 Juan Gris, 'On the Possibilities of Painting', lecture delivered 15 May 1924 to the Société des études philosophiques et scientifiques pour l'examen des idées nouvelles', at the Sorbonne, Paris; in Kahnweiler (1969), op. cit., p. 199.

9 See chapter 6 above.

10 "Moulin à café / levant au travers / Les ailes de ton nez frémissant / Un rhythme lent / Romance / Le ciel tourne / Une roue // Ces lettres sous la porte / Une vie nouvelle / Guerre lontaine / Et mon verre qui fume / Une clarté couronne l'univers". Paul Dermée, 'Deux poèmes, 1', *Nord-Sud,* Paris, no. 12, February 1918, n.p. The second of the two poems takes an Ace of Clubs as its "pretext".

11 See chapter 3, note 53 above.

12 "Sur la table il y avait quelques grains de poudre / ou de café. La guerre ou le repos; mais pourquoi / tout ensemble? L'odeur nous guidait le soir plus / que nos yeux et le moulin broyait du noir, dans / nos têtes". The amendments to the poem were to introduce new images. See Pierre Reverdy, 'Moulin de café', *Au Soleil du plafond,* Paris, 1955. The word-play in this poem is difficult to approximate in English. The phrase "broyer du noir" invokes the grinding of coffee, but can mean to be depressed, to have the "blues". My thanks to Charlotte Green for her help with this translation.

13 Cooper gives the date February 1914 as when Josette became Gris's "compagne". See Cooper, op. cit., 'Eléments biographiques', p. XL. This was confirmed for me by Mme Gris. Conversation with Madame Josette Gris, 20 July 1977.

14 Madame Gris told me that they never actually owned a violin or a guitar. Ibid.

15 See my discussion in chapter 1 above. For Braque and music, see Sophie Bowness, 'Braque and Music', in *Braque: Still-lifes and Interiors,* The South Bank Centre, London, 1990, pp. 57–67.

16 It is given this title in Cooper's Catalogue Raisonné (see no. 21)

17 See Pierre Daix and Joan Rosselet, *Picasso: The Cubist Years,* 1907–1916, *A Catalogue Raisonné of the Paintings and Related Works,* London, 1979, p. 278, no. 462; also p. 268, no. 417 and p. 272, no. 432.

18 The coffee-mill only returns in one *papier collé:* Cooper no. 105.

19 Haviland was the cousin of Picasso's patron Hamilton Easter Field. A friend of the Steins, patron of the sculptor Manolo Hugué at Céret, he was a member of a wealthy family involved in the Limoges porcelain industry. Gris's *The Smoker* (Figure 8) was preceded by a drawing which he gave to Haviland. For further information on Haviland, see William Rubin, 'Appendix: the Library of Hamilton Easter Field' and Judith Cousins, with the collaboration of Pierre Daix, 'Documentary Chronology'; in William Rubin, *Picasso and Braque: Pioneering Cubism,* The Museum of Modern Art, New York, 1989.

20 See chapter 2 above.

21 For contrasting views of the significance of above all the newspaper cuttings that refer to the Balkan Wars, see Patricia Leighten, 'Picasso's Collages and the Threat of War, 1912–13', *Art Bulletin,* December 1985 and David Cottington, 'What the Papers Say: Politics and Ideology in Picasso's Collages of 1912', *Art Journal,* Winter, 1988, pp. 350–59. Leighten was the first to draw attention to the Balkan Wars as an issue in the collages.

22 Cooper no. 61.

23 See Christopher Green, 'Synthesis and the 'synthetic process' in the painting of Juan Gris 1915–19', *Art History,* March 1982, p. 91.

24 See for example Cooper nos. 226 and 244.

25 In fact, Madame Gris told me that *The Pot of Geraniums* is a fictitious subject. She never grew geraniums at 13, rue Ravignan, and the picture does not feature a window that looked out from the rear of the "Bateau-Lavoir". The setting is invented.

26 It is, however, highly abstracted. See Cooper no. 243.

27 Besides giving these details on price rises, Thébaud discusses the development of austerity cuisine in the War. See Françoise Thébaud, *La Femme au temps de la guerre de 14,* Paris, 1986, pp. 211–212.

28 See Michel Augé-Laribé, *L'Agriculture pendant la geurre,* Paris, 1925.

29 See *Letters* (Cooper, 1956), op. cit., pp. 38–9.

30 Maurice Raynal in *Feuilles libres,* no. 31, April 1923; republished in *Anthologie de la peinture en France de 1906 à nos jours,* Paris, 1927, p. 174.

31 Ibid.

32 See chapter 3 above.

33 See the essay by Karin von Maur below where she argues that Gris can also be seen to make this analogy.

34 "Aerienne" can also be translated as light in the sense of light-footed, so that "Merveille aérienne" could well refer to Josette.

35 The crucial texts are Otakar Zich's *Aesthetics of the Art of Drama* and Jan Mukarovsky's 'An Attempted Structural Analysis of the Phenomena of the Actor', both of 1931, Petr Bogatyrev's 'Semiotics in the Folk Theatre' of 1938, and Jiri Veltrusky's 'Man and the Object in the Theatre' of 1940 (the last published in translation in Paul L. Garvin, *A Prague School Reader on Aesthetics, Literary Structure and Style,* Washington, 1964). My analysis here is especially indebted to Keir Elam, *The Semiotics of Theatre and Drama,* London and New York, 1980, pp. 5–9. Altogether, this discussion owes much to Elam, although it is the first to see its implications for reading late Cubist painting.

36 See my discussion of Kahnweiler's theory of the sign in chapter 4 above.

37 Tadeusz Kowzan, 'The Sign in the Theatre' (1968); in *Diogenes,* 61, pp. 52–80. Again, see Elam (1980), op. cit., p. 20.

38 Ibid., pp. 182–4.

39 Raynal (1923); in Raynal (1927), op. cit., p. 174.
40 In Kahnweiler's case, his first monograph on Gris is a clear demonstration. See Daniel Henry (D.-H. Kahnweiler), *Juan Gris,* Leipzig and Berlin, 1929; in French translation in D.-H. Kahnweiler, *Confessions esthétiques,* Paris, 963. Waldemar George's periodical *Formes,* which ran 31 numbers between January 1930 and 1933, was licated to "néo-humanisme".

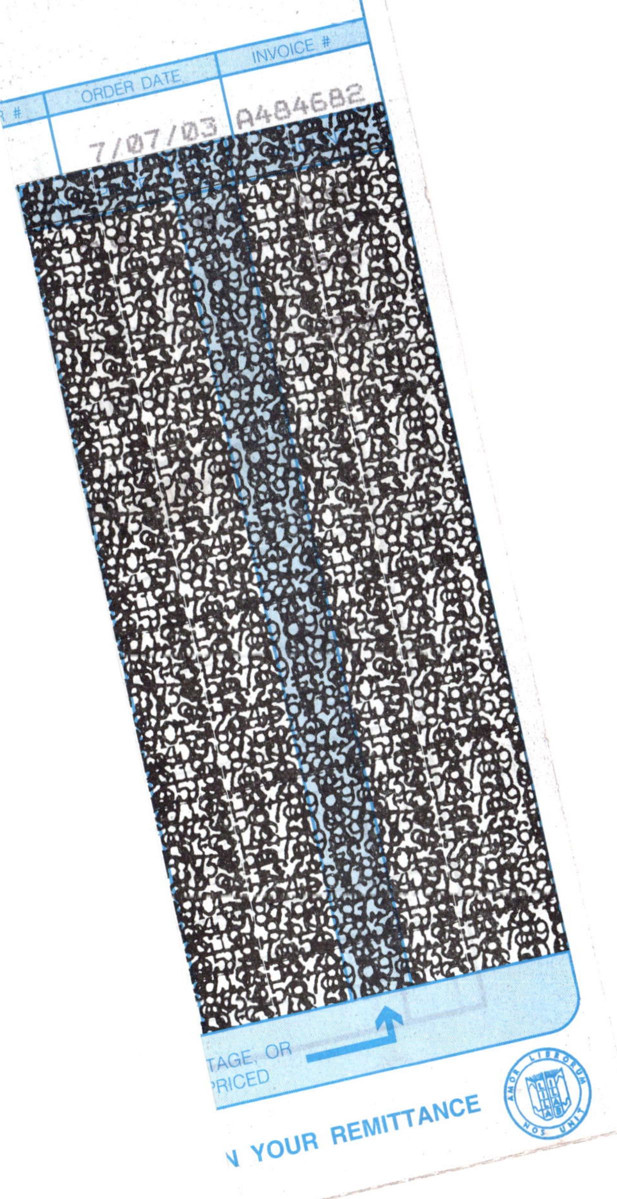

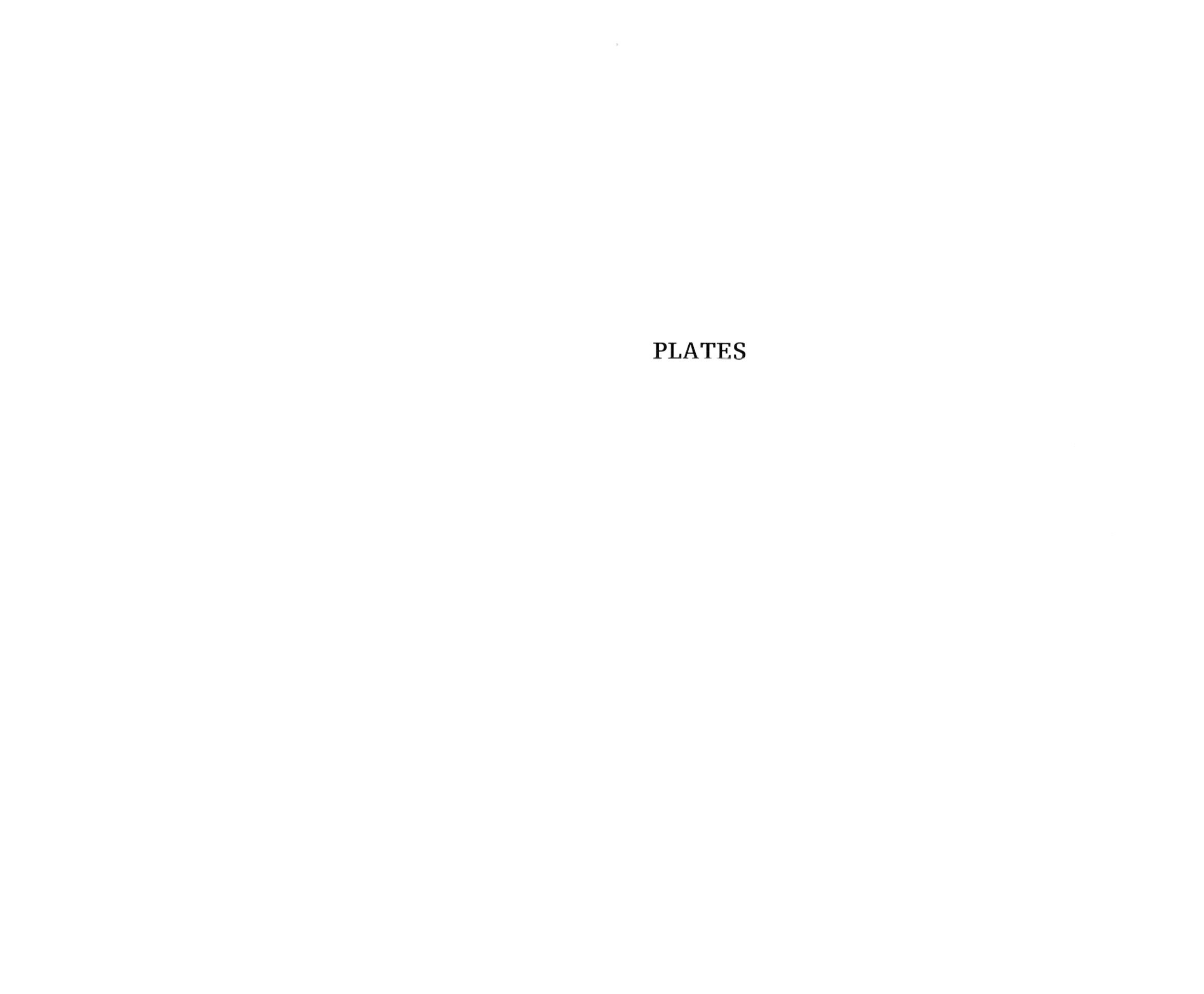

PLATES

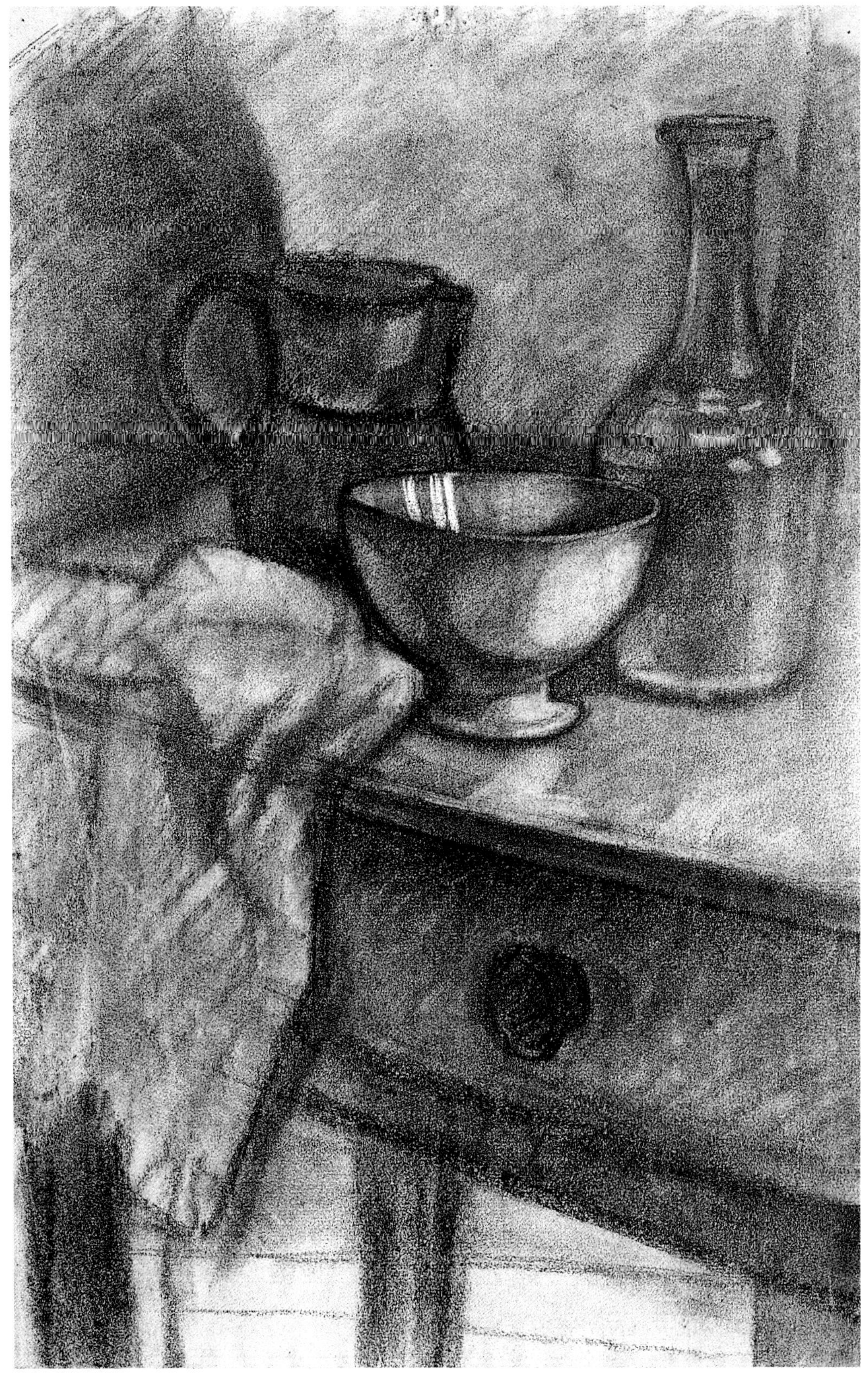

1
Still-life with Bowl,
1910
Charcoal and gouache on paper, 48 x 31.5 cm
Galerie Louise Leiris, Paris

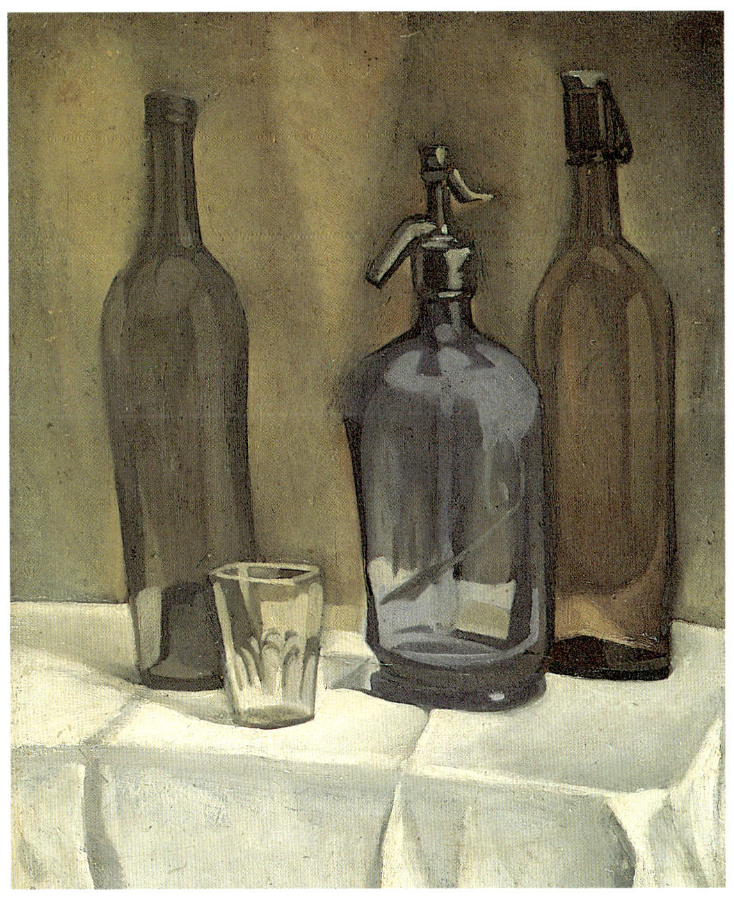

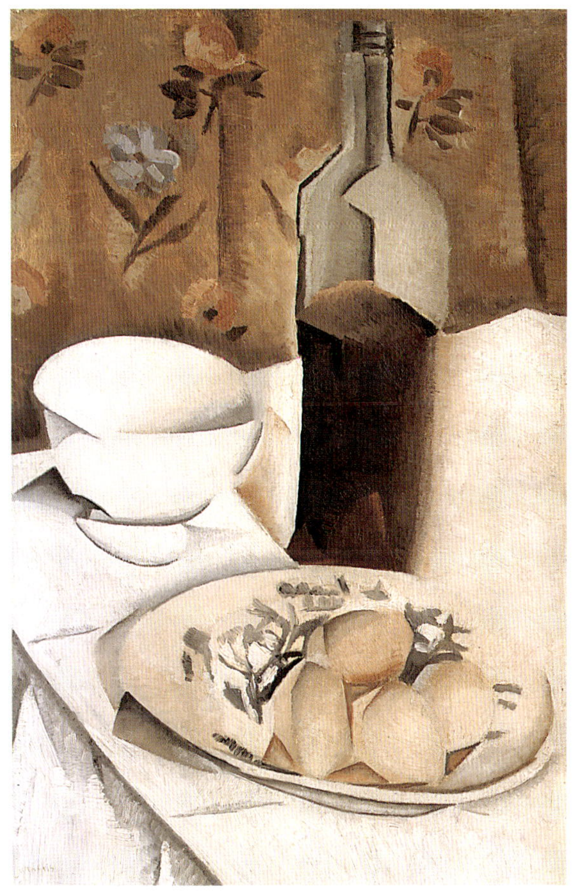

2
Siphon and Bottles,
1910
Oil on board on canvas,
57 x 48 cm
Georges González Gris

3
The Eggs, 1911
Oil on canvas, 57x38 cm
Staatsgalerie Stuttgart

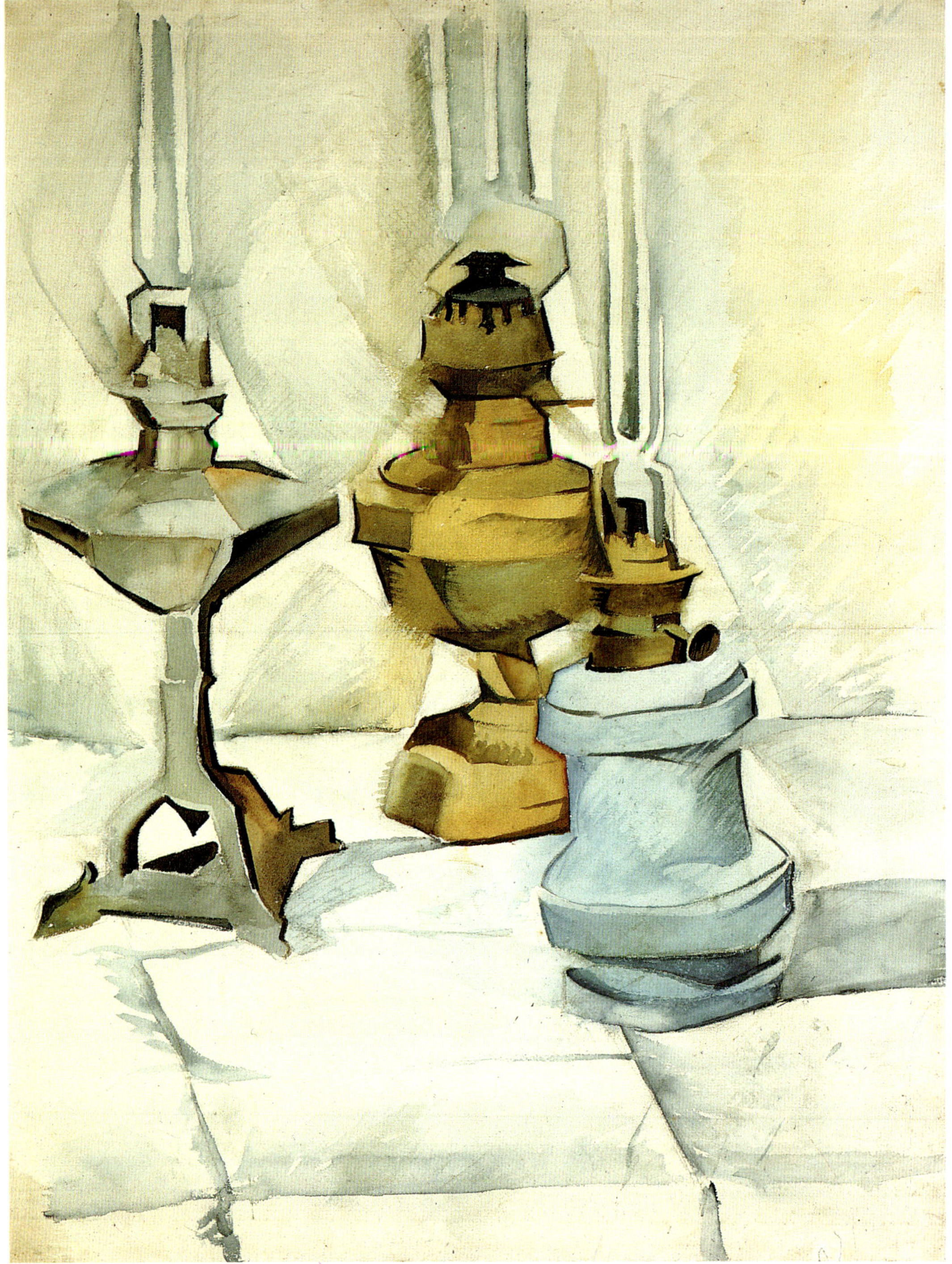

4
Three Lamps, 1910–11
Watercolour on paper,
61.8 x 47.8 cm
Kunstmuseum Bern,
Hermann and Margrit
Rupf Foundation
[London and Stuttgart
only]

5
Still-life with Bottle and Funnel, 1911
Pencil on paper, 47.9 x 31.6 cm
The Museum of Modern Art, New York. Alva Gimbel Fund

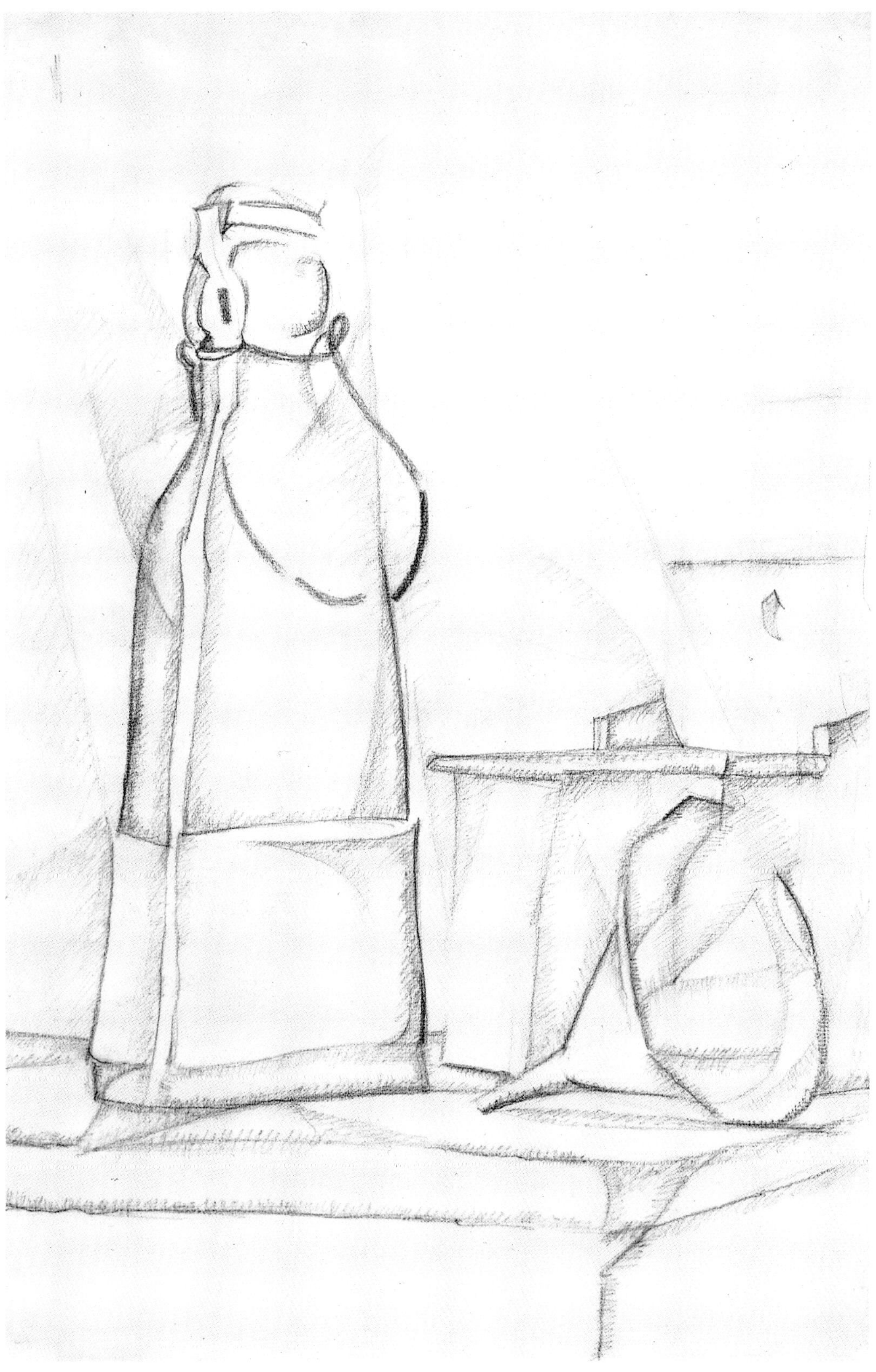

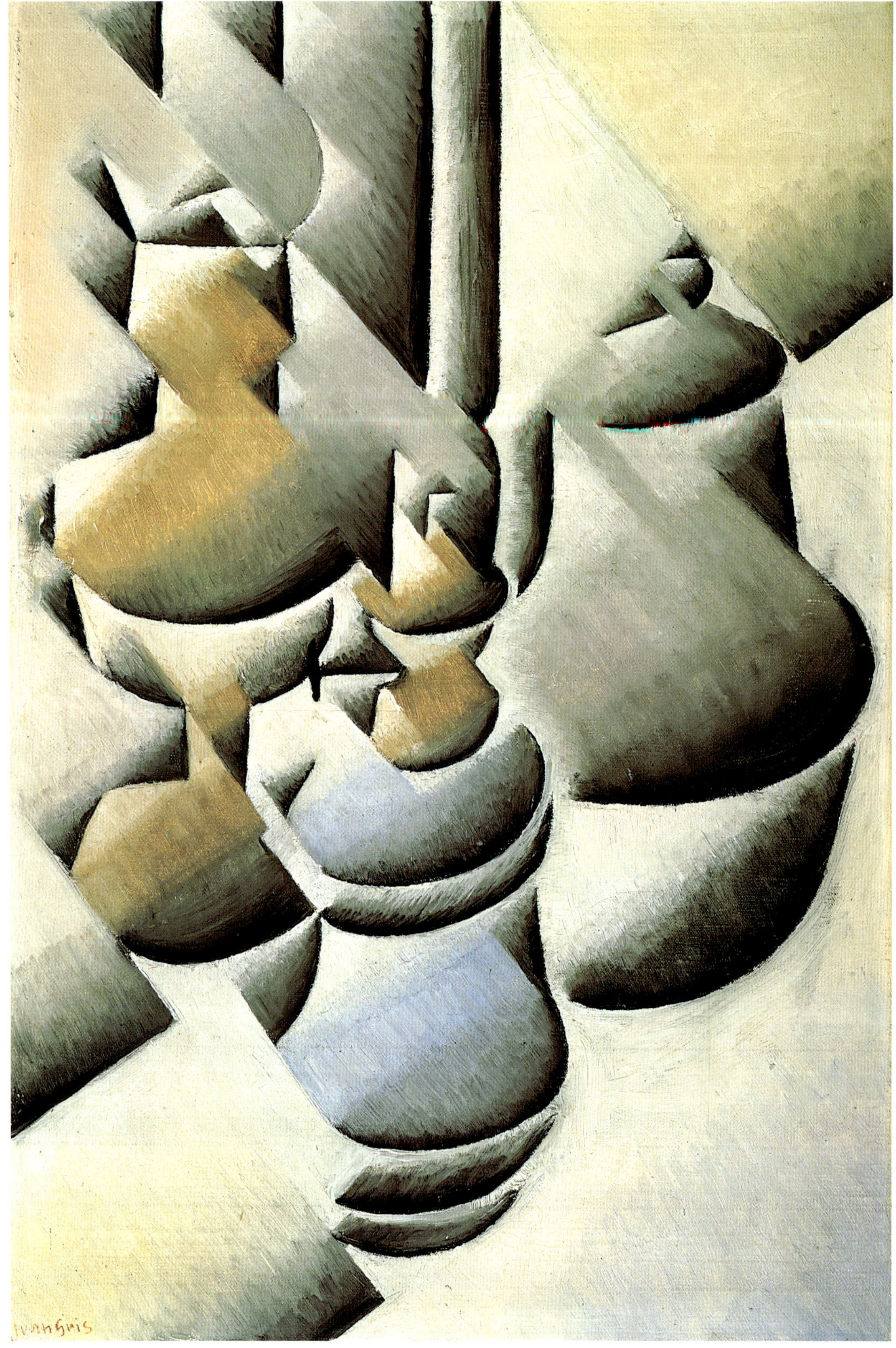

6
Still-life with Oil Lamp, 1911–12
Oil on canvas,
48 x 33 cm
Rijksmuseum Kröller-Müller, Otterlo

7
Bottles and Knife, 1911–12
Oil on canvas,
54.6 x 46 cm
Rijksmuseum Kröller-Müller, Otterlo

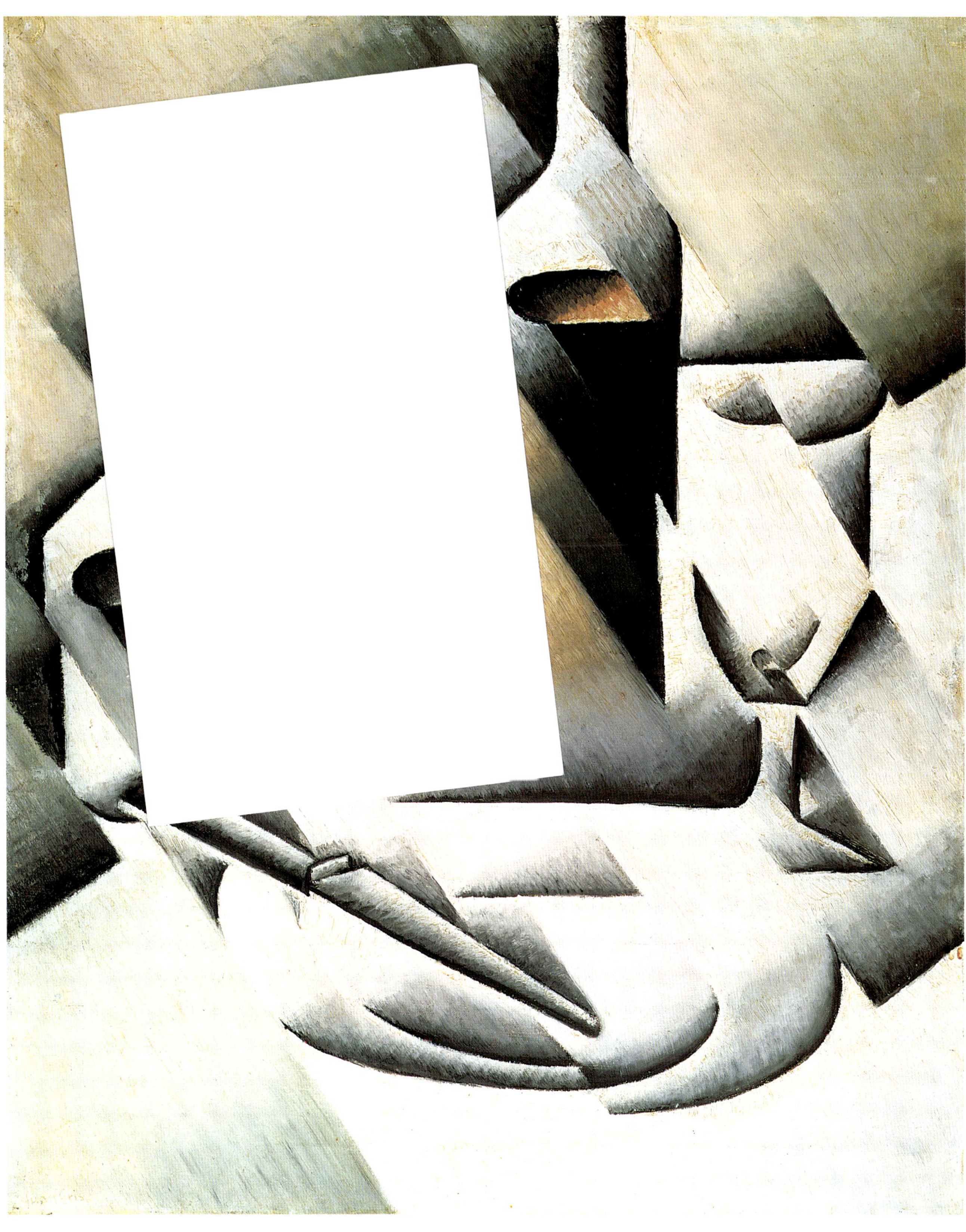

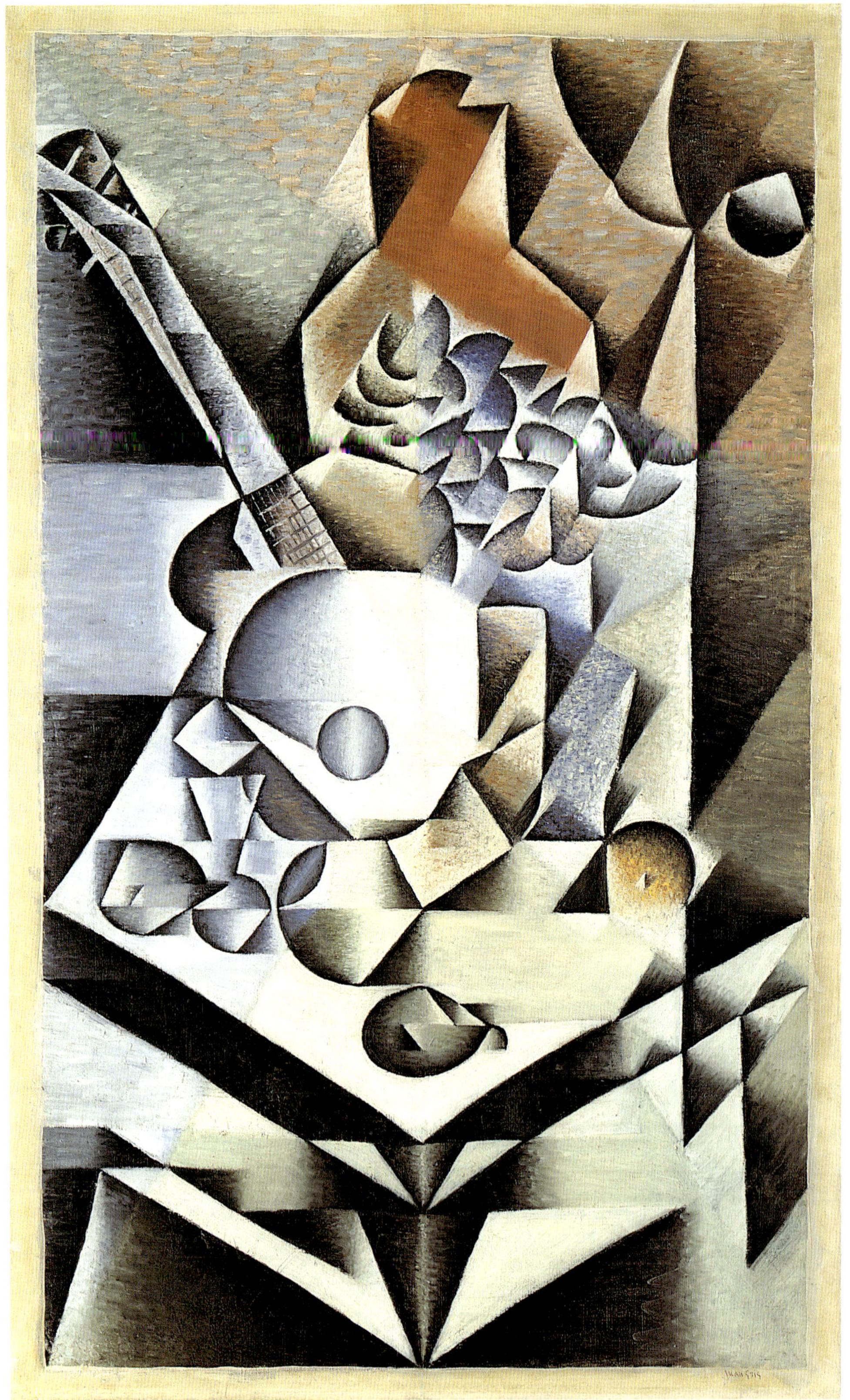

8
Still-life with Flowers, 1912
Oil on canvas, 112.1x70.2 cm
Collection, The Museum of Modern Art, New York. Bequest of Anna Erickson Levene in memory of her husband, Dr Phoebus Aaron Theodore Levene

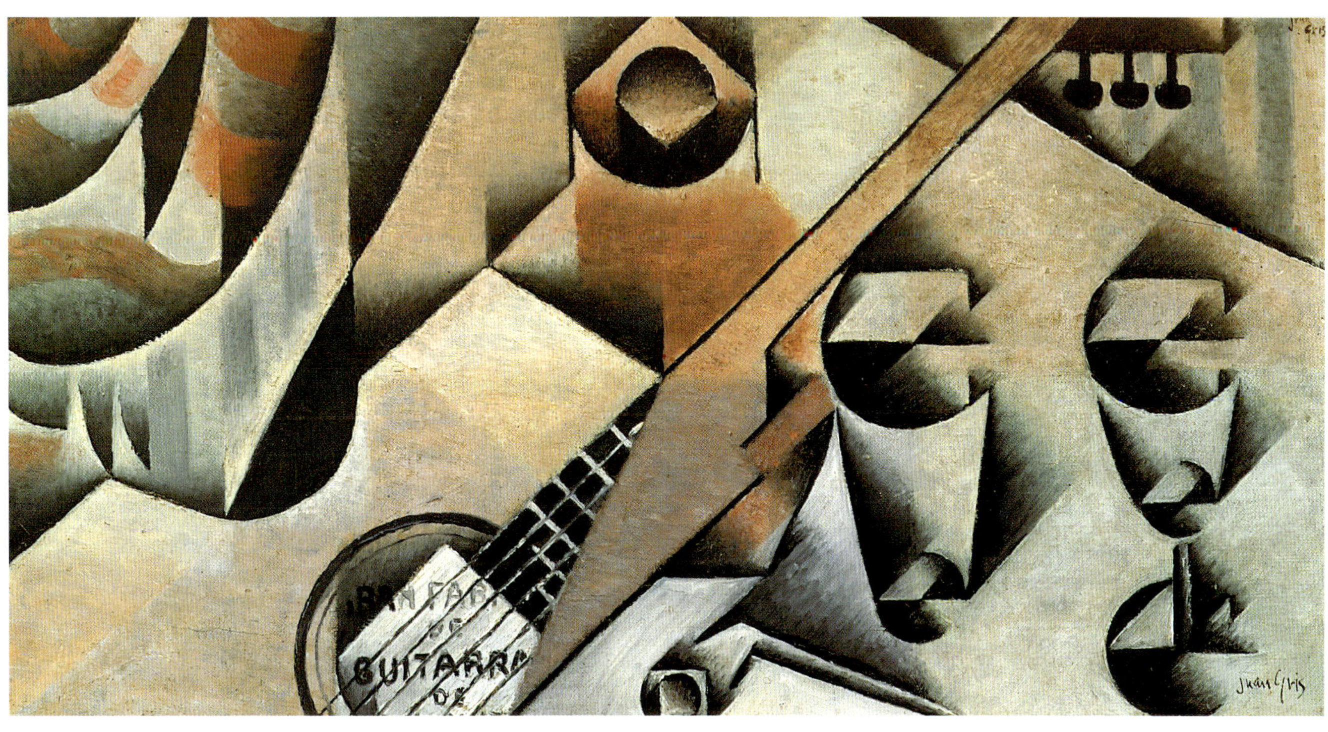

9
Guitar and Glasses
(Banjo and Glasses),
1912
Oil on canvas,
30 x 58 cm
Morton G. Neumann
Family Collection
[Not in exhibition]

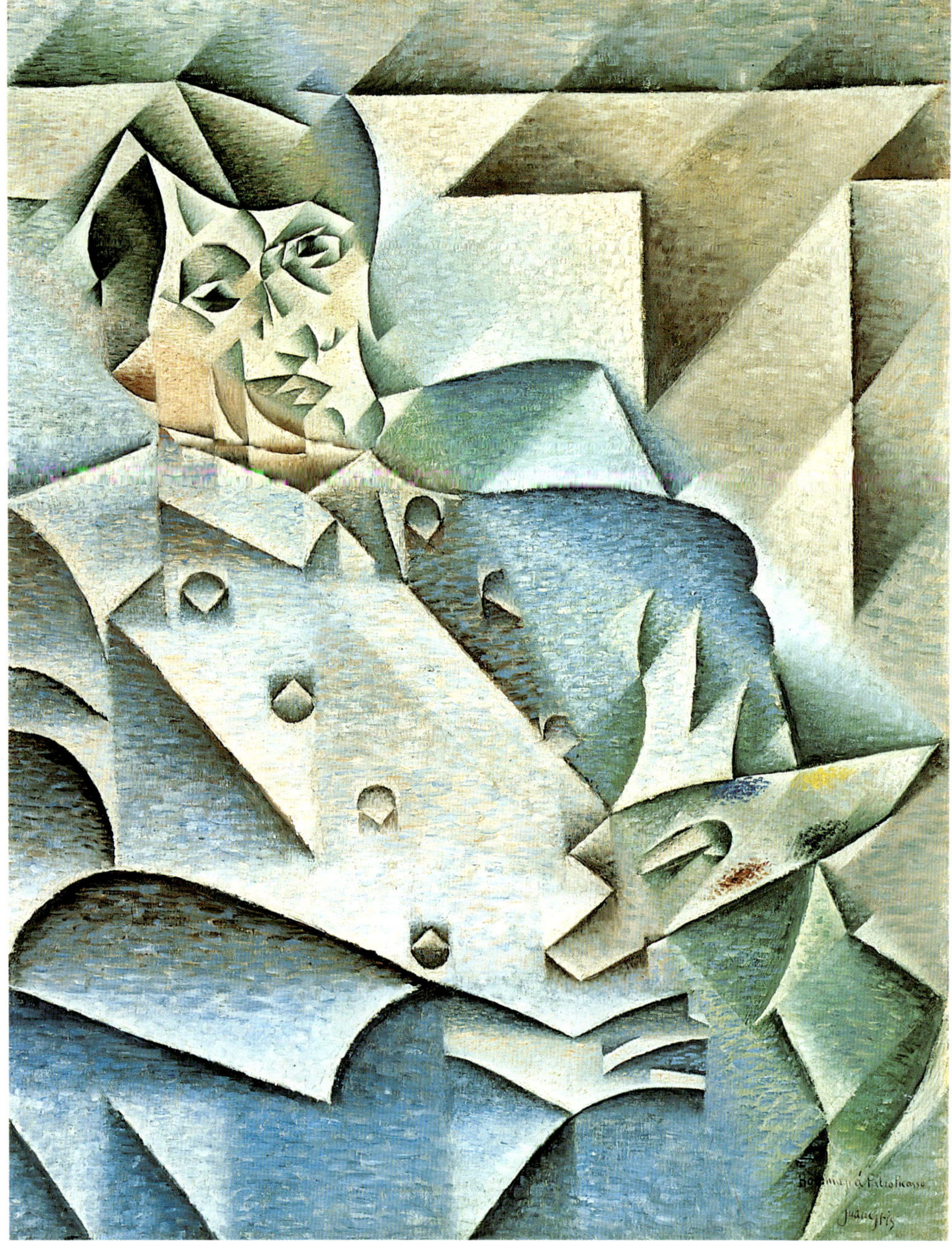

10
Homage to Pablo Picasso, 1912
Oil on canvas,
93 x 74.1 cm
The Art Institute of Chicago. Gift of Leigh B. Block, 1958.525

[Not in exhibition]

11
Portrait of the Artist's Mother, 1912
Oil on canvas,
55 x 46 cm
Private Collection

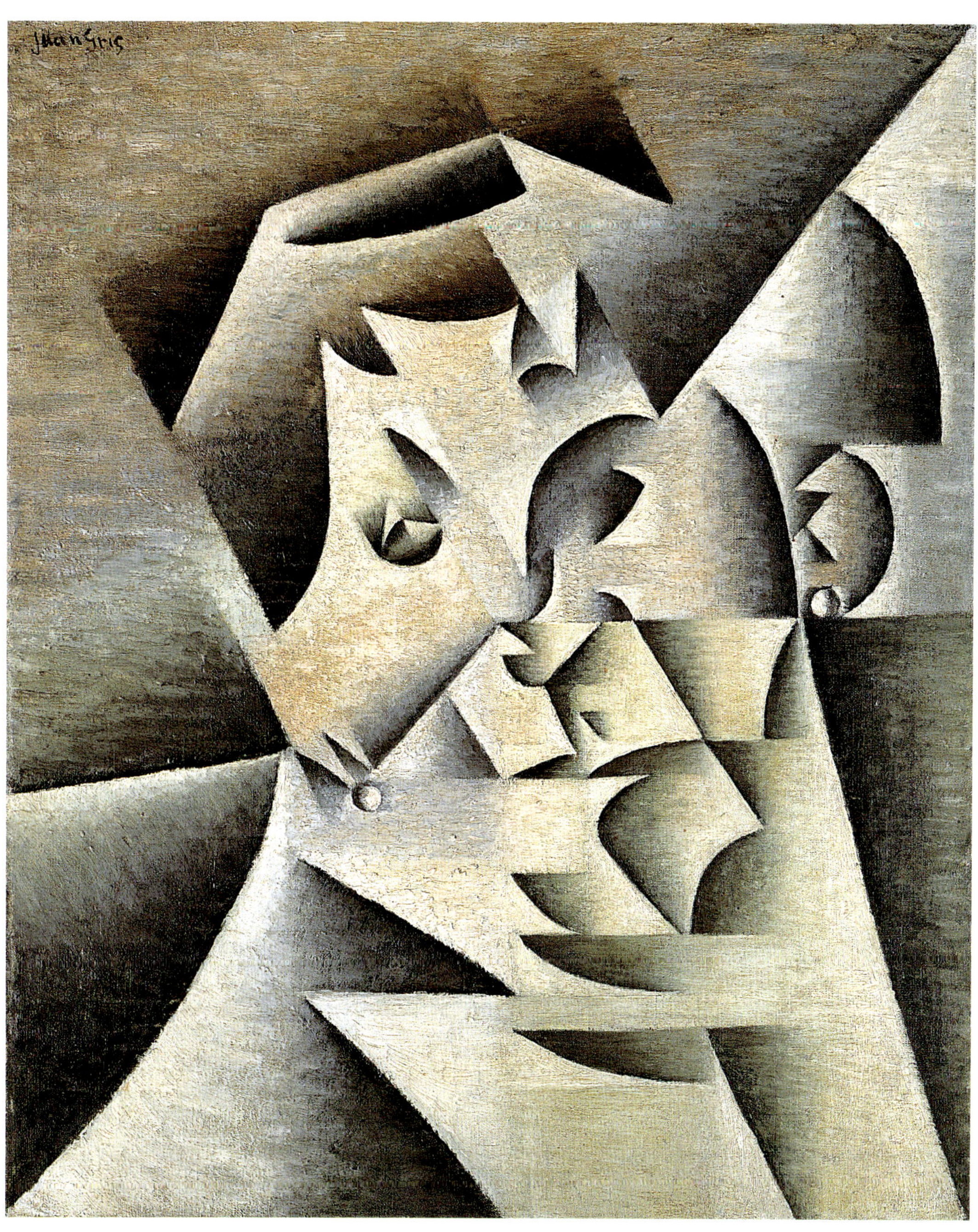

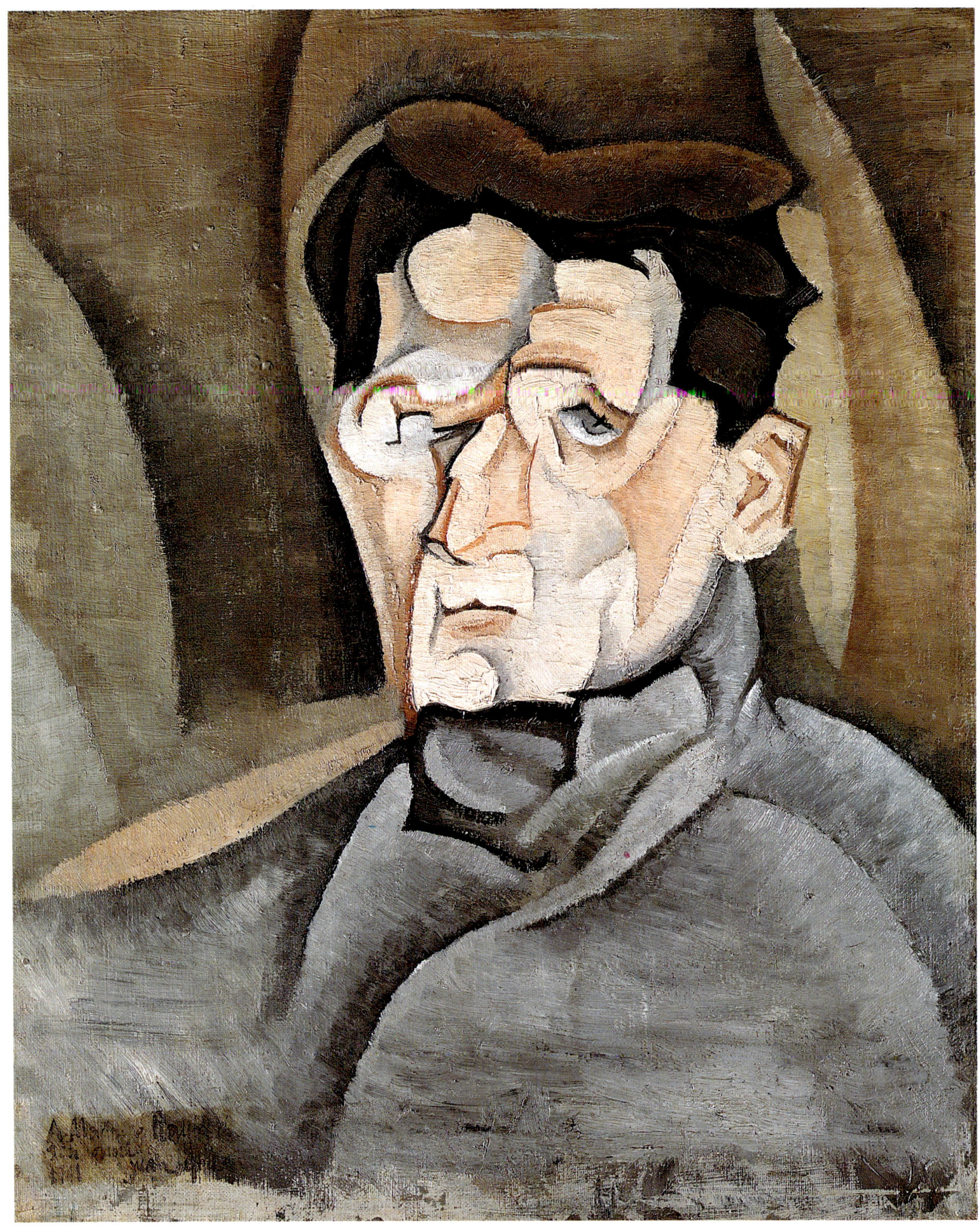

12
Portrait of Maurice Raynal, 1912
Oil on canvas,
55 x 46 cm
Private Collection
(Courtesy of Marc Blondeau, S. A., Paris)

13
Portrait of Germaine Raynal, 1912
Oil on canvas,
55 x 38 cm
Private Collection
(Courtesy of Marc Blondeau, S. A., Paris)

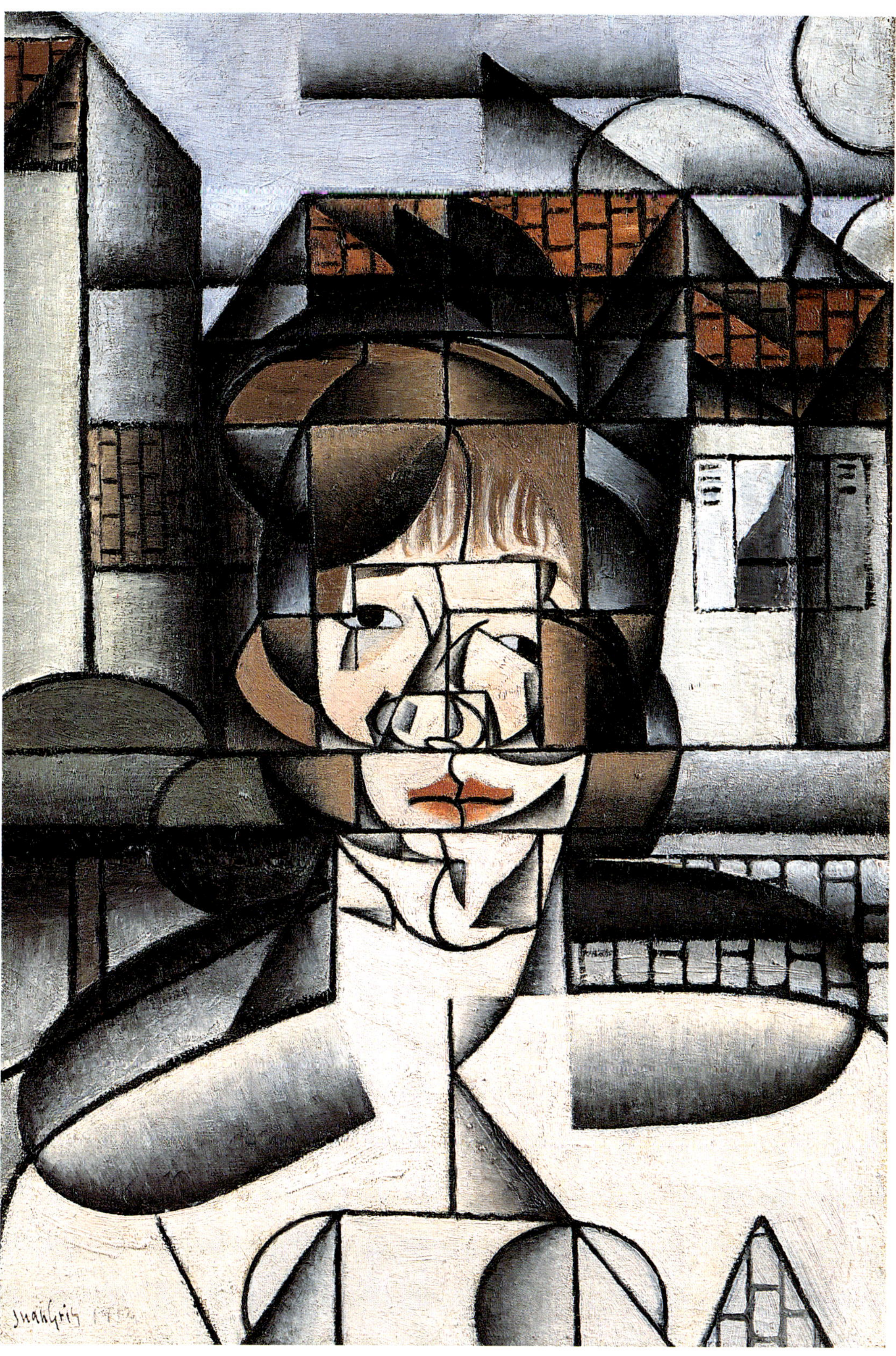

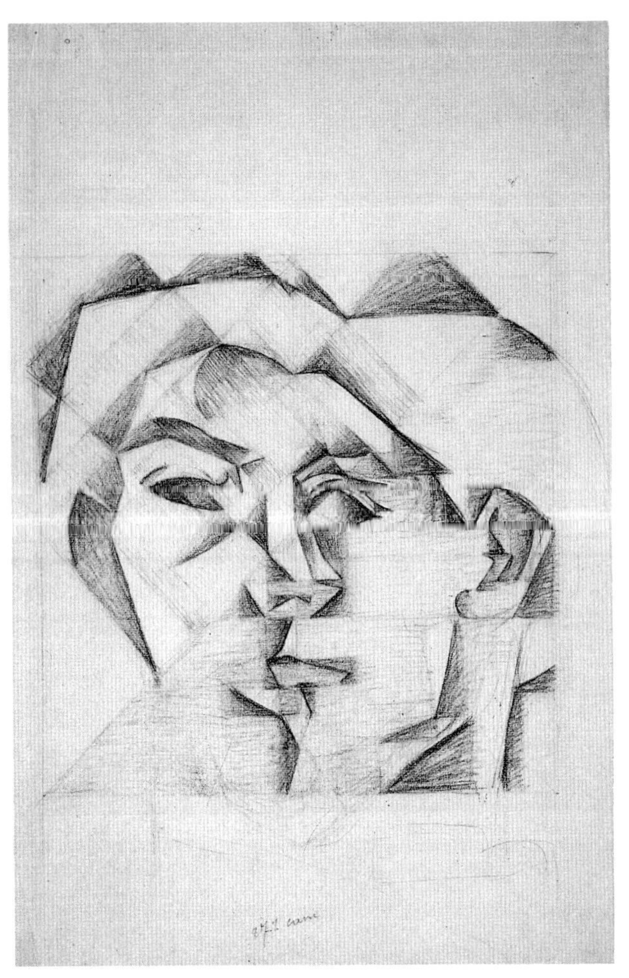

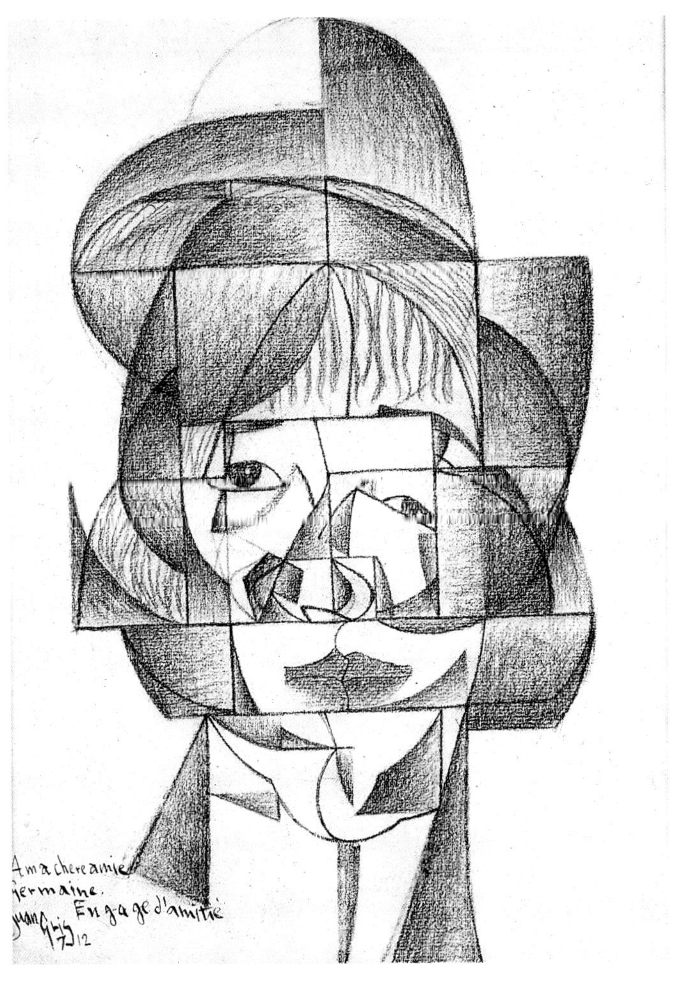

14
Head of a Man (Head of a Woman), 1912
Pencil on paper, 48.1 x 31.5 cm
Öffentliche Kunstsammlung Basel, Kupferstichkabinett

15
Portrait of Germaine Raynal, 1912
Pencil and charcoal on paper, 36 x 26.5 cm
Private Collection (Courtesy of Marc Blondeau, S. A., Paris)

16
Head of Germaine Raynal, 1912
Charcoal on paper, 48 x 31.7 cm
R. Stanley and Ursula Johnson Family Collection

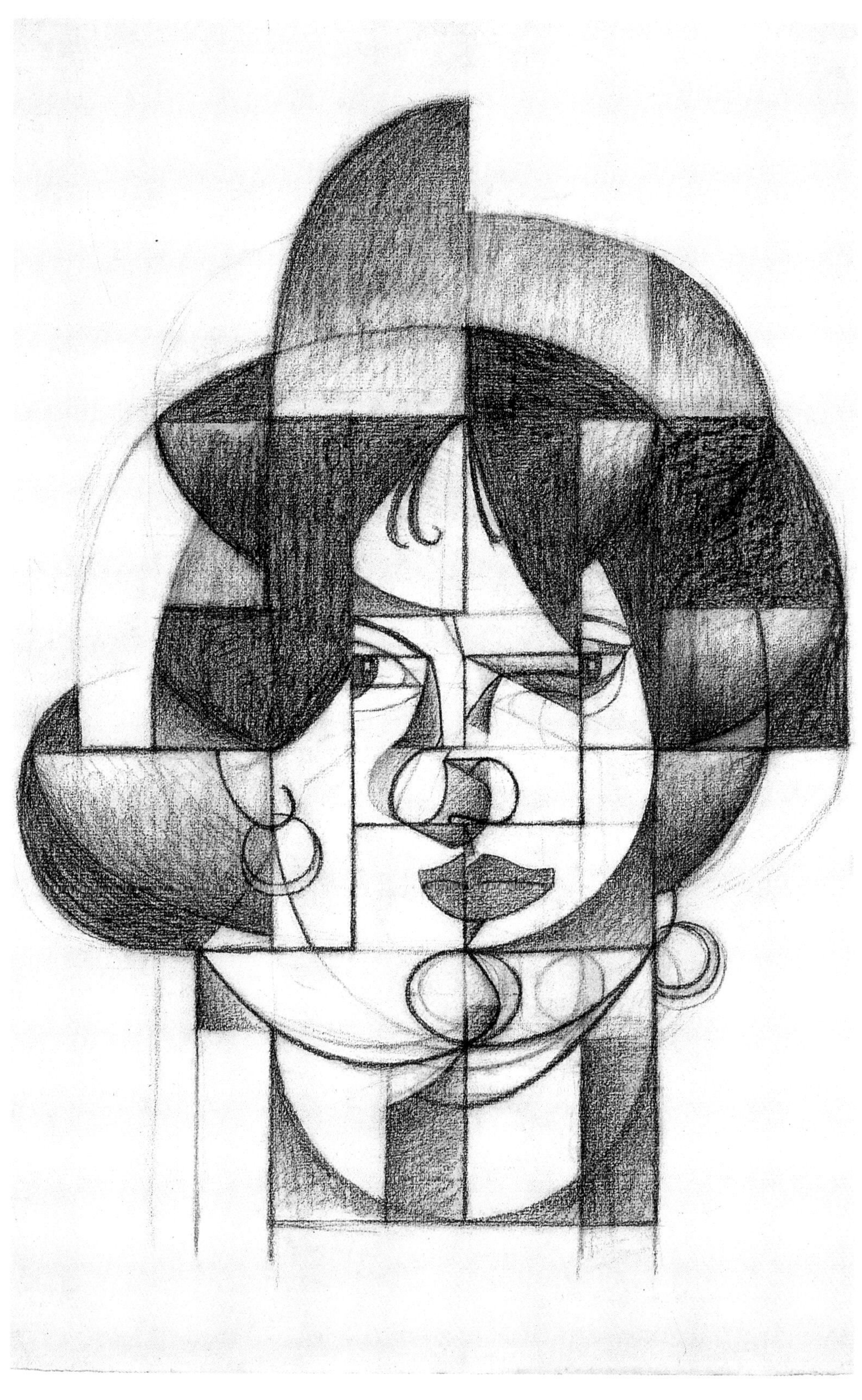

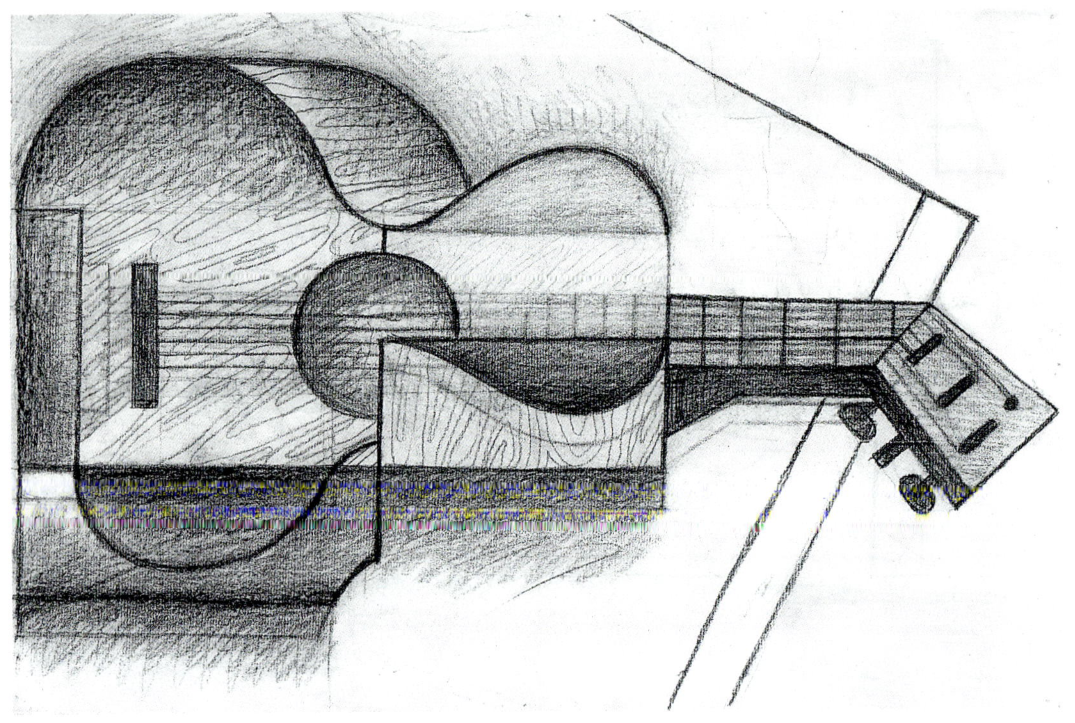

17
The Guitar, 1912
Charcoal on paper,
31.6 x 48 cm
R. Stanley and Ursula
Johnson Family
Collection

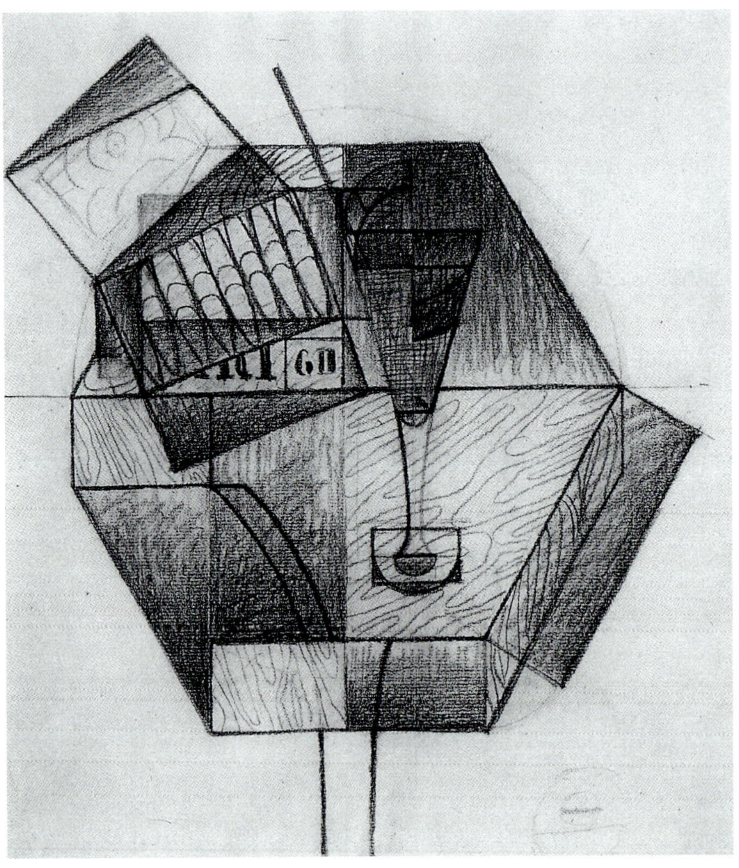

18
Still-life with Box of Cigars, 1912
Pencil on paper,
38 x 31.5 cm
Galerie Louise Leiris,
Paris

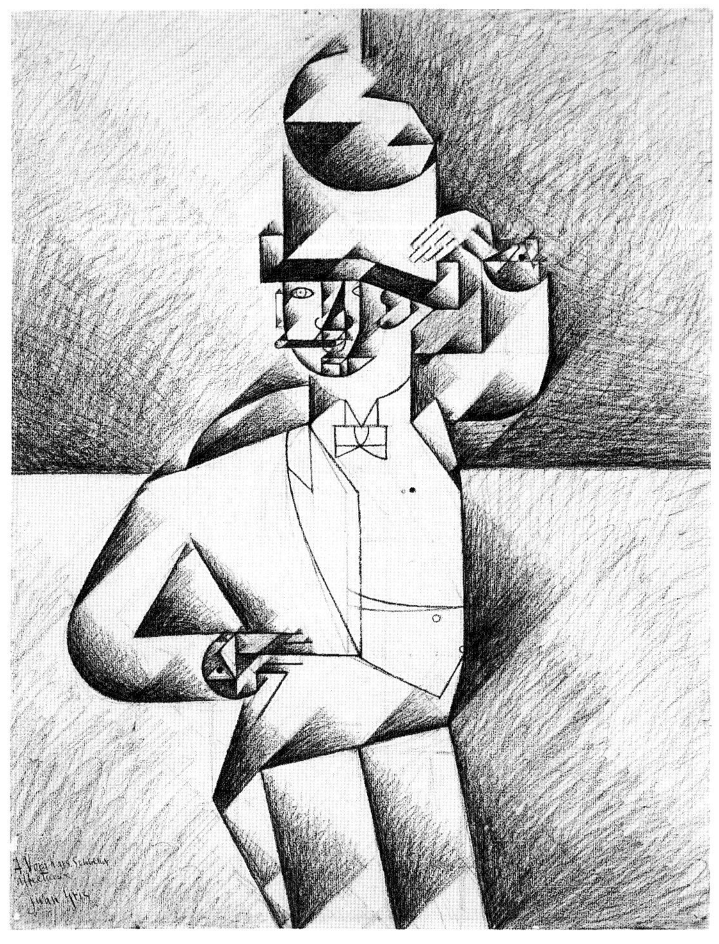

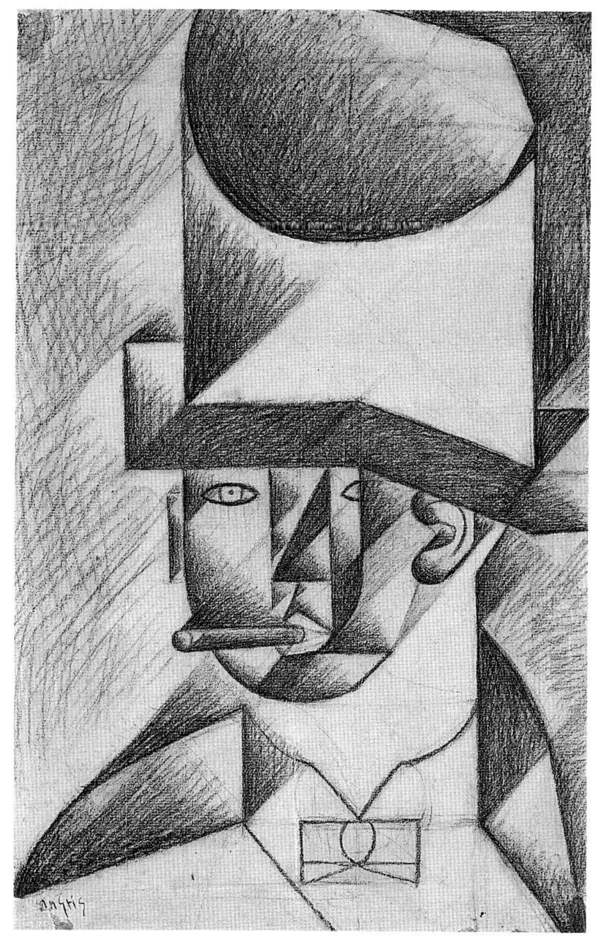

19
Man at Café, 1911–12
Pencil on paper, 55.9 x 41.9 cm
Philadelphia Museum of Art: The A. E. Gallatin Collection

20
Head of a Man with Cigar, c. 1912
Charcoal and chalk on paper, 42.9 x 27.5 cm
The Art Institute of Chicago. Arthur Heun Fund; William McCallin McKee Memorial Collection; John H. Wrenn Memorial Collection, 1955.1024

[Stuttgart and Otterlo only]

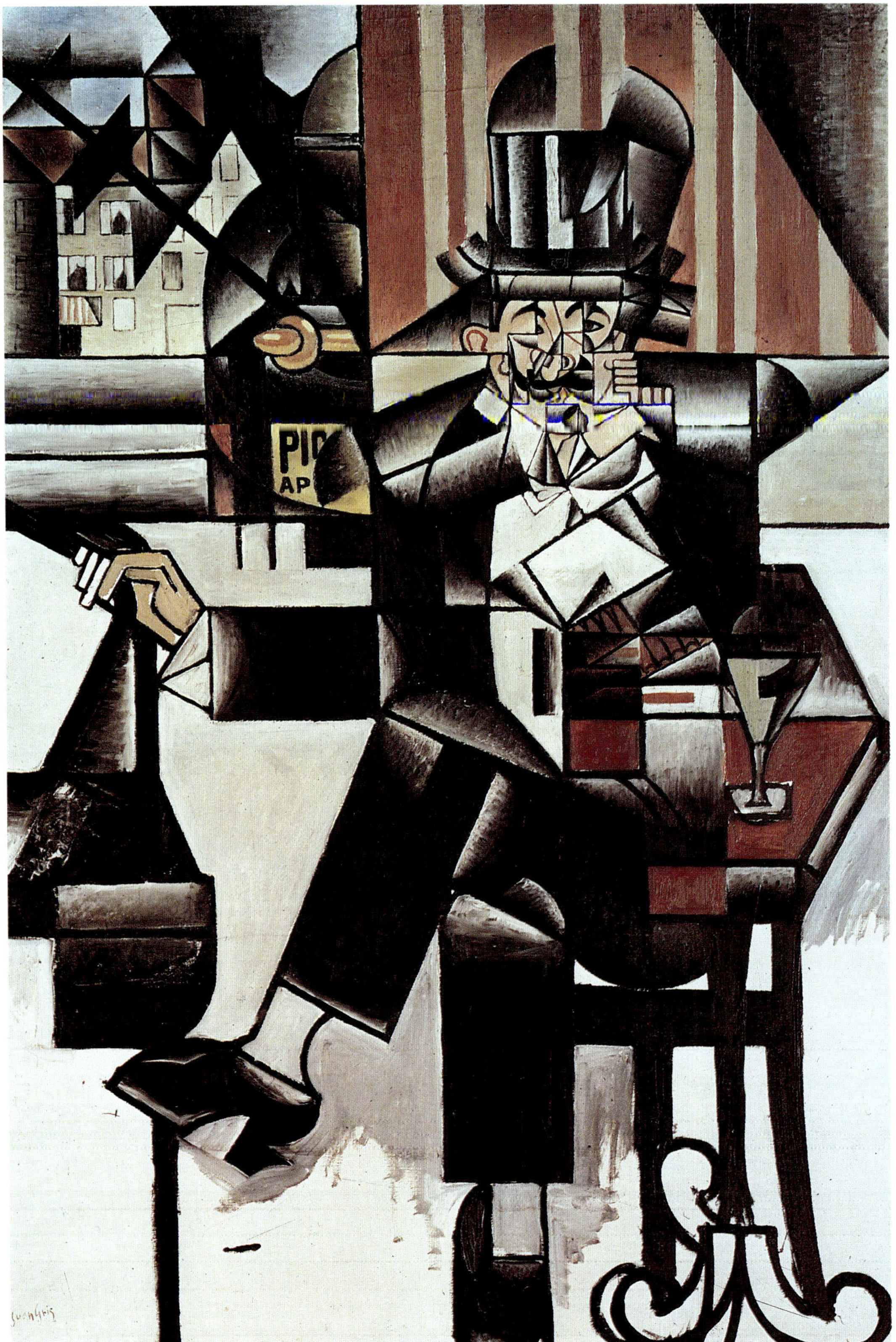

21
Man in the Café, 1912
Oil on canvas,
128.2 x 88 cm
Philadelphia Museum of
Art: The Louise and
Walter Arensberg
Collection

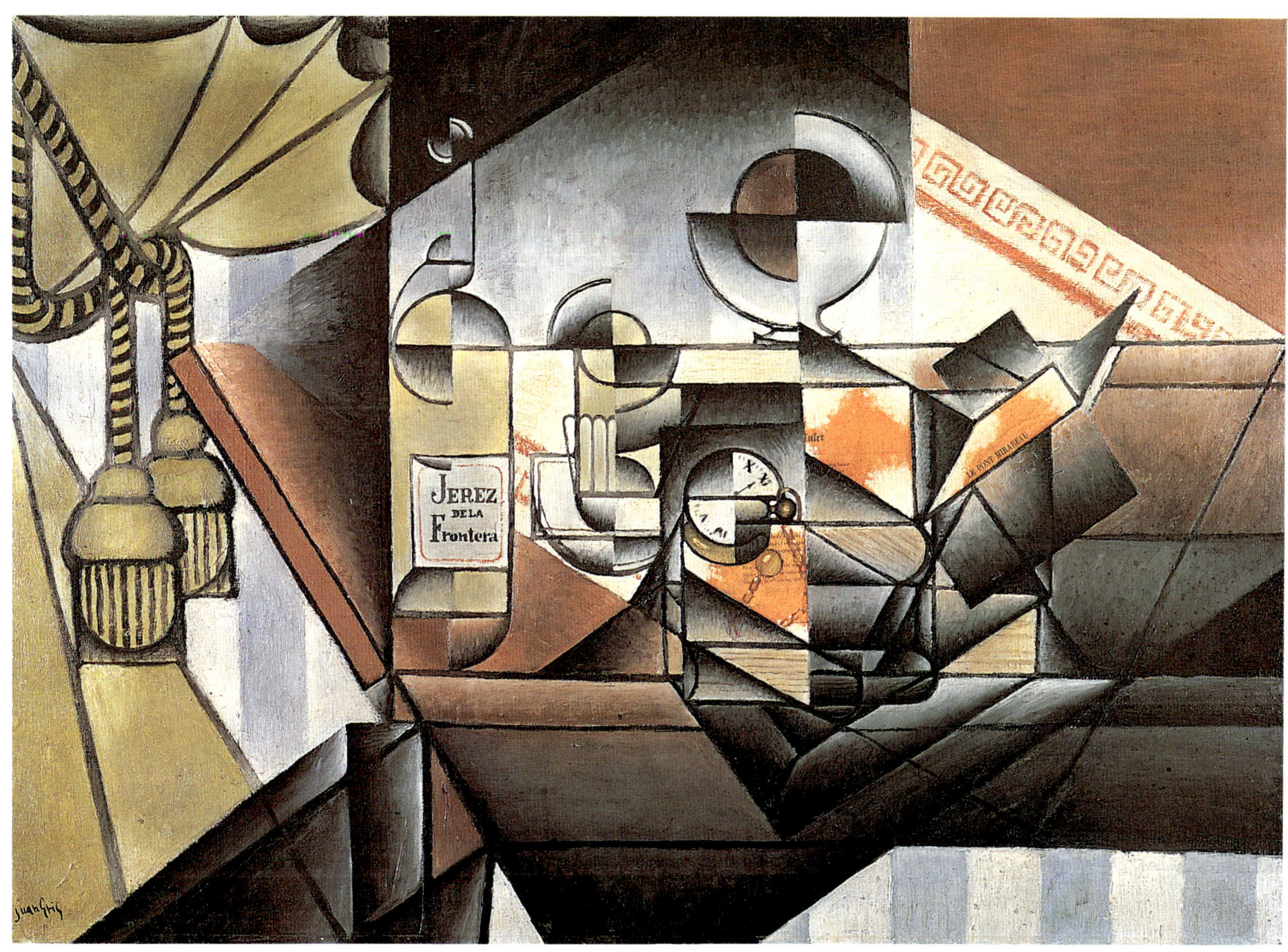

22

The Watch, 1912
Oil and papier collé on canvas, 65 x 92 cm
Private Collection
[Not in exhibition]

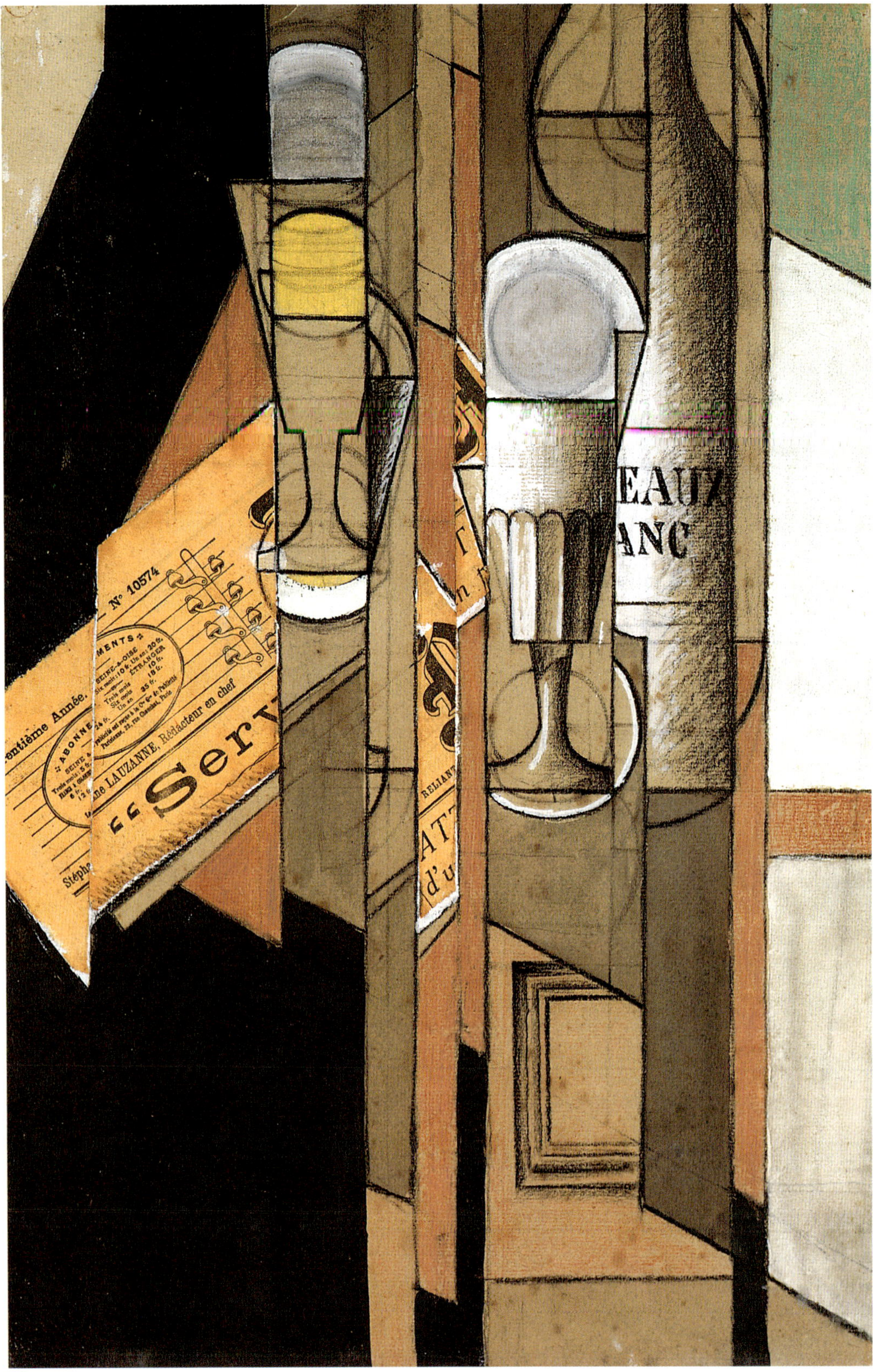

23
Glasses, Newspaper and Bottle of Wine, 1913
Papier collé, gouache, pencil and charcoal on paper, 45 x 29.5 cm
Telefónica de España, S. A.

24
The Book, 1913
Oil and papier collé on canvas, 41 x 33 cm
Musée d'Art Moderne de la Ville de Paris

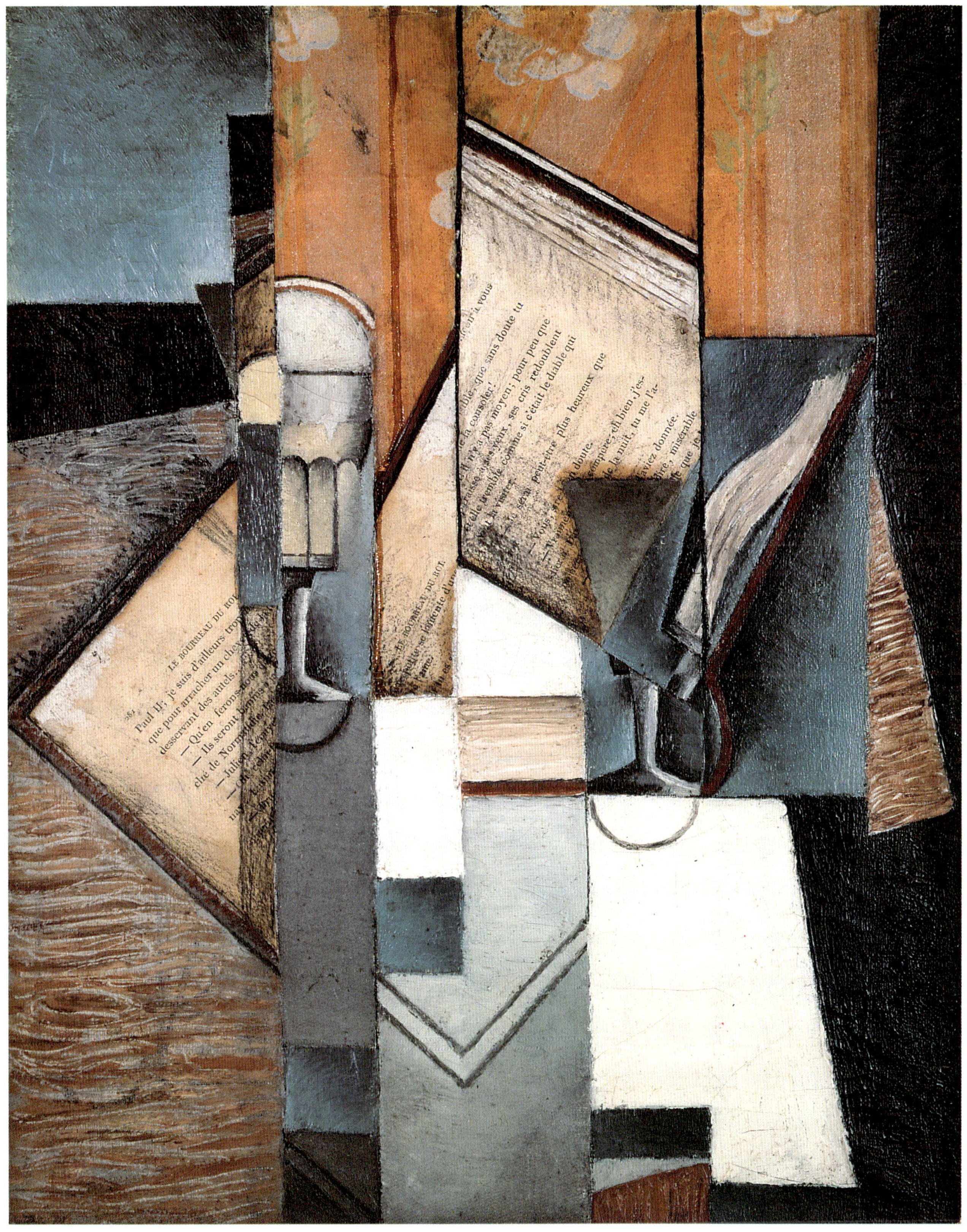

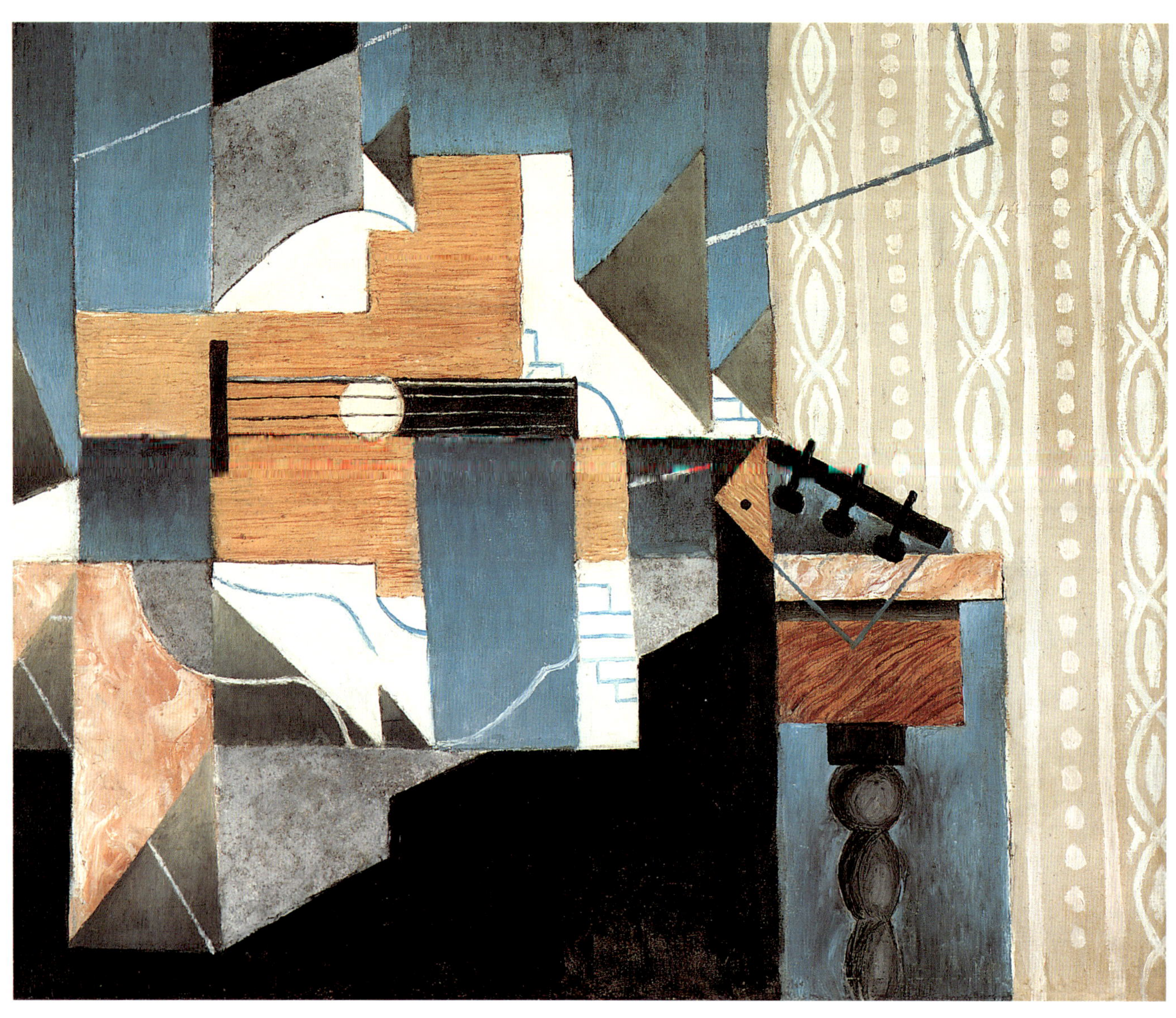

25
Guitar on the Table,
1913
Oil on canvas,
60 x 73.7 cm
Telefónica de España,
S. A.

26
The Siphon, 1913
Oil on canvas, 81x65 cm
Rose Art Museum,
Brandeis University,
Waltham, Massachusetts.
Gift of Edgar
Kaufmann, Jr

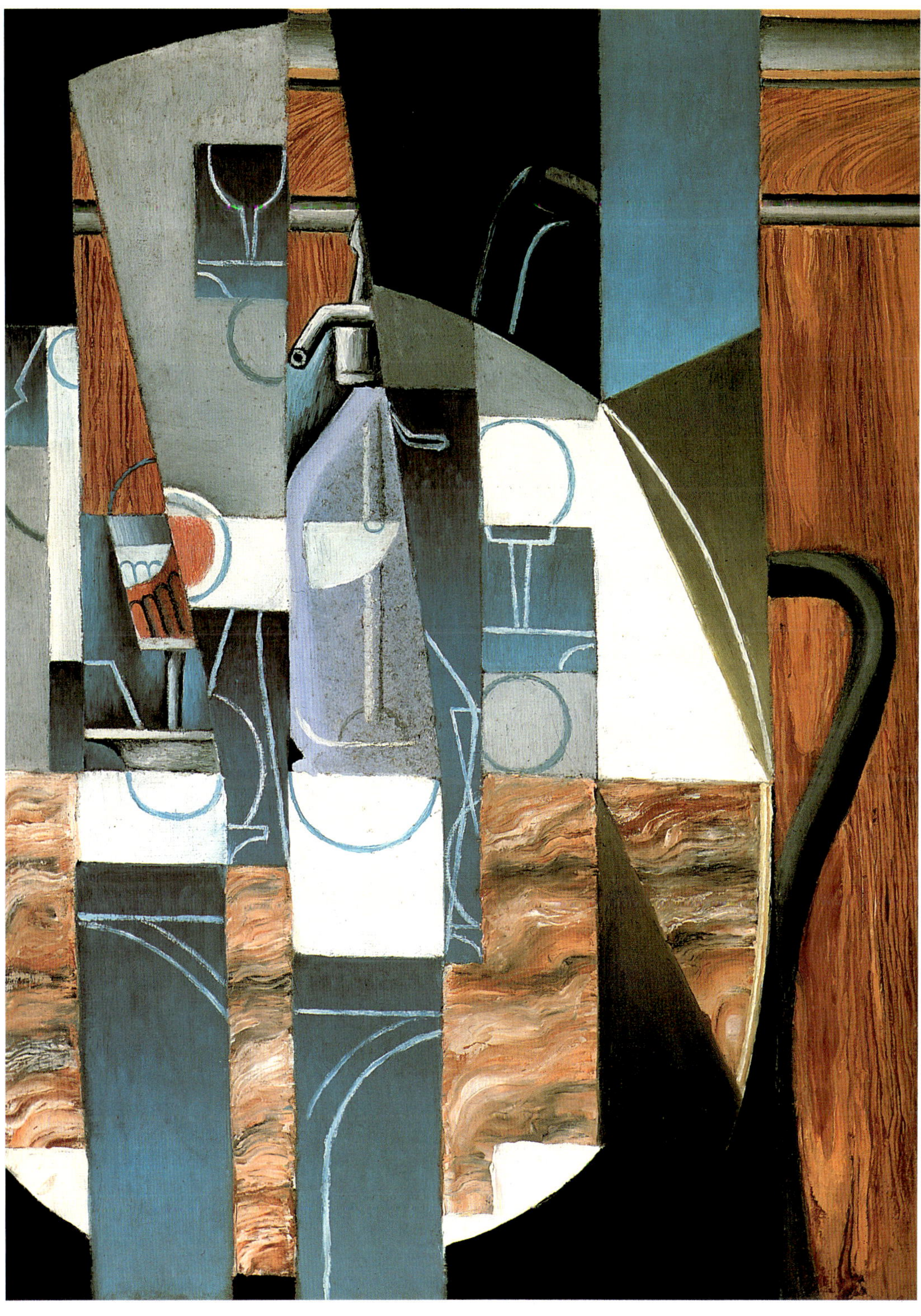

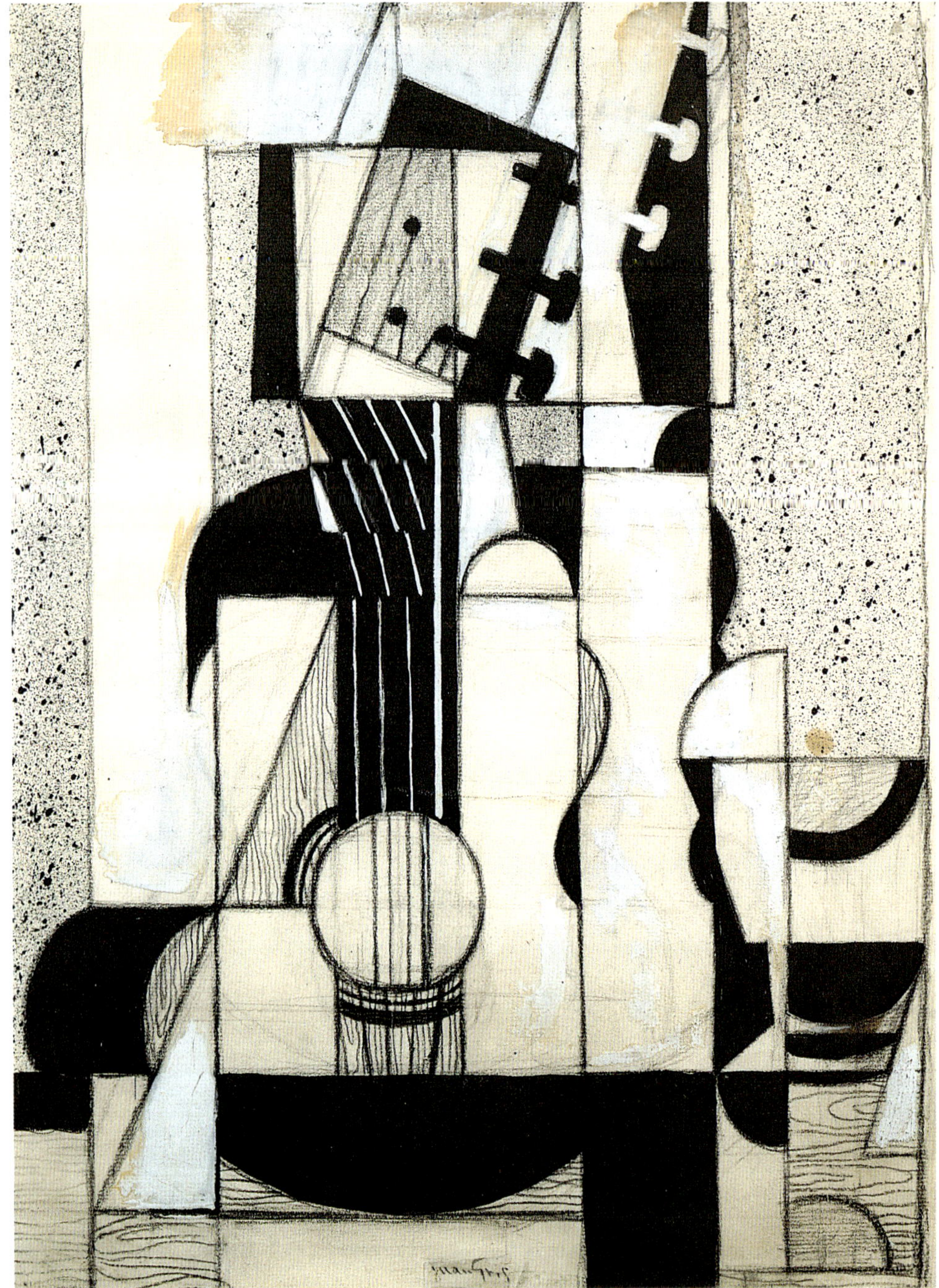

27
Still-life with Guitar,
1912–13
Pencil and gouache on paper, 42 x 31.5 cm
Georges González Gris

28
The Guitar, 1913
Oil and papier collé on canvas, 61 x 50 cm
Musée National d'Art Moderne, Centre Georges Pompidou, Paris. Gift of Louise and Michel Leiris (1984)

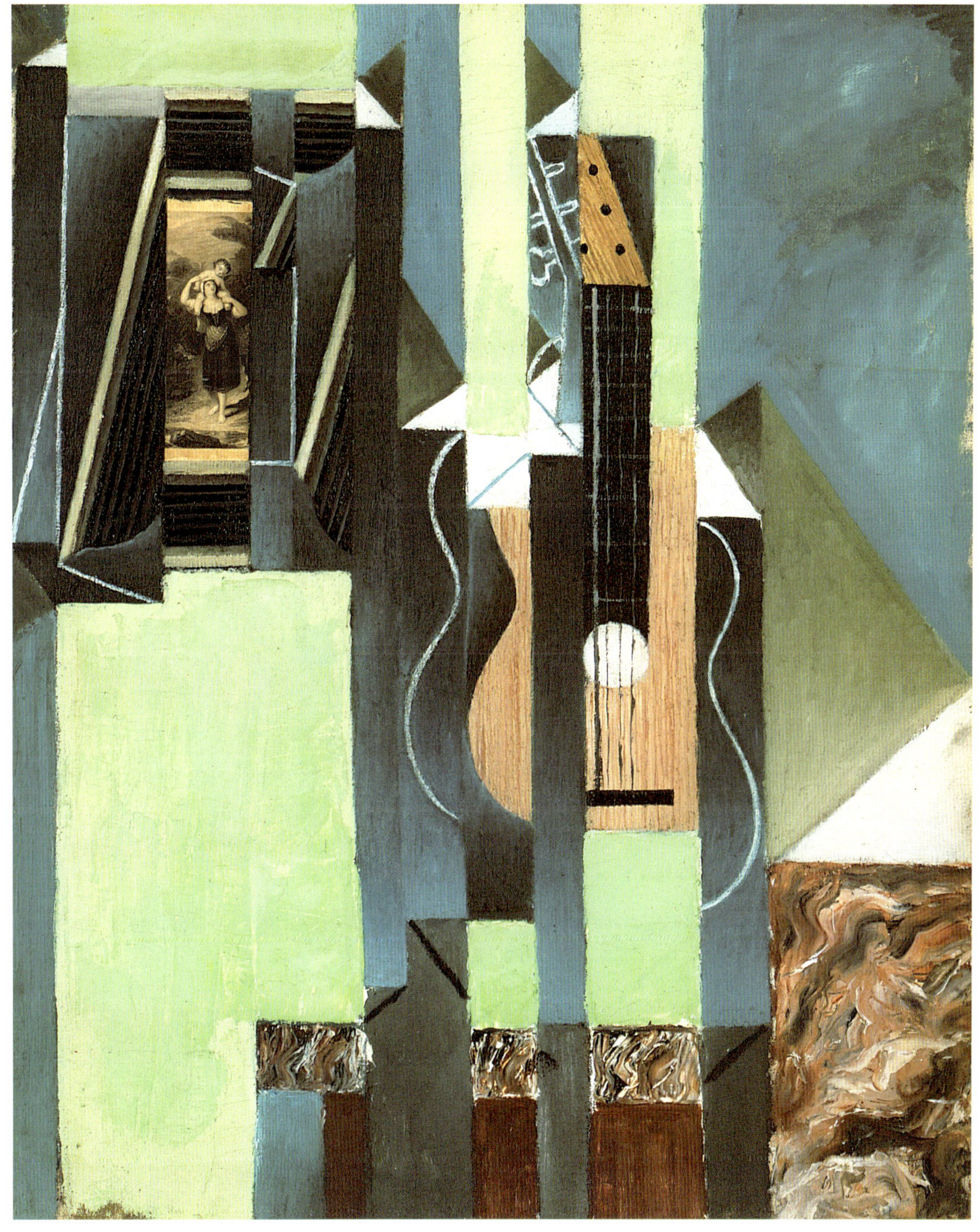

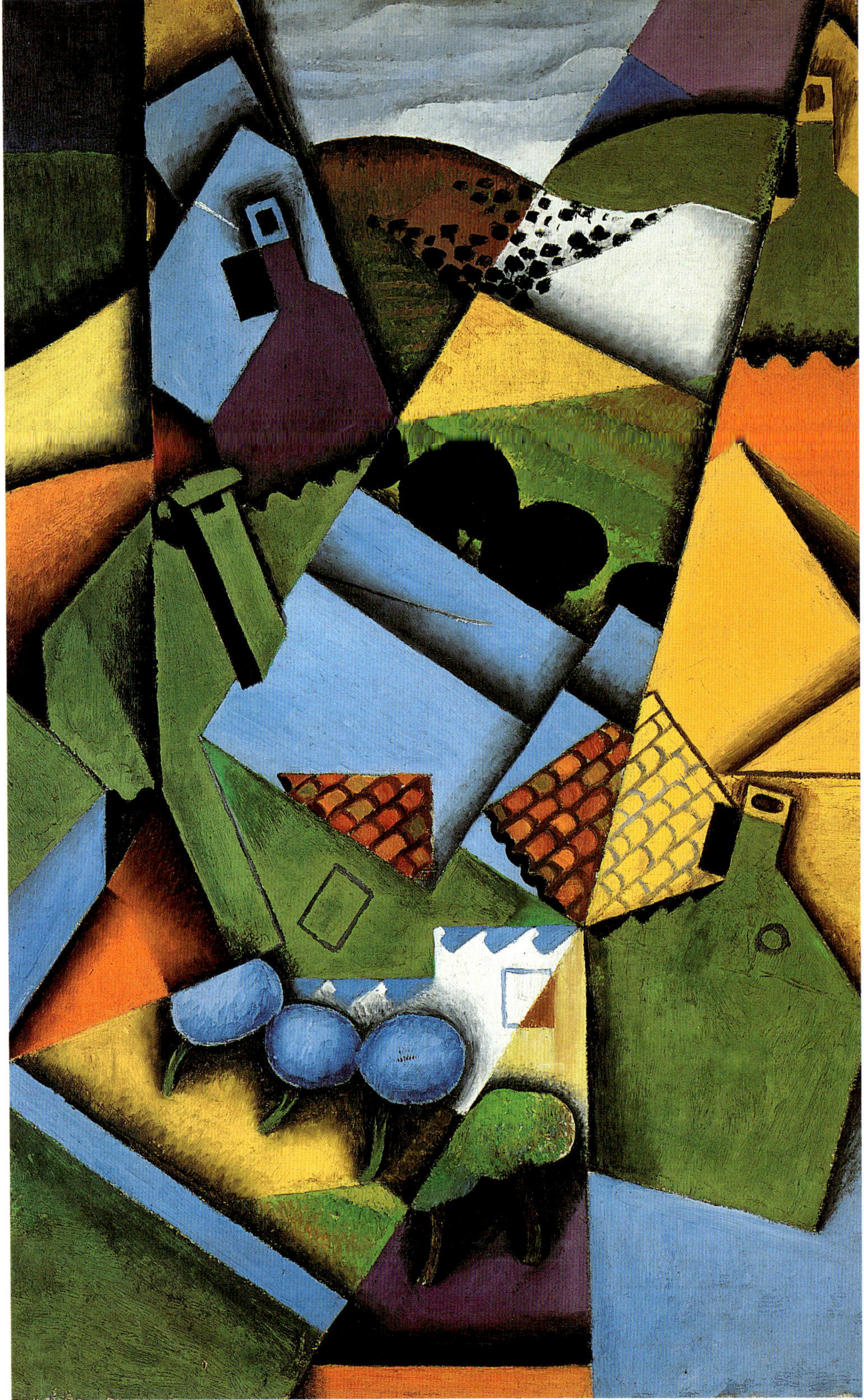

29
Landscape with Houses at Céret, 1913
Oil on canvas,
100 x 65 cm
Fundación Frax
[Not in exhibition]

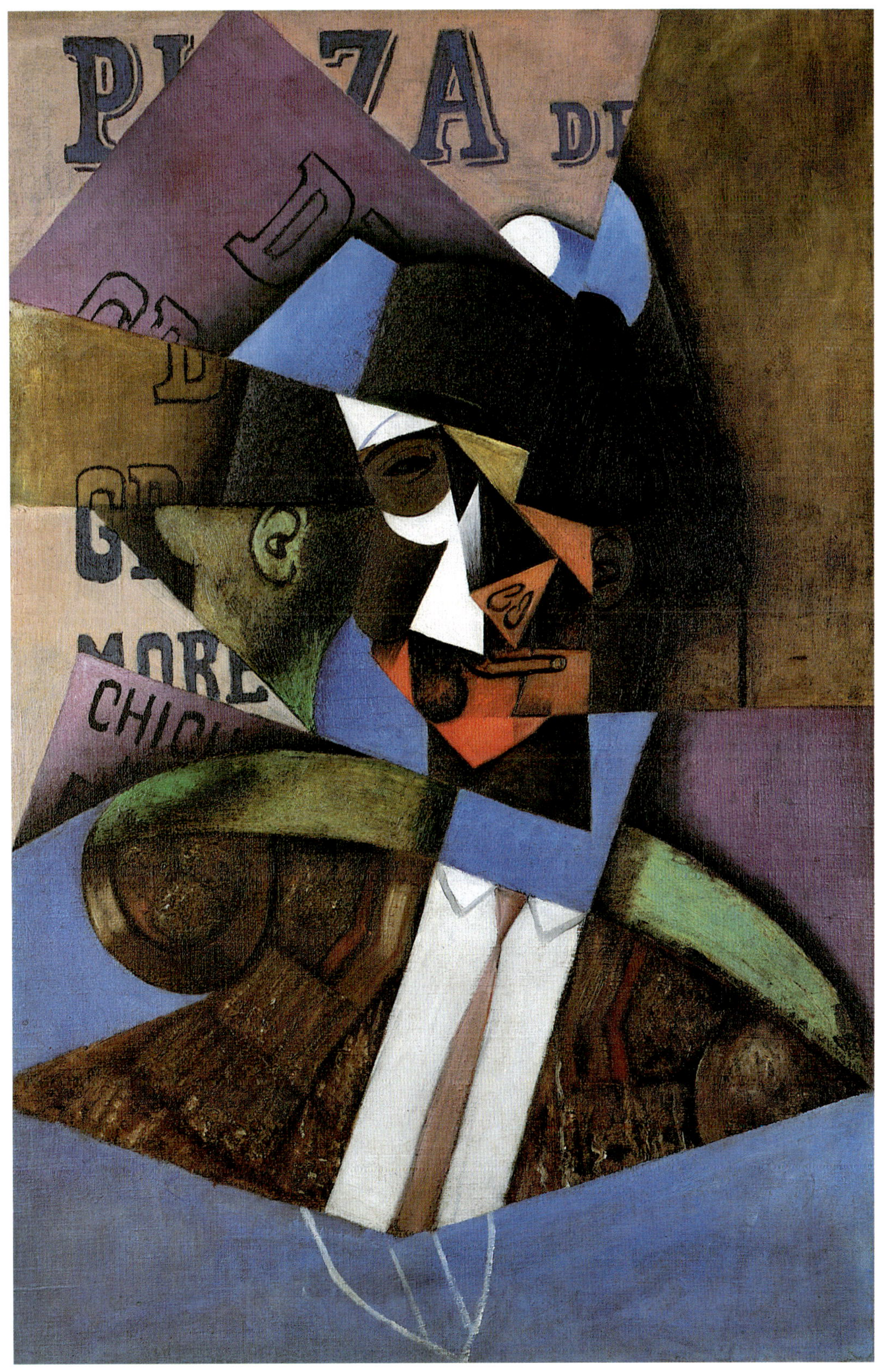

30
The Bull-fighter, 1913
Oil on canvas,
92 x 60 cm
Collection Jose Mugrabi

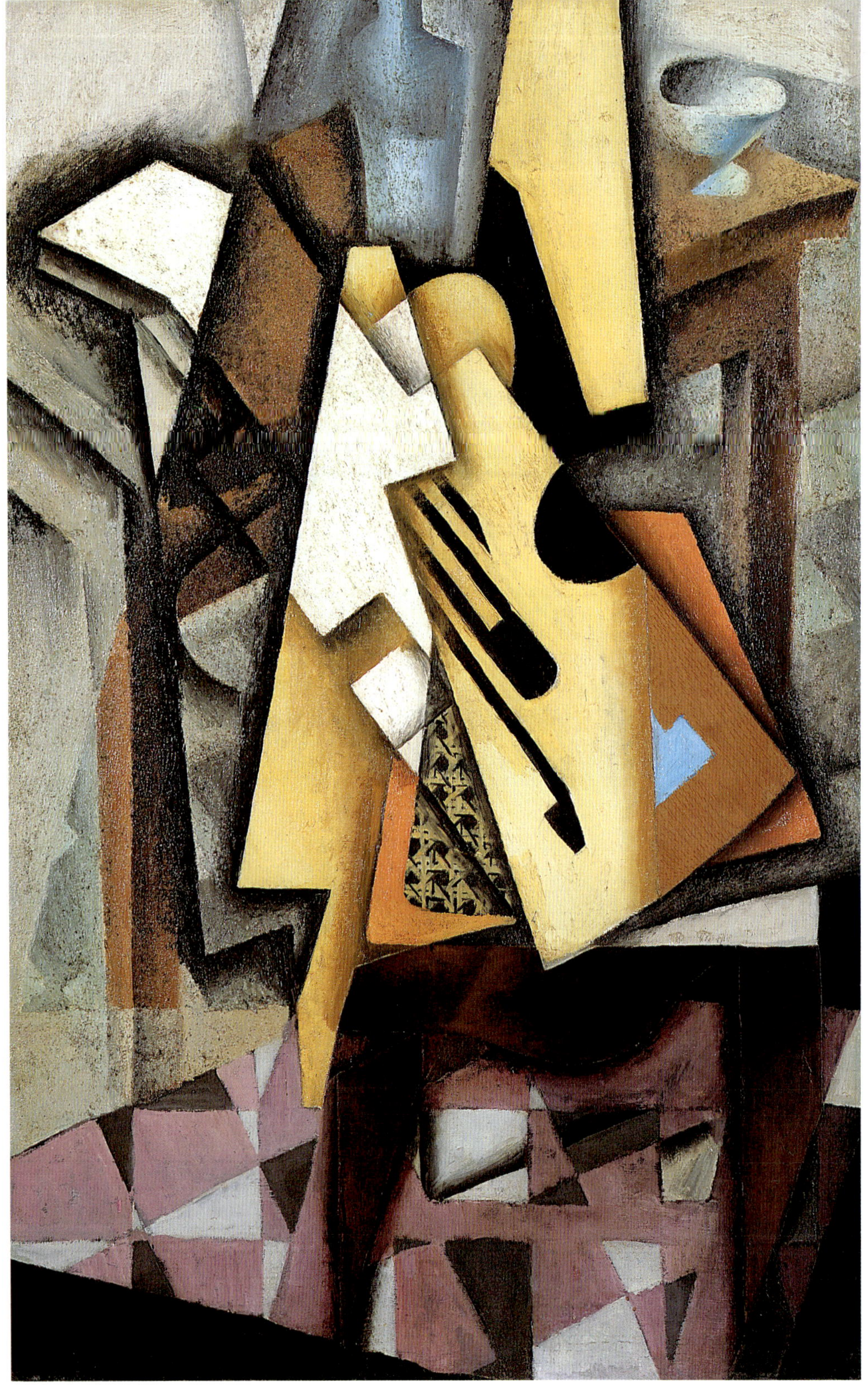

31
Guitar on a Chair,
1913
Oil on canvas,
100 x 65 cm
Private Collection

32
Violin and Guitar,
1913
Oil on canvas,
100 x 65.5 cm
Private Collection
[Not in exhibition]

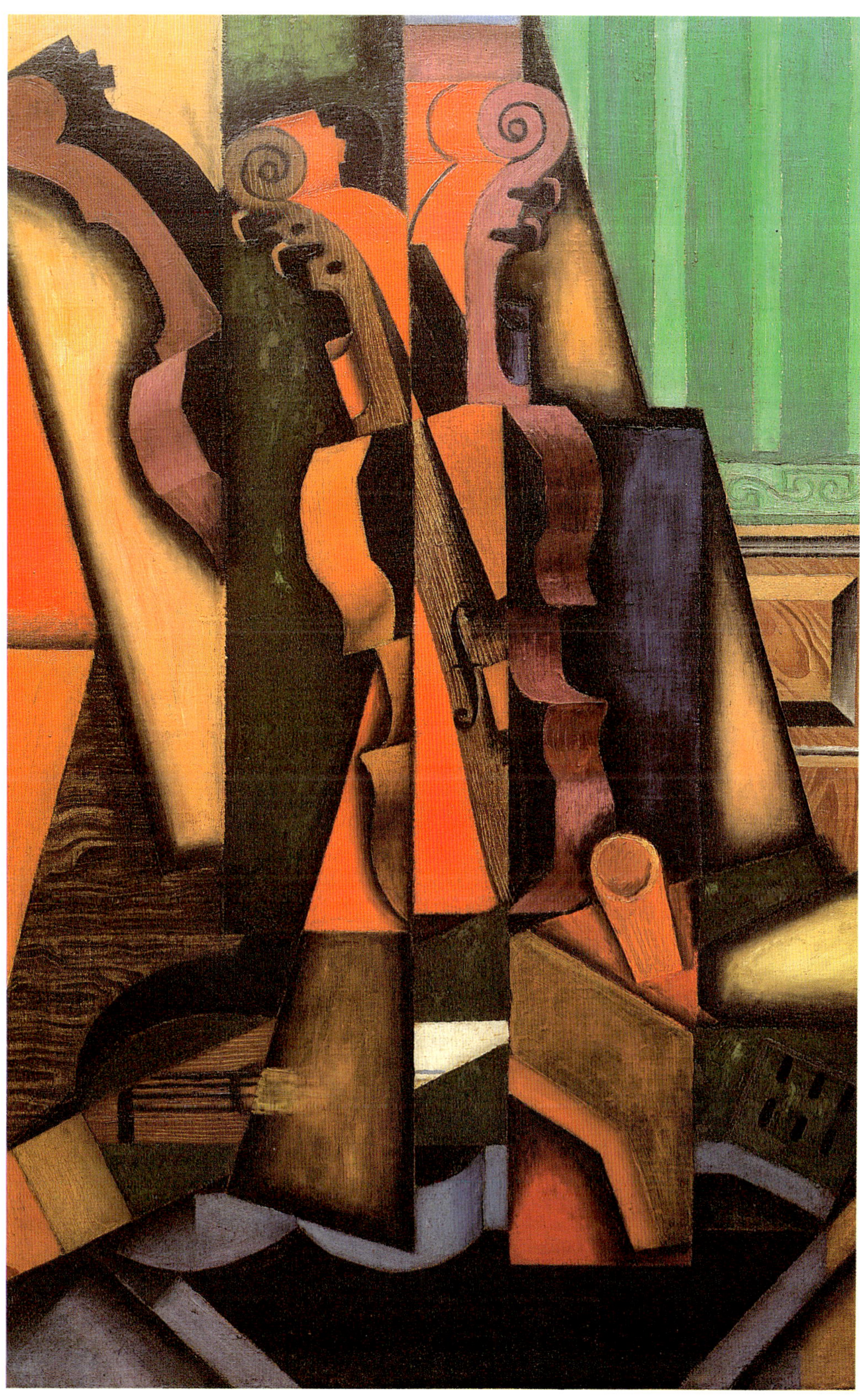

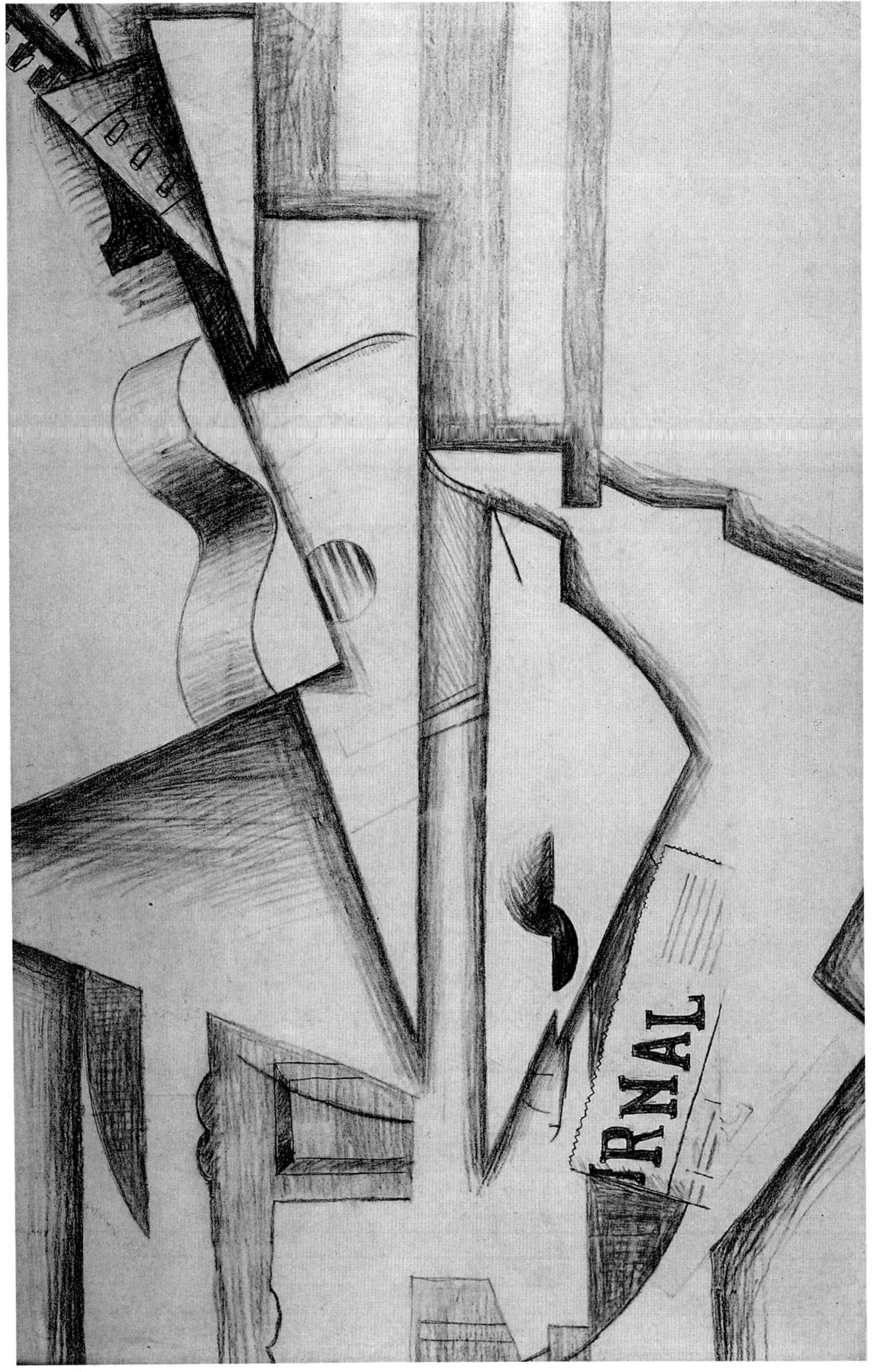

33
Guitar and Newspaper on a Table, 1913
Pencil on paper,
90.2 x 58.4 cm
Private Collection

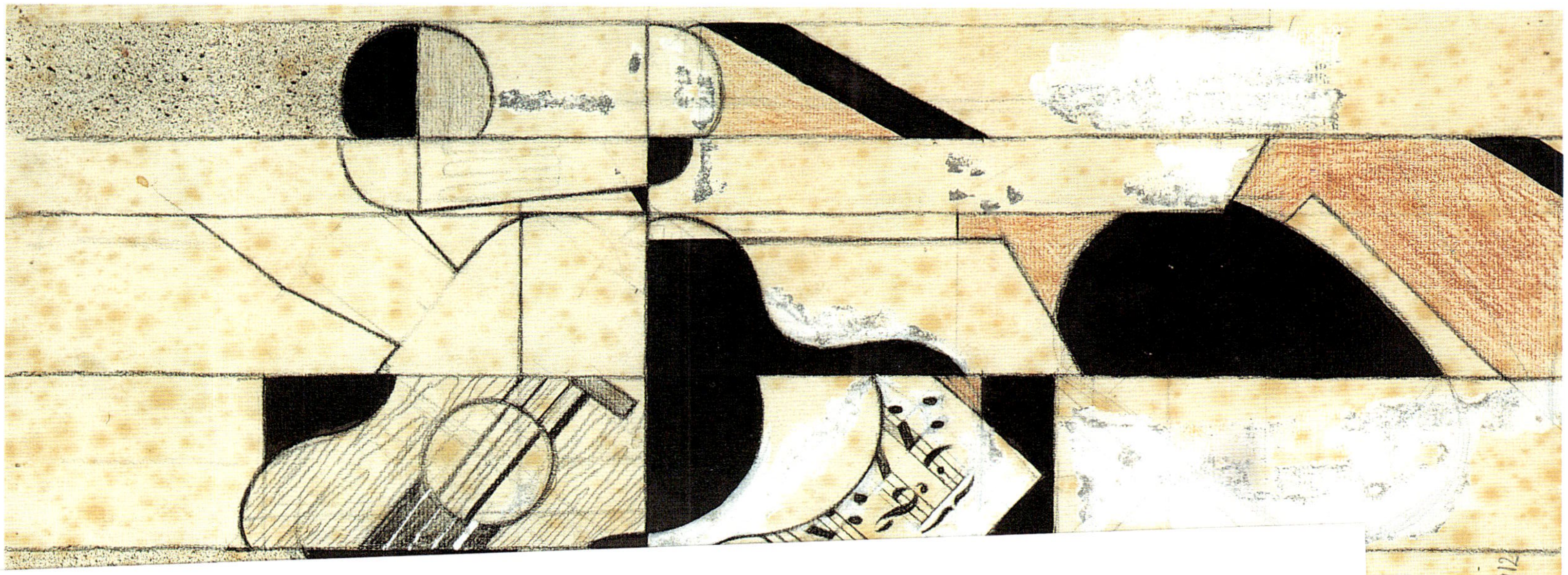

orthogonal

-mutually perpendicular

orthographic projection - ① projection of a single view of an object in which the view is projected along lines perpendicular to both the view and the drawing surface
② the representation of related views of an object as if they were all in the same plane and projected by orthographic projection

golden section

Juan Gris 1912

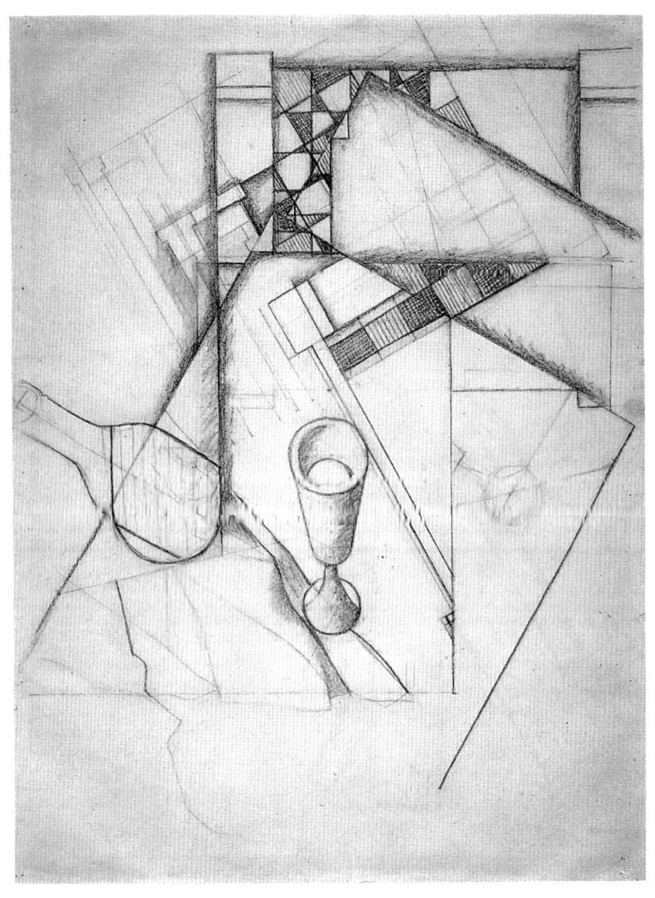

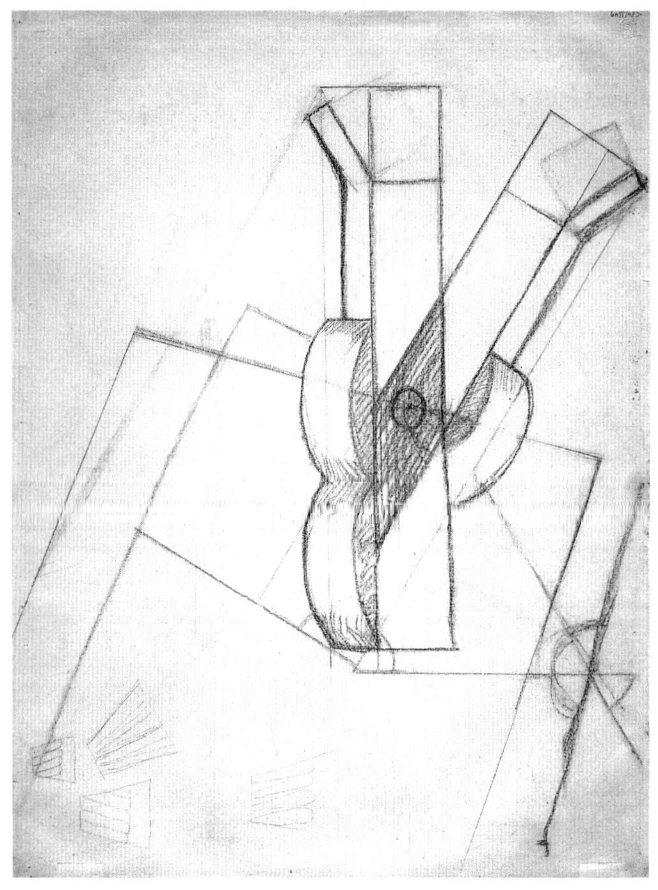

35 and 36
Still-life with Glass and Chequerboard (Guitar verso), 1913
Charcoal and pencil on paper, 60 x 45 cm
Graphische Sammlung Staatsgalerie Stuttgart

37
Glass, Cup and Newspaper, 1913
Oil on canvas,
46.5 x 27.5 cm
Gradowczyk and Garcia
Benitez Collection

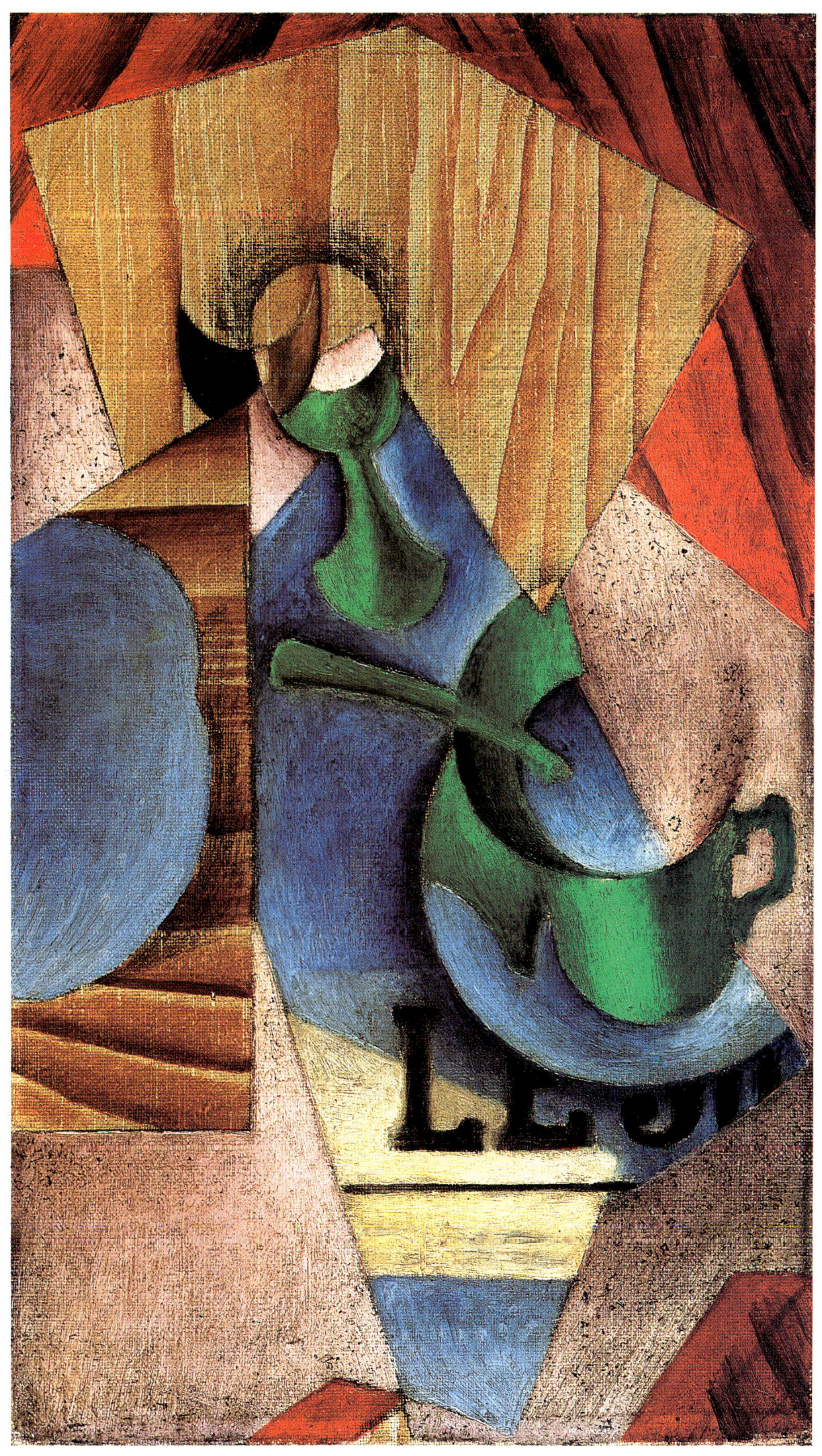

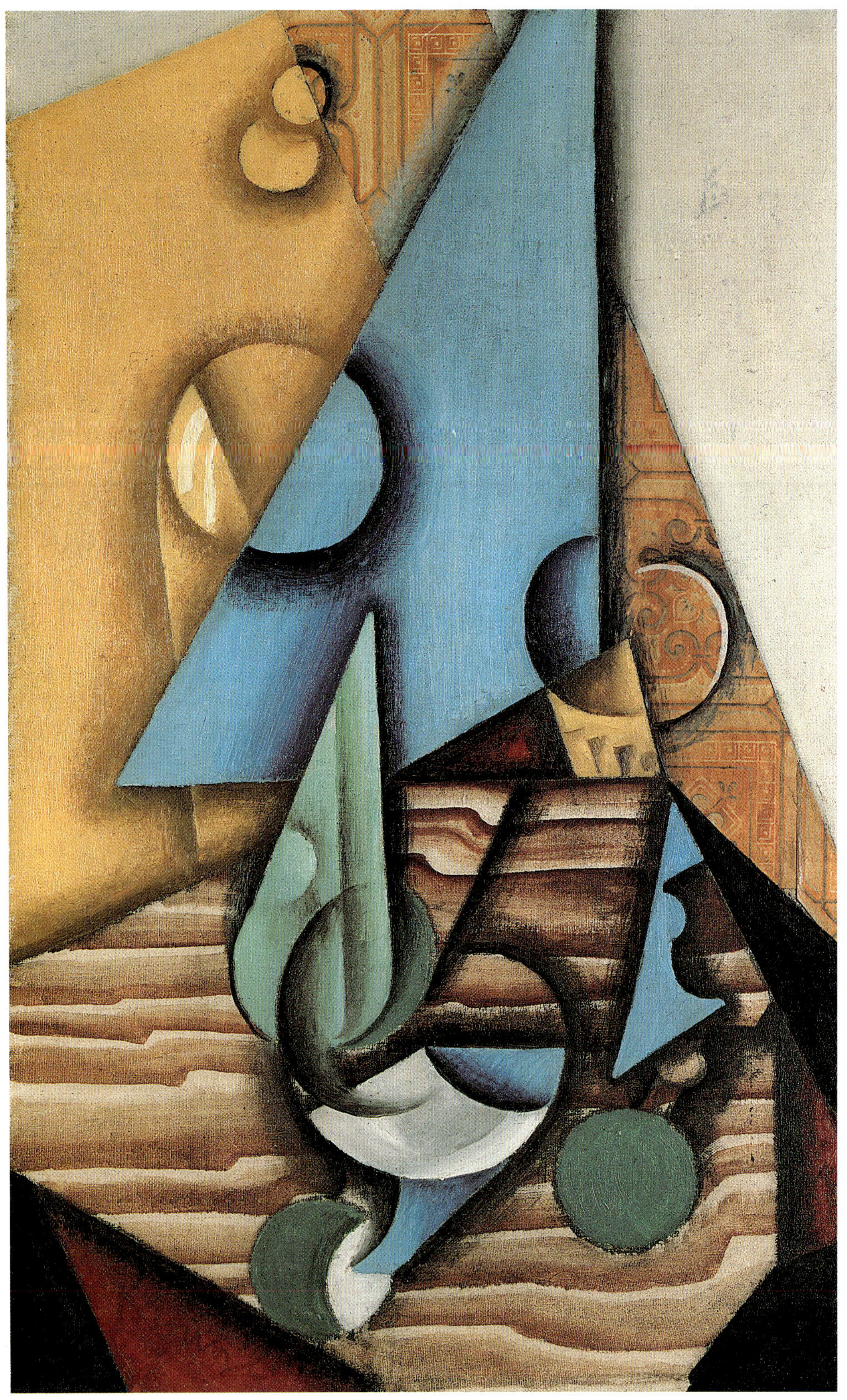

38
Bottle and Glass on a Table, 1913–14
Oil and papier collé on canvas, 61.5 x 38.5 cm
Galerie Jan Krugier, Geneva
[London and Stuttgart]

39
Still-life with Bottle and Glass, 1914
Oil and papier collé on canvas, 46.5 x 38 cm
Staatsgalerie Stuttgart

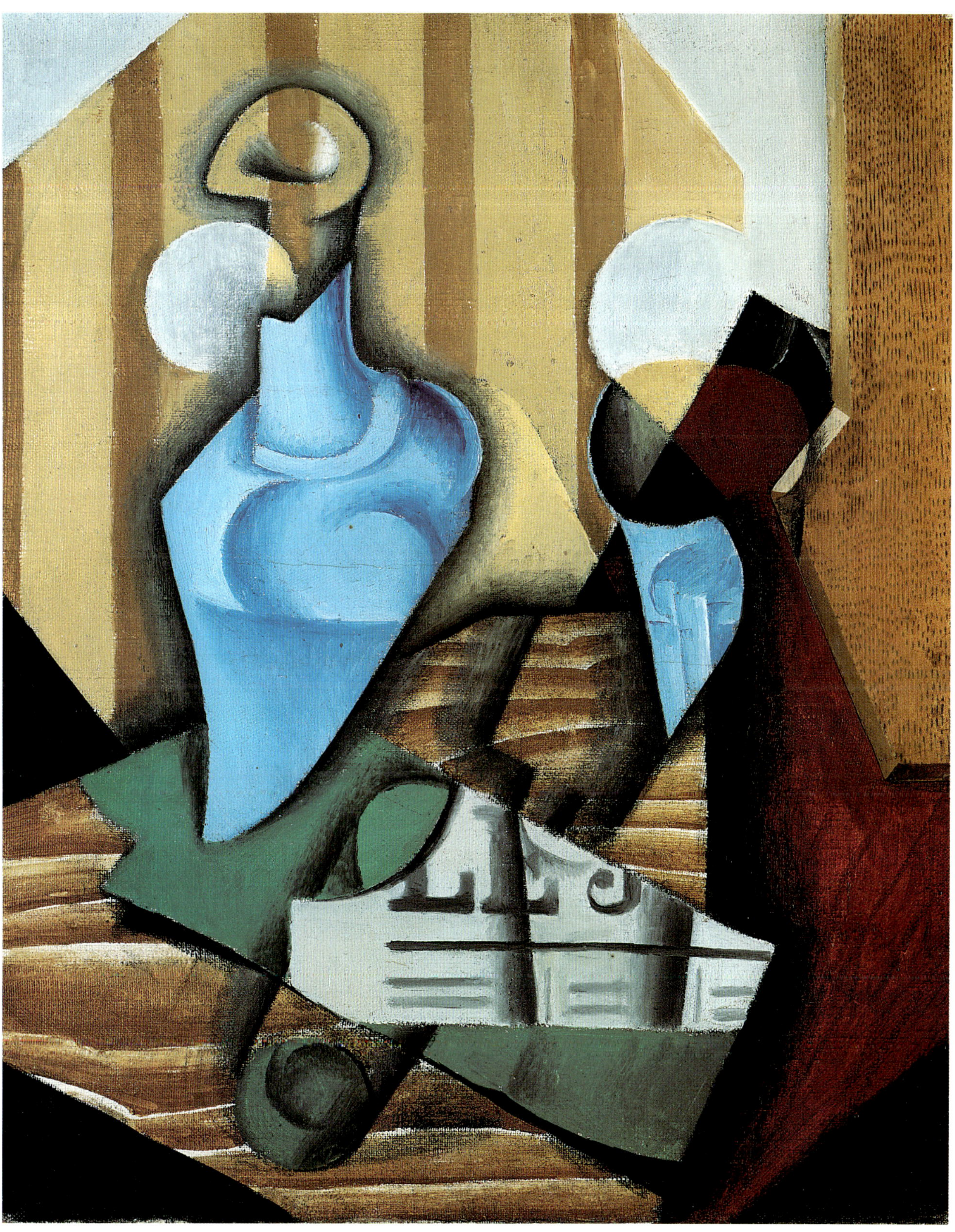

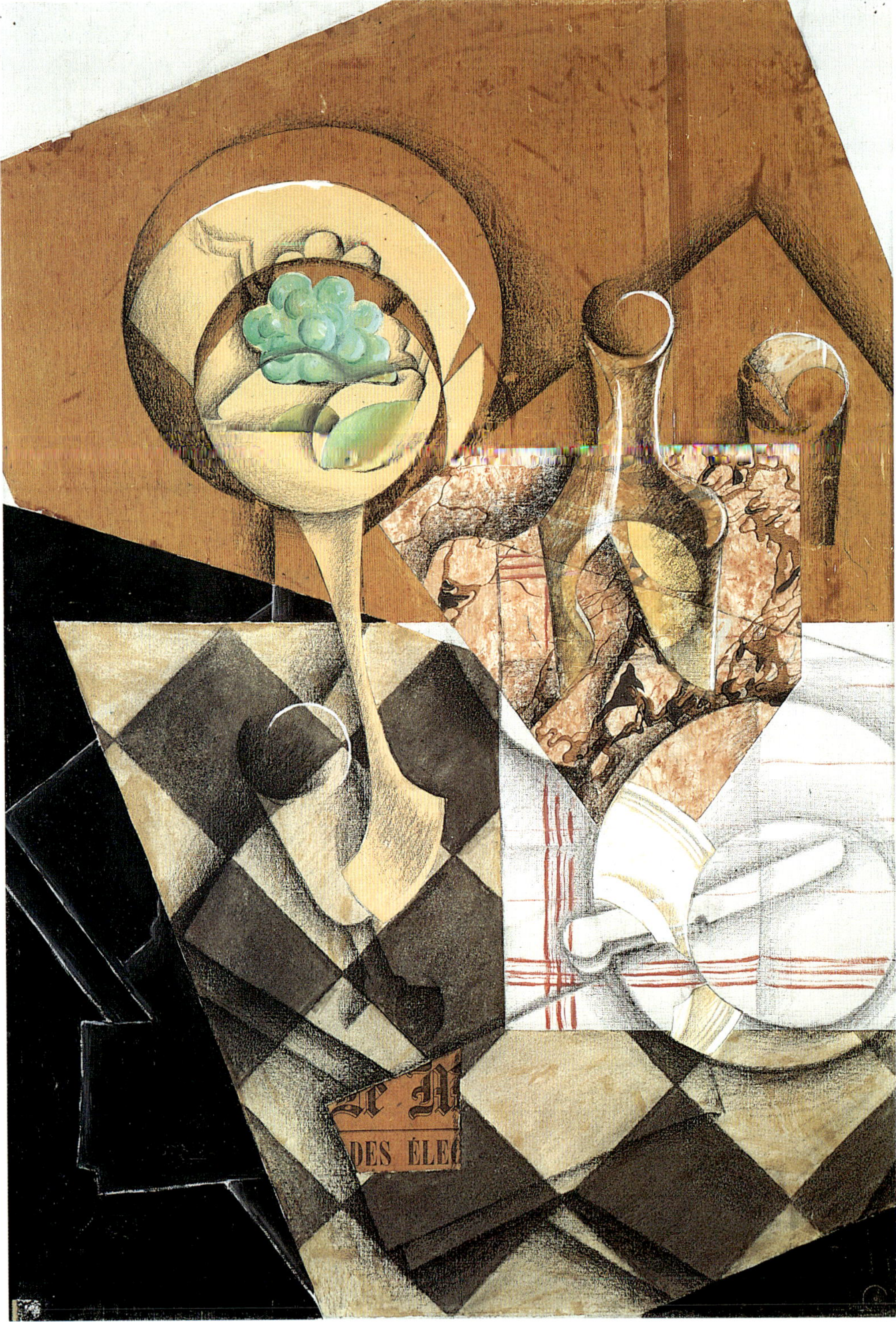

40
Fruit Dish and Carafe, 1914
Oil, papier collé and charcoal on canvas, 92 x 65 cm
Rijksmuseum Kröller-Müller, Otterlo
[Otterlo only]

41
The Packet of Coffee,
1914
Gouache, papier collé and charcoal on canvas, 65 x 47 cm
Ulmer Museum, Permanent Loan of the Land Baden-Württemberg

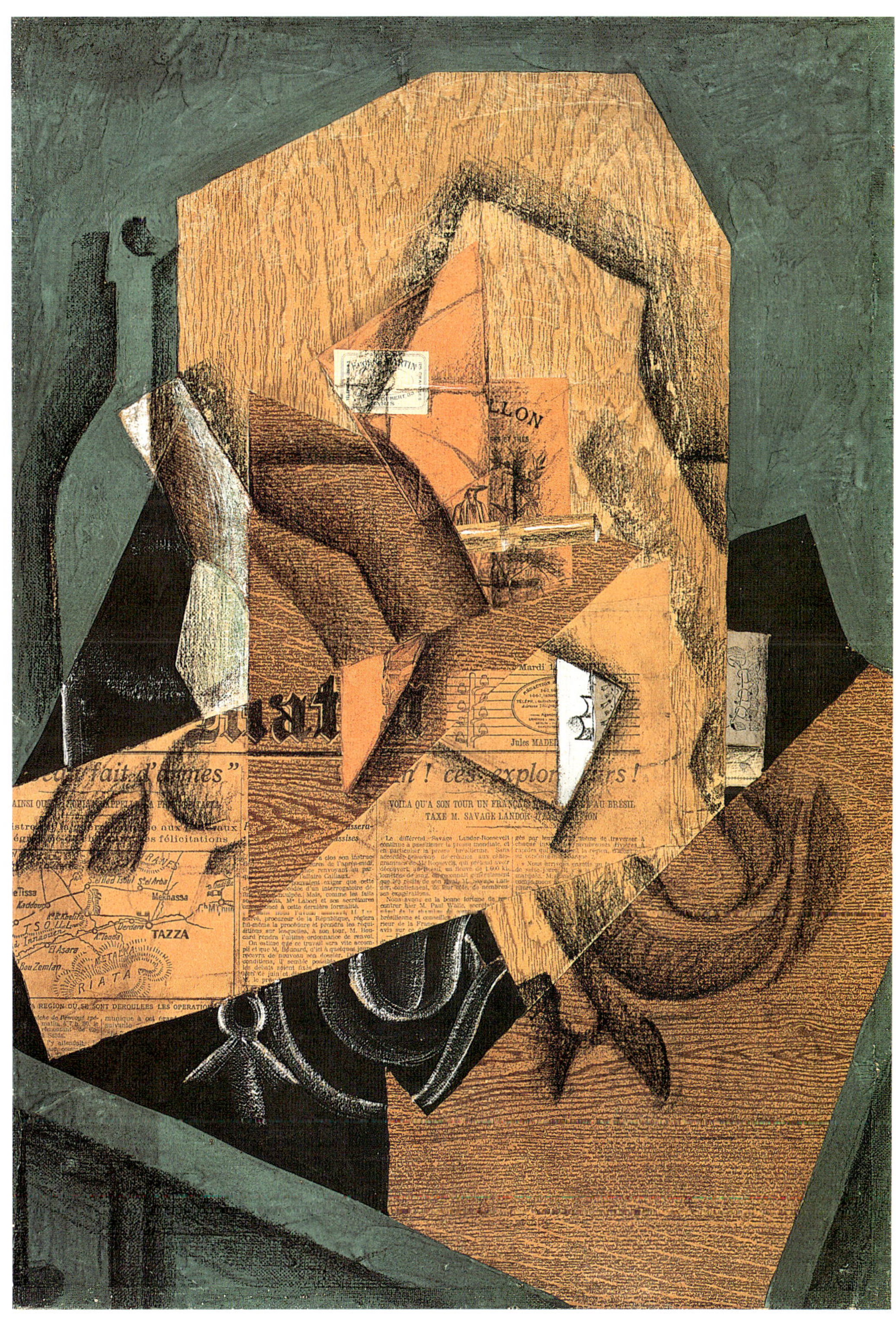

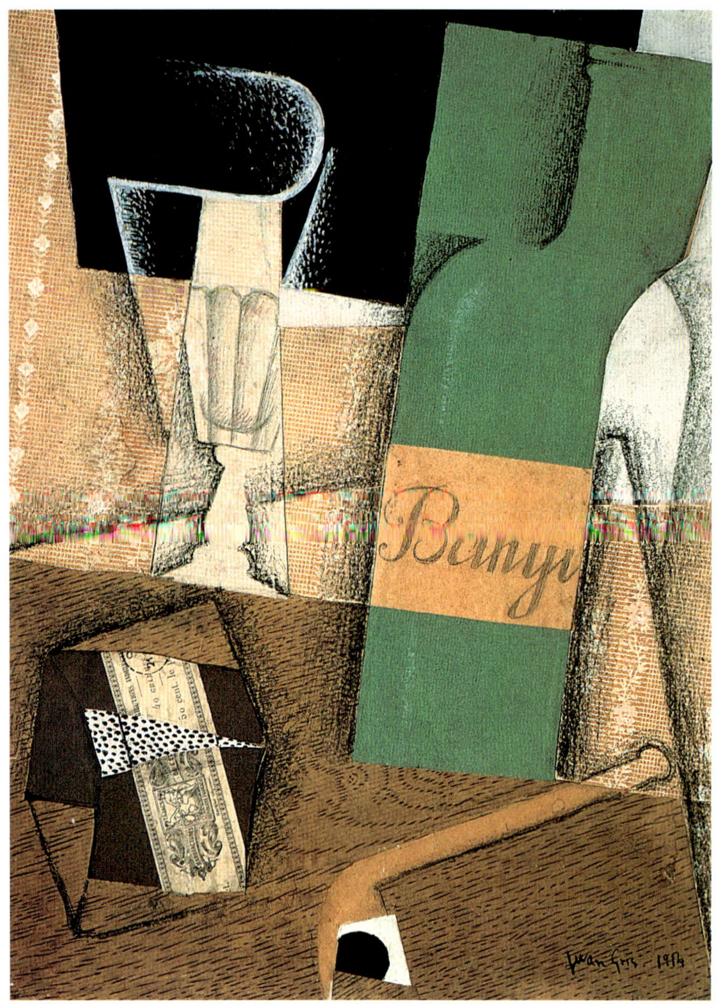

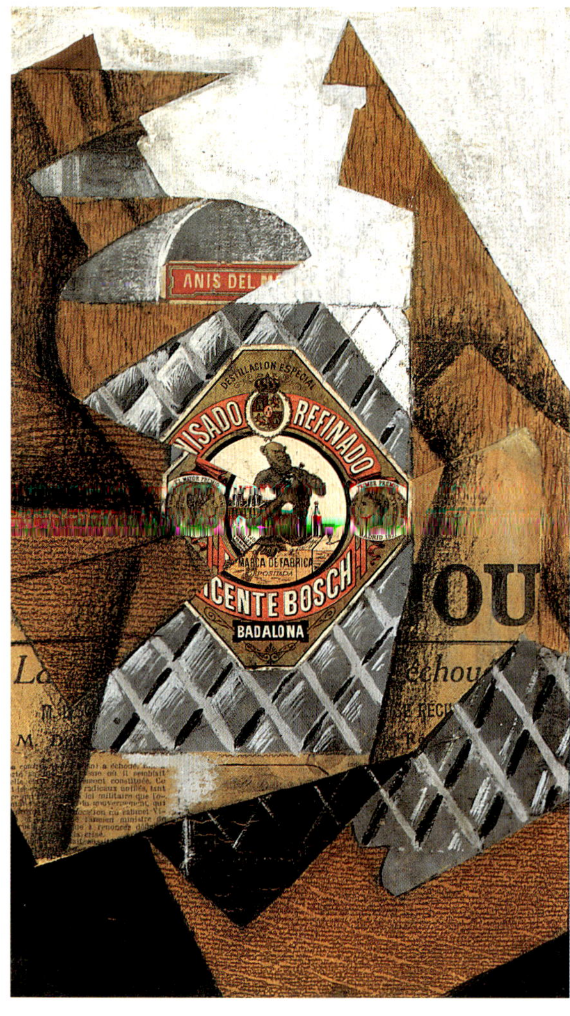

42
The Bottle of Banyuls, 1914
Papier collé, oil and pencil on board, 38 x 28.5 cm
Private Collection, Courtesy Thomas Ammann Fine Art, Zurich

43
The Bottle of Anis del Mono, 1914
Papier collé, oil and charcoal on canvas, 41.8 x 24 cm
Judith Rothschild
[London only]

44
Flowers, 1914
Oil, papier collé and pencil on canvas, 55 x 46 cm
Hester Diamond
[London only]

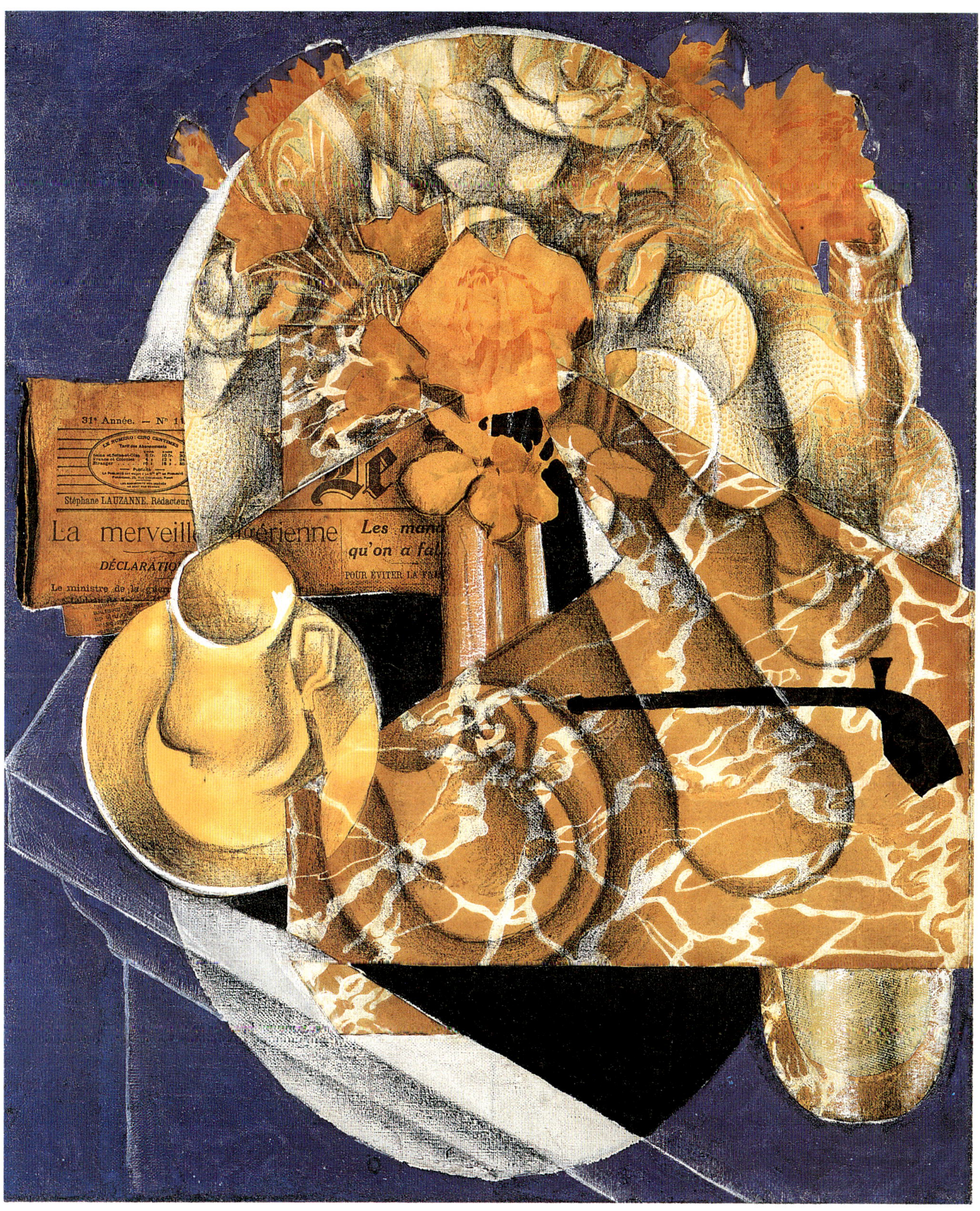
31e Année. —
Stéphane LAUZANNE,
La
Les
qu'on a
POUR ÉVITER LA
Le ministre de la

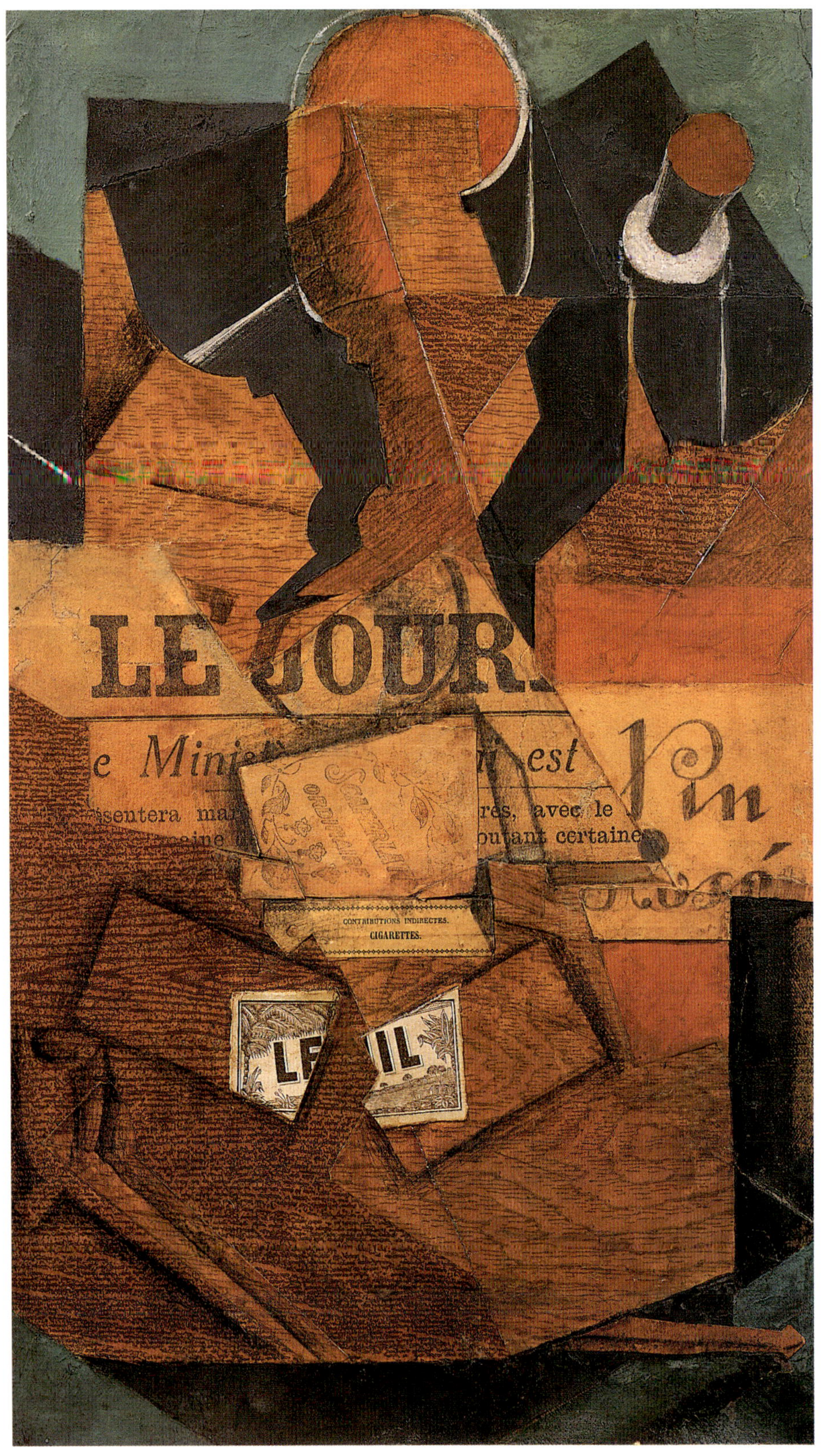

45
Tobacco, Newspaper and Bottle of Wine,
1914
Oil, papier collé and charcoal on canvas,
44.5 x 26 cm
Private Collection

46
Still-life with Checked Tablecloth,
1915
Oil on canvas,
116 x 89 cm
Private Collection
[Stuttgart only]

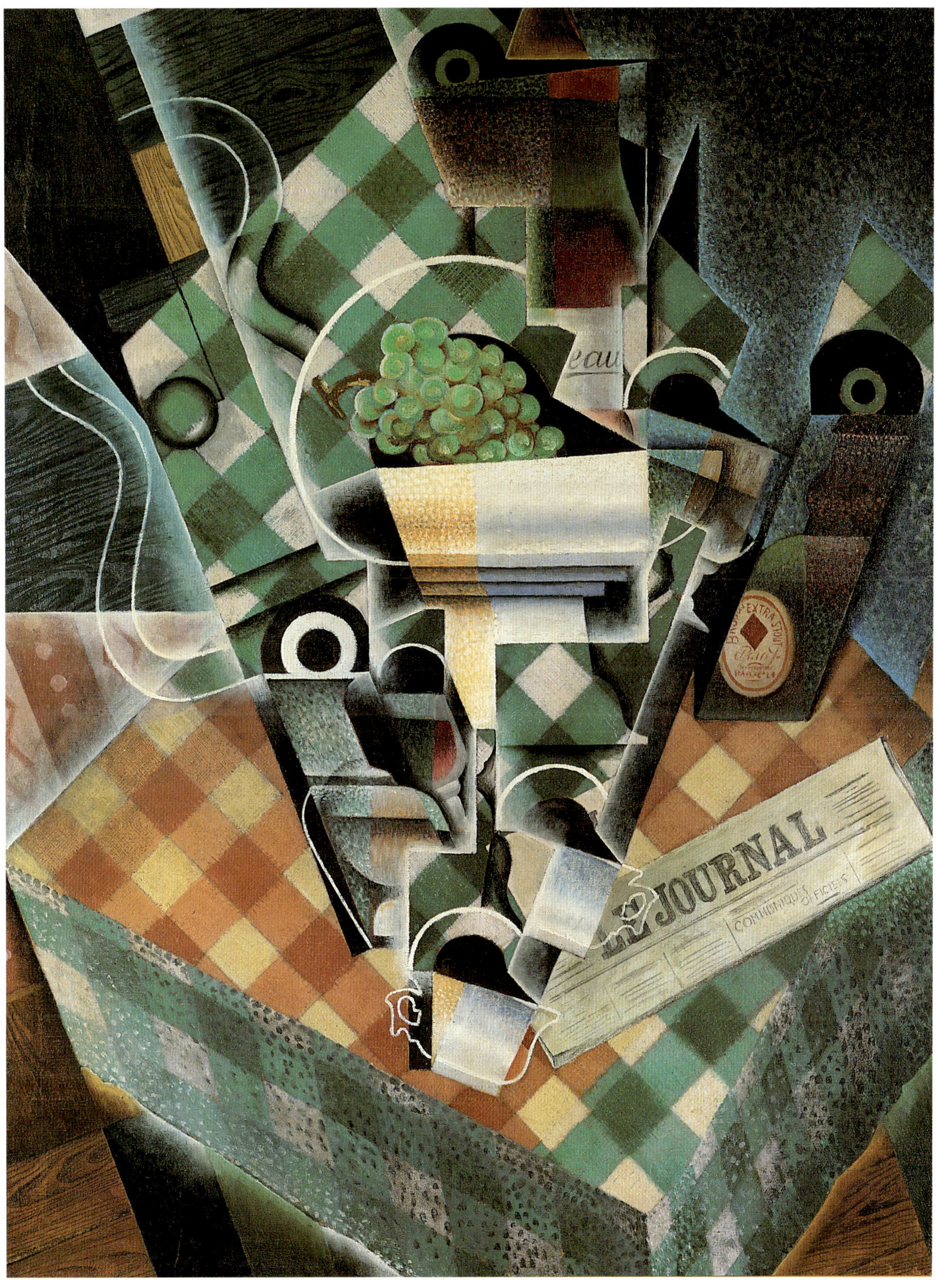
eau
LE JOURNAL
COMMUNIQUES OFFICIELS

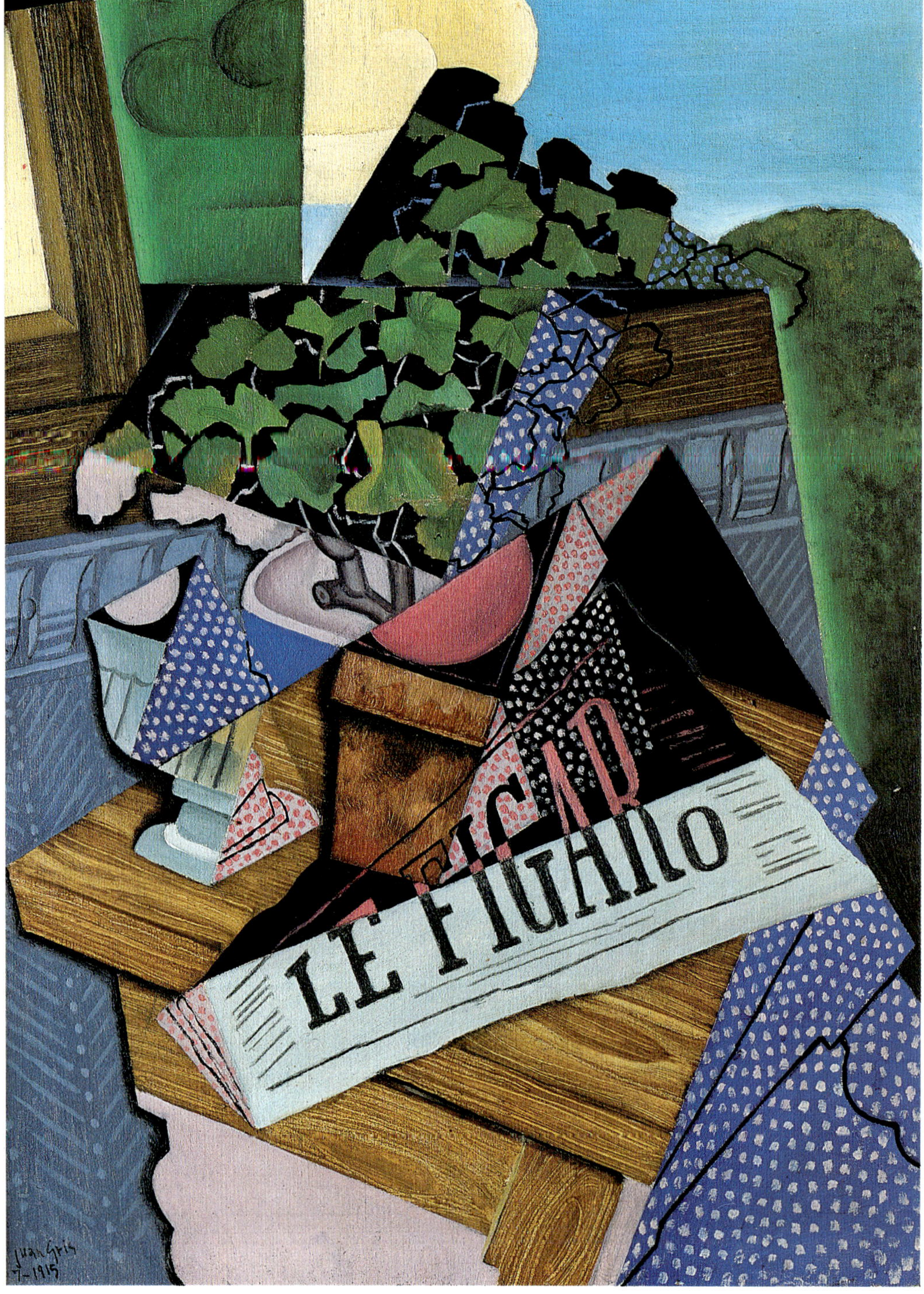

47
The Pot of Geraniums, 1915
Oil on canvas, 81 x 60 cm
Collection S

48
Still-life and Town-scape (Place Ravignan), 1915
Oil on canvas,
114.5 x 89 cm
Philadelphia Museum of Art: The Louise and Walter Arensberg Collection

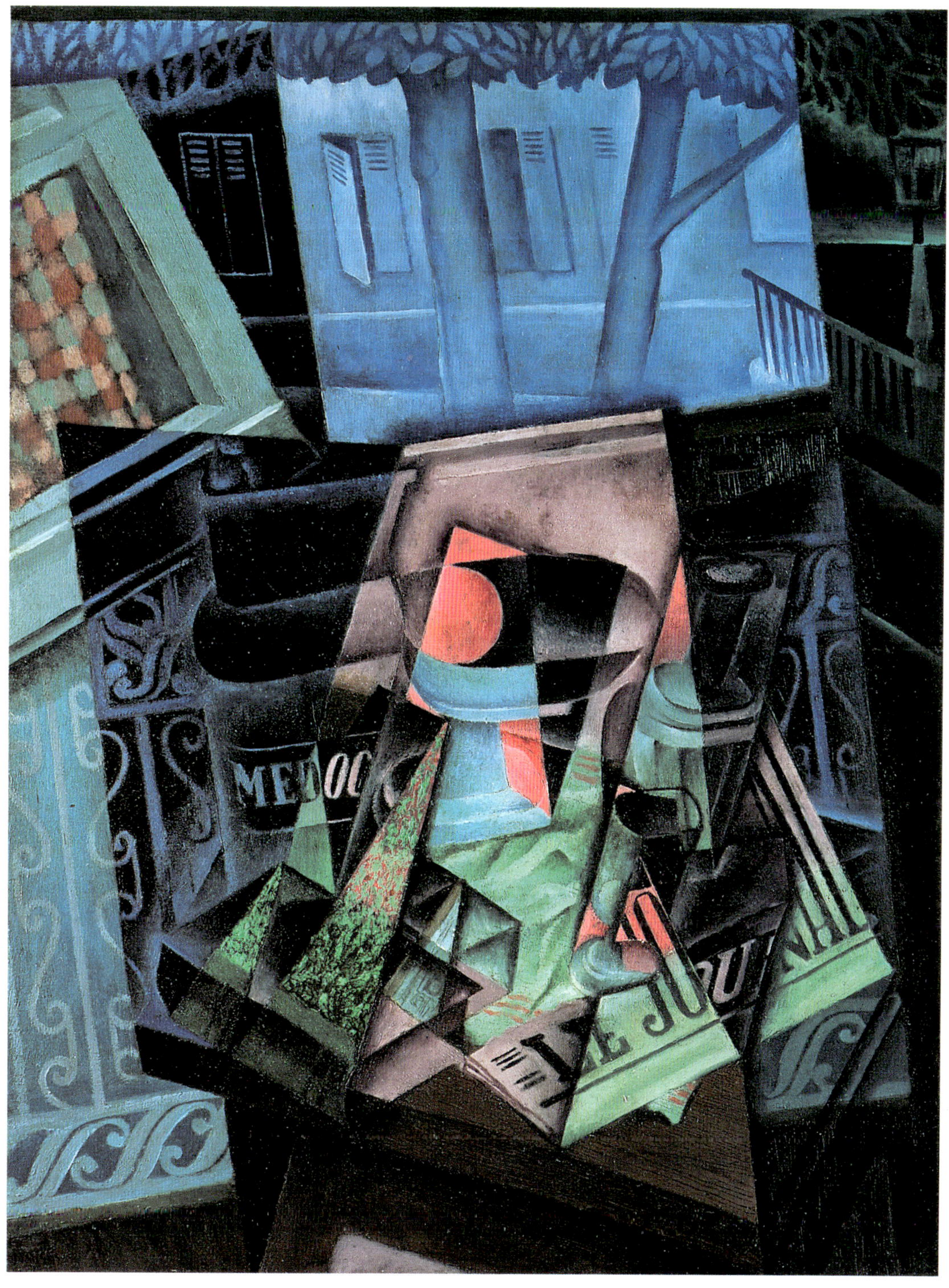

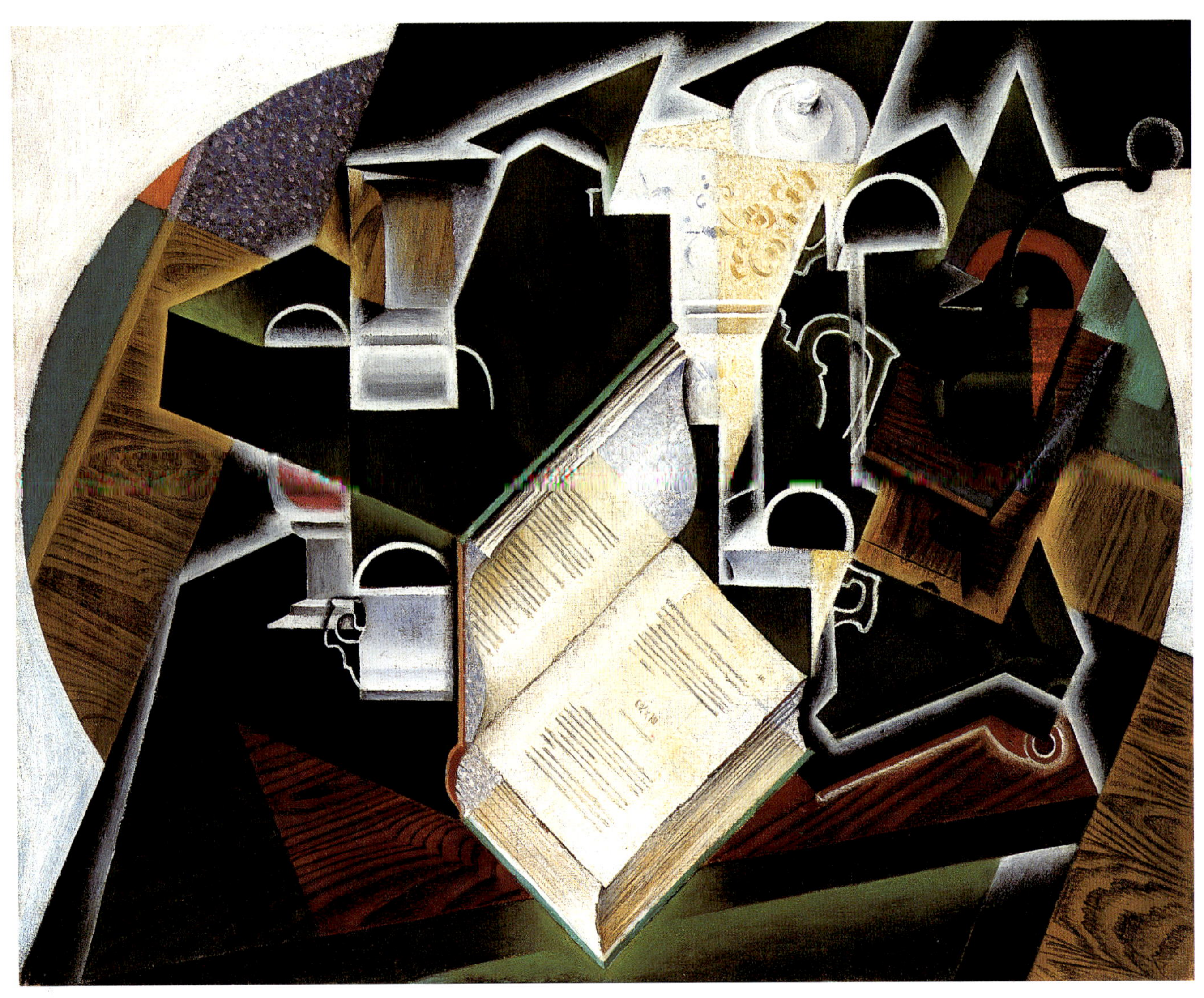

49
Book, Pipe and Glasses, 1915
Oil on canvas,
73 x 91.5 cm
Private Collection
[London and Stuttgart only]

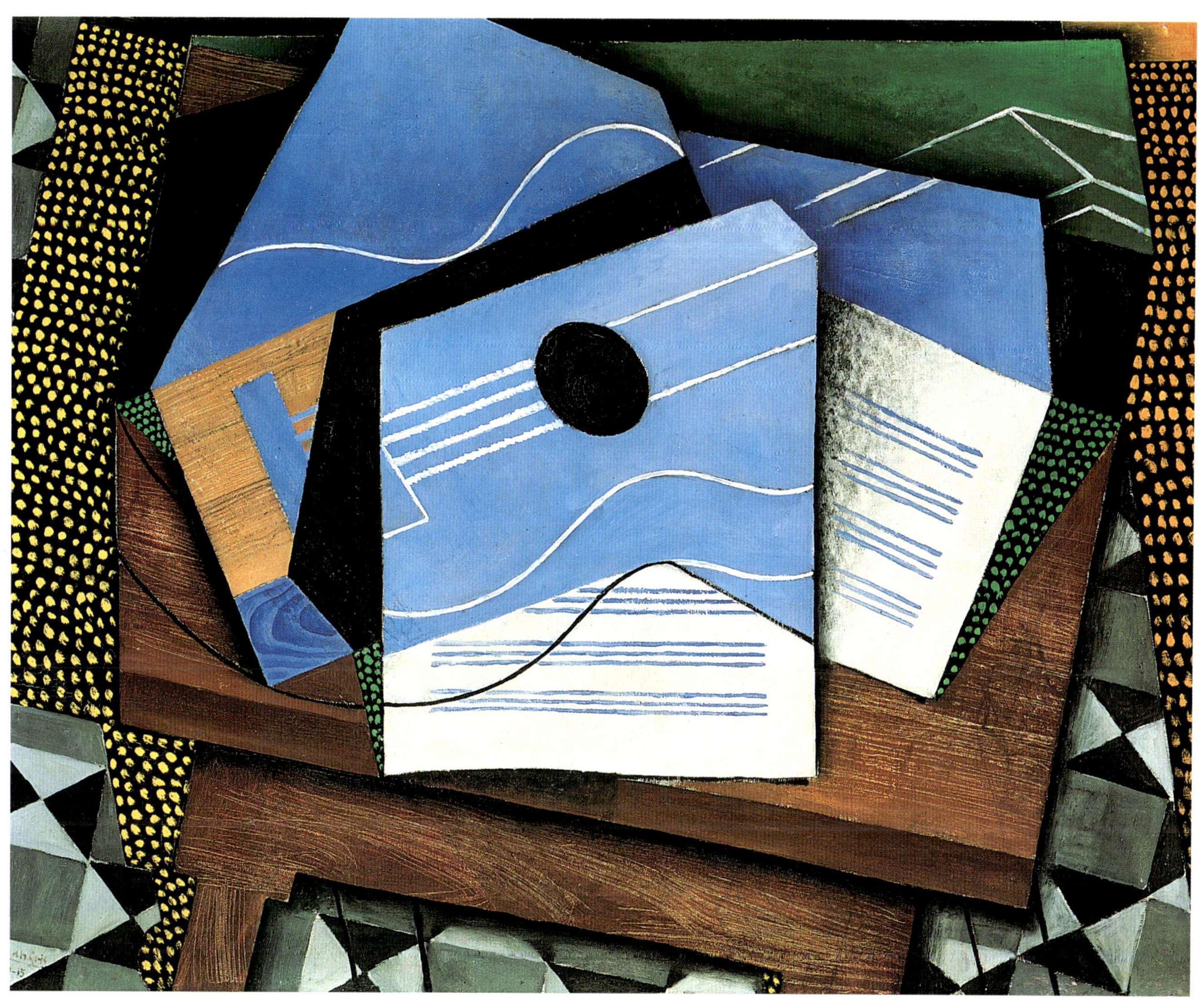

50
Guitar on a Table,
1915
Oil on canvas,
73 x 92 cm
Rijksmuseum Kröller-Müller, Otterlo

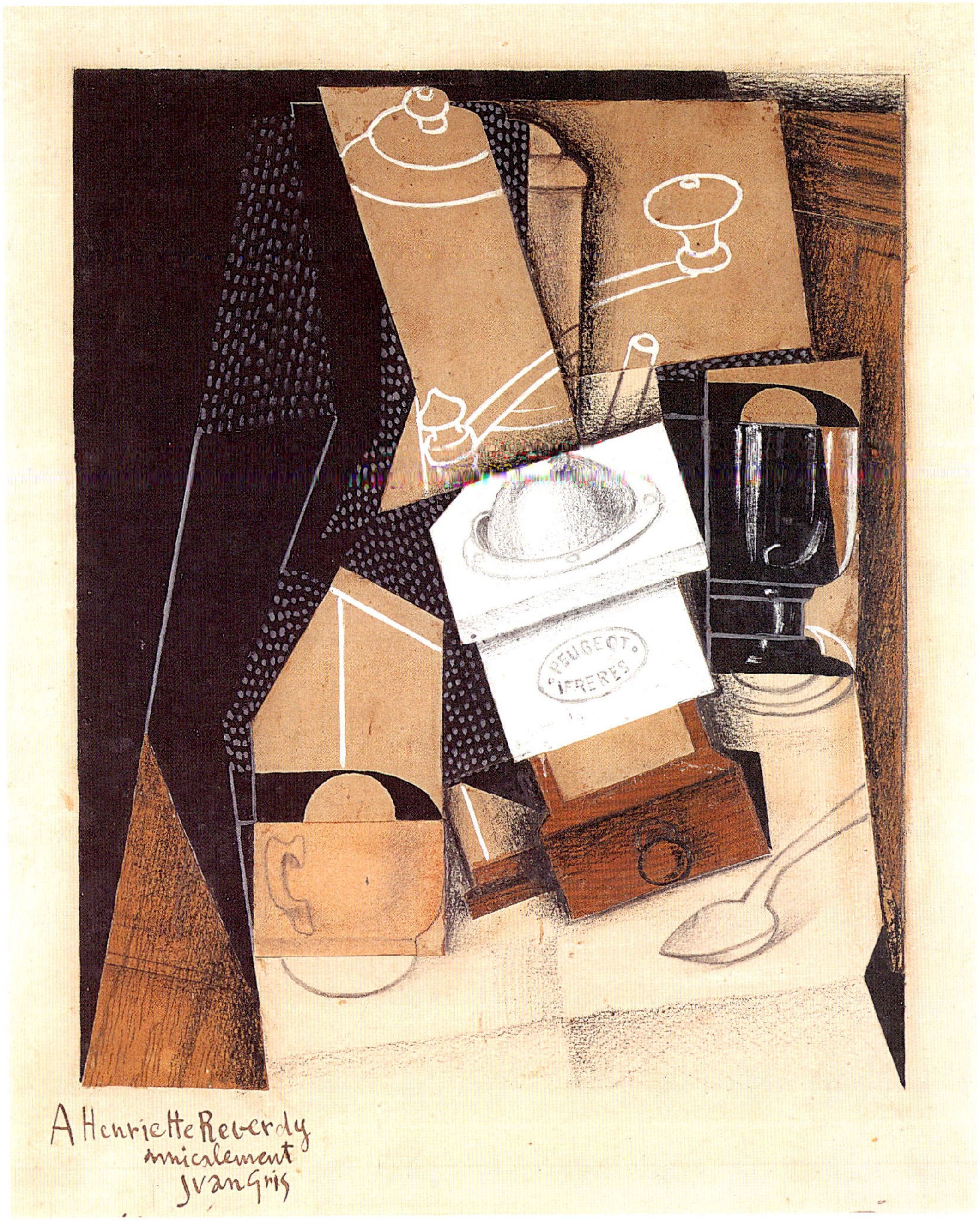

51
The Coffee Grinder,
1916
Oil and papier collé
on paper with poem,
47.6 x 31.8 cm
Judith Rothschild
[London only]

52
Breakfast, 1915
Oil and pencil on
canvas, 92 x 73 cm
Musée National d'Art
Moderne, Centre
Georges Pompidou,
Paris (1947)

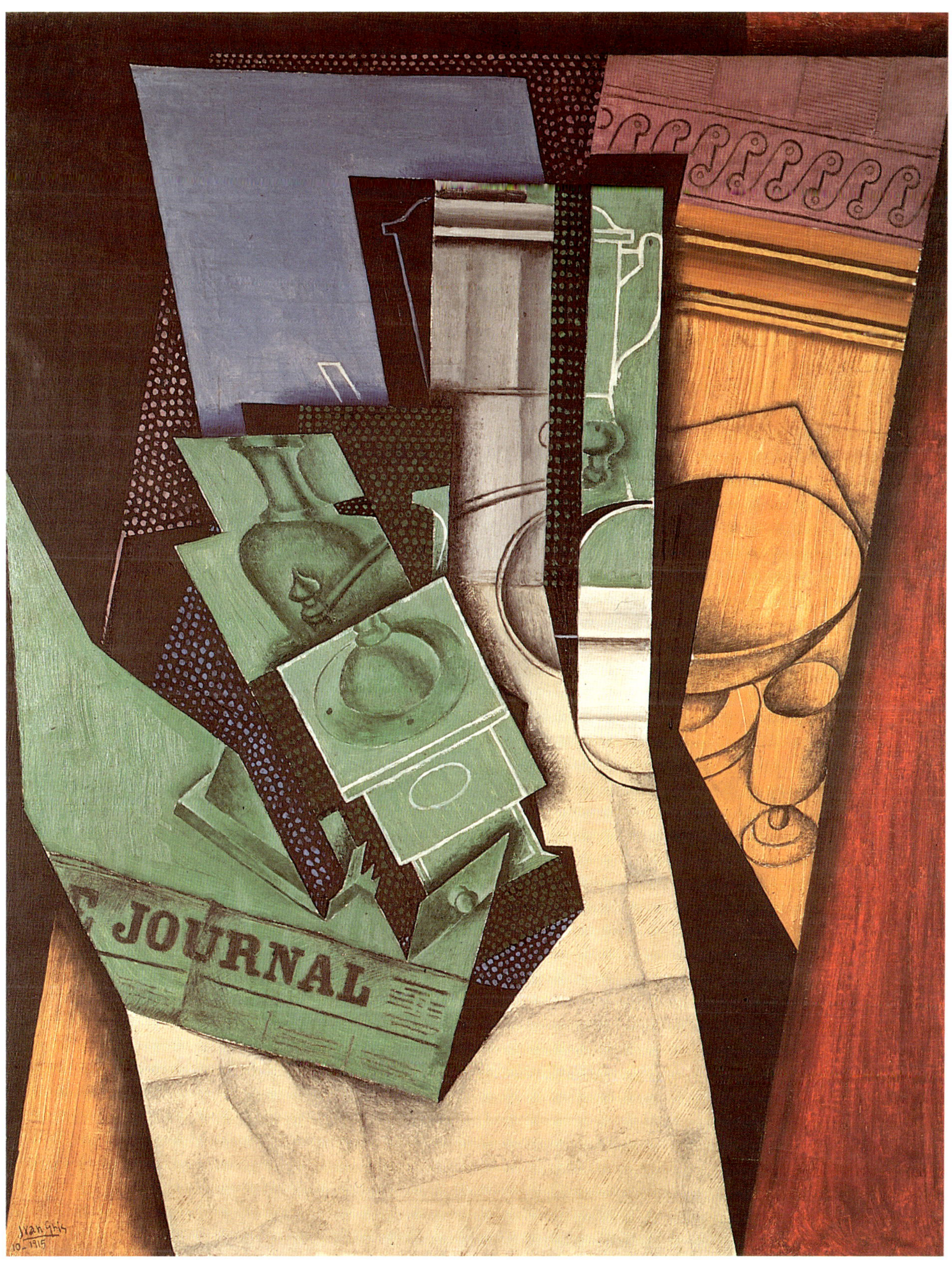
JOURNAL

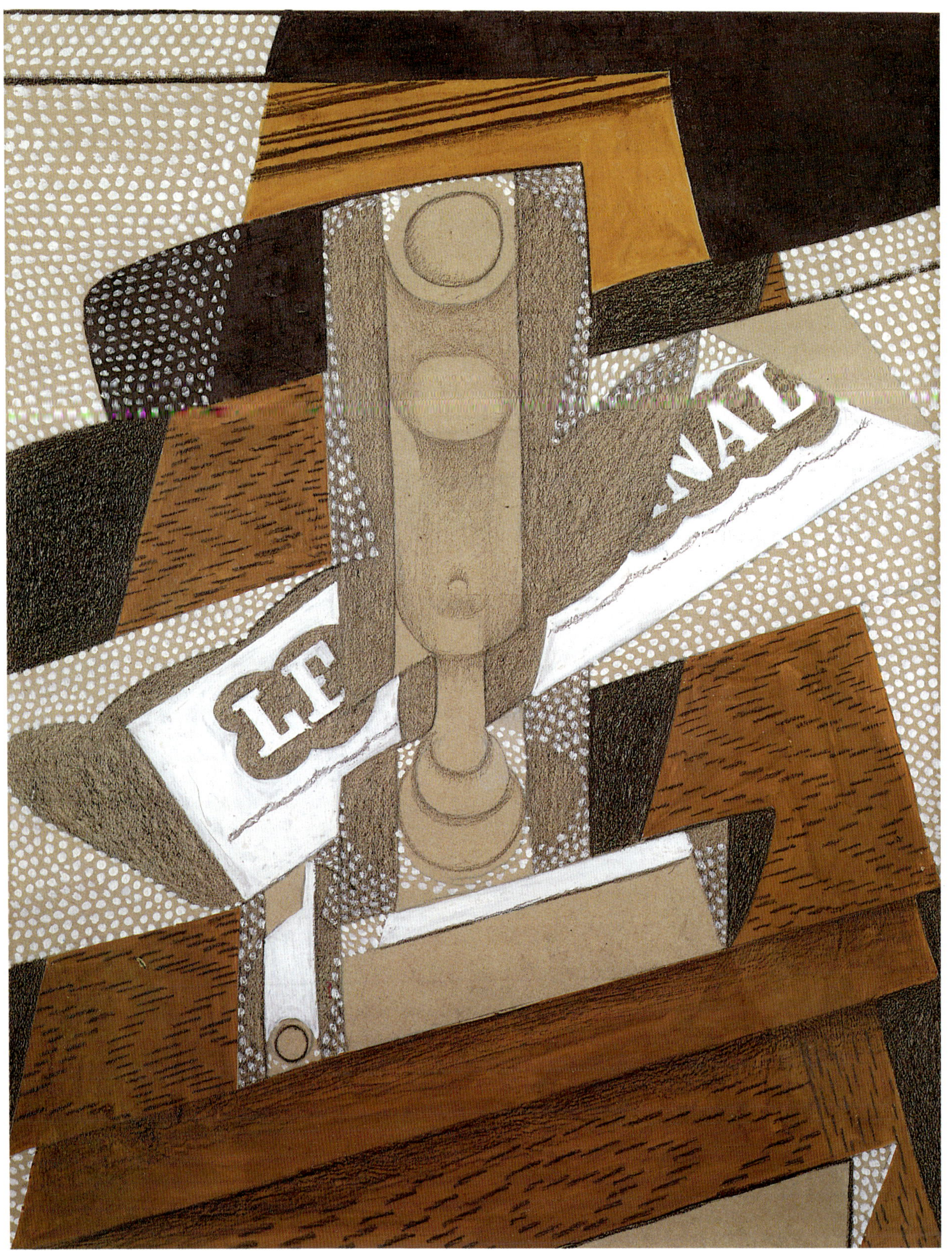
NAL

53
The Pipe, 1916
Gouache on paper,
27.3 x 21.6 cm
Collection Lois and
Georges de Menil

54
Newspaper and Fruit Dish, 1916
Oil on canvas,
92 x 60 cm
Yale University Art
Gallery, New Haven,
Connecticut. Gift of
Collection Société
Anonyme

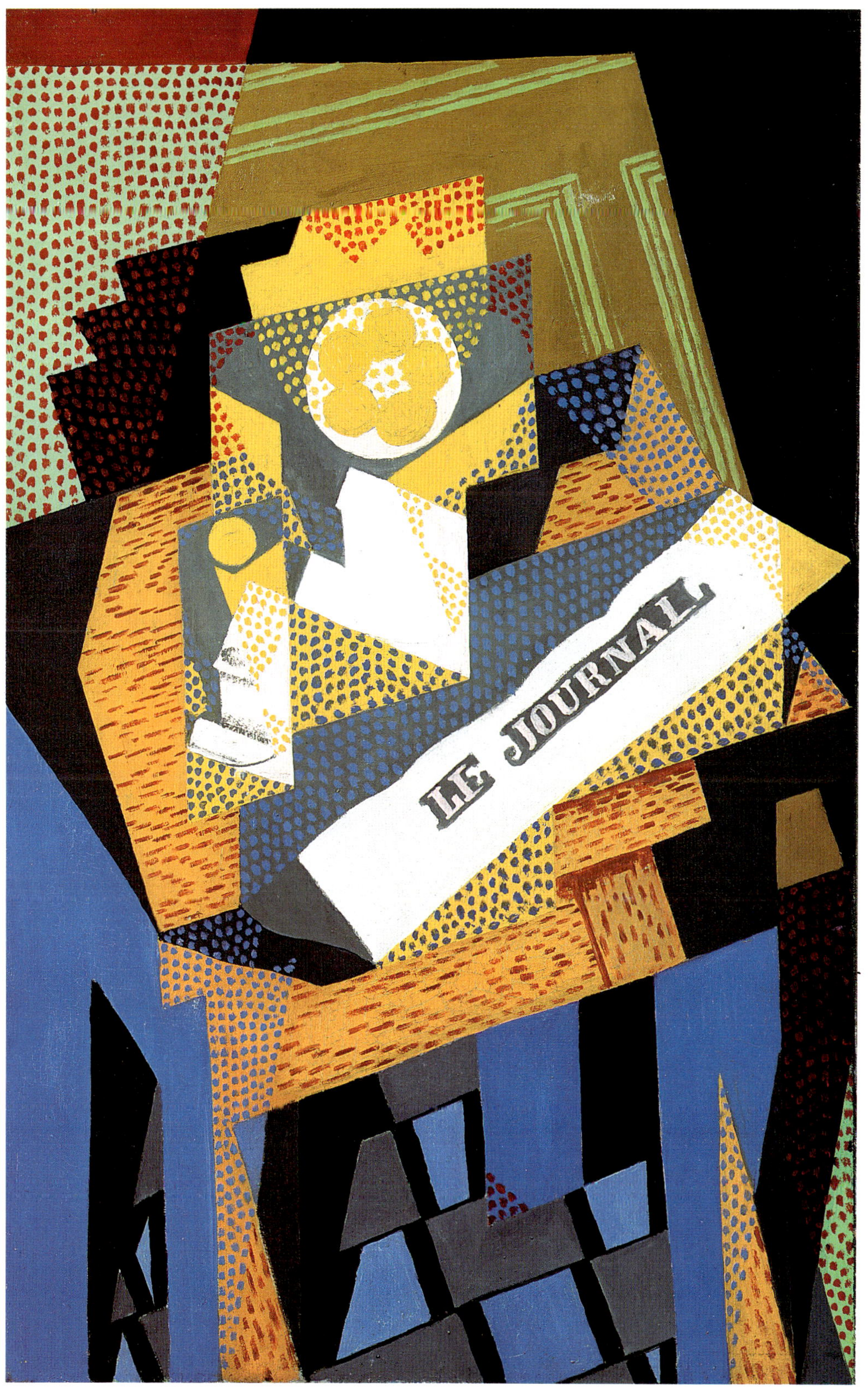

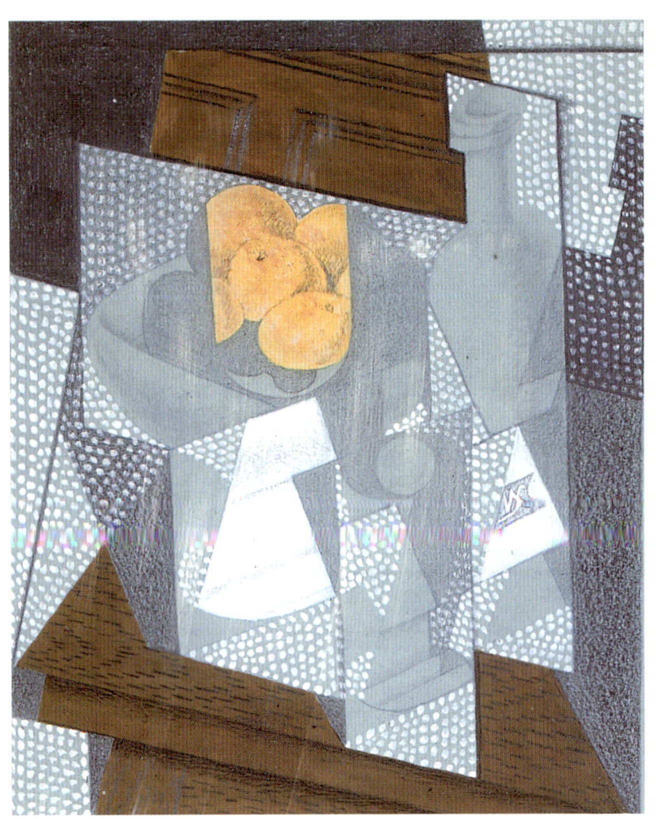

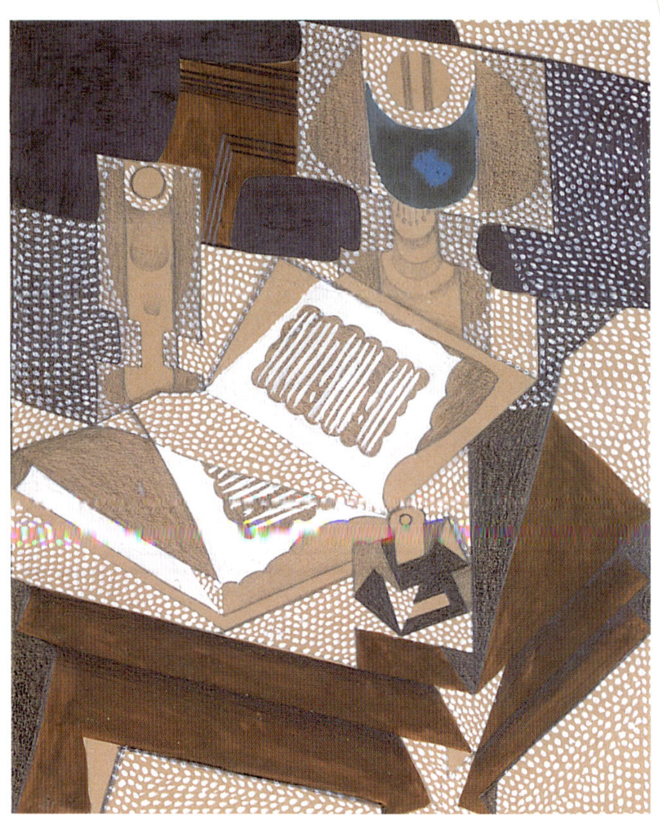

55
The Fruit Dish, 1915
Gouache on paper,
27.5 x 22.5 cm
Judith Rothschild
[London only]

56
The Book, 1915
Gouache on paper,
27.5 x 22.5 cm
Judith Rothschild
[London only]

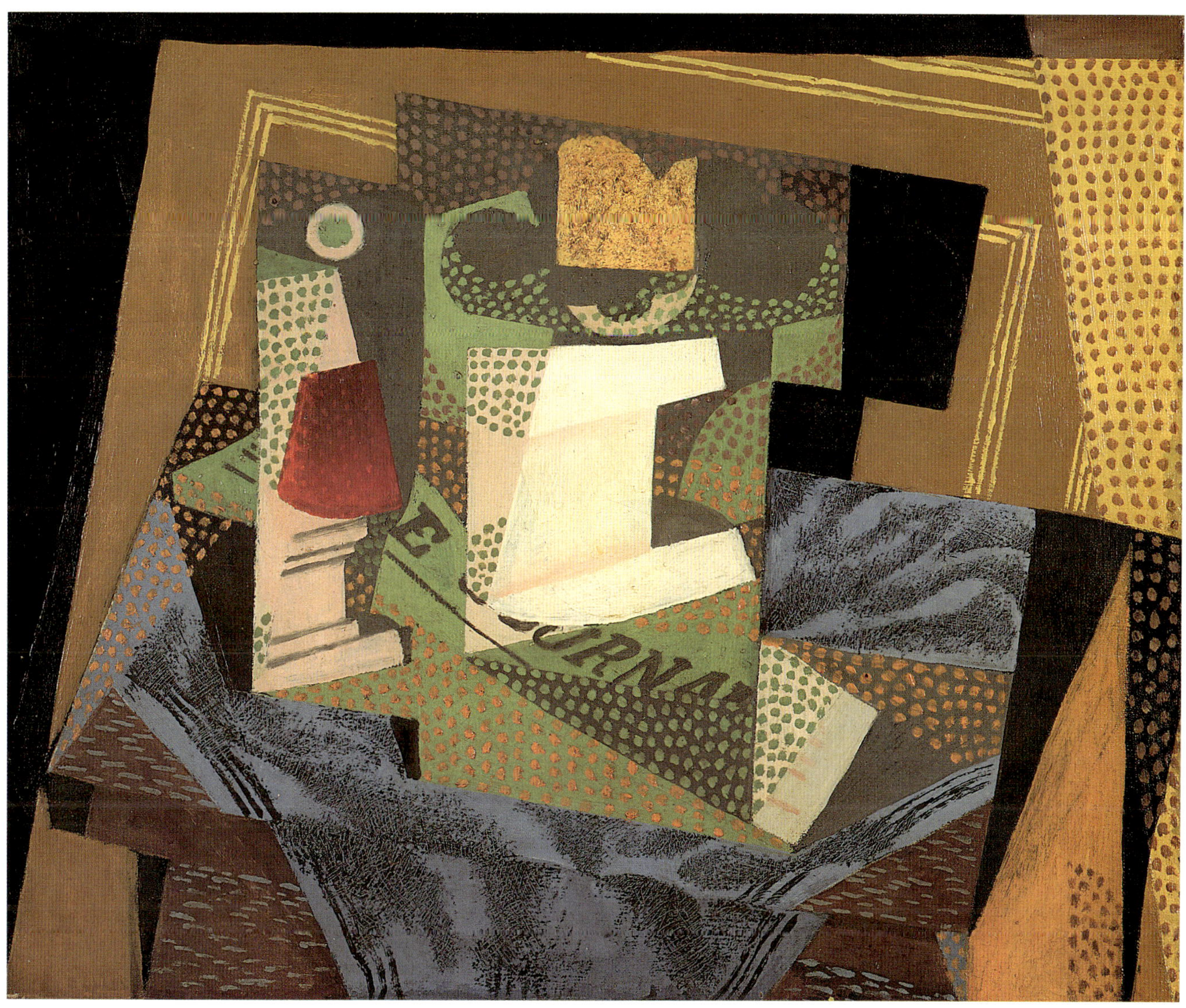

57
Fruit Dish on a Blue Tablecloth, 1916
Oil on canvas,
50 x 61 cm
Moderna Museet,
Stockholm

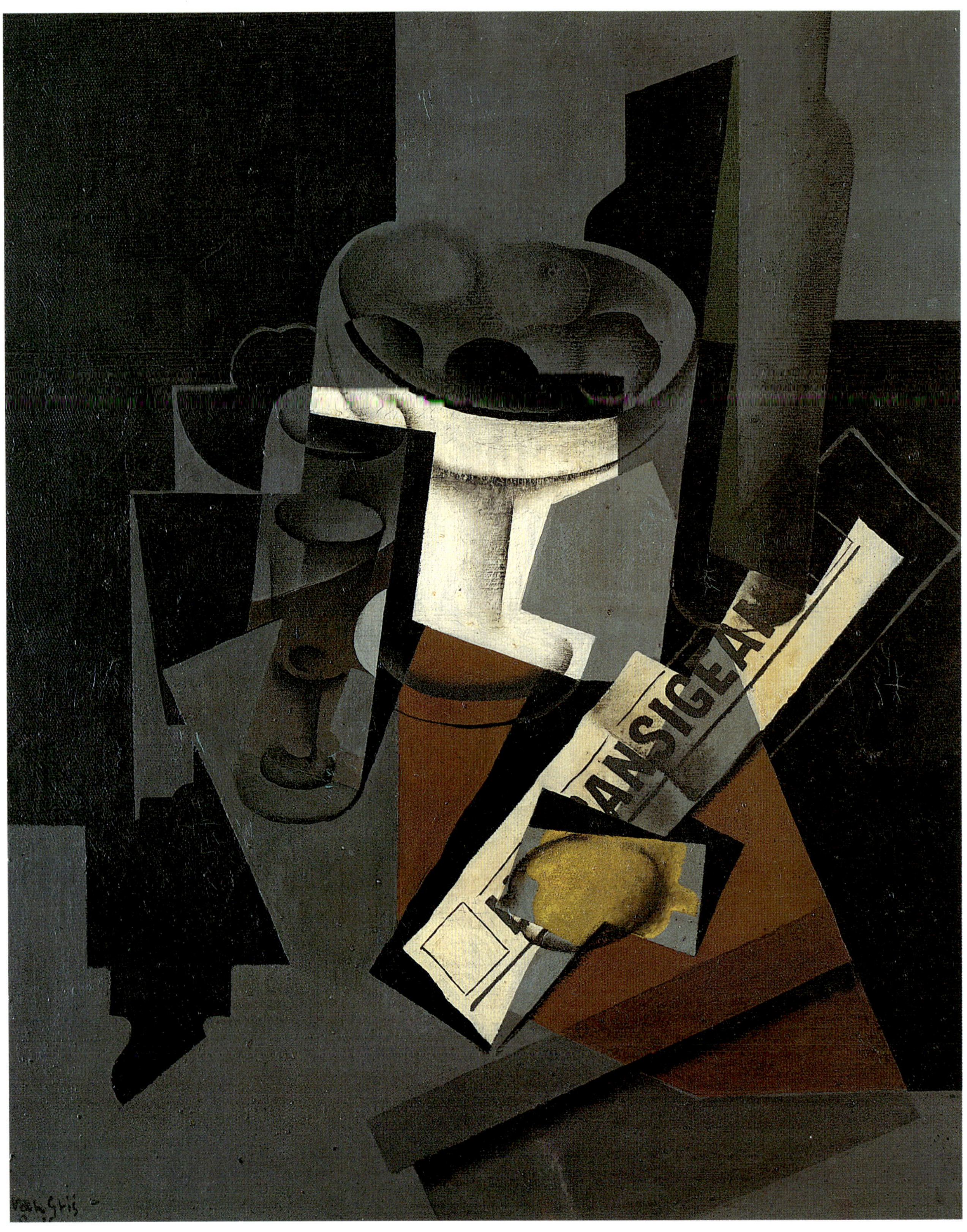
ANSIGEA

58
Fruit Dish, Glass and Lemon (Still-life with Newspaper), 1916
Oil on canvas,
73.6 x 60.3 cm
The Phillips Collection,
Washington, DC

59
Fruit Dish, Glass and Newspaper, 1916
Oil on plywood,
56 x 31 cm
Private Collection,
Courtesy of Thomas Ammann Fine Art,
Zurich

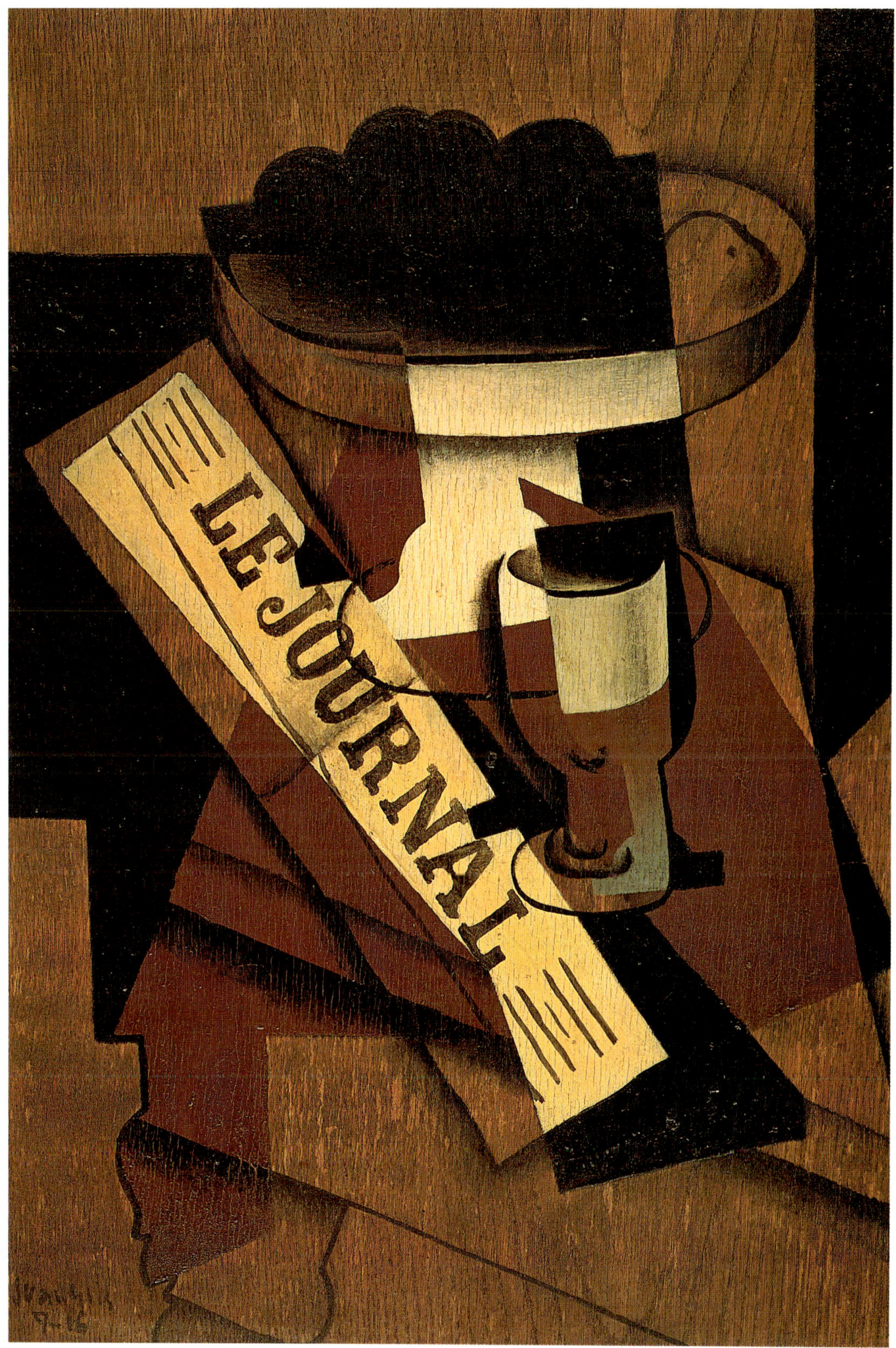

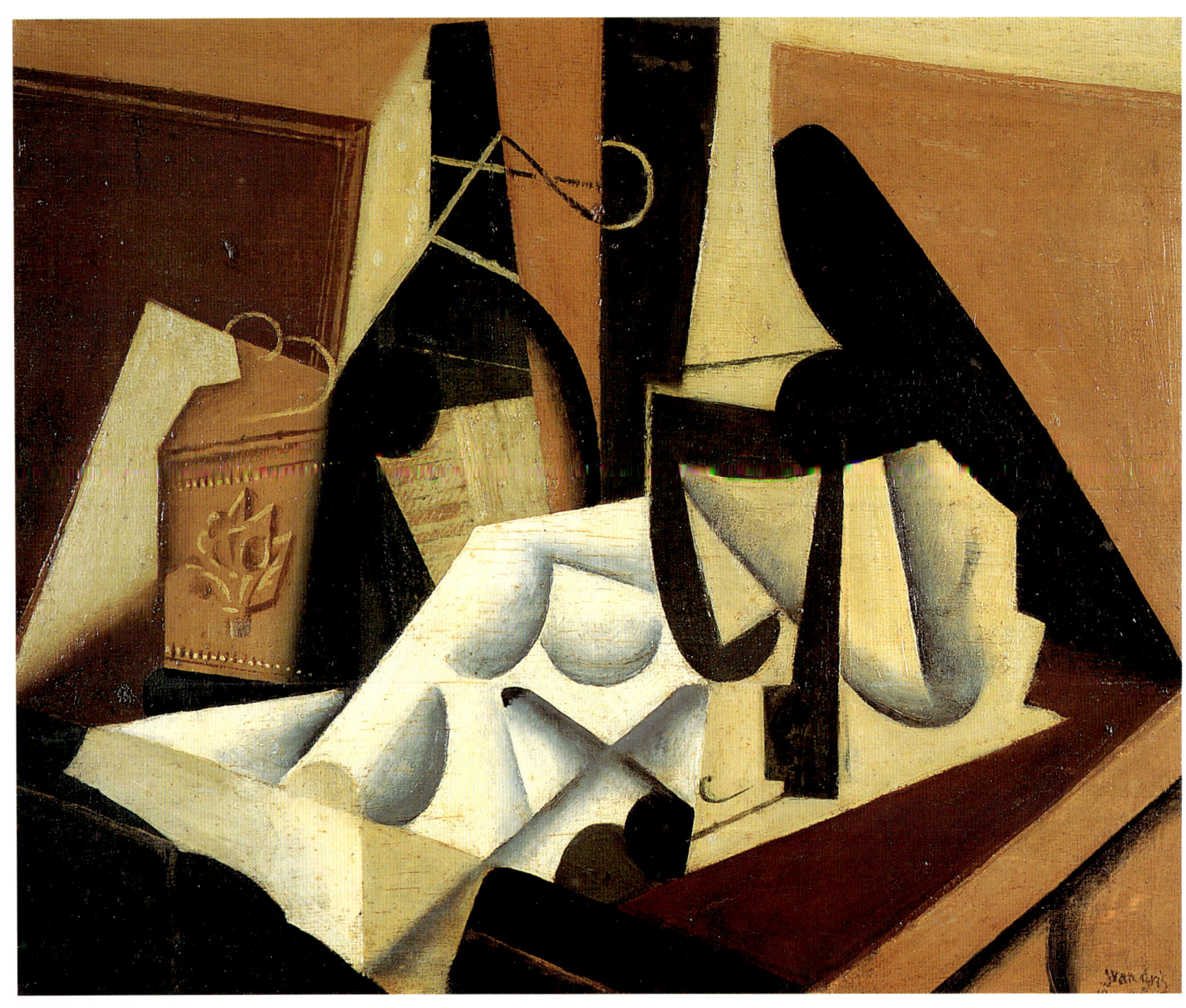

60
Still-life with White Tablecloth, 1916
Oil on canvas, 51x61 cm
Private Collection

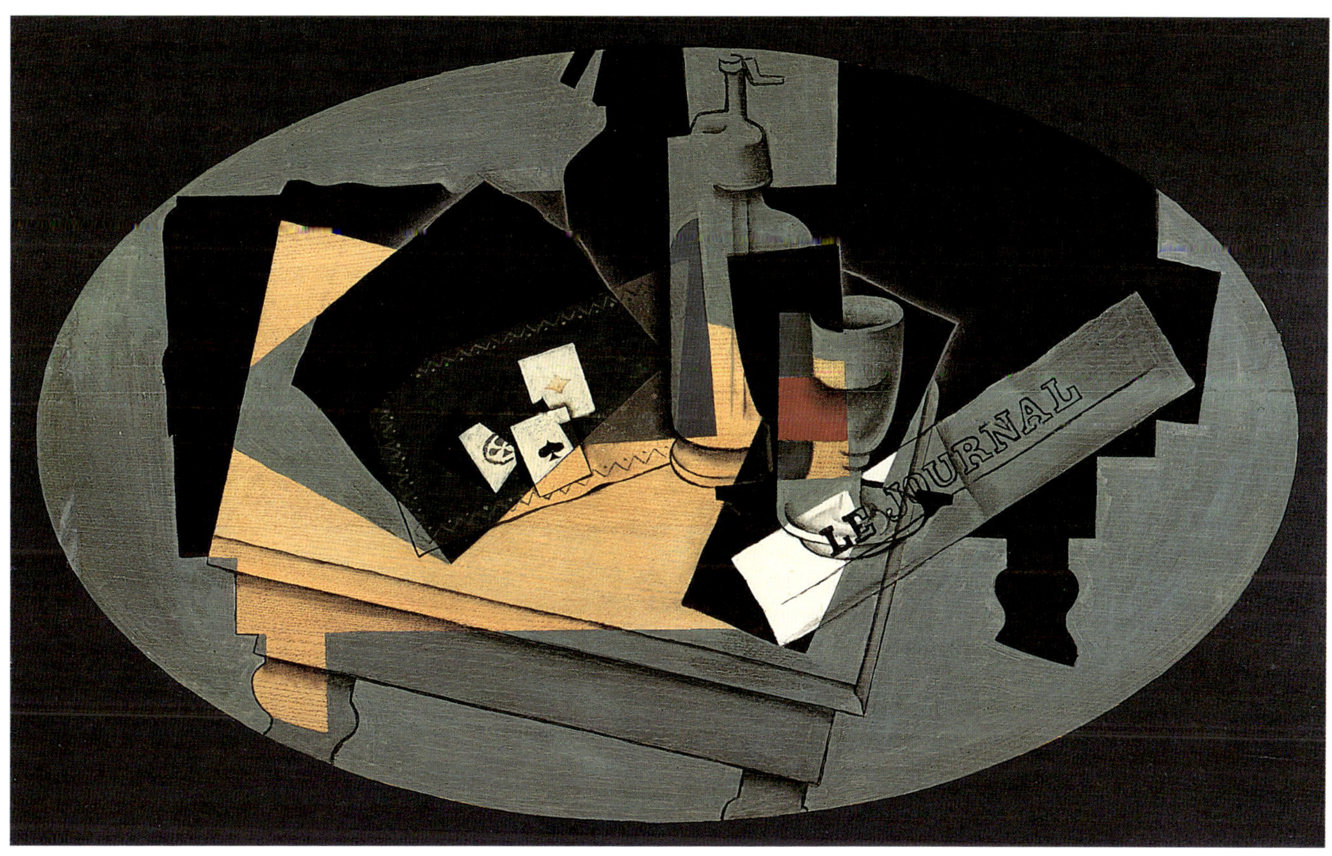

61
Playing Cards and Siphon, 1916
Oil on canvas,
73 x 116 cm
Rijksmuseum Kroller-Müller, Otterlo

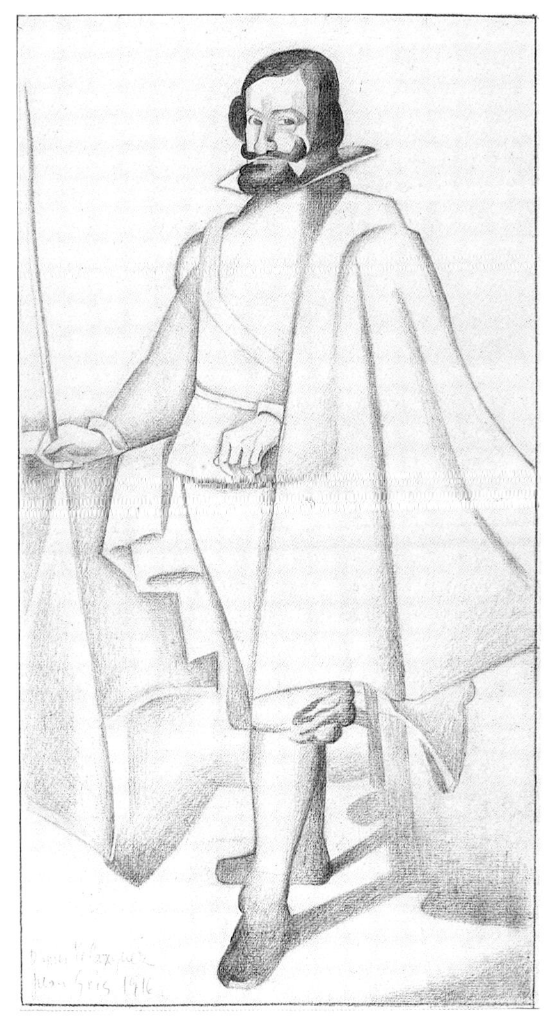

62
Head of a Harlequin (after Cézanne), 1916
Pencil on paper,
25.6 x 20.5 cm
Musée National d'Art Moderne, Centre Georges Pompidou, Paris (1951)

63
Don Gaspar de Guzmán (after Velázquez), 1916
Pencil on paper,
45 x 24.2 cm
Rijksmuseum Kröller-Müller, Otterlo

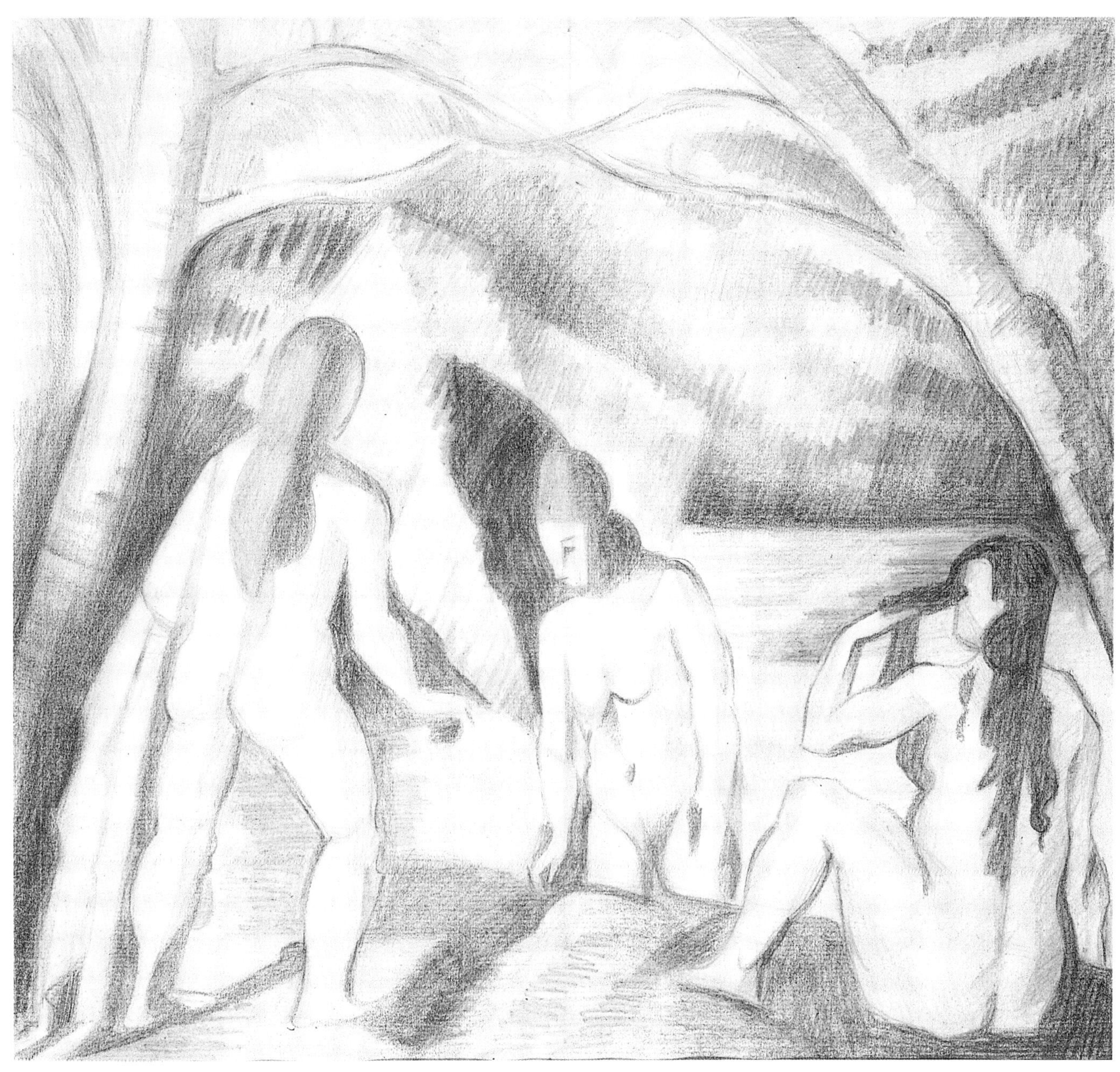

64
Bathers (after Cézanne), 1916
Pencil on paper,
28 x 39.1 cm
Private Collection

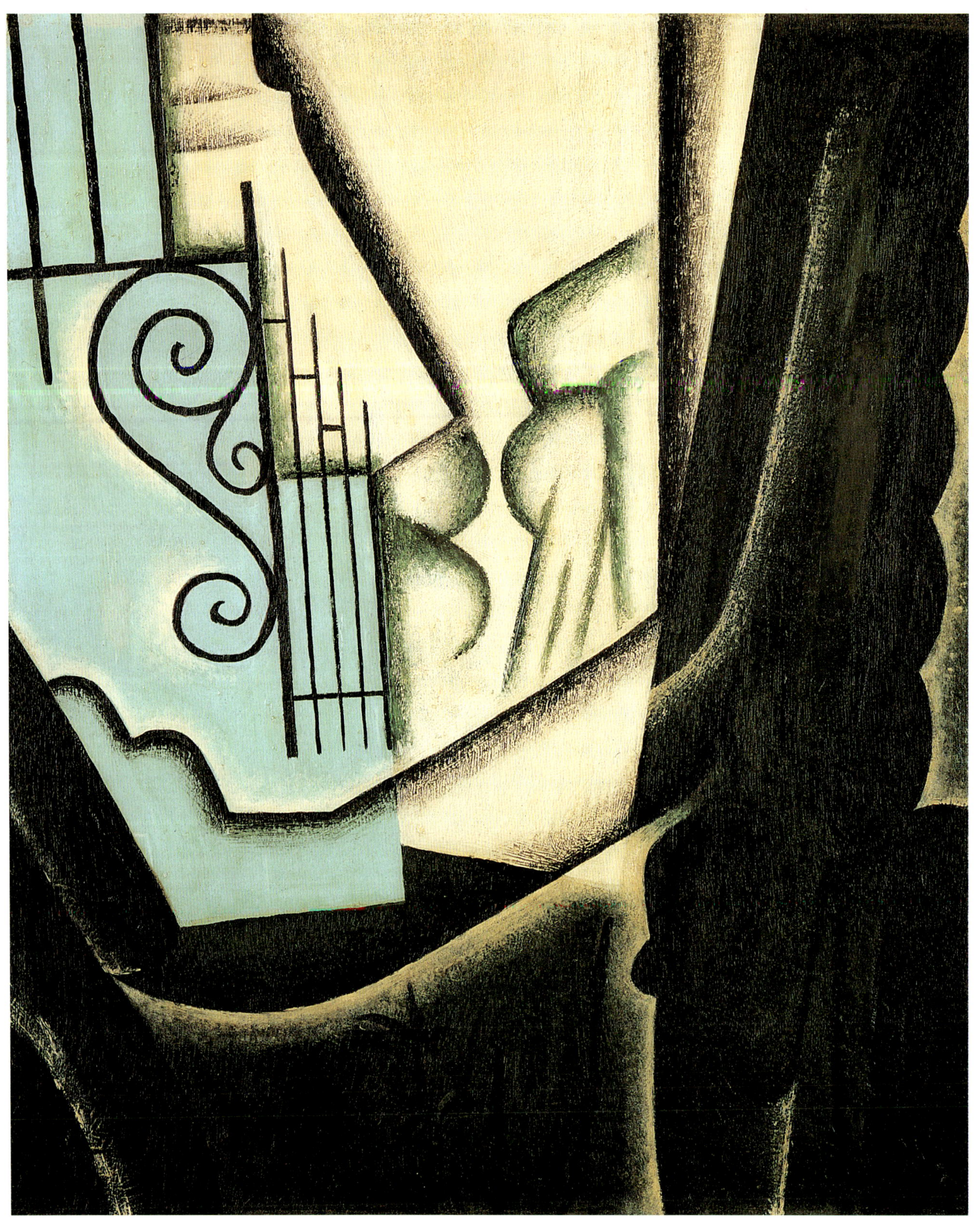

65
The Garden, 1916
Oil on canvas,
65 x 54 cm
Telefónica de España, S. A.

66
Portrait of Madame Josette Gris, 1916
Oil on canvas,
116.5 x 73 cm
Museo del Prado, Madrid

[Stuttgart and Otterlo only]

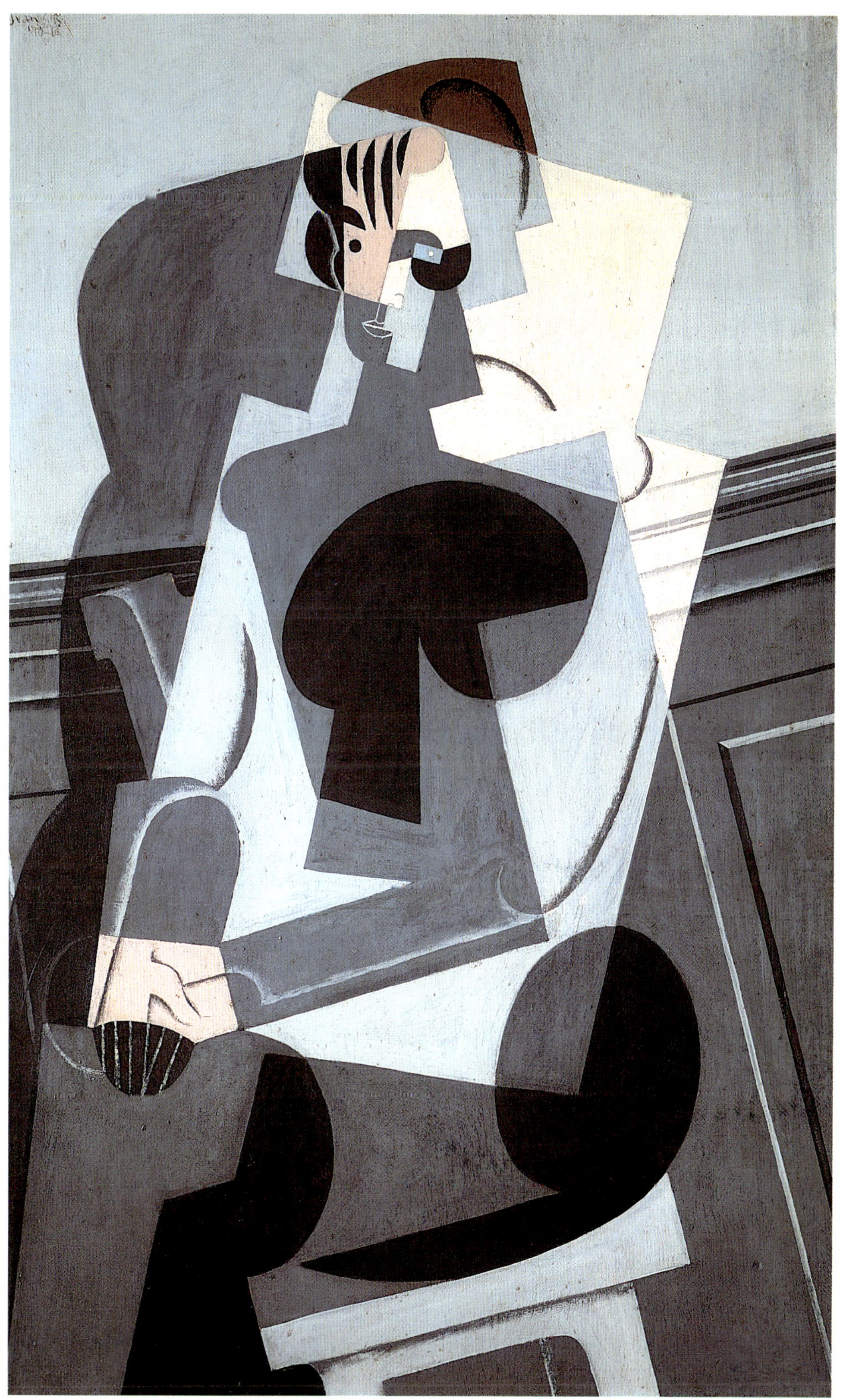

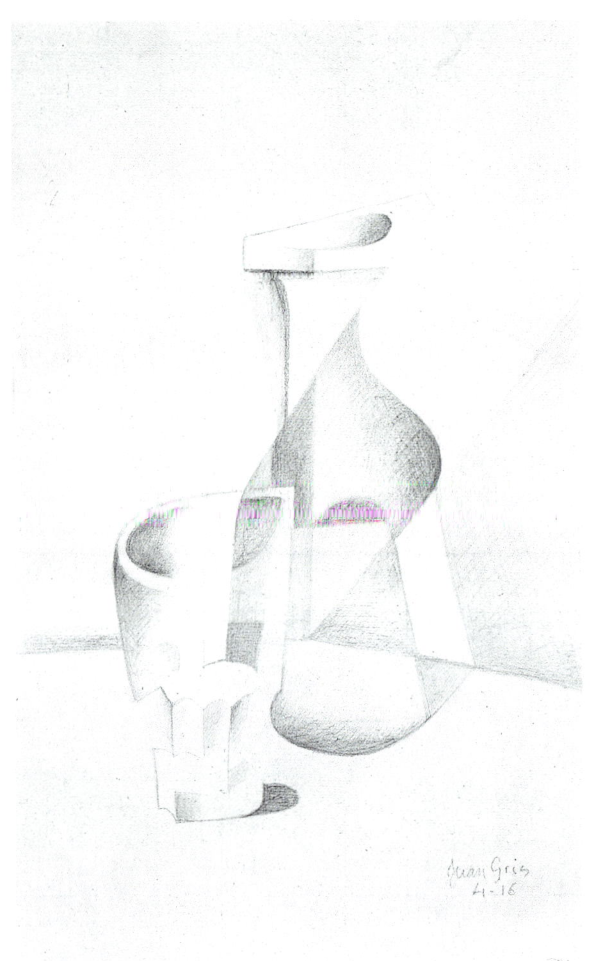

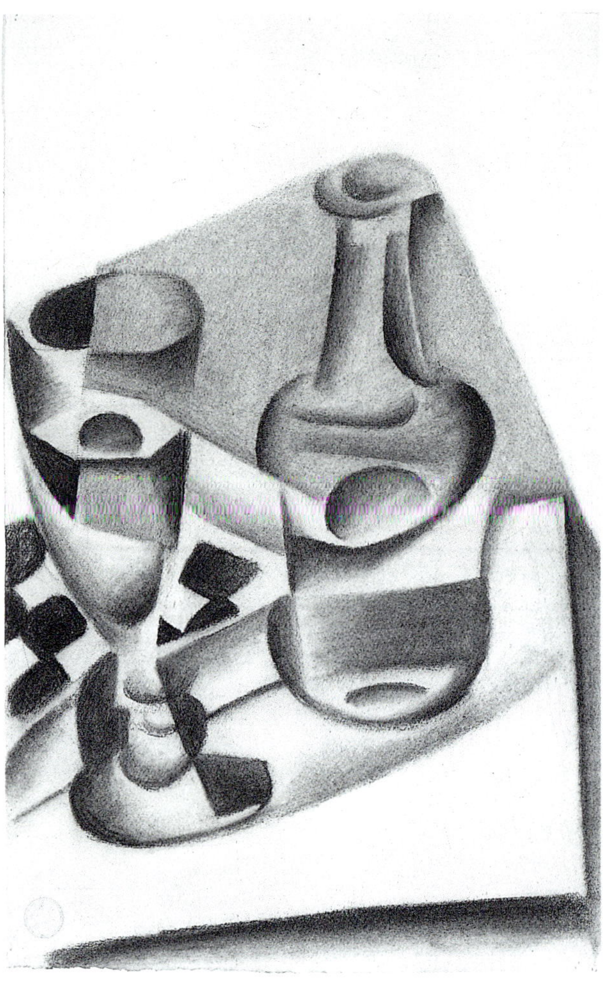

67
Carafe and Glass, 1916
Pencil on paper,
40 x 25.5 cm
Private Collection
[London only]

68
Carafe, Glass and Chequerboard, 1917
Charcoal on paper,
45.7 x 30.5 cm
Private Collection
[London only]

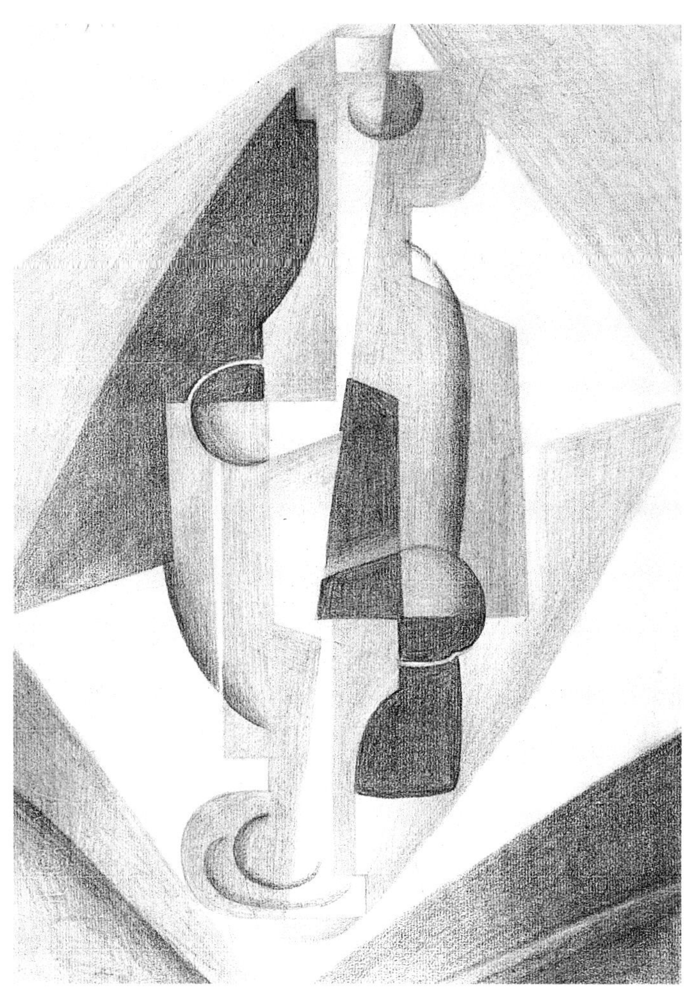

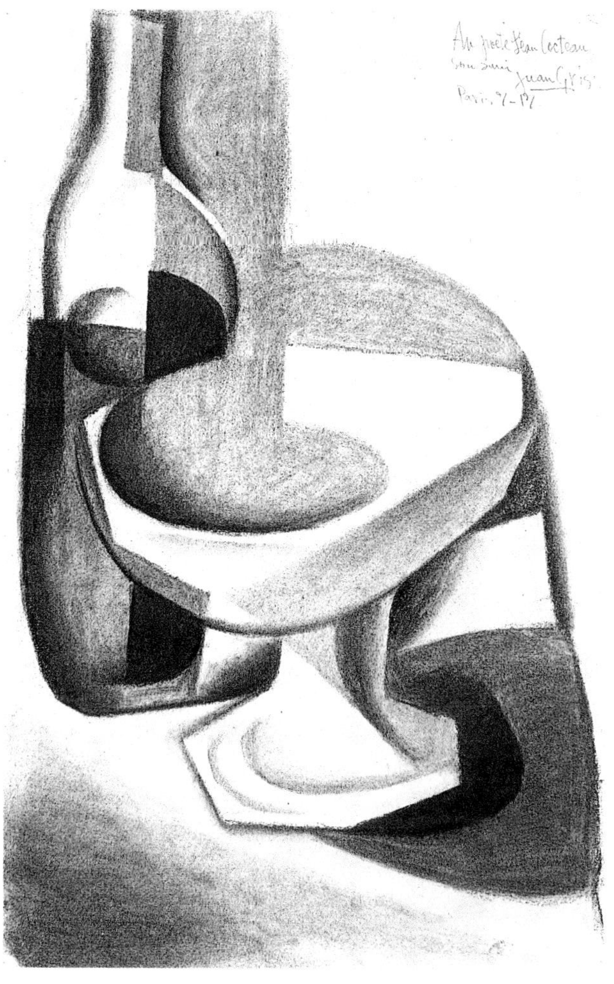

69
Still-life, 1916
Chalk on paper,
37.1x26.5 cm
Rijksmuseum Kröller-Müller, Otterlo

70
Fruit Dish and Bottle,
1917
Conté crayon and
charcoal on paper,
47.6x31.3 cm
Collection, The
Museum of Modern
Art, New York.
Acquired through the
Lillie P. Bliss Bequest

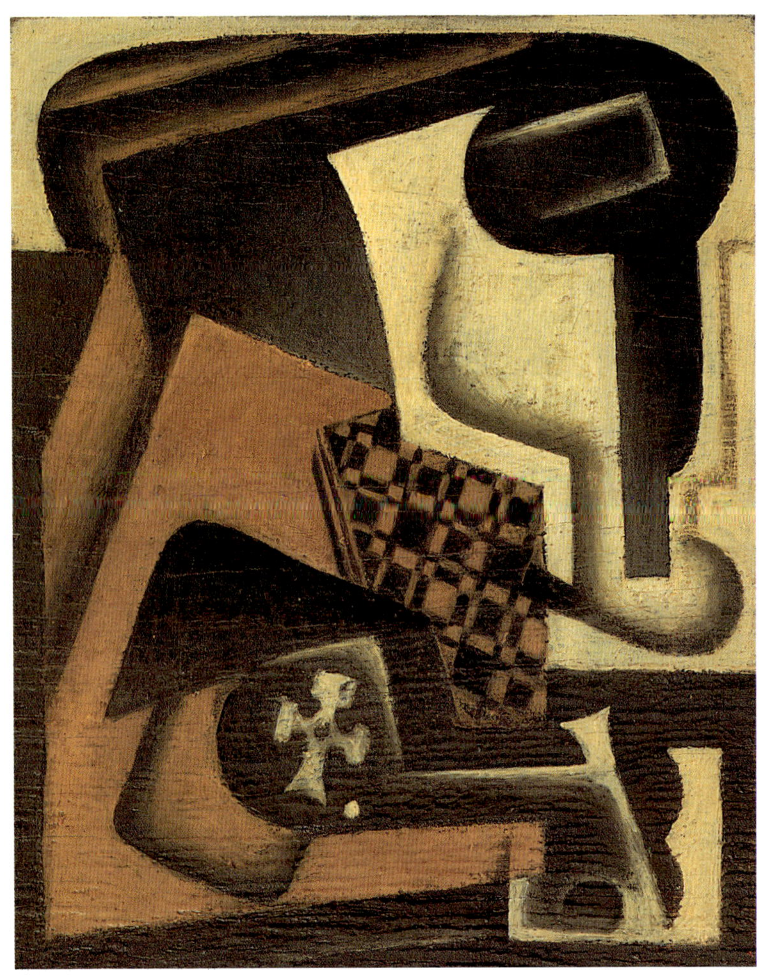

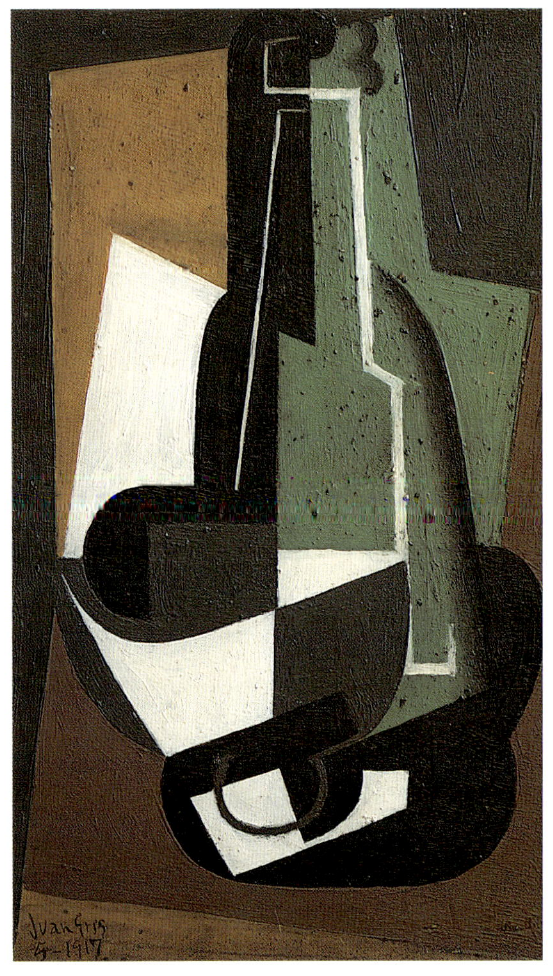

71
The Glass, 1917
Oil on canvas, 27x22 cm
Galerie Louise Leiris, Paris

72
Carafe and Bowl, 1917
Oil on canvas, 41x24 cm
Mr and Mrs Claude Laurens

73
The Packet of Tobacco, 1916
Oil on canvas, 46x38 cm
Collection of Gretchen and John Berggruen

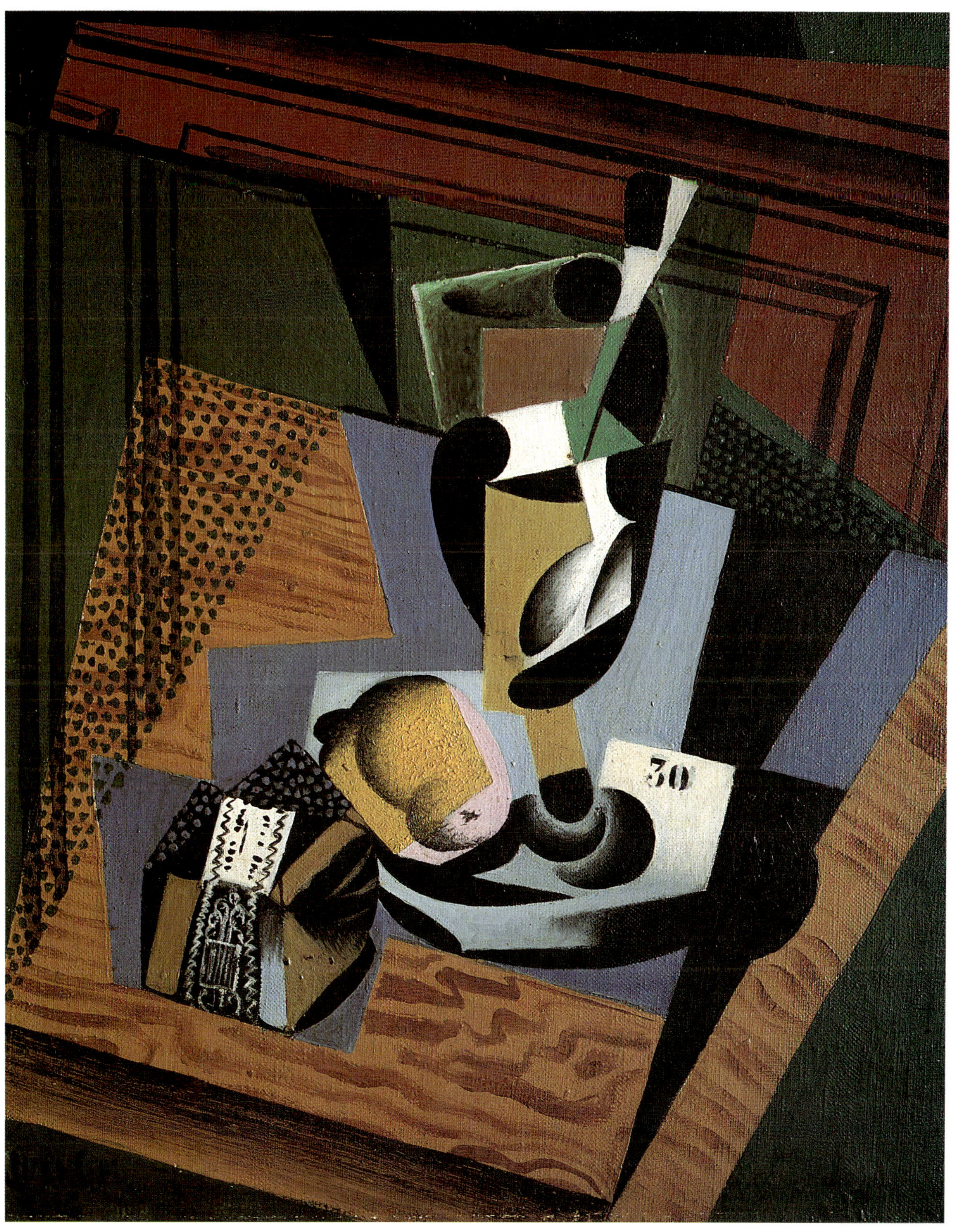
30

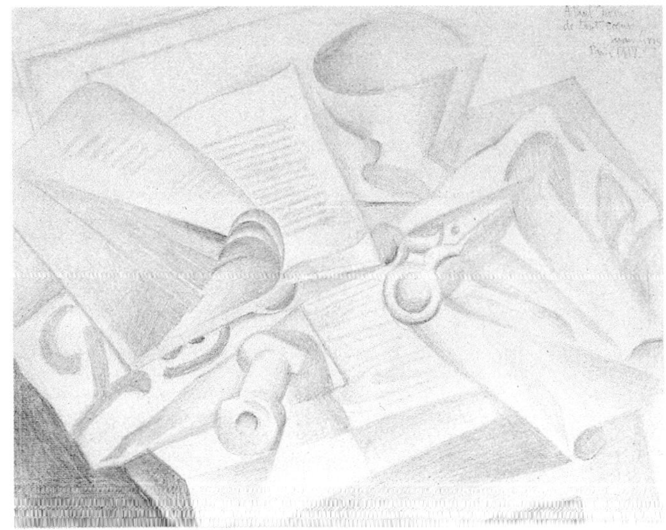

74
The Book, 1917
Pencil on paper,
28 x 35 cm
Galerie Louise Leiris,
Paris

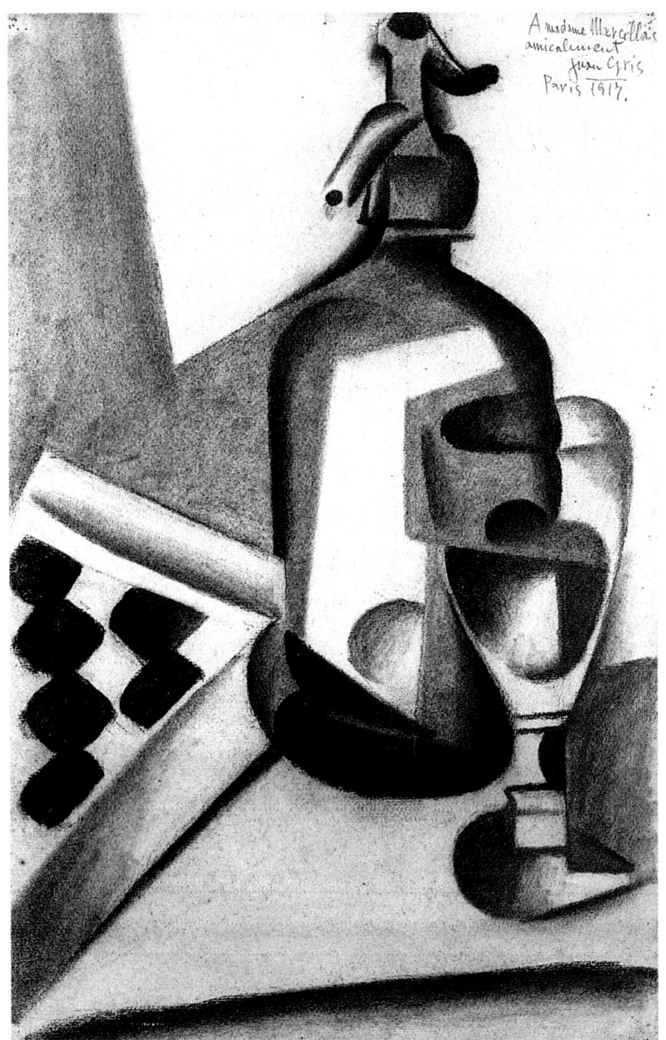

75
Still-life with Siphon,
1917
Charcoal on paper,
47x30.9 cm
The Art Institute of
Chicago. Gift of Mr and
Mrs Leigh B. Block,
1954.1061

[Stuttgart and Otterlo
only]

76
**Portrait of Mme
Huidobro,** 1917
Pencil on paper,
35 x 28 cm
Stephen Mazoh,
New York

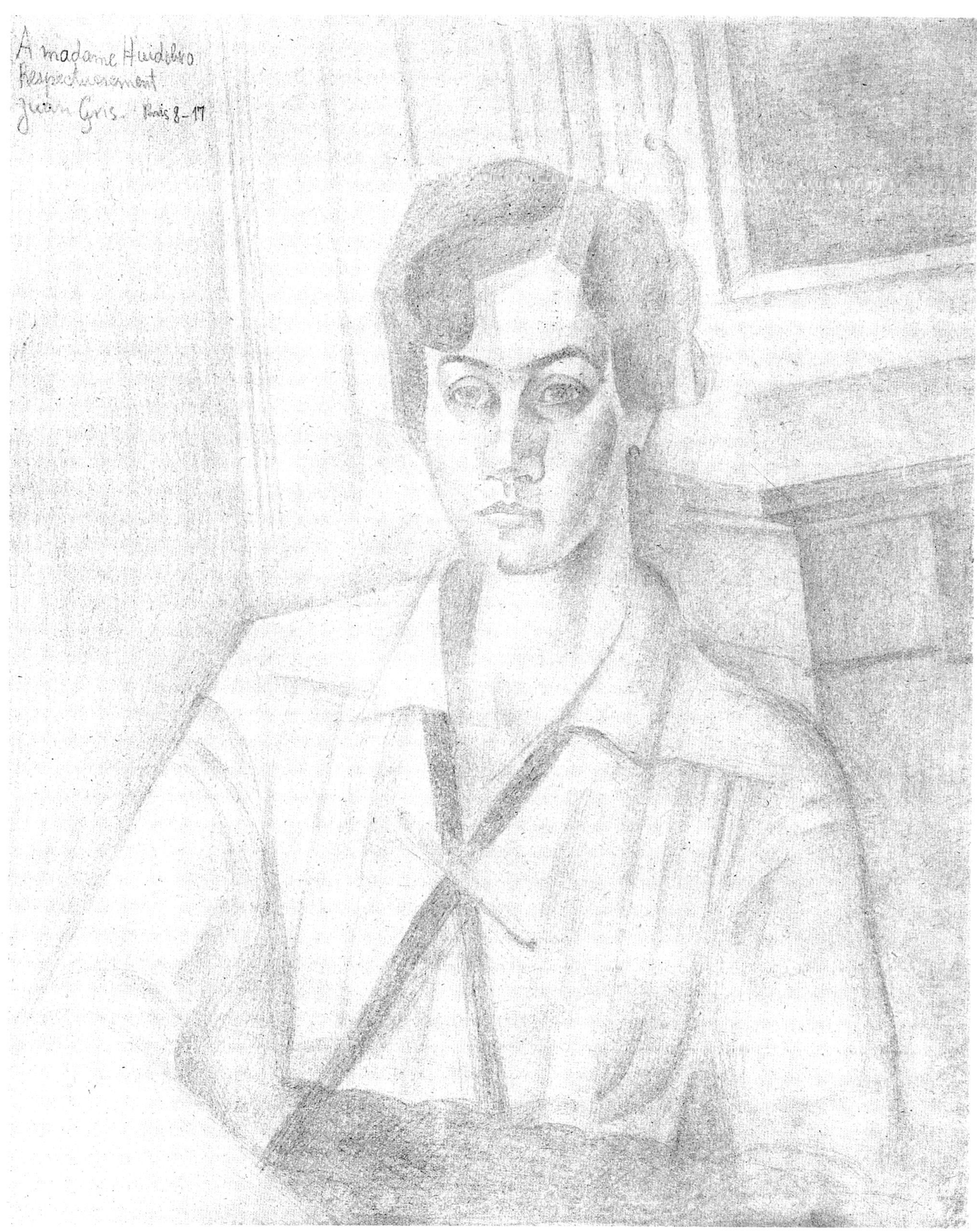
A madame Huidobro
Respectueusement
Juan Gris. Paris 8-17

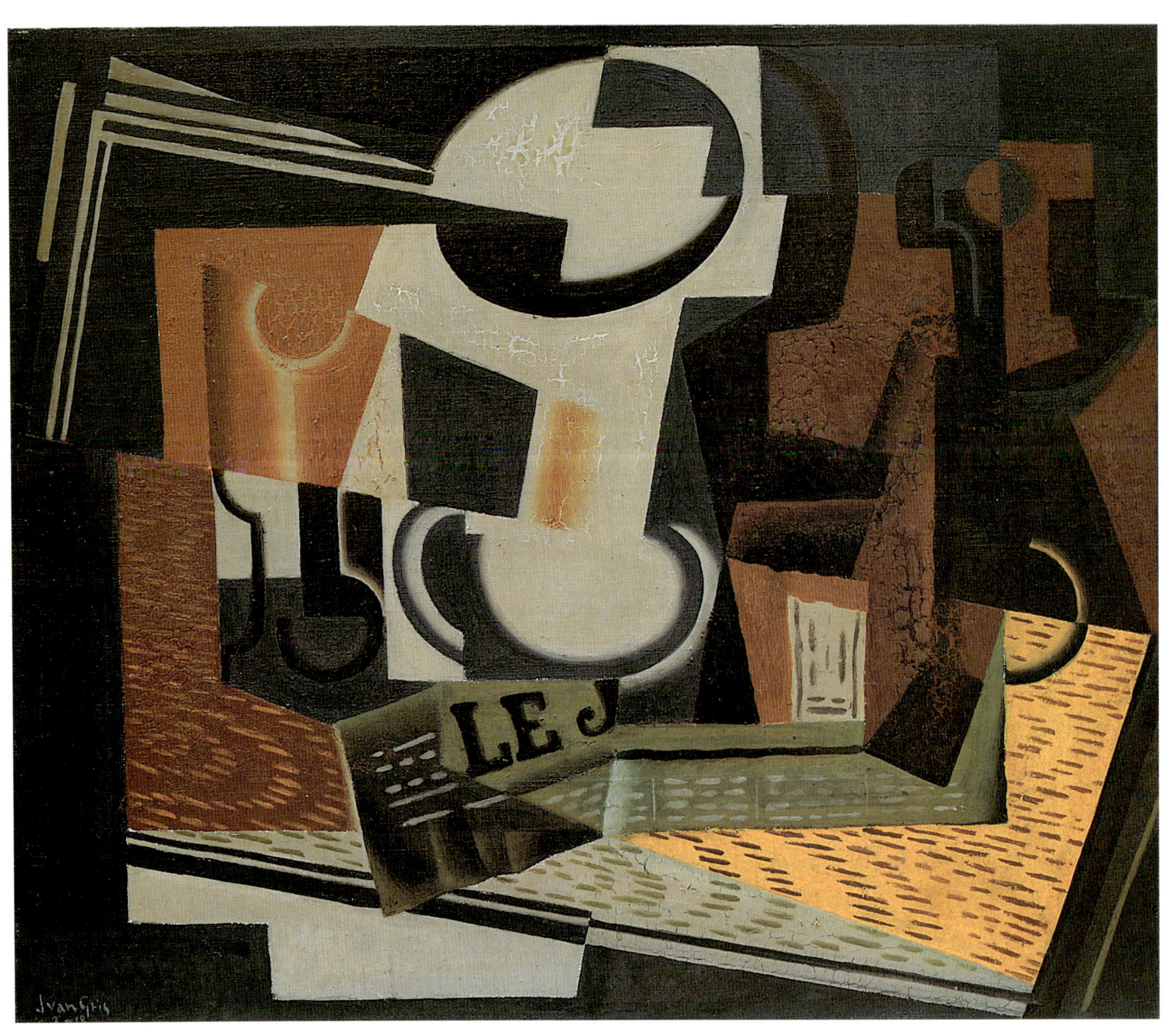

77
Still-life with Fruit Dish, 1918
Oil on canvas,
54 x 65 cm
Staatsgalerie Stuttgart

78
Pipe and Fruit Dish with Grapes, 1918
Oil on canvas, 61x38 cm
Rijksmuseum Kröller-Müller, Otterlo

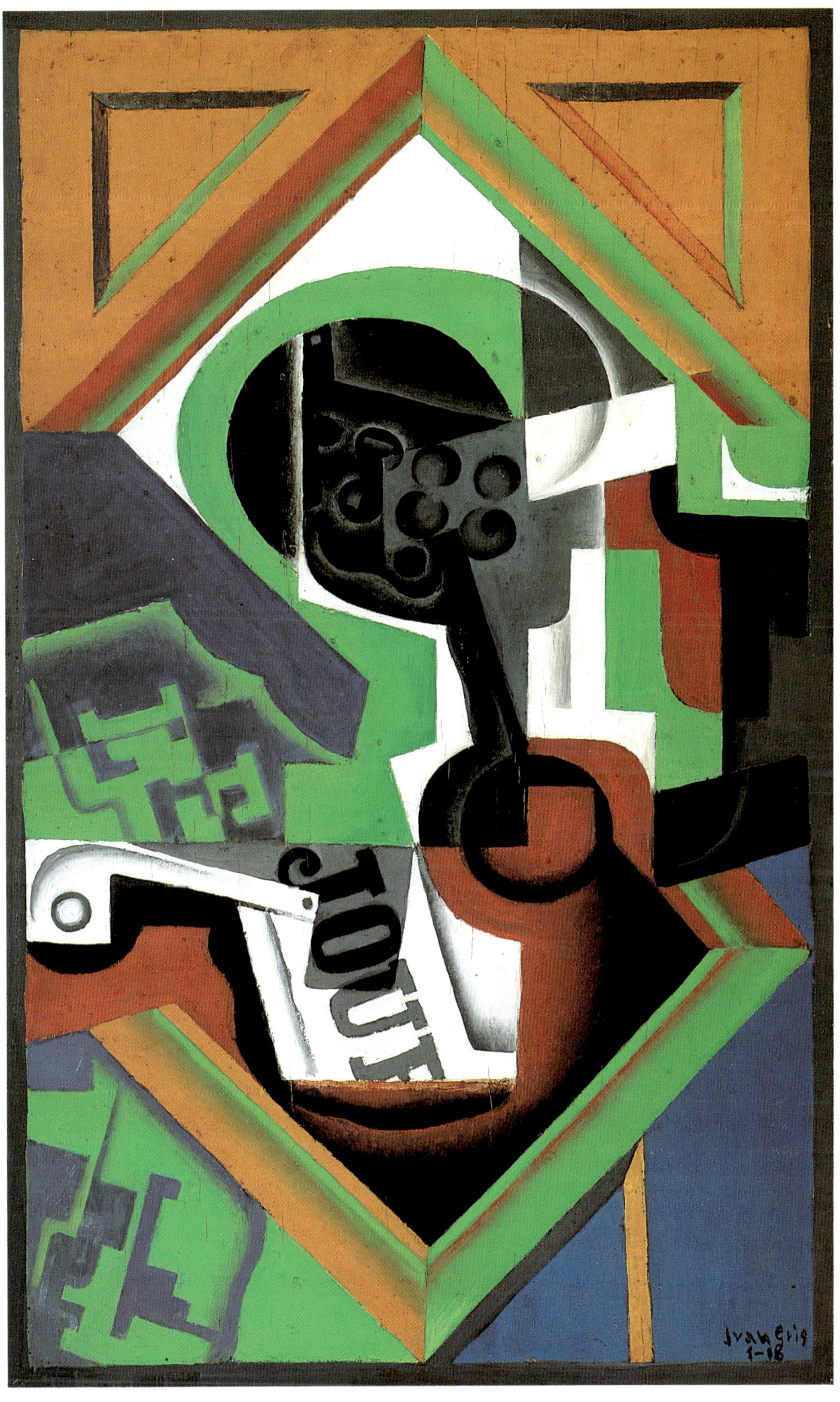

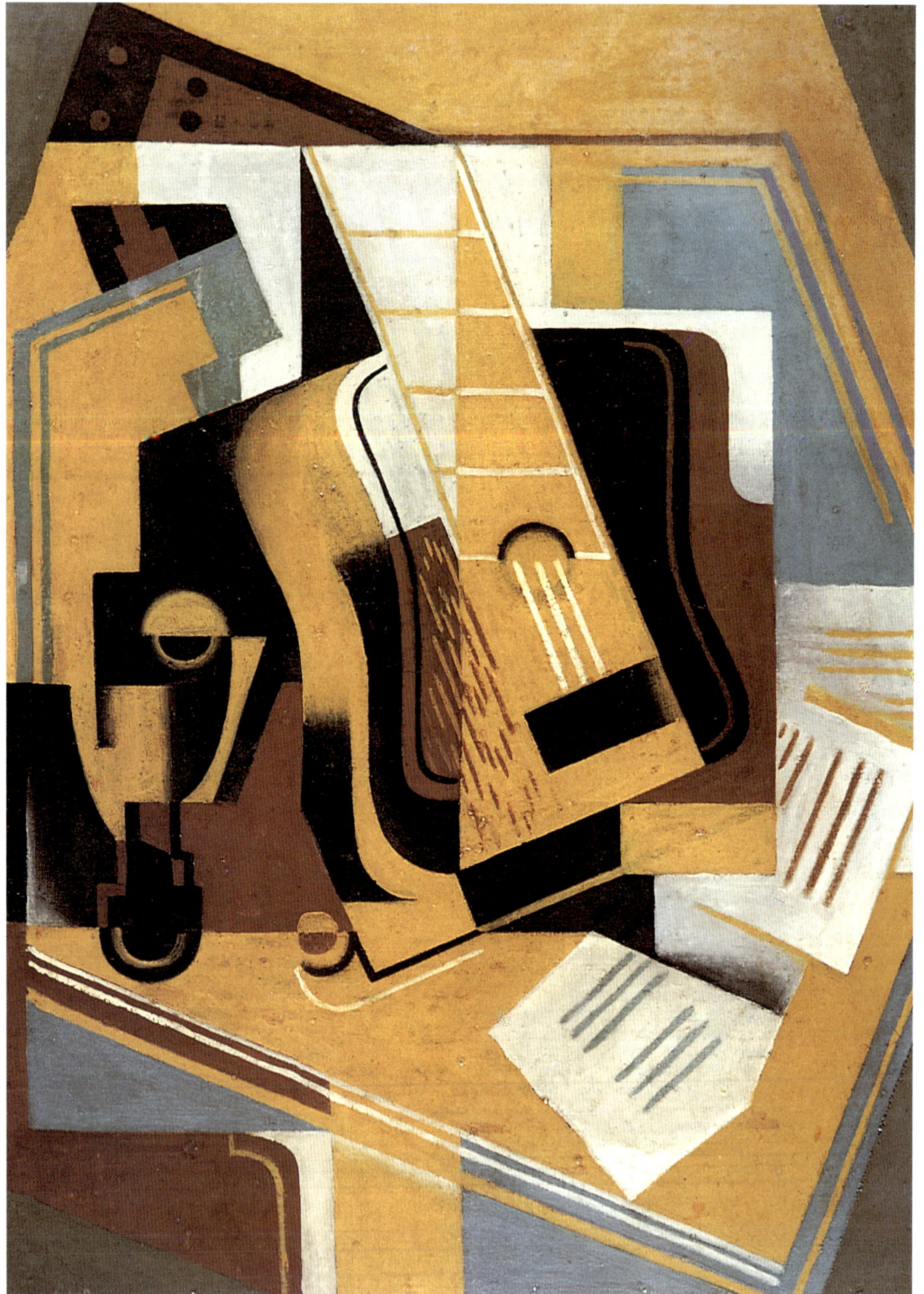

79
The Guitar, 1918
Oil on canvas,
81x59.5 cm
Telefónica de España,
S. A.

80
Violin and Glass, 1918
Oil on canvas,
80.5x65.6 cm
Courtesy of Marc Blondeau, S. A., Paris

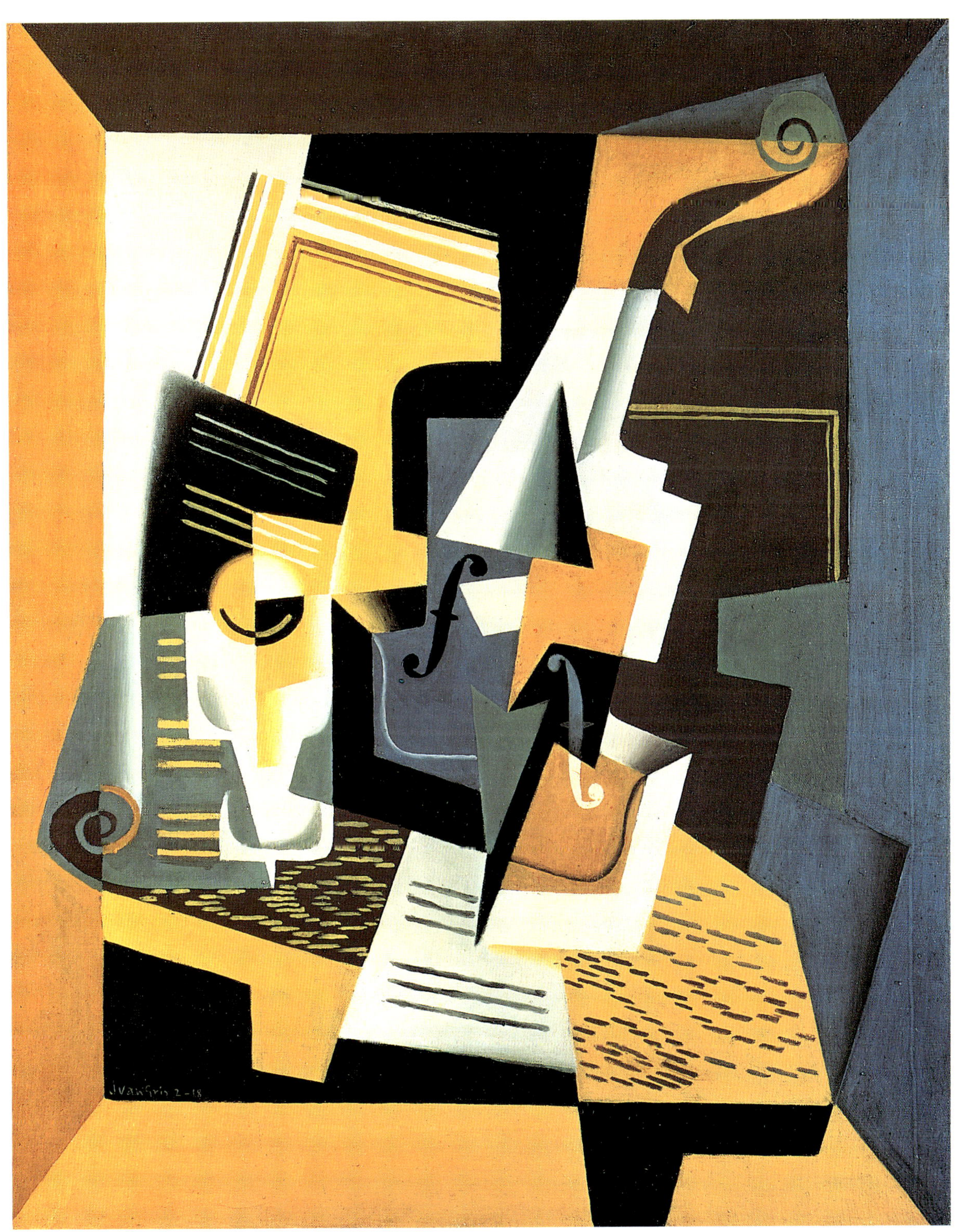
Juan Gris 2-18

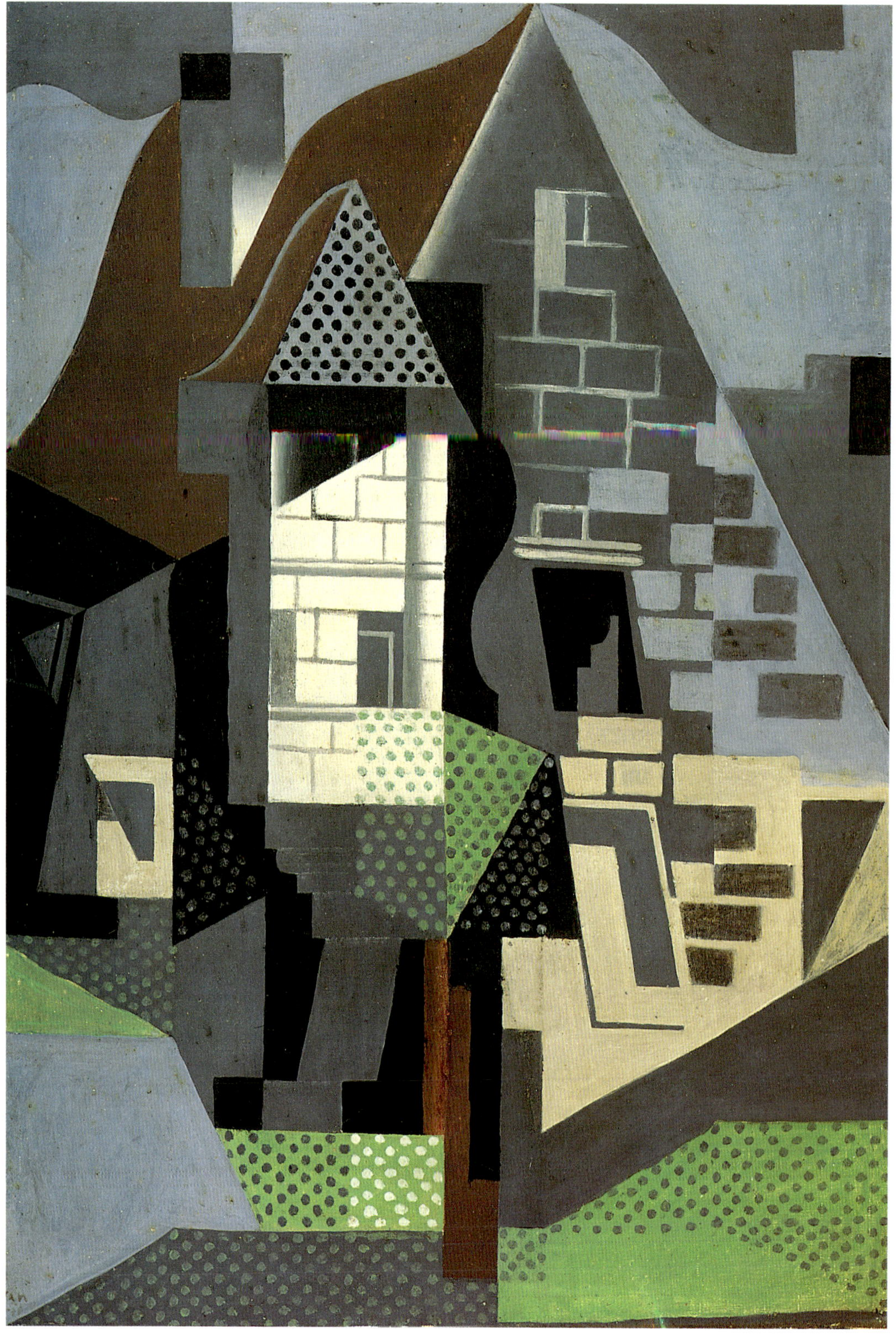

81
Houses in Beaulieu,
1918
Oil on canvas,
90 x 64 cm
Rijksmuseum Kröller-Müller, Otterlo

82
Seated Peasant Woman, 1918
Oil on canvas, 92 x 65 cm
Private Collection

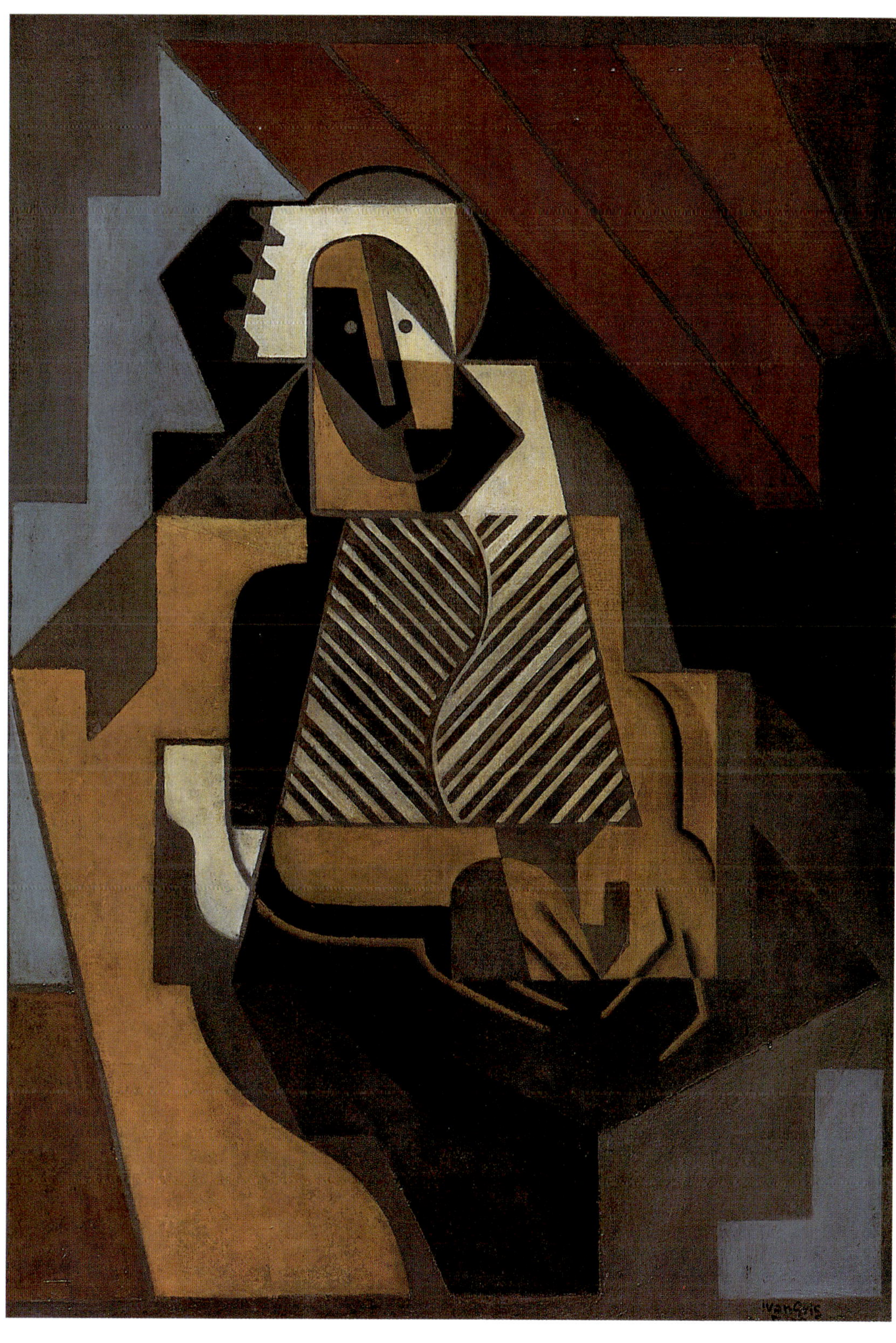

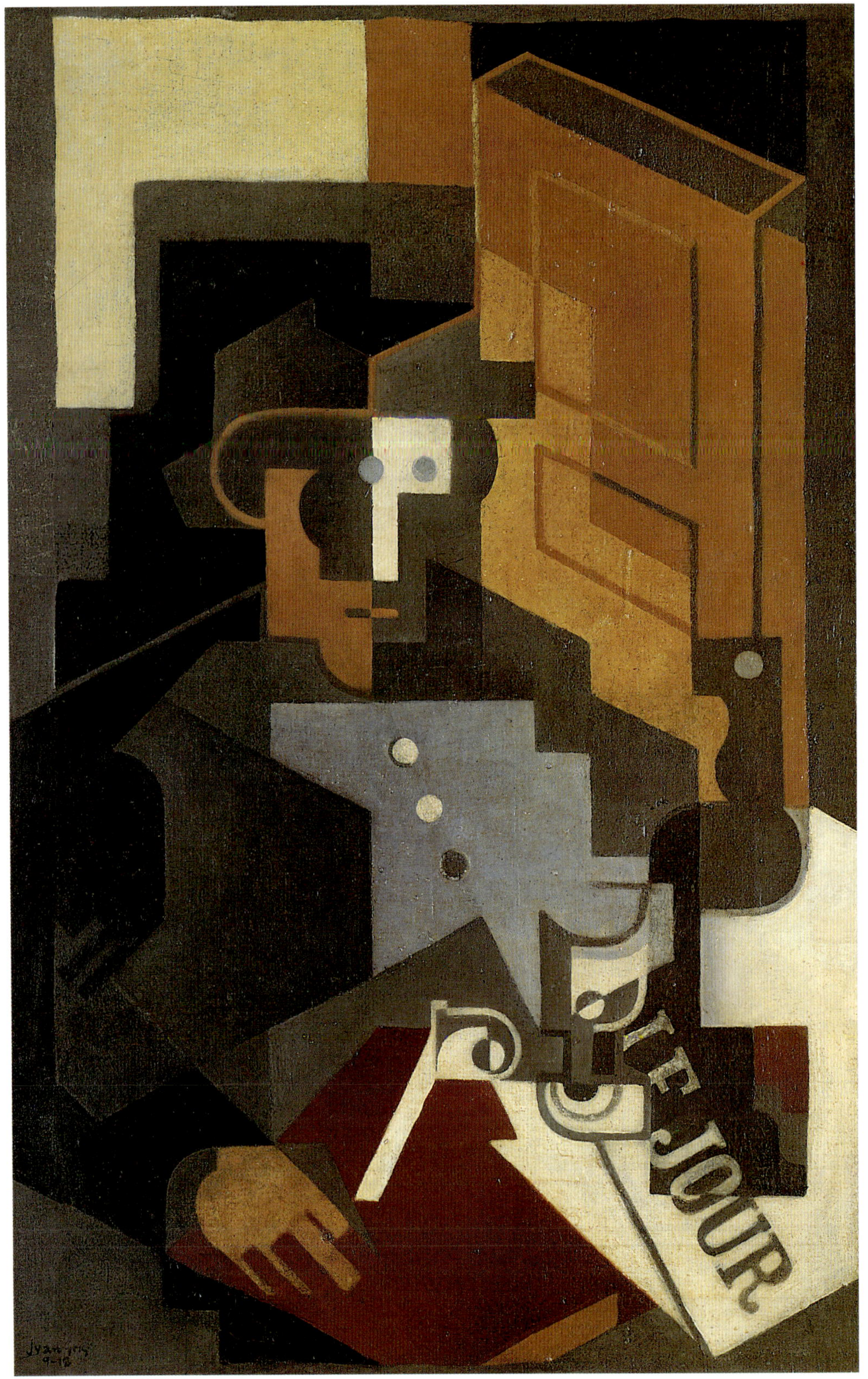

83
The Man from the Touraine, 1918
Oil on canvas, 100 x 65 cm
Musée National d'Art Moderne, Centre Georges Pompidou, Paris. Gift of M and Mme André Lefevre (1952)

84
The Peasant in a Blue Smock (The Miller), 1918
Oil on canvas, 100 x 81 cm
Galerie Louise Leiris, Paris

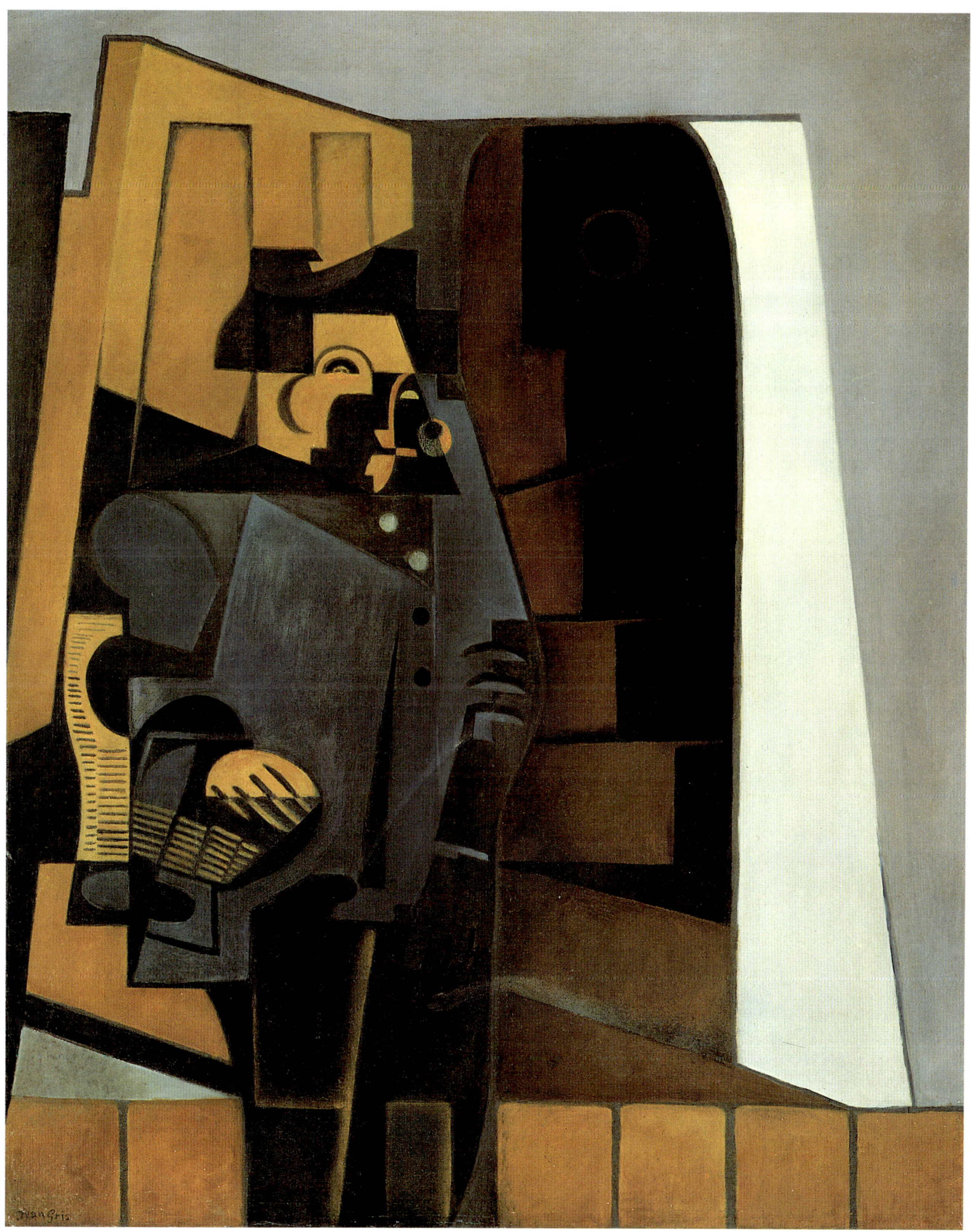
Juan Gris

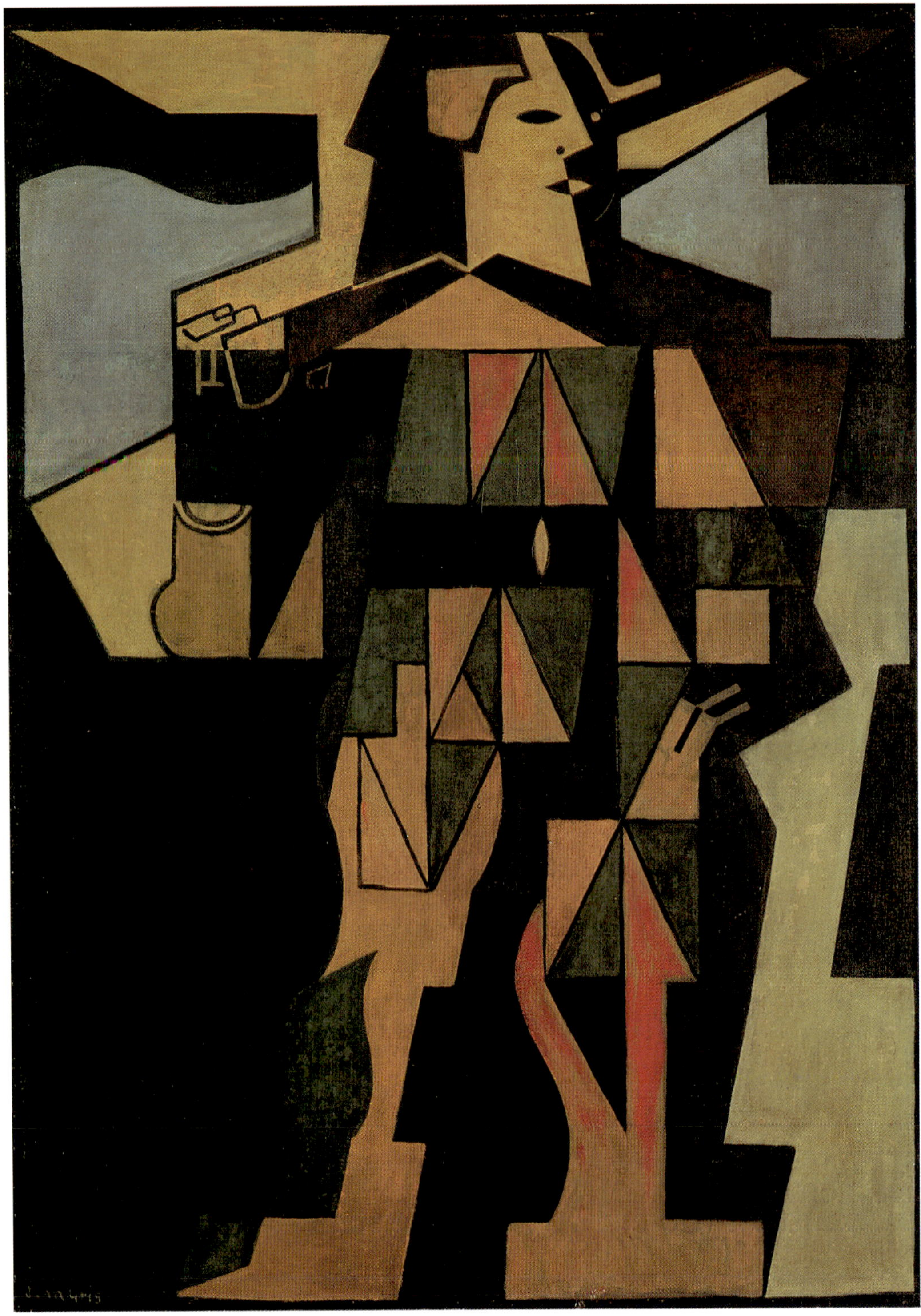

85
Harlequin, 1918
Oil on canvas, 81x60 cm
Telefónica de España, S. A.

86
Pierrot, 1919
Oil on canvas, 101x82 cm
Kunstmuseum Winterthur

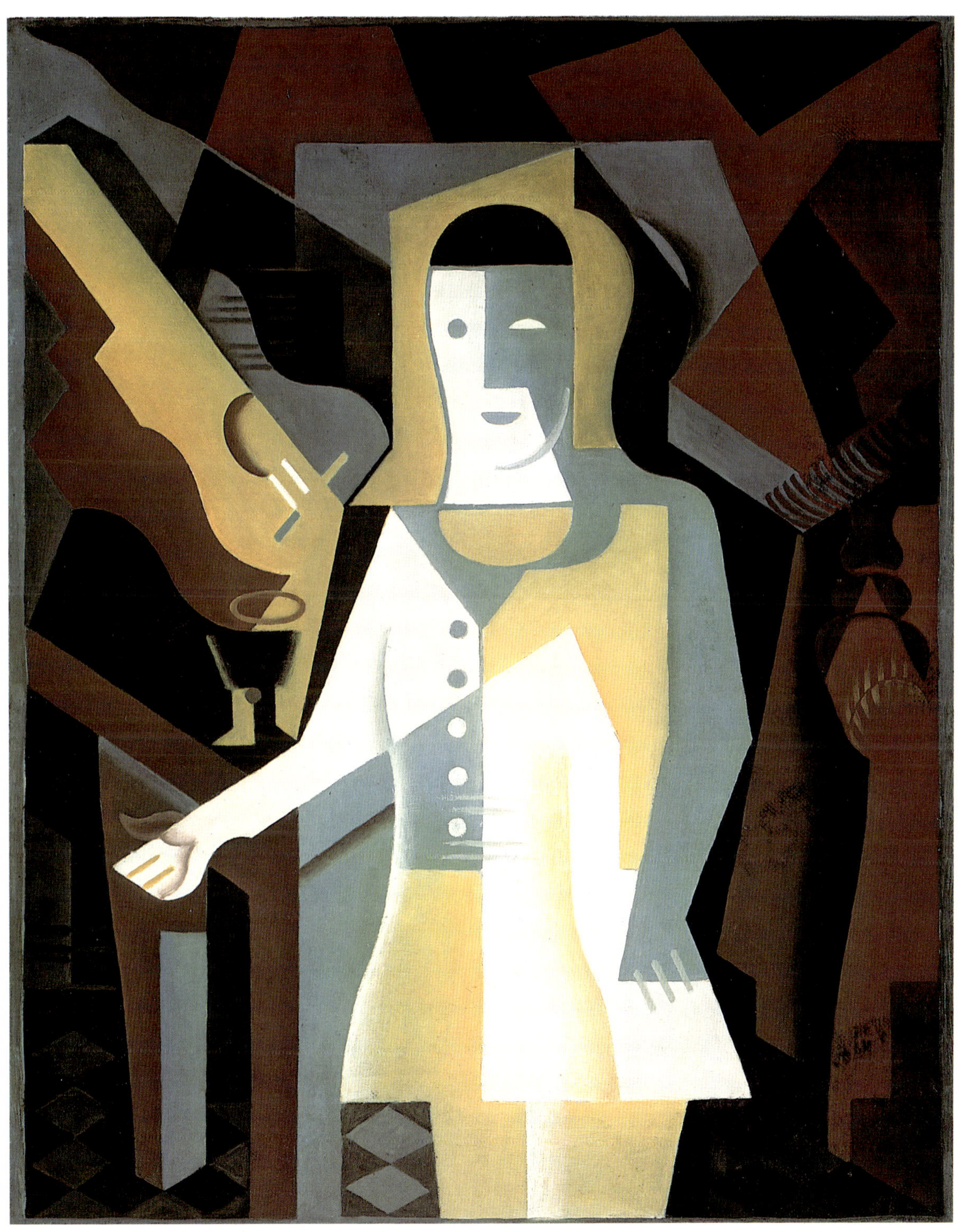

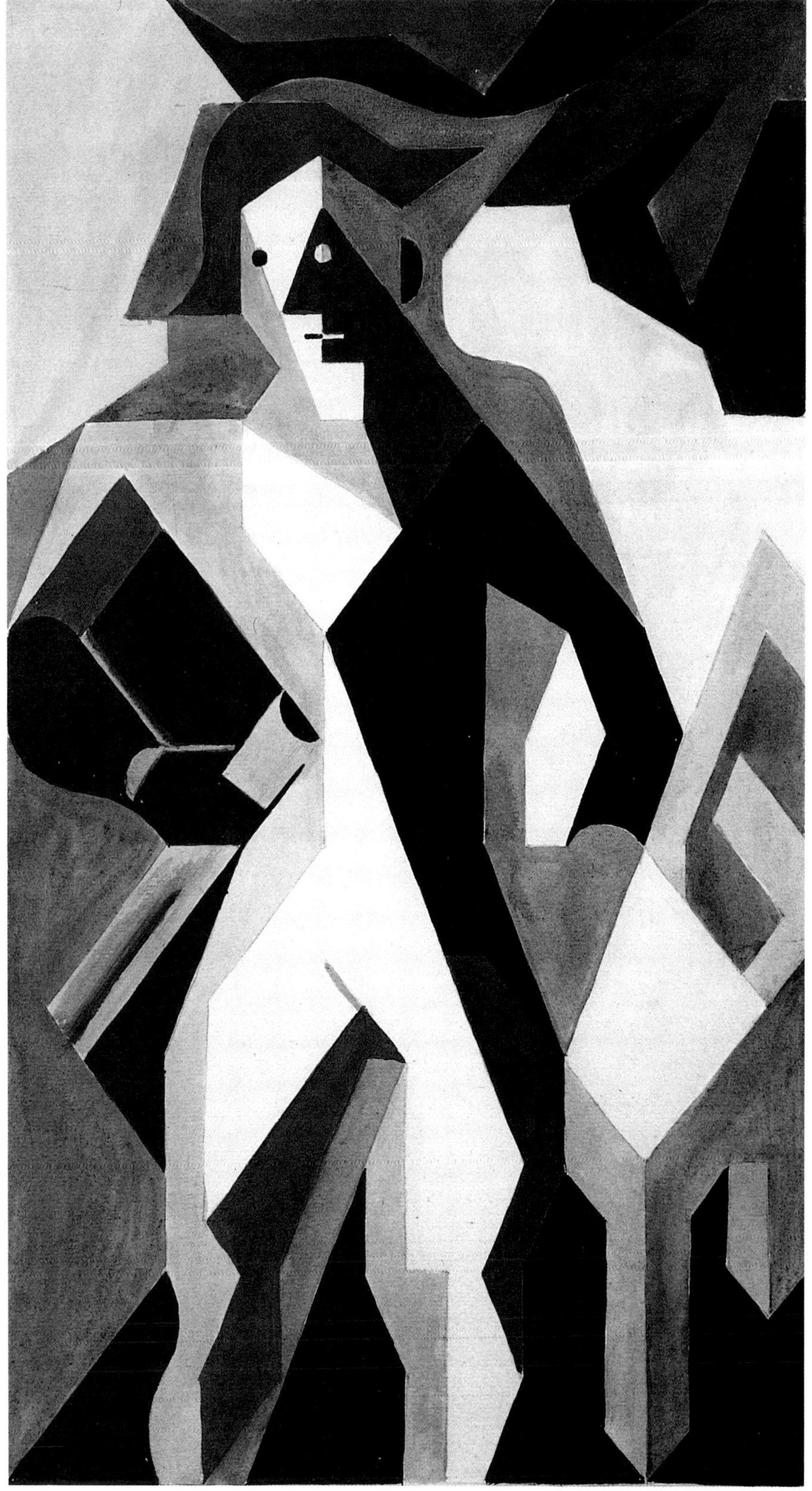

87
Standing Harlequin (Harlequin with a Chair), 1919
Black wash and watercolour on paper, 42.5 x 23.5 cm
Georges González Gris

88
Harlequin at a Table,
1919
Oil on canvas,
101x65 cm
Morton G. Neumann
Family Collection
[Not in exhibition]

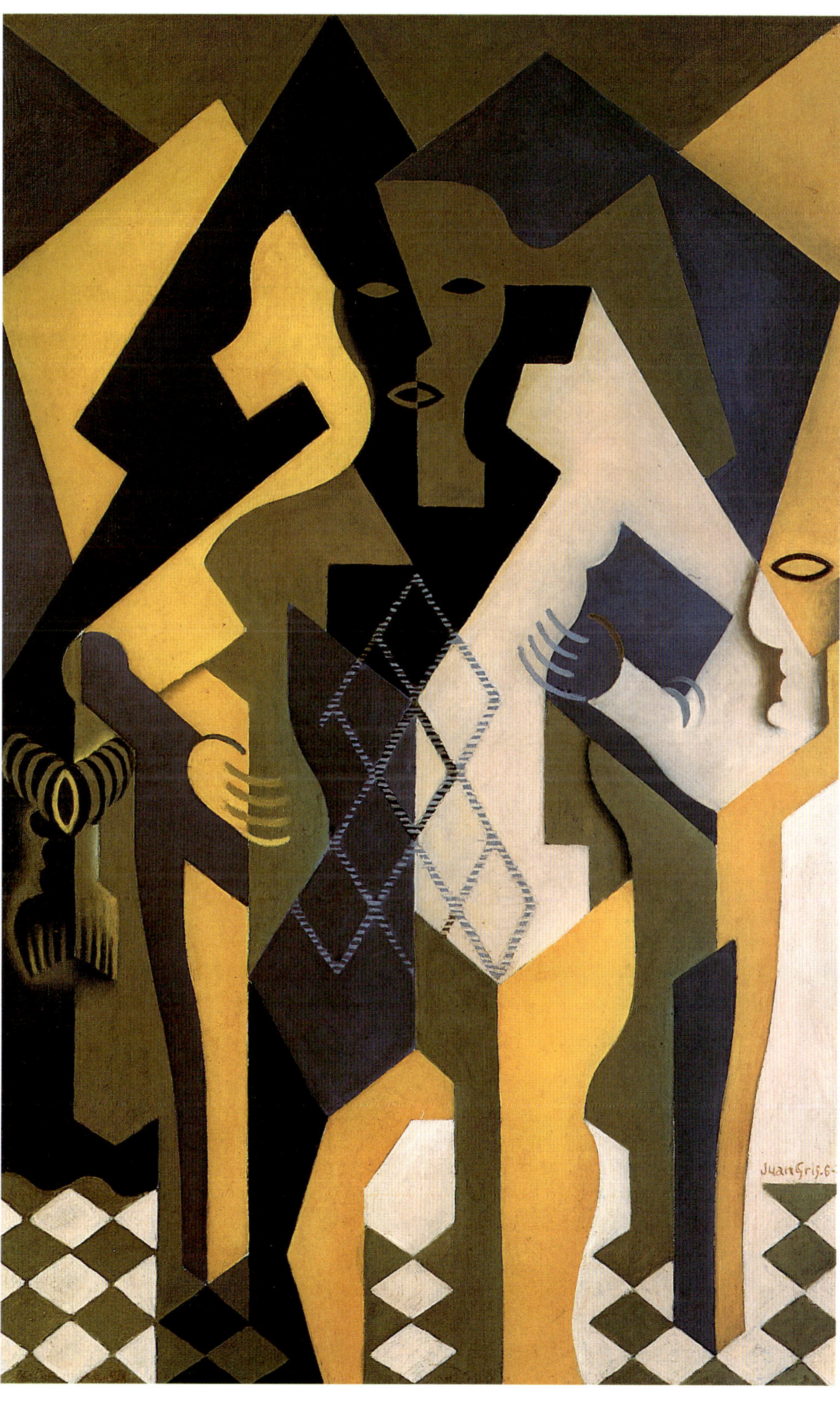

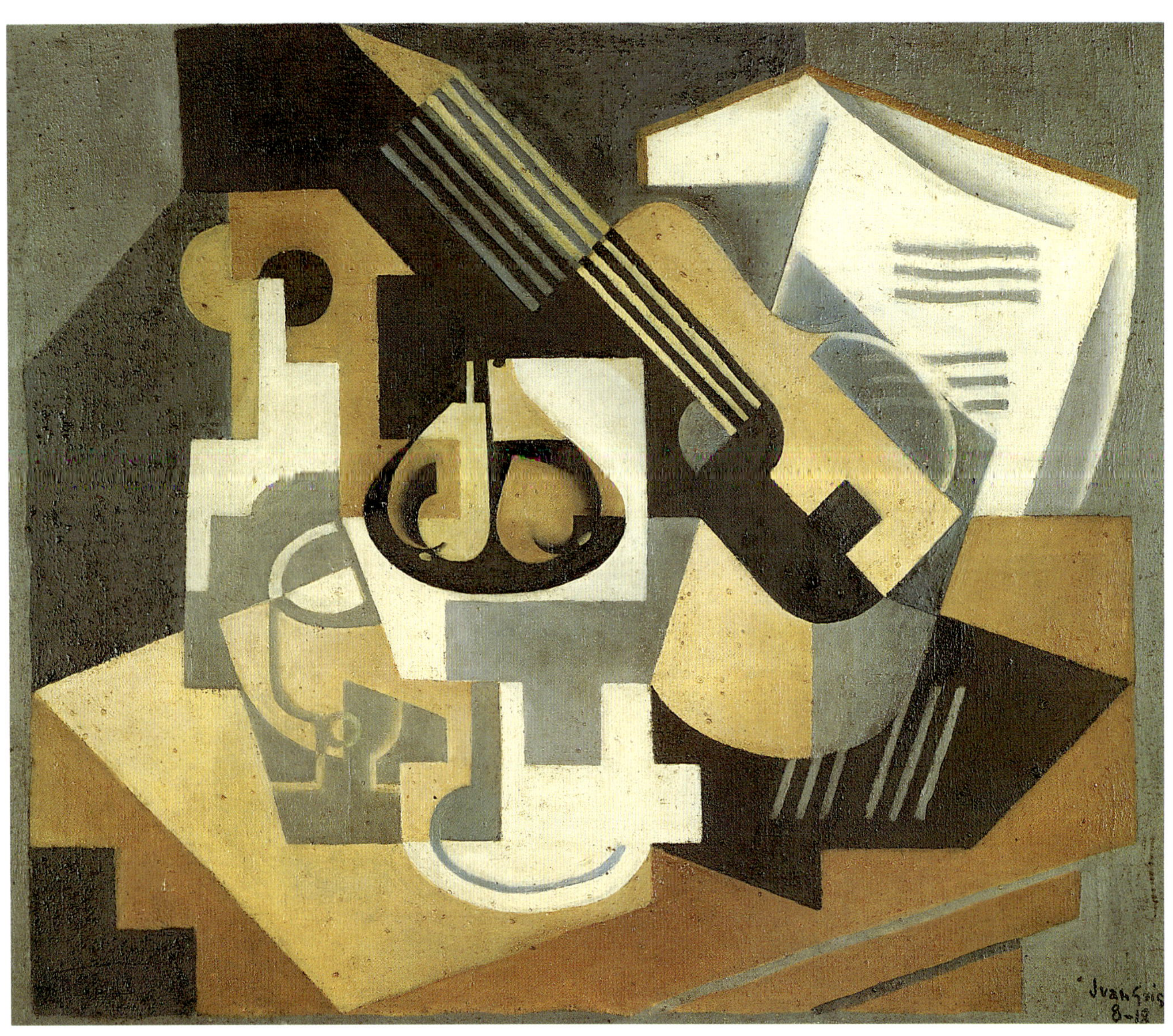

89
Guitar and Fruit Dish, 1918
Oil on canvas, 60 x 73 cm
Öffentliche Kunstsammlung Basel, Kunstmuseum

90
Bottle and Fruit Dish, 1919
Oil on canvas, 74 x 54 cm
Thyssen-Bornemisza Collection, Lugano

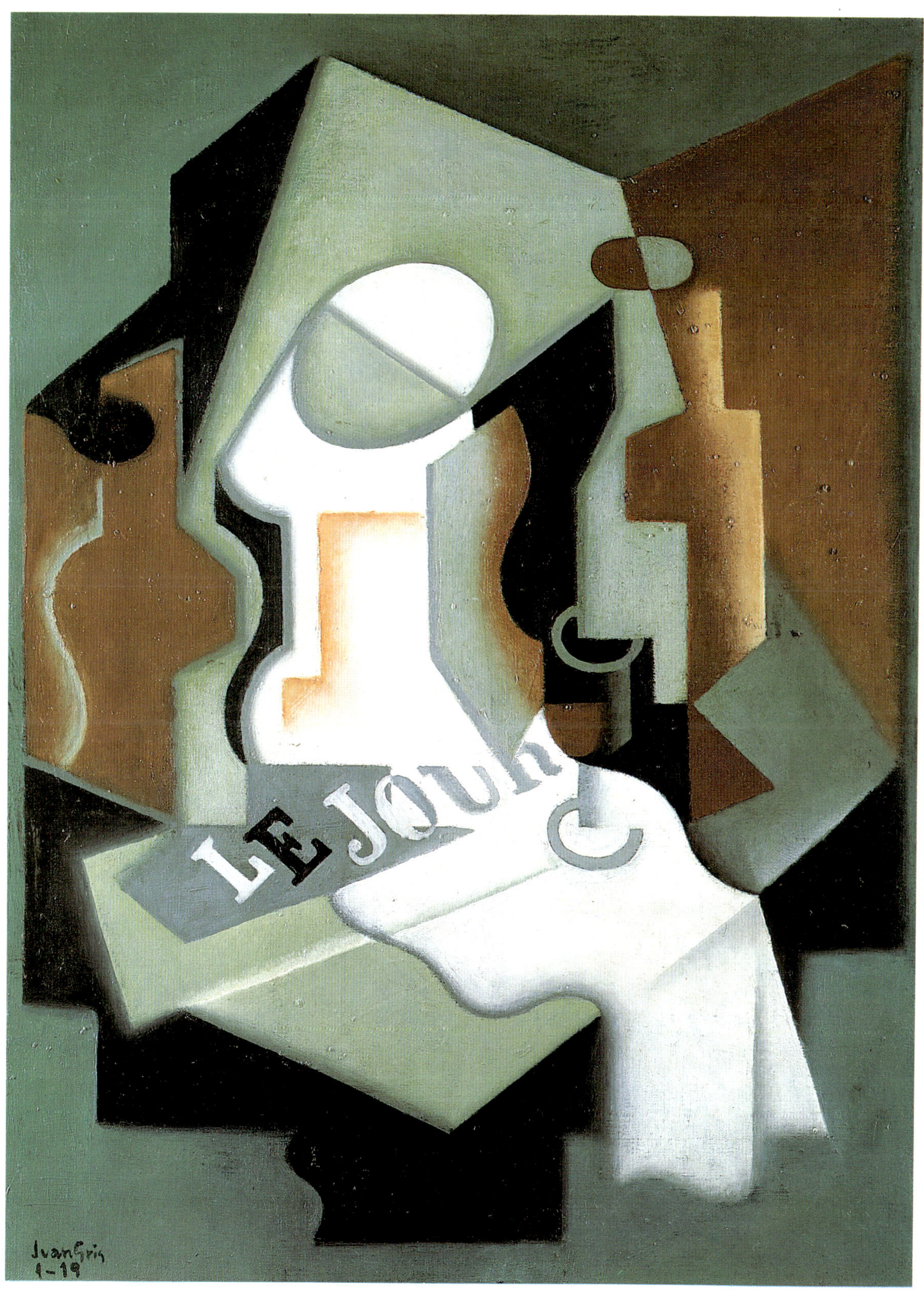
LE JOU
Juan Gris
1-19

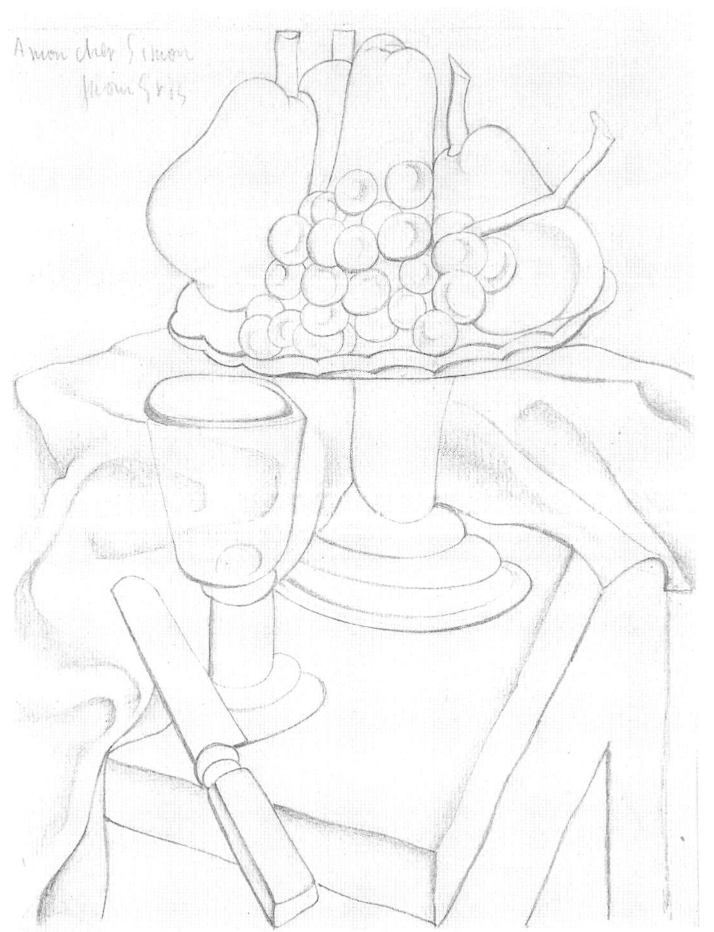

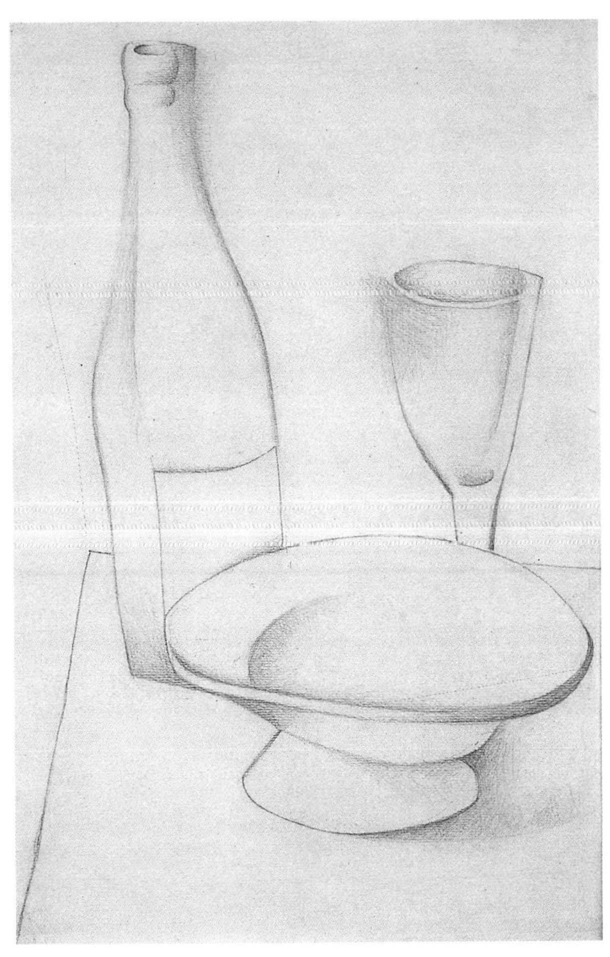

91
Fruit Dish, Glass and Knife, 1919–20
Pencil on paper,
33.5 x 25.5 cm
Private Collection

92
Bottle, Glass and Plate, 1918
Pencil on paper,
48.3 x 31.5 cm
Private Collection

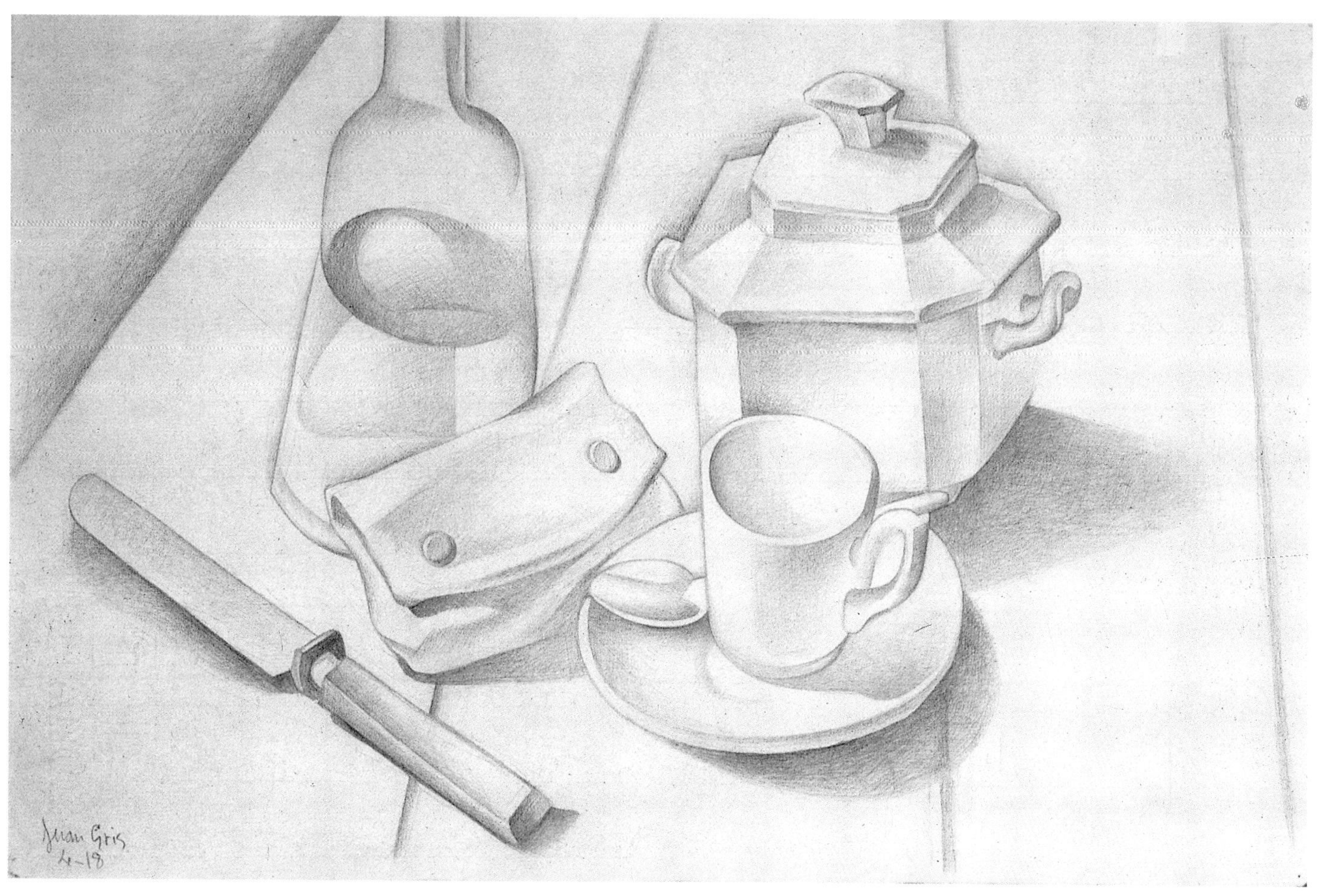

93
The Tobacco Pouch,
1918
Pencil on paper,
28 x 35 cm
Private Collection

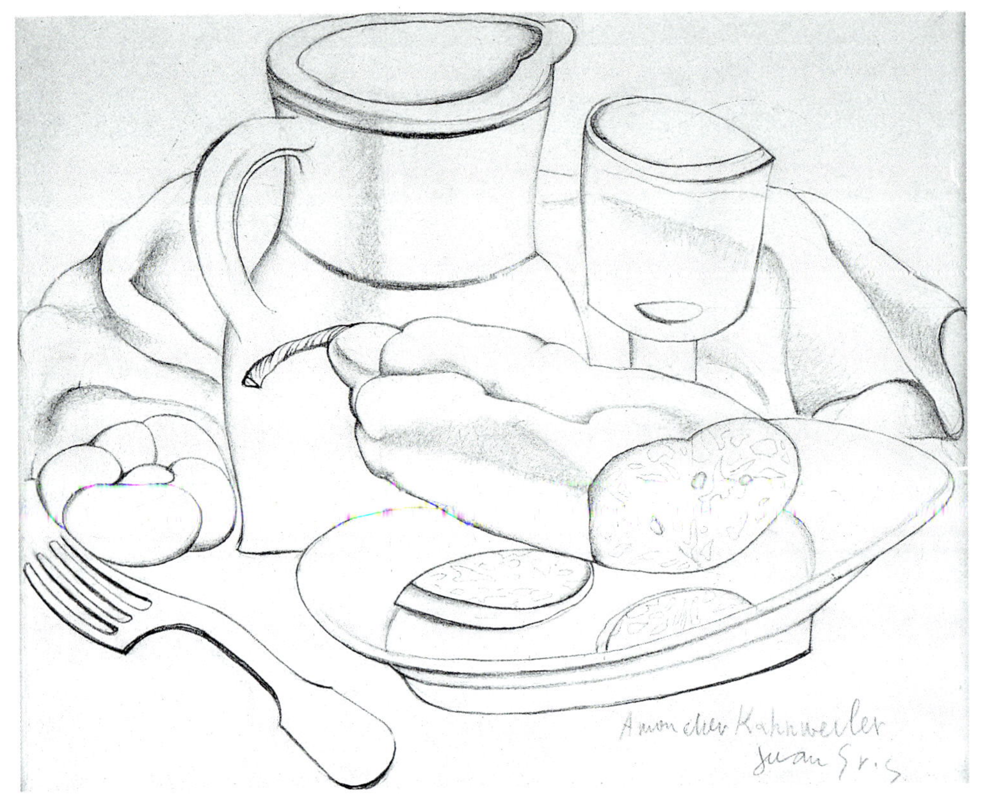

94
Still-life with a Garlic Sausage, 1920
Pencil on paper,
25 x 32.5 cm
Musée National d'Art Moderne, Centre Georges Pompidou, Paris. Gift of Louise and Michel Leiris (1984)

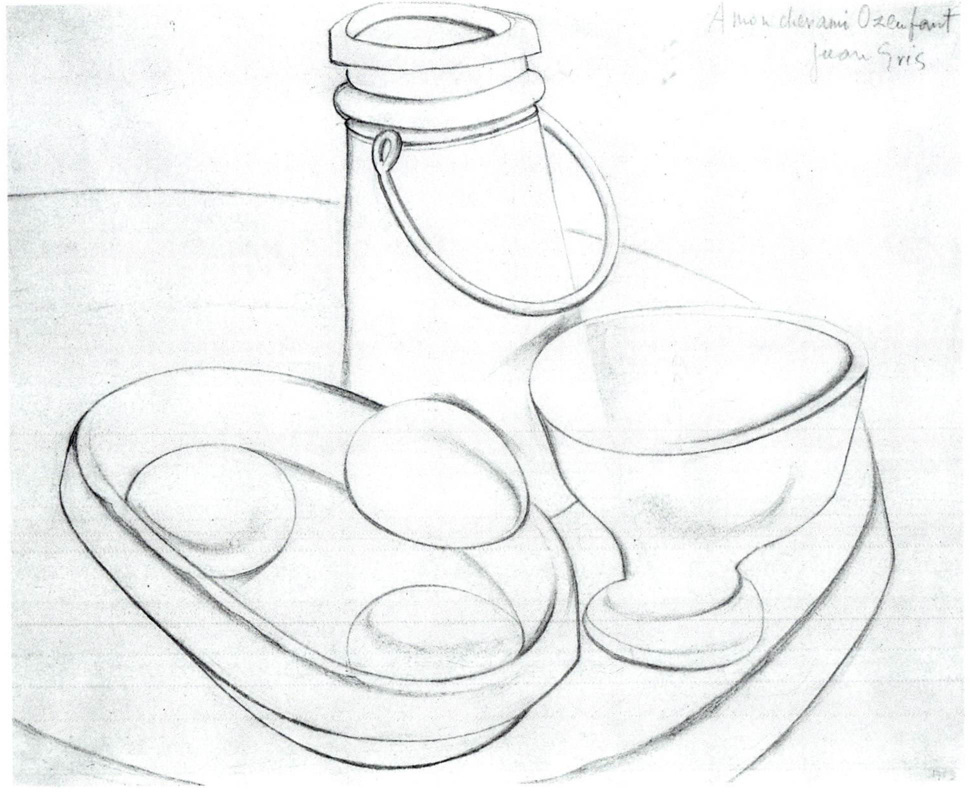

95
Still-life with Eggs, 1920
Pencil on paper,
25 x 31 cm
Private Collection

96
Portrait of Daniel-Henry Kahnweiler, 1921
Pencil on paper,
32.5 x 26 cm
Musée National d'Art Moderne, Centre Georges Pompidou, Paris. Gift of Louise and Michel Leiris (1984)

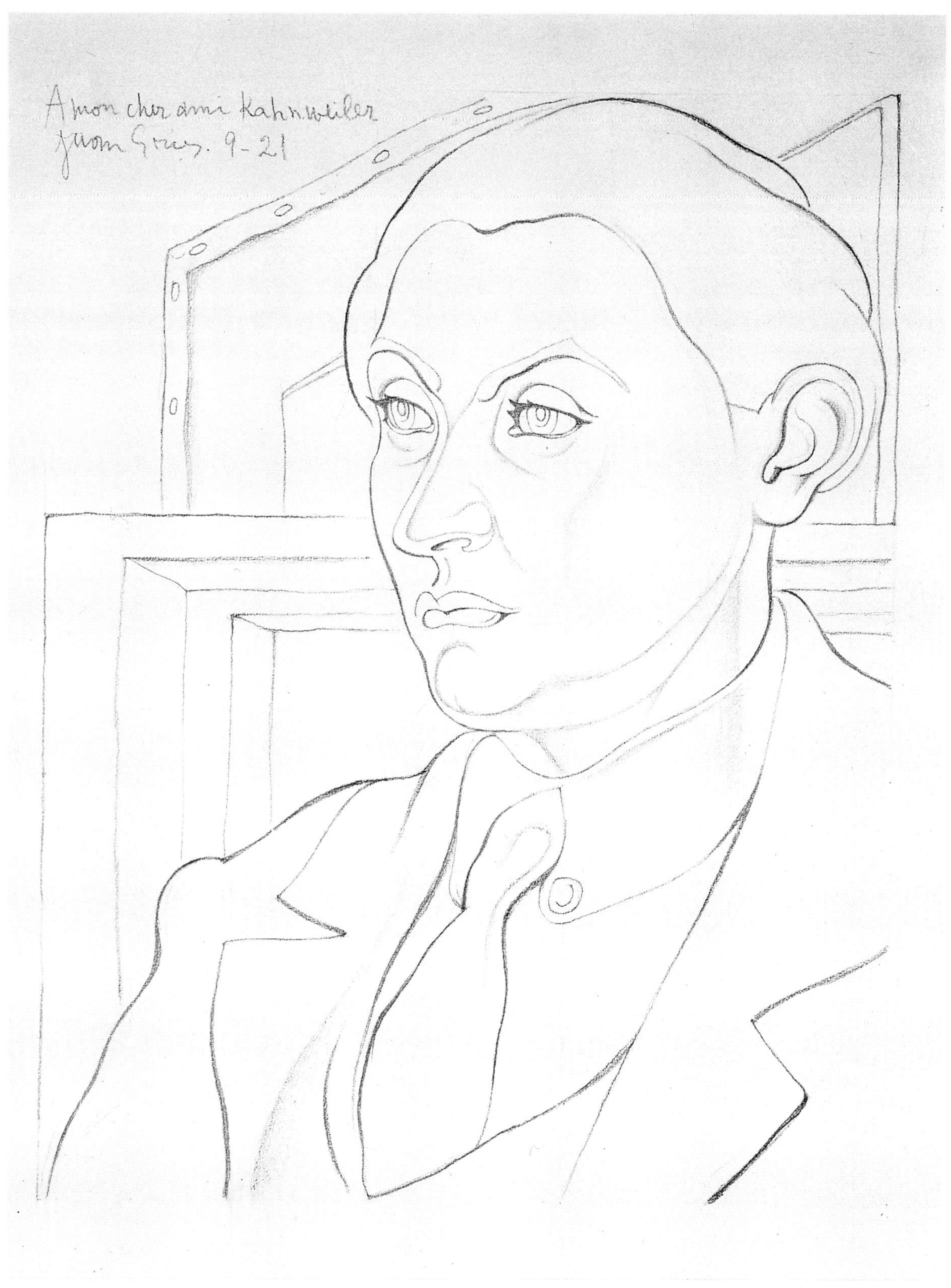
A mon cher ami Kahnweiler
Juan Gris. 9-21

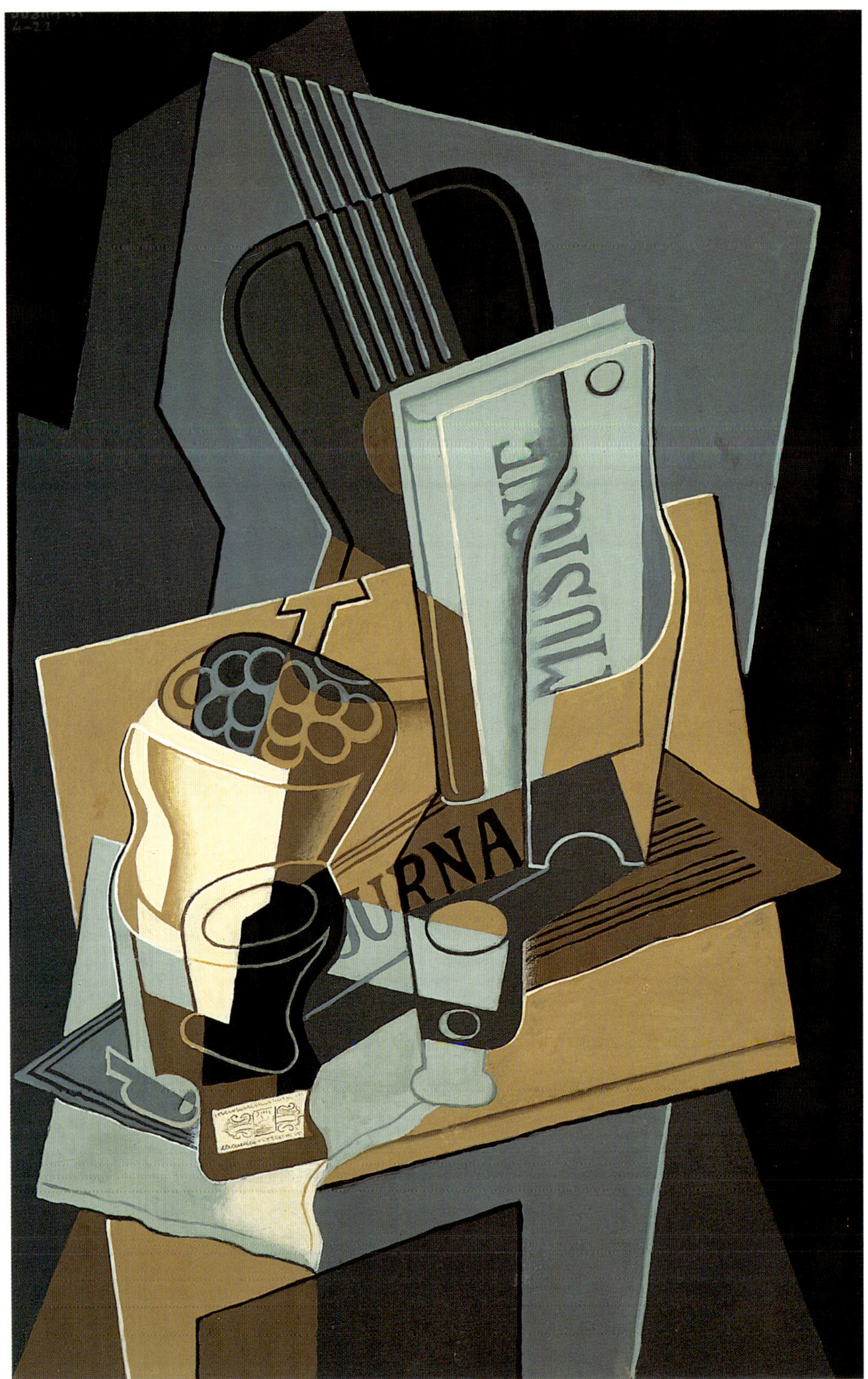

97
The Book of Music,
1922
Oil on canvas,
96x61.5 cm
Museo Nacional Reina Sofia

98
Guitar and Fruit Dish, 1919
Oil on canvas,
92x73.5 cm
Henie-Onstad Kunstsenter, Høvikodden

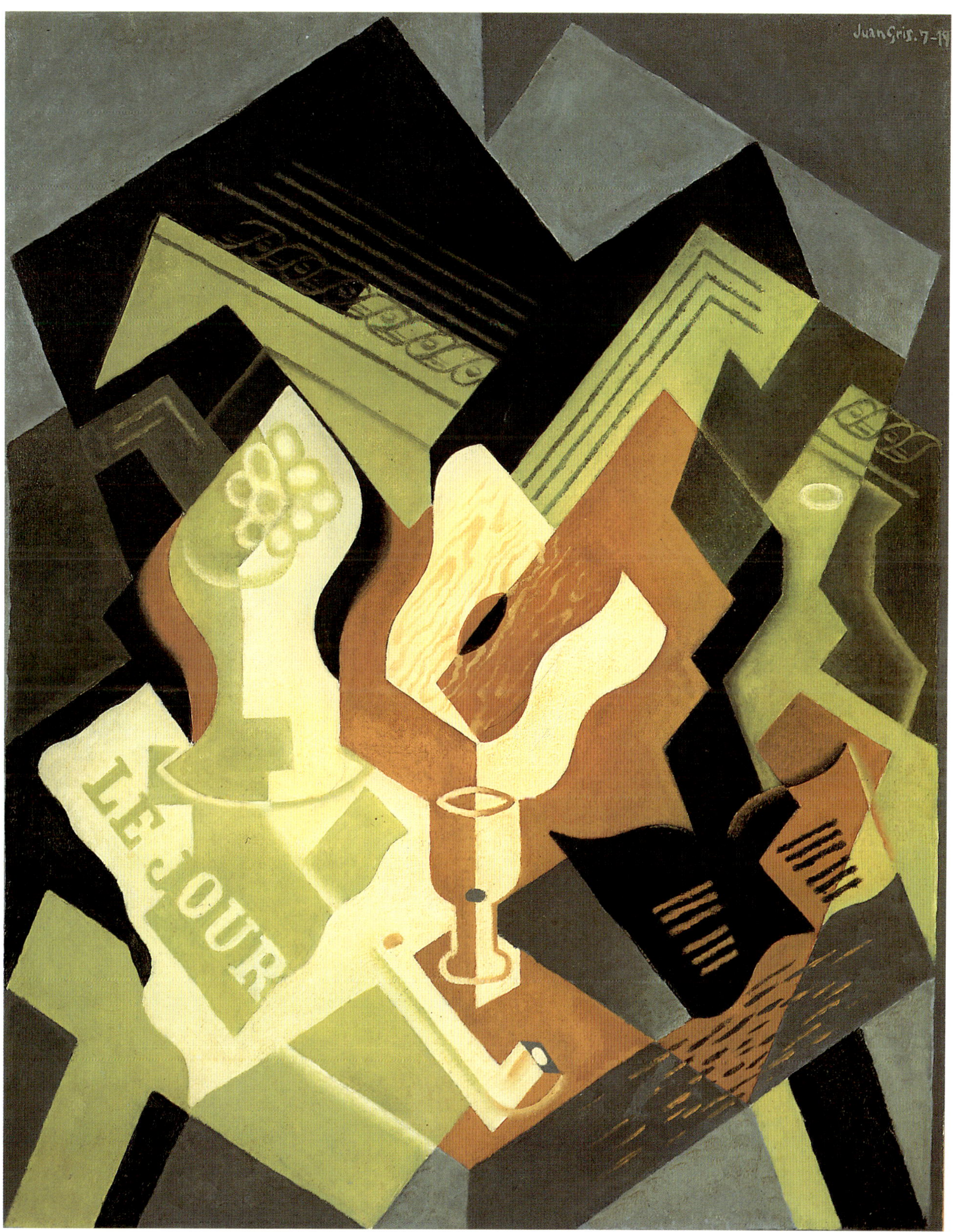
Juan Gris. 7-19
LE JOUR

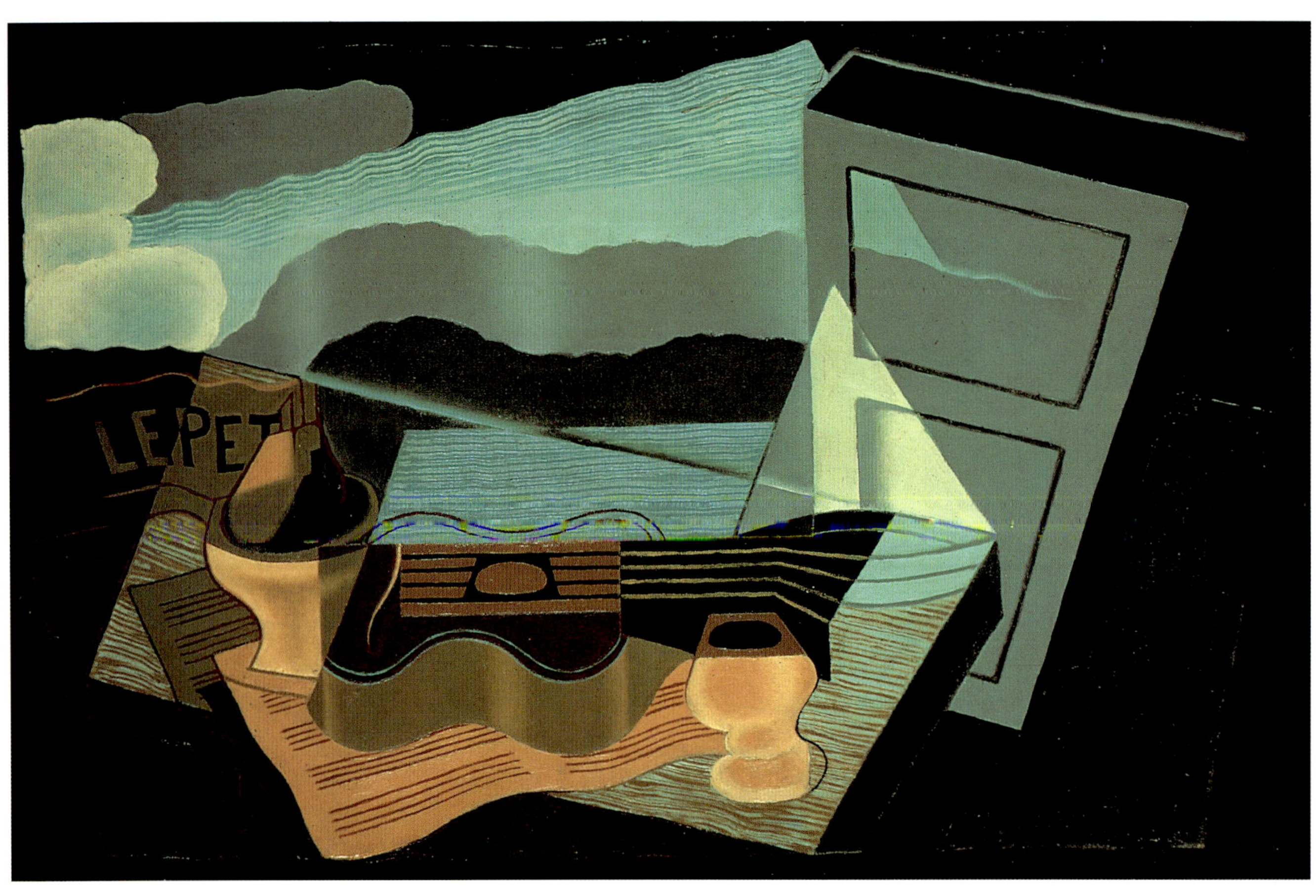

99
The View Across the Bay, 1921
Oil on canvas,
65 x 100 cm
Musée National d'Art Moderne, Centre Georges Pompidou, Paris. Gift of Louise and Michel Leiris (1984)

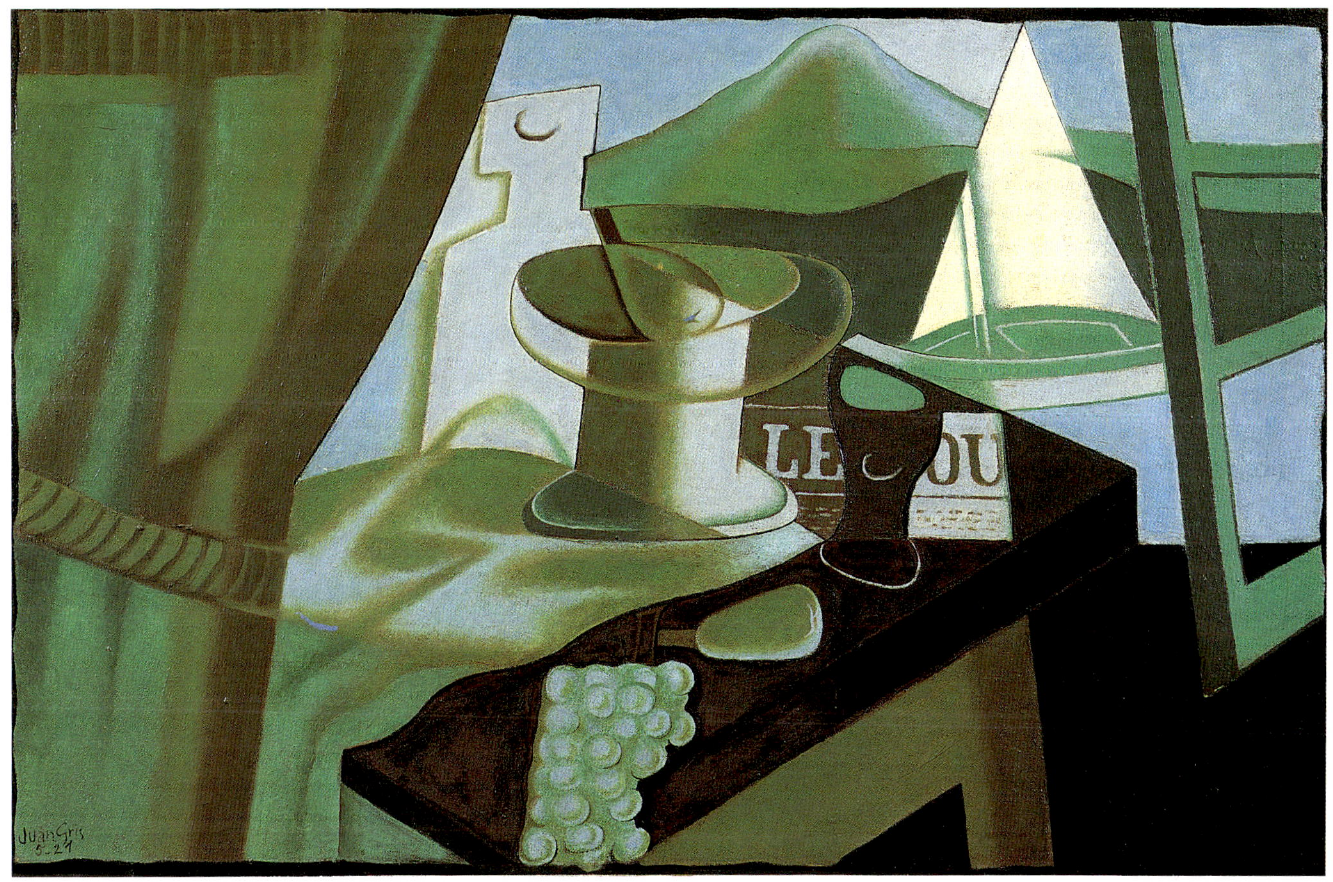

100
The Bay, 1921
Oil on canvas,
68.6 x 97.5 cm
Private Collection

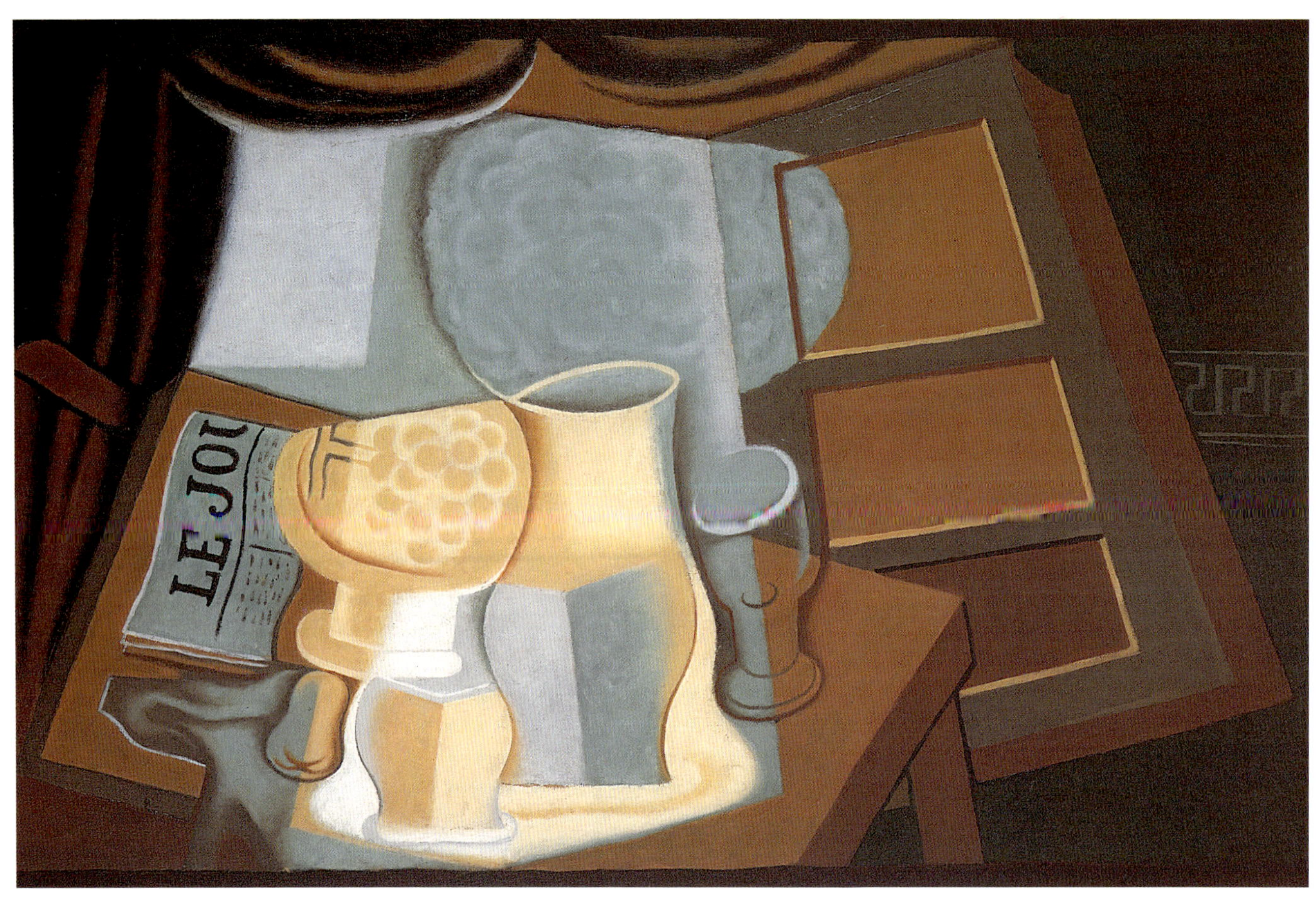

101
The Table in Front of the Window, 1921
Oil on canvas,
65 x 100 cm
Collection of Dr and
Mrs Raymond
R. Sackler

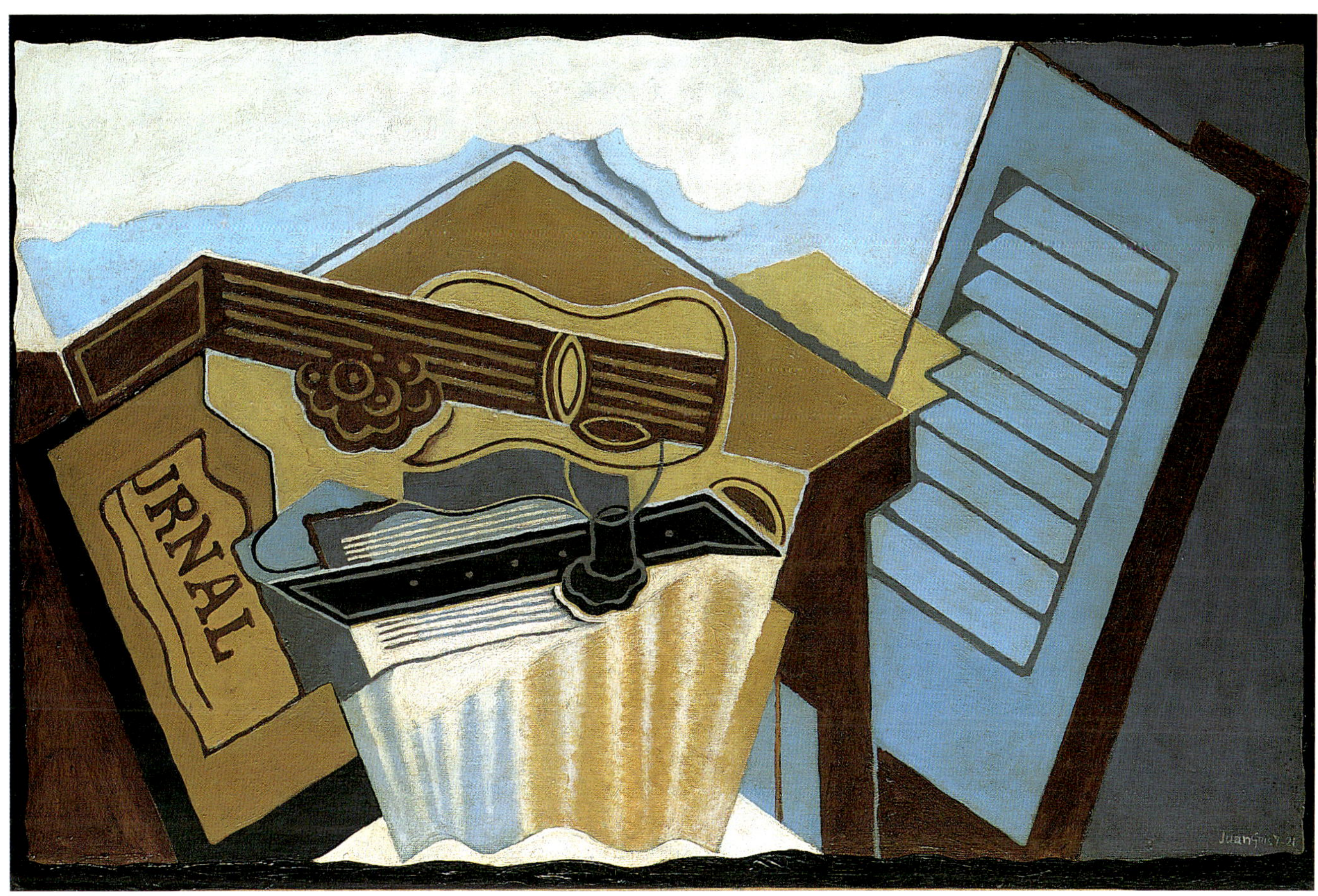

102
The Cloud, 1921
Oil on canvas,
65 x 100 cm
Hamburger Kunsthalle
[London and Stuttgart
only]

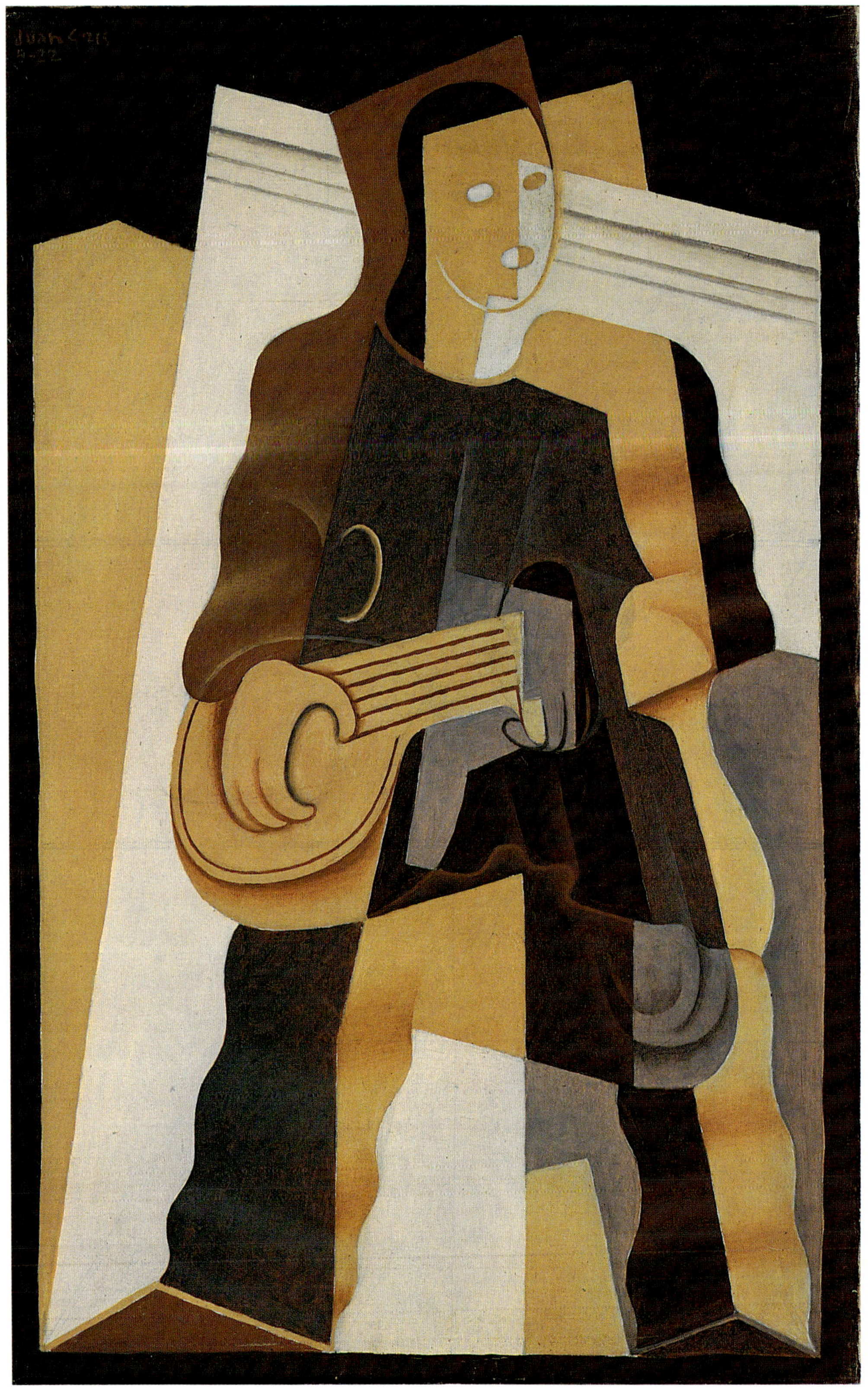

103
Pierrot, 1922
Oil on canvas,
100 x 65 cm
Galerie Louise Leiris,
Paris

104
Pierrot, 1921
Oil on canvas,
115 x 73 cm
The National Gallery
of Ireland, Dublin

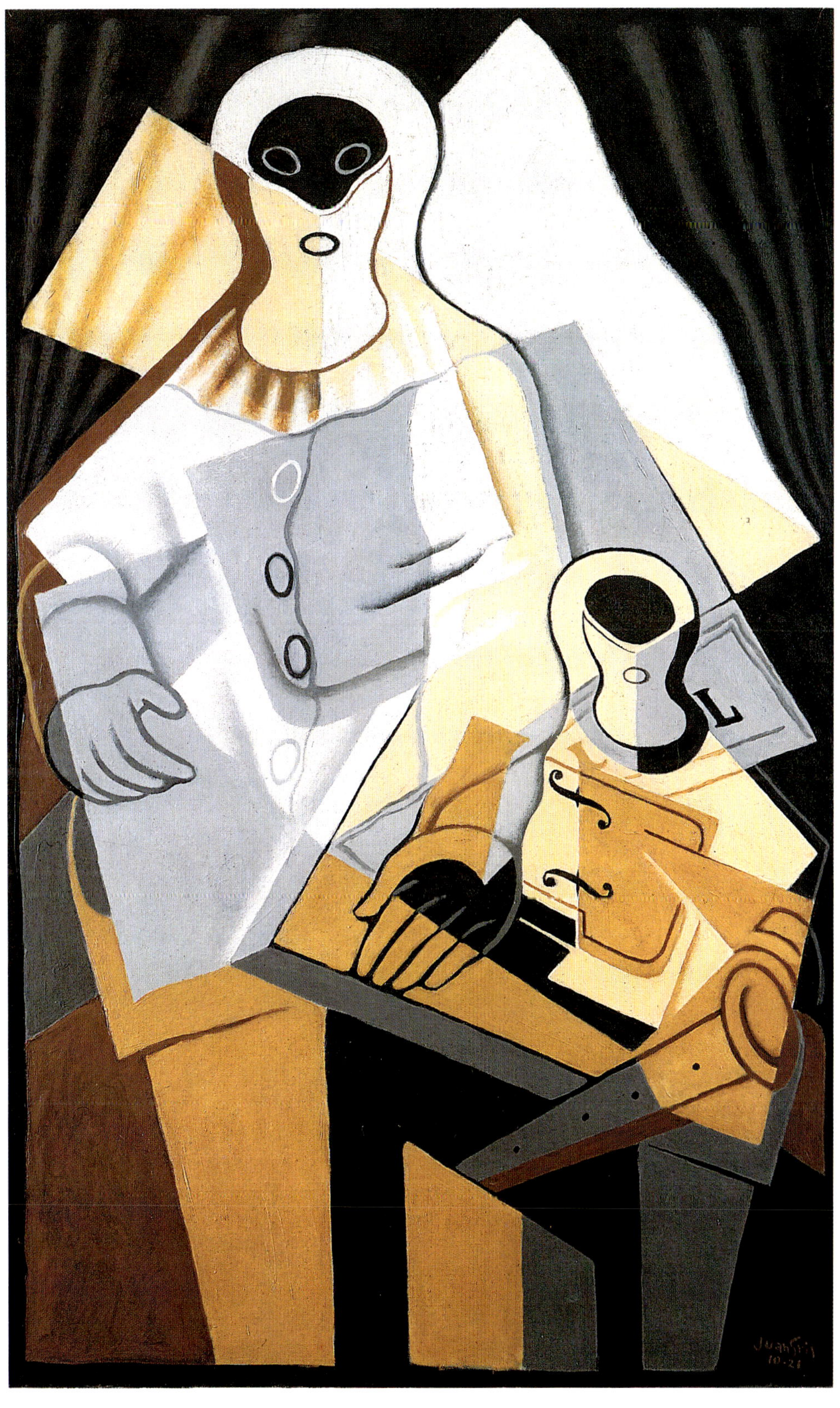

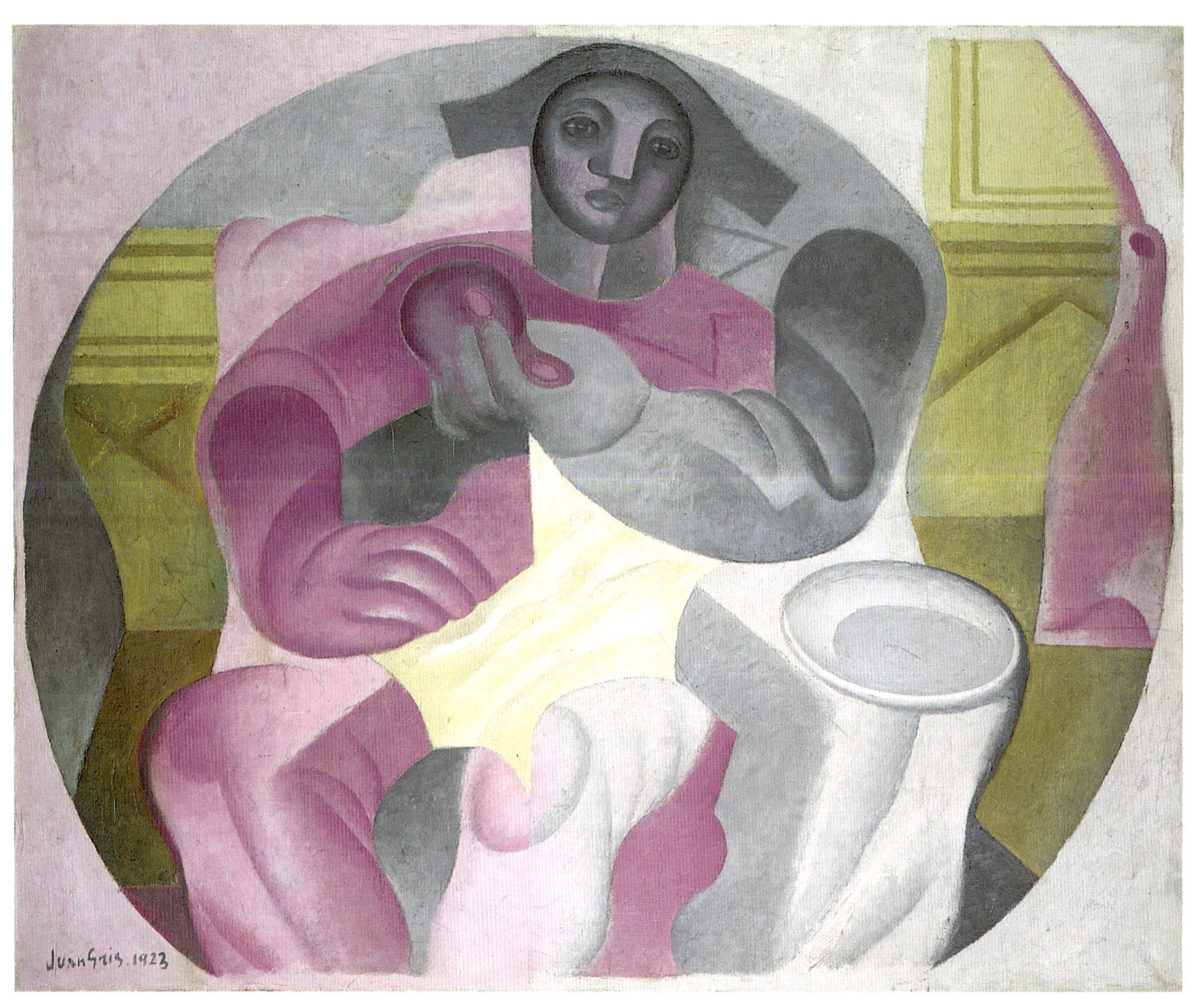

105
Seated Harlequin,
1923
Oil on canvas,
73 x 92 cm
The Carey Walker
Foundation, New York

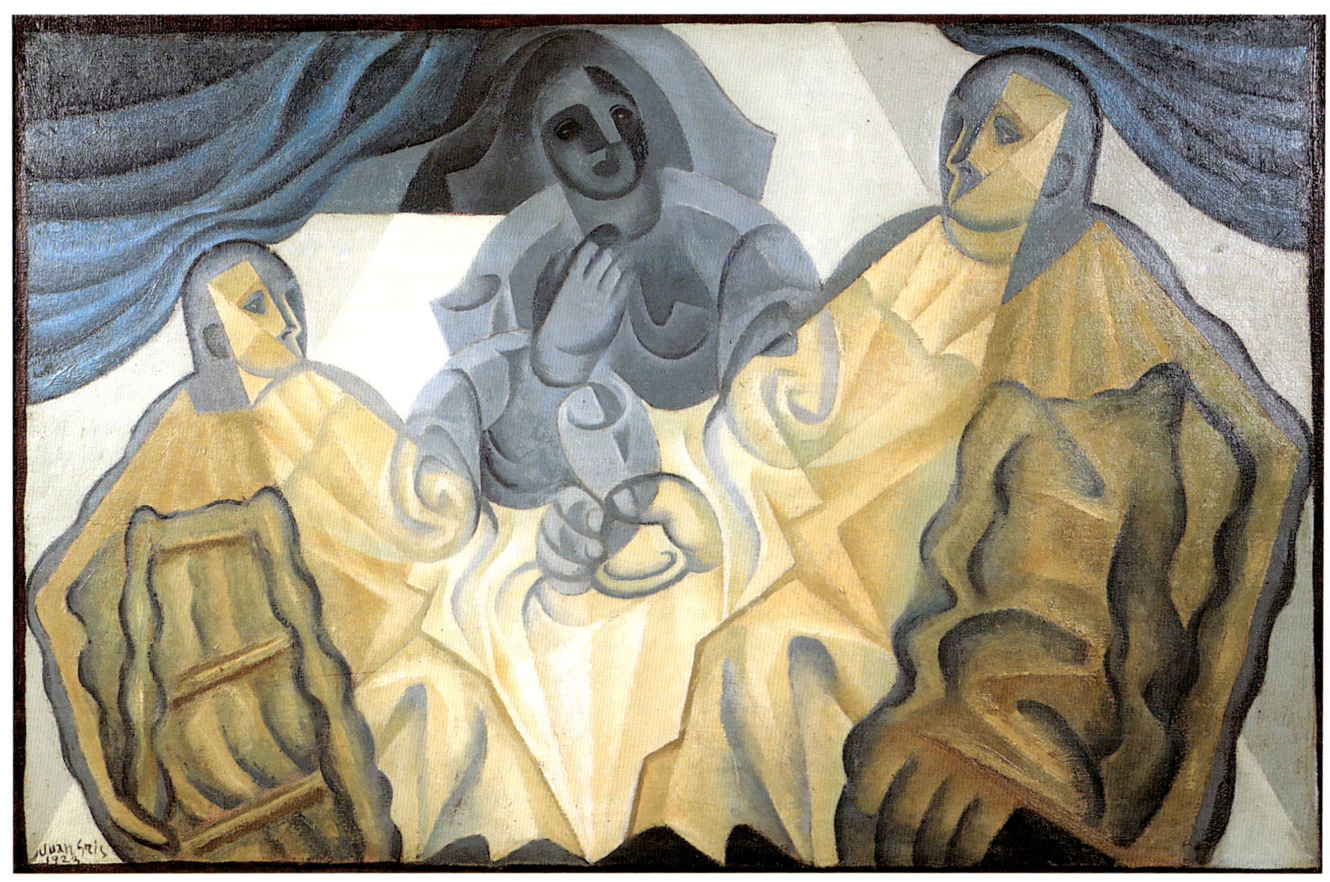

106
The Three Masks,
1923
Oil on canvas,
65 x 100 cm
Private Collection

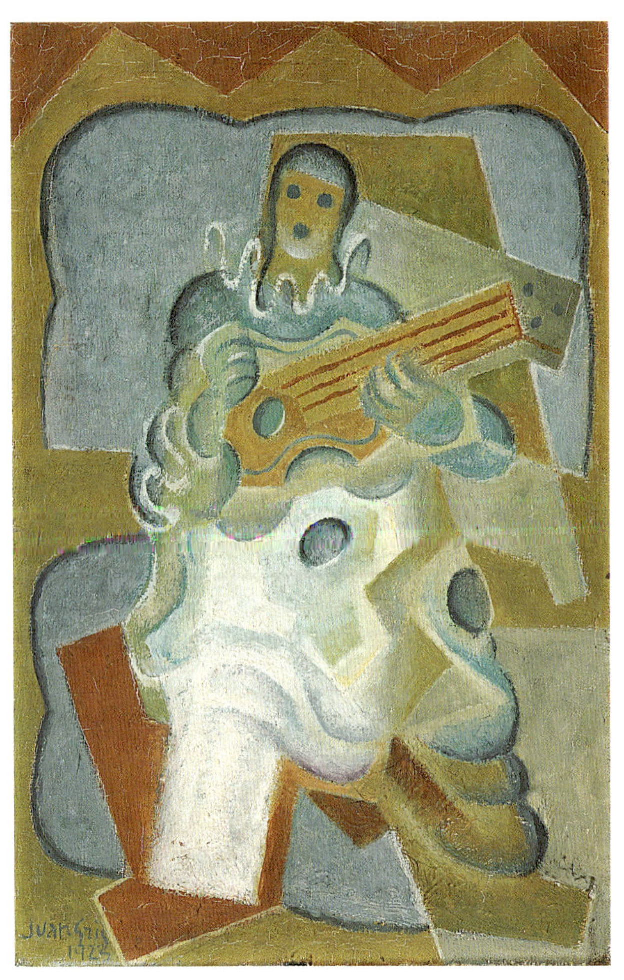

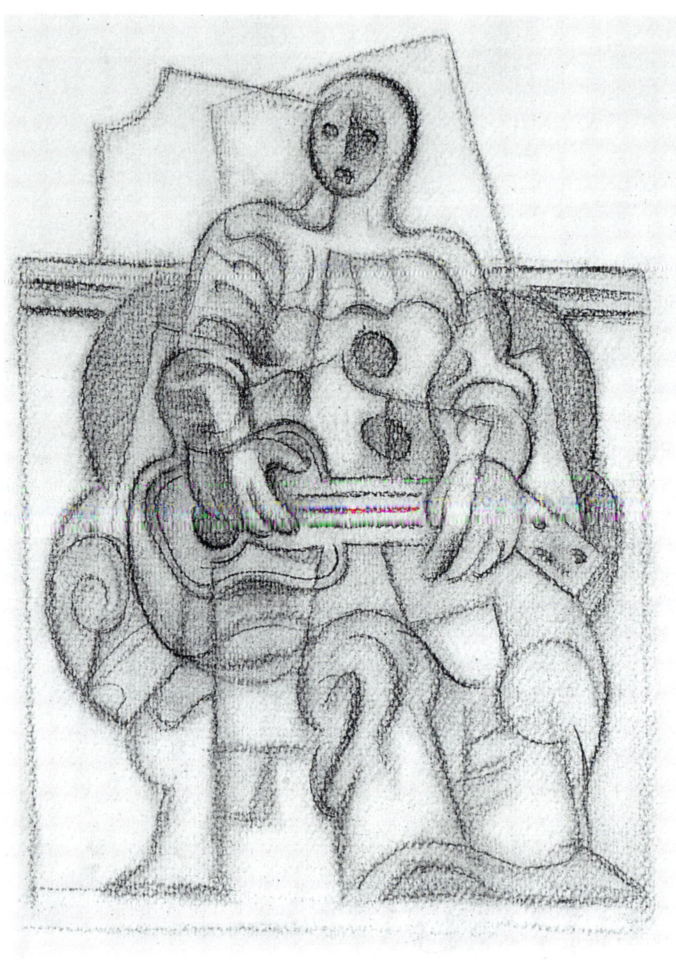

107
Pierrot with Guitar,
1923
Oil on canvas, 41x27 cm
Galerie Louise Leiris,
Paris

108
Pierrot with Guitar,
1922
Charcoal on paper,
32.1x24 cm
Galerie Louise Leiris,
Paris

109
The Bunch of Grapes,
1924
Oil on canvas,
22 x 33 cm
Staatsgalerie Stuttgart

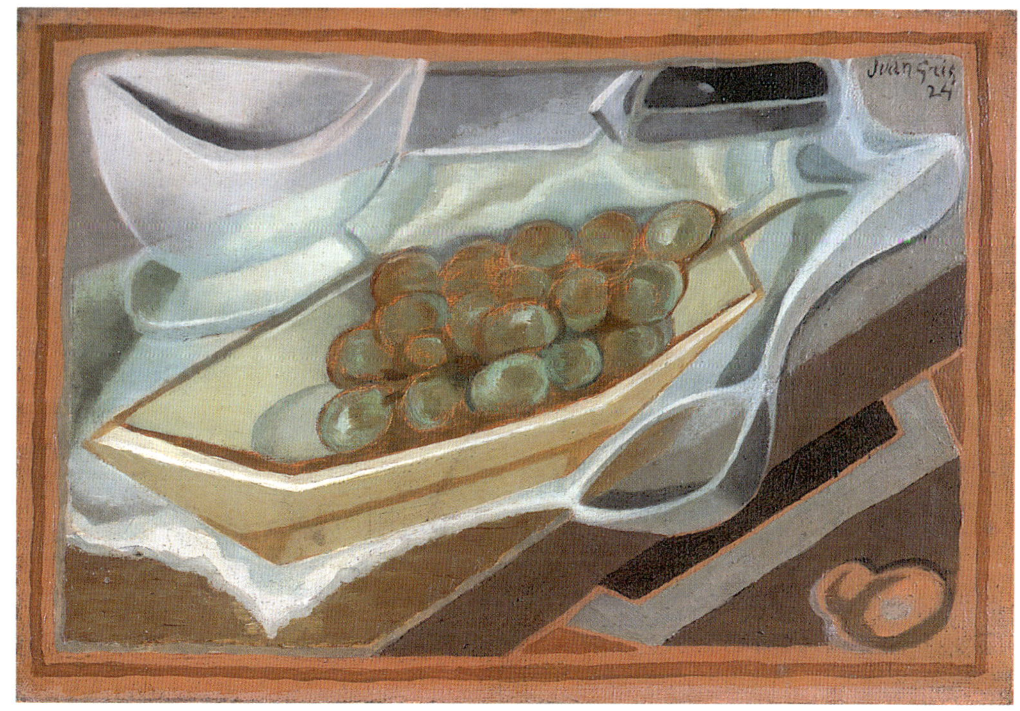

110
The Basket of Pears,
1925
Oil on canvas,
46 x 55 cm
On loan to the Scottish National Gallery of Modern Art, Edinburgh
[London and Otterlo only]

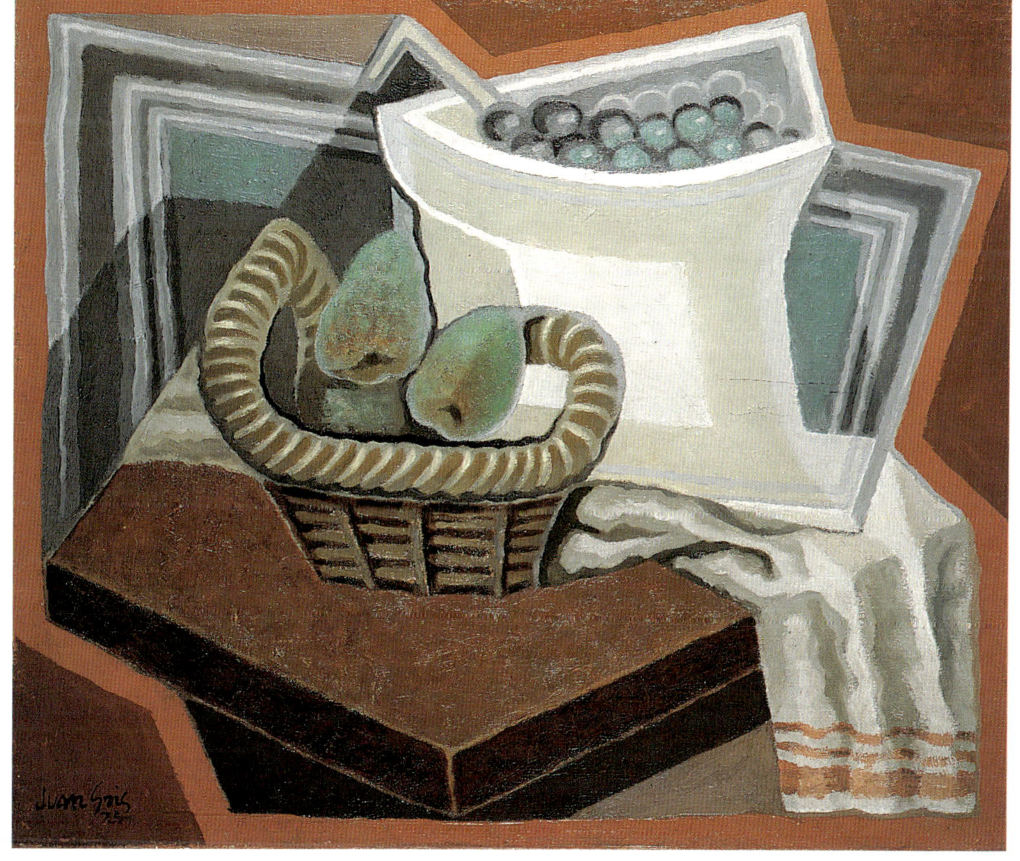

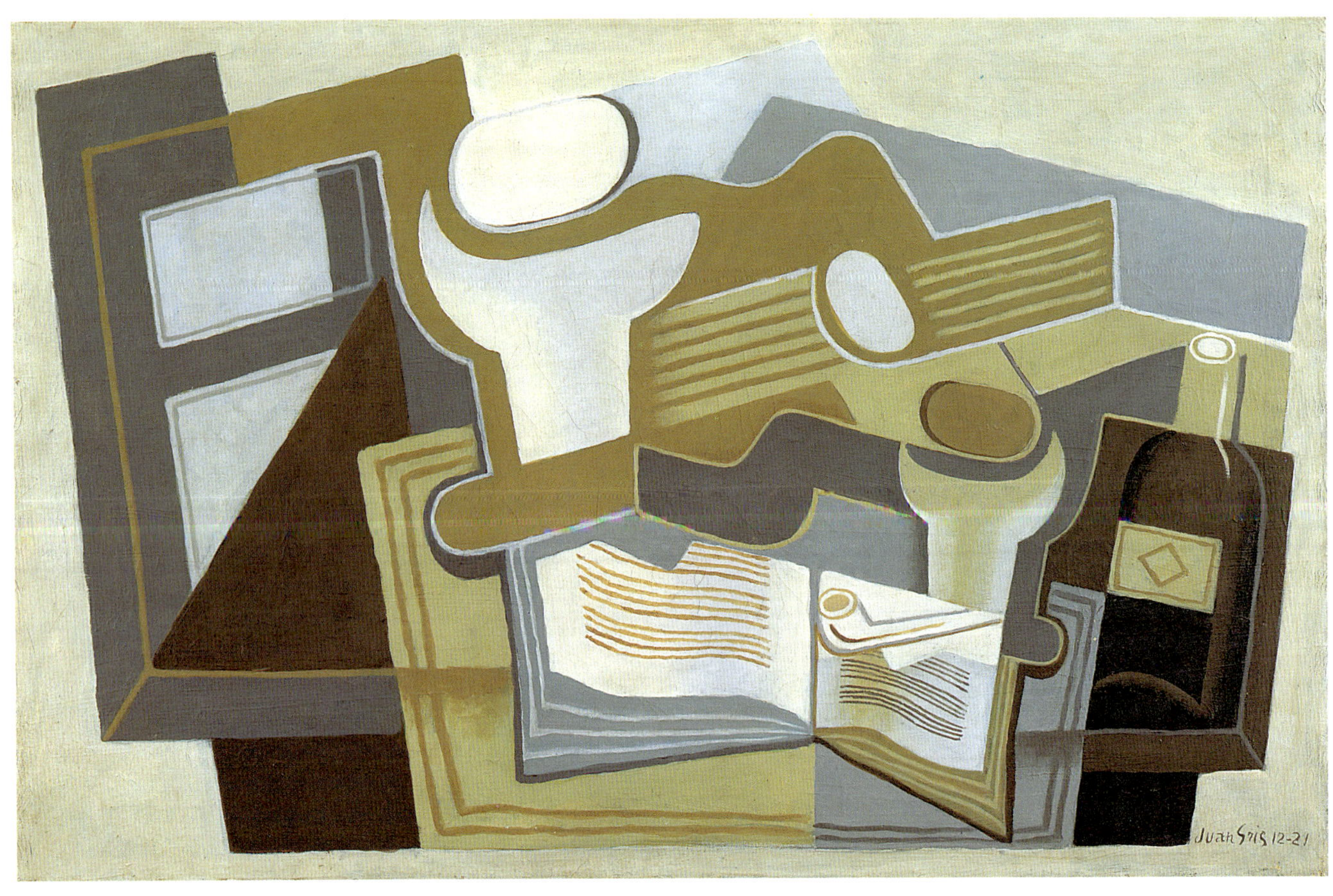

111
Guitar and Fruit Dish, 1921
Oil on canvas,
61 x 95 cm
Mme Georges González Gris

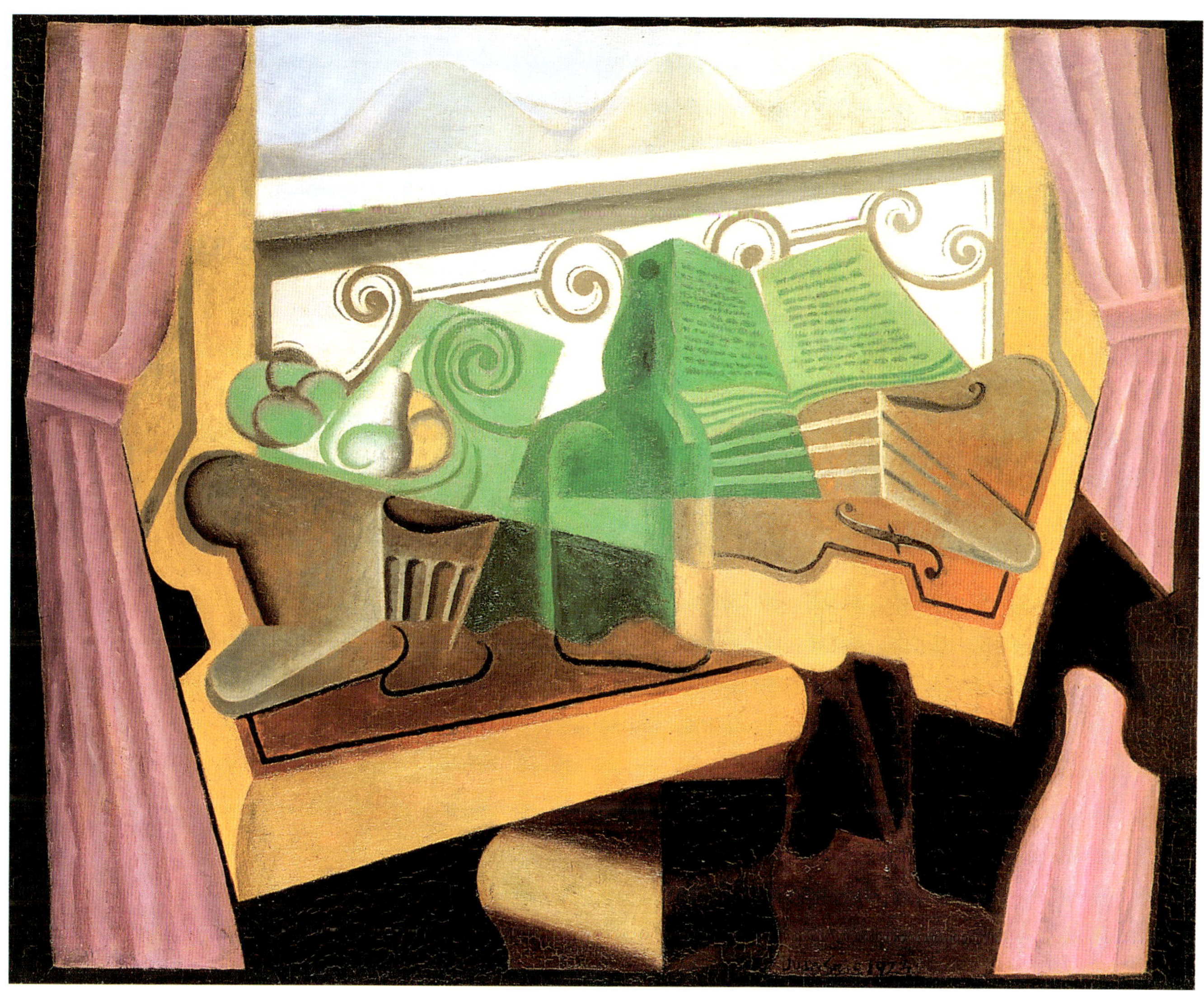

112
Open Window with Hills, 1923
Oil on canvas,
73 x 92 cm
Telefónica de España, S. A.

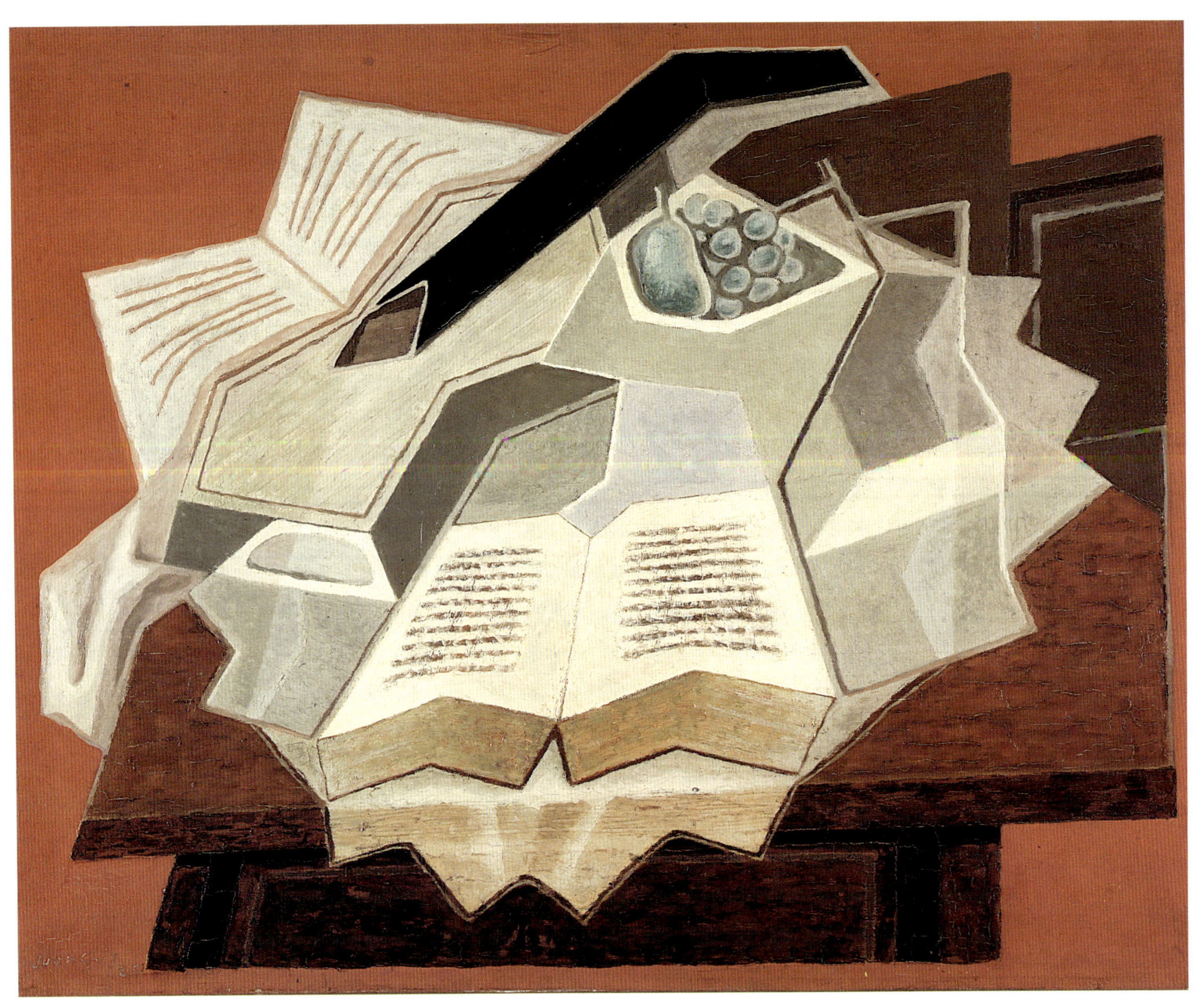

113
The Open Book, 1925
Oil on canvas,
73 x 92 cm
Kunstmuseum Bern
[London and Stuttgart only]

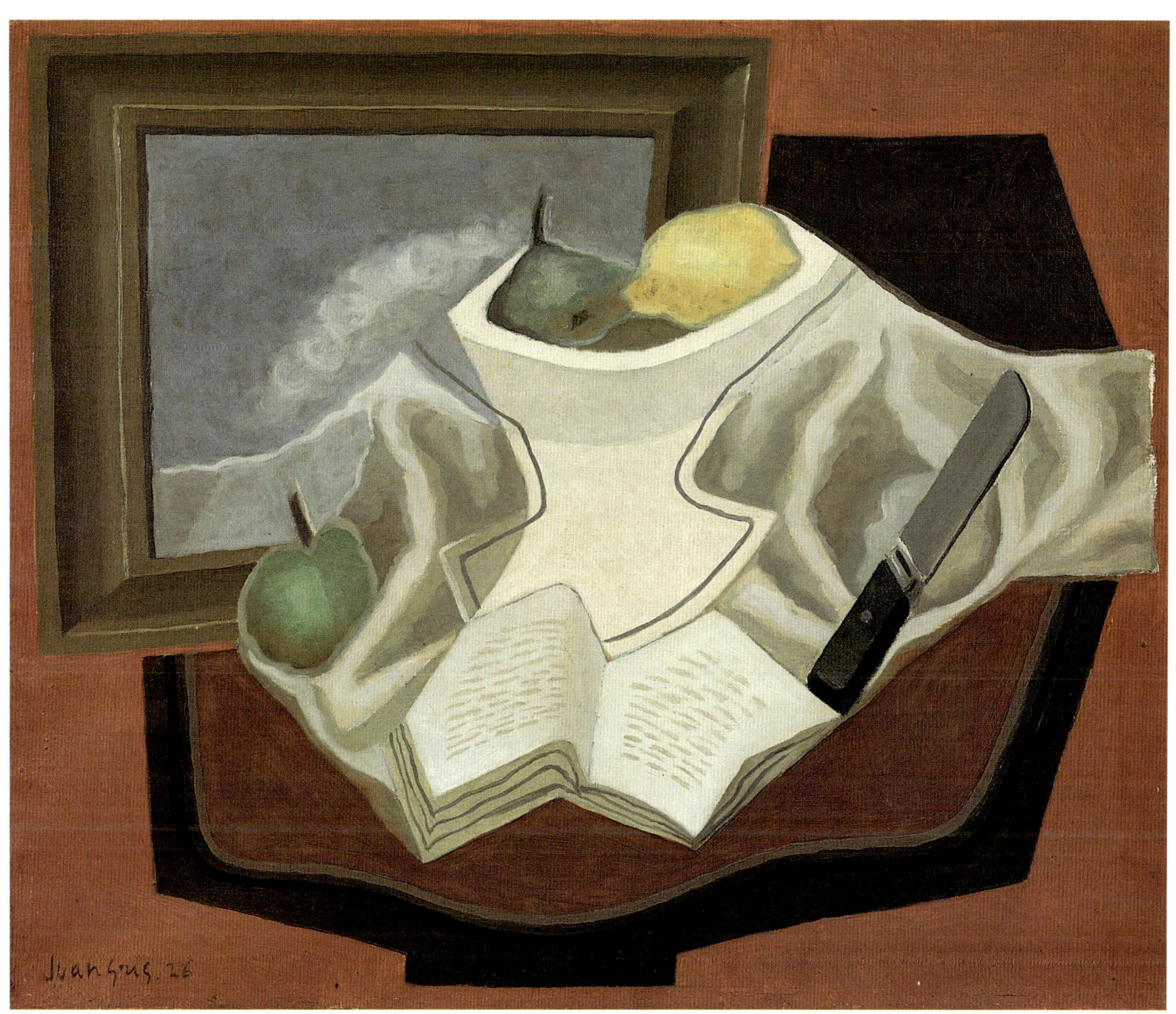

114
The Table in Front of the Picture, 1926
Oil on canvas,
50 x 61 cm
Galerie Louise Leiris,
Paris

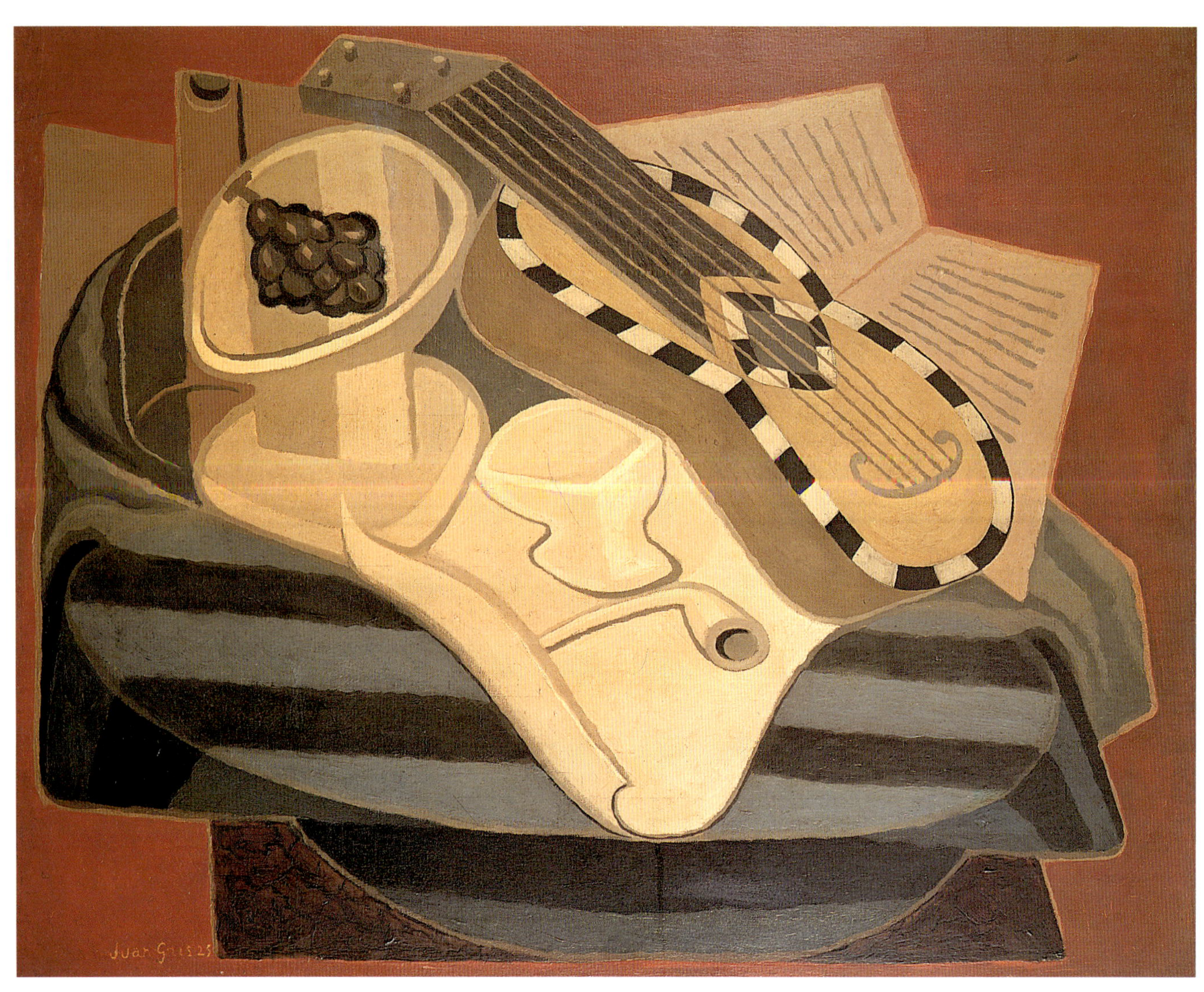

115
The Guitar with Inlay, 1925
Oil on canvas,
73 x 92 cm
Collection Jacques
Hachuel, Madrid

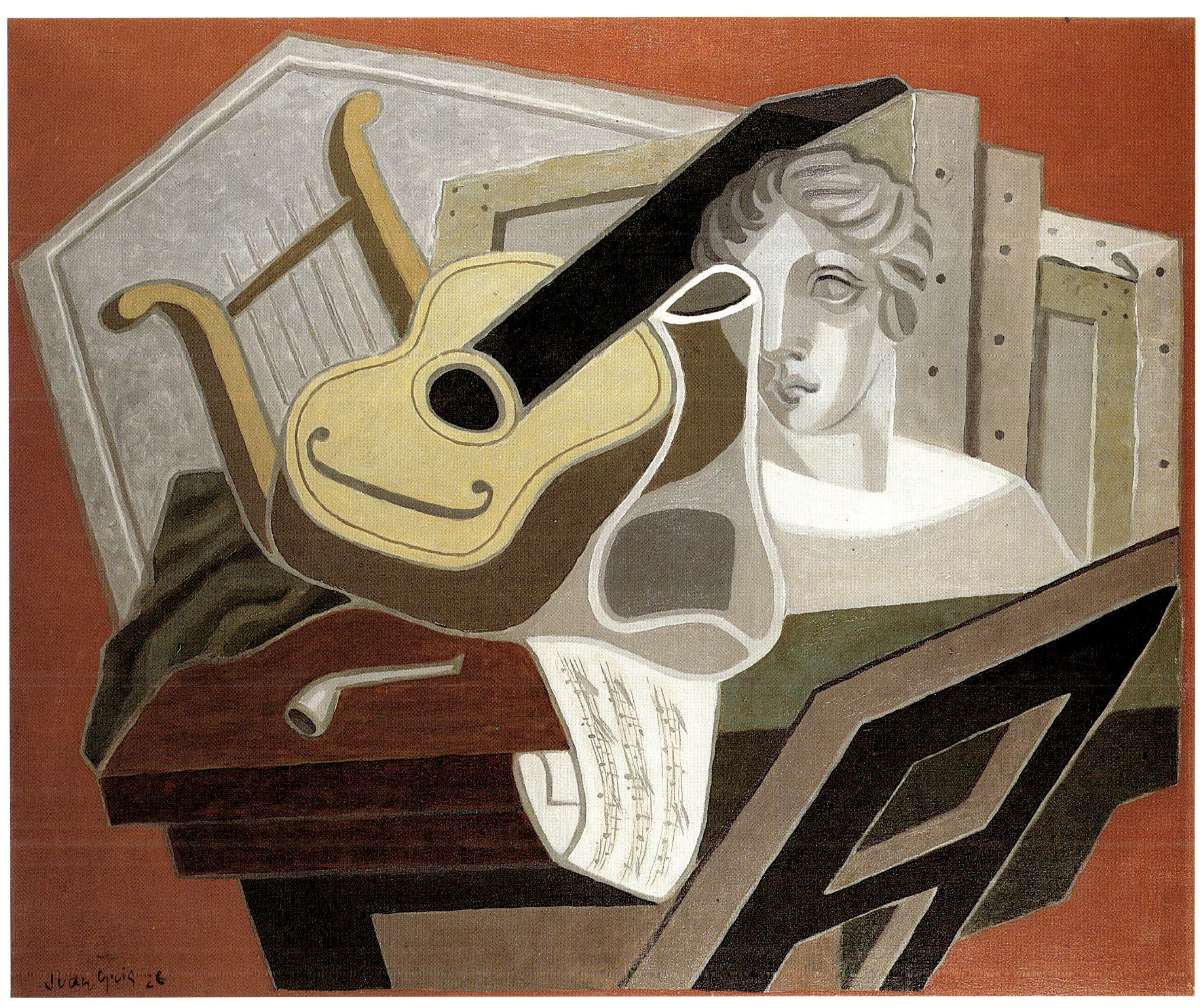

116
The Musician's Table,
1926
Oil on canvas,
81x100 cm
Private Collection
[Not in exhibition]

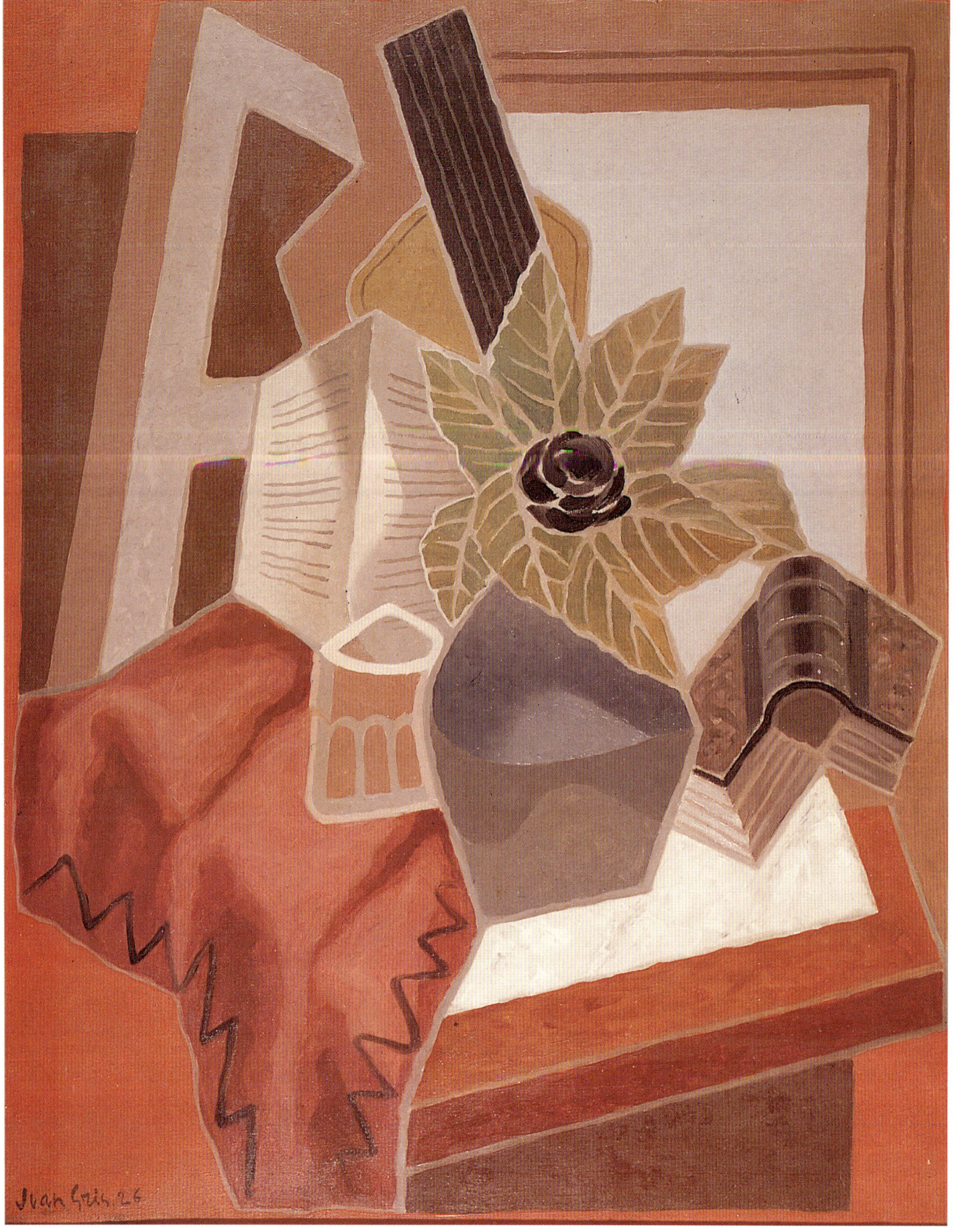

117
The Flower on the Table, 1925–26
Oil on canvas, 92 x 73 cm
Private Collection
[Not in exhibition]

118
The Painter's Window, 1925
Oil on canvas,
100 x 81 cm
The Baltimore Museum of Art: Bequest of Saidie A. May
(BMA 1951.306)

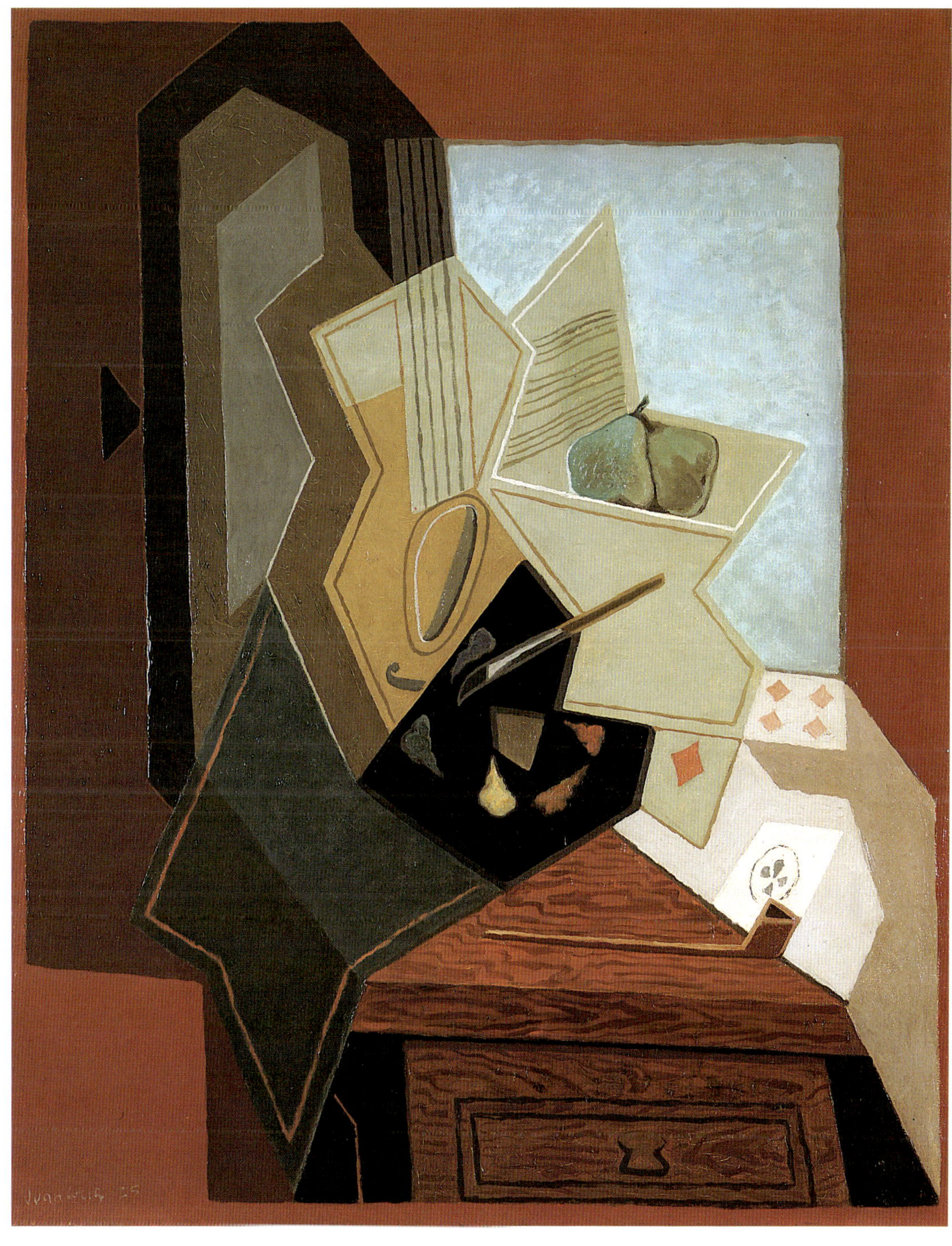

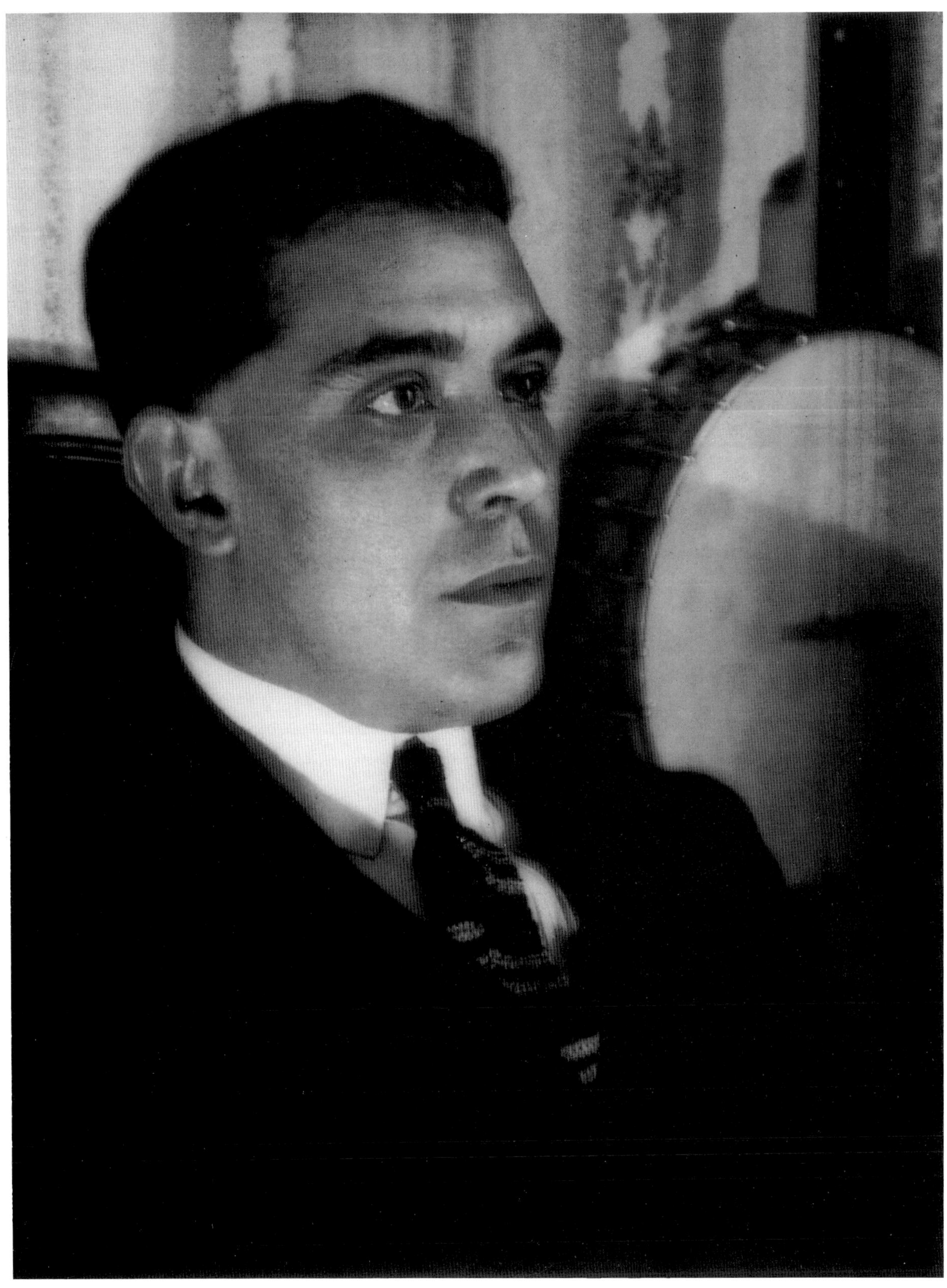

Music and Theatre in the Work of Juan Gris

Karin von Maur

Juan Gris, 1922
(Photograph: Man Ray)

I Musical Structures and Emblems in the Painting

Nowhere in twentieth century painting is there such an evident predilection for musical subject-matter as there is in the work of the Cubists, with their musical-instrument still-lifes and their imagery of *Woman with Guitar.* This applies not only to Picasso and Braque, but also to Juan Gris, their junior by several years who, between 1912 and his untimely death in May 1927, painted no less than 150 pictures in which musical instruments – mainly guitars and violins – play a dominant role.

There has been a tendency to ascribe this iconographic constant in Cubism – and the facetted rendering of space that records perception in terms of a process – to an intense interest in music on the painters' part. This is entirely refuted by a number of statements from the lips of the painters themselves. When asked, Picasso declared that he knew nothing about music[1]. As for Braque, who in 1908 was the first to introduce musical instruments into his painting, and whose work before the First World War frequently included the actual names Bach and Mozart, he accounted for his choice by saying that what particularly fascinated him about instruments was "their sculptural form and their volume". However, he went on to say: "I was already on the way to tactile or, as I call it, manual space; and as an object the musical instrument had the particular quality that touching it could bring it to life"[2].

For Braque, a musical instrument, and a violin in particular, represented the attainment of tangible three-dimensionality; it also stood for the life that springs from touch: vibration, resonance and sound. There was thus a real, if indirect, musical association in his mind. Picasso was probably more interested by the formal ambivalence involved: the analogy between the curves of fiddles and guitars and those of a female body. It was an analogy that he carried to the point of equating the woman, erotically, with the instrument[3].

Gris was an Andalusian on his mother's side and a Castilian on his father's. He had a special love for the guitar, which among other things is, of course, a symbol of the Spanish soul[4]. But he too admitted, in spite of his friendship with the composer Erik Satie: "I don't understand anything about music"[5]. His painting reveals, even so, an intense affinity for stringed instruments, and this is confirmed by a portrait photograph taken by Man Ray in 1922, in which the artist is shown with a banjo (which he could presumably play) hanging on his studio wall (see page 266). The plucked stringed instrument in one still-life of 1912, *Banjo and Glasses* (Plate 9) has always been assumed to be a banjo, in defiance of the autograph inscription "... de Guitarra de ..."; Christopher Green earlier suggests that the circle should be read as the sound-hole of a guitar, which seems considerably more plausible than the traditional reading.

When Gris confessed to musical ignorance, therefore, he was clearly referring to serious music, and to the contemporary compositions of his own musician friends in particular. He was strongly drawn to folk and dance music, not least because he was himself an enthusiastic dancer (from 1921 certainly). With his wife Josette, he never missed an opportunity to practise and perform, with positively professional aplomb, such new dances as the foxtrot, the shimmy, the charleston and the tango; indeed, the couple were good enough to win prizes[6]. We may therefore safely assume that Gris had a discriminating sense of rhythm.

The artists' own assertions did nothing to deter their contemporaries from emphasizing the musical character of Cubist painting. It was an idea that derived not only from the recurrent imagery of musical instruments but, above all, from the visual rendering of a time-factor: that of perception as a step-by-step process of approaching and exploring. The relationship between object and space, hitherto seen as static, had been opened up and set vibrating. The object – the instrument – was no longer set down bodily, as it were, as a finished object seen from a single viewpoint: it was constructed on the canvas out of component signs. The close interweaving of the perceptual process with the artist's record of it set up an intricate tissue of objective, planar and spatial structures that was likened to the musical principle of polyphonic composition.

The notion of polyphony, and the analogy with Johann Sebastian Bach, made their appearance very early on in the discussion. "Picasso's paintings grow into veritable structures of Bach polyphony", proclaimed the Czech art historian and collector Vincenc Kramá in his book on Cubism, published in 1921[7]. One year before, Paul Erich Küppers, the director of the Kestner-Gesellschaft in Hanover, wrote in positively euphoric tones of the kinship between Cubist painting and the structure of a Bach fugue: "Out of pale harmonies of colour, lines ascend; prisms thrust themselves up, grow towards us, spring back, hew out steps in spatial infinity, lead upwards and into depth, spread out, multiply, cluster into chords, are energized by rhythm, and dance amid the absolute music of space. This transcendental dynamism is experienced in the same way as the remote counterpoint of Bach's fugues . . ."[8].

In his book on Cubism, *Der Weg zum Kubismus* (published in the same year, 1920), Daniel-Henry Kahnweiler steered clear of musical analogies (presumably in order to avoid misunderstanding); but in his later monograph on Gris he dwelt at length on this very connection. In a chapter entitled "Polyphony", he declared: "The works . . . suggest a comparison with another art: the majestic musical compositions of Johann Sebastian Bach . . . In employing the term 'polyphony' to define the construction of Gris's works at this period, I am not merely inventing an ingenious label. It is worth examining some of these 'architectures' closely. In these 'double compositions', which can be found in Gris's works from the start, it is no affectation to talk of 'independent voices'. Thus, one can describe Gris's method as 'contrapuntal'"[9].

Although unable to cite any direct evidence that Gris regarded himself as influenced by Bach, or that he had any music in mind at all, Kahnweiler went on to draw an additional parallel with Arnold Schoenberg and other composers of serial music. In his last chapter, under the heading "Finale", he declared: "Their conception of 'the series of twelve notes', whose intervals are the nucleus of the whole work, is reminiscent of the 'proportions' and 'relationships' at the basis of every painting of Gris. And I do not think it exaggerated to compare their austere technique of variation, recurrence, inversion (which is fundamental in twelve-note musical composition) with Gris's 'rhymes'"[10].

He went on to refer to the relationship between atonal music, with its compositional techniques of "the simultaneous unfolding of a number of autonomous, 'horizontal' melodic lines", and the principles of Bach's polyphony and counterpoint.

Figure 1
Violin Hanging on the Wall, 1913
Oil on canvas, 92 x 60.5 cm
Philadelphia Museum of Art: The A. E. Gallatin Collection

Others saw Igor Stravinsky as the best point of musical comparison for Cubism. Jean Cassou, for instance, wrote in his monograph on Braque: "In the same way, in contemporary music we are witnessing the progressive demolition of tonal coherence and a rejection of melody, and even of notes themselves, at least insofar as they immediately give rise to other notes. Hence the tendency to approximate more closely to noise, and to abandon melody and harmony in favour of raw rhythms, and then of the rhythms of rhythms. There is an evident analogy between such music, as it has evolved since Stravinsky, and the pictorial syncopations of Cubism"[11].

What emerges from such analogies is a striking contrast between intention and effect. Both Picasso and Braque denied that any musical interest played a part in their choice of motifs, or in the genesis of Cubism – although Braque, in particular, went out of his way to stress his musical allusions with a profusion of actual notes, composers' names, and such generic terms as "valse", "sonate", "rondo", "duo", "étude" and "aria". Gris, too, although in a different context, proclaimed, as we have seen, his lack of knowledge of the sister art; which did not deter his ally, Kahnweiler, from drawing detailed comparisons between Gris's compositional technique (in the painterly sense) and polyphonic and serial forms in music.

Not all contemporaries shared this view; some, indeed, came to diametrically opposite conclusions, as is shown by a comment that Guillaume Apollinaire made about Gris: "His painting avoids the musical, that is, it seems to aim, above all, at scientific reality"[12]. And yet in the very book from which this sentence is quoted, *Les Peintres cubistes* (1913), Apollinaire himself had already drawn attention to the role of music as an inspiration for painting[13].

At first sight, it is true, Apollinaire's verdict on Gris appears entirely plausible – especially by comparison with Braque who, in the facetted structures, subtle modulations and weightless, vibrant space of his pre-war painting, had achieved a musical lightness and immateriality very different from the Spaniard's solid, high-contrast compositions. As the idea of musicality tends mostly to be identified with Mozart, Braque might be likened to him, while Gris, with his strict pictorial structures, suggests the "musical architectures" of Bach (as invoked by Kahnweiler). There is, however, a whole succession of paintings and collages by Braque in which the letters of the name J. S. Bach appear far more often than those of Mozart.

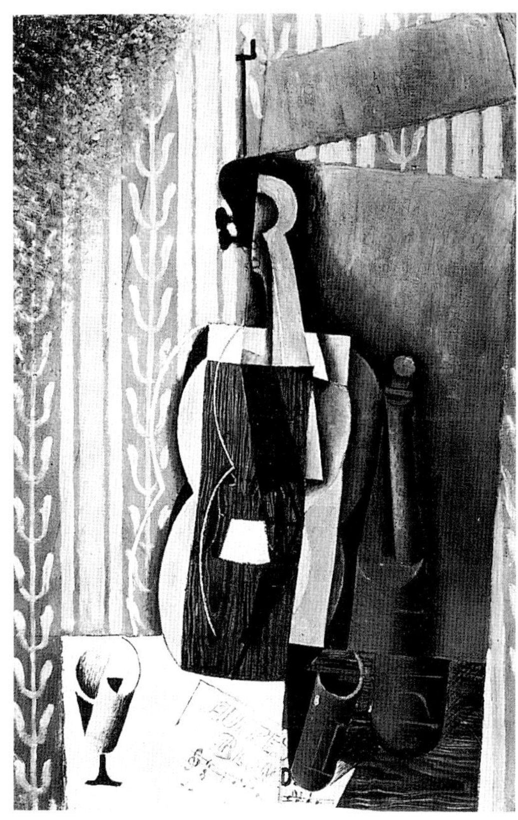

The advent of Cubism, in the early years of this century, coincided with a major revival of interest in Bach. Long dismissed as merely "fit for conservatoire exercises"[14], Bach had emerged in a new light as part of a reaction against the prevailing cult of Wagner. He now stood revealed as the absolute antithesis of Wagner, a musical "Constructivist", who stood for a strictly ordered musical aesthetic governed by counterpoint and by the laws of

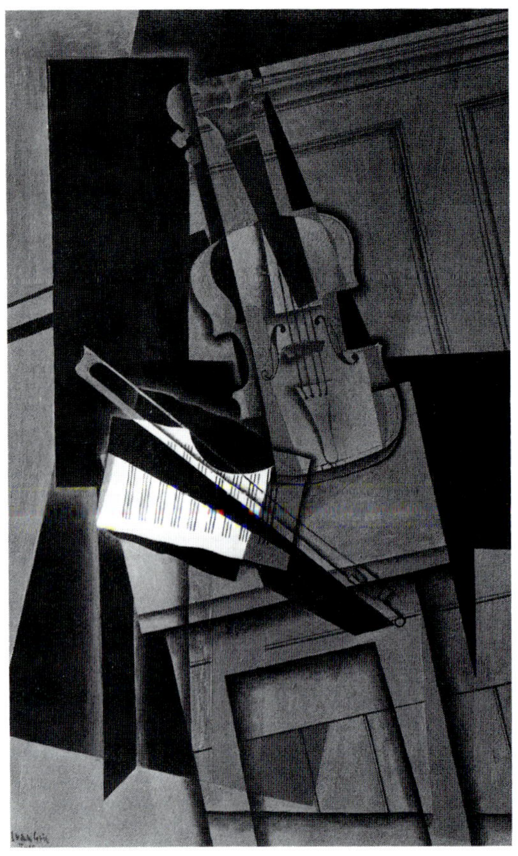

Figure 2
The Violin, 1916
Oil on wood,
116.5x73 cm
Öffentliche Kunst-
sammlung Basel,
Kunstmuseum

fugue. After Mendelssohn's celebrated revival of the St Matthew Passion in 1829, the works most performed were the great oratorios and Passions, with huge choral forces; but after 1900 there was a gradual shift of emphasis towards the more intimate cantatas and keyboard works, and there was an endeavour to gain a hearing for an authentic Bach, purged of all accretions[15].

In France, Albert Schweitzer's monograph on Bach (first published in French in 1905) and Romain Rolland's essay on the St Matthew Passion brought a new understanding of polyphonic compositional structure. Stravinsky, in his treatise on *Musical Poetics,* was one of those who acclaimed the fugue as a "perfect form, in which music signifies nothing beyond itself"[16].

But it is not very likely that Bach was, as it were, the presiding genius of Cubism. The tendency to genuflect in his direction is rather to be interpreted as a confirmation of the Cubists' own desire for system and law. For by 1912, when his name began to appear in a variety of works by Braque, the phase of Analytic Cubism, in which the object disintegrated into an array of emblematic signs, had already passed its peak.

It was then that paintings – including many by Gris – began to incorporate elements of musical notation, sometimes collaged as an *objet trouvé,* sometimes painted. This made the connection between painting, score and music more explicit; and at the same time musical signs came as a welcome addition to the range of prefabricated patterns already in use: wallpaper, wood-graining, scraps of newspaper, brand labels and the like. In his painting *Pen and Pipe* (Cooper 41) of 1913, for instance, Gris has placed a musical score in the centre. We find ourselves trying to decipher it, but on inspection there prove to be only three lines on the stave, and those out of kilter with each other.

Another painting of the same year, *Violin Hanging on the Wall* (Figure 1), incorporates in fragmentary form the title and (apparently) the first bars of a song: "Auprès [de ma] blonde". But even here, where even a treble clef and the (rather unusual) time signature 4/8 are supplied, the musical enthusiast is doomed to disappointment, and is hardly likely to extract the well-known *chanson* (or any other tune, for that matter) from the few notes given, again on only three lines.

This apart, *Violon Hanging on the Wall* is a work in which the identification of the instrument with the beloved (to which the *chanson* title also alludes) is more overt than it usually is with Gris; the fiddle, placed upright above the music, unmistakably recalls a female figure[17].

From 1914 onwards, the music sheets are more often blank, with three – or at most four – lines that take on a particular graphic importance, as for instance in *Guitar, Glass and Bottle* (Cooper 94), or in the famous work now in Basel, *The Violin* (Figure 2) of 1916. The

Figure 3
Guitar and Music-sheet,
1926–27
Oil on canvas,
65 x 81 cm
Private Collection

light-catching surface of the painted paper, with its three black lines interrupted at rhythmic intervals, sets up a succinct and forceful pattern that also "rhymes" with the parallel lines of the violin or guitar strings, usually shown in a diagonal position. Here, too, the artist is not concerned with realistic accuracy, but with the allusive sign and its accurate placing within the context of his composition; he mostly restricts himself to four lines for the strings, whether the instrument is a four-stringed fiddle or (as it much more often is) a six-stringed guitar.

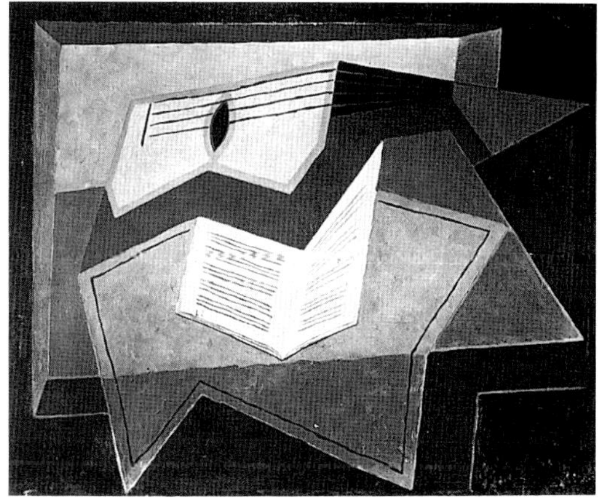

The "wrong" number of lines on the stave and of strings on the guitar is a clear sign that – like Picasso and Braque – Gris is scrupulously avoiding realistic depiction and detailed accuracy. Like the other objects shown, such as bottles, glasses, cups, bowls and tables, the instruments are used primarily as elements of colour and form, subordinate to the whole. Gris, as he himself explained, is practising a "deductive painting", in which such pictorial elements as line, form, colour, lighting, contrast and correspondence are set down on the canvas in initial disregard of their depictive relevance to any object whatever. Only later does the artist "read" objective motifs into the basic compositional outline. No wonder certain standard motifs – musical instruments among them – crop up again and again; for the artist knows them "by heart". And in the process he gives his preference to those object-signs that approximate to basic geometrical forms: circle, ellipse, triangle, square, sine curve, etc. The undulating outlines of the violin and the guitar make them particularly suitable for the interweaving of different planes and layers of depth, and also for instilling rhythm and depth into the pictorial structure.

In Gris, the way in which the outlines of the instruments are drawn – in soft curves or in harsh and jagged forms – gives the beat, as it were, to the whole composition. This emerges, for instance, from a comparison between two paintings of the 1920s. In *The View Across the Bay* (Plate 99) of 1921, the guitar and the sheet music, alternating rhythmically between wavy curves and tight fourfold strips (strings and staves), are "echoed" by the landscape; by contrast, in *Guitar and Music-sheet* (Figure 3; one of his last paintings, done in 1926–27), the jagged, zigzag lines of the musical manuscript paper and the guitar create an austerely ascetic composition of lapidary density and conciseness, entirely built up of triangles, quadrilaterals and pentagons in a few contrasting colours. In both these cases – as in many others – the instrument "sets the tone", not only rhythmically, but in the actual tonal quality of the colour.

Interpolated sheet music can also melodiously recapitulate the principal lines and rhythms of a painting, as happens in the still-life *Guitar, Glass and Carafe* (Figure 4) of 1917.

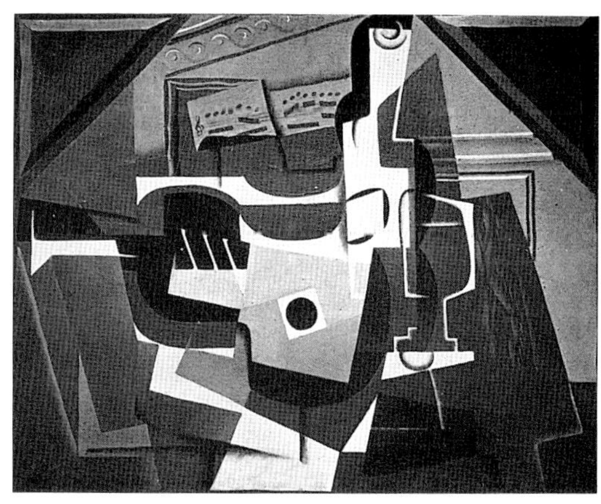

Figure 4
Guitar, Glass and Carafe,
1917
Oil on canvas,
73 x 92 cm
Private Collection

The rhythmic principle is similarly manifested in Gris's figure paintings, in which, again, guitars often appear. Although in these cases the pictorial content suggests music-making, what dominates is not the activity, but the synthesis of figure and instrument. In 1916, inspired (like Picasso) by Corot, he painted his magnificent paraphrase of the *Woman with a Mandolin (after Corot)* into a structure of contrasts in colour and form. In 1918–19 there followed a first series of Harlequins, mostly playing the guitar, but sometimes singing or playing drums; these were followed in 1922 by a softer, brighter, more Baroque phase of Pierrots, some of whom were playing instruments. Paintings such as *Seated Harlequin with Guitar* (Figure 5) of 1919, or *Pierrot with Guitar* (Cooper 410) of 1922, are classic examples of the sculptural integration of the musician with his instrument, and of the metamorphosis of both into a lively, rhythmic, two-dimensional arrangement of angles and curves, zigzags and undulations, light and dark, "loud" and "quiet" colour tones, correspondences and contrasts in syncopated alternation.

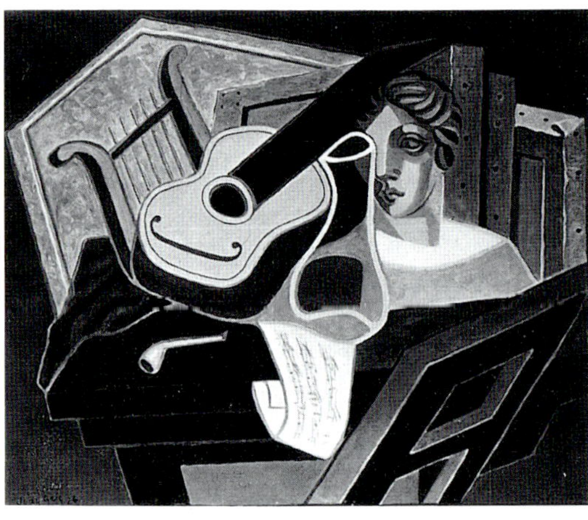

Figure 6
The Musician's Table, 1926
Oil on canvas, 81 x 100 cm
Private Collection

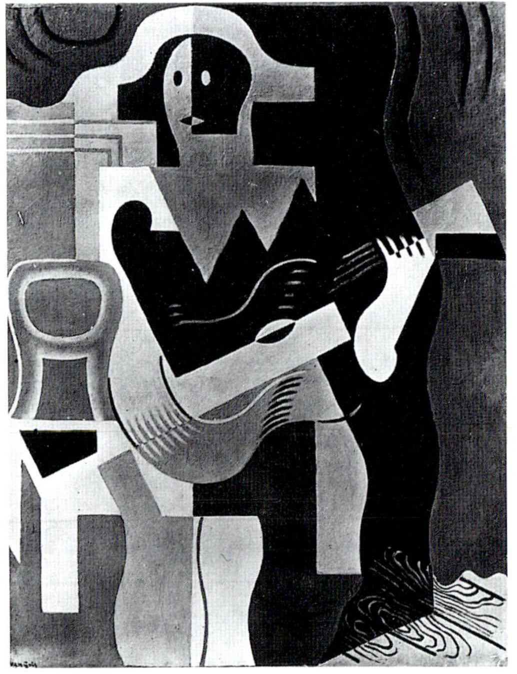

Figure 5
Seated Harlequin with Guitar, 1919
Oil on canvas, 116 x 89 cm
Musée National d'Art Moderne, Centre Georges Pompidou, Paris. Gift of Louise and Michel Leiris (1984)

The composition of Picasso's *Three Musicians* of 1921, now in New York, seems like an echo of Gris's *Seated Harlequin with Guitar* projected onto a monumental scale. Like Picasso's musicians, the guitar-picking Harlequin of his younger contemporary is a static, seated figure; like them too he is instilled with a sense of rhythm that recalls the Spanish culture of Flamenco, and also Gris's affection for the Argentine tango and for the modern dances that go with jazz.

The iconography of musical instruments in Gris's work is also emblematic: it stands not only for the arts and creative activity in general, but above all for the sister art whose element is not space but time, not the visible and the objective but the invisible and the immaterial. How strong this emblematic element can be is exemplified by *The Musician's Table* (Figure 6) of 1926 which belongs to the ancient tradition of the still-life of studio and musical objects.

The instrument still-life was no novelty in European art: one has only to think of the virtuoso decorative arrangements of lutes, violins, flutes and sheet music that were the speciality of the seventeenth century painters of Bergamo, Evaristo Baschenis and his circle[18]. With their consummate *trompe-l'œil* rendering of stereometric volume, and of such materials as polished wood, these artists were extraordinarily successful in achieving tactile effect and a sense of closeness to solid reality.

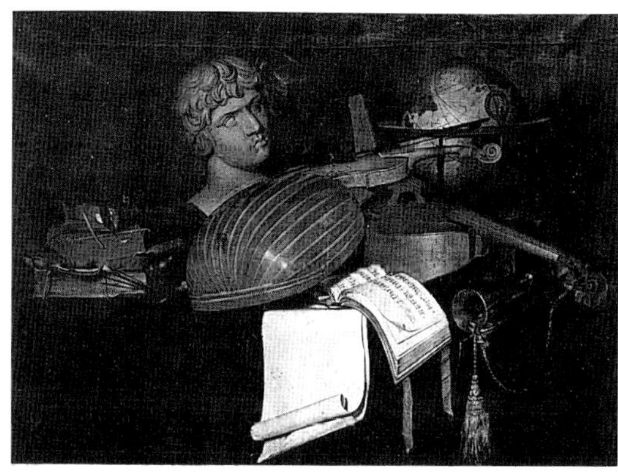

Figure 7
Bartolomeo Bettera
Vanitas, c. 1670
Oil on canvas,
125 x 170 cm
Private Collection

At the same time, they aimed to evoke associations with musical sound and harmony; and they also belonged to the emblematic tradition of the *Vanitas*. Music, as an art that has its existence in time, is in itself a symbol of transitoriness; and instruments lying idle might be allegorically interpreted as dead bodies, which only a musician could bring to life again.

The Musician's Table is astonishingly reminiscent of one particular Bergamo *Vanitas* still-life, ascribed to Bartolomeo Bettera (Figure 7). In both, a decorative arrangement of instruments is combined with a sheet of music and an antique bust, which is there primarily as an allegory of sculpture (in Bettera's case, its elegiac facial expression might also be a reference to melancholy)[19]. In the Gris, the sculpture is accompanied by a stretcher to serve as an allegory of painting. The bust embodies the classical element in art, in keeping with the idea of a "call to order" after the War; and this is also emphasized in the symmetrical balance of the composition as a whole[20].

In such paintings as *The Musician's Table* and *The Book of Music* (Plate 97) of 1922, Gris is unmistakably making an allusion to music. The idea behind this is undoubtedly that music – being freed from mimetic ties to reality – is an art that can follow no laws, but its own laws of harmony. This freedom and this absoluteness were precisely the qualities that painters were fighting hard to win for themselves; and in this the Cubists had achieved a decisive breakthrough. This also meant, of course, that artists' own creative methods and laws required very close scrutiny before being applied in the total assurance that they would hold good in the absence of a bridge to the world of objects.

Gris, with his "deductive method", was already practising a technique that Kahnweiler likened to musical counterpoint. This interpretation has been confirmed, in the context of later scholarship, by Ernst Strauss, who writes at the end of his study of Gris's "technique picturale": "In Gris's painting, the precisely distinguished elements of form, colour and light can be likened to the voices or parts that unite in a musical 'setting'. And just as the ear hears the independently laid-out parts in a polyphonic composition as a single whole, the eye never experiences the separate elements in Gris's paintings in isolation from each other but as the means of rendering the structure of the work transparent"[21].

To sum up, it may be said that, both in iconographic and in structural terms, music plays a vital – even if not an explicit or intentional – part in the work of Gris.

II Gris, Diaghilev and the Ballets Russes

Gris came into contact with music in another way in the work he did for the *Ballets Russes* in collaboration with Diaghilev. In April 1921, Gris was staying with his wife at Bandol when a telegram came from the Russian impresario offering him the commission to design costumes and sets for the Spanish folk ballet *Cuadro flamenco*. Gris was surprised and gratified, but at first he hesitated to accept, as he did not want to take time away from his painting. He eventually agreed, moved by the hope of wider appreciation and a spontaneous public response to his work.

The initial consequence was a bitter disappointment. By the time Gris reached Monte Carlo, one week later, Diaghilev had already made other arrangements. It seems that Picasso had stolen a march by promptly submitting his own designs, and the commission had gone to him[22]. By way of compensation, Gris was commissioned to make portrait drawings of the two soloists in the ballet, Tadeo Slavinsky and Maria d'Albaïcin, and later also of the painter Mikhail Larionov and of Diaghilev's assistant, Boris Kochno, for the *Ballets Russes* programme booklet.

After that, he heard no more from Diaghilev for a long time. A year and a half later, at the end of 1922, Gris was at Boulogne-sur-Seine when he suddenly received an offer to design a ballet to the music of a long-forgotten composer, Michel de Montéclair (1666–1737). This time Gris wasted no time in indecision, but hurled himself into his work and into the atmosphere of the "Grand Siècle".

In the midst of preparations for the ballet, which later received the title *Les Tentations de la Bergère* (Temptations of the Shepherdess), Diaghilev came along with another project on which he wanted Gris to work; this was a gala evening in the Galerie des Glaces of the Château de Versailles. The event, dubbed by

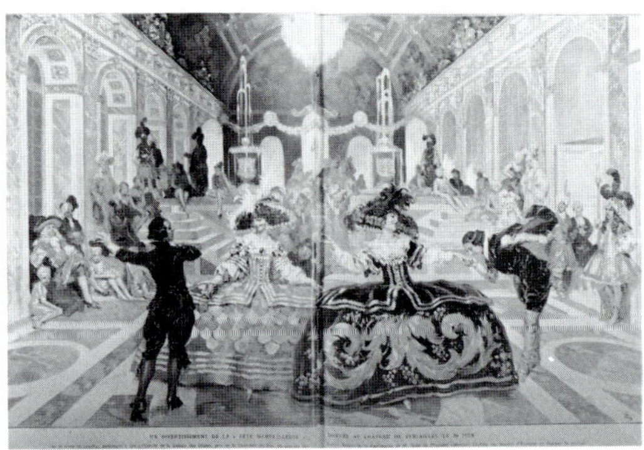

Figure 8
La Fête Merveilleuse in the Château de Versailles on 29 July 1923. Watercolour by René Lelong reproduced in *L'Illustration*

the French government the *Fête Merveilleuse*, was planned for 29 June 1923. Its purpose was to raise funds for the restoration of the Château. Diaghilev and Gabriel Astruc were engaged to devise the evening's programme, and Gris was to design the staging. This was something of a challenge, in a room more than seventy metres long and only ten metres wide, with an elaborate décor of mirrors designed to reflect the windows, together with marble columns, huge crystal chandeliers and ceiling paintings.

Gris succeeded brilliantly. At one end of the gallery he built a podium flanked by a pair of stairways and divided in the centre by a deep and wide central stairway (Figure 8). *Le Figaro* described the effect with enthusiasm: "With the collaboration of the Keeper and the Architect of the Château, Juan Gris has created a décor worthy of Mansart. Imagine a great staircase, covered in mirror from Saint-Gobain, and completely embellished with glittering adornments: spun-glass fountains, baskets, flowerbeds, dazzling swags and garlands – all leading gradually to a stage some ten metres square, on which the ballets were to be performed. In front of all this was a low fountain with mirror representing the water in the basin, and more spun-glass jets, catching the light of the great chandeliers . . ."[23]. Those chandeliers were not the originals but copies, made especially to take electric lamps; this was the first time that electric light had ever been used in the Château de Versailles. Stravinsky waxed enthusiastic: "The famous Gallery was

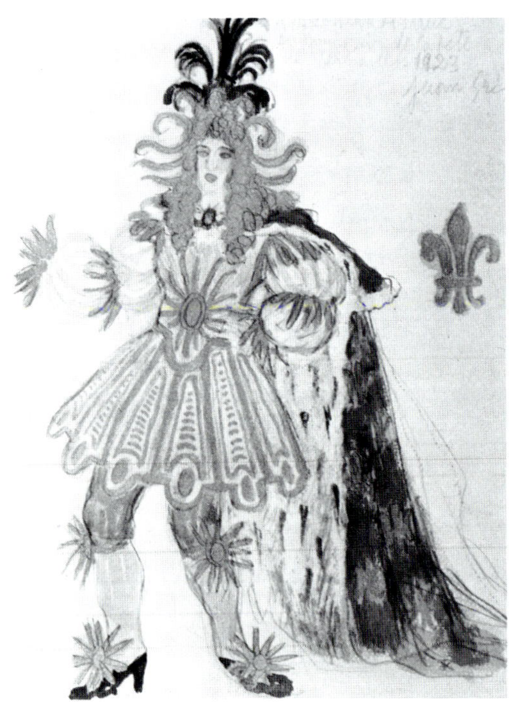

Figure 9
Sketch for the Costume of Louis XIV, 1923
Pencil and watercolour on paper, 31 x 23 cm
Kunstbibliothek, Staatliche Museen Preußischer Kulturbesitz, Berlin

Figure 10
Costumes for the Sun King and the Two Heralds for *Les Tentations de la Bergère* first performed at the Théâtre de Monte Carlo on 3 January 1924

flooded with light. The jewels of the top ladies of fine society sparkled under it"[24]. On the lateral steps and on the stage itself, members of the Comédie Française were grouped in historical costume. After a fanfare by Rameau, the master of ceremonies – a celebrated baritone from the Opéra comique – delivered an oration in period style and announced the Tchaikovsky ballet *Le Mariage d'Aurore* (The Sleeping Beauty). One of the two heralds was Boris Kochno, dressed by Gris in a costume reminiscent of Roman armour; it was Kochno's one and only appearance on any stage.

Vocal interludes such as the aria *Queen of the Night* from Mozart's *Magic Flute* took turns with dances like the majestic Pavane presented by princesses and princes in magnificent costumes designed by José-Maria Sert. It culminated in a grand finale, the Apotheosis of Louis XIV, to the strains of Rameau's *Hymne au Soleil* (Hymn to the Sun). Choreographed by Diaghilev and costumed by Gris, the Sun King solemnly ascended the mirror stairway, and twenty black pages hastened to spread out across the steps his 35-metre, blue, ermine-trimmed train, embroidered with gold fleurs-de-lys. Frenetic applause followed, and as the Monarch departed through the central door a lavish firework display began in the park. This went on for half an hour, during which time the guests moved into the Galerie des Batailles, where a candlelight supper was prepared, every dish named after one of the notabilities of Louis XIV's court.

Of Gris's much-praised set design nothing remains, but the faint impression given in a drawing by René Lelong, published in the magazine *L'Illustration* (Figure 8)[25]; but his costume design for the Sun King still exists to convey some idea of the brilliancy of the whole occasion (Figure 9). In his designs for this palace festival, Gris laid aside the normally spare and astringent style of his own paintings and hurled himself into the world of the Baroque.

And there, for the time being, he stayed; for the ballet *Les Tentations de la Bergère*, which

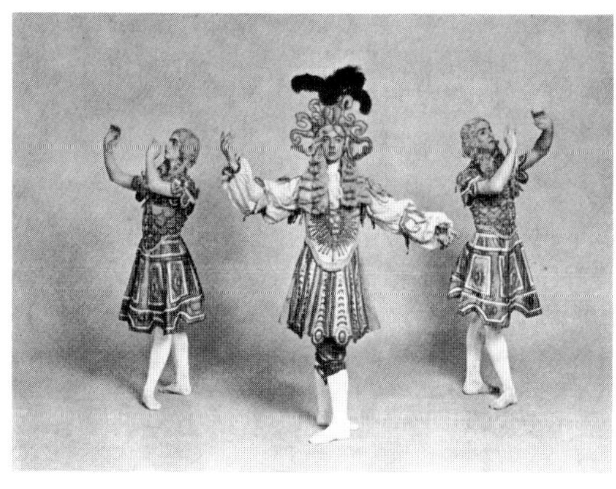

he had to complete after the hectic weeks of work for Versailles, was set in almost exactly the same period setting. A number of the costumes, including those of the two heralds and that of the King (with some minor modifications and without the long train), were available for reuse in the pastoral ballet (Figures 9, 10 and 11).

Ever since the triumphant production of the Tchaikovsky ballet *The Sleeping Beauty* in London in 1922, the experimental side of the Diaghilev ballet, as represented by such scan-

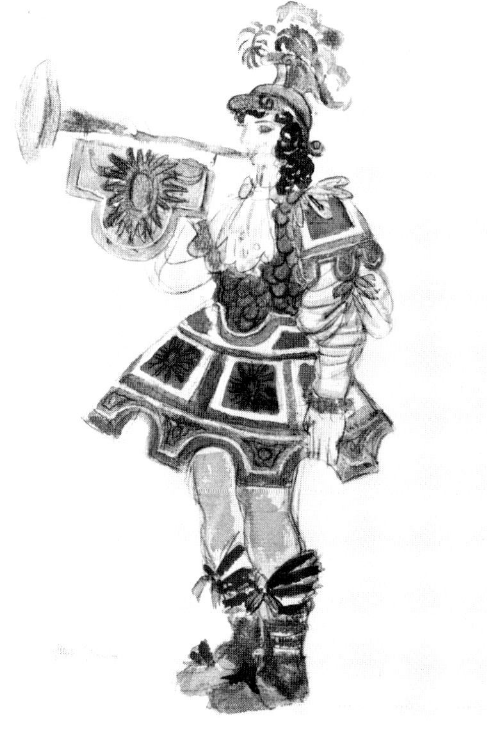

Figure 11
Sketch for the Costume of a Herald, 1923
Pencil, watercolour, gouache and metallic paint on paper, 34.3 x 30.5 cm
Wadsworth Atheneum, Hartford, CT. The Ella Gallup Sumner and Mary Catlin Sumner Collection

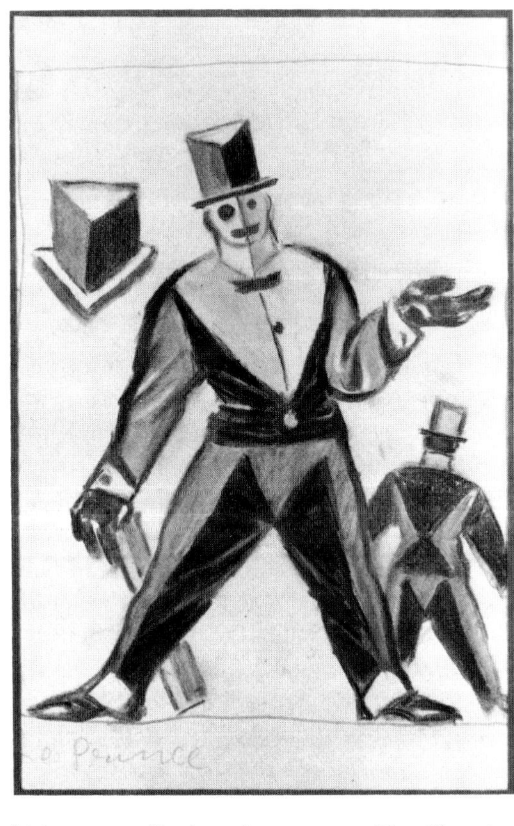

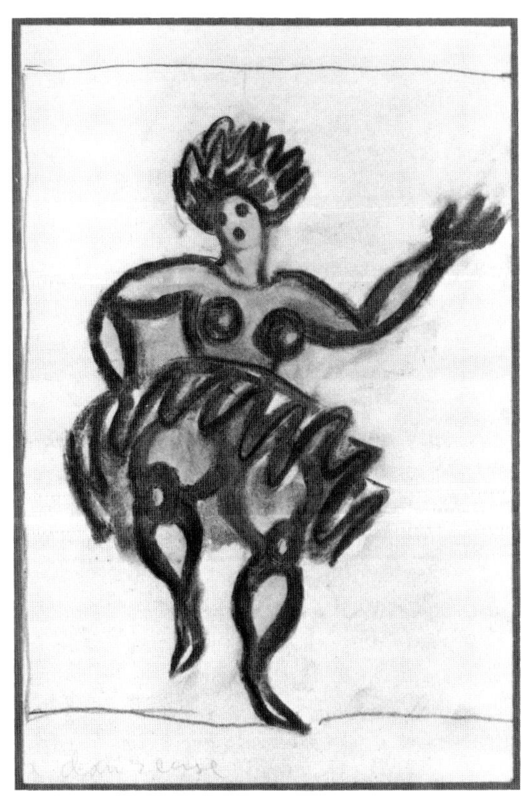

Figures 20 and 21
Caption see page 279

hitherto ascribed to the operetta *Une éducation manquée*, must have been made at about the same time; so it too may well have been intended for the Casino ballet, subject unknown (Figure 22).

There is an alternative hypothesis: for, in spite of his distaste for the theatrical milieu, Gris did agree to work with Diaghilev just once more. This was on the décor and costumes for a Red Cross Festival, held at a Paris department store, Les Grands Magasins du Printemps, on May 28, 1924. Perhaps one day sources will be found to permit a more certain identification of Gris's two Modernist stage designs, the deck of the liner and the drawing-room with the Paris skyline.

A retrospective view of the years 1921 and 1923–24, in which Gris concerned himself with dance, music and theatre, reveals that in commissioned work, he conformed to the period requirements laid down for him; but his own theatrical inventions were entirely contemporary. There is, unfortunately, no telling what kind of music he had in mind for, say, the Pierrot project. He was friendly with a number of Modernist composers, including Satie, Milhaud and Georges Auric, although he does not seem to have discussed music with them very much. His ballet scenario makes no mention of music as such; however, the mere fact that a car was supposed to come on stage and sound its horn suggests the need for a thoroughly modern score, with affinities to *musique concrète*: the sort of thing that Satie and

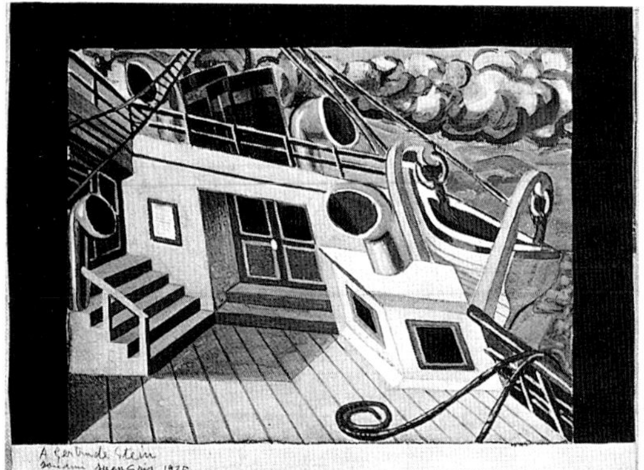

Figure 22
Set with the Bridge of a Trans-Atlantic Steamer, 1924
Gouache on paper, 17x24 cm
Private Collection

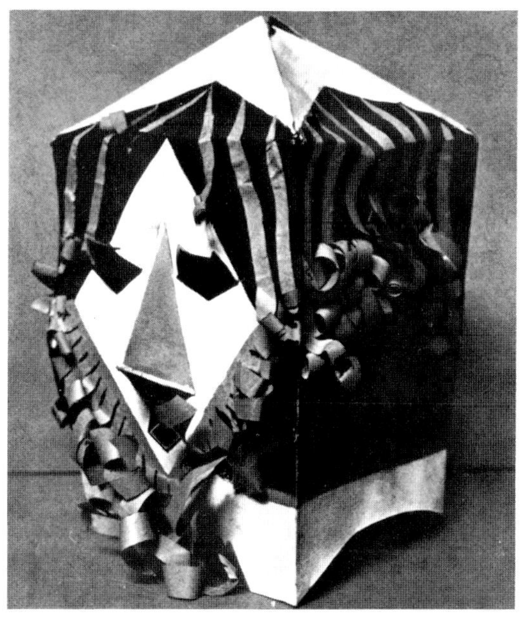

Figure 23
Cubist Paper Mask for a Bal Suédois, 1923
Painted paper and cardboard, height 34 cm
Private Collection

his friends would have been entirely suited to supply.

Gris's year in the theatre had left him richer in experience, but it had also shown him that the theatre world – at least in the form that was on offer from Diaghilev – was not for him. His public successes do not seem to have meant very much to him; he must have known only too well how little of his own, innovative talent had gone into the work.

How different his theatrical ideas looked when he was not working to order is shown by the five little figures that Gris cut out of sheet metal and painted at the beginning of the 1920s – alongside his work for the *Ballets Russes* – and by the Cubist paper masks that he and Kahnweiler wore to a masked ball in 1923 (Figures 23 and 24).

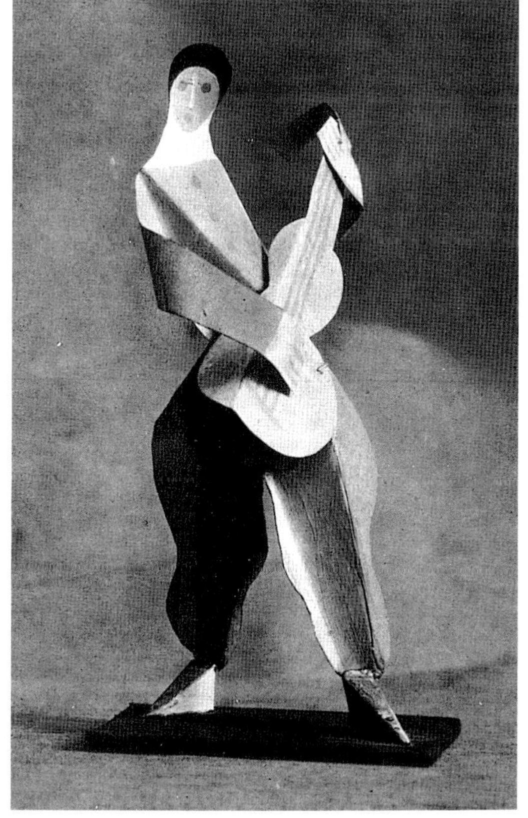

Figure 24
Harlequin, 1923
Painted metal,
29.5 x 12 x 10 cm
Musée National d'Art Moderne, Centre Georges Pompidou, Paris. Gift of Louise and Michel Leiris (1984)

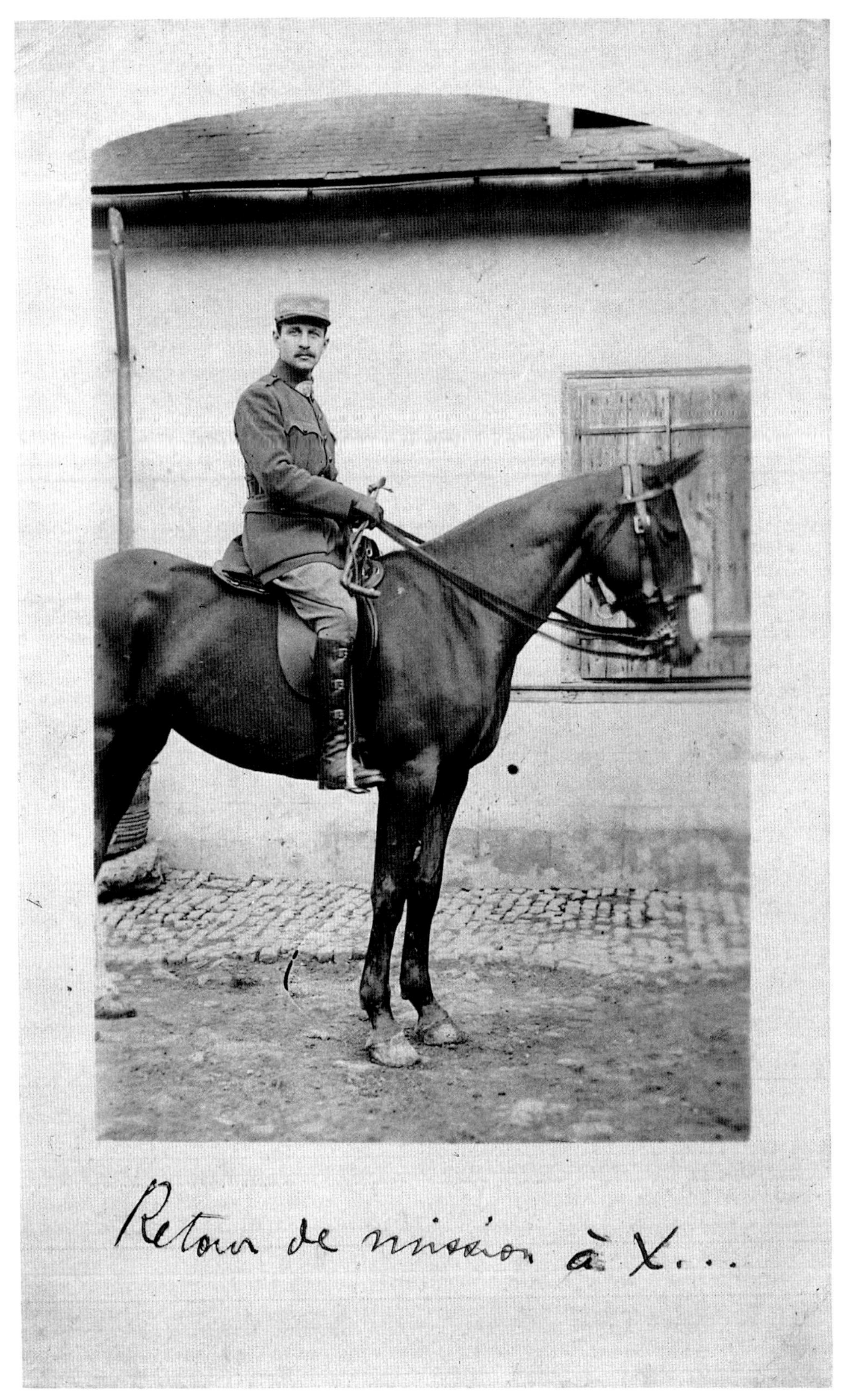
Retour de mission à X...

Juan Gris: A Correspondence Restored

Christian Derouet

Throughout his short life – 1887 to 1927 – Juan Gris was in all things the perfect gentleman. The rectitude of his conduct and the probity of his art won him the admiration and regard of Gertrude Stein and Daniel-Henry Kahnweiler. In difficult circumstances, the latter wrote a monograph on him, published in 1946, which cast fresh light on the painter's personality and ensured his place in the evolution of Cubism. Douglas Cooper transformed the impact of this partisan biography with the publication in 1956 of Gris's correspondence (the authorized text, but transposed into English for the benefit of an élite few), and in 1977 by the publication of a monumental *catalogue raisonné* of his paintings. Intelligently presented and sympathetic, with a flavour of aristocratic brevity, this exemplary work of documentation left very little else to be added.

There nevertheless remained a lacuna, precisely circumscribed, which altered the sense of this apparently objective account. This was the intervention of Léonce Rosenberg. It was known that between 1915 and 1920 there had been an exchange of letters between the two, but no one seemed concerned to restore these letters – or even the recollection of them – to their context. That has now been done: we might say that Léonce Rosenberg's heirs kept us waiting for the privilege. For my part, I am merely astonished that, seventy years on, in spite of the damage inflicted on the assets of the Jewish community in France during the Second World War, we can today read letters and financial records that guaranteed a painter's income and governed his rate of production for more than five years. Fresh light is shed on these five years of "maturity", in the life of a man who lived for only forty years: Gris met Rosenberg at twenty-seven, and left L'Effort Moderne at the age of thirty-three.

This material, new to the historians of Cubism, provides the justification for an updated edition of Juan Gris's letters requested by his son, Georges González Gris, which has been promised for the near future. To the collection made by Douglas Cooper and Daniel-Henry Kahnweiler, a number of short notes will be added which were excluded from the first edition. The text will remain faithful to the original language, that is to say it will be in Spanish or French, and will respect errors of spelling and syntax, as well as the author's Spanish turns of phrase.

The Gris-Rosenberg correspondence, with its 197 items copied from various archival deposits, slots in between the last letter to reach Gris from Kahnweiler, in December 1915, and the first letter of their resumed correspondence, dated 22 August , 1919. Of all the various correspondences conducted by Gris during the war years, it is far and away the most extensive; so indeed the painter indicated to Rosenberg on 2 October, 1916, when he wrote "you apart, no one writes to me".

This correspondence consists, from Gris to Rosenberg, of 44 short notes, 75 letters, 3 contracts, and 40 receipts issued by Gris to Rosenberg, plus 35 letters and circulars addressed by Rosenberg to Gris. The communications vary, as may be imagined, in frequen-

Léonce Rosenberg on horseback: "Return from the Mission at X..."

cy, in length and in interest, depending on the correspondents' absences. As it stands, we can count 11 communications in 1915, 60 in 1916, 50 in 1917, 39 in 1918, 15 in 1919, 16 in 1920, 3 in 1921.

Some estimate also has to be made of the proportion lost. There are references to postcards and mail of which no trace has been found. It is not therefore possible to recreate the interchange of letters, for Gris and his family have preserved only a few of Rosenberg's missives. And when the latter was at the front or in barracks, he could not keep duplicates of those he sent to his painters, contrary to his later practice. But, fundamentally, Rosenberg's letters would be no more than useful but minor details, if we did not have the essential at our disposal, namely, the letters sent by the painter.

Between a scrupulous artist and a dealer inclined to split hairs, there can be no question of a delightful literary correspondence. What we have here are rudimentary business letters, the accompaniment to a regular pattern of acquisitions; the use of "Mon cher ami" (My dear friend) barely softens the other aspects, the figures for contracts, lists of works, prices, acknowledgments. Fortunately, interspersed among these are numerous references to small services rendered, meetings, and – below the surface – to other considerations which are of the greatest possible interest, if one knows how to read between the lines. That can be done by comparing these letters with those addressed by Gris to his other correspondents, specifically Maurice Raynal; also by cross-checking with the letters Rosenberg exchanged with other artists, Georges Braque, Henri Laurens, Jacques Lipchitz and Pierre Reverdy.

In performing this small task of external criticism, one quickly perceives the importance of the correspondence between Gris and Rosenberg, certainly the most extensive, and also the most detailed: it enables us to reassign works chronologically and clarifies the meaning of the other correspondences. It is thanks to the artist who lives in seclusion that we arrive at a better understanding of the community of artists gravitating around Rosenberg. Scarcely noticed events become fundamental, as for example the preparation and performance at the Théâtre du Châtelet of the ballet *Parade*. The information Gris gives about this ballet illuminates even the use of stage business.

This correspondence transforms empty years of virtual silence into years filled with gossip – even if the gossip is nothing to do with Gris, but relates to others. Gris spends his time passing on small items of news, but says too little – from our point of view – about what interests us, his own painting.

As we follow his fine handwriting, careful and legible, with no crossings-out, no corrections, no blots – he writes in pen – we discover through a vocabulary that is simple, banal even, unencumbered by the jargon peculiar to painters, an admirable man, an honest artist who is quite at sea amid the wheeler-dealing of his colleagues; and we follow the slow analysis of the disintegration of Cubism, or rather, of a particular form of Cubism.

The whole is expressed in a tone at first cautious, then confident, almost friendly, but which then plunges abruptly into resentment when Gris perceives at the Armistice of November 1918 that he has been duped by his correspondent.

Exempt from military service by reason of his Spanish nationality, Gris finds himself one of the few Cubist artist-painters regularly at work throughout the whole of the period of hostilities. André Level wrote on 1 June, 1915 to Apollinaire that after the mobilization of the painter Auguste Herbin – all the other French painters, Derain, Braque, etc. having already been mobilized – there remained only the two Spaniards, Picasso and Gris. It is those three, Level and the two others, who are to persuade Rosenberg to pledge himself to the salvation of Cubism – that much Rosenberg acknowledges in a letter addressed to the painter and critic Jacques-Emile Blanche, on 27 January,

1919: "before leaving for the front and, at the insistence of Monsieur André Level, connoisseur of Cubism's first hour, and also at the insistence of Picasso and Juan Gris, I determined to constitute myself the adoptive father of abandoned Cubism, and when the war is over, its promoter" (Figure 1). From reading this sentence, we understand that Rosenberg confirms Gris's role as a "saviour" of Cubism. At the same time, from the bombastic tone adopted by Rosenberg, we can tell what it is that sets our two correspondents so radically apart.

The first, Juan Gris, lives for the most part in a modest studio at the "Bateau-Lavoir", 13,

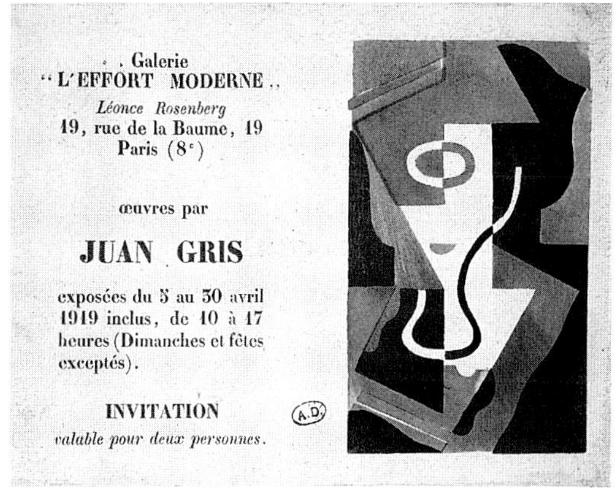

Figure 1
Invitation to the exhibition 'Works by Juan Gris' held at the Galerie de l'Effort Moderne from 5–30 April 1919

rue Ravignan (now place Émile-Goudeau), and occasionally at Beaulieu-lès-Loches, Touraine. He is an unassuming and credulous man; but a lucid, intelligent artist. Reticent about his financial problems, it is with complete trust that he enters into an agreement with his dealer that is at first tacit, from April 1915 onwards, and then written, on 20 April, 1916 – although its validity is subject to certain conditions. This treaty is consolidated on 15 October, 1917, and its terms grudgingly improved in codicils dated 5 December, 1918 and 8 May, 1920. Its modest provisions, of 700 francs per month, are to be eaten into by the inevitable devaluations of the gold franc. Although this has ceased in fact to be gold a few months after fighting begins, it remains the standard for financial transactions which exist over a period of six years between, on the one hand, a creative artist in full spate, and on the other, a promoter who, constrained by his military commitments, finds it impossible to publicize his artist's products. There is a coolness and embarrassment that neither party dares admit.

Gris shows loyalty every time Rosenberg asks it of him to do so, whether in banning an exhibition, or over a recommended restriction on the distribution of the drawings, which remain the artist's only (but nevertheless vital) means of earning a living in which he expresses himself freely. Gris, although it is he who is meant to be the recipient of Rosenberg's assistance, often plays the part of the humble assistant. In all his letters he maintains a low profile: always tactful and demonstrating submissiveness, holding back, avoiding anecdotes which would lead to over-long explanations, preserving the appearances of friendship, writing considered replies to absurd suggestions, responding to his employer's military tirades. To satisfy the regimental fantasies of their "master", Gris, together with Laurens and Léger, good-naturedly manufactures trifles in the shape of the heraldic devices and placards that mobilized Cubism for the victory celebrations of 1918 (Figures 2 and 3).

He does so the more willingly because during these years he has had bitter experience of xenophobia; on the one hand, indeed, it ensures him the rather heavy-handed attentions of the French authorities. In Paris, in the artists' canteens, people are wary of him because he has done business with a German dealer, Kahnweiler; and on his arrival in Beaulieu-lès-Loches, José González (better known as Juan Gris) is subjected to an officious interview by the regional commandant of police before the town hall of Ferrière-sur-Beaulieu is authorized to issue his certificate of registration as a foreign resident, dated 1 September, 1916. It will come as no surprise that he could write to Rosenberg (24-5-16) that he has "turned down a drawing for

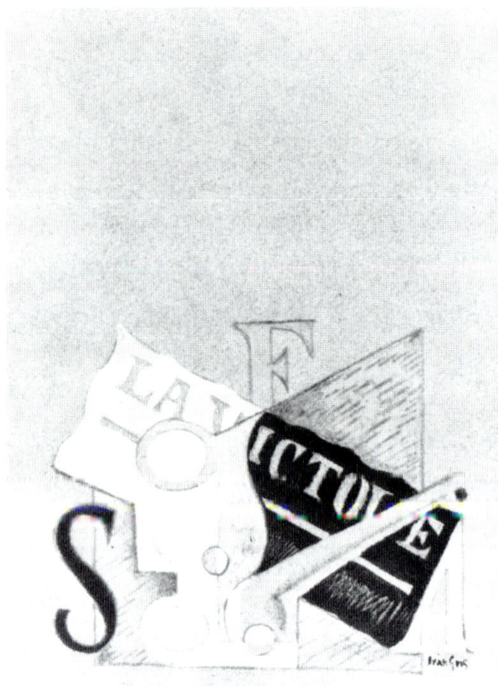

Figure 2
"La Victoire" S.F.A., 1918
Gouache on paper, 31.5 x 24 cm
Whereabouts unknown

L'Elan, and also an invitation to exhibit in a coming exhibition at Madame Bongard's", pleading that as a foreigner "he did not want to 'put himself forward during the war'".

On the other hand, it is not without emotion that he sees now his dealer, now his friend Maurice Raynal return to the front at the end of every leave. One sometimes wonders how the history of Cubism could have neglected, to the point of being oblivious, the sheer oppression of this war which threatened Paris daily for four years. In Gris's case at least, the newspapers succeed in forcing their presence upon the hypothetical variations of the Cubist still-life. He respects and admires the "combatant" tatus of Braque and Léger when they return from the front, and concedes that their claims on the Galerie de l'Effort Moderne are on that account superior to his own.

Three times he goes to ground near Loches in Touraine, the family home of his companion Josette (Charlotte Herpin). There he can escape the artistic rivalries, the shortages and bombs afflicting the capital, preferring to immerse himself in his work. His first visit (1 September, to 28 October, 1916) helps him recover from the disturbance provoked by the first quarrel with his friend Pierre Reverdy. The second much longer visit (2 April, 1918 to early December of the same year) transforms him into the leader of an improvised community of artists: it comprises initially the two Lipchitzes, Jacques and Berthe, the Huidobros, María Blanchard and, for a few weeks from 21 June to the end of July, Jean Metzinger, his wife and daughter. He rents a vast manor house deep in the heart of the country, where he disposes of a rudimentary comfort, but also spacious accommodation where he has ample room to set up a studio. He does more than transpose Cubism to a country setting, he also immerses himself, at a time of pronounced nationalism, in French values, copying Cézanne and Ingres after postcards that are sent to him, concentrating in particular on artists from the region, such as the painter Jean Fouquet, and reading Alfred de Vigny. In 1920, for a period of convalescence, he returns to Les Fourneaux in Beaulieu for the third and last time.

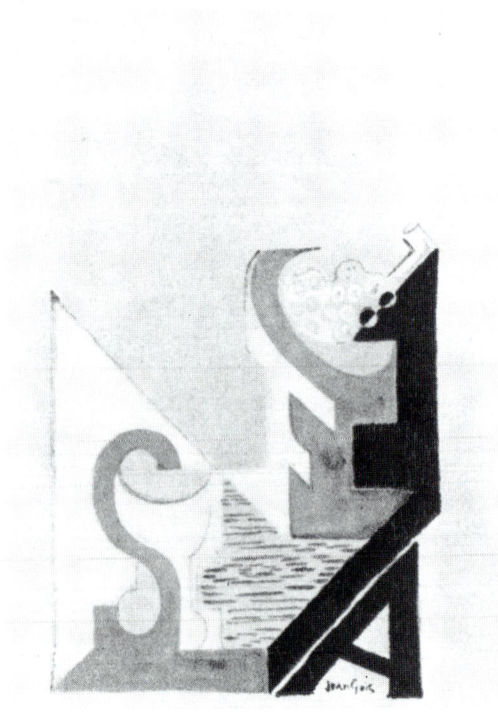

Figure 3
(Pipe and Grapes) S.F.A., 1918
Gouache on paper, 31 x 24 cm
Whereabouts unknown

His correspondent, Léonce Rosenberg (1879–1947) serves with the colours. He has a uniform, and military postcodes, which impress Gris the more as the dealer has the gall to usurp the glamour attaching to the name "volunteer". His feats of arms are restricted for the most part to garrison postings at the aerial surveillance bases of Chalais-Meudon and Nanterre-La-Folie. His acts of valour consist in serving for a time as interpreter to the English expeditionary force at the front, on the Somme, from May 1916 to March 1917, at which time he is "evacuated to the second line by hospital X, which declared me unfit for service in the advanced line". He then serves at Le Havre, and returns to Nanterre, where he waits until he can open his gallery at long last. This he plans to do in November 1917. Starting with Herbin, he embarks on an ambitious series of exhibitions in March 1918, but is obliged to discontinue them because of the threat of shelling hanging over Paris. While waiting for a lull in hostilities, he lends his painters works of military theory by Commander-in-Chief Foch, and in March 1918 invites them to produce occasional pieces for a projected Cubist exhibition *Retour du Front,* to which Léger, La Fresnaye and Gris pledge their support; this explains Braque's indiscreet comment to Kahnweiler (8-10-19): "I found Gris in the middle of doing patriotic pictures, 'our little 75', servicemen's heads, and all in Cubism [sic]".

Rosenberg is a sensitive man, but easily invites ridicule. At the same time, he is appalled by expense and extravagance. He has a sordid sense of thrift. He shows imagination in cost-cutting, notably where picture-framing is concerned. He is the "epileptic" of the family, a volatile and sometimes cowardly man, over-inclined to displays of boldness and magnanimity, but at heart no more than an irritable fault-finder.

It is in his hands that Gris places his destiny. Over this period, Rosenberg buys all his paintings, to wit, 195 canvases, and only 53 drawings. Between April 1915 and March 1920, Gris delivers to him 9 size 50 canvases, 11 size 40s, 28 size 30s, 22 size 25s, 19 size 20s, 16 size 12s, 26 size 10s, 11 size 8s, 13 size 6s, 7 size 5s, 14 size 4s, 9 size 3s. But he was never allowed the chance to do annually "a canvas bigger than a 60 format but not more than a 100, what one might call somewhat ironically a Salon canvas".

In exchange Rosenberg disburses to his painter a regular monthly sum, erring on the mean side but enough to enable him to pose as "master of his own house". Rosenberg assumes full responsibility and control. Under the fallacious pretext of holding exclusive rights, he advances only negative proposals, no positive strategy. He makes mistakes, turning down offers made by Brenner and confirmed by Gris in the course of negotiations with a nebulous America, on 25 November, 1916, in the person of Coady and Brummer; these latter go bankrupt, and place on the open market, at the Anderson sale of 29 July, 1918 in New York, an unsecured stock of Cubist canvases. The sanctimonious tittle-tattle which Rosenberg dispatches to "his" painters, to combat the boredom of garrison life, barely conceals the extent of his total incomprehension of the work of those who believed they had found in him an enlightened promoter.

This antiquarian specializing in remote antiquity was no more progressive in his views than one would expect of a connoisseur of the "noble style" – a style appealing to the more or less conventional, not to say old-fashioned, criteria of the "prevailing taste", as determined by a few sagacious collectors. By means of a few abusive circulars (5-7-17, 3-9-17), he manages to pump his painters for information, to acquire a veneer of Cubist culture by establishing at their expense collections of *Soirées de Paris,* etc. He is alas influenced by "what people will think", and blurts out a betrayal of his painters to Ozenfant of *L'Elan*; he conducts reprehensible conversations and intrigues with the poet Jean Cocteau and even the retardataire critic Louis Vauxcelles, with whom he pointlessly crosses swords during the years 1918–19 in *Le Carnet de la semaine*. Rosenberg is pitiful when he grovels before Reverdy, who publishes in *Nord-Sud* his translation of the article "On Cubism" and his reflective piece "Why change", or before Paul Dermée, in the hope he will accept further of his aphorisms. Granted, on that lost cause, to his credit, he risked his own money, but his lack of discrimination additionally brought about a spontaneous generation of artists, late converts, whom the movement's true representatives could well have done without, who tip Cubism over into that mawkishness which is denounced by Apollinaire in a letter to Derain of 20 February, 1916, written after calling on Rosenberg: "Well, they are working, that's the main thing, but they are working towards vulgarity". When in January 1918 Rosenberg begins to review his spoils of war, setting down in his inventory by order of size the purchases that have piled up in his cellars, he is quite incapable of distinguishing the excellent from the merely flatulent. All this Gris discovers abruptly on an abortive trip to Paris in November 1918: Cubism has long been adrift, but he can at least be grateful he has not been too badly compromised.

The break cannot be immediate or complete because of the terms of the official contract, but it is accomplished in his own mind at the Armistice. Gris cannot understand that Rosenberg fails to appreciate his worth. He discovers that the friendship he has born this person throughout their correspondence has been poorly served. The frost between them intensifies in a letter of 26 November, 1918, for Gris is too shy to express his anger out loud. He does not regain his composure until Kahnweiler's return, when life resumes its normal pattern. Let it be said in Rosenberg's favour that he does not, in 1921, send to the Hôtel Drouot his store of works by Gris, in the same way as – off-handedly and contrary to his own interests – he disposes of works from his stock bearing the signatures of Lhote, María Blanchard, Lipchitz, Rivera and Zarraga.

What emerges on the plus side of this close, but scarcely profound relationship is an improved acquaintance with the artistic circle with which they are associated. The friendships and feuds shift and change from one letter to the next.

Gris introduces to Rosenberg the sculptor Gargallo, from whom the dealer purchases some small masks; he recommends to him the painter Henri Hayden, giving him his address (27-3-17). But Rosenberg manipulates Gris, believing he has found in him the best person to intervene on his behalf with Pablo Picasso. The latter is difficult to pin down, he replies only in short, curt notes to advances made by Rosenberg, who had purchased a large Harlequin from him on 3 November, 1915. But Picasso sets his prices too high for Rosenberg's liking. He dares not offer him a contract and is furious when in June 1917 a dealer's consortium joined by his brother Paul Rosenberg overtakes him in the race for the "genius". Gris in fact has no more than occasional meetings with Picasso, and yet remains close to him; he attends Eva's funeral in December 1915. He finds it hard to understand his compatriot's indifference, his eagerness to move away and associate himself with the artificial activities of Diaghilev's *Ballets Russes,* leaving with Cocteau for Rome on 2 March, 1917; he is nevertheless very honoured to be visited by him in his studio on his return. "Picasso got back the day before yesterday, came to see me. We spent the evening together. I told him what you wrote to me about the two paintings he did in Rome... I showed him my latest stuff and he doesn't seem to think too badly of it. I was really pleased because, as you well know I'm always inclined to think everything I do is dreadful". Once again Gris is given the task of mediating between them, for one last time, as Léonce Rosenberg writes to Picasso (27-7-17): "I imagine your friend Gris has delivered the various messages I gave him for you when I was on leave in Paris ...".

Gris also greatly admires Braque, and on 2 June, 1916 writes to Rosenberg recommending Picasso and Braque as "the only two who are indispensable, truly indispensable, for anyone wanting to have a firm grasp on this movement in painting... If the one has considerable authority, which needs to be capitalized on, the other needs help to achieve the reputation and authority he deserves for his talent and the significance of his oeuvre. That is the advice of a painter who values these masters and would like no more than to be linked with them again." At one point, Gris is confident of Braque's friendship. He writes (18-9-16), "I get on well with Braque, we write to one another"; also, Gris belongs to the organizing committee for the Braque dinner, which is to take place at the home of Marie Wassilieff on 17 January, 1917. Subsequently, there is a coolness on Braque's part, when he takes Reverdy's side in the affair of the article "One Night on the Plain", published in *Nord-Sud*, no. 3, April 1917.

Beyond these two great names, Gris's circle is of limited extent; it corresponds to the list he passes to Rosenberg, at his request (10-7-17), in which he mentions those individuals to whom he has given drawings or paintings bearing dedications: among them we find the names of Picabia, one small painting, 1912; Poiret, one drawing, 1912; Dorival, one drawing, 1917; Paul Guillaume, one drawing, 1917; La Serna, collage, 1915, one drawing, 1916; Matisse, picture executed in Touraine, 1916; and also Laurens – Madame Laurens, one drawing, 1912. It is the sculptor Henri Laurens who sometimes photographs Gris's pictures in an emergency, and it is to Laurens's home that Gris and Lipchitz go to eat pancakes at Candlemas in February 1917.

His friendship with Lipchitz (Madame Lipchitz, one drawing, 1917) is warmer. At first, as Rosenberg likes to remind him, Gris had to overcome a certain suspicion of this sculptor, who arrived back in Paris with Diego Rivera in 1915, and also of María Blanchard. But it is in his company that Gris learns his way around Montparnasse. These outings on the Rive Gauche are a running theme from one letter to the next. Gris writes to Rosenberg (29-1-17): "I often see Lipchitz. We get on very well together and I like him a lot"; or (19-4-17): "I don't see many people, every Sunday I go to Lipchitz's in Montparnasse and there I see a few friends"; or again (15-5-17): "I often go to Montparnasse and there Lipchitz and I take the air on the Rotonde terrace". He allies himself with him against Reverdy following the publication of the article "One Night on the Plain"; he makes a sculpture under his supervision, and proposes to Rosenberg (25-10-17) an edition of it in terracotta. The Lipchitzes join him at Beaulieu, together with María Blanchard, from 28 April to 4 September, 1918. And Gris recommends him to Kahnweiler (2-7-19): "Perhaps of all the younger ones, the sculptor Lipchitz is the one with the sweetest nature, and the most serious-minded. In my opinion he has a great future for he is developing very well and has made great progress in a short time...". 1917 and 1918 are the Lipchitz years, and this special relationship has to be taken into account in arriving at a better understanding of the development of Gris's painting.

Relations with Jean Metzinger (three drawings, 1912) are sporadic and hard to pin down. It seems they see a lot of each other. In January 1915, Metzinger secures Gris's name, together with those of Gleizes and Jacques Villon, for a book on Cubism which he plans to publish in New York with the help of his brother. Then from March 1915 to October 1916, Metzinger is mobilized as a medical orderly at the Hôpital Saint-Charles at Sainte-Menehoud. On his discharge, and following Gleizes departure for New York, he passes as the intellectual of the movement. He is anti-Reverdy in the Rivera affair, anti-Apollinaire at the time of *Les Mamelles de Tirésias*. He spends the months of June and July 1918 with Gris at Beaulieu and on his return is guilty of a few indiscretions to Louis Vauxcelles about the direction Gris's work is taking.

A coolness develops between Gris and his close friend Pierre Reverdy (drawings, 1913, 1914 and 1915), the reason for which is unclear, unless it be the exhibition organized by André Salmon in 1916. He writes to Rosenberg from Beaulieu (10-9-16): "Even in my best friend Reverdy I have felt the frost of hostility and malice". But the main thing is the incident between Rivera and Reverdy which takes place at a dinner organized by Rosenberg for his painters at Lapérousse's. Rosenberg has just been sent back from the front for health reasons – not, like Apollinaire and Braque, returning from the front bearing the glorious scar of some dreadful wound. He too, however, claims to be celebrating with his friends his return from active service. Later, after the dinner, the poet and painter fall to blows in André Lhote's salon. Gris notes brusquely (21-3-17), referring to the incident of the Monday: "I have been too long associated with Reverdy not to take his side... Personally I shall base my conduct on Reverdy's". And when Reverdy's article "On Cubism" appears in *Nord-Sud*, no. 1, 15 March, 1917 – the partial cause of the brawl – Gris agonizes to Rosenberg (5-4-17): "You see that the painters were wrong to get worked up about Reverdy's article, which is not aggressive and does no more than set out a few ideas with which one can either agree or disagree". On the other hand, when Reverdy puts forward his version of events in the form of a cautionary tale, which he publishes without alerting anyone in issue no. 3 of this review, under the title "One Night on the Plain", Gris is devastated, and writes as much to his dealer (23-5-17): "The thing that really upset me in issue no. 3 is Reverdy's article. This story 'à clef' is purely and simply the account of our dinner at Lapérousse's and the incident at Lhote's place. I think it is unworthy of a poet to lower his pen to personal revenge, even if it is in veiled form". He models his position on that adopted by Lipchitz and Metzinger, and (29-5-17) notes that "this affair has made me more miserable than angry for it deals perhaps the final blow to my long-standing friendship with Reverdy, which has become so much cooler of late. Too bad for me, and too bad for him, and yet I would have liked to be his friend always". Reverdy, for his part, gives his version of events to Rosenberg at the end of March, citing the Mexican painter's dishonesty towards Gris: "As for Rivera, he is a mercenary greaseball whom I have seen committing the most vile acts against Gris, when he needed Gris to plagiarize his painting and gain an entrée with you, and then once he had done that, I observed how he adopted a disgustingly provocative manner towards his two patrons". This second altercation does not last, and both sign a contract with Rosenberg on 15 March 1920 for an edition of *Entre les quatre murs*.

The estrangement from Apollinaire (one picture, 1916) is equally prejudicial. The poet used to pride himself on having got Gris and Léger onto Kahnweiler's books practically by force, and now, because of the performance of Apollinaire's play *Les Mamelles de Tirésias* on 27 June, 1917, what does he find but Gris (together with Metzinger, Severini, Diego Rivera, Henri Hayden, Lipchitz and Kisling) signing a petition in protest against the way certain theatre designers debase their art. Outraged, Apollinaire notes to Reverdy, the other outcast from the group, on 28 June, 1917: "In short, they have given me the opportunity to make a break with commercial Cubism, which I want nothing to do with. I shall therefore stay with Cubism's great painters and abandon the rest of them. I'm sorry about it in Gris's case, but he shouldn't have acted in this matter, where Cubism wasn't in jeopardy...". As for Gris, he attempts to justify himself to Rosenberg (1-7-17): "I am very upset because of that note, which you must have read, protesting against *S.I.C's* displays. I signed it in solidarity with my friends and in no way frivolously, for I do not enjoy these sorts of public protests".

With Jean Cocteau (one drawing, 1917) there are also frictions. Rosenberg, having warned him to beware of this schemer, tells him to support a number of his intrigues, the most honorable of which is the defence of the musician Erik Satie, who has certain difficulties with the law. Gris indicates to Rosenberg (6-8-17): "This very morning I went to see Cocteau to try to find out what needs to be done". And Max Jacob writes in August 1917 to the gossip-loving couturier Jacques Doucet: "Juan Gris saw Cocteau yesterday morning, Monday, and according to him Satie has grounds for appeal;... we have the Préfet de Police with us, through his son, who is a particular friend of Juan Gris". The son of the police chief in question is Louis Aragon. Later, on the occasion of the Gris exhibition of 5-30 April, 1919, held at Rosenberg's premises in the rue de la Baume, the dealer does not consult the artist before imposing his choice of Jean Cocteau for the poetry reading on Sunday 27 April, 1919; Gris feels very bitter about this, or so at least he writes to Maurice Raynal, his own candidate.

A friend of long standing, Raynal (several drawings and one painting, 1912) is the critic with whom Gris enjoys talking shop. Time and again he has arranged for him to meet Rosenberg, and is naturally delighted when the latter asks Raynal to take charge of his programme of publications. In June 1919, Rosenberg plans to launch a review and almanac called *L'Effort Moderne*, but he has over-estimated the strength of his financial position and is obliged to withdraw. (It is with the trio of Dermée, Ozenfant and Jeanneret, the editors of *L'Esprit Nouveau*, that Raynal is eventually to find a proper platform.)

Only with Max Jacob does Gris have no known dealings – beyond doing him the favour of retrieving from Ozenfant the Picasso drawing which the poet wishes to have stereotyped, to illustrate a booklet of poetry.

Of the poet Vicente Huidobro (portraits in pencil and one drawing, 1917) Gris has little to say to Rosenberg, beyond (23-5-17): "He is a young boy of 23, Chilean, who writes in Spanish and has already had 6 or 7 volumes printed". The Huidobros join him at Beaulieu in 1918, and a correspondence survives between him and Vicente, which is to be included in the new edition of his writings.

For Gris, the whole affair blows apart in 1918 with the scandalous attitude adopted by Diego Rivera. Picasso has become the patron of a colony of Hispanic artists centred on Rosenberg, who by this means is transformed into a sort of impotent money-lender in his dealings with Rivera, Ortiz de Zarate, María Blanchard, etc. Rivera, having already played the spectre at the feast when he slapped Reverdy at Rosenberg's dinner in March 1917, is by 1918 openly plotting against the L'Effort Moderne group. Together with André Lhote, he passes into the camp of the reactionary critics, the guiding spirit among them being Louis Vauxcelles ("Pinturrichio" of *Le Carnet de la semaine*), whom he keeps supplied with titbits of gossip. Léonce Rosenberg expresses his astonishment to Picasso (3-9-18) at finding words penned by his adversary which he said to Rivera only a short while before: "This sentence was said by me to Rivera, alone, a year ago: 'Fernand Léger' – he declares to all-comers – 'is a modern Fragonard, but... better constructed'". Léger, Braque and Gris try to calm the dealer's rage and urge him to remain silent, but Rivera does not let up with his provocation. Gris, losing patience, writes to Rosenberg from Beaulieu (25-10-18): "I have just been diverting myself by reading the letters of Messieurs Lhote and Rivera. If the former's letter is merely grotesque, the second's is idiotic, clumsy and blundering in its effrontery. Really, that man is an impudent humbug – he himself couldn't have believed what he said in his letter. These are the real dates: in 1912 he was doing Zuloagas, in 1913 Le Fauconniers, in 1914 (Salon des Indépendants, the last) Metzingers, then Gris up to 1916, when he started doing Picassos, and, totally demoralized, gives that up and falls back on Cézanne, thinking he is easier, and believing he has discovered I know not what wonderfully descriptive and geometrical methods of displacement which the great Cézanne never thought of because he was a painter. He would not dare tell me those lies to my face since, for nearly two years, all he did was avail himself of my discarded methods. As I was the tailor, I knew perfectly well that the suits I gave my customer were cast-offs. This I say to you in confidence because I don't want anyone to think I am battling to lay claim to methods I despise (for it is only talent that counts), or that I'm being pretentious. I can at least say this, I can work on my own without contact with him or Braque or Picasso, while he, as soon as he lost contact with Picasso and me, collapsed in the most pitiful fashion".

In his correspondence with Rosenberg, Gris sometimes has occasion to refer to painter friends who play no part in Cubism: Galanis (one drawing, 1914), a volunteer who was naturalized after mobilization; and Kisling, whose wedding he attends in August 1917.

He sometimes suffers from moods, periods of depression, in which he abandons his brushes and is content merely to draw. But he cannot announce plainly to his dealer that he has had a surfeit of Cubist embellishment, of a process of mass production designed to meet a fixed quota of canvases. By means of new combinations of the solid and transparent, the opaque and the translucent, he seeks to transcend the Cubist stereotypes recycled by all those around him, and he is in no doubt that he is maintaining what is best in his aesthetic and ethical position by reconciling composition and tradition. Drawing is at this time his preferred line of investigation, large-scale pencil sketches, highly wrought and self-contained pieces, still-lives and portraits of an extreme perfection, very 'Prix de Rome' – one of his companion Josette which is recorded as a portrait of Madame Léonce Rosenberg because it is dedicated "to my friend Léonce Rosenberg/ Juan Gris/ Paris 7-1917" (Figure 4). He sees painting and drawing as two clearly distinct activities, or so at least he writes on 13 May 1918 to Paul Dermée: "Work is going well, and I am busy painting for eight or nine hours a day, apart from two hours in which I do drawings from nature".

In the determined effort to resurrect the Rosenberg archive, it never formed part of the intention to raise a memorial to the memory of a dealer who, when all is said and done, served as no more than an epistolary sounding-board for his painters, who is no more than an occasionally irksome, but still entirely secondary factor in this dissolution of an avant-garde which called itself then and is still called Cubism. But a reading of the following selection of letters from Gris, all of which date from his second stay at Beaulieu-lès-Loches in 1918, which appear here in translation for the first time, having been published previously in the catalogue of IVAM, Valencia, will demonstrate how indispensible it is in the writing of art history to impose upon oneself the preliminary task of assembling and establishing reliable and significant sources, even if these are confidential – not merely to provide the usual props with which the historian buttresses an argument, but because they bring us into the painter's intimate circle.

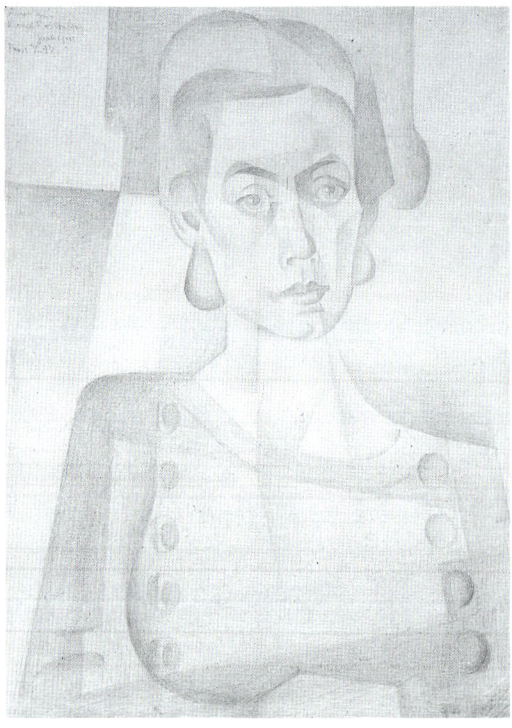

Figure 4
Portrait of Madame Josette Gris, 1917 (formerly known as *Portrait of Madame Léonce Rosenberg*), 1917
Pencil on paper, 39.5 x 28.3 cm
Tel-Aviv Museum

Juan Gris to Léonce Rosenberg. Beaulieu, 4-4-18. (Archive: MOMA; Léonce Rosenberg no. 1. Rosenberg register: letter no. 729, received 7-4-18)

Beaulieu 4-4-18
My dear friend,
We arrived here the day before yesterday quite tired after the journey because we had to spend the night in Tours without having a bed to sleep in.
There wasn't a hotel room free where we could spend the night. Tours is packed but full of crowds, with a life and bustle which doesn't exist in Paris.
The house I have here, more than two centuries old, is like a mill interior. The cost of living is less than in Paris and apart from paraffin and tobacco, which are scarce, we can get everything else. I think I shall be able to work well here, especially as I have a fine well-lit room with lovely white-washed walls.
With Josette's best wishes to you, yours, Juan Gris
Beaulieu-près-Loches (Indre-et-Loire)

Juan Gris to Léonce Rosenberg. 20-5-18. (Archive: Paul Getty Museum, Los Angeles 850255. Rosenberg register: letter no. 803, received 21-5-18)

Beaulieu-près-Loches, Indre-et-Loire 20-5-18
My dear friend,
I was very pleased to receive your letter. Lipchitz has indeed passed on to me the 520 francs, for which I thank you. That friend's kindness towards me has perhaps given the impression this picture is very good, although in my opinion it is simply a little bit better than the rest. It is almost finished, and I am working at the same time on a landscape which is certainly more successful than the one you have from last time.
Without being content with what I do, I nevertheless think that these two things mark quite a considerable advance on the ones before.
I also did a portrait in coloured crayons of Madame Lipchitz, which I'm not satisfied with at the moment. I am doing one of my wife which promises well. In black pencil. I'm thinking of making a picture of it.
Looking forward to your news. Accept, dear friend, the good wishes of your Juan Gris.
Good wishes from my wife and greetings to Madame Rosenberg.

Juan Gris to Léonce Rosenberg. 27-5-18. (Archive: MOMA; Léonce Rosenberg no. 2. Rosenberg register: letter no. 813, received 28-5-18; reply: 28-5-18, no. 20, 486)

Beaulieu-près-Loches, Indre-et-Loire, 27-5-1918
My dear friend,
I hope that in your new duty you are no worse off than before. I am about to set to work on making the placards with heraldic devices and I am trying to get hold of engravings from which I can copy the decorations you told me about.
Also tell me please, is it only the text you wrote that is the one to be included [?] [and the lanyard: erasure] As soon as they are done I will send the placards.

Enclosed is a letter I received from Switzerland asking me to reproduce my drawings in a review. I am writing at the same time to this Monsieur Tzara telling him to address himself to you about this. I am still working hard and am not too unhappy with it.
With Josette's greetings, very much your friend.
Juan Gris.

Juan Gris to Léonce Rosenberg. 4-6-18. (Archive: Institut Néerlandais, Fondation Custodia, Paris 1972, A40. Rosenberg register: letter no. 929, received 4-6-18)

Beaulieu-prés-Loches, Indré-et-Loire 4-6-18
My dear friend,
The placards with heraldic devices were finished yesterday and I think the gentlemen will be happy with them. I haven't sent them off to you because the post office wouldn't accept them. They measure 40 cent[imeters] on their longest side and the post office only takes up to 35. So I don't know what to

do. Do you want me to go to Paris and take them to you? I will bring the pictures at the same time. Would you prefer that I try to get them to you by rail? I was counting on sending you the placards by post and going to see you in Paris on the fifteenth but with the post office's refusal to take them and circumstances as they are, I don't know what to do. Do please give me instructions about what to do. Do please give me instructions about what is best. Tell me if I must bring the trip forward or whether I should defer it or whether you prefer sending by train. After all, you ought to know better than me what is most advisable at the moment. I will fit in with whatever you say.
I have three completed pictures. One size 40, the peasant in a blue smock. One 25 (Harlequin) and one 20 (landscape). I also have three crayon drawings (2 portraits and a still-life).
Eagerly anticipating your reply, accept the good wishes of your Juan Gris.
My respects to Madame Rosenberg and hello from my wife. Greetings to Mademoiselle Burray.

Juan Gris to Léonce Rosenberg. 10-7-18. (Archive: Institut Néerlandais, Fondation Custodia, Paris 1971, A172. Rosenberg register: letter no. 895, received 11-7-18)

Beaulieu, 10-7-18
By the same post I am sending you, registered, the placard for the doctor. It is smaller than the previous ones because of the post office which only takes up to to 35 cent[imeters] on the longest side. I am pleased about your letter of yesterday and to know from today's that the business with the young man worked out. I have partly been prevented from working these last few days as I'm rather tired. A few small pictures which I finished recently have satisfied me more than some others, as I think the brushwork is better, that is to say, they are painted in a more supple and lively manner. One size 30 picture of a peasant woman is not badly composed, but I would like to be able to make it come alive through the actual paint. I am fed up with laying on the colours in a cold and mechanical way and I would like to be able to produce brushwork: in the countryside I see such solid and delectable tones of pigment and such perfect harmonies that they carry within themselves a far greater power than all the combinations drawn from the palette – I wish I could work with them. A walk in the country is not only a source of elements but also of means. And I promise you, the more I understand the countryside the more I like it. Once the dazzle of the picturesque has disappeared, its perfect, solid relationships are even more enhanced. And without any need to be a landscape painter, to understand the relationships there is [sic] in a field is to extend and verify your painting.
Looking forward to good news from you soon my dear friend and with greetings from my wife, best wishes from your Juan Gris. My respects to Madame Rosenberg.

Juan Gris to Léonce Rosenberg. 22-8-18. (Archive: MOMA; Léonce Rosenberg no. 7. Rosenberg register: letter no. 970, received 23-8-18)

Beaulieu, 22-8-18
I am not surprised the article you sent me should have been inspired by the people you think. Impossible to say exactly which quality they possess the most of, whether [it is] malice or ignorance. To think that just because I mention brushwork and making a colour sing means I am denying Cubism is really idiotic.
Using brushwork, modulating a colour is not the same thing as modelling an object by one's use of brushwork.
What is more, it is only a device, which passes as a technical and not an aesthetic device. I know for them that is something that doesn't exist as Cubism has never been for these people any more than a technique, or a genre at the most. That is why they have become bored with it, as one always gets tired of doing a set genre of painting which does not correspond to any need. For those of us who work seriously, Cubism is an aesthetic emerging out of a mental attitude that is very profound, very human and very much of its day. All aesthetics [erasure]

have been based either on a religious attitude or a need for sensuality or luxury or some other mental attitude. Thus they will have acted in vain, it will achieve nothing.
By the same post I address you an Ecole des Beaux-Arts review in which there is an article which I have marked for you in blue crayon and which will demonstrate to you how [that so much: erasure] even that old grave of painting feels the need for something strong and new, modern. As for the pains Monsieur Rivera puts himself to in order to sustain his painting, I am sorry for him. He reminds me of another painter, also barbu as well as barbed, whose name is Le Fauconnier, now vanished, who did not succeed in spite of all the skill he deployed to make his pictures good.
For my part, I have no thought of bestirring myself and using my person to set off my oeuvre. If my pictures are bad they will founder as they deserve and if they are worth something they will always find disinterested persons to support them. I hope, thanks to you, I will increasingly be able to live far away from the artistic community where artistic politics are more indulged in than art, and even for as long as possible far away from Paris.
As for Vauxcelles, he plays his part and one shouldn't bear him a grudge. If one didn't want his praises it [is] because they were of no significance, so his attacks shouldn't be either.
With my respects to Madame, dear friend, sincere good wishes from your Juan Gris.
Best wishes from Josette and the friends.
I am deeply upset that Metzinger has blundered over our affairs in spite of the fact that I repeatedly urged discretion upon [him].

Juan Gris to Léonce Rosenberg. 6-9-18. (Archive: Paul Getty Museum, Los Angeles 850 255. Rosenberg register: letter no. 994, received 9-9-18)

Beaulieu 6-9-18
My dear friend,
Really, Vauxcelles and his inciters go too far. What do they hope to achieve with all this? If Vauxcelles thinks his malicious attacks will discourage anyone who takes an interest in our painting then he is deceiving himself. Your reply is very good but we must [fait] avoid you being dragged into a slanging-match in the newspapers. We must never desert the artistic ground and if one day I have the chance I shall say anonymously or somehow let it be known what I think about painting and what I think about these gentlemen. It is amazing the way ignorance and lack of intelligence are almost always allied with unscrupulous ambition. They have at the most that small intelligence that comes from the head, like the voice of a bad singer, but never that other profound sort which thrusts up from the chest and is the only one that is creative. I am very touched by the Foch book and I like the clarity and precision it displays. Accept, my dear friend, together with my thanks the good wishes of your Juan Gris. My respects to Madame Rosenberg. Good wishes from Josette and the friends. You haven't yet written to say whether you received the placards I sent you a week ago.

Juan Gris to Léonce Rosenberg. 6-9-18. (Archive: MOMA; Léonce Rosenberg no. 9. Rosenberg register: letter no. 1008, received 17-9-18)

Beaulieu 15-9-18
My dear friend,
It seems to me that there was nothing else to be done in the Rivera affair but what you did. The situation was too tense and his attitude appeared too hostile – judging anyway from what I have learned of it, as it is almost three years since I had anything to do with that gentlemen. I cut myself off from him as soon as I noticed his massive ambition to succeed. If you sell off his pictures at the Hôtel you run the risk that this is something he has anticipated and that it would be more to his advantage than his detriment. On one occasion the pictures of Van Dongen were sold off at the Hôtel and you could buy them for ten or fifteen francs, but that made him well-known where before he wasn't known.
I ask nothing better than [to] send you my pictures but I am very much at a loss as you don't want me

to send them rolled. I'll give them to Lipchitz so that he can take them to you, all he can manage. I can also have a crate made to send them to you by rail but apart from the fact that I don't know if they would take it express I'm afraid to send them at present [given] the great congestion in the stations at present.
As for my return to Paris, I don't envisage it being just at the moment for several reasons. First because I work more comfortably here than in the Paris studio, given that I have a number of rooms in this house. Then because, with the money at my disposal I can manage a bit better here than [back] there. And finally, because I'm scared of all the aggravation in artistic circles, as all I think of is work. Rest assured nevertheless that if you needed me [to] return for some reason or you judged it opportune I would respond immediately to your arguments and your summons. Accept dear friend the sincere good wishes of your Juan Gris.
I have just received the 800 francs from the bank. Of them I acknowledge receipt and to you I offer my thanks. Greetings from Josette.

Juan Gris to Léonce Rosenberg. 26-11-18. (Archive: Paul Getty Museum, Los Angeles 850 255. Rosenberg register: letter no. 1154, received 26-11-18)

Sunday
My dear friend,
On another occasion I would have feared the consequences of this letter but in the state of demoralization and weariness I find myself in, the consequences are a matter of indifference to me.
You spoke to me yesterday of someone who is unscrupulously ambitious. If you had extended your adjective to a number of other people you would not [have] been far wrong. For here am I, I have never protested or made any demands, and I find myself being submerged by these gentlemen.
I am not the one who can say whether my pictures are good or bad but what I can say without fear of contradiction is that they are definitely by me.
However the bizarre fenomenon [sic] exists that the G[alerie] E[ffort] M[oderne] pays as much or even more for fake Picassos, fake Braques and fake Gris as for genuine Gris. You understand my dear friend that this isn't calculated to encourage me in the purity of work, and although I am not a money-grubber I can[not] say I enjoy seeing myself become the Cinderella or the ragamuffin of the G.E.M. All I say to you is addressed to you as a friend, for with you as a dealer I have a signed treaty which brooks no appeal.
I therefore say this to you to bring to your attention an injustice which, absorbed by other preoccupations, you have overlooked. If I speak to you in a letter it is because of my shyness at handling business verbally.
Looking forward to the favourable response that your honesty and sense of justice will dictate, very much your friend. Juan Gris.

Translated from the French by Jane Brenton

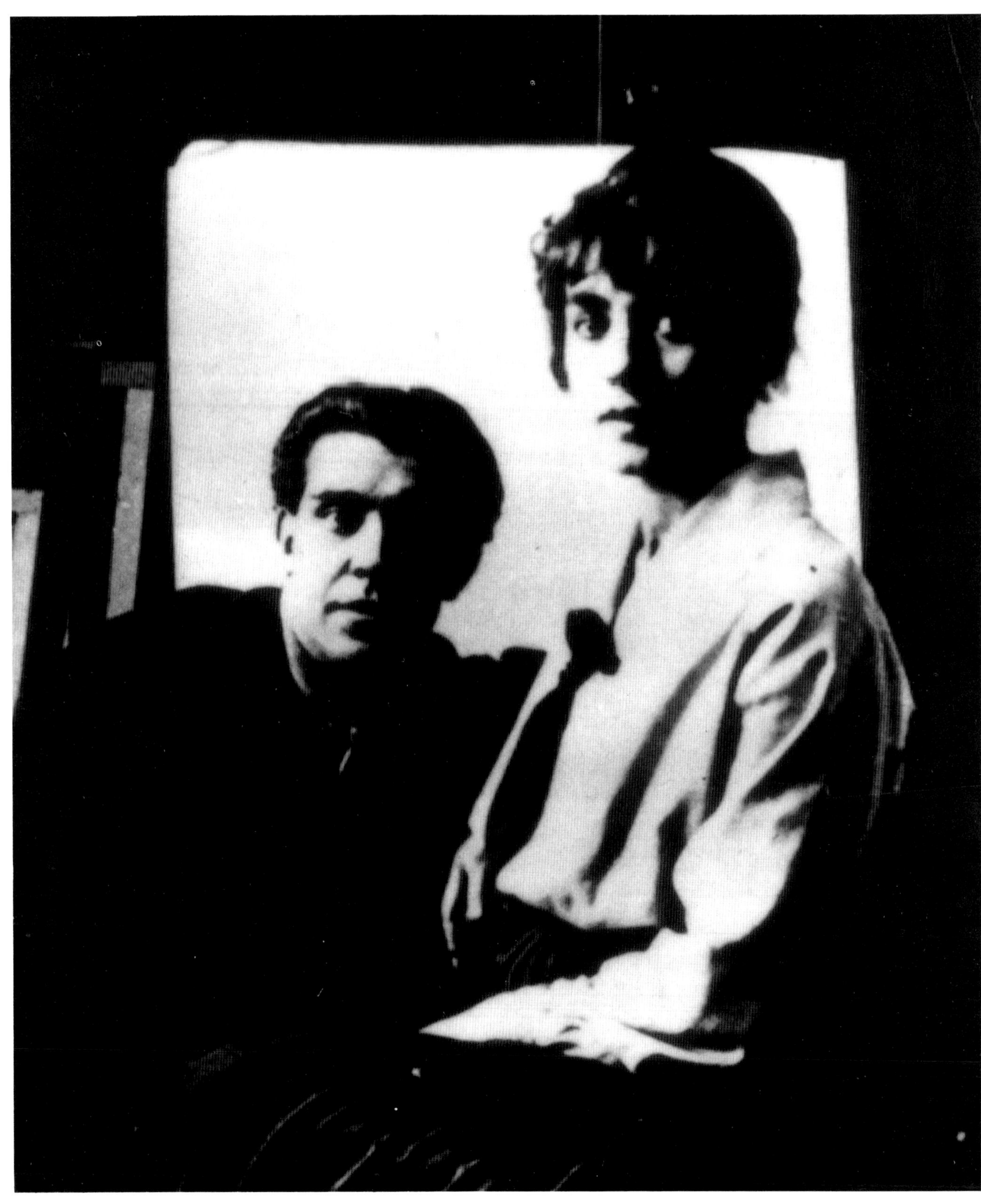

Biography

Compiled by Christopher Green

José Victoriano Carmelo Carlos González Pérez (who later called himself "Juan Gris") was born on 23 March 1887 at 4, Calle del Carmen in Madrid. He was the thirteenth of fourteen children. His mother was Isabel Pérez Brasategui (from Malaga); his father was Gregorio González y Rodríguez (from Valladolid). Gregorio was a well-off merchant whose fortunes declined during Gris's childhood and youth.

Gris studied at the Escuela de Artes e Industrias in Madrid between 1902 and 1904. It is unclear what the curricula were, but it is likely that he studied mathematics, the natural sciences and engineering to at least elementary standard. In 1904 he decided on a career as an artist and was taught for a while by the academic painter José Moreno Carbonero. Despite later reports that he published drawings while attending the Escuela de Artes e Industrias, no drawings are known from before 1905 when he published in the two numbers to appear of the Villaespesa review *Renacimiento Latino*. Mostly his drawings here are *ex libris* vignettes for poets and artists, among them Ruben Dario and Angel Zarraga. Already in a few he signed himself "Juan Gris". In 1906 he illustrated *Alma América*, a book of poems published in Madrid by the Peruvian José Santo Chocano, again signing himself "Juan Gris". His flat, fluid use of line and surface in the drawings of 1905–6 identify them as "Modernista"; they are stylish additions to the sum of international Art Nouveau/Jugendstil.

Juan Gris with Josette in the artist's studio at the "Bateau-Lavoir" on 1922 (Photograph: Daniel-Henry Kahnweiler)

He moved to Paris in September 1906, following his friend the painter Daniel Vázquez Diaz (another contributor to *Renacimiento Latino*), who met him off the train at the Gare d'Orsay. He was never to return to Spain, since he faced criminal charges there for evading military service. Between 1907 and 1914 he worked actively as a caricaturist and illustrator, publishing in such magazines as *Le Charivari, Le Rire, L'Indiscret, Le Témoin, Le Frou-Frou* and especially *L'Assiette au beurre*, and sending drawings for publication in the Barcelona magazine *Papitu*. He was a prolific caricaturist, publishing well over 400 drawings and dozens of vignettes. His drawings continued to be published in the caricature magazines until 1914. In Paris his work as a graphic artist is more satirical than decorative. It is comparable with such caricaturists as d'Ostoya and Gris's friends Gallanis and Paul Iribe (editor of *Le Témoin*).

On arriving in Paris, Gris lived in the Hôtel Caulincourt in Montmartre. Vázquez Diaz, another resident there, introduced him to Pablo Picasso, and he moved into the studio building at 13, rue Ravignan (the so-called "Bateau-Lavoir") as Picasso's neighbour, probably by 1908. Picasso was to move out late in 1909, but to take a studio there again in 1911–12. In 1910 Gris decided to become an avant-garde painter. He was one of a small Montmartre group, which included, besides Picasso, Georges Braque and the writers Guillaume Apollinaire, André Salmon and Max Jacob. After two years of studies and experimental paintings, exploring the possibilities opened up by Picasso and Braque, he exhibited first as a painter in January/February 1912 at the Montmartre gallery of Clovis Sagot (15 works). This was followed by the showing of 3 paintings, including *Homage to Pablo Picasso* and probably *Still-life with Flowers*, at the Salon des Indépendants in March 1912. There were positive critical responses from Salmon and Apollinaire; both mentioned his *Homage to Pablo Picasso* and Apollinaire called his contribution "integral Cubism". In April 1912 he was included in the Cubist exhibition held at the Galerias Dalmau in Barcelona (5 paintings and 3 drawings). Later that year, he showed 13 pictures at the Salon de la Section d'Or, organised expressly as an exhibition of artists associated with "Cubism". Among them were *Man in the Café* and *The Watch*. The critic Maurice Raynal, writing in the single issue to appear of the review *La Section d'Or*, stressed his importance as a *collagist*; Raynal became a close friend. Gris was now in contact with the Cubists who had grouped together at the Indépendants of 1911 in "Salle 41", among them Jean Metzinger, Albert Gleizes and Fernand Léger.

The dealer Daniel-Henry Kahnweiler, who began buying from Picasso and Braque in 1907–8, had met Gris at the "Bateau-Lavoir" in 1908. In October 1912, persuaded by his showing at the Salons, he decided to give him a contract. It was drawn up and signed in February 1913 and gave Kahnweiler the exclusive right to his production in return for a regular income. Alongside Picasso and Braque, as one of Kahnweiler's Cubists, Gris explored a range of new idioms and techniques, including *papier collé* in 1913–14. In the summer of 1913 he worked at Céret; Picasso was briefly there with him. In February 1914 Charlotte Augusta Fernande Herpin, known as Josette, moved in with him at 13, rue Ravignan. An earlier relationship had given him a child, Georges, in 1909 who, when the mother (Lucie Belin) left, had been dispatched to Madrid to be brought up by Gris's sister Antonieta. The relationship with Josette was to be childless, but long-lasting.

The declaration of war in August 1914 found Gris in Collioure, near the Spanish border where, in friendly contact with Henri Matisse, but anxious about his status as a foreigner, he stayed until the end of October. Following Kahnweiler's exile from France (as a German), Gris was left without material support, although Gertrude Stein and the American dealer Michael Brenner tried to help. In January 1915 Léonce Rosenberg, a dealer who had bought Cubist work before the war, visited him on the advice of Picasso, and a contract was signed with him in 1916 (18 April); it was modified in 1917 (15 October) and 1918 (December). During the war Rosenberg became the dealer for all the leading Cubists, including Picasso and Braque (although Picasso did not sign a contract), and in the six months immediately following the Armistice of 11 November 1918 he put on a series of major Cubist exhibitions including one of Gris's war-time production (5–30 April 1919). About 50 works were shown.

Gris spent most of the war in Paris. By 1916–18 he was a recognised leader among Léonce Rosenberg's Cubists. He was a close friend of the poet Pierre Reverdy, another Montmartre neighbour, who edited the influential little magazine *Nord-Sud* through 1917–18. The title of the magazine referred to the Metro line that joined Montmartre to Montparnasse, and Gris was seen more often in the Montparnasse studios and cafés. Alongside Reverdy, he was close to the poet Paul Dermée and especially to the Chilean poet Vicente Huidobro and the sculptor Jacques Lipchitz. He helped Huidobro translate his poetry from Spanish into French and even made an attempt at Reverdian composition himself. He provided illustrations for Huidobro's *Horizon carré: Poèmes* (1917) and

Tremblement de la terre (undated), Dermée's *Beautés de 1918* (1919) and Reverdy's *La Guitare endormie* (1919), as well as a series of gouaches for *pochoir* reproduction in a projected book of Reverdy's prose poems which were not to appear until the edition of Reverdy's *Au Soleil du plafond* published by Tériade in 1956. His friendship with Picasso continued and in 1917 Picasso arranged for him to see rehearsals of the ballet *Parade* for which he had designed the sets and costumes. Put on by Serge Diaghilev's *Ballets Russes,* it opened on 18 May at the Théâtre du Châtelet with Gris in the audience.

To escape Paris, Gris spent two extended wartime stays at Beaulieu-lès-Loches in the Touraine, the home-town of Josette, where they rented rooms found for them by her grandfather in a country house at Les Fourneaux. The first stay was in September-October 1916, during which he painted the *château-fort* of Loches and, most notably, his *Portrait of Madame Josette Gris.* The second stay was between April and December 1918; it was instigated by the bombardment of Paris by "Big Bertha", which caused a mass exodus from the city. Gris and Josette were joined at Beaulieu for varying periods by Lipchitz, Metzinger and Huidobro with their wives, as well as the Spanish Cubist María Blanchard. While there he painted local peasants and landscapes alongside still-lives. He also drew regularly, using a meticulous quasi-"naturalist" manner, a practice he had begun in 1915 and had substantiated with variants on Cézanne, Corot and Velázquez done from postcards in 1916.

Rosenberg's Galerie de L'Effort Moderne Cubist exhibitions of 1918–19 were followed early in 1920 by a co-ordinated group showing of Cubist painters at the Salon des Indépendants and a revival of the Salon de la Section d'Or. Gris was acknowledged as a leading contributor to both. The modification at the end of 1918 of the terms of Gris's contract with Rosenberg led to a cooling of relations between them. Gris and Kahnweiler were back in touch in 1919, and after Kahnweiler returned to Paris (February 1920) Gris decided to paint only in formats that were not specified by his agreement with Rosenberg so that he could sell again exclusively to his pre-war supporter. Both as friends and as intellectual allies they were to remain very close until Gris's death.

In early May 1920 Gris fell ill. He was thought to have pneumonia, which developed into "pleurisy". He was hospitalized for two months before convalescing at Beaulieu-lès-Loches, where he began to work again. His recovery was sustained from late 1920 until mid-summer 1921 at Bandol on the Mediterranean, where a brief affair with a local woman, Marcelle Brune, led to a temporary estrangement from Josette. Back with Josette, Gris spent the period between November and early spring 1922 at Céret. He was highly productive at this time. At Bandol he produced lithographs for an illustrated edition of Max Jacob's *Ne coupez pas, Mademoiselle, ou les erreurs des P.T.T,* and a series of portrait lithographs, both published by Kahnweiler's Galerie Simon, and at Bandol and Céret he painted an ambitious suite of open window still-lives.

When Gris and Josette returned to Paris from Céret, they moved into an apartment found for them by Kahnweiler above a plumber at 8, rue de la Mairie (now rue de l'ancienne Mairie), Boulogne-sur-Seine. Kahnweiler and his wife lived at number 12. Sundays at Kahnweiler's became a regular part of Gris's life. Among those invited from around 1924 were the writer Armand Salacrou, the poet Michel Leiris and the painter André Masson (who was involved with Surrealism from its inception in 1924). They all became friends.

Kahnweiler's Galerie Simon put on a major solo exhibition of Gris in 1923 (20 March – 5

April). Despite a savage attack by Charles Hiver in *Montparnasse*, the 1923 exhibition was generally well received. Another mark of emerging public recognition was Gris's collaboration with Diaghilev's *Ballets Russes* between 1922 and 1924. He designed the sets for a ballet based on music by Michel de Montéclair, which opened at Monte Carlo on 3 January 1924 with the title *Les Tentations de la bergère*. Diaghilev gave him the commission at the end of 1922, and followed it by asking him to design the costumes and setting for a reception and ball, dubbed the *Fête merveilleuse*, held in the Galerie des Glaces of the Château de Versailles on the evening of 30 June 1923. Gris also designed the costumes and sets for productions of Charles Gounod's *opéra-comique La Colombe* and Emmanuel Chabrier's one act *operetta Une Education manquée*, both of which opened at Monte Carlo in January 1924. His final collaboration with Diaghilev was on a Red Cross gala held at Les Grands Magasins du Printemps on 28 May 1924.

1924–25 were years of stability, working in Boulogne-sur-Seine and holidaying in the summers, first in a mill-house at Nemours with the Salacrous and the Massons, and then on a river boat down the Seine to Le Havre with the Salacrous. In 1924 he illustrated Salacrou's *Le Casseur d'assiettes*, following this with illustrated editions of Tristan Tzara's *Mouchoir de nuages* (1925), Gertrude Stein's *A Book Concluding With As A Wife Has A Cow A Love Story* (1925) and Raymond Radiguet's *Denise* (1926). Kahnweiler's Galerie Simon was the publisher. Gris's reputation was enhanced by the lecture he delivered on 15 April 1924 at Dr René Allendy's *Société des études philosophiques et scientifiques pour l'examen des idées nouvelles* in the Sorbonne. By January 1925 it had appeared in English, Spanish and German. Also in 1925 the major collectors Alphonse Kann and Dr G.F.Reber of Lausanne began to buy his work. A new interest was Free Masonry into which he was initiated on 2 February 1923, being elevated to the grade of "companion" in January 1924 and "master" on 1 May 1925.

Gris's health showed serious signs of decline in winter 1925–26, persuading him to go south to Toulon where he stayed until April 1926. Among his friends and visitors there were Gertrude Stein and the American writer Ford Madox Ford. In spring 1926 his son Georges came to live with him at Boulogne-sur-Seine, staying until his death. Gris's worsening condition forced him south to Hyères in November. High blood pressure led to cardiac asthma. He moved to Puget-Theniers, hoping that the altitude would help. It did not, and he returned to Boulogne-sur-Seine on 24 January 1927. His final decline was rapid. He died there on 11 May and was buried in the cemetery of Boulogne-sur-Seine on 13 May 1927. At his funeral the chief mourners were Georges González Gris, Lipchitz, Raynal, Picasso and Kahnweiler.

A Selected Bibliography

Note: This bibliography is confined to the literature specifically by or on Juan Gris. It is highly selective and does not include the numerous discussions of Gris's work in more general writings on twentieth century art and Cubism. It is in two parts: writings by and interviews with Juan Gris and writings on Juan Gris. Part I is organised chronologically according to publication dates. Part II is alphabetical by author (or equivalent) covering all types of publication from books and catalogues to newspaper articles. A great deal of bibliographical information on Cubism and on broader cultural, social and political contexts is to be found in the footnotes above. Useful bibliographies on Gris are to be found in Part II nos. 37 and 66 below, although the first necessarily does not go beyond the late 1960s and the second is relatively selective.

Part I: Writings by and interviews with Juan Gris

1. Statement, *Valori Plastici*, Rome, February-March 1919, p. 2. (trans. in (II) no. 37)
2. Statement (in answer to an *enquête* on "art nègre"), *Action*, no. 3, Paris, April 1920, p. 24 (trans. in (II) no. 37)
3. Untitled biography and statement of Gris's "aesthetic" signed "Vauvrecy" (the pseudonym of André Ozenfant), *L'Esprit Nouveau*, no. 5, Paris, February 1921, pp. 533–4; reprinted as 'Zu Meinen Schaffen' in (ed) Paul Westheim, *Künstlerbekenntnisse*, Berlin, 1924 (?) (trans. in (II) no. 37)
4. 'Notes sur ma peinture', *Der Querschnitt*, nos. 1–2, Frankfurt, Summer, 1923, pp. 77–8 (trans. in (II) no. 37)
5. Interview published in Georges Charensol, 'Chez Juan Gris', *L'Intransigeant*, Paris, 25 April 1924
6. Lecture, 'Sur les possibilités de la peinture'; delivered at the Société des études philosophiques et scientifiques in the Sorbonne, 15 April 1924, published in: *Transatlantic Review*, Paris, vol. 1, no. 6, June 1924, pp. 482–8 and vol. 2, no. 1, July 1924, pp. 75–9 (English); *Alfar*, La Coruña, no. 43, September 1924 (excerpts in Spanish); *Der Querschnitt*, Berlin, vol. 1, January 1925, pp. 32–40; *Cahiers d'Art*, Paris, nos. 5–6, 1933, n.p. (excerpts in French) (trans. in (II) no. 37)
7. Statement (in answer to an "enquête" entitled 'Chez les cubistes'), *Bulletin de la vie artistique*, Paris, 6th Year, no. 1, 1 January 1925, pp. 15–7 (trans. in (II) no. 37)
8. Statement, *Europa-Almanach*, Potsdam, 1925, pp. 34–5; reprinted in French with a preface by Carl Einstein under the title 'Juan Gris: texte inédit' in *Documents*, Paris, 2nd Year, no. 5, 1930, pp. 267–73 (trans. in (II) no. 37)
9. Statement published in Maurice Raynal, *Anthologie de la peinture*, Paris, 1927 (trans. in (II) no. 37)
10. Letters published in (ed.) Douglas Cooper, *Letters of Juan Gris, 1913–1927*, collected by Daniel-Henry Kahnweiler, translated by Douglas Cooper, London, 1956

11. Letters published in (ed.) Christian Derouet, *Juan Gris: Correspondance, Dessins 1915–1921*, IVAM Centre Julio González, Valencia and Musée National d'Art Moderne, Centre Georges Pompidou, Paris, 1990–91

Part II: Writings on Juan Gris

1. ANON. (probably Carl EINSTEIN), 'Exposition Juan Gris' (Berlin, Galerie Flechtheim), *Documents*, Paris, 2nd Year, no. 4, 1930, p. 243
2. Guillaume APOLLINAIRE, 'Juan Gris'; in *Méditations esthétiques: Les peintres cubistes*, Paris, 1913
3. Manuel ABRIL, 'El pintor Juan Gris', *Alfar*, no. 34, La Coruña, November 1923
4. Manuel ABRIL, 'Juan Gris', *La Gaceta Literaria*, Madrid, 1 June 1927
5. ARTE VIVO, special number dedicated to Juan Gris, Valencia, May-June 1959
6. BADEN-BADEN (Kunsthalle), catalogue of the exhibition *Juan Gris*, 1974; texts by Jean Leymarie, Man Ray, Gertrude Stein, Daniel-Henry Kahnweiler, Will Grohmann, Georg Schmidt, Joachim Büchner, Herta Wescher and reprinting of Gris's writings
7. BALAŸ et CARRÉ (Galerie), catalogue of the exhibition *Juan Gris*, Paris, 1938
8. BERN (Kunstmuseum), catalogue of the exhibition *Juan Gris*, ed. with contributions by Douglas Cooper, 1956
9. Juan Manuel BONNET, 'Juan Gris, en su alba', *Diario*, 9 January 1988, pp. IV–V
10. BOULOGNE-BILLANCOURT (Musée Municipal de Boulogne-Billancourt), catalogue of the exhibition *Juan Gris et les dimanches de Boulogne*, 1987–88; essays by Claude Frontisi, Raymond Bachollet, Michèle Lefrançoise-Agis Garcin and Emmanuel Bréon
11. CAHIERS D'ART, special number dedicated to Juan Gris, 8th Year, no. 5–6
12. William A.CAMFIELD, 'Juan Gris and the Golden Section', *The Art Bulletin*, March 1965
13. E.A.CARMEAN JR., 'Juan Gris "Fantomas"', *Arts*, vol. 51, no. 5, January 1977
14. Douglas COOPER (under the pseudonym Douglas Lord), 'Juan Gris', *Axis*, Autumn, 1936, no. 7, pp. 9–12
15. Douglas COOPER, *Juan Gris ou le goût du solonnel*, Geneva, 1949
16. Douglas COOPER, *Juan Gris: Catalogue Raisonné of the Painted Work*, compiled with the collaboration of Margaret Potter, Paris, 1977
17. Douglas COOPER, 'A Juan Gris Discovery', *Burlington Magazine*, London, vol. 126, no. 971, February 1984, p. 91
18. Gerardo DIEGO, 'Devoción y meditación de Juan Gris', *Revista de Occidente*, Madrid, vol.5, August 1927, pp. 160–80
19. Enrique ECHEA, 'In Memoriam. Juan Gris', *La Esfera*, Madrid, vol. 14, 4 June 1927
20. Enrique ECHEA, 'En la ruta de la celebridad. Juan Gris', *ABC*, Madrid, 28 August 1951
– Carl EINSTEIN, see ANON.
21. Frank ELGAR, *Gris; Still Lifes*, New York, 1961
22. Alfred FLECHTHEIM (Galerie), catalogue of the exhibition *Gedächtnissausstellung Juan Gris*, Berlin, 1930
23. Sebastià GASCH, 'Ha mort Juan Gris', *L'Amic de les arts*, Sitges, vol. 3, 31 May 1927
24. José A.GARCIA-DIEGO, *Antonio Machado y Juan Gris: Dos artistas masones*, Madrid, 1990
25. Juan Antonio GAYA NUÑO, *Juan Gris*, Barcelona, 1971 (trans. London, 1975)
26. Waldemar GEORGE, 'Juan Gris', *L'Amour de l'art*, Paris, vol. 2, no. 11, November 1921, pp. 351–2
27. Waldemar GEORGE, *Juan Gris*, Paris, 1931
28. John GOLDING, 'Juan Gris at Bern', *Burlington Magazine*, London, vol. 97, December 1955, pp. 384–6
29. Christopher GREEN, 'Synthesis and the 'Synthetic Process' in the Painting of Juan

Gris', *Art History*, London, vol. 5, no. 1, March 1982, pp. 87–105
30. Christopher GREEN, 'Purity, Poetry and the Painting of Juan Gris', *Art History*, London, vol. 5, no. 2, June 1982, pp. 180–204
31. Georges GONZÁLEZ GRIS, 'Jean, mon père'; in *Hommage à Juan Gris (1887–1927)*, Grand Orient de France, 6 bis rue Cadet, 75009 Paris, 1987, pp. 5–6
32. Guy HABASQUE, 'L'Atelier de Juan Gris', *L'Œil*, Paris, no. 37, January 1958, pp. 28–35
33. L.ISHI-KAWA, *Aproximación a Gris: ocho marchos para once cuadros*, Fundación Arte y Technología for Telefónica d'España, S.A., 1990
34. J.J (Josep Junoy?), 'Juan Gris', *La Publicitat*, Barcelona, 4 April 1912
35. Daniel-Henry KAHNWEILER, 'Der Tod des Juan Gris', *Der Querschnitt*, vol. 7, July 1927, p. 558
36. Daniel-Henry KAHNWEILER (under the pseudonym Daniel Henry), *Juan Gris*, Leipzig and Berlin, 1929
37. Daniel-Henry KAHNWEILER, *Juan Gris: Sa Vie, Son Oeuvre, Ses Ecrits*, Paris, 1946; *Juan Gris: His Life and Work*, translated by Douglas Cooper, London, 1947; new enlarged edition, London and Stuttgart (German edition), 1968–69
38. H.A.L., 'A note on Juan Gris and cubism', *Broom*, New York, no. 5, 1923, pp. 32–5
39. LA BROSSE, 'Silhouettes: Juan Gris', *Paris-Journal*, Paris, 22 June 1912
40. LEIRIS (Galerie Louise), *Jean Gris: Dessins et gouaches, 1910–1927*, Paris, 1965; preface by Daniel-Henry Kahnweiler
41. The LITTLE REVIEW, New York, Autumn-Winter, 1924–5, vol.10, no. 2, special number dedicated to Juan Gris (includes no. 52 below)
– MADRID, see TINTEROW
42. MARLBOROUGH FINE ART LTD, *Retrospective Exhibition*, London, 1958; texts by Daniel-Henry Kahnweiler and John Russell
43. Benedict NICHOLSON, 'Cubism and Juan Gris', *Horizon*, London, no. 99, March 1948, pp. 225–7
44. PARIS, Réunion des Musées Nationaux, *Juan Gris*, 1974; introduction by Jean Leymarie
45. Elliot PAUL, 'A Master of plastiç rela-tions', *Transitions*, New York, 1927, pp. 163–5
46. Maurice RAYNAL, 'L'Exposition de la "section d'or" (Juan Gris)', *La Section d'Or*, Paris, 9 October 1912, pp. 2–5 (trans. in Edward F. Fry, *Cubism*, London, 1966, pp. 97–100)
47. Maurice RAYNAL, 'Juan Gris', *L'Esprit Nouveau*, Paris, no. 5, February 1921, pp. 533–5
48. Maurice RAYNAL, 'Les Arts: Exposition Juan Gris', *L'Intransigeant*, Paris, Sunday 1 April 1923
49. Maurice RAYNAL, 'Juan Gris et la métaphore plastique', *Les Feuilles libres*, vol. 5, no. 31, March-April 1923; reprinted in no. 52 below
50. Maurice RAYNAL, 'Juan Gris', *Bulletin de l'Effort Moderne*, Paris, no. 16, June 1925, pp. 1–16; also in *Das Kunstblatt*, Vol.5, 1925, pp. 364–72
51. Maurice RAYNAL, 'La Mort de Juan Gris', *Art Vivant*, Paris, 1 June 1927, pp. 431–2
52. Maurice RAYNAL, 'Juan Gris'; in Raynal, *Anthologie de la peinture en France de 1906 à nos jours*, Paris, 1927 (includes (I) no. 9 and no. 49 above)
53. Mark ROSENTHAL, *Juan Gris*, University Art Gallery, Berkeley, California and Abbeville, New York, 1983
54. André SALMON, 'Juan Gris', *Paris-Journal*, 21 January 1912
55. Georg SCHMIDT, *Juan Gris und die Geschichte des Kubismus*, Baden-Baden and Stuttgart, 1957
56. Georg SCHMIDT, 'Juan Gris', *Das Kunstwerk*, vol.11, no. 7, January 1958, pp. 3–14
57. Ethlyne and Germaine SELIGMAN, 'Of the Proximity of Death and its Stylistic Acti-

vations – Roger de la Fresnaye and Juan Gris', *Art Quarterly*, New York, vol. 12, no. 2, 1949, pp. 147–55

58. Kenneth E. SILVER, 'Eminence Gris', *Art in America*, New York, May 1984

59. James Thrall SOBY, *Juan Gris*, New York (Museum of Modern Art), 1958

60. Gertrude STEIN, 'Juan Gris', *The Little Review*, New York, vol. 10, no. 16, Autumn-Winter, 1924–5

61. Gertrude STEIN, 'The Life and Death of Juan Gris', *Transition*, New York, no. 4, July 1927, pp. 159–62; German trans. in no. 22

62. Ernst STRAUSS, 'Über Juan Gris' "Technique picturale"', *Amici Amico: Festschrift für Werner Gross*, Munich, 1968

63. Ernst STRAUSS, 'Über Juan Gris als Zeichner', *Pantheon*, no. 33, 1975, pp. 334–42

64. E.TÉRIADE, 'Juan Gris', *Cahiers d'Art*, vol. 3, nos. 5–6, 1928

65. THEO (Galería), *Juan Gris*, Madrid, 1977

66. Gary TINTEROW (ed.), catalogue of the exhibition *Juan Gris*, Salas Pablo Ruiz Picasso under the auspices of the Ministerio de Cultura and the Banco de Bilbao, Madrid, 1985; essays by Marilyn McCully, Pierre Daix, Lewis Kachur, Kenneth E.Silver, Mark Rosenthal, Julián Gállego, René de Costa, Christopher Green, texts also by Francesco Calvo Serraller, Gerardo Diego, Juan Larrea, Paul Eluard, Elise Goldstein, Rosario Maseda and Anne M.P.Norton

67. Guillermo de TORRE, 'Juan Gris y Robert Delaunay: Reminescencias personales', *Minorías y Masas en la Cultura y el Arte Contemporáneos*, Barcelona, 1963, pp. 231–40

68. Joaquin TORRES-GARCIA, 'Juan Gris y el cubismo' (signed August 1936); in Torres-García, *Universalismo Constructivo*, Buenos Aires, 1944

69. Daniel VÁZQUEZ DIAZ, 'Juan Gris o la creciente vocación', *ABC*, Madrid, 5 May 1957

70. Daniel VÁZQUEZ DIAZ, 'Primeros dibujos en la prensa de Paris', *ABC*, Madrid, 18 March 1966

71. Daniel VÁZQUEZ DIAZ, 'Juan Gris y nuestra vieja amistad', *ABC*, Madrid, 27 September 1926

72. Christian ZERVOS, 'Juan Gris et l'inquiétude d'aujourd'hui', *Cahiers d'Art*, Paris, vol. 1, no. 10, 1926, pp. 269–74

73. (C)hristian (Z)ERVOS, 'Juan Gris', *Cahiers d'Art*, Paris, vol. 2, no. 6, 1927, pp. 170–2

Catalogue

Direction
Gerd Hatje
Design
Kate Stephens and
Tanja Van Steenkiste
Coordination
Tanja Van Steenkiste
Production
Dr. Cantz'sche Druckerei, Stuttgart

Photography
Christopher Green, London
Colorphoto Hans Hinz, Allschwil
Courtesy Acquavella Galleries, Inc., New York
Courtesy Dallas Museum of Art
Courtesy E.V. Thaw & Co., Inc., New York
Courtesy Fondazione Thyssen-Bornemisza, Lugano
Courtesy Fundación Arte y Tecnología, Madrid
Courtesy Galería Theo, Madrid
Courtesy Galerie Jan Krugier, Geneva
Courtesy Galerie Louise Leiris, S.A., Paris
Courtesy Georges González Gris
Courtesy Hamburger Kunsthalle
Courtesy Henie-Onstad Kunstsenter, Høvikodden
Courtesy John Berggruen Gallery, San Francisco
Courtesy Kunstmuseum Bern
Courtesy Kunstmuseum Winterthur
Courtesy Marc Blondeau, S.A., Paris
Courtesy Museo del Prado, Madrid
Courtesy Museo Nacional Reina Sofia, Madrid
Courtesy Öffentliche Kunstsammlung Basel
Courtesy Philadelphia Museum of Art
Courtesy Photothéque des Musées de la Ville de Paris
Courtesy Rheinisches Bildarchiv Köln
Courtesy Rijksmuseum Kröller-Müller, Otterlo
Courtesy Rose Art Museum, Brandeis University, Waltham, MA
Courtesy R.S. Johnson Fine Art, Chicago
Courtesy Scottish National Gallery of Modern Art, Edinburgh
Courtesy Service photographique du Musée National d'Art Moderne, Centre Georges Pompidou, Paris
Courtesy Staatsgalerie Stuttgart
Courtesy Statens Konstmuseer, Stockholm
Courtesy Stephen Mazoh & Co., Inc., New York
Courtesy Tarica Ltd., Paris
Courtesy Tate Gallery, London
Courtesy The Art Institute of Chicago
Courtesy The Baltimore Museum of Art
Courtesy The Museum of Modern Art, New York
Courtesy The National Gallery of Ireland, Dublin
Courtesy The Phillips Collection, Washington, DC
Courtesy The Solomon R. Guggenheim Foundation
Courtesy Thomas Ammann Fine Art, Zurich
Courtesy Ulmer Museum
Courtesy University of Michigan Museum of Art, Ann Arbor, MI
Courtesy Van Abbemuseum, Eindhoven
Courtesy Yale University Art Gallery, New Haven
Michael S. Tropea, Chicago
Photostudio Saas, Lausanne
Prudence Cuming Associates Ltd., London
Zindman/Fremont, New York

Lenders to the Exhibition

Collection Jose Mugrabi
Collection S
Dr and Mrs Raymond R. Sackler
Galerie Jan Krugier
Galerie Louise Leiris
Gradowczyk and Garcia Benitez Collection
Gretchen and John Berggruen
Hamburger Kunsthalle
Henie-Onstad Kunstsenter, Høvikodden
Hester Diamond
Jacques Hachuel Collection
Judith Rothschild
Kunstmuseum Bern
Kunstmuseum Winterthur
Lois and Georges de Menil Collection
Marc Blondeau, S.A.
Moderna Museet, Stockholm
Mr and Mrs Georges González Gris
Mr and Mrs Claude Laurens
Musée d'Art Moderne de la Ville de Paris
Musée National d'Art Moderne,
Centre Georges Pompidou, Paris
Museo del Prado, Madrid
Museo Nacional Reina Sofia, Madrid
Öffentliche Kunstsammlung Basel,
Kunstmuseum and Kupferstichkabinett
Philadelphia Museum of Art
Rijksmuseum Kröller-Müller, Otterlo
Rose Art Museum, Brandeis University, Waltham, MA
R. Stanley and Ursula Johnson Family Collection
Scottish National Gallery of Modern Art, Edinburgh
Staatsgalerie Stuttgart
Stephen Mazoh
Telefónica de España, S.A., Madrid
The Art Institute of Chicago
The Baltimore Museum of Art
The Carey Walker Foundation
The Museum of Modern Art, New York
The National Gallery of Ireland, Dublin
The Phillips Collection, Washington, DC
Thyssen-Bornemisza Collection, Lugano
Ulmer Museum
Yale University Art Gallery, New Haven, CT
and other private collectors who wish to
remain anonymous